# The Scramble for America

# The Scramble for America

*How the United States Conquered a Continent*

Clement Knox

WILLIAM COLLINS

William Collins
An imprint of HarperCollins*Publishers*
1 London Bridge Street
London SE1 9GF

WilliamCollinsBooks.com

HarperCollins*Publishers*
Macken House, 39/40 Mayor Street Upper
Dublin 1, D01 C9W8, Ireland

First published in Great Britain in 2026 by William Collins

1

Copyright © Clement Knox 2026

Clement Knox asserts the moral right to be identified as the author of this work in accordance with the Copyright, Designs and Patents Act 1988

A catalogue record for this book is available from the British Library

ISBN 978-0-00-844727-4

All rights reserved. No part of this publication may be reproduced, stored in a retrieval system, or transmitted, in any form or by any means, electronic, mechanical, photocopying, recording or otherwise, without the prior permission of the publishers.

Without limiting the exclusive rights of any author, contributor or the publisher of this publication, any unauthorised use of this publication to train generative artificial intelligence (AI) technologies is expressly prohibited. HarperCollins also exercise their rights under Article 4(3) of the Digital Single Market Directive 2019/790 and expressly reserve this publication from the text and data mining exception.

Set in Minion Pro
Printed and bound in the UK using 100% renewable electricity at CPI Group (UK) Ltd

To my father Raymond

> The Almighty setteth up; and he casteth down: He breaks the Sceptre, and transfers the Dominion: He has made Choice of the present Generation to erect the American Empire.
>
> WILLIAM HENRY DRAYTON, 1776

> Our colonial system did not begin with the Spanish war; the United States had had a colonial history and policy from the beginning of the Republic: but they have been hidden.
>
> FREDERICK JACKSON TURNER, 1901

# Contents

INTRODUCTION: 'The Decisive Fact in the Modern World' — 1

## PART I
### THE OHIO COUNTRY

| | |
|---|---|
| Mr Washington Goes to Ohio | 11 |
| All He Surveyed | 30 |
| Long Knives | 37 |
| The Bloody Grounds | 55 |
| Cutting the Knot | 73 |
| Ideal Lines | 86 |
| Quelling the West | 99 |
| Ohio Fever | 110 |

## PART II
### LOUISIANA

| | |
|---|---|
| The Door to the House | 125 |
| Thomas Jefferson Dreams of an Empire of Liberty | 135 |
| This Affair of Louisiana | 145 |
| Committing Louisianicide | 158 |
| Filling in the Map | 166 |
| Everything Shifts | 177 |
| The Broom of Destruction | 192 |

## PART III
### THE FLORIDAS

| | |
|---|---|
| A Pistol Pointed at the Heart of the Republic | 209 |
| The Original Lone Star State | 217 |
| Enter Jackson | 227 |
| Two Trips to London | 245 |
| Alabama Fever | 250 |
| Jackson Redux | 261 |
| Giant Steps | 272 |
| The Widower | 289 |

## PART IV
### THE OREGON COUNTRY

| | |
|---|---|
| Consider the Otter | 309 |
| The Shape of a Problem | 328 |
| Into the Pacific | 343 |
| Oregon Fever | 358 |
| The Pioneers and the Politicians | 377 |
| Careering Towards Compromise | 390 |

## PART V
### TEXAS, CALIFORNIA AND THE SOUTHWEST

| | |
|---|---|
| The Runaway Scrape | 411 |
| Marching Alone | 422 |
| Fortuna in a Frolic | 434 |
| From Intrigue to War | 454 |
| The Mexican Polka | 462 |
| The Ordeal of Peace | 481 |
| Gold Fever | 496 |
| Trying Conclusions | 508 |
| Mesilla, USA | 518 |

## PART VI
### ALASKA

| | |
|---|---:|
| Young Russia Greets Young America | 533 |
| Winning Walrussia | 547 |
| CONCLUSION: The Scramble for America | 563 |
| Notes | 573 |
| List of Illustrations | 637 |
| Acknowledgements | 639 |
| Index | 641 |

INTRODUCTION

# 'The Decisive Fact in the Modern World'

> In America, the geography is sublime, but the men are not;
> the inventions are excellent, but the inventors one is
> sometimes ashamed of. The agencies by which events so
> grand as the opening of California, of Texas, of Oregon, and
> the junction of the two oceans, are effected, are paltry,
> – coarse selfishness, fraud and conspiracy; and most
> of the great results of history are brought about by
> discreditable means.
>
> RALPH WALDO EMERSON

It is often said that America is an idea, not a country. For seven years after the Declaration of Independence in 1776, that was quite literally the case. In that period, the United States had no internationally recognized boundaries, no exact limits, no defined territory over which it was sovereign. It had claims, of course – but many would-be states have claims. The United States was still an aspiration, not a territorial entity.

Then something remarkable happened. In 1783, the United States not only obtained borders but it began to expand at an astonishing rate. In the years between 1783 and 1867, the United States went from an idea to a country of some 3.6 million square miles.[1] Averaged out, the United States grew at a rate of 42,000 square miles a year, adding territory equivalent to the land mass of Bulgaria each year, every year, for eighty-four years. Put another way, the United States expanded by 115 square miles a day for some 31,000 days. In the process, it exploded out of its original confines on the eastern seaboard, breaching the Appalachians, the Mississippi Valley, the Great Plains, the Rockies, and extending its reach to the Rio Grande, the Florida Keys and the Bering Strait, eventually straddling two oceans and commanding some of the most agriculturally, mineralogically and strategically valuable lands on the planet.

Was the United States' expansion unprecedented? For many countries expanded in the eighteenth and nineteenth centuries. Belgium claimed control of the Congo, which was eighty times the size of its colonizer. Britain established an empire in India of some 1.8 million square miles. Over the course of several centuries, Imperial Russia – the country that contemporaries most frequently compared to the United States for its geographical sprawl – expanded eastwards at a rate of twenty square miles a day, commanding at its peak 8.8 million square miles, stretching from Warsaw to Vladivostok.

But the United States' achievement was not just to expand its borders but to *settle* the vast new lands it acquired. There are few Belgians in Congo today or Britons in India. The Russian far east is almost empty. There are 38 million people living between Kamchatka and the Urals. That many people live in the state of California alone.

Even those countries where European powers made conscious attempts to settle large white populations could not compete with the United States. In 1900, 10 million people lived in Canada, New Zealand and Australia combined. That same year, 76 million people populated the United States, 48 million of them living in states and territories that had not been a part of the Thirteen Colonies.

Today the United States is the pre-eminent global power. Its economy is the largest and the most dynamic. Its military is the most powerful and the best-equipped. It has exported not just its technologies and its corporate brands, but also its manners, norms and habits of commercial, political and economic organization. The United States' pervasive influence has made English the global vernacular and has brought American fashions, cinema, music and food to every corner of the planet. It has become the arbitrator of international affairs. In the twentieth century alone, the United States determined the outcome of two world wars, confronted and ultimately faced down the Communist bloc, rebuilt Europe via the Marshall Plan and brought it peace through NATO. Elsewhere the United States' influence has been less benign but no less decisive. For better or for worse, it remains today the only nation capable of projecting power anywhere in the world.

In its ambition, influence and sheer scale, the modern United States might feel far removed from the world of the nineteenth century, when settlers travelling by foot and on horseback, in wagons and on rafts, spread out across the North American continent. But the one could not exist without the other. The creation of the continental United States in the nineteenth century was the necessary precondition for the United States' emergence as a global superpower in the twentieth. For that reason alone, the expansion of the United States between 1783 and 1867 was arguably the most consequential development of the modern era. The story of those eighty-four years is the subject of this book.

This massive upheaval was once recognized as one of the most remarkable events in history. In an Independence Day speech given in 1870, Vice President Schuyler Colfax summarized what the United States had achieved:

> From a territorial area of less than nine hundred thousand square miles, the Union has expanded into over four millions and a half\*
> – fifteen times larger than that of Great Britain and France combined – with a shore-line, including Alaska, equal to the entire circumference of the earth, and with a domain within these lines far wider than that of the Romans in their proudest days of conquest and renown.

Walt Whitman, reflecting on these words in *Democratic Vistas* (1871), marvelled at this 'copious, sane, gigantic offspring' of the American Revolution.

What made the achievement even more awe-inspiring was that it seemed to have been prophesied. On the eve of the revolution, Philip Freneau had foreseen, in his ode 'The Rising Glory of America', the day when Americans would 'spread Dominion to the north, and south, and west/Far from th' Atlantic to Pacific shores'. A decade later, with independence won, Thomas Jefferson was already telling friends that 'our

---

\* Colfax misspoke and added an additional million square miles to the United States.

confederacy must be viewed as the nest from which all America, North and South is to be peopled'. Gouverneur Morris, who wrote the preamble to the Constitution, agreed, declaring his belief that 'all North America must at length be annexed to us – happy, indeed, if the lust of dominion stop there'.[2]

And it happened.

In 1872 Uriah Smith documented the stages by which this process had unfolded since America first established its borders in 1783. There was the 900,000 square miles of the Louisiana Purchase, obtained in 1803. Florida – 60,000 square miles – acquired from Spain in 1821. Oregon, partitioned between Britain and the United States, brought 300,000 square miles into the Union. Texas, California, New Mexico and Arizona, together some 945,000 square miles, taken from Mexico between 1845 and 1854. Alaska, bought from the Russian Empire in 1867, added another 585,000 square miles. In less than a century, the United States had grown to encompass 3.6 million square miles – or, as Smith put it, 'about four-ninths of all North America, and more than one-fifteenth of the whole land surface of the globe'.

Even sober minds could not restrain their wonder at what America had accomplished. 'Three hundred years is a brief interval in the long epoch of human history,' historian Charles Morris wrote in 1899, 'yet within that short period the United States has developed from a handful of hardy men and women, thinly scattered along our Atlantic coast, into a vast and mighty country, peopled by not less than seventy-five millions of human beings ... It began as a dwarf; it has grown into a giant.' Overseas observers were no less impressed by the speed and scale of America's growth – and did not miss its implications. German Chancellor Otto von Bismarck declared the settling of the North American continent to be 'the decisive fact in the modern world'.

In the twenty-first century, this history has been obscured by the United States' successful coherence as a nation. America is so confident that it carries itself with an air of inevitability, as though it is only natural that it should occupy so vast a land mass. History tells a different story. But accessing this history requires us to look at the map with new eyes. The modern continental United States did not spring into existence in 1776 fully formed. It was assembled in discrete phases over the course of a century and at the expense of other powers and other peoples. To understand this history and to appreciate its significance requires us to disassemble the United States into its component parts and to study each in turn. This disrupts a conventional chronological narrative, but it also deepens our understanding of one of the great developments in global history.

Titles matter, and the title of this book has a double meaning which captures the fact that this immense historical process took place at two levels – high and low – at the same time, and that these dual forces worked upon one another to propel America's epochal continental expansion.

The familiar use of the word 'scramble' refers to imperial rivalry for land and pre-eminence, most famously used to describe the territorial feeding frenzy that occurred in Africa in the late nineteenth century. The term can be usefully applied to what happened in North America in these years. Although the United States' westward expansion would subsequently be whitewashed and presented as preordained by Fate and Providence, the reality is that it was contingent. For the better part of a century, American politicians, diplomats and generals worked to push their nation's borders outwards. They used all the means at their disposal while they wrestled with forces beyond their control. The mechanics of this process – the battles, the bush wars, the endless diplomatic negotiations, the scrutinizing of maps and charts, the legislative dramas, the financial crashes, the unlikely influence of distant crises on local circumstance, the peculiar mix of grand impersonal forces with personal foibles and random chance – are recognizably the same as those which have hastened the rise and fall of empires throughout history.

Those dead statesmen, could they talk to us now, might protest that they were building a nation, not an empire. I leave it to the reader to judge. But viewing it through an imperial lens is useful because the United States operated in a world of empires. All the principal actors on the world stage were empires and acted accordingly. Situating the creation of the continental United States within this global, imperial context allows us to see vividly how territorial expansion was moulded by decisions in London, Paris, St Petersburg and Madrid, as well as those in Washington.

Watching the young nation navigate the shoals and eddies of European great-power politics might lead us to conclude charitably that the United States acted imperially out of necessity rather than desire – but it acted imperially by choice, as well. As will become apparent over the course of this book, Americans used the language of empire, wielded the tools of imperialism and realized the creation of an American imperium. In many ways, the American achievement was so successful that it set the bar for subsequent imperial gambits. The Scramble for America foreshadowed the Scramble for Africa.

The Zulu king Cetshwayo kaMpande is supposed to have said of the British imperial process that 'first comes the trader, then the missionary – then, the Red Soldier'. His analysis on the creeping, incremental nature of empire as seen from the ground holds true in North America, as does the variety of imperial actors. But to this cast we must add a fourth figure: the settler.

The United States was a settler empire first and foremost. And on the American frontier the scramble was not a metaphor. It was just that: a wild rush for land whose violence and avarice impressed itself upon everyone who was witness to it. No description of the pell-mell manner in which the American frontier was discovered, settled and advanced can compare with Pierre-Clément de Laussat's account of what he saw in early-nineteenth-century Louisiana:

> Wherever the Anglo-Americans settle, land is fertilized and progress is rapid. There is always a group of them who act as trailblazers, going some fifty leagues in the American wilderness ahead of the settlers. They are the first to migrate to a new area. They clear, populate it, and then push on again and again without any purpose other than to open the way for new settlers. Those who thus forge ahead into unknown places are called backwoodsmen. They set up their temporary shanties, fell and burn trees, kill the Indians or are killed by them, and disappear from this land … relinquishing to a more stable farmer the land which they had begun to clear. When a score or so of such new colonists have congregated into one location, two printers arrive – one a federalist, the other an antifederalist – then the doctors, then the lawyers, and then the fortune seekers. They drink toasts, nominate a speaker, set up a town, and raise many children.

Finally, they advertise the sale of vast tracts of land, attracting and deceiving as many land buyers as possible. They exaggerate the population figures so that they quickly reach the sixty thousand souls entitled to form an independent state and be represented in Congress. And so another star appears on the flag of the United States!

It is useful to encounter Laussat's summary of the settler dynamic now, as we shall see what he describes play out many times in the chapters ahead. What Laussat captures that is absent from many literary, cinematic and romantic accounts of the American West is the connection between settlement, land accumulation and political organization.

It would be possible to write a history exclusively about the settler experience of continental expansion. Similarly, it would be possible to write a history exclusively about the diplomatic and political dimensions of America's territorial growth. But this would create an artificial distinction between the two. The reality, as Laussat recognized, was that the two were mixed in with one another. Settlers were soldiers, political actors and diplomatic pawns. The arrival of American settlers in any great numbers – even the prospect of their arrival – was almost always the prelude to a geopolitical crisis of some kind. 'Where others send invading armies,' one Mexican official observed in 1830, '[the Americans] send their colonists.'

At the same time, American generals, diplomats and politicians were not above the fray. Far from being isolated from the chaotic world of the frontier, many if not most of the major figures in the first century of American life (and many of the minor ones too) were profoundly involved in and shaped by the process of continental expansion. Some fought in the wars of American expansion. Some profited through speculative land schemes. Some represented western states and furthered western interests. Some of the most famous names in American history – George Washington, Andrew Jackson, Abraham Lincoln – did all three.

The frontier was where the United States' fortunes as an independent power and its future as a superpower were determined. It was also peopled by Americans who were both aware of their world-historical role and completely absorbed in the business of personal advancement. It is in their stories, as well as in the stories of the native peoples,

Mexican civilians, French furriers, South American revolutionaries, British Marines and black slaves who were drawn into the vortex of continental expansion, that we can find the humanity and the dynamism, as well as the pity and the tragedy, of the Scramble for America.

In the final telling, this is a book about land. For that reason, it is organized by geography rather than by strict chronology. Linear chronological histories of American expansion have their merits. But by prioritizing place over time, my hope is that we can gain a deeper appreciation of why and how America came to occupy its now familiar shape. It is organized into six parts, with each representing a geographical focus of American empire-building. It begins with the first swathe of territory the United States coveted and incorporated – the Ohio Valley, secured in 1783 – and ends with the last – Alaska, purchased in 1867. In between, we will look successively at Louisiana, Florida, Oregon and finally the Southwest, and so will be moving continuously forward in time even as we delve back to uncover the deep history of America's continental empire.

# PART I

# THE OHIO COUNTRY

Whoever takes control of the Ohio and the Lakes will become sole and absolute lord of America.

JAMES MAURY, 1750S

# Mr Washington Goes to Ohio

As dawn broke and first light began to trickle through the dripping forest canopy, a tall young man emerged out of the gloom onto a rocky outcrop. His black tricorn hat and red and blue coat marked him out as an officer of the Virginia Regiment. His round, complacent features signalled his youth and inexperience. The fatigue in his eyes spoke of the long, soaking march he had just completed. In the woods around him fifty men took up position. From the high ground, the officer looked down into the hollow beneath, where a French camp was stirring to life. Some of the soldiers still lay wrapped in their blankets; others were lighting fires and preparing breakfast. As darkness lifted, they became aware of their encirclement. Muskets were readied, words exchanged. What happened next is not clear. In the British account, the French fired first. In the French telling, their commander, Ensign Jumonville, attempted to parley with the Virginians, only to be silenced by a volley of bullets. Whatever the exact order of events, within minutes both sides were firing, the crack and whistle of musketry shattering the silence of the forest. The French had the worse of the exchange and soon broke and fled into the treeline. As they scattered into the woods their path was intercepted by the Virginians' Indian allies, who charged out of cover with their tomahawks raised. The French soldiers fled back into the glade and begged the Virginians for quarter. Several were killed and scalped while they pleaded for mercy. Presently the Virginians restored order. The massacre had left eight Frenchmen dead and twenty-two taken prisoner. Identifying the Virginian commander, Jumonville began to remonstrate with him. His party was there, he insisted, for peaceful purposes. The Virginians had attacked a diplomatic mission. What, if anything, his counterpart said in response is not known. But their discussion was summarily concluded when one of the Indians stepped out of the forest and approached the French officer. He was Tanaghrisson, a Seneca who held the title of Half King. Tanaghrisson knew Jumonville. 'Thou art not yet dead, my father,' he said to the young Frenchman. Then, in the words of one of the colonial soldiers present, the Half King lifted his tomahawk and 'split the head of the French Captain ... took out his brains, and washed his hands with them and then scalped him'.

It was 28 May 1754 and George Washington had just started a world war.[1]

## THE WESTERN WORLD

The fateful meeting of Ensign Jumonville, the Half King Tanaghrisson and Major George Washington took place deep in the forests of western Pennsylvania, fifty miles south-east of the forks of the Ohio and in the dead centre of a geopolitical crisis. At the forks, the Allegheny River flows in from the north-east from its headwaters in central Pennsylvania. There it is joined by the Monongahela, approaching from the south-east and its own origins in the Appalachians. At their juncture, they unite to form the Ohio River that rolls south-west across the American continent for a thousand miles until it reaches the Mississippi.

The Ohio was one of the wonders of the eighteenth-century world. The French called it the Beautiful River for its stately pace and charming setting. The British prized its navigation. Broad, deep and even, the Ohio was navigable for boats of any shape and size. For all its inhabitants the Ohio was a great meeting place of waters. As it rolled out of western Pennsylvania towards the Mississippi, along a path that encompasses the modern states of West Virginia, Ohio, Kentucky, Indiana and Illinois, the Ohio welcomes into its channel a host of other waterways. From the north flow in the Muskingum, the Scioto, the Miami and the Wabash; from its southern bank enter the Great Kanawha, the Kentucky, the Cumberland and the Tennessee. Combined, the Ohio and all its tributaries drain 200,000 square miles. Its waterways connected the Mississippi Valley with the Appalachian Ridge, the Great Lakes with the Gulf Plain. In between, watered by the innumerable creeks and streams that fed this great river system, lay some of the most fertile land on the planet, covered with inches of pristine top soil, unploughed, unspoiled and, in the imaginations of the Europeans hovering about its fringes, uninhabited. On its plateaus grew ash and oak, hickory and walnut. In its meadows were cherry and beech, elms and aspen. Fish filled its rivers and in the great hunting grounds of Kentucky roamed deer, turkey and buffalo.

'No part of the globe is blessed with a more healthful air, or climate,' wrote one Englishman, than 'the country on both sides of the Ohio.' Another described it as 'the most healthy, pleasant, commodious, and fertile spot of earth known to European people'. The French and the British called it the Ohio Country. The Americans called it simply 'the western world'.[2]

In Paris and London the Ohio posed a problem. By 1750 the eastern half of the American continent was split between the French and the British. The French possessions were divided between Louisiana – which stretched along the path of the Mississippi River from New Orleans to a patchwork of trading posts in Illinois – and New France

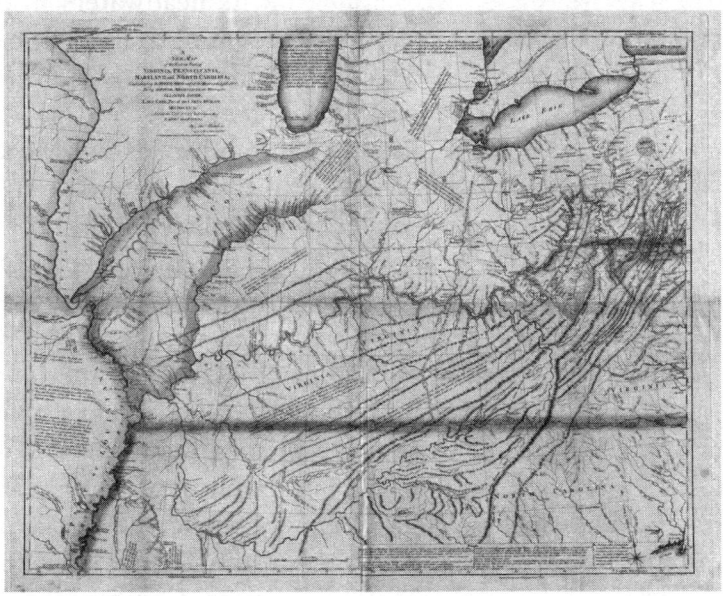

*William Hutchins' map of the western world with the Ohio River at its centre.*

(what is now Canada) where colonists had settled along the St Lawrence and had begun to fan out across the Great Lakes.

In between the French settlements was the Ohio Valley. And the only thing separating the Ohio from the British settlements along the Atlantic coastline were the Appalachian Mountains. This was a formidable barrier. Stretching along the back of the British settlements, the Appalachians had only two natural passes – the Mohawk River in New York and the Cumberland Gap in south-western Virginia – and were otherwise impassable for boats and wagons. And there should have been no need for the British to cross the mountains. Twenty years before, they had scarcely left the tidewater. But as Benjamin Franklin had observed in 1751, the colonies were booming. Their population doubled every twenty-five years. As the coast was settled, the frontier had pushed westwards to the foothills of the Appalachians. If, as seemed inevitable, the British began moving in numbers across the mountains, they would naturally head to the forks of the Ohio. Once established there, the British would flood the valley with settlers and drive a wedge between Louisiana and New France. The loss of the forks would be the prelude to the loss of French America. An entire continent was at stake.[3]

British fears were the mirror image of French ones. In London, French dominance of the Ohio Valley was intolerable for several reasons. By uniting their possessions in New France and Louisiana, the French would become a permanent threat to their interests on the continent. Additionally, the rationale for holding the American colonies was to have a captive market for British manufactures. If the tide of settlement was halted at the Appalachians on account of the French, then, so the theory went, the colonists 'would be compell'd to convert their attention and industry to manufactures'. In so doing, the once passive consumers of domestic industry would become competitors with the mills of Lancashire and Derbyshire. This would upset the entire system of imperial finance and, in the dismal reasoning of the day, spell the doom of the British Empire. For the British as well as the French, the fate of their empire would be determined at the forks of the Ohio River.[4]

* * *

Caught in between, as the ambitions and interests of the two great powers converged on their homeland, were the native peoples of the Ohio Valley. The region had been settled for two millennia. In the eighteenth century, the peoples of the Ohio were still processing the trauma of European contact which had severely depopulated the Ohio Valley. But by mid-century it was the scene of native immigration from all sides. Cherokee came northwards out of the Smoky Mountains into Kentucky. Mascouten and Kickapoo arrived from the west, settling along the Wabash River alongside the Miami from Michigan. The Wyandots emerged from the Great Lakes and settled on the Sandusky. The Shawnee settled in central Ohio along the Scioto, while the Delaware – who arrived fleeing the arrival of Europeans in Pennsylvania – settled near the forks. In addition, there were large numbers of Iroquois (called Mingo in the Ohio Valley), as well as scatterings of tribes from the Great Lakes: Ottawa, Ojibwe, Abenaki, Potawatomi and Chippewa.

For all their diversity, in absolute numbers the Indians of the Ohio Valley were relatively few. By one (generous) estimate, the entire Ohio Country could supply 10,000 warriors. Some of the larger tribes had only 500 warriors. Many of the smaller tribes amalgamated into confederacies to prevent their disappearance altogether. This did little to reduce the complexity of Indian politics. In theory, the Iroquois controlled the Ohio Country through designated Half Kings like Tanaghrisson. In practice, Iroquois control was notional and local tribes acted independently. There were also divides among native populations and differing degrees of acculturation to European life. Moravian missionaries worked the valley, and by 1750 hundreds of Ohio Indians lived in Christian communities like that at Gnadenhutten and practised European-style agriculture. Most Indians still kept to the old ways: hunting in Kentucky in the autumn and winter and tending to gardens of beans, squash and pumpkins in the spring and summer.

All native peoples, however, used European guns, European powder and European textiles. The unscrupulous traders that provided these goods were the beachhead of European influence in the Ohio Country and a salutary reminder of the costs of European infiltration into the valley. If there was one belief that united all the Indians along the Ohio, it was that both the French and the British had to be resisted. As one Iroquois explained to a Frenchman in 1750, the Indians 'on the beautiful river' were 'a Republic composed of all sorts of Nations' formed of Indians who once 'lived near you'. They had fled into the Ohio Valley to escape European encroachment. Now they found themselves in the teeth of a great-power conflict whose origins and purpose they only vaguely understood. 'You tell me to distrust the English; the English say the same to me of you,' the speaker noted, 'and this has led me to remain neutral.'

This sentiment was typical of native attitudes. As a matter of course the Ohio Indians avoided long-term alliances with either side, instead preferring to let the Europeans fight among themselves. It was illogical to fight and die to help one or other party settle their country. What they wanted was to be left alone.[5]

The Indians watched with close interest as the British and the French raced to secure the forks. The French moved first, dispatching an officer named Blainville to explore the country in 1749. The British claim was pushed most actively by Virginia. In 1750, the Virginians built a storehouse at Wills Creek on the eastern flank of the Appalachians, one hundred miles from the forks of the Ohio. The next year they blazed a trail across the mountains to Redstone Creek on the Monongahela. That same year a veteran Virginia backwoodsman named Christopher Gist went on two consecutive tours of the Ohio Valley. Gist visited Indian villages across the region, marching in behind the British flag, handing out gifts and inviting the residents to attend a conference he was organizing the following spring. That meeting went ahead at Logstown in May 1752 and produced a treaty which granted the Virginians the right to build a fort at the forks of the Ohio. In 1753, the Virginians crossed the mountains and built a storehouse on Redstone Creek. The forks were now in sight.

The arrival of the Marquis Duquesne as governor of New France in 1752 reinvigorated the French. In the spring of 1753 Duquesne began building a series of forts along the approaches to the forks of the Ohio. When London learned of the French actions, the governor of Virginia, Robert Dinwiddie, was given instructions to check the French advance. Dinwiddie responded by writing a strongly worded letter reminding the French that 'the lands upon the River Ohio' were 'notoriously known to be the property of the Crown of Great Britain' and requesting their departure from the King's territory. Dinwiddie was casting around for a messenger to carry the letter into the Ohio Country when, in October 1753, George Washington rode into Williamsburg and volunteered for the mission.[6]

## AMBITION AND NECESSITY

On Halloween 1753, Washington left Williamsburg in the company of Jacob van Braam, his interpreter for the coming encounter with the French. It took them two weeks to travel up to Wills Creek. This obscure stream emptying into the Potomac in the far north-west of Maryland was the key to the Ohio Country. Nestled in the eastern flank of the Appalachians, Wills Creek was close to an important mountain pass. 'This Gap is the nearest to Potomac River of any in the Allegheny Mountains,' Christopher Gist had written in his account of the country the year prior, 'and is accounted one of the best.' The mountains along the route were considerable and the path still 'very full of old Trees & Stones', but it offered a direct path to the Monongahela River and 'with some Pains might be made a good Waggon Road'. Gist was at the storehouse on Wills Creek when Washington arrived and was recruited into his party along with four other men who would serve variously as guides, bodyguards and servants for the twenty-one-year-old Virginian. Washington would depend heavily upon them. He had never gone across the mountains. And although he held the rank of major in the Virginia militia, he had never seen war or led men in battle. He was about to march through ice and snow into an unknown country filled with suspicious Indians and hostile Frenchmen. The little party departed Wills Creek on 15 November. Travelling west, they climbed up to 3,000 feet and within twenty miles had left the Potomac watershed behind and crossed the Appalachian Ridge. George Washington had entered the western world.[7]

Their immediate destination was the Great Crossing of the Youghiogheny River, the principal tributary of the Monongahela, and only thirty-four miles from Wills Creek. Reaching it on the 17th, they ignored its northerly course and continued westwards, climbing again across Laurel Ridge until they reached a plateau known as the Great Meadows. Continuing onwards, they crossed the Youghiogheny again before coming to the mouth of Turtle Creek on the Monongahela, at a site where a frontiersman named John Frazier had established a smithy.

They pressed on. The smaller streams had frozen but the Monongahela was swollen. On 23 November Washington emerged from the forests and gazed upon the forks of the Ohio.

'A fort at the forks,' he wrote in his journal, would 'have the entire command of the Monongahela, which runs up to our settlements and

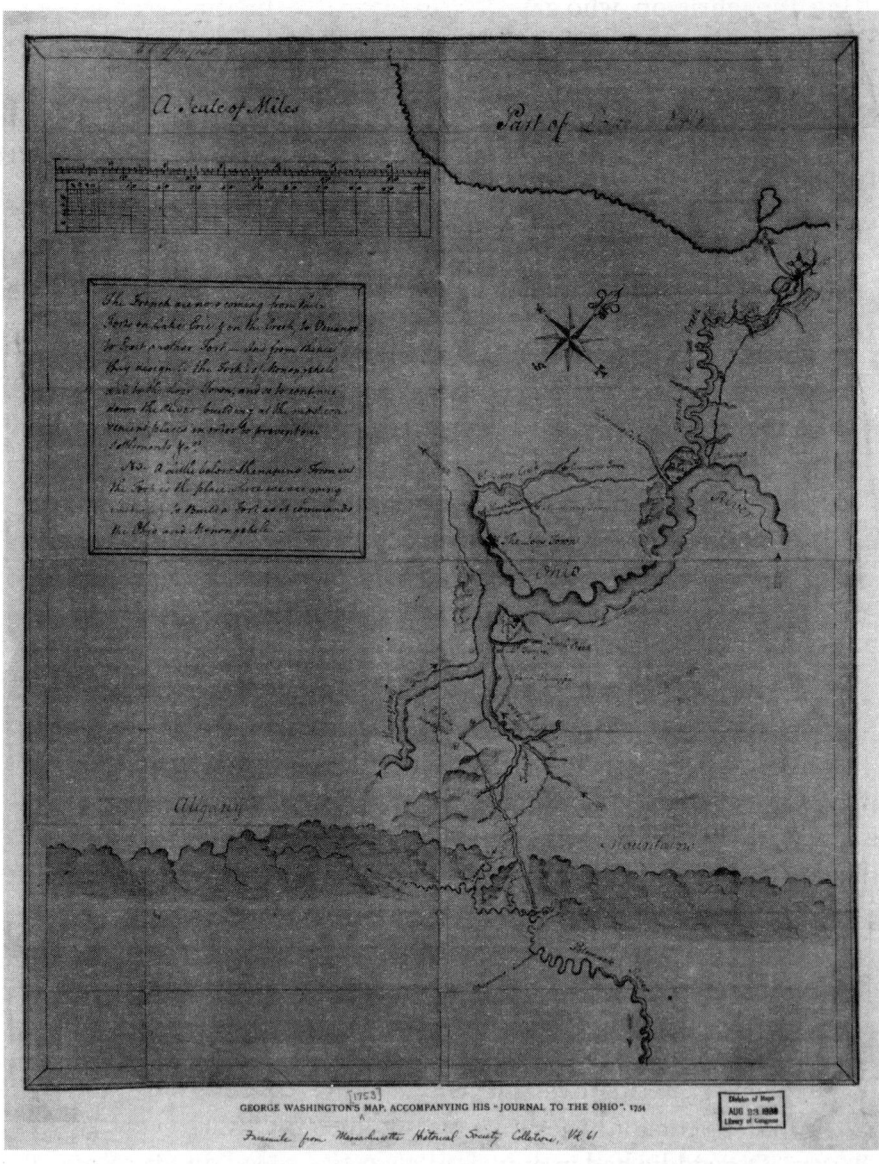

*A map of the Ohio Country drawn by George Washington in 1754.*

is extremely well designed for water carriage as it is of a deep, still nature.' But all this was still theoretical. A few miles south of the river was Logstown and the real power in the country: the Indians of the Ohio Valley. At Logstown he was ushered into a longhouse, where he explained his mission to the chiefs present. Among them was the Half King Tanaghrisson, who gave Washington a fascinating account of his dealings with the French. He had visited the French fort at Venango and reprimanded them for their intrusion. The Ohio, he explained, had been designated as the 'place of residence' for the Indians by the 'Great Being above'. He gave the French commander a belt of wampum and asked him to withdraw. 'Child, you talk foolish,' the officer replied, flinging the wampum belt to the ground. 'It is my Land, and I will have it.'

They stayed a week at Logstown and it was not until 30 November that Washington, Tanaghrisson and the rest of the party departed for Venango. Four days later they sighted the French colours. The men there said he would have to deliver his message to their commander at Fort Le Boeuf, upriver. That evening they treated the young colonial officer to dinner and liberal quantities of wine. In their cups they revealed to Washington 'that it was their absolute Design to take Possession of the Ohio, and by G— they would do it', and do it soon. A week later he was at Fort Le Boeuf, where he delivered his letter. While he waited for a response, Washington counted two hundred canoes stacked by the riverbank outside the palisade – proof that the French would soon make their play for the forks.

Two days later the French gave their reply in the form of a sealed letter for Dinwiddie's eyes only. Washington hastened back to Virginia. On his return over the mountains Washington came across a Virginian named William Trent and a train of packhorses bound for the forks. They carried with them construction materials for the fort the Indians had said they could build at the Treaty of Logstown. The race for control of the Ohio was entering its final furlong.[8]

By mid-January, Washington was huddled with Dinwiddie in Williamsburg, poring over the French letter. The French reply was a foregone conclusion: they had no intention of ceding the Ohio to Britain. Dinwiddie had in any event already decided on his own course of action. William Trent was already across the mountains. The French were on the verge of moving on the forks. Washington had done his bit to scout out the French position and to go through the motions of diplomacy. Now it was time for war. Dinwiddie made Washington a lieutenant colonel and sought to recruit several hundred men for an expedition to the forks. He dispatched officer's commissions to men already in the Ohio Country, including a captaincy for Trent, with instructions 'to keep possession of His Majesty's lands on the Ohio'. He sent out letters to the other colonies calling for support. He prepared for a new round of treaty negotiations with the Ohio Indians. When Washington had trouble raising the regiment, Dinwiddie authorized a grant of 200,000 acres of land to be distributed among men who enlisted for the mission.[9]

On 2 April, Washington marched out of Alexandria at the head of 160 men. Dinwiddie had assured him more would come in the following months. In the meantime he was under instructions to 'restrain' anyone who might obstruct Trent's construction work at the forks, 'and in case of resistance to make prisoners of or kill and destroy them'. By 22 April they were at Wills Creek, where they learned from Ensign Edward Ward that the contest was already over. The French had won. Ward had been with Trent at the forks when, on 17 April, 500 Frenchmen in canoes and pirogues arrived with eighteen cannon in tow. Heavily outnumbered, Ward surrendered the fort and led his men back to Virginia. The French destroyed the British fort and replaced it with a new structure, Fort Duquesne. There was a tantalizing detail appended to this otherwise gloomy report. Trent and Ward had been aided at the forks by Tanaghrisson. In a bid to secure his friendship, they had given him the honour of laying the first plank when construction began. He was with them when the French evicted the Virginians from the fort, and as they departed, Tanaghrisson 'stormed greatly against the French' who had humiliated him once more.[10]

If the Half King's pride was bruised, so too was Washington's. 'The heroic spirit of every free-born English man' was offended by the French action, he wrote from Wills Creek, and it now fell to Virginia to 'rescue from the invasions of a usurping enemy, our Majesty's property, his dignity and land'. Washington led his force across the mountains, reaching the Great Crossing of the Youghiogheny on 23 May. As soon as he re-entered the western world the pace of action quickened.

Reaching the Great Meadows, Washington met Christopher Gist, who had spotted signs of French incursions in the area. Missives from Tanaghrisson began to pour in with intelligence on French movements. Then, on the evening of 27 May, Tanaghrisson sent another letter. He had traced a French raiding party to 'a gloomy hollow' only a few miles from Washington's position. Washington immediately broke camp and headed for a rendezvous with the Half King. Marching in the black of night through a furious downpour, they held council with Tanaghrisson and then set out in search of the French. As dawn broke they arrived at the rocky outcrop overlooking the French camp. The Americans readied their muskets. Their Mingo allies circled round the French camp and took up their position in the woods.[11]

What exactly Washington thought as he watched Tanaghrisson wash his hands in the brain matter of Ensign Jumonville later that morning is unclear. But an examination of the documents on Jumonville's body quickly revealed that he had, in fact, been on a peaceful mission to deliver a letter to the Virginians – much as Washington had done the previous winter. Washington had just presided over the murder of a captive diplomat. His immediate course of action was to retreat back to the Great Meadows, where he oversaw construction of a fort. Small, poorly built and poorly situated, the meagre structure was deservedly named Fort Necessity.

In late June, Coulon de Villiers, brother of the murdered Jumonville, set out with 700 men to seek vengeance. By this stage, Washington's men were so run down that barely three-quarters of his force was fit to fight. When, in early July, the French finally appeared at the Great Meadows, they outnumbered the Virginians two to one. De Villiers moved his men into the woods, where they harassed the Virginians from cover. As the fort was too small to house them all, the majority of Washington's men fought from shallow trenches outside the palisade. In the driving rain these trenches were soon half flooded. The Virginians' powder dampened and would not fire. They could not even see their enemy, who 'from every little rising, tree, stump, stone and bush kept up a constant, galling fire upon us'. Thirty men died and the rest expected to be massacred when the final assault came. Around sunset, discipline broke and some of the men raided the supply of rum and began to get drunk. Night fell; Washington mulled his options.

Then, around eight in the evening, an unexpected summons to parley came from the French lines. De Villiers was low on ammunition and supplies and fearful of being surprised by Indians loyal to England. He decided to extract Washington's submission on paper. By the light of a candle Van Braam translated the French terms, as Washington sat in his makeshift fort, cold, damp and surrounded by inebriated militiamen. Washington signed and the next morning – 4 July – his men marched out behind the British colours. As a courtesy De Villiers let them keep their muskets and a single artillery piece. The rest of their supplies were abandoned. The French had shot all their horses the day before, and so the ragged survivors of Washington's first military campaign traipsed back to Virginia on foot. While they made their way over the mountains the French demolished all remaining traces of English presence in the region. Fort Necessity, the storehouse at Red Stone Creek, even John Frazier's smithy – all were put to flame. When Dinwiddie learned of the debacle, he disbanded the Virginia Regiment and offered Washington the rank of captain in a smaller outfit. Washington declined. Instead he returned to Mount Vernon, where he minded his farm, organized his affairs and wrote long self-exculpatory letters justifying his disastrous turn in the Ohio Country.[12]

## DISASTER AND REDEMPTION

News of the humiliation at Fort Necessity reached London in September 1754. 'All North America will be lost if these practices are tolerated,' declared the prime minister, the Duke of Newcastle. Britain would not suffer France's claim to the continent to go unchallenged. Newcastle opted for massive retaliation. A grand expeditionary force was assembled. Several thousand men aboard three ships of the line and a flotilla of transports were readied off the coast of Ireland. At stake 'in so great an affair', one contemporary wrote, was nothing less than 'the settling [of] the boundaries in North America'.[13]

The man chosen to lead this fateful venture was holidaying in Italy when he received news of his appointment. Little in the biography of Major General Edward Braddock marked him out as the obvious choice for a campaign on the American frontier. The son of a career officer, Braddock had followed his father into the Coldstream Guards as a teenager. It took him twenty-six years to make the rank of captain and thereafter he had purchased his commissions. Now aged sixty, Braddock should have been preparing for retirement. Instead, on Boxing Day, 1754, he found himself in Cork, endowed with the title of commander-in-chief of all British forces in North America, carrying instructions to 'vindicate our just rights and possessions' on that continent, and preparing to board a vessel bound for Virginia. This would be Braddock's first time in America. He travelled there at the head of the largest conventional force ever sent to the colonies, with orders to clear the French out of the Ohio Country.[14]

Braddock landed in Hampton in late February 1755, where he passed a month organizing his force, squabbling with colonial officialdom and dealing with the horde of petitioners that swarmed his entourage. Among them was George Washington. Although still smarting from the indignity of his surrender at Fort Necessity, Washington could not resist the chance to burnish his reputation by association with what everyone assumed would be a swift and successful campaign against the French. His efforts were rewarded with an unpaid position as an aide-de-camp. Such matters kept Braddock in Alexandria until April, when he finally began the march west. Procuring supplies, however, proved near impossible and almost led to the expedition's abandonment. Then a celebrity came to the rescue. Marching through Maryland, Braddock ran into Benjamin Franklin, who had come from Philadelphia with 150 wagons with horses and drivers, a gift from the Pennsylvania assembly. Braddock granted him an audience during which he sketched his plan of marching over the mountains to the forks of the Ohio. 'The only danger I apprehend of obstruction to your march is from ambuscades of Indians,' Franklin observed; 'and the slender line ... which your army must make, may expose it to be attack'd by surprise in its flanks.' In his memoirs he recalled the general's response. 'He smil'd at my ignorance, and reply'd, "These savages may, indeed, be a formidable enemy to your raw American militia, but upon the king's regular and disciplin'd troops, sir, it is impossible they should make any impression."'[15]

Braddock's march on the forks was a monument to methodical soldiering and imperial hubris. At a meeting with the Ohio Indians at Wills Creek (where a new fort, Fort Cumberland, had recently been built), Braddock managed to alienate the assembled warriors, telling their leader, the Delaware Shingas, that 'the English should inhabit and inherit the land' the tribes lived on. As a consequence, when Braddock's 2,200-strong army marched out of Fort Cumberland on 10 June there were only eight Indians among them.[16]

In London Braddock had been told that the distance from Fort Cumberland to Fort Duquesne was fifteen miles. It was only after his arrival in Virginia that he learned the true distance was 120 miles. It was one thing for small groups to cross the mountain trail; it was quite another for several thousand men, hundreds of wagons and two dozen artillery pieces to make the journey. Braddock threw bodies at the problem. Hundreds of men were given axes and orders to push back the treeline. Boulders were blown up with gunpowder. Wagons and cannon were dragged up and down mountains. Visibility in the lush forest often fell to less than twenty metres, adding to the confusion and disorientation of the men on the march. Soon the army was strung out across the trail and moving painfully slowly. In exasperation, Braddock decided to split his force. He would push on with a flying column of 1,200 men while the rest of the army under Colonel Dunbar followed.

It still took this lighter force another three weeks to hack their way through the forest and over the mountains, a journey that took them across the Great Crossing of the Youghiogheny, past the ruins of Fort Necessity and near the site of Jumonville's death. This army was not just a shambling mass of men and materiel but a snapshot of colonial America and an intimation of the United States. Travelling in the vanguard with the native scouts were Christopher Gist and George Croghan, old frontier hands. In the main column were British regulars marching alongside colonials from New York, Virginia and the Carolinas. Among them was Robert Orme, Braddock's aide-de-camp, who would marry the sister of Charles Townshend, the Chancellor of the Exchequer who imposed the duties of the same name that inflamed the revolutionary crisis in the 1770s. Nearby was Thomas Gage, a junior officer in the 44th, who would be governor of Massachusetts during the Boston Tea Party and whose actions would trigger the clashes at Lexington and Concord. Elsewhere in the column was Horatio Gates, then a captain, who would defeat Burgoyne at Saratoga twenty-two years later. Further back, in the wagon train, was Daniel Morgan, a lowly teamster who would rise up to the rank of brigadier general in the Continental Army and defeat Banastre Tarleton at the Battle of

Cowpens in 1781, a pivotal juncture on the road to Yorktown. Riding alongside him was Daniel Boone, the North Carolina backwoodsman who would come to embody the spirit of the American West.[17]

George Washington was not among their number. Struck down with dysentery, he hung back from the main army and made his way across the mountains in the back of a wagon. In early July his fever broke and he hastened up the trail. He caught up with the column on 8 July, still so weak from his illness that he rode into camp with pillows strapped to his horse to keep him in the saddle. Washington's timing was fortuitous. By Braddock's reckoning they were now two days from Fort Duquesne.[18]

On the morning of 9 July, Braddock's army crossed the Monongahela, the final obstacle on the approach to Fort Duquesne, now only ten miles away. If the French were going to attack, it would be here. But to the tune of the Grenadier's March, the column crossed the river unmolested, passed the ruins of John Frazier's smithy and began to march northwards to the forks. The forest thinned and the trail passed through a pasture bordered by woodland. The soldiers moved easily through the grass and the column stretched out to over a mile in length. They were marching as they ever had, with gangs of axemen clearing out a path before the main trunk of the column, when just after midday they marched right into the approaching French force.

After some confused skirmishing, the English formed up into a line. The 250 Frenchmen and their 650 native allies – mainly Great Lakes Indians with a scattering of Iroquois and Delaware – split and ran along the flanks of the column, effectively enclosing the English in the open ground along the trail while they fired from cover in the woods. The effects were devastating. The Indian riflemen targeted the English officers, killing or wounding fifteen of eighteen in the advance party in the opening minutes of the battle. The front of the column fell back under fire and was met by the rear of the column rushing forward towards the enemy. As the ranks compressed, army discipline held, with men lining up to shoot in regular formation – in many cases shooting their own side at point-blank range. A few inconsequential salvos of artillery were fired into the treeline before the Indian sharpshooters shot down the gunners. Within an hour Braddock's army was trapped in a killing zone, enveloped in smoke, outflanked by the enemy and powerless to respond to fire from cover. Survivors later recalled that they never saw a single French or Indian soldier over the course of the entire engagement. They fought in this manner for three hours until Braddock was shot off his horse. At this point, with most of the officers dead or wounded and their commander fatally injured, discipline broke. The column fell back to the river in disarray.

As they retreated, the Indians emerged from the forest to take scalps. For English soldiers the effect was terrifying. A retreat became a rout. They 'broke and [ran] as sheep before the hounds', Washington later wrote. The men of the 44th abandoned their regimental colours, which were retrieved under fire by their chaplain. The wounded officers were left for dead, with several last seen pleading to be shot rather than left for the Indians. Among them was Braddock, who asked to borrow George Croghan's pistols so he might shoot himself. Instead, Washington came to the rescue. Using Braddock's general's sash, Washington had him lifted onto a tumbril and organized a rearguard to escort him off the battlefield and back across the river.

As the sun descended, the battle dissipated into an inglorious melee. The English continued to flee blindly back down the trail. The Virginians, who had more experience of Indian warfare, tried to conduct a fighting retreat. Meanwhile, some of the French and Indians broke into a captured supply of rum and began to celebrate their victory while their comrades took scalps from the dead and wounded. They did not press their advantage and instead retreated back to Fort Duquesne to continue the festivities. A Pennsylvanian named James Smith who was being held captive at the fort recalled seeing the victorious soldiers return loaded with booty. 'I beheld a small party coming in with about a dozen prisoners, stripped naked, with their hands tied behind their backs, and their faces and parts of their bodies blackened,' he later wrote. 'These prisoners they burned to death on the bank of the Allegheny River.'[19]

That same evening, somewhere in the forest south of Fort Duquesne, Washington rode through the night to make contact with Dunbar's reserve column. The woods were perfectly black and filled with the sounds of the wounded and the dying. 'The shocking scenes which presented themselves in this night's march are not to be described,' Washington told a biographer many decades later. The 'lamentations and cries along the road of the wounded for help … were enough to pierce a heart of adamant'. At dawn the next day he ran into Dunbar's column, informed him of the battle and conveyed instructions from

Braddock. He stayed in camp as, over the next two days, the remainder of Braddock's army drifted into camp, along with the general himself, alive but fading. Although they were not being pursued, the decision was taken by Dunbar to retire to Fort Cumberland. Before they left they destroyed their supplies, to stop them falling into enemy hands. 'Nearly 150 wagons were burnt,' one officer reported, 'the powder casks staved in a spring, the cohorns broke or buried and the shell bursted; the provisions were scattered abroad on the ground.' Once this was complete, the column continued its retreat.

On 13 July they paused at the Great Meadows. Braddock called his aides to his side. He gave Washington his sash and pistols, spoke a few final words and died. The next day Washington chose a spot for his grave and organized his funeral with all the honours the defeated army could muster. Once Braddock was lowered into the ground Washington had the entire army march over the grave to conceal it from enemy trophy hunters.[20]

On 17 July, the remnants of Braddock's army arrived back at Fort Cumberland. Now the danger was past, Washington had time to reflect. He was lucky to be alive. Several horses had been shot from beneath him during the battle and there were bullet holes in his hat and coat-tails. His fellows had been less fortunate. Two-thirds of the ninety officers at the Battle of the Monongahela were killed or wounded. Fully a third of Braddock's flying column were killed that day and another third reported injured. George Washington emerged from this American Isandlwana not just unscathed but elevated in stature. His unquestionable bravery on the battlefield and his role in organizing an orderly retreat in the days following had washed away the ignominy of Fort Necessity.[21]

Washington's redemption was timely. Braddock's defeat was the starting shot for a general war on the frontier. Along a front stretching from New York to North Carolina, Indians began raiding the settlements. In Virginia, Dinwiddie responded by appointing Washington to the command of the Virginia Regiment. From his base at Winchester, Washington was responsible for mounting a defence of the frontier. The challenge was daunting. Fort Cumberland was periodically cut off. Raiders sometimes came within twelve miles of Washington's headquarters. By day soldiers stationed at the forts could see the plumes of smoke rising in the distance as nearby farms were burned by Indian soldiers. To sow fear, native warriors would often kill their victims in the woods and then move their bodies to roads where they would be discovered. The mutilation of these corpses – one Pennsylvania captain discovered the body of one of his sergeants 'scalped and entirely stripped, and shamefully cut, so much so that his bowels were spread upon the ground' – multiplied the effect. Such methods produced terror but also deepened the enmity. 'Desolation and murder still increase,' Washington wrote in the spring of 1756, but as a last resort he knew he could depend on the 'insatiate revenge' of the backcountry populace to take the war to the Indians on their own terms. Virginia offered generous scalp bounties to civilians who killed Indians. Soon bands of scalp hunters were killing any Indian they found. This catalogue of violence broke the old pattern of social relations all along the frontier, creating lasting enmity between communities who, one settler recalled, had once been 'daily familiars'.[22]

This brutal, messy war in the colonial backcountry was far removed from the seats of power in the European capitals but would ultimately be decided in them. Remarkably, news of Braddock's defeat did not immediately precipitate a general war between France and Britain. Britain did not formally declare war on France until May 1756, almost exactly two years since Washington, Jumonville and Tanaghrisson had met in the forests of western Pennsylvania. Yet that encounter was the opening volley in a conflict that in 1756 erupted into a global war.

The Seven Years War saw a dozen combatants engage in battle over five continents as France and Britain clashed in places as far afield as India, Senegal, Cuba and the Philippines. Under the leadership of William Pitt, Britain strung together a series of victories that transformed Britain's global position. In 1759, the *annus mirabilis* of the British war effort, Pitt was unbeatable in every theatre from Madras to Guadeloupe – including in colonial America. The strategy in North America was a rerun of the Braddock campaign: secure the forks of the Ohio and then drive the French from the Great Lakes and Quebec.

In 1758 Pitt unleashed his generals on the continent. Once again Washington was summoned to serve in another British campaign in the Ohio Country, this time under Brigadier General John Forbes. As ever, Washington sought to ingratiate himself with the new British commander, presenting himself as one 'who would gladly be distinguished in some measure from the common run of provincial officers'. Washington was integrated into the war effort as a colonel leading one of the Virginia regiments, reporting to Forbes's trusted aide, Colonel Henry Bouquet. By May 1758 he was back at Fort Cumberland, where an army of 7,000 was amassing to make another assault on Fort Duquesne. Forbes and Bouquet had learned from Braddock's mistakes and over the summer and autumn of 1758 worked on the new road while also working to win over the Ohio Indians. That October the strategy bore fruit when, at the Treaty of Easton, the bulk of the Ohio tribes, including Shingas's Delaware, defected to the British. With their native allies gone, the French withdrew from Bouquet's approaching army. On the night of 24 November, the French blew up Fort Duquesne and withdrew into Canada.

The next day Washington was among the men sent to inspect the smoking ruins of the fort at the place he had been trying to conquer for four years. In a letter to Francis Fauquier, Dinwiddie's replacement as governor, Washington outlined the benefits to their colony now that the forks were in British hands. If Virginia moved swiftly to build up its presence along the Braddock Road, then it could secure the Ohio Country to itself. But 'although none can entertain a higher sense of the great importance of maintaining a post on the Ohio than myself', Washington continued, his part in the struggle for the Ohio was, for now, complete. Within a year Britain would have conquered the entirety of French North America and expelled France from the continent forever. But with Fort Duquesne in rubble, and the new Fort Pitt already rising from the ruins, Washington's war was over.[23]

# All He Surveyed

After resigning his commission in December 1758, Washington would not serve again until 1775. He was considered and ultimately chosen as commander of the Continental Army purely on the basis of his accomplishments two decades prior. The contest in the Ohio Valley seeded Washington's identity as a soldier, and Washington would carry himself as a military man for the rest of his life. That war was the moment when Washington burst into public view fully formed in the role he would diligently perform for the next forty years.

But there was another side to George Washington. While the French and Indian War was the occasion for his arrival as a public figure, Washington emerges in the documentary record almost a decade before. The first entry in the fourteen-volume collected works of George Washington is a journal he kept in the spring of 1748. It records a journey up the Potomac River in the company of some neighbours and acquaintances from his family home in Westmoreland County, Virginia. Washington was sixteen at the time; this was his first time travelling west. The party set out up the river and over the Blue Ridge Mountains, the young George in awe of the 'richness of the land' around them. As they moved further into the interior he was exposed to life on the frontier. In the afternoons they shot wild turkey, ate around the fire with (to his shock) 'neither a Cloth upon the Table nor a Knife to eat with', and slept in tents beneath the stars. One evening they were visited by an Indian war party and Washington saw his first scalp. They continued westwards, exploring the waterways near Cumberland and wandering in the eastern foothills of the Appalachian Mountains.

It was a short trip. After four weeks Washington was back at home. But the journey was filled with significance. Not only had Washington had his first taste of the frontier, not only had he walked in places that he would revisit again and again over the course of his life, but he had gained valuable experience in a profession that shaped his life and would – quite literally – shape the future United States. For his travels west were not done for pleasure but as a part of a surveying party.[1]

## A TRUE RELATION

Before Washington was a soldier he was a surveyor. The work of the surveyor, as one eighteenth-century manual put it, was to oversee 'the division and separation of *Land*'. It was hard work, requiring physical stamina and complex mathematics. Surveyors used cutting-edge technology. Washington was familiar with the surveyor's tools as his father kept a set at home. The principal instrument was Gunter's chain, named after its inventor, the seventeenth-century English polymath Edmund Gunter. The chain was an ingenious device. Made up of one hundred eight-inch links, a full chain was 66 feet long. Ten chains square enclosed one acre. Eighty chains were equal to a mile. A square mile enclosed 640 acres. The mathematics of the chain meant that surveyors could work in decimal to measure imperial.[2]

A surveyor would not do the chain work himself. A surveying party typically consisted of two chain men, a marker (who would mark trees in the area to advertise the completion of a survey) and a guide. To the surveyor was reserved the task of calculating the exact size of a plot of land. He would stand in the middle of the plot being surveyed and then use a device (normally a circumferentor) to determine the angles. The surveyor then used arithmetic to triangulate the distance between points and calculate the size of the area surveyed. Once this was done, he would write up his findings on a plane table. First he would create a 'plat', a drawing of the surveyed area with relevant topographical features marked out to scale. On the back of the plat he wrote a report which contained information including the date, the total acreage, the location and jurisdiction of the plot, and any other relevant information, which he would then sign, vouchsafing with his own name and reputation the soundness of the completed survey.

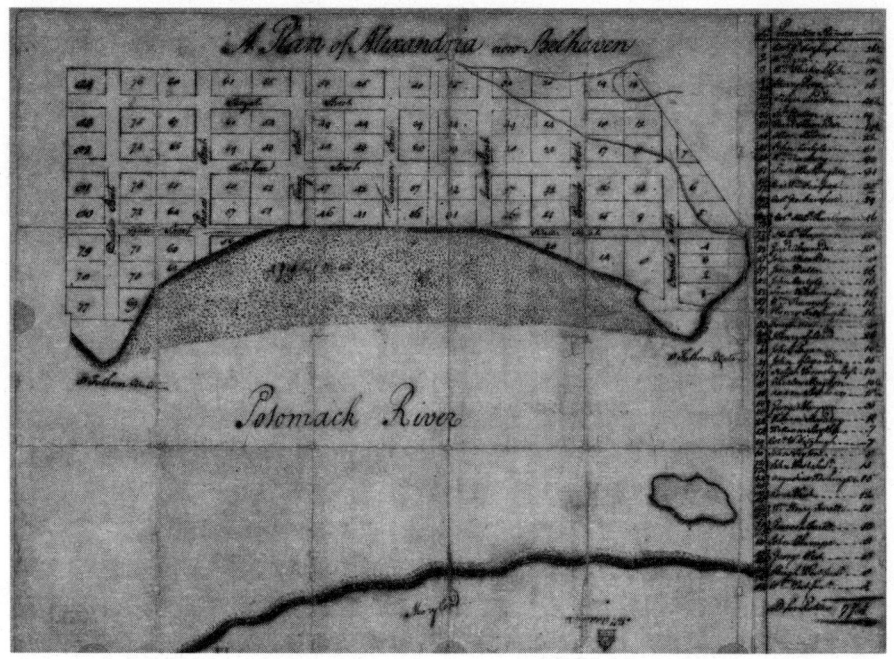

*A plan of Alexandria, Virginia produced by George Washington in his capacity as assistant surveyor.*

Washington took to surveying as a teenager, practising on his brother's turnip field. By the time he was sixteen he was being paid for his surveys and this led to the invitation to join the surveying party heading west in March 1748. That summer he returned up the Potomac for another survey. Not long afterwards he acted as assistant surveyor to John West, who was laying out the town of Alexandria. In 1749 he secured an appointment as surveyor of newly organized Culpeper County. Washington spent months at a time out in the woods conducting surveys. He had by now grown to be a sturdy young man, over six feet tall, strong, resilient, an excellent horseman – all traits that served him well as he ranged about the frontier. He enjoyed the work, though life as a surveyor on the Virginian frontier was thoroughly unglamorous. In a letter to a friend Washington complained of living 'amongst a parcel of Barbarians and an uncouth set of people' in conditions offensive to his rank and stature. 'I have not sleep'd above three Nights or four in a bed,' he wrote, 'but after walking a good deal all the day lay down before the fire upon a Little Hay Straw Fodder or bearskin whichever is to be had with Man Wife and Children like a parcel of dogs or cats & happy is he that gets the berth nearest the fire.'³

Washington endured these hardships for a reason. The surveyor's art was fundamental to sustaining and perpetuating the social order – an order into whose higher ranks Washington had been born. 'The Beame and Chaine balke no Truthes, nor blaunch untruthes,' wrote one early English surveyor. 'Take away Number, Weight, Measure, you exile Justice, and reduce and haile-up from Hell the olde and odious Chaos of Confusion.'

By establishing 'a true relation' between the dimensions of a plot of land and its legal owner the surveyor created a permanent and objective record of ownership that men of property could depend upon. Not by accident, the surveyor came to the fore as the rate of enclosure picked up in Britain. Surveyors helped landowners mark out plots and transform the commons into private property. 'He loves to see the bounds of his boundless desires,' wrote one critic of enclosure. 'Enclosures make fat beasts and lean poor people.' Defenders of enclosure saw matters differently. They described unenclosed land as 'wastes' and 'deserts', economically unproductive barrens that cried out for 'improvement' and ordered exploitation. Surveyors were the sharp edge of this process – agents of a state-sanctioned mission to make the land legible and prepare it for cultivation. 'For how could Men set down to Plant,' asked one seventeenth-century treatise on surveying, 'without knowing some Distinction and Bounds of their Land?'

All of this dovetailed neatly with the biblical injunction to be 'fruitful in the land' and with the emerging secular doctrines of the Enlightenment. In the first of his *Two Treatises of Government* (1689), John Locke defined property as something an individual had taken 'out of the state that nature hath provided' and then 'mixed his labour with'. He used the example of land, writing that 'as much land as a man tills, plants, improves, cultivates, and can use the product of, so much is his property'. Surveyors were instrumental to this process, for they converted what had been produced by the 'spontaneous hand of Nature' into something ordered and rational. Surveyors enabled the commoditization of the earth's surface. But this process was not merely economic. Locke claimed that the purpose of government was 'the preservation of property', and it followed that only men of property could participate in government. In Britain only male freeholders could vote and hold office. Political influence flowed out of ownership. 'Property is power,' as Burke would write. Civilization itself arose out of this relationship between the organized ownership of land and the orderly government of society.[4]

These ideas had special resonance in America. From the earliest days of settlement the continent was described as a 'vacant place', a 'desert Wildernesse', a 'howling desart Land ... where lands lye wast and free'. Although the language was alarming, the appeal was magnetic. Whereas 'Europe is generally full settled,' Franklin wrote in 1751, land was 'plenty in America, and so cheap as that a laboring man ... can in a short time save money enough to purchase a piece of new land sufficient for a plantation, whereon he may subsist a family.' In America a man had a route to property and political recognition.

This was especially the case in Virginia. The Puritans moved to New England and the Quakers moved to Pennsylvania to create godly communities. Men moved to Virginia for economic opportunity. In the north, land distribution was tightly controlled and farms tended to be smaller. In Virginia, land was claimed and settled with little oversight and farms tended to be expansive. In the north, the focus was on growing cereals and rearing livestock on the same plots of land. In Virginia, the focus was on cultivating tobacco, a cash crop that rapidly exhausted the soil, requiring the acquisition of new tracts of land to replace the old.* The Virginia model was attractive. In 1700 the population of the colony was 62,000. By 1770 it had grown to 583,000 – by far the largest colony and accounting for almost a quarter of the population of the Thirteen Colonies combined.[5]

This influx of settlers, combined with the prevailing pattern of landholding and land usage, pushed the frontier westwards. When George Washington's great-grandfather John Washington, the first American Washington, arrived in Virginia in 1657, settlement was still focused on

---

* Philip Fithian, a Yankee who worked as a tutor on a Virginia estate, remarked upon the wastefulness of local farming practices: 'Their Method of farming is slovenly, without any regard to continue their Land in heart, for future Crops – They plant large Quantities of Land, without any Manure, & work it very hard to make the best of the Crop, and when the Crop comes off they take away the Fences to inclose another Piece of Land for the next years tillage, and leave this a common to be destroyed by Winter & Beasts till they stand in need of it again to plough.'

the tidewater, in particular on the three peninsulas or 'necks' that jut out into Chesapeake Bay. Each neck was formed by rivers: the Virginia Peninsula was enclosed by the James and the York, the Middle Peninsula by the York and the Rappahannock, and the Northern Neck – where John established himself – by the Rappahannock and Potomac Rivers. As the population grew, settlers streamed along these rivers into the interior. As they made their way up these waterways, they encountered a peculiarity of Virginia's geology. The bedrock of eastern Virginia is softer than that in the west. At a certain point all the rivers flowing eastwards encounter this geological transition point, which over the course of millennia of erosion became marked by rapids or falls. Virginians called this the 'fall line' and the country above it the Piedmont.

By the time Washington's grandfather Lawrence died, settlers had crossed the fall line and had begun to settle the Piedmont. The Piedmont was itself bordered to the west by an even more formidable geological barrier: the Blue Ridge Mountains. But in the 1720s, when Washington's father, Augustine, was a young man, the tide of settlement crested the Blue Ridge and flowed into the Shenandoah Valley, beyond which lay the Appalachians. At the time George Washington was appointed surveyor of Culpeper County, the Shenandoah Valley was still being peopled. But Washington knew that it was only a matter of time until the Appalachians were breached and settlers began to cross into the Ohio Valley.

Washington knew this because it was the story of his family. The Washingtons were not just farmers but speculators in land and their speculations had kept pace with the frontier. As settlers arrived and went west for land, they did not find the land unclaimed. Instead, wealthy men had already purchased and surveyed the land. Once the frontier reached their landholdings, they either leased land out or sold parcels on at a profit to the new arrivals. The Washington family, like all elite Virginia families, had been engaged in this business for several generations. John had established his landholdings in the tidewater, Lawrence had added to them in the Piedmont, and Augustine had witnessed (though not participated in)* the stampede across the Blue Ridge. George understood

---

* Augustine Washington's son Lawrence, George Washington's elder brother by fourteen years, did participate in the blizzard of speculative activity in the Shenandoah Valley.

from a young age that his generation would push on and make their fortunes across the Appalachians. It was what Washingtons did.

Washington's surveying funded his early speculating in land. Washington's first survey in Culpeper County was for a tract of 400 acres owned by Richard Barnes, for which he was paid £2 3s. This was the beginning of three lucrative years of surveying work. In a single month's surveying in the spring of 1750 Washington earned £140 – a princely sum. Over the course of several years Washington took in approximately £400 from his surveying duties. He reinvested this income into the very same regions he had come to know so well through traipsing through the woods calculating angles and acreages. Soon he was ready to start buying. In October 1750 Washington purchased Dutch George's, a tract of 453 acres in the Shenandoah Valley. A few weeks later he purchased another 550 acres in Frederick County, in western Maryland. Before the year was out, Washington had returned over the Blue Ridge to purchase another sizeable tract on Bullskin Run, a tributary of the Shenandoah. Within eighteen months of becoming a surveyor Washington had bought 1,459 acres of land along the western frontier. This was just the beginning of a years-long spree. By 1752 – when he was still only twenty-one years old – Washington owned a total of 4,291 acres, an estate that did not put him at the pinnacle of the Virginian landholding elite but certainly placed him among its foothills. Washington wanted to continue scaling the mountain. That meant breaking new ground across the Appalachians.[6]

This accounts for Washington's decision in 1753 to volunteer to go west as Dinwiddie's emissary. He was motivated by more than service to the British Empire. He wanted to go west to glimpse the lands he hoped to claim for himself. His participation in the subsequent campaigns was similarly inspired. And standing on the smouldering ruins of Fort Duquesne in 1758, he looked down the river on which he sought to make his fortune – a fortune that now felt within his grasp. He was not alone. When the Seven Years War came to an end in 1763 land speculators across the country had ample reason to believe that their time had come to profit from the newly opened lands in the Ohio Valley. To their surprise and mortification, they would snatch defeat from the jaws of victory.[7]

# Long Knives

In late January 1763, news reached America that a treaty had been concluded ending the Seven Years War. The Treaty of Paris represented an extraordinary achievement for the British Empire and reformulated the balance of power across the globe. In North America Britain's dominance was now total. France ceded all its Canadian possessions to the British and agreed to hand over its forts in the Illinois Country and across the Great Lakes. The entire continent north of Florida and east of the Mississippi was now British. The contest for the Ohio Country was over.

What was a triumph for the British amounted to a disaster for the Ohio Indians. When one Delaware leader learned of the peace terms he 'was Struck dumb for a considerable time', and when he was finally convinced the news was true, commented only that the 'English [were] grown too powerful & seem'd as if they would be too Strong for God himself'. 'The Indians seem under great Concern at the Advantage the English has Gain'd, by the peace,' one merchant wrote in his journal, noting the atmosphere of distrust and anger that had pervaded the Ohio Valley ever since its inhabitants had learned of the British victory.[1]

The tension spilled over to produce a new war. On 7 May 1763, an Ottawa leader named Pontiac led an assault on Fort Detroit. The attack on Detroit signalled the beginning of a coordinated campaign to drive the British out of the Ohio Valley that became known as Pontiac's War. Blindsided by the renewed hostilities, the British commander-in-chief Jeffery Amherst instructed his subordinates to use every method available 'to Extirpate this Execrable Race'. Bouquet considered using bloodhounds to hunt the Indians. Amherst wondered whether disease might be purposefully spread among them. At Fort Pitt William Trent attempted just that. When some Indians came to meet with his commander he gave them 'two blankets and a handkerchief out of the smallpox hospital'.[2]

Such methods did nothing to slow the tempo of violence. The war continued into 1764 with raiding along the Virginia frontier and deep into Pennsylvania. The frontier reeled eastwards. The region around the forks was abandoned. Carlisle, the principal town in the south central portion of the colony, was flooded with refugees from across the Susquehanna Valley. In a particularly notorious episode, a schoolhouse in modern-day Greencastle, Pennsylvania – only one hundred miles north-west of Baltimore – was stormed by four warriors. Eight students, none yet teenagers, were killed. The schoolmaster was found dead, still clutching his Bible. Incidents like this inflamed white sentiment across the state. Having botched their original response to the fighting, the Pennsylvania legislature started offering scalp bounties in the hope of cultivating a 'spirit of enterprize against the savages'. Predictably this led to the formation of mobs of vigilantes who indiscriminately massacred any Indians they found to claim their reward – which in turn drove more Indians to take up arms in self-defence.

One group of Indians who refused to take part in the violence were the Delaware Moravian converts living at Nain and Wechquetank. They were convinced pacifists. 'If it should happen that white people want to kill us,' one told a missionary, 'I will not defend myself at all.' That August several were murdered by militiamen. As threats of violence increased in the autumn, they moved to Philadelphia for protection. For a while they seemed safe, but that winter reports arrived in the city that a militia group called the Paxton Boys had massacred some peaceful Conestoga Indians in Lancaster County. The Paxton Boys then marched on Lancaster, killed some Conestoga refugees quartered in the local jailhouse and declared their intention to travel to Philadelphia to kill the Moravians. In early February, the Paxton Boys appeared on the outskirts and for a few days the city was in turmoil, in full expectation of street-to-street fighting between the frontier posse and the city's garrison. In the end a peace was brokered and the Paxton Boys agreed to return home. In exchange, they asked that a record of their grievances be published and circulated at the city's expense. A pamphlet entitled 'A Declaration and Remonstrance of the Distressed and Bleeding Frontier Inhabitants' appeared shortly afterwards. It was a document saturated in the blood spilt by the explosion of violence produced by Pontiac's War. It called frankly for the sacrifice of the Moravians to assuage 'the Fury of the brave Relatives of the Murdered' settler families. What did it matter that these Delawares were pacifists who abjured the violence of their countrymen? 'Who ever proclaimed War with a part of a Nation,' they reasoned, 'and not with the Whole?'[3]

Pontiac's War was a desperate attempt to restore the balance of power in the Ohio Country. For decades the Ohio Indians had preserved a space between the French and the British by playing the two sides against the other. The disappearance of the French had produced total British dominance. The uprising of 1763 was a reminder that the Ohio River still belonged to native people. Many Indians believed that the British had promised the valley to them in exchange for their support during the war. One Indian negotiator recalled that fact at a meeting in August 1761. 'You know there is a line made between you & us,' he said, 'and we desire that none of the English would settle on the other side of that line.' Pontiac's War was fought to redraw that line between English and Indian settlements in British North America.[4]

The irony was that even as the war broke out, British ministers in London were contemplating just such a line. Having recently completed an immensely expensive war, they were in no mood to fund another conflict in North America. Instead they sought to conciliate the Native Americans. The British proposed drawing a line down the ridge of the Appalachian Mountains. West of it to the Mississippi River would be reserved for the Indians. No white settler could live beyond that line. No colony could grant lands beyond that line. No individual could privately negotiate with the Indians for land beyond that line. Trading with the Indians could continue under certain conditions. For the most part, the document represented a singular victory for the Indians and a galling setback to any American looking to make their fortune westwards. King George III signed the Royal Proclamation of 1763 into law that October. Within weeks it was circulating in the colonies. Its articles were read aloud at a meeting of British officials and Indian leaders at Niagara the following summer. Runners were sent across the interior with copies to distribute among the tribes. The message from London was clear: the American West still belonged to the Indians.[5]

## A NOBLE ESTATE

George Washington had emerged from the war with landholdings just short of 10,000 acres. This was a considerable amount – but Washington wanted more. The Proclamation Line did nothing to curb his enthusiasm for land accumulation. Washington's eyes remained fixed on the Ohio Country. These were lands he knew well. These were lands he had spilt blood over. As far as Washington was concerned, these lands were his birthright. More importantly, these were lands he needed. Like so many Virginia planters, Washington emerged from the war financially straitened. Tobacco prices were in the doldrums and he owed £2,000 to his British factors. All his cash had been 'swallowed up' by the costs entailed in maintaining his farms, and that still left piles of debt owed to foreign creditors. These were years of retrenchment and hard choices – and they made Washington push his land claims all the harder.[6]

The basis of Washington's principal land claim was the 1754 Dinwiddie Proclamation. The Dinwiddie Proclamation was an ironclad commitment to reward military service with land bounties. Under its terms Washington was owed between 10,000 and 15,000 acres. Of course these lands also lay beyond the Proclamation Line, but Washington was optimistic that this would not be a permanent barrier. 'I can never look upon that Proclamation in any other light (but this I say between ourselves) than as a temporary expedient to quiet the Minds of the Indians,' Washington wrote to a land agent in 1767. 'Any person therefore who neglects the present opportunity of hunting out good lands and in some measure marking and distinguishing them for their own (in order to keep others from settling them) will never regain it.'

Washington expanded on these remarks in a letter to his friend and neighbour John Posey in the summer of 1767. To Posey Washington observed that precisely *because* the lands along the Ohio had been declared formally off-limits by the Crown they should be pursued with increased energy. Surely Posey understood 'how the greatest Estates we have in this Colony were made'? In every generation Virginians had strayed into forbidden Indian territory, fought wars with the native inhabitants and eventually seized their lands for their own. The 'first takers up of those Lands' had built their fortunes by taking risks out west. This was their generation's chance. 'There is a large Field before you – an opening prospect in the back Country for Adventurers,' Washington wrote, 'where an enterprizing Man with very little Money may lay the foundation of a Noble Estate in the New Settlements upon Monongahela for himself and posterity.' Move to the backcountry, Washington exhorted, 'where there is a moral certainty of laying the foundation of good Estates to your Children'.[7]

Washington certainly acted like a man convinced that the opening-up of the West was a moral certainty. A few months after his letter to Posey he wrote another, this time to William Crawford, who lived on the Youghiogheny River. Crawford was a Virginian, a veteran of the Braddock and Forbes campaigns, and a backcountry entrepreneur. Now established near Pittsburgh, Crawford was on the ground with access to the latest news and knowledge of the best land opportunities. Washington offered him a partnership. He could provide Crawford with political cover and social connections, and train him up as a surveyor. In turn, Crawford could find and obtain lands for Washington in the Ohio Country. Washington's letter proposing the arrangement is as good a document as survives of the machinations of western land speculation in these years. Washington wanted a tract of between 1,500 and 2,000 acres in a contiguous plot, somewhere along the Youghiogheny or one of its tributaries. He made clear his need of quality land: 'It will be easy for you to conceive that Ordinary, or even middling Land would never answer my purpose ... No: A Tract to please me must be rich ... good and level.' He then moved on to the more delicate matter of seeking out 'valuable Lands in the King's part', which he desired 'notwithstanding the Proclamation that restrains it at present & prohibits the Settling of them'. Washington knew that he was now engaging Crawford in a criminal conspiracy. In exchange for his assistance and discretion in staking, he offered him 'a very handsome quantity' of his own 'without any Costs, or expenses'. 'I would recommend,' he concluded, for 'you to keep this whole matter a profound Secret'.

Crawford's response was prompt and eager. Within a year he had located a tract on the Youghiogheny and Washington was at work securing title to what would become his first tract of land west of the mountains.[8]

\* \* \*

Washington and Crawford's partnership took on new significance in 1768. That year Washington's prediction that the 1763 Proclamation Line was simply a 'temporary expedient' was vindicated. In the autumn 3,000 Iroquois met in council with British officials at Fort Stanwix in New York. The Iroquois wanted to protect their settlements around the Finger Lakes from settlers flowing in from the Mohawk Valley. They offered to cede the Ohio Country, where very few Iroquois lived, in order to divert the flow of settlers away from the Iroquois heartland. In November they did just that. In exchange for twenty boatloads of gifts and £10,000 cash, the Iroquois agreed to move the Proclamation Line west. The new line ran from Pittsburgh along the path of the Ohio River, opening up everything south of the river to settlement. North of the Ohio remained in possession of the Indians. Crucially, the line then continued northwards in such a manner as to shield the Finger Lakes entirely from settlement. The Iroquois had saved themselves by selling off the lands belonging to the Ohio Indians. Henceforth settlers would be legally permitted to settle in Kentucky – the long-standing hunting grounds of the Shawnee, Cherokee and others, none of whom had been present at Fort Stanwix.[9]

The Treaty of Fort Stanwix was one of several treaties signed in the late 1760s that revised the Proclamation Line westwards. After a five-year hiatus on settlement and speculation, a good portion of the West – essentially all of the modern states of Kentucky and West Virginia and parts of Tennessee – was reopened for both. Washington seized the opportunity to advance his claims under the Dinwiddie Proclamation. Much of 1769 was spent securing the grant in the House of Burgesses and wrangling with the other claimants – his fellow soldiers from the inglorious 1754 campaign. The upshot was that Washington was put in charge of locating, surveying and securing title to 200,000 acres of land somewhere south of the Ohio River. To aid in this, Washington had William Crawford appointed surveyor for the claimants. Concurrent with this public campaign to win lands for Virginia's veterans, Washington was working privately to maximize his share of the bounty. He tried to convince Jacob van Braam – the translator at Fort Necessity – to part with his 9,000-acre share for a mere three cents an acre. This was not an isolated occurrence. In the years leading up to the revolution Washington had agents across Virginia on the lookout for veterans willing to sell their land bounties on the cheap. Ultimately he would buy tens of thousands of acres of land claims in this manner.[10]

By 1770 the Dinwiddie grant was confirmed and the claimants corralled into order. All that remained was to travel up to the Ohio and see the lands that Crawford had scouted. In October Washington headed up the Potomac to Cumberland, and then across the mountains along Braddock's Road. While travelling to Pittsburgh he stopped off to visit tracts of land on the Great Meadows and along the Youghiogheny that Crawford had reserved for him. One plot was next to the site of Braddock's ambush on the banks of the Monongahela. Signs of the slaughter still lingered. Trees were gouged with grapeshot. Cannonballs, bullets and metal fragments were scattered in the undergrowth. The skulls of the dead, many showing signs of having been scalped, lay unburied in the woods. If these reminders of the carnage twenty years before moved him, he made no note of it. In his journal he wrote only that the tract consisted of 'exceedingly fine land'.

At Pittsburgh, Washington and Crawford hired some men and canoes and headed down the Ohio. As they travelled westwards Washington remained intently focused on the quality of the land. He liked what he saw. As the Ohio dipped southwards from Pittsburgh, his diary recorded his rising enthusiasm: 'abounding in very fine bottoms', 'exceedingly good lands', 'a large bottom of good land'. They travelled as far as Point Pleasant, at the mouth of the Kanawha River, and then headed upstream to visit tracts Crawford had in mind for the Dinwiddie claimants. To Washington's expert eye the land here was inferior to that found along the Youghiogheny but it had the advantages of being plentiful, well watered and vacant. They spent ten days that November inspecting plots on the Kanawha and its tributaries before returning back up the river to Pittsburgh.

By 1 December he was back home in Mount Vernon. Crawford remained in the Ohio Country, busy surveying land. Crawford's surveys would be the basis for land claims that Washington would put before the claimants and the House of Burgesses. The process ground on for another two years, testing even Washington's considerable reserves of patience – 'What inducements have men,' he lamented at one point, 'to explore uninhabited wilds but the prospect of getting good lands?' – but they eventually paid off. In December 1772 the Burgesses formally approved the grants, eighteen years after Dinwiddie had offered land in exchange for military service in the Ohio Country. Washington secured five tracts, much of it along the Great Kanawha and other streams in West Virginia.

His final tally from the grant came to 24,100 acres, a haul that had taken nearly two decades to obtain but which at a stroke more than tripled his landholdings and brought the size of his estate to nearly 40,000 acres.[11]

## TROUBLESOME NEIGHBOURS

In the spring of 1773, a congregationalist minister named David McClure crossed the Appalachians, heading home to New England after a season spent spreading the gospel in the Ohio Valley. As he went east along the road between Pittsburgh and Fort Ligonier he met wagons heading westwards carrying families from the mid-Atlantic colonies bound for new lives in the western world.

'I noticed, particularly, one family of about 12 in number,' McClure wrote. 'The man carried an axe and gun on his shoulders – the Wife, the rim of a spinning wheel in one hand, and a loaf of bread in the other. Several little boys and girls, each with a bundle, according to their size. Two poor horses, each heavily loaded with some poor necessaries, on the top of the baggage of one, was an infant rocked to sleep in a kind of wicker cage, lashed securely to the horse. A Cow formed one of the company, and she was destined to bear her proportion of service, a bed cord was wound around her horns, and a bag of meal on her back.' This humble family was a representative example 'of the greater part of the poor and enterprising people, who leave their old habitations and connections, and go in quest of lands for themselves and children, & with the hope of the enjoyment of independence, in their worldly circumstances, where land is good & cheap'. What McClure glimpsed on the road that April was the human face of an impersonal demographic phenomenon that was in the process of transforming Britain and America – and was now about to transform the Ohio Country.[12]

In the fifteen years between the Treaty of Paris and the American Revolution the rate of immigration to America tripled to almost 15,000 arrivals each year, with the overwhelming majority coming from Britain. In a single decade, roughly 3 per cent of the population of Scotland and 2 per cent of the population of Ireland decamped across the Atlantic. They were fleeing high rents, exploitative landlords and an economic downturn. They were also drawn by dreams of a better life in the New World. When John Harrower arrived in Tidewater Virginia in 1774 after an arduous journey from his home in the Shetland Islands, he was amazed at the quantity of food Americans ate – even newcomers like himself who came (as half of all British migrants did in this period) as indentured servants. In America he dined on coffee, warm corn bread and butter at breakfast, bacon, ham and greens at supper, and had ready access to rum and 'good strong beer'. '[I] am only afraid of getting fat,' he wrote home to his wife. Cross the ocean, he told her, and he would 'make you a Virginian Lady among the woods of America … [and] make you eat more wheat Bread in your old age than what you have done in your Youth'. Accounts like Harrower's circulated across the straitened British Isles. America soon won a reputation as 'the best poor man's country in the world'.[13]

Not all of the new migrants headed directly to the frontier, but those who did had a special character. In the wake of the Stanwix Treaty the frontier decisively crossed the mountains. By the end of the decade 10,000 families lived in the region around Pittsburgh, and by the time of the revolution it was thickly settled. In the same period settlers began heading down the New and Greenbrier Rivers into the Kanawha Valley and along the Holston, Clinch and Watauga Rivers into eastern Tennessee. As they flowed into these unsettled regions they brought with them a particular way of life. It was not to everyone's taste. McClure described the backcountry settlers around Pittsburgh as 'hospitable & prodigal', visibly drunk at religious services and indifferent to his summons to sexual chastity,* they were 'much addicted to drinking parties, gambling, horse race & fighting'. 'Drinking, debauchery & all kinds of vice reign,' he wrote, 'in this frontier of depravity.' 'The whites on the extensive frontiers of Virginia,' he concluded, 'are generally white Savages.' McClure's assessment was widely held. British officials referred to them variously as 'white Indians', 'lawless ruffians', 'lawless banditti', 'the very dregs of the people', 'the lowest vilest Scum of Mankind' and 'the outcasts of all nations, and the refuse of mankind'. They were sometimes referred to more neutrally as 'borderers', 'frontiersmen' or 'our back inhabitants'. Over time they would come to be called the Scots-Irish.[14]

---

* As evidenced in this anecdote about Daniel Boone and his daughter Susan: 'When Hays came to Boone for his daughter, Boone told him it would not suit, she would cuckold him. Hays wavered all apprehensions, and they were married. The thing was realized. Hays came and complained to Boone. Boone replied, "Didn't I tell you she would cuckold you. Trot father, trot mother, how could you expect a pacing colt?"' In *Border Life: Experience and Memory in the Revolutionary Ohio Valley*, Elizabeth A. Perkins.

The Scots-Irish accounted for the largest single British population group that emigrated to the Thirteen Colonies. Perhaps a quarter of a million of them moved to North America over a 150-year period, with the great majority arriving between 1713 and 1775. As David Hackett Fischer observed in *Albion's Seed: Four British Folkways in America* (1989), the designation 'Scots-Irish' was misleading. The borderers actually came from the Scottish Marches, the disputed lands between Scotland and England that were the scene of six hundred years of continual violence. The borderers became renowned for their fighting ability and their clannishness. In the Marches one's loyalty was to a clan and to a name. ('Are there no christians here?' asked a visitor. 'Na,' came the response, 'we's a' Elliots and Armstrongs.') And when there was no war to be had, clans fought among themselves and this incessant raiding between them resulted in a culture of feuding. The temper of the borderers can be gathered from the words they left to the English language: blackmail, red-handed, bereaved. But perhaps their most characteristic contribution was the term 'hot trod'. Under this practice, any victim of raiding had six days in which the offending party was considered 'hot trod', meaning that the crime was fresh enough to warrant summary justice. In this period a man was legally permitted to ask his neighbours to join him in pursuit of his stolen property and his neighbours were legally required to join him in the effort. This practice exacerbated the violence in the Marches, leading to cycles of raids and counter-raids. Feuding families took to declaring open season on entire bloodlines. When the Scotts raided Tyndale in 1594 they murdered every man named Charlton they could find. One feud between the Kerrs and the Herons lasted eighty years and saw violence spread as far afield as York. On the border, one English official wrote, 'I see none other than revenge for revenge and blood for blood.'[15]

In the seventeenth century, the borderers began to migrate to Ireland and then on to America. Upon their arrival in the colonies, British officials recognized their warrior pedigree and decided to put it to good use on the frontier. For a century the Scots-Irish migration was deliberately channelled to an arc of backcountry settlements extending from Maine to the Carolinas. The intention, as one Virginia official put it, was to 'strengthen the colony in its weakest parts' and form a buffer between the Indians in the interior and the towns on the coast. In these isolated communities the Scots-Irish retained their old ways. They gave their new settlements the same names – Westmorland, Antrim, Carlisle, Donegal – as their old homes in Britain. They constructed fortified buildings, and in periods of danger whole communities would 'fort up' for protection. They kept up their reputation for drinking and dancing and racing and fighting. They kept, too, their traditions of feuding – although in this new world their enemies were no longer the Charltons and the Kerrs but the Shawnee and the Delaware.[16]

Of all the misfortunes to befall the Native Americans of the Ohio Valley perhaps the most unlikely and the most disastrous was that several hundred thousand members of northern Europe's last surviving warrior culture should be relocated 4,000 miles across the Atlantic Ocean to settle along the fringes of their homelands. However violent the Indians could be, the Scots-Irish always matched them. When the Indians raided farms, the whites would ride 'hot trod' after them. When the Indians took scalps, the whites did likewise. When the Indians tortured captives, the whites responded with horrific mutilations of their own. When the Indians laid siege, forcing the settlers to fort up, the whites would wait until the siege was lifted and then launch punitive raids on Indian towns. This violence intensified after Pontiac's War. That conflict, more than any other event, destroyed whatever residual goodwill existed between the Scots-Irish and their Indian neighbours. The Paxton Boys' rampage against the Conestoga and the Delaware was the symptomatic episode. Recruited from among the backcountry Scots-Irish settlers,* the Paxton Boys expressed sentiments in their 'Remonstrance' to the civil authorities of Philadelphia that were essen-

---

* Their notional leader was John Elder, a Presbyterian minister who was nicknamed the 'Fighting Parson'. Elder conducted services with one musket at his side in peacetime and a second during times of war. Armed clerics and armed worshippers were not unusual in rural Presbyterian communities. At Sinking Spring in western Virginia, 'the men never went to church without being armed', including the priest, who entered the church with a shot pouch slung over his shoulder and a musket in his hand. He would put down both at the pulpit, but his congregation listened intently, 'each man with his rifle in his hand'. As a rule, Presbyterianism was well suited to the militant ways of the frontier. 'I was bred to war,' wrote one Pennsylvania minister, 'the world being a warfare, and my sword is therefore ready to push at all the opposers of the true word of God.' Among the Scots-Irish settlers, one Virginian wrote, 'singing [the Psalm book] old Rouse, rebellion and being plundered, were synonymous terms'.

tially the exterminatory logic of the blood feuds of the Marches' applied to the native inhabitants of Pennsylvania.

And so although Pontiac's War technically ended in 1766, the killing never stopped. Instead, the Ohio Valley descended into a state of brigandage with individuals, gangs and sometimes entire communities targeting the native population. In the first six months of 1766, twenty murders of Indians by white settlers were recorded by British officials, the majority happening near Fort Pitt. In a particularly horrifying episode in January 1768, two frontiersmen killed six Indians who they were hosting in their house. The next day they killed four more, including two girls and a baby, apparently in a bid to keep the earlier murders secret. They were apprehended and detained in Carlisle, only for a posse to descend on the town from the frontiers and break them out. Neither the murderers nor their rescuers were ever punished. 'I have not Words to Convey fully to thee,' one Quaker told Benjamin Franklin apropos of the incident, 'the Prevalence of a Disposition in the Inhabitants of Cumberland County to support All persons who kill Indians.'[17]

The settlers were not just indulging in mindless violence. Their intent was to clear Indians off the land they coveted. Almost all Americans held landowning as their highest aspiration; among the Scots-Irish this tendency was exaggerated. They were never content with what land they already possessed but were always looking westwards at new, unclaimed territory. This nomadism was inspired by a homespun libertarianism and a marrow-deep desire to be left alone. Daniel Boone, the paragon of the Scots-Irish mentality, claimed that he felt cramped if he had a neighbour within a hundred miles. Another backcountry native claimed that 'no man ought to live so near another as to hear his neighbour's dog bark'. This mindset kept the Scots-Irish on the crest of the wave of settlement as it swept west.

By the early 1770s, the Scots-Irish had swarmed over the mountains and were blazing trails and establishing settlements throughout the Ohio Valley. This mass of newcomers caused chaos in Indian communities. A Delaware leader told white officials that since the Stanwix Treaty – a treaty the Delaware did not recognize – 'great Numbers more of your People have come Over the Great Mountains and settled throughout this Country'. They were evidently 'very fond of our Rich Land' and had no interest in respecting Indian claims to it. The settlers were unmoved by their complaints. Many harboured grudges dating from Pontiac's War and earlier. All subscribed to a folk version of the Lockean beliefs that justified settlement more generally. In the common saying of the backcountry, land 'was to be had here for taking up'. One settler spoke for many when he told a British official that 'it was against the laws of God and nature that so much land should be idle while so many Christians wanted it to labor on'. They had not fled landlordism and rack-renting in Britain to be stymied in their desire to own and settle land by a few thousand Indians. David McClure captured a sentiment widespread among the frontiersmen when he described the Indians as 'lazy lords of the wilderness'. In their minds, Indians were analogous to the great landowners of Scotland and Ireland: men who neither toiled nor spun but grew fat off the land. Although this same logic was also applied to the great land speculators east of the mountains who laid claim to the acreage the settlers squatted on – men like George Washington.[18]

William Crawford kept Washington well informed of goings-on around the forks, which included an account of the arrival of thousands of land-hungry settlers. Sure enough, they were soon crowding around lands Crawford had claimed for Washington. 'There are such numbers of people out now looking for land,' Crawford wrote, 'and one taking another's land from him. As soon as a man's back is turned another is on his land.' The solution was to try and build cabins, fences and other improvements to establish the claim and to keep employees on the property whenever possible. 'Nothing will do now but possession,' he wrote, 'and hardly that.' A few months later, Crawford provided an update on proceedings along the Youghiogheny. A new crop of men had arrived who did not pretend to have title 'but took your land, and say they will keep it. I could drive them away, but they will come back immediately as soon as my back is turned.'

Washington read these letters with concern and excitement. Concern, as he had to double- and triple-check his title was sound. Excitement, as the presence of the frontiersmen augured the maturing of his land-speculation schemes. His entire investment plan depended on the arrival of settlers willing to buy or lease land at multiples of what he had paid for it. The turbulence attending the arrival of the Scots-Irish was indicative of a more orderly mass of settlers not far behind. As early as 1773 Crawford reported that this first wave of squatters were beginning to vacate the forks for lands further down the Ohio along Wheeling and Grave Creeks and along the Kanawha and Elk Rivers. Washington's lands were about to become massively profitable – if he could hold on to them long enough.[19]

### LAST DAYS OF THE COLONIAL FRONTIER

As 1772 turned to 1773, George Washington was riding high. The confirmation of his land claims had buoyed his confidence, his finances and his social status. He began to spend lavishly: on immense orders of luxury items from London; on an expansion of Mount Vernon; on an elaborately designed pew in his parish church. All this liberality was underwritten by the belief that his lands across the mountains were about to become working assets. In the same period he was advertising land for sale and seeking out tenants to work plots he wished to retain. He also decided to follow Crawford's advice and establish possession the easiest way he knew how: buy labour and send it to the Ohio Valley to settle and work his lands. To that end, he spent £110 on four indentured servants, four convicts and an enslaved husband and wife who, along with ten domestic servants already in his employ, he sent to his property along the Kanawha. They would join the two dozen men and women Washington already had labouring on his plantations on the frontier. Overall, Washington's finances remained parlous. He still struggled under debts and these new outlays only worsened his total position. But he could take some succour from the belief that once his landholdings began to pay out, better days would lie ahead.[20]

And then, slowly at first and then with startling speed, the bottom fell out of all his plans.

David McClure witnessed one of the first signs that the British government was intent on upsetting the schemes of George Washington and other land speculators. In October 1772 he was in Pittsburgh, where Fort Pitt was being dismantled and the garrison was preparing to decamp eastwards. The decision, he noted, was a 'matter of surprise & grief to the people around, who have requested that the fortress may stand, as a place of security to them, in case [of an] Indian invasion'. By contrast, the Indians he spoke to 'could not conceal their joy at this event. The Fort had been a bridle upon them hitherto, to restrain their murders &

depredations on the frontiers.' The Ohio Indians had repeatedly stated to McClure 'their extreme resentment at the encroachments of the white people'. Now, with the most visible expression of British power being removed from their lands, they had reason to hope that the broader trend of settlement might also be reversed. But perhaps the most revealing aspect of the episode came when McClure approached one of the British officers in charge of the withdrawal. 'I asked [him] the reason of their destroying a Fort, so necessary to the safety of the frontiers? He replied, "The Americans will not submit to the British Parliament, and they may now defend themselves."'[21]

The decision to withdraw from the Ohio Valley – which in the 1750s the British had fought so hard to secure – was the product of several interconnected lines of reasoning. After 1763 the British had struggled to find ways of making the empire pay for itself in America. Proposals that would have introduced new taxes on the colonists (most famously the Stamp Act of 1765) resulted in a massive backlash and an embarrassing reversal in policy. At the same time, settlers had ignored the Proclamation Line of 1763 and flooded into the Ohio Valley, stoking tensions with the Indians. This gave rise to the prospect of a costly Indian war. From London this looked like gross hypocrisy: the Americans expected Britain to protect lawless settlers violating the King's proclamation, but would riot when asked to fund their own defence. Moreover, there was little merit in westward expansion. In a departure from previous policy, London now felt that there was no value in having settlements too far from the coastal core. If America was to be settled, the population should hug the coast, not scatter into the interior. Finally, the Indians were not Britain's enemy. In so far as London needed anything from them, it was peltries for the fur trade. The empire gained nothing from permanent war with Native Americans. In fact, they might be better placed to police the frontier than the British army – which was having a hard time policing Boston and New York.

It fell to General Gage to execute the British withdrawal and he did so with 'great pleasure'. Gage considered the 'liberty mad' Americans as guilty of 'scandalous behaviour and ingratitude' for their refusal to pay taxes, and was appalled by the violence on the frontier. In his opinion the Scots-Irish settlers were 'too numerous, too lawless and licentious ever to be restrained' and the government should stop trying to do so. Ending the military presence in the interior would also be a means of punishing out-of-control frontiersmen by abandoning them to whatever justice the Indians would have. 'Let them [the settlers] feel the consequences,' Gage wrote with relish, 'we shall be out of the scrape.' By the end of 1773 the British had withdrawn to forts at Niagara, Detroit and Michilimackinac and maintained a small force at Kaskaskia, deep in the Illinois Country. Otherwise the Ohio Valley had been returned to the Indians.[22]

The British decision to withdraw from the West was not sufficient to destroy Washington's plans, but it was indicative of a turn in British thinking. In the early 1770s London began to reassess its entire policy with respect to the American West. At a fundamental level, ministers started to wonder whether 'the spirit of emigration' that had inspired large chunks of the British population to move across the ocean to America was actually in the national interest.* A desire to curb emigration led British authorities to actively intervene in colonial schemes to encourage settlement. It also produced a new drive towards centralizing control of American land sales, to end the system of massive grants that had enriched speculators for decades.

Apart from these considerations, but not disconnected from them, was the matter of colonial administration. There were still question marks lingering over the legal status of lands outside the formal limits of the Thirteen Colonies. There was also the matter of how best to administer Quebec. All of these policy discussions were informed to a greater or lesser degree by the escalating revolutionary crisis. America had been aflame ever since the Stamp Act. In the 1770s the crisis spiralled further. The summer of 1772 saw the *Gaspee* affair, which left Rhode Island in a state of insurrection. The Tea Act of 1773 resulted in the Boston Tea Party in December of that year. Revolutionary sentiment spread the length of the continent in 1774, and that was the year that saw Washington, long a moderate, drawn into the revolutionary maelstrom. The British government, he told his neighbour George Fairfax in June, was 'endeavouring by every piece of Art & despotism to fix the Shackles of Slavery upon us'. By August Washington had been chosen as one of Virginia's seven delegates to the First Continental Congress, meeting in Philadelphia that September. That winter he

---

* As one Irish landowner put it, 'if the numbers of inhabitants constitutes the riches of a state ... Ireland will soon be the poorest country under the canopy of Heaven.'

began organizing, training and reviewing volunteer militias preparing to raise arms against the King.[23]

The period of Washington's political radicalization coincided with the collapse of his land schemes. In February of 1774 the Privy Council issued new guidelines on American land sales. Colonial governors could no longer make discretionary land grants. Instead, they would have to survey numbered lots of between 100 and 1,000 acres, which would then be mapped, advertised for public sale and auctioned off to the highest bidder. The measure destroyed the value of the claims Washington had acquired through participation in various land schemes over the previous two decades.

Then, in April, London issued another edict, this time informing the governor of Virginia, Lord Dunmore, that colonial veterans were not eligible for land under the Proclamation of 1763. The land warrants that Washington had trawled Virginia to acquire were now so much worthless paper.

But it was in June that the most galling development occurred. That month Parliament passed the Quebec Act. Designed to make special accommodations for Francophone Canada, the Act expanded the territorial limits of Quebec to include the entire region north of the Ohio River. This new, enlarged Quebec encompassed almost the entirety of the Great Lakes, the whole of the modern Midwest, as well as an enormous swathe of Canada. At a stroke the British government had ended the long debate over which American colony held true title to the Ohio Valley. Westminster had ruled that none of them did. The north bank of the Ohio now belonged in perpetuity to Quebec – which was controlled by the same French-speaking Catholics that the colonists had fought against during the French and Indian War. London had reasonable grounds for enacting the law. But ministers also made no secret of the fact that part of the Act's purpose was to limit westward expansion. By expanding Quebec, London hoped to 'confine the inhabitants [of America] ... according to the ancient policy of the country, along the line of the sea'.

The Quebec Act was one of those rare laws that managed to offend almost everyone. It upset the colonies with land claims north of the Ohio. It angered land speculators and merchants with interests in the region. And it enraged Americans of all stripes who feared and loathed Catholicism – which was practically the entire population.[24]

But it was not until 1775 that the final hammer blow landed on Washington's schemes. At the end of March, Washington heard a disturbing rumour. Apparently, Lord Dunmore was revoking the land grant made under the Dinwiddie Proclamation of 1754. Scarcely able to believe it, Washington asked the governor for confirmation. On 18 April he received a terse response. Dunmore had indeed annulled the entire 200,000-acre grant, including Washington's 24,000-acre tranche. The official reason was that William Crawford had never formally qualified as a surveyor, invalidating the plats and reports produced for the claimants. Whether this was the real reason for the claim's abrogation is hard to know. But it says something about Washington's character that he would expect the Crown to honour a discretionary land grant in an Indian reserve at a time when he was actively involved in organizing armed militias to wage war on the King's representatives.

In any event, Washington never replied to the letter. The day after it was written shots were fired at Lexington and Concord and almost exactly two months later, on 16 June 1775, Washington accepted command of the Continental Army.[25]

# The Bloody Grounds

The American Revolution is not usually thought of as a western affair. In the classic telling its origins lay in disputes over taxation and representation – debates concentrated in towns and cities along the Atlantic seaboard. But there was a western dimension to the revolutionary cause and it was felt most strongly in the colony that mattered most: Virginia.

The largest, the oldest and the most populous colony, Virginia was the indispensable participant in the events of the 1770s. Had Virginia not thrown its weight behind New England in 1774, the revolution might have sputtered out. But Virginia did join the revolution and Virginia did play a major role in the revolutionary era. And Virginia cared deeply about the fate of the American West. This was in no small part because the Virginian elite were heavily invested in frontier lands. George Washington was not an outlier in his land speculations: he was typical. And while it would be reductive to narrow down his motivations to land, it would be naive to remove them from his thinking entirely. The same was true for men like George Mason, Patrick Henry, Edmund Pendleton, Thomas Jefferson, Richard Henry Lee and many others who played leading roles in the revolutionary drama.

If their frustration over the Crown's interventions in Indian affairs, land sales and westward migration are not always obvious, it is because they were blended into a larger set of grievances that they held in common with revolutionaries in other colonies. Look closer and this peculiarly Virginian set of concerns is found hiding in plain sight. They are, in fact, right there in the Declaration of Independence. Among the allegations levelled against King George was that he had 'endeavoured to prevent the population of these States; for that purpose ... refusing to pass [laws] to encourage their migration hither, and raising the conditions of new appropriations of lands'. Further down, Jefferson took aim at the Quebec Act, describing it as a measure aimed at introducing 'absolute rule into these Colonies', and defended the old colonial charters as 'our most valuable Laws'.

What did these men expect to gain through the revolutionary struggle? In its early days, the revolution was conceived of as spanning the entirety of British North America, including Canada and the Floridas. Consequently the revolutionaries laid claim to all the lands won by the Crown at the Treaty of Paris in 1763. This meant that at a minimum the United States would stretch to the Mississippi and encompass the Ohio Valley. How exactly the Ohio Country would be divided, administered and sold off was not clear in 1776. But everyone believed that the republic would assume control over its destiny. There would be no more bowing and scraping in London for land. There would be no more petitioning royal governors for grants. There would be no more arbitrary lines of settlement drawn across the frontier. The states would manage the administration and sale of their territory as they saw fit. In a period of uncertainty and dissension, this vision, at least, was one that unified all Americans. Everyone from the humblest frontier settler to the grandest tidewater landowner could take heart in the prospect of an independent United States, sovereign over its borders, and liberal in its land policy.[1]

Once the war began in earnest, the question of land became central to the revolutionary cause. The reason was noted in the diary of Nicholas Cresswell, an Englishman of loyalist sympathies, who found himself stranded in Alexandria, Virginia, as the colony slid into war in the winter of 1775. In a November entry he described a novelty produced by the revolution: paper money. These new notes, issued for lack of gold and silver, came adorned with symbols and slogans. The three-dollar bill featured an eagle fighting a crane with the inscription *Exitus in dubio est*: 'The event is uncertain'. The six-dollar bill showed a beaver gnawing a tree trunk and the motto *Perseverando*: 'By perseverance'. The seven-dollar note depicted a pitch-black storm cloud and the promise *Serenabit*: 'It will clear up'. 'The Congress have issued two million of

Dollars in these bills for the support of the present War,' Cresswell wrote. 'It is to be sunk by the sale of Land, in Terra Incognita.'[2]

Cresswell was rightly sceptical of the value of these new bills. The United States was born bankrupt. It had little specie, few financial institutions and no government body to marshal the young nation's meagre resources. What it did have, as Cresswell observed, was land. Land was the only asset that could underwrite the issuance of paper money, and land was the only asset the republic had to pledge as security against loans.

The problem was that there was not enough vacant acreage east of the Appalachians. The solution would have to be found west of them. 'The Western Lands ought to be held up to View as an encouragement for your soldiers,' exhorted one Connecticut delegate to the Continental Congress. They would also be held up as an encouragement to the United States' bankers and creditors – and indeed to anyone who put their faith in the new currency festooned with beavers, eagles and storm clouds. If the United States wanted an army, a currency and a financial system – if it wanted, in short, a future – it would need to win the West.[3]

## 'A PEOPLE NOT TO BE DEPENDED UPON'

The war for the West began with an attempt to win back the favour of the Ohio Indians after yet another conflict. In 1774 the last royal governor of Virginia, Lord Dunmore, had provoked a war with the Shawnee. Dunmore's goal was to secure Shawnee acknowledgement of the Treaty of Fort Stanwix and so open Kentucky to Virginia settlers and to major land speculators, including Dunmore himself. To this end, he had given permission for surveyors to enter the Great Kanawha Valley and installed a belligerent commander at Fort Pitt. When a surveying party was murdered on the Kanawha that spring, the familiar tit-for-tat cycle of raids and murders resumed, climaxing with the massacre of a Mingo family on Yellow Creek, near Pittsburgh. At Yellow Creek a settler named Daniel Greathouse lured a family across the river with the promise of alcohol, then proceeded to butcher them with the help of several others. The victims, one of whom was pregnant, were relatives of Logan, a well-known Mingo leader. The grief-stricken Logan went on the warpath and his raids along the frontier drew in the Shawnee, led by Cornstalk. In response, Dunmore sent two armies into the Ohio Valley.

The Virginians won a victory at Point Pleasant, at the mouth of the Kanawha, on land that George Washington had secured two years prior. (Washington was well informed on the campaign, not least because William Crawford served in it as an officer.) Cornstalk was brought to terms and the Shawnee submitted to the Fort Stanwix Treaty.

Lord Dunmore's War was the final outing of the old colonial system of land acquisition. For one last time British administrators joined hands with Virginia planters and frontier settlers to extract more land from the Indians. The irony was that within months of the war's end, this alliance would unravel and both the British and the Virginians would be scrambling to secure the support of the Indians they had just defeated.

Just how hard it would be to reach an understanding was discovered by James Wood. Wood was tasked with travelling into the Ohio Country to inform the tribes of Virginia's proposal. Wood spent several weeks travelling around the region. What he found in the villages troubled him. The Indians had a remarkably accurate knowledge of the breach between the revolutionaries and the King, but they struggled to make sense of what the revolution meant for them. Some Indians seemed to think that Virginia now stood alone and was an easier target. Others had clearly been in contact with the British and had been warned that the Virginians 'only wanted to deceive them and take their lands'. One Delaware reported that a British officer in Detroit had told him that the Virginians were 'a people not to be depended upon' and that they would 'take the whole country' from the Indians if they did not ally with the British.

In this tense environment violence loomed over every interaction. In one village Wood encountered Logan and several Mingo who had been held hostage at Fort Pitt. They had been drinking. Wood made his speech and then moved to a camp outside the town to await their response. That evening, 'one of the Indians came and stamped upon my head as I lay asleep'. He awoke to find himself surrounded by men with knives and axes. One of them said they intended to kill him. Wood fled into the forest, where he remained until the next morning, 'when we returned again into the town [where] Logan repeated in plain English the manner in which the people of Virginia had killed his mother, sister and all his relations during which he wept and sung alternately and concluded with telling me the revenge he had taken. He then told me that several of the Mingos ... wanted to kill us and asked me whether I was afraid to which I answered I was not.'

Logan promised to guarantee their safety and Wood continued on his circuit. But episodes like this showed how hard peace would be to come by in the Ohio Valley.[4]

Under the leadership of the Shawnee chief Cornstalk, a deal was brokered between Virginia and the Ohio tribes. The Virginian commissioners secured recognition of the Fort Stanwix Treaty and formal native neutrality in the revolutionary conflict. In exchange, they guaranteed that the Ohio River would be the permanent boundary between American and native lands in the West.

Few believed that the peace would hold, and by the summer of 1776 regular raiding on the frontier settlements had resumed. One of the most storied events in the history of the Kentucky frontier transpired that tense summer of 1776 when a Shawnee and Cherokee party kidnapped three teenage girls from Boonesborough, among them Daniel Boone's daughter Jemima. Boone set out hot trod after the raiders, catching up with them three days later. The Indians were killed and the women rescued – an unusually satisfactory outcome from the settlers' perspective in a period filled with dread of Indian attacks.* Officers posted at the two frontier forts – Fort Randolph at Point Pleasant and Fort Henry at Wheeling – sent letters up the river begging for supplies of lead and powder. At Fort Pitt new regiments were formed, including the 7th Virginia, under the command of William Crawford. Yet even amid this charged atmosphere there was opportunity for those who saw it. Crawford continued to conduct surveys and settlers continued to mark out tomahawk claims up remote streams. Some settlers frankly welcomed war, if it meant new lands to occupy afterwards. If an open rupture with the Indians should come, John Harris wrote from the Pennsylvania frontier a few weeks after the publication of the Declaration of Independence, then 'let the war be pushed on with the Greatest Vigour into their own Country ... [for] Surely their Territory of the best lands in America is a fine prize for our Warriors to fight for.'[5]

---

* This incident was the inspiration for *The Rescue*, a sculpture by Horatio Greenough, which from 1853 to 1958 stood outside the Capitol building by the steps where presidents gave their inaugural addresses.

Against all odds, the treaty held into 1777. It was not until autumn that the final, devastating blow landed. In mid-September Cornstalk visited Fort Randolph. He delivered a speech filled with 'strong protestations of friendship' but also noted that the Delaware were about to move against the Americans and that the Shawnee would likely join them. The commander understood this as a threat and detained him. A week later Cornstalk's son came to protest his arrest and was also imprisoned. Raiding around Fort Randolph continued. And the Indians were still being held in November when two soldiers named Gilmore and Hamilton ventured across the Kanawha to hunt deer. A short while later men at the fort heard gunshots and screaming. They set out across the river in a canoe and found Hamilton alive and 'the corpse of Gilmore ... scalped and covered with blood'. They loaded the body aboard and returned to the fort. 'The canoe was scarcely landed in the creek,' one witness later wrote, 'when the cry was raised let us kill the Indians in the fort and every man with his gun in his hand came up the bank pale as death with rage.' Hearing the men approach, Cornstalk turned to his terrified son and 'encouraged him [and] told him not to be afraid, for the great Spirit above had sent him there to be killed. The men advanced to the door, the Cornstalk arose and met them, seven or eight bullets were fired into him, and his son was shot dead as he sat upon a stool.'[6]

With Cornstalk's death the tenuous peace between the Americans and the Ohio Indians finally snapped. News of his murder reverberated across the country. With his death all the tribes went to war. On the American side, it was immediately recognized as a diplomatic and military disaster. Governor Patrick Henry, sounding a great deal like the British colonial officials he had replaced, raged that the government had ceded control over war and peace to the frontier. 'Shall this Precedent establish the Right of involving Virginia in War whenever any one in the back Country shall please?' Henry wrote. 'No Man but an Enemy to American Independence will do it [i.e. provoke an Indian War], and thus oblige our People to be hunting after Indians in the Woods, instead of facing General Howe in the field.'

By that time it was far too late to stop what was coming. Within weeks of Cornstalk's death commanders on the frontier were reporting signs of war parties and rumours that 'all the Western Nations had taken up the Tomahawk against the Americans'. In the New Year the violence reached a new pitch. 'From the East branch of the Susquehanna to the Kiskismenitas Creek upon the Ohio & from thence down to Kanawha River,' a British Colonel observed from Niagara in February 1778, 'an extent of many hundred miles is now nothing but an heap of ashes.'[7]

## 'THE SAME WORLD WILL SCARCELY DO FOR THEM AND US'

The fury of Indian warfare fell hardest on Kentucky, and in turn Kentucky produced the most celebrated of the United States' western commanders. George Rogers Clark was born in the Virginia Piedmont in 1752, not far from the family home of Thomas Jefferson. As a young man he qualified as a surveyor and in 1773 he went west and found himself among the deluge of squatters and land speculators who descended on the Great Kanawha Valley after Fort Stanwix. He was still there a year later when Lord Dunmore's War broke out and served as a captain. In 1775 he found work as a surveyor with the Ohio Company and joined a party heading into Kentucky. The region enchanted him. 'A richer and more beautiful country than this I believe has never been seen in America,' he told his brother in a letter encouraging his family to migrate. 'I am convinced that if he once sees ye country, he never will rest until he gets in it to live.'

Kentucky was at this point in the very earliest stage of development. It was only as recently as 1768 that Daniel Boone had blazed a trail across the Cumberland Gap, scrambled up the Pinnacle Rock and 'saw with pleasure the beautiful level of Kentucke'. Still, fully fledged migration did not begin for another couple of years. It was not until April 1775 that Boone escorted the first wave of settlers across the mountains, establishing a path, known as the Wilderness Road, that ran across the Cumberland Gap and through the forests to newly founded Boonesborough on the Kentucky River.[8]

By the time Clark appeared in Kentucky, the Cherokee were preparing to go to war. 'You have bought a fair land,' the Cherokee warrior Dragging Canoe had told the settlers, 'but there is a cloud hanging over it; you will find its settlement dark and bloody.' Not long afterwards the Shawnee offered Dragging Canoe the war belt, a symbol that the two tribes should unite against the Americans, telling him it was 'better to die like men than to dwindle away by inches'. Dragging Canoe accepted the belt and the two tribes went to war on the Kentucky settlements. The settlers responded by sending George Rogers Clark to Williamsburg to request that Kentucky be annexed to Virginia and that supplies, arms and money be sent to secure the frontier. Virginia happily complied and sent Clark back to the stations with five hundred pounds of gunpowder and a commission as a major.[9]

Clark returned to Kentucky in early 1777. Only twenty-four, he was now the ranking officer in the region as it entered its darkest hour. Dragging Canoe was as good as his word. The Cherokee and the Shawnee put the Kentucky settlements under siege. By March the settlers had consolidated into three fortified stations at Harrodsburg, Boonesborough and St Asaph's, the remnants of a larger population who had fled eastwards rather than face the depredations of Dragging Canoe's warriors. Across all three stations the militia could probably muster fewer than 200 men. When Indians laid siege to the stations, the militia would instruct the women to dress up in 'hats and hunting shirts to appear as men and git up on the top of the wall and as they might appear as a great many men'. Women ran musket balls in frying pans and occasionally took up arms. But drafting women into the ranks could not protect the settlers from the Indians' scorched-earth tactics. Fields of wheat and corn were burned. Livestock were slaughtered and horses stolen. There was nothing to eat – no bread, no fruit, no vegetables – nothing apart from deer or buffalo meat, assuming the hunters came back alive. Men, women and children huddled inside cramped forts alongside their hogs and horses. One survivor of these years recalled 'the whole dirt and filth of the Fort, putrified flesh, dead dogs, horse, cow, hog excrements and human odour'. Sickness swept through the stations. The Indians did not need to risk direct assault on the walls to wear down and kill off their defenders.[10]

Under Clark's leadership the stations survived the year, but Clark was quite sure they could not survive another. Without action the settlers faced annihilation and Kentucky would be abandoned. But Clark had the presence of mind to situate the Indian war in Kentucky within a larger geopolitical landscape. Dragging Canoe and others were not acting in isolation but were supported by the British at Detroit. If Detroit could be captured, pressure on the frontier would ease. In October 1777 Clark went to Williamsburg to sell an audacious scheme to Patrick Henry. Clark would raise an army and proceed down the river to the Illinois Country. Clark would seize the poorly defended French settlements, make peace with the tribes and then stage an assault on the British at Detroit. In a stroke the Indian war on the frontier would be cut off and the Ohio River would be opened up for trade down to New Orleans. Governor Henry approved the plan. Clark was promoted to lieutenant colonel and given permission to raise the men he needed.'[11]

Clark moved fast. By July 1778 his little army had taken Kaskaskia and by the end of the summer he had rolled up the surrounding settlements: Prairie du Rocher, Cahokia, Saint Phillips and Vincennes. Over the next few weeks he summoned the nearby tribes to his camp. His manner was the same with each. Clark would show them the peace belt and the war belt. He did not care, he said, if they chose the latter, for 'we should soon see which of us would make it the most bloody'. The tribes chose peace.

As winter approached, Clark was obliged to withdraw to Kaskaskia. He had neither the men nor the supplies to take Detroit or even to hold Illinois. Then he heard that the British commander in Detroit, General Henry Hamilton, was on the march with several hundred men, gathering native allies as he descended from Lake Erie down the Maumee and Wabash Rivers into Illinois. By mid-December, Hamilton was at Vincennes, where he found the American colours flying over the town. Clark, with his native decisiveness, knew he had to act. If he let Hamilton see out the winter and then reassemble his army, Kentucky would be overrun the following spring. Moreover, he loathed Hamilton. Across the frontier he was known as the 'Hair-Buying General', due to the widespread belief he paid Indian raiding parties for white scalps they delivered to Detroit. Hamilton's death or capture would represent long-overdue justice for the suffering Kentucky settlers. Whatever its merits, Clark knew this was a gamble. 'I know the case is desperate,' he wrote to Patrick Henry, but 'we must either quit the country or attack Mr. Hamilton ... Great things have been effected by a few men well conducted. Perhaps we may be fortunate.'

In February 1779, Clark struck out. Vincennes was 240 miles away. Between them lay the Wabash – the third-largest tributary of the Ohio – and several smaller streams. The ice had begun to thaw and the rivers had burst their banks and amalgamated into one continuous mass of water. Clark led his men across these 'drowned lands' along paths concealed beneath the deluge. They spent days wading through the high water on half rations. When they reached the final river crossing before Vincennes, Clark put on black warpaint, started roaring a popular song and marched by himself into the water. His men followed, in the words of one witness, 'without saying a word, like a flock of sheep'. Not long afterwards, Clark surprised Hamilton at Vincennes. When the British officer refused to surrender, Clark began murdering some Indian captives he had taken (one of them was Pontiac's son) in sight of the walls. One by one, the Indians sang their death song before being tomahawked in the head and thrown in the river. The British watched aghast as one man was thrown into the water alive 'and suffered to spend still a few moments of life in fruitless struggling' with a noose around his neck. Clark then ordered one of his men to begin scalping another captive while the rest watched. The man would take off a small portion of the scalp, then Clark would order him to stop, then signal for him to proceed, and then stop once more, and so on. Eventually, amid a clamour for mercy, Clark spared the semi-scalped man, who later committed suicide while imprisoned in Virginia. Clark now appeared before the gate, covered in blood, and asked to continue his negotiations with Hamilton. 'I agreed to meet him and treat of the surrender of the garrison,' Hamilton reported. 'He spoke with rapture of his late achievement, while he washed off the blood from his hands stained in this inhuman sacrifice.' Clark told him frankly that if they did not surrender, he would kill them all once the fort inevitably fell. Clark also confided that he 'expected shortly to see the whole race of Indians extirpated, that for his part he would never spare man, woman or child of them on whom he could lay his hands'. Hamilton duly surrendered. The American colours were once again lifted over the Illinois Country and the hated 'Hair-Buying General' was sent back to Williamsburg under armed guard.[12]

Clark returned to Kentucky a hero. The Virginia legislature awarded him a specially made sword to honour his victories and granted him and his men 150,000 acres of land as a token of their appreciation. But in 1780 the Shawnee resumed raiding across the frontier. Boats and rafts were ambushed on the Ohio. Outlying stations were besieged and sometimes overrun. A clamour for a new campaign against the Shawnee went up. Thomas Jefferson, who had replaced Patrick Henry as governor, joined the chorus. In a letter to Clark he observed that the Shawnee and their Mingo and Wyandot allies were 'troublesome thorns in our sides' and deserved 'extermination'. 'The same world,' Jefferson wrote, 'will scarcely do for them and us.'[13]

That August Clark led 1,000 militiamen across the Ohio into the Shawnee heartlands. Clark encircled and bombarded the Shawnee town of Piqua and, after a spirited defence, the Shawnee fled into the forest. Clark decided not to pursue them and instead he ordered his men to destroy the fields surrounding Piqua. Hundreds of acres of corn, as well as gardens filled with beans, squash, pumpkins and potatoes, were destroyed over the next two days. As they worked their way through the fields, the men found Indians who had been left behind in the retreat. A father and son were beaten to death. One female prisoner was killed 'by ripping up her Belly & otherwise mangling her'. All of these were also scalped. Indeed, such was the hunger for scalps – which by Virginia law had bounties attached to them – that Clark's men opened up the tombs in the Piqua cemetery and scalped the dead. Before they left, Clark had his own dead buried beneath the ashes of Piqua's razed buildings to try and conceal the site of American graves. Then his men returned across the river to Kentucky. His campaign had been an inglorious success but the frontier war raged on regardless. Not long after the Battle of Piqua, the Shawnee returned to the settlement and burned alive several American prisoners at the site of their old township. They also found the graves of Clark's men and scalped their corpses. As 1780 turned to 1781 this was fast becoming the true face of the revolutionary West: a war of extermination, revenge and symbolic violence which spared neither the living nor the dead.[14]

## 'A ROBBING, PLUNDERING, MURDERING SCHEME'

By 1781 the war for the Ohio Valley was organized around two poles of military activity: Detroit and Pittsburgh. Successive campaigns against Indian settlements north of the Ohio had emptied much of the valley of its native inhabitants. Those that remained were clustered around the great fort at Detroit, especially along the Sandusky, Maumee and Miami Rivers on the approaches to the British stronghold. Renewed raiding had driven many American settlers back east. Those who remained clung on stubbornly in the Kentucky stations and in settlements near Forts Wheeling and Randolph. The only reliably safe place was Pittsburgh, where the Continental Army was garrisoned. The country between Detroit and Pittsburgh was practically a no man's land. Wyandot, Shawnee and Delaware raiding parties journeyed eastwards through it to raid the frontier. Ambush parties along the Ohio River surprised supply ships and rafts carrying soldiers and settlers downriver. Forts and stations along the southern bank of the Ohio were struck with hit-and-run attacks. The Continental Army responded with search-and-destroy missions aimed at the Indian home front, razing homes, burning thousands of acres of crops and manufacturing a refugee crisis that overwhelmed the British garrisons. These formal campaigns by American regulars were supplemented by ad hoc militia and volunteer actions and small-scale, opportunistic raids by frontier settlers.

It was a war that continued to escalate even as campaigning on the Atlantic seaboard began to wind down. After the surrender at Yorktown in October 1781, major operations in that theatre ceased. But the conflict ground on pitilessly in the West. 'The Indian war is now more general than Ever,' Clark wrote to Washington in the middle of the year, 'any attempts to appease them Except by the Sword will be fruitless.'[15]

Caught in the middle were the pacifist Moravian Indians, mostly Delaware converts who lived in picturesque towns along the Muskingum River in eastern Ohio. The Moravian settlements of Salem, Schonbrunn and Gnadenhutten ('huts of grace') were a well-known feature of the Ohio Valley. Pre-revolutionary visitors to the region almost always passed through them and left vivid accounts of life in these quiet religious communities. When Nicholas Cresswell visited in 1775, he described 'a pretty town' of about sixty clapboard houses laid out along three streets. At the centre was a meeting house 'built of logs sixty foot square covered with Shingles, Glass in the windows and a Bell, a good plank floor with two rows of forms. Adorned with some few pieces of Scripture painting.' In the daytime, the Moravians worked in the fields and mills surrounding the town. In the evening, they attended lengthy religious services conducted in a mixture of English, German and Lenape. Cresswell went to a service and was moved by the beautiful singing of the Moravians, who sang German hymns translated into their native language. Life in these towns was tranquil. The Moravian Indians did not drink alcohol and kept apart from the unconverted tribes. Their rejection of violence was as sincere as their reflexive Christian charity. For their fellow Indians, it was these virtues that made them objects of suspicion. The other tribes in the region despised the Moravians for submitting to a foreign faith. One Delaware chief observed that, whatever the Bible might say, 'it was not in their interest to appear so friendly to the white people who had already crowded too fast upon their land'. Christianity, he said, simply made them 'easy prey' for unscrupulous white men who coveted their territory.

It was the Indians who struck the Moravian villages first. In August 1781 an Indian war party appeared on the Muskingum. They informed the Moravians that they had to leave their settlements. 'You live in a dangerous place,' a Wyandot leader told them. 'Two powerful and mighty spirits or gods are standing and opening wide their jaws toward each other to swallow, and between the two angry spirits, who thus open their jaws, are you placed.' 'It is not advisable for you to remain here longer,' he concluded, 'for here must you all die.' The Moravians were forcibly relocated to the Sandusky, where they were left 'in the wilderness, where there was no food to be found and no game to hunt, and many among our brethren had nothing left to eat'. Hunger set in and throughout that winter groups began to steal back to their old homes on the Muskingum.[16]

In February Wyandot raiding parties began striking the frontier. That month a party attacked the home of Roger Wallace while he was away. Wallace came home to find his farm plundered and his wife and children vanished. Wallace travelled to the nearest settlement, rounded up a posse and went hot trod after the Indians. In early March, the pursuing party made a grim discovery. On the banks of the Ohio they found the bodies of Mrs Wallace and her infant child. Both had been impaled, the child on 'a Stake which was run up from between its Leggs until the Neck, with its belly to the Indian Country & its Face towards the Settlement over the River'.

Meanwhile, the Wyandots they were following had continued westwards and had stopped off at the Muskingum settlements, where about ninety Moravians were now living. The warriors told the Moravians of their exploits and warned them that the borderers were almost certainly in pursuit. They then left town. By great misfortune, however, during the same period another party of Indians came through the villages with American captives. During their stay one of their captives managed to escape. He travelled back to Pittsburgh with news that the Moravians were providing safe harbour to Indians raiding American settlements.[17]

At once the communities around Pittsburgh took up the cry for revenge. An expedition was advertised under the command of David Williamson and volunteers directed to meet at Mingo Bottom on 4 March. On 7 March, Williamson's posse entered Gnadenhutten. The militia disarmed the Moravians, separated them by gender, robbed, stripped and bound them, and then locked one group up in the meeting house and the other in a cooper's shop. When the villagers from Salem arrived, they were similarly treated. That evening Williamson and his men, in a parody of a courtroom trial, began putting charges before their captives. Had the Moravians not been 'furnishing' parties 'going and returning from war' with the Americans? Had they not 'harboured the warriors'? The Indians tried to rebut these allegations, but their 'proofs of innocence would not satisfy' the Americans.

When it became clear that the Americans would kill them, the Moravians asked if they could 'beg a day's time for the purpose of praying and preparing for death', and when this was granted 'they fell on their knees praying and singing hymns'. That night, with the chorus of the Moravians ringing in their ears, the posse met to decide how best to kill them. Someone found a cooper's mallet and suggested it might do.

The next morning the killing began. One by one the Moravians were beaten to death with the mallet, and then scalped. One woman who spoke English fell on her knees before Williamson and begged for her life, 'but got for answer that he could not help her'. 'Prisoners said that the militia themselves acknowledged and confessed they had been good Indians,' one Moravian later wrote. 'They prayed and sang until the tomahawks struck into their heads.'

Ninety-six Moravians were killed in this manner. Forty of them were children. After the killing was complete, Williamson had the towns ransacked for plunder and then razed. The posse returned east weighed down with booty. Outside Pittsburgh they killed several more friendly Delaware before returning to their farms. Two Indians, however, had lived through the carnage. A boy named Thomas woke up on the killing floor having survived his scalping. He ran into the forest, where he found another survivor. This second boy had been kept with the women and they had managed to smuggle him into the cellar beneath the floor. The posse began slaughtering the women in the room above, and he crouched there in silence as 'the blood began to stream down between the boards' onto him. He was able to escape through a ventilation hole before the building was burned down.

The two boys travelled west to the Sandusky, carrying the news of the massacre with them. Accounts of the killings were soon circulating among the Ohio tribes and within weeks were being reported by British officers in Canada. The fact that the frontiersmen had massacred converts confirmed the worst suspicions of the Ohio Indians. The white missionaries, one Indian reasoned, 'sought to make the Indians tame, so as to have them then killed by the white people'. The slaughter caused a crisis of faith in at least one of the surviving Moravians, a man named Augustus. 'On the Muskingum the white people have at last attained their purpose, murdering so many of our friends,' Augustus told his brother Samuel. 'Therefore will I keep far enough from them … [and] nevermore will I come to you and live with you; I will hear nothing about the Saviour … My forefathers have all gone to the devil; there will I go also; where they are there will I also be.'[18]

These events marked a new, yet more severe phase in the war. No sooner had the posse returned from Gnadenhutten than the country was agitating for another raid, this time on the Indian towns of the Sandusky. On 5 April, less than a month after the massacre, General Irvine, the ranking Continental Army officer at Fort Pitt, met the local militia commanders, among them David Williamson. They called for a new campaign against the Indians. In one account, they said they wanted to 'exterminate the whole Wyandot tribe'. According to another, they claimed they wanted to complete the work of Gnadenhutten by destroying the remainder of the Moravians along the Sandusky. In May the expedition was sanctioned by General Irvine. His only request was that the campaign be led by the most experienced militia commander in the region: William Crawford.[19]

In May 1782, Crawford was fifty years old. He still retained the position of colonel in the local militia and was also the county surveyor. He had three children, several slaves and legal title to thousands of acres of land. He was a successful and respected man. He could probably have excused himself from participating in the expedition but offered to serve. In mid-May, Crawford wrote his will, said goodbye to his wife and children and headed to the rendezvous point. On 24 May, 500 men assembled at Mingo Bottom. They rode for a week across central Ohio, arriving at their destination on 3 June. The next day, scouts stumbled across a Delaware party and by mid-afternoon Crawford's men were engaged in a firefight with a mixed group of several hundred Delaware, Mingo and Wyandot soldiers. On 5 June, the fighting continued, this time with the Indian force supplemented by Shawnee warriors. Outnumbered, that evening Crawford ordered a fighting retreat. Over the next two days the militia fell back, pursued by Indians. They rode through marshlands, where their horses sank up to their haunches and had to be abandoned. Men became separated. Soon all discipline was lost and the force broke up into dozens of little groups fleeing for their lives through the forest. The survivors met again at Mingo Bottom on 13 June. They had lost fifty men. William Crawford was missing.[20]

For several weeks Crawford's whereabouts were unclear. Then, on 4 July, a skeletal figure emerged from the forest. It was Dr John Knight, the surgeon who had accompanied the expedition. It would later emerge that Knight had spent three weeks in the forest living off 'green gooseberries, nettle tops & green May apples'. For now he could barely talk. He was delirious, his jaw severely swollen, and when he tried to speak an acquaintance noted that 'his Scottish dialect was much broader than it had been when I knew him before'. After some time, he recovered and related what had happened.[21]

During the retreat Knight had been in a group with Crawford, who had stayed behind trying to find his son-in-law. They were captured by the Delaware. Knight and Crawford were taken together to Pipe's Town on the Sandusky River. Their faces were painted black and Crawford was brought before a group of Indian leaders. They spoke good English and many of them had met Crawford before. This made no difference, however. 'The blood of the innocent Moravians,' they told him, 'calls aloud for *revenge*.' Crawford would satiate it.

The Virginian was stripped naked and beaten by the villagers. Then his arms were bound behind his back and his hands were attached by a length of cord to a tall stake. The warriors stepped forward and took turns scorching his skin with gunpowder. At some point Crawford's ears were cut off. Then a fire was built a few feet away from the stake. Hickory sticks were placed in the flames and when red hot were pressed into Crawford's flesh. The rope was long enough that Crawford could move around the post and his tormentors began to pursue him around the stake. This went on for some time until the women stepped forward holding trays covered with 'burning coals and hot embers', which they threw all over him until 'he had nothing but coals of fire and hot ashes to walk upon'. Crawford begged one of the Indians he knew to shoot him but he refused. For two hours he remained conscious, walking back and forth across the coals, until at length he collapsed into the embers. 'They then scalped him,' Knight said, 'and repeatedly threw the scalp in my face. An old squaw ... got a board, took a parcel of coals and ashes and laid them on his back and head after he had been scalped; he then raised himself upon his feet and began to walk around the post: they next put a burning stick to him, as usual, but he seemed more insensible of pain than before.' Knight was taken away. The next morning he was led past 'the spot where the Colonel was burnt ... I saw his bones laying amongst the remains of the fire, almost burnt to ashes, I suppose after he was dead they had laid his body on the fire.' Knight was told that he would meet the same fate at a nearby Shawnee village but was able to escape and make his way back to Fort Pitt.[22]

It fell to General Irvine to tell Washington what had come of his old business partner. 'The unfortunate colonel,' he wrote in a letter to his commanding officer, 'was burned and tortured in every manner they could invent.' The Delaware who had presided over the execution had told Knight that 'not a single soul should in future escape torture; and gave, as a reason for this conduct, the Moravian affair'. A few weeks later Washington sent his reply. 'I lament the failure of the [Sandusky] Expedition – and am particularly affected with the disastrous fate of Colonel Crawford,' he wrote. 'No other than the extremest Tortures which could be inflicted by the Savages could ... [be expected] by those who were unhappy enough to fall into their Hands ... For this reason, no person should at this Time, suffer himself to fall alive into the Hands of the Indians.'[23]

Raiding continued. In mid-July Hanna's Town, thirty-five miles east of Pittsburgh, was overrun. Hamlets along the Monongahela and Allegheny were attacked, whole families killed and their farms destroyed. Terror gripped the settlers. 'I much fear our settlements will break,' one militiaman reported, noting that the shambolic campaign to the Sandusky had emboldened the Indians. Others understood that they were paying the price for the Gnadenhutten Massacre. 'The murder committed on the Moravians is every day retaliated,' another officer wrote.

In the meantime the carnage unleashed at Gnadenhutten had reached Kentucky. As raiding resumed that August, almost 200 Kentucky militiamen, among them Daniel Boone, set out to avenge a recent attack on a station. On 19 August, just after crossing the Licking River in pursuit of their quarry, they were ambushed by a much larger Indian and British force. Within minutes the American line broke and the Kentuckians were massacred as they fled to the riverbank. Survivors later wrote that the Indians took no prisoners. Those that fell into their hands were later 'found at the crossing of the Creek tied & Butchered with knives & spears', quite possibly killed in imitation of the Moravians at Gnadenhutten.

After what became known as the Battle of the Blue Licks, Kentucky was subject to waves of raiding. In September the American garrison at Wheeling was besieged, with the attackers attempting to storm the walls four times. When they were repulsed, they moved on to another fort and attempted the same. Retaliation came in October when George Rogers Clark, in one of the last campaigns of the Revolutionary War, led a column against the Shawnee settlements on the Miami River. His men destroyed seven villages and burned 10,000 bushels of corn before returning home.

By this juncture the peoples of the Ohio Valley were overwhelmed by bloodshed, saturated in violence and numbed by endless war. 'We can scarcely Behold a spot of Earth but what reminds us of the fall of some fellow adventurer, Massacred by Savage hands,' Daniel Boone told a Virginia official. 'If something is not speedily done we no doubt will wholly be depopulated.' The despair was mutual. 'If we had the means of publishing to the World the many Acts of Treachery & Cruelty committed by [the Americans] on our Women & Children,' a Seneca commander told the British at conference in Niagara, 'it would appear that the title of Savages would with much greater justice be applied to them than to us.'[24]

And then the violence began to drop off. As Christmas approached, raiding decreased. Word came down from Washington that Americans should halt further campaigning. As 1782 turned to 1783 there were rumours of impending peace with Britain. It was not until May that the news reached the frontier. The American Revolution was over. A few months before, a treaty had been signed in Paris.

# Cutting the Knot

There has always been a tension between the United States as an abstract proposition and its existence as a nation with a homeland. Never was that tension felt more strongly than during the revolution, when it fell to a small group of American diplomats in Europe to establish the boundaries of the new country. America was to be an example to the world, like a city on a hill. But how big a city? How large a hill?

An easy solution to the question of the United States' territorial limits was offered by the 1763 Treaty of Paris. At that negotiation British and French diplomats had referred to the Mitchell Map when discussing territorial matters. The Mitchell Map was the most up-to-date map of North America and it dramatically illustrated British claims on the continent. It showed the boundaries of Georgia and the Carolinas stretching to the Mississippi. It had Virginia sprawling across the Ohio Valley. It was an image of a large, confident British America that touched the Atlantic, the Mississippi, the Gulf of Mexico and the Great Lakes.

The Mitchell Map was an obvious point of reference for American territorial claims during the revolution. Britain had claimed these limits for the colonies; surely the colonies could now claim them for themselves. But this was to assume moderation on the part of the Americans and graciousness on the part of the British. Infected by revolutionary zeal, the Americans sought more than just the Mitchell Map. 'As long as Great Britain shall have Canada, Nova Scotia, and the Floridas,' John Adams insisted, 'so long will Great Britain be the enemy of the United States.' The only tolerable outcome, one Rhode Island delegate claimed,

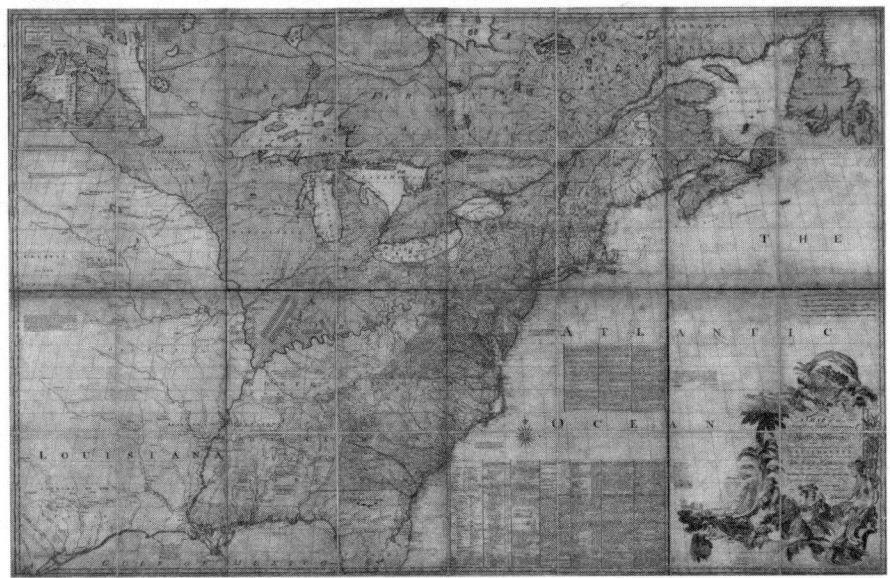

*The Mitchell Map.*

was 'the divesting of Britain of every foot upon this Continent'. Nor did their territorial ambitions stop at the water's edge. For a period some members of the Continental Congress hoped to make the Bahamas and Bermuda American.[1]

These claims were wildly optimistic. For most of the war it looked as though the Americans might have to settle for smaller quarters. Out west, the American dream of a western border at the Mississippi River was beset from all sides. Although George Rogers Clark was hailed as the 'Conqueror of the Northwest', he was nothing of the sort. At best, Clark had averted the total destruction of American settlements west of the Appalachians. This was no small feat but it hardly amounted to a territorial claim by right of conquest. By comparison, Britain had a number of cards to play – not least its promise to its native allies to preserve the integrity of their homelands. Nor were the United States' woes limited to the lands beyond the Appalachians. Throughout the revolution the British retained control of swathes of territory along the Atlantic seaboard. It would have been quite normal for a peace settlement to be reached on the basis of *uti possidetis*, a legal term meaning that belligerents could claim in peace such land as they had won in war. At various times, this meant that Britain would have kept Savanna,

Charleston, East Florida, New York, Long Island, Rhode Island and much of Georgia – not to mention the entirety of Canada. And this assumed the United States survived the conflict. Washington spent much of the war in despair at the American position. Only months before Yorktown he declared that the Americans were 'at the end of our tether' – unable to feed, fund and equip a fighting force.[2]

For much of the war, then, the territorial limits of the United States were in flux. In moments of optimism, the republic claimed the entire continent. In moments of despair, it vanished from the map entirely. The United States was everything and nothing. Its future outlines would depend on the exertions of its leaders, the liberality of Great Britain and – perhaps most importantly – the capriciousness of its allies.

## EUROPEAN CALCULATIONS

The War of Independence is principally remembered for the great engagements between Redcoats and Continentals on the American mainland, but it was from the outset a global conflict. As early as July 1775 the Continental Congress had declared that in the event of a rupture with Britain 'foreign assistance is undoubtedly attainable'. No one doubted which countries the United States would look to. 'Independence, Confederation and Negotiations with foreign Powers,' John Adams wrote the next year, 'particularly France, ought to go hand in hand, and be adopted all together.' 'It is next to infatuation and madness,' a British MP told Parliament that spring, 'to suppose that we can have an American without a French and Spanish war.' Few missed the irony: American independence from Britain would be dependent on foreign, specifically French, support.[3]

France provided that support with relish. French policy was in the hands of Charles Gravier, Comte de Vergennes, minister of foreign affairs. A career diplomat, Vergennes had spent over three decades representing France abroad and was a redoubtable figure. Hard-working, alert and realistic, Vergennes was the guardian of French interests and the defender of French honour. Both were at a low ebb. France had been humbled in the Seven Years War. Vergennes's ambition was to overturn 'the deplorable peace of 1763' and restore France to primacy. Vergennes combined this ancient animosity towards Britain with an innovative analysis of the wellsprings of British power. Since their humiliation in

1763, French diplomats had spent considerable time analysing British dominance. Britain, they concluded, represented a new kind of power that acted globally and used a combination of financial, mercantile and naval power to dominate the world. For the French, Britain's control of North America was the *beau idéal* of this policy. Some even concluded that British supremacy was built upon an American base. 'We must not deceive ourselves,' one French diplomat wrote. 'The true balance of power really resides in commerce and in America.' The Thirteen Colonies, wrote another, 'draw in their wake the balance of power in Europe'. The conclusion was obvious: if France could break the transatlantic nexus, it could cut down the British colossus.[4]

Accordingly, the French watched the burgeoning revolutionary crisis with interest. As early as 1765, during the Stamp Act furore, agents were dispatched across the Atlantic to gauge the temper of the colonists. This foray into American affairs was premature. But the French were well prepared for the events of 1776. By the winter of that year Benjamin Franklin was in Paris, representing the colonies, and the Franco-American courtship was afoot. But it was not until 1777 that the French started sending significant quantities of gold, munitions and supplies to the Americans, and not until March 1778 that informal support of the revolution solidified into a formal treaty between the two countries. That treaty was a remarkable occurrence. The spectacle of a French absolute monarch extending support to republican insurgents was unusual in itself. More unusual still was that, in exchange for becoming the first major power to recognize American independence – and thus assuming the burden of fighting a global war with the British Empire – Vergennes asked for nothing. The terms of the treaty explicitly stated that the French sought no territorial acquisitions in North America as a consequence of the war – including Canada, which was majority French-speaking.

This decision to forgo conquest was congruent with the overall priority of shattering the unity of the British Empire. It was curious nonetheless. France wanted to upset British hegemony. The United States simply wanted independence. Their policies had no connection except their origins in a shared hatred of Britain. France tried to ensure harmony of action by insisting that the treaty include a guarantee that neither party would pursue a separate peace with Britain – although it was not obvious how this could be enforced. Such matters were lost in the wave of war enthusiasm that washed over France in 1778. Although Vergennes was an icy realist, the sons of the French ruling class were filled with zest for the American cause. Young men flocked to arms and clamoured after commissions in the army and navy. In salons and spa towns all the talk was of Boston and Philadelphia. 'The courage displayed by these new republicans procured for them, throughout Europe, the esteem and the good wishes of every friend of justice and humanity,' the Comte de Ségur recalled. 'The rising generation' found in revolutionary America what they could not in France, 'and every heart beat with the desire of retrieving the disgrace of the last war, of taking the field against England, and of flying to the aid of America'.[5]

Less enthusiastic were the Spaniards, who the French brought with them into the war with Britain. Spain and France were joined by a family alliance and tended to act in concert. Having run into an American alliance ahead of Spain, the French now had to drag the Spanish into the war effort behind them. The Spanish proved less than pliable. After studying the matter the Spanish foreign minister, the Conde de Floridablanca, came to the conclusion that though the break-up of the British Empire was desirable, the establishment of an American one so close to Spain's imperial possessions in the western hemisphere was not. He told his French counterpart early on that Spain's preferred policy was one that brought America 'to a sort of anarchy', with a state of 'perpetual war' between the colonies and Britain. As it looked as though that could be achieved without Spanish involvement, Floridablanca declined participation. A desperate Vergennes tried to bribe his counterpart with territory. He refused all his advances. In the end Vergennes gave Floridablanca a blank cheque. The Spaniard demanded Minorca, Honduras, the Floridas and Gibraltar. Vergennes submitted, and in June 1779 Spain joined the conflict against Britain. But Floridablanca remained tepid on the Americans. Where Vergennes was liberal, Floridablanca was parsimonious. The Spanish did permit supplies to flow up the Mississippi and Ohio Rivers, but that was about the extent of their direct material support. The few hundred thousand dollars they made available in loans and subsidies were dwarfed by the millions lent by France. Unlike the French, the Spanish saw the danger in promoting republicanism merely to spite Britain. Floridablanca was suspicious of the aims and ideals of the Americans. In line with this fundamentally sceptical view of their cause, Spain refused to recognize

American independence and the two countries never signed a formal alliance.⁶

The Continental Congress entrusted its diplomatic fortunes to four men. It fell to them to navigate the treacherous waters of European diplomacy in pursuit of a settlement to end the war and establish the United States among the nations of the world.

The least consequential of the group was Henry Laurens. A Charleston merchant and slaver, Laurens departed Philadelphia on the *Mercury* in August 1780, bound for the Netherlands and discussions with Dutch bankers for a $10 million loan. Off the coast of Newfoundland, the *Mercury* encountered a British frigate. When the British boarded, Laurens attempted to dispose of a bag of confidential material by throwing it overboard; the bag filled with air and bobbed back up to the surface. The British retrieved its incriminating contents and arrested him on suspicion of espionage and treason. Laurens was taken to England and imprisoned in the Tower of London, where he remained for fifteen months.

In contrast to Laurens, John Jay was able to get to his post at Madrid unmolested but he also found himself a virtual prisoner in Europe. A brilliant lawyer, if a slightly unassuming man ('He is as plain as a Quaker,' wrote Abigail Adams, 'and as mild as New Milk'), Jay came from a New York mercantile dynasty and went about diplomacy with business-like efficiency. His instructions authorized him to negotiate with the Spanish for loans and diplomatic recognition. He was also charged with trying to persuade Floridablanca to accept an American border on the Mississippi. To the Spanish, Jay gave the frankest exposition of American claims in the Ohio Valley. 'The Americans, almost to a man, believe that God Almighty had made that river a highway for the people of the upper country to go to the sea by,' he said, '[and] that this country was extensive and fertile [and] that the General [Washington], many officers, and others of distinction and influence in America, were deeply interested in it.' Jay's arguments fell on deaf ears. The Spanish ignored him for eighteen months, leaving the New Yorker disillusioned with the prospects of an entente with absolute monarchies of Catholic Europe.

The other lawyer in the group, John Adams, experienced frustrations of his own. Originally ordered to Paris in 1777, Adams was recalled home in 1779, only to be sent back across the ocean a few months later to serve as minister to the Netherlands. Possessed of a brilliant mind and a commensurate measure of pride and arrogance, the imperious Adams never failed to impress his sense of his own superiority on others. Unrelenting in his advocacy for American claims but frosty and puritanical in his manner, Adams was an effective envoy but an imperfect diplomat. 'He can't dance, drink, game, flatter, promise, dress, swear with gentlemen, and small talk and flirt with the ladies,' one of his many critics once said of him. 'In short, he has none of the essential arts or ornaments which make a courtier.'

Famously sharp-tongued, Adams was venomous in his criticism of his colleague Benjamin Franklin, who had in abundance the qualities Adams lacked. By dint of both time served and years lived Franklin was the senior diplomat in Europe. Since 1776 he had been in Paris garnering support for the American cause. Franklin loved Paris and Paris loved him. Parisians 'saw in Franklin a sage of antiquity come back to give austere lessons and generous examples to the moderns', one Frenchman recalled. 'They personified in him the republic of which he was the representative.' Already famous before the war, Franklin's celebrity reached new heights during the revolutionary years. A fixture at Versailles and a favourite at the salons, Franklin was also honoured by an audience with Voltaire, who kissed him on both cheeks, sealing the embrace between France and the United States. Franklin's popularity in France made him a better beggar, for much of his time was spent pleading for loans and subsidies. But Franklin was besotted with France to a degree that muddied his diplomatic judgement.\* Franklin forcefully advocated for the maintenance of a united front with France and insisted that the United States' long-term interests required a close working partnership with Versailles. He would not countenance talk of a private settlement with Britain. 'If we were to break our faith with this nation [France], on whatever pretence,' he insisted, 'England would again trample on us, and every other nation despise us.'[7]

---

\* 'This is the civilest nation upon earth,' he once declared, and 'a delightful people to live with'. He went even further in a 1779 letter to Josiah Quincy: 'I think the French have no national Vice ascrib'd to them. They have some Frivolities, but they are harmless ... there is nothing wanting in the character of a Frenchman.'

Everyone who saw Franklin at work in Paris feared that his love of France had blinded him to the realities of European great-power politics. Both Jay and Adams had their own episodes of Francophilia, but ultimately neither man forgot that French policy was not guided by love of American liberty. Both men feared Spanish influence in Versailles and were unnerved by persistent rumours that Madrid wanted to deny the United States control of the Ohio Valley. More broadly, they perceived the fundamental mismatch in interests between the United States and the Bourbon family alliance. One wanted independence, the other wanted to bloody the British nose. They might simply let the Revolutionary War grind on forever without resolution. (As Adams put it vividly, the French might agree to hold 'our chin to prevent us from drowning, but not to lift our heads out of water'.) Conversely, they might seek a separate peace with Britain that would satisfy European needs at the expense of American ones. This almost happened in 1781. Labouring under the weight of war-related debt, Vergennes made overtures to Britain. He proposed a general peace settlement which would have ended the war on the basis of *uti possidetis*, granted chunks of the Ohio Valley to Spain and secured independence for a mutilated and likely ungovernable United States. Luckily for the Americans, King George refused the offer and a few months later Lord Cornwallis surrendered at Yorktown.[8]

## 'INDEPENDENCE OF FRIENDS AND FOES'

There were more Frenchmen than Americans at Yorktown, and had it not been for a last-minute intervention, a French admiral would have taken Cornwallis's surrender rather than General George Washington. This reflected a fundamental truth of the American war effort. For six years the Continentals had been armed, clothed, fed and equipped by the French. France's navy escorted American merchants and French ports provided safe havens to American privateers. French gold filled American coffers and French officers trained and led American soldiers. Some of the American cannon even had Louis XVI's monogram engraved on them. Yorktown was the zenith of the Franco-American alliance; it was ultimately the occasion for its betrayal. When news of the defeat reached Britain the embattled ministry of Lord North collapsed and a new government, led by the Earl of

Shelburne, was established with a mandate to make peace with the rebellious colonies.[9]

If the Americans had good reason to distrust their allies, they had every hope of fair treatment from the man now at the helm of the British state. Shelburne had been a soldier in the Seven Years War before entering Parliament as a Whig. In Westminster he had been a vocal critic of the Stamp Act. When Pitt formed a ministry, he put Shelburne in charge of North American policy, where he proved himself a dogged supporter of American rights. In 1768, the Pitt ministry collapsed and Shelburne went into opposition until 1782. Like many Whigs, Shelburne was aghast at the spectacle of war with the Thirteen Colonies. Although he longed for reconciliation and dreaded the permanent loss of Britain's American possessions, he ultimately judged it preferable to 'see America forever severed from Great Britain than restored to our possession by force of arms or conquest'. On becoming prime minister, Shelburne thought that his liberal stance towards the Americans might have earned him enough goodwill to effect a rapprochement. Once disabused of this notion, he settled for the next-best outcome. Influenced by the free-trade theories of Adam Smith, and not wanting to let the French succeed in permanently alienating America from Britain, Shelburne arrived at a counterintuitive conclusion. If the United States was to be independent, he reasoned, it was better that its independence should be established such 'as to avoid all future Risque of Enmity', and he sought a settlement that would be 'the Foundation of a new Connection better adapted to the present Temper and Interest of both Countries'. In practice this meant a large, dynamic United States filled with consumers hungry for British exports. Spain and France could never compete with the mills and manufactures of industrializing Britain. The United States would have to buy from Britain, but Britain would no longer have to pay for the defence and administration of the colonies. In Shelburne's view, Britain could have the milk without paying for the cow.[10]

Shelburne's pick to lead peace negotiations reflected these ambitions. Richard Oswald was an elderly Scottish merchant with extensive interests in the United States. Aside from owning property in Virginia, the Floridas and the West Indies, Oswald operated a slave-trading business in Charleston, South Carolina, in partnership with none other than Henry Laurens. It was Oswald who posted bail for his old friend, and after Laurens's release from the Tower the two men went to the seaside town of Margate together for a short break. A friend of Adam Smith's, Oswald was committed to Shelburne's policy of setting the fledgling Anglo-American relationship on a footing conducive to transatlantic trade. 'The more these States extend themselves in population and cultivation, the better it will be for England,' he wrote in his journal. 'While they have such immense expansion of vacant lands behind them ... they will never become manufacturers ... the States will, therefore, for centuries to come, continue extending themselves backwards, and according as they produce, they will consume.' If Britain was at hand to serve this expanding market it would 'never fail to profit' from America's flourishing. Oswald and Shelburne were of one mind. Both men saw the value in going easy on their former subjects. Oswald's mission, Shelburne stated, was to 'to regain the affections of America' – not to argue over every comma and full stop. 'Our earnest wish for peace,' Shelburne wrote, was such that he was willing to 'purchase it at the price of acceding to the complete independence of the Thirteen States'. His envoy eagerly fulfilled this brief. When Oswald arrived in Paris, Franklin was scarcely able to believe his good luck. After several meetings in which Oswald conceded to almost every American demand, Franklin wrote to London expressing his satisfaction with their choice of diplomat. 'I desire no other channel of communication between us than that of Mr. Oswald,' he told Shelburne, 'which I think your Lordship has chosen with much Judgment.'[11]

Franklin now summoned the other three diplomats to Paris. Jay abandoned his doomed mission to Madrid and arrived in late June. At this juncture his faith in the French alliance was still intact and when Franklin insisted they follow France's lead in negotiations, Jay agreed. Then, in August, Franklin was struck down by bladder stones and took to his sickbed. The management of the negotiations fell to Jay alone, both Adams and Laurens still being absent.

That month Jay met with the Spanish ambassador to Paris, the Conde de Aranda, to discuss borders. With a copy of the Mitchell Map sprawled over a table, Aranda began to draw lines across the American continent. Refuting American claims west to the Mississippi while asserting Spanish ones, Aranda drew a line which in its essentials was the Royal Proclamation Line of 1763. Jay was appalled and stated that such a boundary was unacceptable. Aranda turned to the French. Vergennes dispatched his private secretary, Rayneval, to mediate between the Spaniard and the American. Over the next few weeks, the fate of the American West hung in the balance as Rayneval and Aranda marched red lines back and forth across the Mitchell Map. Had some version of the French and Spanish ministers' line come into effect, America would have forfeited almost the entire Ohio Valley.

The scales now fell from Jay's eyes. 'Our allies don't play fair,' he wrote; 'they want to play the western lands, the Mississippi, and the whole Gulf of Mexico into the hands of Spain.' Jay now grasped the fundamental contradiction in the Franco-American alliance. 'We can depend upon the French only to see that we are separated from England, but it is not in their interest that we should become a great and formidable people.' The final straw came later that month when he learnt that a senior French diplomat had secretly visited London. Jay had no intention of being France's dupe, still less of sacrificing his country's future. He now decided to cast off his instructions to cooperate with Vergennes and to initiate independent discussions with the British. 'We had only to cut this knot of independence,' Jay told Oswald, and the two countries would be 'sure of recovering and preserving a solid and beneficial friendship'.[12]

Oswald and Shelburne seized the moment and over the course of September a deal took shape. Britain made concessions on fishing rights and the status of loyalists; America dropped the demand for Canada and the Floridas. The result was a strong and expansive United States containing the entirety of the Ohio Valley. That river, one British observer noted, would be like 'a trading coast at the back of the American Colonies' where British merchants could hawk their wares for decades to come. Britain would profit from American greatness. There were, inevitably, last-minute hiccups. Risen from his sickbed, Franklin decried the betrayal of their French ally. He was shouted down by Adams – finally arrived from Amsterdam – who had long considered their instructions to work with Vergennes to be 'servile and intolerable'. 'It is glory to have broken such infamous orders,' he wrote. Their deal with Britain was 'the triumph of stubborn Independence – Independence of Friends and Foes'. Not all their arguments were among themselves. The drawing of the Canadian line produced a brief and vicious spat over the Maine–Nova Scotia boundary (a region Oswald described as 'a little spot of cross frosty land, which an Empress of Russia would give away at breakfast'), but after laboured negotiations they settled on the now familiar lake and river border. At the last hour, Henry Laurens arrived from London, still gaunt and sickly from his stay in the Tower, but in time, at least, to sign the final document at Oswald's rooms in the Hotel Muscovite on 30 November 1782. 'Thus drops the curtain upon this mighty tragedy,' Adams wrote to his wife. 'It has unravelled itself happily for us. And Heaven be praised.'[13]

The end of the war and the creation of the United States met with mixed reactions in Europe. In Britain Lord North wondered at the 'extremely generous' deal Shelburne had brokered with a crew of rebels and traitors. 'We have flung away men, money and thirteen provinces,' lamented Horace Walpole. 'Our glory is gone, our constitution gone, our sense gone.' The prime minister was unmoved. 'We prefer trade to dominion,' Shelburne remarked, coolly dispensing with pride and sentiment in favour of a commercial logic that would profit Britain immensely. Within twenty years a fifth of all British exports would go to the United States.

France, by contrast, profited little from the peace. It had spent a billion livres on a war that had failed to destroy the British Empire. France was bankrupt, Britain defiant. Vergennes bridled at American ingratitude. 'If we may judge the future from what has passed here under our eyes,' he wrote, 'we shall be but poorly paid for all we have done for the United States, and for securing them a national existence.' He could not have imagined how catastrophic the final bill would be. As the Comte de Ségur later observed, the Bourbon monarchy had sent a generation of young men to America, 'whence they were to bring back into France, the seeds of a lively passion for the establishment of political liberty, and independence'. Fifteen years later, the debts incurred in that struggle forced Louis to summon the Estates General, resulting in a revolution that swept away his regime.

The Spanish recognized at the time the dangerous sequence of events they had set in train. 'This federal republic has been born a pygmy,' the Conde de Aranda told Charles III, 'and it needed the support of two states as powerful as France and Spain to win its independence. The day will come in which it grows and turns into a giant, even a frightening colossus, in that region. It will then forget the benefits it has received from the two powers, and it will think only of its own expansion.'[14]

These words would prove prophetic. But for now the Americans were exultant. The war was over; the West was won. And after the peace settlement was announced in the spring of 1783, George Washington could finally relinquish his command of the Continental Army. On 8 June, from his headquarters in Newburgh, New York, Washington accompanied the announcement of his resignation with a farewell letter to his countrymen. He was bound for Virginia and Mount Vernon. But he encouraged Americans to look westwards. 'The Citizens of America,' he wrote, were 'placed in the most enviable condition, as the Lords and Proprietors of a vast Tract of Continent, comprehending all the various soils and climates of the World, and abounding with all the necessaries and conveniences of life ... They are, from this period, to be considered as Actors on a most conspicuous Theatre, which seems to be particularly designated by Providence for the display of human greatness and felicity.'[15]

# Ideal Lines

At the close of the revolution, Washington claimed 40,000 acres of land in the Ohio Valley, most of them on account of Dinwiddie's Proclamation in 1754. And in September 1784 – exactly thirty years since that grant – he headed west to visit them. As ever, Washington kept a journal and, as ever, his entries were terse. Departing Mount Vernon on 1 September, his party crossed the Appalachians at Cumberland two weeks later. When he had come there as a young man it was unspoiled. Now there were taverns along the road near the Youghiogheny and traders travelling in groups down to Pittsburgh. As before, he visited the site of Fort Necessity and, as before, the scene made no apparent impression upon him. He simply noted the quality of the grass and remarked that it was a promising location for a guesthouse. At Laurel Mountain he stopped for dinner at the house of Christopher Gist's son Thomas. Here he learned that his journey would have to be cut short. Over half of the lands Washington had come to visit were along the Great Kanawha. Gist told him that renewed Indian raiding made the journey impossible; he would not be able to travel beyond Pittsburgh. Washington had won independence for his country but he could not travel safely across it.

Thwarted, he turned his focus on his holdings nearby. These were some of his best, surveyed for him by William Crawford before the revolution. But as Crawford had noted at the time, these tracts had also been claimed by Scots-Irish settlers. These settlers – squatters, in Washington's eyes – had proved troublesome. Washington might have been a national hero, but to these men he was an absentee landlord with an old and tenuous claim to lands they had long been farming. On 14 September, Washington rode out to Miller's Run to meet them. They were a dozen or so men, proud and insistent on their claim to the land. Washington wrangled with them for a week but they held fast. Unable to strike a deal, Washington now had to gird himself for court.* He rode to the surveyor's office to gather information supporting his claim. The office was a log cabin – a single room with a bed, a desk and a mass of paperwork. Washington installed himself at the desk and began to pore over old land surveys and examine ledgers filled with sales records. His presence attracted a crowd and the room filled with curious frontiersmen. Washington interviewed each of them, gathering local knowledge of land matters, noting down the history of property transactions and recording any other snippets of information that might support his claim. That night he slept in the sole bed while his entourage wrapped themselves in blankets and buffalo hides and lay on the floor around him. A few days later he began the journey home. The trip had been a failure. He had been unable to see his lands on the Great Kanawha and had not managed to resolve his land disputes along the Ohio.

At the same time, the visit to the frontier had stirred old feelings inside him. His affairs might have been uncertain, but the West was still filled with promise. Washington had always seen his future in the West. Now he married his own ambitions with those of the country. The Treaty of Paris had 'given bounds to a New Empire' across the mountains. The United States' destiny was to settle it. His own travels had confirmed that this process had begun. 'I say not withstanding this disappointment I am well pleased with my journey,' he wrote at the close of his journal, 'as it has been the means of my obtaining knowledge of facts [concerning] the temper and disposition of the Western Inhabitants.'[1]

What were the facts? In brief, that the West was filling up fast. The road to Pittsburgh and the trail through the Cumberland Gap were packed with wagons heading west. Army officers at forts along the Ohio River

---

* Washington requested that they be polled individually and asked each one to speak for himself. The result was a unanimous rejection of his offer. He then removed a red handkerchief from his pocket and announced, 'Gentlemen, I will have this land just as surely as I now have this handkerchief.'

reported dozens of boats crammed with families, farming equipment and livestock passing by each week bound for Kentucky. Only a decade before Daniel Boone had lived in Kentucky alone with his family. Now the population was estimated to be 30,000. By the end of the decade it would double. Washington had seen the tide of migration with his own eyes during his 1784 visit.

But while he was pleased to see the western country fill up, he feared the chaos that would ensue if every settler heading west experienced the same frustrations buying land that he had faced himself. If the frontier remained a place filled with overlapping claims, conflicting surveys and tense stand-offs between squatters and legal claimants, it would be neither happy nor prosperous. As a young man Washington had taken advantage of the confused and chaotic condition of the frontier to buy up tracts of land for himself. Now as an elder statesman he wanted the government to impose order on the land and to manage and regulate its sale to ensure the Ohio Valley was populated by 'useful citizens'. And it would have to move fast. 'The spirit for emigration is great, people have got impatient,' he wrote to Richard Henry Lee shortly after his return, 'and tho' you cannot stop the road, it is yet in your power to mark the way; a little while and you will not be able to do either.'[2]

## 'REGULARLY AND COMPACTLY'

Look out the window as you fly across the United States today and you will see the solution that Congress struck upon as they grappled with how to manage the survey, sale and settlement of the vast lands that the Treaty of Paris had brought into the Union. Compared to Europe, where fields are divided according to ancient and often eccentric customs, the American landscape is strikingly regular. As you pass over open farmland you will see the land divided up into a series of squares and rectangles, which in turn contain other squares and other rectangles. The effect is not quite fractal, but suggestive of a repeating logic at work. Above all, it is rectilinear. The natural topography – the bend of rivers, the boundaries of pine forests – has been ignored. The land conforms to a rational human scheme. Perpendicular lines have been drawn across the continent corresponding to no geological or astronomical logic but only to the planner's whimsy. In the eighteenth century, they were called 'ideal lines' and they represented the triumph of order over chaos and man over nature. What you are looking at is the product of one of the great achievements of the Enlightenment: the Land Ordinance of 1785.[3]

Passed in May 1785 by the Continental Congress, the Land Ordinance dictated how the West would be surveyed and sold. The act was downstream of the revolutionary struggle. The terms of the Treaty of Paris had delivered the Ohio Valley into the Union; now Congress had to determine what to do with it. The question of land had also figured in the internal politics of the fledgling United States. Some states had large land claims in the West and some did not. All states needed land to pay soldiers and to collateralize their debts. Consequently there was a fundamental inequality between the states. This caused a cleavage so profound that Maryland refused to sign the Articles of Confederation until 1781, and only did so once the states with western lands agreed to cede them to Congress. This cession resolved another outstanding issue. While the states had raised loans individually, Congress had also borrowed on behalf of the United States. After the war, these debts were somewhere around $80 million, a vast amount at a time when Congress had scarcely any revenue powers. But with the land cessions the Congress would have some 220 million acres of land at its disposal. The solution was apparent: sell the lands to pay off the debt.

Under the terms of the ordinance, land had to be surveyed before it could be sold, and surveying had to be done in a precise manner. Each survey would begin with the marking-out of a baseline running from east to west. From this line would then be drawn a series of meridians running from north to south. The distance between meridians was six miles and so the intersection of baselines and meridians created rectangles of land called 'ranges'. These ranges were then divided into stacks of squares, each six miles wide and six miles tall. These were called 'townships'. Each township was thirty-six square miles, or 23,040 acres. Accordingly, each township was subdivided into thirty-six 'sections' of one square mile, or 640 acres. From here it was easy to continue subdividing the sections into smaller plots: a half section (320 acres), a quarter section (160 acres), a half quarter section (80 acres), and even a quarter quarter section (40 acres).

Why these numbers? Thomas Jefferson proposed an alternative scheme that would have used the decimal system, and had Jefferson got his way the American West would have been divided into factors of ten.

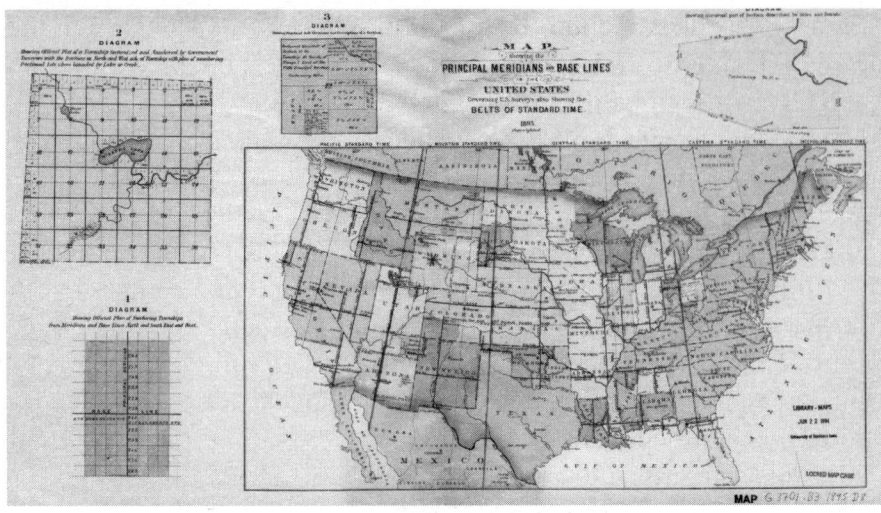

*A map of the United States featuring the components of the public land system: baselines, ranges, townships, and sections.*

And Jefferson's was only one of several competing schemes. The final plan won out for a simple reason: Gunter's chain. The language of the Land Ordinance provided for the use of the chain and, viewed from the perspective of Gunter's chain, the one-mile-square section and the six-mile-square township were perfectly logical. Eighty chains to one side of a section; 480 chains to one side of a township. A trained survey team would be able to survey lands in this manner quickly and easily. In as much time as it took the chainmen to ply their trade, the West could be transformed into a grid of ranges, townships and sections, each numbered, surveyed, platted and ready for sale. The system of measurement that George Washington had once practised in his brother's turnip field would now be applied to the entire American West.

The Land Ordinance was a long-term triumph and a short-term disappointment. It created a logical schema for land management that was so simple and intuitive that it ended up being adopted across the western United States. In a sense, the American West *was* the section and the township. The lines laid out by government surveyors influenced railroad construction and were later used in the creation of the Interstate Highway System. The units of land that the survey system defined became totemic. Generations of American farmers would think in factors of forty and dream in parcels of six miles square. The principle of prior survey, the use of a rectilinear grid and the practice of numbering sections, townships and ranges all made the prospects of emigrating west significantly more appealing. Under the previous system, land acquisition had been a lengthy and uncertain proposition. The West was a tangle of overlapping land claims, conflicting surveys and disputatious frontiersmen. Now the would-be settler could travel safe in the knowledge that what he bought he would own.

At the same time, by assuming the roles of surveyor and salesman, the American government hoped not only to generate revenues but to control the pattern of migration itself. Through the management of surveys and sales, the government would be able to channel settlers into certain regions and away from others. Western settlement would advance 'regularly and compactly', in Washington's words. The New Englanders in Congress went further, arguing that, by encouraging dense settlement, the Land Ordinance would establish virtuous communities on what had once been a frontier of depravity.

They did not see, or perhaps chose not to see, how closely their schemes resembled those put forward by the British colonial authorities just prior to the revolution which had then seemed so onerous. Those with longer memories might have seen echoes of the Proclamation of 1763 in Washington's paean to limits, regularity and compactness. Now the West was theirs, the Americans meant to tame it – not turn it over to people and forces beyond their control.

It was this impulse that led to a decision that hamstrung this first attempt at managing western settlement. Congress included in the ordinance a minimum price per acre of one dollar and a minimum tract size of 640 acres. In other words, only someone with at least 640 dollars in ready cash could actually buy land out west. Adding to the difficulty, land could only be purchased at a government land office, of which there was just one – in New York City, hundreds of miles from the frontier.

Despite these shortcomings, Congress pressed ahead with the ordinance, eager to see revenue from land sales. In September 1785 a team of surveyors led by Thomas Hutchins met at Pittsburgh. They headed down the river to the place described in the ordinance as 'the point of beginning'. This was an unassuming spot on the west bank of the Ohio where the modern states of Ohio, Pennsylvania and West Virginia meet. The intention was to mark out a baseline forty-two miles wide, corre-

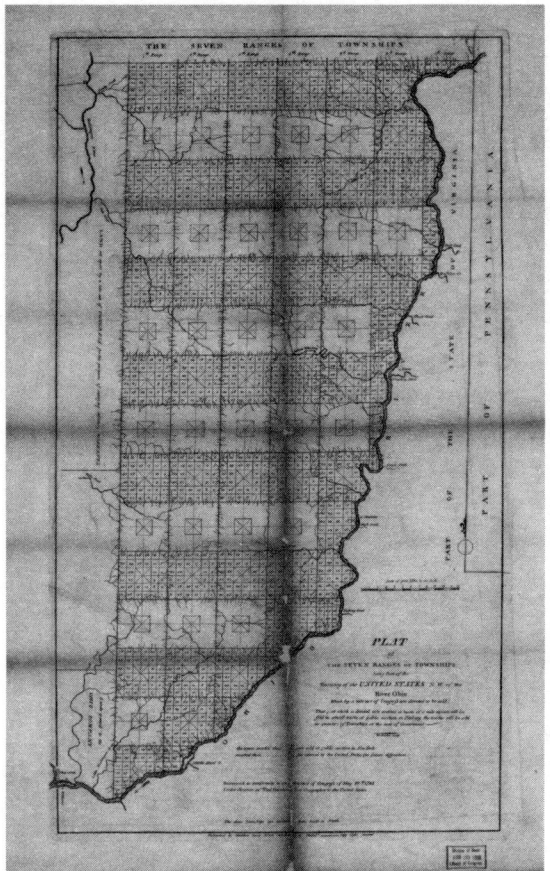

*A plan for the 'Seven Ranges' in Ohio, the first part of the United States surveyed under the Land Ordinance Act.*

sponding to the seven ranges envisioned in the ordinance. These ranges would extend southwards until they hit the Ohio as it swept around the eastern flank of the state and flowed on into Kentucky. Had the entirety of the seven ranges been surveyed, then approximately seventy-five townships, or 1.7 million acres, would have been thrown open to settlement. In the event, the survey was hampered by the outbreak of hostilities with the Shawnee.

Over the next two years, Hutchins continued his work in fits and starts but was only able to complete four of the seven ranges. He submitted these surveys to Congress in April 1787. In September of that year the first and only auction of public lands held under the Congress of the

*The first land warrant ever issued made out to John Martin on 4 March, 1788.*

Confederation took place in New York. The first plot of land patented under this new regime of land sales was issued on 4 March 1788. It recorded the sale of section twenty of township seven in range four to John Martin for the price of $640. For all the historical significance of this first transaction, the auction as a whole was a failure: 108,431 acres were sold for only $117,108. The Congress had envisioned the West as 'this fine fund for extinguishing the public debt'. It had proved to be no such thing – at least not yet. For even as these disappointing results were coming in from the land auctions, transactions of greater import were afoot. A new constitution was being written for the nation and a new scheme of government was being drawn up for the West.

## A TEMPLATE FOR EMPIRE

While Washington welcomed a system for ordered land surveys and sales, he knew it solved only half the problem the country faced in the West. Americans wanted land but they also wanted liberty. The revolution had unleashed a raucous and defiant political culture that enjoyed almost total popular support. Americans expected to enjoy the same rights and freedoms in the Ohio Valley as they would on the Atlantic seaboard. They expected the same institutions that guaranteed those rights and freedoms east of the mountains to be established west of them. During the revolution the problem had been partially solved south of the Ohio River when Virginia annexed Kentucky. North of the river the situation was very different. The Treaty of Paris had delivered the Ohio Valley to the United States but in the Northwest there was almost no government presence at all. There wasn't even a name for the country, let alone a coherent vision for how it would be administrated.

Washington grasped the danger of allowing this condition to persist. His own journey to the West convinced him that if the United States government did not create a system of government palatable to the people in the western world, they would create a system of their own. He had no expectation of automatic loyalty from the Scots-Irish settlers streaming west. The revolution, after all, had proclaimed as its founding principle the right of self-determination. The Thirteen Colonies had effectively seceded from the British Empire in order to satisfy their yearnings for self-rule. There was no reason the westerners might not do the same. 'The Western settlers ... stand as it were on a pivot,' he wrote; 'the touch of a feather would almost incline them any way.' The United States had to offer them good reasons to stay in the Union.*

The issue was not simply one of abstract political theories but of national survival. Washington was keenly aware that the young country was surrounded by enemies – Britain in Canada and Spain in Louisiana – who wanted the republican experiment to fail. If Congress could not keep the westerners content, America's foreign rivals would tempt them with alternatives. Establishing republican government over the mountains would draw settlers into these empty lands. At a time when the United States Army had fewer than a thousand soldiers under arms, settlers could do far more to assert American sovereignty in the West than Congress with its meagre resources. Washington wanted to 'plant a brave, a hardy and respectable race of people' in the Ohio Valley. These would be the 'advanced post' of American power who, by extending the range of American settlement, would 'banish forever the idea of our Western territory falling under the dominion of any European power'.[4]

Proposals for how best to govern the Northwest were discussed throughout the first half of the 1780s. Most demonstrated the same New England preference for ordered settlement that had moulded the 1785 Land Ordinance. The intention was to impose 'regularity' on the Northwest and avoid 'the desultory way' that the western frontier had been settled when the Scots-Irish pioneers had led the charge. Key to this was establishing a connection between land sales, settlement and self-government. In areas which the United States claimed but which were largely unsettled the government would impose rule directly. But in territories which were marked out for survey and settlement there would be a path to statehood.

---

* James Madison expressed the same fears in vivid terms in a March 1785 letter to Lafayette: 'Will the settlements which are beginning to take place on the branches of the Mississippi be so many distinct Societies, or only an expansion of the same Society? so many new bodies or merely the growth of the old one? Will they consist of a hostile or a foreign people, or will they not be a bone of our bones, and flesh of our flesh? Besides the confederal band, within which they will be comprehended, how much will the connection be strengthened by the ties of friendship, of marriage and consanguinity? ties which it may be remarked, will be even more numerous, between the ultramontane and the Atlantic States than between any two of the latter.'

The plan for how this would work in practice began to take shape in July 1786 when a committee that had been formed to consider the matter reported its findings to Congress. The committee proposed the creation of the Northwest Territory, a new governmental organization encompassing all the lands north of the Ohio River. And the Northwest Territory bore the hallmarks of its Yankee designers. In this new land civil liberties and religious freedom would be guaranteed, slavery would be forbidden and tracts of land would be set aside for educational institutions. The governmental architecture of the territory would be as rational and well built as the system of rectilinear survey lines that organized its land mass. It would be perfect for the 'enlightened people' its promoters expected to settle it.

Moreover, its government would evolve with the pace of settlement. The proposal envisioned that the territory would pass through a three-stage process of political maturation. In the first phase, the unsettled lands would be ruled by decree by a governor appointed by Congress. Once the population reached 5,000 white adult males, the form of government would change. The region would become a territory, a brand-new legal condition in American law, which would have defined boundaries and a more sophisticated government apparatus. The territory would still be ruled by a governor, but he would be advised by a legislative council and an elected house of representatives. This status would last until the free male population reached 60,000. At that point the territory was deemed large enough to be eligible for statehood. To do so, it would first have to hold a constitutional convention to decide the fundamental law of the proposed state. The only requirement was that 'the constitution and government so to be formed, shall be republican'. This draft constitution would then be sent to Congress, who would vote on whether to allow the new state to enter the Union. If it did so, the new state would join the compact of states with the same rights, responsibilities and standing as existing states. The plan envisioned that between three and five states would be carved out of the Northwest Territory on this basis.[5]

Congress adopted the Northwest Ordinance on 13 July 1787. Under its auspices five states – Ohio, Indiana, Illinois, Michigan, Wisconsin – were ultimately formed out of the lands north of the Ohio River. Indeed, the Northwest Ordinance established a process by which nearly all of the thirty-seven states that joined the United States after independence found their way into the Union. Its success proved that the United States could extend its founding principles into new lands. It was the blueprint for a new kind of republican imperialism, one which collapsed the old imperial relationship between periphery and core and created a new paradigm in which all the component parts of the United States were given equal standing within it. The original thirteen states would not hoard their republican principles; they would seek to extend them into the American West. There would be no periphery in this new American empire, only an expanding core of liberty.

It would be an empire all the same. While the ordinance conjured up an image of gradual progression towards equal participation in the Union, it was at its heart a scheme for imperial management. The basic unit of this American empire was the newly invented territory. James Monroe, who sat on the committee who drafted the ordinance, described the document as built 'upon colonial principles'. Thomas Jefferson said the Northwest Territory was 'highly tinctured with Aristocracy and monarchy' and essentially a reconfiguration of 'our old English Colonial Governments', in which the territorial governor was 'clothed with all the power of a British Nabob'. Just like colonial Virginia, a territory had an appointed governor, a council, an elected chamber – and was effectively subject to a faraway legislature in which it had no voice.

The fact that this condition was meant to be temporary could not disguise its essentially dictatorial nature. Congress would decide the pace of expansion, settlement and accession to the Union. This was where the Land Ordinance of 1785 and the Northwest Ordinance intersected. Congress held all the land as part of the public domain. Congress decided when the land was surveyed and sold. Congress could effectively regulate the population growth and so calibrate the political status of its outlying provinces. Fundamentally, Congress retained the right to veto entry into the Union altogether. Would-be states could be kept in territorial limbo in perpetuity. Guam and Puerto Rico have been United States territories for well over a century. Not by coincidence, it was often regions with large non-European populations that were kept as territories for longest. Implicit in the language of the ordinance was the right to reserve political rights to white men. Naturally, the expansion of the state system would come at the expense of the Native Americans. But it was also understood that the territories might house other undesirable populations whom Congress might want to discriminate against. In the 1780s these were largely French and Spanish Catholics on the western edge of the Ohio Valley. But over the next decades the United States would expand to encompass new lands and new peoples. The Northwest Ordinance provided a comprehensive system for managing ethnic outsiders and controlling their access to political power.[6]

The Northwest Ordinance assumed the existence of a dynamic, well-funded central government capable of administrating a vast system of bureaucrats, soldiers and surveyors. At the time of its passage this central government did not exist. But in the background one was being created.

At the same time as the Northwest Ordinance was being debated in New York, the Constitutional Convention was in progress in Philadelphia. The aim of the Constitution was to create a muscular federal government capable of raising taxes and asserting sovereignty at home and abroad. Alexander Hamilton, one of its chief architects, wrote that the sheer size of the United States was 'the strongest argument in favor of an energetic government; for any other can certainly never preserve the Union of so large an empire'. His vision prevailed and in March 1789 the Articles of Confederation were superseded by the Constitution of the United States. On 30 April of that year, George Washington was inaugurated as president of the United States. One of the first actions of the new regime was to re-enact the Northwest Ordinance. The lofty visions of both the Northwest Ordinance and the Land Ordinance of 1785 were now complemented by a government administration capable of funding and effecting them. The Constitution, one booster of the Northwest Territory wrote, would prove to settlers that 'the government of the United States was not a mere shadow'. Guarded by a powerful and responsive federal system, Americans on the frontier would 'grow up in habits of obedience and respect – they would learn to reverence the government; and the countless multitudes which will be produced in that vast region would become the nerves and sinews of the Union'. In the short term almost the exact opposite would be the case. Within a few years of Washington's inauguration, the capacity of the federal government to manage the West would be challenged once more.[7]

# Quelling the West

Fort Harmar was established in 1785 on the west bank of the Muskingum where it flowed into the Ohio. For many years the small garrison there did little else than count the number of keelboats heading down to Kentucky. Upstream were the old Moravian towns, and occasionally Indians came in to trade. On the other bank of the Muskingum was a large tumulus, a remnant of an ancient native civilization that had once lived there. Otherwise the main company for the small group of American soldiers were owls and deer and the immense sycamores that lined the banks of the river.

Then, shortly after midday on Monday, 7 April 1788, a small flotilla pulled in from the main current of the Ohio and went ashore on the east bank of the Muskingum. The lead boat was a large, well-made galley named the *Mayflower*, and from it disembarked Rufus Putnam and several dozen men. The arrival of Putnam and the first batch of settlers on the Muskingum marked a new epoch in the history of the Ohio Valley. For several decades pioneers had been establishing farms in the Ohio's southern watershed. Now, for the first time, American settlement had crossed the river.

## A HAPPY WORLD

The settlement of the Northwest Territory would be different from the settlement of Kentucky and western Virginia. These were not Scots-Irish adventurers looking to escape into the wilds. They were Yankees, descendants of the Pilgrim Fathers who had founded Plymouth Colony two centuries before. They had not come into the Northwest Territory to flee authority but to establish it, and everything they did spoke to a vision of ordered, rational settlement. Putnam and a team of surveyors laid out a town which they called Marietta, in honour of Marie Antoinette and the Franco-American alliance that had secured the Ohio Country to the United States. At the centre was the Campus Martius, a fortified wooden bastion erected on a piece of high ground, around which they laid out smaller residential lots along a grid. Over the next couple of months they worked in teams clearing the land and planting gardens.[1]

Work came to a halt on 4 July, a warm wet day, when the settlers at Marietta and the soldiers at Fort Harmar dined together at tables sixty feet long. As significant as this first Independence Day was, the settlers looked forward to another, more momentous day. 'May he soon arrive,' prayed James Mitchell Varnum in his celebratory speech before the feast. 'Thou gently flowing Ohio, whose surface, as conscious of thy unequaled majesty, reflecteth no images but the grandeur of the impending heaven, bear him, oh, bear him safely to this anxious spot!'

'He' was Arthur St. Clair, the first governor of the Northwest Territory. Born in Caithness, St. Clair had come to America as a soldier during the Seven Years War and never left. A tall, good-looking man

The seal of the Northwest Territory. The Latin phrase (meaning 'He has planted one better than the one fallen') celebrates the conquest of the wilderness by American settlers.

with great 'suavity of manners', he married into one of the grandest families in Boston. During the revolution he served with Washington at Valley Forge and Trenton. To the settlers at Marietta, St. Clair's coming bore immense significance. When he duly appeared to the sound of a thunderous artillery salute on 9 July, they rejoiced as they had for the nation's birthday. 'This is, in a sense, the birthday of this Western World,' one settler wrote in his journal. The people of Marietta did not seek the unruly freedom of the Kentucky frontier. As they put it in an ecstatic letter of welcome to St. Clair, they wanted to 'become a people voluntarily subjected to government and ... uniform regularity, among whom peace and justice, unanimity and friendship will ever delight to dwell!'

This wish was granted a few days later when, with great ceremony, St. Clair proclaimed the formal creation of the Northwest Territory. After his address, his secretary, Winthrop Sargent, read out the text of the Northwest Ordinance. Over the coming weeks, the citizens of Marietta looked on with glee as St. Clair and his assistants went about establishing the infrastructure of civil government. Laws were published, courts set up, oaths of office written. Ohio's first county – Washington County – was organized. Judges and clerks were appointed, profanity was outlawed and rules for the 'sacred observance of the Christian Sabbath' were put in place. 'Those people appear the most happy folks in the world,' wrote one soldier who witnessed the rapturous response of the citizenry to the arrival of St. Clair and the Northwest Territory's authority to Marietta. This atmosphere of solemnity and self-congratulation infected everyone, even the soldier-bureaucrat St. Clair. 'Reducing a country from a state of nature to a state of civilization ... fills the mind with delectable ideas,' he told the citizens of Marietta. Seeing 'vast forests converted into arable fields, and cities rising in places which were lately the habitations of wild beasts, give a pleasure something like that attendant on creation; if we can form an idea of it, the imagination is ravished, and a taste communicated of even the "joy of God to see a happy world"'.[2]

If the Northwest Territory was to be a new Eden, then there was a snake in the garden. Only a few weeks after St. Clair arrived in Marietta, a blockhouse a few miles upriver was attacked by Indians. This was one of many. Every week the men at Fort Harmar and Marietta saw dozens of families on the river heading for Kentucky. They also saw the aftermath of devastating Indian ambushes on keelboats heading downriver. Boats were found adrift, their passengers missing. Sometimes the raiders would scalp whole families and float their corpses down the Ohio. St. Clair was keenly aware that his job was to oversee the sale and settlement of the Northwest Territory in order to raise revenue for the federal government. If settlers felt insecure and the Ohio tribes felt emboldened, he would surely fail. 'It was always my Fear that our western Territory, instead of proving a Fund for paying the national Debt, would be a Source of Mischief,' St. Clair wrote to John Jay in December 1788. If 'the Possession and Sale of the western Territory is an Object with Congress … they must prepare to chastise the western Nations seriously'. Congress agreed with his assessment. Within a year of his triumphant arrival in Marietta, St. Clair would abandon idle talk of the joy of creation and commit to war.[3]

## THE ROAD TO FALLEN TIMBERS

The tribes of the Ohio Valley had not been consulted during the negotiations in Paris. As had happened twenty years before, their land had been traded away by European diplomats thousands of miles distant from their homelands. When the news reached them they reacted with disbelief. One British officer at Niagara reported that the Indians 'could never believe that our king could pretend to cede to America what was not his own to give, or that the Americans would accept from Him what he had no right to grant'. The Americans relished telling them of their betrayal by their former British allies. 'Your Fathers the English have made Peace with us for themselves,' one man told a group of Shawnee, 'but forgot you their Children, who Fought with them, and neglected you like Bastards.' The Indians remained dependent on the British and still looked to Detroit for supplies and support. The British kept the connection alive but made it clear that they were finished fighting the Americans. The tribes were left to contend with the Americans alone.

In peacetime Congress took a hard line and sent envoys – among them the unrelenting George Rogers Clark – to impose punitive treaties on tribes they claimed were a 'conquered people'. Within two years of the war's ending, all the Ohio tribes had signed treaties with the

Americans acknowledging their sovereignty over the entire valley. For almost twenty years the Ohio River had been the boundary between American and native lands. Now this barrier had been torn down and the shrinking remnants of the Indians' territory was picked over by soldiers, surveyors and settlers.[4]

These treaties were so manifestly unjust and so clearly intolerable to the mass of Indians, that nobody with any experience of the region believed they would endure. When Washington learnt of them, he expressed surprise at the severity of their terms. Yet even if the Indians had been willing to accept the unacceptable, the actual conditions of the frontier did not permit for peace. Scarcely a year after the Shawnee signed their treaty with the Americans, the Kentucky militia crossed the Ohio into their lands. Entering a village where an American flag flew, they were greeted by Moluntha, the tribal elder who had convinced his people to make peace with the Americans. Moluntha approached the horsemen, holding aloft a copy of their treaty. The militiamen hacked him to death and then scalped him. Moluntha's death, like that of Cornstalk before him, convinced the Shawnee that peace with the Americans was impossible. Most of the tribe retreated to villages in north-west Ohio and north-east Indiana along the Maumee, Wabash and Miami Rivers, where they lived among Wyandot and Delaware who had also fled the encroaching Americans.

A Shawnee named Blue Jacket emerged as their leader. A veteran of the Battle of Point Pleasant and the slaughter at Blue Licks, Blue Jacket set about forging a new confederacy of Ohio and Great Lakes Indians to resist the United States. The Shawnee message was simple but compelling. They had to resist American settlers and the very notion of settlement. These were not things that could be haggled over. 'God gave us this country,' the Shawnee insisted. 'We do not understand measuring out the lands. It is all ours.' They would not stand idly by while the Americans began the process of settling the north bank of the Ohio. They intended to 'take up a Rod and whip them back' to the southern shore of the river. By the end of the decade, the Shawnee and their allies were at war once again.[5]

This was the situation General St. Clair sailed into in the summer of 1788. Washington – who wanted a more accommodating Indian policy – had charged him with revising the treaties signed a few years before and winning back the goodwill of some of the tribes. St. Clair was unconvinced. The Indians, he told the secretary of war, were 'embarrassed' at the idea of further negotiations 'and were determined on War'. Besides, St. Clair was there to secure the Northwest to the United States, not to return it to its original inhabitants. Fundamentally, there was little he could offer the Indians. The only remaining course of action, in St. Clair's opinion, was an assault on their villages in northwest Ohio. His lobbying was successful and in 1790 Washington authorized a 'sudden stroke' against Blue Jacket and his allies.

In October, General Josiah Harmar set out from his base at Fort Washington near Cincinnati. After burning villages and farms along the Maumee River, Harmar set course for home. On the return journey, part of his force was lured into combat and sustained devastating losses at the hands of Blue Jacket's men. In the aftermath of Harmar's bungled campaign, the Indians were further emboldened. In January, a party of Delaware and Wyandot attacked settlers just upriver from Marietta. Shortly afterwards, another station was besieged and a settler tortured to death within sight of its walls. Settlement in the valley stalled. One land speculator noted 'the panic running through this country' occasioned by 'the repulse of our army'. At Marietta, Rufus Putnam was even less sanguine. 'Unless [the] Government speedily sends a body of troops for our protection,' he wrote, 'we are a ruined people.'

These were not simply the complaints of worried settlers. The cash-strapped federal government needed money from land sales. As Alexander Hamilton observed to Washington, war in the Northwest would undermine land values and undercut the credit of the United States at a crucial moment in its economic development. Washington was outraged on all accounts. Facing national insolvency, bound by the misguided Indian policy of his predecessors and let down by Harmar (who he accused of being a drunkard),* he turned to a man he thought he could trust to bring Blue Jacket to heel: Arthur St. Clair.[6]

Much of 1791 was spent in organizing St. Clair's punitive expedition into the Wabash Country. Congress almost tripled the size of the army, spending tens of thousands of dollars in the process and sending

---

* Secretary of War Henry Knox informed Harmar, 'It would be deficiency of candor on my part were I to say your conduct is approved by the President of the United States, or the public.'

recruiters across the eastern seaboard looking for volunteers. Washington looked on nervously as the mustering and supply of St. Clair's army dragged on into the summer and then beyond. For all the lethargy of the young army, morale remained high. 'I hope we shall give the Indians a thorough drubbing,' Jefferson wrote, 'and then change our tomahawk into a golden chain of friendship.' Washington's letter to Blue Jacket reflected the mood of confidence. 'The United States are powerful, and able to send forth such numbers of warriors, as would drive you entirely out of the Country,' he wrote. Resistance 'would occasion some trouble to us, but it would be absolute destruction to you, your women and your children'. The tribes were unmoved. Rufus Putnam reported from Marietta that Blue Jacket's men were in good spirits, joking that they would send their women to fight the Americans, 'and threatened there should not remain a smoke on the Ohio by the time the Leaves put out'.[7]

After months of anticipation, St. Clair's army finally marched out of Fort Washington in mid-September. The column was roughly 2,000 strong, including 1,500 soldiers, over a hundred teamsters with their hundreds of mules, some 200 women – wives, prostitutes and washerwomen – and two dozen children. At its head was Arthur St. Clair, appointed major general for the occasion, and suffering from a severe case of gout. Under his command were both (there were only two) regiments of United States infantry and a battalion of artillery. The remainder of the army were volunteers on short-term contracts, hurriedly trained over the summer. They were led by experienced men – Colonel William Darke had marched with Braddock and Washington on Fort Duquesne forty years earlier – but were described damningly by St. Clair's own adjutant general as having been 'picked up from the offscourings of large towns and cities'.[8]

This unruly army proceeded to hack its way through the forest towards the Indian settlements near the headwaters of the Wabash. They moved slowly, sometimes only several miles a day, and the want of discipline and proper provisioning soon began to show. The men walked on broken shoes and slept in tents designed for summer use. Flour ran out and the army marched on half rations. St. Clair neglected to post scouts and Indians began to steal horses and pick off stray soldiers. The recruits deserted by the dozen and St. Clair had to start hanging offenders to try and impose order. After two months they had marched less than a hundred miles. Winter arrived and the men suffered in the frost, hail and snow. St. Clair was so stricken with gout he travelled in a wagon. On 3 November, this bedraggled and demoralized mass of men stopped south of the forks of the Wabash and set up camp on a piece of high ground. Some Kentucky militiamen bivouacked in the forest on the opposite bank of one of the creeks that curled around St. Clair's flanks.

At daybreak the next morning a terrific noise went up from the surrounding forest. Survivors compared it to the ringing of hundreds of bells; veterans of the frontier recognized it as the Indian war cry. Without realizing it, St. Clair's army – reduced to perhaps a thousand fighting men – had stumbled into an equal number of Indian warriors led by Blue Jacket. Shortly afterwards, the Kentucky militiamen streamed out of the forest and into the main camp. Suddenly the treeline exploded with musket fire. The attack caught St. Clair in bed and he emerged from his tent wearing an overcoat and tricorn hat over his pyjamas, his long grey hair flowing around his face, and tried to take control of his men. He managed to get the artillery formed up but they were quickly silenced by lethally accurate fire from the trees. The gout-ridden general had, with great difficulty, got into the saddle of three horses and had all three shot from beneath him. After a fourth was killed, he drew his sword and tried to lead on foot. By this stage the fire was so dense that St. Clair's coat was riddled with bullet holes and a musket ball had shot off locks of his hair. The smoke given off by the American guns smothered the battlefield, giving Blue Jacket's men the chance to advance 'from one tree, log, or stump to another'. 'The Indians seemed to brave everything,' Ebenezer Denny, a veteran of the Continental Army, recalled, 'and when fairly fixed around us they made no noise other than their fire, which they kept up very constant and which seldom failed to tell, although scarcely heard.'

Under this withering fire, St. Clair's flanks crumbled and the Indians began to envelop the panicked Americans. As the lines gave way and Indians broke through into the main camp, the scene became chaotic. 'I wish I could describe that battle, but I lack the power,' one survivor recalled. 'As I look back on it now, it seems like a wild, horrible dream, in which whites and savages, friends and foes, were all mixed in mad confusion. They melted away in smoke, fire, and blood, amid groans, shouts, shrieks, yells, clashing steel, and exploding firearms.' Men fought toe to toe with hunting knives and axes. Major Jacob Fowler recalled that at the height of the battle the Indians 'were so thick that we could do nothing with them'. His men launched bayonet charges to prevent encirclement, only to find themselves surrounded once more. Fowler ended up climbing up a tree and shooting Indians, until the lock of his gun came loose. He discarded it, took a rifle from a corpse and kept fighting. The American commanders fought bravely, with senior officers, including St. Clair, personally leading bayonet charges. But discipline among the volunteers and militiamen broke completely. Survivors recall how many of these men seemed to be in a kind of fugue state, wandering around the battlefield 'stupefied and bewildered'. Fowler discovered a mass of them inside the officers' tents eating breakfast while the Indians laid down volleys of fire into them. 'Some of the men were shot down in the very act of eating,' Fowler wrote. The panic was even greater among the women and children trapped as the lines buckled under the weight of Blue Jacket's attack. One recruit recalled seeing several hundred civilians 'in a state of excitement bordering on distraction. Some were running to and fro, wringing their hands and shrieking out their terrors; some were standing speechless, like statues of horror.'[9]

After three hours of fighting, St Clair ordered a retreat, to prevent the army from being cut off. Officers practically had to beat their dumbstruck men off the battlefield. Those with their wits still about them sprinted for safety. The wounded and the vast majority of the women were left behind. 'The whole Army ran together like a mob at a fair,' Colonel Darke wrote. Major Fowler recalled the scene as he fled for his life. Looking back as the Indians closed in, he saw the bodies of the American dead: 'The freshly-scalped heads were reeking with smoke, and in the heavy morning frost looked like so many pumpkins through a cornfield in December.' The rump of the army fell back in utter disarray, leaving guns and cartridge boxes littering the road back to Cincinnati. Blue Jacket did not pursue them. His men ransacked the American camp and returned to their villages loaded down with scalps, captives and loot. That evening they celebrated in fine style, dressing up in the uniforms of the defeated army. 'They looked like an American Army in Masquerade,' one captive recalled. Another saw an Indian wearing the dress coat of an artillery officer 'with silver epaulets on his shoulders and a watch suspended from each ear'.[10]

St. Clair rode into Cincinnati on a packhorse to find the remains of his army getting roaring drunk. The army stayed there for days while survivors limped in, some without their pates. St. Clair retreated to his bed and did not leave it for a fortnight. In the meantime, Ebenezer Denny was sent to Philadelphia to convey the news to Washington. The president could not escape the magnitude of the disaster. Six hundred Americans were dead or missing, and a further 300 were wounded. Blue Jacket lost fewer than thirty men dead and forty wounded. By comparison, at Custer's Last Stand at the Little Bighorn eighty-five years later – which is typically remembered as the greatest Indian victory over an American force – fewer than 300 men died. Moreover, in 1876, the 7th Cavalry was eminently replaceable. In 1791, Blue Jacket did not just defeat an American army – he defeated the *only* American army. For Washington, his own biography provided a ready parallel to St. Clair's catastrophic defeat. 'I think the slaughter far greater than Braddock's,' Colonel Darke concluded in his own account of the battle. Almost forty years after that fateful expedition into the Ohio Valley, the western tribes had proved they could still best American soldiers in the field.[11]

St. Clair's Defeat proved to be the high-water mark of native resistance. In the immediate aftermath, Congress and the country were so appalled by the humiliation that for a period it seemed as though the entire project of western expansion would be reconsidered, or at least significantly curtailed. There was talk of creating a permanent Indian barrier state in the Northwest and of limiting the range of American settlement. Overtures of varying sincerity were made to Blue Jacket and other prominent Indian leaders. All were rebuffed. Riding high after their victory, the Ohio tribes had no desire to treat with the duplicitous Americans.

Congress acted to repair the damage. A professional, standing army of 5,000 men was planned and provided for with a million dollars in congressional spending. In 1794 another attempt was made on the Wabash. This time General Anthony Wayne led several thousand well-armed and well-trained professional soldiers into the Northwest. Wayne met Blue Jacket in battle at a place called Fallen Timbers in north-western Ohio on 20 August 1794. When the Indians failed to envelop the Americans, Blue Jacket and his men were beaten from the field. In the weeks that followed, Wayne pillaged their farmlands in the Auglaize and Maumee valleys, burning vast cornfields and laying waste to towns and villages. Abandoned by the British and with no means to continue fighting, Blue Jacket submitted. At the Treaty of Greenville, signed in the summer of 1795, the tribes agreed to sweeping land cessions across the Ohio Valley. 'We must think of war no more,' Blue Jacket told his men. At the end of the signing ceremony he turned to the American representatives and said it was his great wish to meet 'our elder brother, general Washington ... for your younger brothers have a strong desire to see that great man and to enjoy the pleasure of conversing with him'.[12]

These sentiments were not reciprocated. The federal government was finished with Indian diplomacy. It had other matters to attend to. Within a year of the Treaty of Greenville, Congress passed a new land act further liberalizing access to western territory. The floodgates of settlement were opened once more. 'All Kentucky and the back parts of Virginia and Pennsylvania are running mad with expectations of the land office opening in this country,' one speculator reported from Cincinnati. 'Hundreds are running into the wilderness west of the Great Miami, locating and making elections of land.'

The war for the West was over; the scramble for Ohio had begun.[13]

# Ohio Fever

George Washington died in his bed on 14 December 1799, at home in Mount Vernon. His death triggered an outpouring of public grief. Up and down the country his passing was discussed at length in newspapers, observed in public ceremonies and made the subject of eulogies that were then printed and circulated throughout the nation. These eulogies helped define Washington for future generations. In life, Washington had been stoic, imperturbable and reserved. In death, these virtues came into their own, making him amenable to a cult of veneration that has lasted to this day. The Washington of marble statuary and prose encomia was a blank to which everything noble could be ascribed. He became, in the words of his most famous eulogist, Henry Lee, 'first in war, first in peace, and first in the hearts of his countrymen'.

Lee's eulogy became the template for how Washington was remembered, or rather *which* Washington was remembered. Lee's Washington was essentially a man of the tidewater. The moments in Washington's career he chose to dwell on – Boston, Morristown, Princeton, Trenton – occurred on the Atlantic seaboard. Washington's legend was formed along the old line of settlement, far from the frontier. Lee did mention his role in Braddock's defeat and he noted in passing his role in ending the threat posed by 'Indian tribes' in 'distant forests' during the wars of the 1790s – but these were westward detours. Washington was an eastern figure. This became the general structure of the countless eulogies given in the days and weeks after his death: a few nods across the mountains but otherwise a strict focus on the scenes of Washington's life that played out against a mid-Atlantic backdrop.

Eulogies tell one story; probate documents tell another. Washington's last will and testament was recorded at Virginia's Fairfax County Courthouse on 20 January 1800. Washington's net worth was roughly $780,000. Two-thirds of this, $486,000, was in land whose values he had calculated a few months before his death. The schedule of his landholdings offers a rather different account of Washington's career. Aside from his holdings in Virginia, Washington owned 1,100 acres in western Maryland, 5,000 acres in Kentucky, 3,000 acres along the Miami River in the Northwest Territory, and 234 acres at the Great Meadows in south-east Pennsylvania near the site of Fort Necessity. In addition, he listed 9,744 acres along the Ohio River and the Little Kanawha. But the single largest line item in his accounts was his 23,341 acres along the Great Kanawha River. These lands, secured for himself under the Dinwiddie Proclamation fifty years and another country prior, were worth $200,000 dollars, or a quarter of the total dollar value of his estate. 'I have found distant property in land more pregnant of perplexities than profit,' Washington had written in a letter a few years before his death. They had at least been profitable perplexities. Washington had achieved his youthful ambition of leaving a noble estate to posterity. He also left a great example to his contemporaries. Washington died worth approximately $30 million in today's money.* By some calculations he was the richest man in the country. The East had made him a national hero; the West had made him wealthy. Generations of Americans would model themselves on him and head to the frontier to find their fortune. And at the time of his death, the frontier at hand was the Ohio Valley.[1]

## THIS WESTERN CANAAN

In a rare moment of effusiveness in the summer of 1785, Washington outlined his highest hopes for the American West. 'My first wish,' he wrote, 'is, to see this plague [war] to Mankind banished from the Earth; & the Sons & daughters of this World employed in more pleasing & innocent amusements than in preparing implements, & exercising them

---

* Measurements of Washington's wealth vary widely. This figure comes from https://measuringworth.com. A figure of $400 million is often cited. Some metrics go as high as $1.5 trillion.

for the destruction of the human race. Rather than quarrel about territory, let the poor, the needy, & oppressed of the Earth; and those who want Land, resort to the fertile plains of our Western Country, to the second Land of promise, & there dwell in peace.' Washington's reference to the 'land of promise' was significant. In the early years of the republic it was common to refer to the lands over the mountains as 'this western Canaan', the American analogue to the biblical land beyond the River Jordan that was promised to the Israelites. In scripture, Canaan was famous as 'a land which floweth with milk and honey'. The American Canaan was no less wondrous. The perch that swam in the Ohio were so large that they could provide lunch for seven men and still have plenty left over. The sycamores that towered over the riverbanks were so immense that thirteen horsemen could ride abreast in their hollows, with space for more still. There were crawfish as big as lobsters, nuts as big as hen's eggs, and peach trees that shot up so fast they bore fruit a mere three years after planting. So bounteous was this land, so fertile and so health-giving, that it was common for men to live to over eighty, and there were reports of one man living to the age of one hundred and forty.

Americans believed. More than that, they wanted to believe. The idea that the West would somehow end want, redeem their life's toils and set everything right was congruent with scripture, with the trajectory of American history and with their innermost yearnings.* Inevitably, Americans wanted to see Canaan with their own eyes. Ohio Fever took hold and within months of the Battle of Fallen Timbers the wagon roads across the mountains were packed and boats left Pittsburgh every day heading downriver. This torrent of humanity kept flowing west for decades. 'We have now fairly turned our backs on the old world, and find ourselves in the very stream of emigration,' one British traveller wrote as he joined the train of emigrants heading over the Appalachians. 'Old America seems to be breaking up, and moving westward.'[2]

---

* One of the most popular anecdotes of the time was of a Methodist preacher from the Ohio Valley touring in another state. Standing before an audience, burning up with religious fervour as he described the joys that awaited the faithful after death, the preacher, approaching the climax of his paean to the pleasures of the hereafter, and having exhausted his reserves of metaphors and similes and florid biblical phrases, hit on an example of paradise closer to home and exclaimed: 'In short, my brethren, to say all in one word, heaven is a Kentucky of a place!'

In June 1801, a French botanist named François Michaux went west to see the Ohio Valley for himself. He departed from Philadelphia along the old Forbes Road, reaching the foot of the Appalachians at the end of the month. On 1 July, he joined the wagon road heading over the Allegheny Mountains. The road itself was famously bad, single-track and strewn with large rocks. At times so steep that descending wagons had logs strapped to the back to prevent them from careering off, it was packed full of wagons heading west and herds of cattle, oxen and hogs heading east. It took Michaux three days to cross Laurel and Chestnut ridges. By 3 July, he was on the road to Pittsburgh when a heavy shower obliged him to take shelter in a farmhouse near the Monongahela. When the weather cleared, the owner offered to show the Frenchman a site of local historical interest. '[He] informed us that this was the spot on which the French, in the Seven Years War, had completely defeated General Braddock: he showed us several trees which were damaged by the balls.'[3]

The next evening Michaux rode into Pittsburgh. For many years, he noted, the forks of the Ohio had been considered 'the key of the Western Country'. But now that the Indian threat had passed, its purpose had changed. The garrison had been reduced and the fort left to decay. Pittsburgh was a rapidly growing commercial and industrial hub. The roads approaching it were lined with 'handsome villages' inhabited by industrious and law-abiding settlers. Factories producing glass, nails, rope and hats had sprung up along the Monongahela and Youghiogheny Rivers. Open-pit coal mines pockmarked the hillsides. Its greatest industrial enterprise was shipbuilding. At the wharfs and jetties near Pittsburgh were a vast range of river-going craft. 'The first thing that strikes a stranger from the Atlantic,' one traveller wrote, 'arrived at the [Pittsburgh] boat-landing, is the singular, whimsical, and amusing spectacle, of the varieties of watercraft, of all shapes and structures.' There were single-man canoes, larger pirogues that could hold four men, roofed skiffs or bateaux, with (or without) masts, and fitted with oars, as well as barges, ferryflats, sleds, dugouts, schooners and keelboats that could be poled upriver as well as sailed down and could hold upwards of a hundred passengers.

By far the most characteristic Ohio vessel was the flatboat, known variously as a Kentucky boat, a Kentucky flat, a broadhorn, a family boat or an ark. These were flat-bottomed rectangles, made entirely of wood and piloted by a steersman at aft with a large paddle. They had a roof, and one witness described them as looking like waterborne pigsties, although they more properly resembled floating log cabins. These craft could be lashed together at Pittsburgh for forty dollars, used to transport cargo to their destination and then sunk in the river. They were also the favoured mode of transport for families relocating to the frontier. It was not uncommon to see three generations of a family with their livestock and all their earthly possessions wheeling off down the river from the confluence of the Ohio. Michaux recalled seeing these 'large square boxes ... which, abandoned to the current, presented, by turns, their ends, their sides, and their corners' as they spun downstream. 'These people abandoned themselves in this manner,' he marvelled, 'for several hundred miles to the current of the river, probably without knowing the place where they might stop.'[4]

In mid-July, Michaux set out overland on the bridle path connecting Pittsburgh to Wheeling through a country filled with mills, prospering farms and smart country churches. Wheeling was a 'rising town', profiting much as Pittsburgh had, and was home to seventy frame houses and a dozen stores. Here he bought a twenty-foot-long canoe cut from a single tree, pushed off from the shore and within twelve miles had crossed into Ohio. A few days later he arrived in Marietta, which had now grown to two hundred buildings. Like Wheeling and Pittsburgh, Marietta was booming. The north bank of the Ohio around Marietta was filled with expatriate New Englanders whose tidy farms lined the river as Michaux continued downstream. On 1 August he reached Limestone, Kentucky, after travelling 350 miles in ten days since leaving Wheeling.[5]

Limestone was an inland harbour of thirty or forty frame houses whence merchandise from Pittsburgh and Wheeling was transported into central Kentucky. Michaux struck out south on foot down country roads and over crude log bridges slung over creeks. A few days later he strolled into Lexington. This region, which a few years before had consisted of heavily armed stations and blockhouses filled with cowering settlers, was now the heartland of the famed Bluegrass Country, the richest land in the state. Lexington was girded with large plantations where gangs of slaves grew hemp and tobacco. The wealth produced by their labour was spent in Lexington, a town of 3,000 with two newspapers, two rope-walks, a library and several tanneries. Lexington,

Michaux noted, was essentially an outgrowth of Virginia and its inhabitants retained 'the manners of the Virginians. With them, a passion for gaming and spirituous liquors is carried to excess ... They meet often at the taverns ... [and] they pass whole days there. Horses, and the lawsuits, are the usual subjects of their conversation.'

Michaux hired a horse and rode south from Lexington, past Danville and Harrodsburg, to the Barren River, which he followed through the open meadows (or barrens) of south-central Kentucky. Straying from the road to water his horse, Michaux got lost and came across a farm 'in a deep and narrow valley' and fell in conversation with the woman who lived there. 'She told me that she had lived three years in these barrens; that for eighteen months she had not seen any person; that, weary of living in this sequestered manner, her husband had been gone about two months to look for other lands towards the mouth of the Ohio. Such was the pretext for this change of residence, which would be the third, since the family had left the back settlements of Virginia.' This roving family of five was typical of the southern backcountry, and the counterpoint to the fabulously wealthy planters of the Bluegrass Country. Still, Michaux observed they were 'very abundantly supplied with maize and milk', and so were doing better than surviving. The woman directed him back to the road and Michaux continued south along the river, across a landscape of scattered plantations and remote homesteads.

On 27 August he rode into Tennessee. 'The first habitation I met with on entering Tennessee,' Michaux wrote, 'belonged to a person named Cheeks, of whom I conceived a very bad opinion from the conversation he was holding with seven or eight of his neighbours, with whom he was drinking whiskey immoderately.' A fearful Michaux pressed on to find safer quarters.

Ahead lay Nashville – the most southerly point on Michaux's western adventure – on the very edge of the Ohio basin. Here, 1,500 miles from Philadelphia, was a flourishing town of 120 buildings, grown rich off the cotton trade. The planters of Nashville largely sold their crop in Europe, but when Michaux arrived there were plans in train to have bales of cotton poled up the Cumberland and Ohio Rivers on keelboats to Pittsburgh. 'Thus those parts of the western states which are farthest asunder, are cemented by commercial relations, of which cotton is the basis, and the Ohio the link of communication.'

Michaux could not dally in Nashville and turned east on the road to Knoxville. This was a heavily wooded land, filled with thick reeds and canebrakes that hid the numerous farms scattered in the forest. After several days, he arrived at a plantation owned by William Sampson on the Cumberland River. This, he learned, used to be the site of Fort Blount, constructed about eighteen years before, to protect the emigrants from the Cherokee. But since the peace, 'the population [of Tennessee] being greatly augmented, [the Indians] are incapacitated from doing them any further injury, and the fort has been destroyed'. The Cherokee had not gone altogether. Leaving Sampson's, Michaux crossed the Cumberland Mountains, following a path marked by crude wooden signs. On the second day in, they met some Cherokee, who they lavished with gifts. These were the only Indians Michaux recorded seeing in his entire time west of the mountains.

At the end of the trail was the federal garrison at Fort Southwest Point, built at the confluence of the Clinch and Holston Rivers, and thirty-five miles beyond that lay Knoxville, then larger than Nashville and the entrepôt for goods entering Tennessee from Richmond, Baltimore and Philadelphia. Here Michaux stayed the night at the George Washington tavern, a decent hotel but to his mind too expensive. 'This high price arises from a desire of getting rich in a short time,' he grumbled in his journal, 'a desire which is general in the United States, where every man who exercises any profession or art whatsoever, is anxious to get a great deal by it, and is not contented with a moderate profit, as in Europe.'

Riding north-east out of Knoxville, Michaux travelled through the Holston River Valley to Jonesborough, on the North Carolina border. This region, which during the revolution had been raw frontier, was now packed with farms, log cabins and apple and peach orchards. At a farm he met two families of emigrants heading west to Tennessee. 'Their torn garments, and the bad plight of the children, who followed barefooted, and in their shirts, were indications of their poverty.' These destitute pilgrims into Canaan were drawn onwards by the dream common to every frontiersman: landownership. 'The riches of the inhabitants of the western country does not ... consist in money,' Michaux wrote, 'but each man lives on his own freehold.' He had, however, spent enough time among the land speculators in Nashville and Lexington to know that even this small wish would likely be denied to these barefoot travellers. Wealthy men had already engrossed almost all the good land as far west as the Mississippi. They would welcome these people as tenants; let them clear, plant and improve the land; let them boost its value while paying their rent in kind; and then shift them off westwards to make way for the wealthier settlers sure to come in their wake. For these pauper migrants, as a Virginian named Moses Austin noted when passing through the same region in 1796, what lay ahead was 'a goodly land ... but to them a forbidden land'.[6]

Michaux rode on, into the hollows of the Ridge-and-Valley Appalachians of western North Carolina, wandering among forests of oak and ash, covered in streams, carpeted with wild peas and filled with black bears. At some point along the trail he crossed the ridge of the mountains and passed out of Canaan and into the old Atlantic settlements.

The Ohio Valley was changing rapidly in these years and Michaux's journal was necessarily a snapshot in time. A few years before, the scene had been very different. Pittsburgh was still dotted with blockhouses, its citizens were still scarred by the recent Indian wars, and the coal in the surrounding hills was still in the ground. Downriver, Wheeling and Limestone were 'trifling hamlets', while Marietta was all farmers, Cincinnati was a seedy garrison town and there was scarcely a log cabin on either side of the river from these settlements to Louisville – then an 'inconsiderable village' with a single stone building. A decade after Michaux's tour, the scene was transformed. Pittsburgh had become 'the Birmingham of America', famous for the 'stygian' smog that hung over it, the product of a hundred smokestacks and ironworks and open-pit mining operations.

And as went Pittsburgh, so went the Ohio Valley. Wheeling, Marietta, Cincinnati, Louisville – all boomed. Limestone morphed into Maysville, and Cleveland, Columbus, Canton, Akron and Chillicothe sprang up on the Ohio's northern tributaries. The once bare banks of the Ohio's main channel became thickly settled. 'Thirty years ago, the whole country on the banks of this river was almost an entire wilderness,' noted one traveller in 1815. 'When I descended, I found its banks studded with towns and farm-houses, so close that I slept on shore every night.' Between Maysville and the Falls of the Ohio, another traveller observed twenty new towns. In Louisville, he recorded, 'all is life, activity and motion'.

Change, perpetual change, was the essence of western life. An outsider 'can have but a faint conception of the rage existing at the west for "improving" the country', proclaimed one visitor. 'New farms, new towns, new railroads and new canals, are continually projecting, and you cannot fall upon a knot of a half dozen persons anywhere, but the burden of their conversation is of some new project or other. Indeed, the whole ... west is racy.'[7]

Some constants did emerge. By 1800 the Ohio River had become the boundary between two societies. South of the river, slavery flourished and hemp, tobacco and cotton enriched the slave-owning few, while the mass of poor whites were forced to the periphery. Kentucky was a replica of Virginia. Its politics retained some of its frontier flavour, but it was soon dominated by landowners, slave-owners and Lexington lawyers. The mass of the free white population, as one Kentucky radical had prophesied, was 'wheedled out of our just rights, by flattery, grog, [and] the wag of a ruffled hand'.

The political power of the slave-owners south of the Ohio produced an exodus of non-slave-owners to its northern shore. The Northwest Territory became a Promised Land within a Promised Land. The Ohio River ran 'like Jordan, between [Kentucky] and the Canaan of liberty on the other side'. If Kentucky was opulent, oligarchical and stained by slavery, society on the north shore of the Ohio was tolerant, temperate and democratic. Ohio became associated with New England in much the same way that Kentucky was linked to Virginia. Cincinnati became the Boston of the West and spawned universities, colleges, charitable institutions, temperance societies and the first western abolitionists. To its promoters, the true West – the West consonant with America's founding principles – was in these Yankee regions of the Ohio Valley.[8]

If the Ohio Valley was divided by slavery, it was united by a common pursuit: land speculation. As the scramble for Kentucky lands predated the Land Ordinance of 1785, the land there had been claimed through squatting, marking trees and building higgledy-piggledy 'improvements' to demonstrate settlement. Over the years, these claims overlapped and concatenated to produce a morass of titles, deeds and pretensions that kept Kentucky's lawyers in business for decades. In some places the same tract was claimed by ten people. 'Whoever purchases there,' wrote one frustrated Kentucky claimant, 'is sure to purchase a lawsuit.' Lengthy and expensive legal actions favour the rich, and in Kentucky, as in Virginia, the majority of land passed into the hands of the burgeoning Bluegrass aristocracy. The pattern was repeated in Tennessee and Appalachian Virginia and – despite the more orderly manner of survey and sale – north of the Ohio too. Huge chunks of land there were claimed by speculators and land companies. As the tide of immigration increased, old speculative schemes matured and new ones were hatched. 'Land speculations are carried on to a degree of madness,' one writer reported from the frontier. 'Were I to characterise the United States,' wrote an English traveller, 'it should be by the appellation of the land of speculation ... Surely there never was a country where that passion was so universal, or had such unbounded scope.'[9]

This was no country for the old Scots-Irish pioneers. 'I was raised on the frontiers of Kentucky,' recalled one of them many years later, 'in the midst of the Indian war, where men were only respected in proportion to their valor and skill in fighting Indians, and killing wild beasts.' The time for such men was past. The Ohio Valley, in the words of one of its eulogists, had become 'the empire of the cultivator's axe and plough'. The newcomers had never met a Shawnee or survived a winter in a stockade. They disdained the unruly mass of backcountry settlers; their arrival drove up prices, scared off game, and ended the independence of the frontier.

Perhaps the most famous victim of this process was Daniel Boone. Thirty years after settling in Kentucky, Boone found himself surrounded by farms and unable to hunt for want of game. This was intolerable for the old Virginia long hunter. During the revolutionary years, he once said, 'you would not have walked out in any direction for more than a mile without shooting a buck or a bear. There were then thousands of Buffaloes on the hills in Kentucky; the land looked as if it never would become poor; and to hunt in those days was a pleasure indeed.' By the end of the 1790s the buffalo were gone and deer were scarce. In 1799, the man later praised as 'the instrument of opening the road to millions of the human family ... to a Land flowing with milk and honey' left Kentucky and headed west to Missouri, hoping to find land, game and peace.

The Scots-Irish went with him, scattering into Indiana, Illinois, Michigan and beyond. One traveller found himself far up a tributary of the Miami River on the Indiana frontier and, though the land was 'poor and ridgy soil, I could hear on all sides the settler's axe resounding, and the dogs barking, sure indications, that the land had been, as the phrase is, "taken up"'. As the Scots-Irish moved west, the great cycle of settlement began anew. Soon, as one Illinois settler wrote, one could speak not just of 'the Ohio fever', but also 'the Illinois, or Michigan, or Wisconsin fevers'. 'The spirit of emigration pervades the world,' one Yankee lamented. 'It has loosened the foundations of society, severed the ties of the kindred and set mankind afloat as it were, upon a tumultuous sea, without any settled destination.'[10]

## CANAANITES

In 1791, the population of the entire Northwest Territory was 4,280 people. A decade later, the population of Ohio was 45,000, and by 1810 the population had quadrupled to 230,000. In 1820, the population had almost tripled to 581,000. By 1860, Ohio was the third-largest state in the Union. Cincinnati was the sixth-largest city in the country and the largest settlement west of the Appalachians. Five million people lived along the banks of the Ohio, and the entire river and all its tributaries probably contained a quarter of the United States' population. 'The progress of this great state has no parallel in the history of colonies,' one contemporary enthused. 'No records can be found of equal advancement of population, national wealth, strength and improvement of every sort, by the unforced progress of immigration and natural increase ... The whole scene has at first view the aspect of fable and enchantment.' Canaan had flourished.[11]

In the Old Testament, Canaan was the promised land of the Israelites – but it was not an empty land. Canaan was home to the Canaanites. Part of the biblical instruction to the Israelites was to go into Canaan and 'cast out many nations before thee ... [and] save alive nothing that breatheth'. 'Thou shalt utterly destroy them ... as the Lord thy God hath commanded thee.' To Americans steeped in scripture the parallel was clear. 'I rather consider the American Indians as Canaanites,' Ezra Stiles, president of Yale, wrote in 1783, 'and the extirpation of the Canaanites ... [as] of God.' What was believed by the president of Yale was self-evident on the frontier. The settlers 'represented the Indians as Canaanites', one frontier missionary recorded, 'who without mercy ought to be destroyed from the face of the earth, and considered America as the land of promise given to the Christians'.[12]

By 1860 that injunction had been fulfilled. That year the census recorded the number of Native Americans living in the Ohio Valley. The total native population of states directly bordering the Ohio River was 392: 290 in Indiana, 33 in Kentucky, 32 in Illinois, 30 in Ohio, 7 in Pennsylvania. Of the old tribes that had once given law to the Ohio Valley there was no trace. Settlers would occasionally plough up an axe or an arrowhead. Sometimes an old Indian would appear and camp by his former lands for a time. Shortly after the turn of the nineteenth century, a few Shawnee came to Mount Sterling in north-east Kentucky. It was an old man and his two grandsons. When they saw Pilot Knob, a settler named Jesse Daniel recalled, 'they gave great demonstrations of joy'. They 'visited several licks about there', Daniel said; 'seemed to know them all. I soon found by his chat, he seemed to be acquainted with the ground he was on.'

But these appearances were unusual. If Shawnee were talked of at all, it was to scare children into good behaviour. The long and bitter Indian wars had become the stuff of folklore and gothic romance.* The only reminder of centuries of Indian habitation were in the names given to the land itself. Mingo Creek. Shawnee Lookout. Cherokee Run. Seneca Rocks. Tuscarora Mountain. Chillicothe. Piqua. Coshocton. Muskingum.

But occasionally the past would surface. In August 1812, a teenager was at Burgettstown, Pennsylvania, on the Ohio line, where volunteers were mustering for a planned invasion of Canada. The mood was festive and as the crowd grew larger, the whiskey began to flow. As he moved through the mass of people, he came across a very drunk old man 'who was singing maudlin songs, when some person said, "Now, Uncle Sol, show us how they killed the Indians." ... At once the old fellow's whole manner changed from the gay to the grave, and he began crying and cursing the cowards who killed women and children. Presently he ran forward, making motions as if throwing a rope over the heads of those in front of him, and then running backwards as if dragging an object after him, seized the large stick held in his hands, and began beating an

---

* An English author who visited Braddock's Field in the 1830s wrote that 'there are a few superb oaks still standing which ... must enhance the value of the place with all faithful ghost-believers and pious lovers of the marvellous – the dim form of the red savage, with the ghostly spectre of his pallid victim shrinking before it, it is said, may be seen gliding at times among the hoary trunks.'

imaginary object, all the time howling and cursing like a demon, when somebody pulled him away, saying it was a shame.' Confused by the spectacle, the boy asked one of the other spectators what had transpired, 'and learned that Uncle Sol had been at the Moravian Massacre, and when in his cups, as he had seen him, would show how they killed the Indians, but when sober could not be induced to open his mouth upon the subject'.[13]

# PART II

# LOUISIANA

The Greater Mississippi Basin is the continent's core, and whoever controls that core not only is certain to dominate the East Coast and Great Lakes regions but will also have the agricultural, transport, trade and political unification capacity to be a world power – even without having to interact with the rest of the global system.

'THE GEOPOLITICS OF THE UNITED STATES', STRATFOR

# The Door to the House

The first European to stand on the banks of the Mississippi River had no way of knowing what he was really looking at. Hernando de Soto travelled from Havana to Tampa Bay in the spring of 1539 with 600 men. In Spain he had met Álvar Núñez Cabeza de Vaca, a survivor of an earlier attempt to explore the American Southwest, who described it as 'the richest country in the world'. In Cuba he had been told by captive Indians that 'there was much gold in Florida'. Now, in the finest tradition of the conquistadores, he had arrived to claim these riches for the Spanish Crown – and for himself.

There was no gold. But there was much else. For two years, Soto roved around the continent, through Florida, Georgia and South Carolina, at some point crossing the southern tip of the Appalachians and entering Alabama, Mississippi and Tennessee. The land was thickly peopled. He stumbled across towns set in fertile fields and surrounded by high walls. He encountered the monumental temple mounds of the ancient Mississippi culture. He met bands of soldiers with 'their bodies, legs, and arms painted and ochred, red, black, white, yellow, and vermilion in stripes … Some wore feathers, and others horns on the head, the face blackened, and the eyes encircled with vermilion, to heighten their fierce aspect.' He made contact with the Creek, the Caddo, the Choctaw and the Apalachee, and he brought violence and disease with him wherever he went.

In 1541 he was directed to a settlement named Quizquiz.[1] As his band marched towards it the landscape began to change. There was water everywhere. It was deep enough to swim in, but just shallow enough for their horses to wade through. It was also covered with trees – walnut, mulberry and plum – and filled with game and fish. Near Quizquiz, they found a 'great river' and began cutting down trees to build pirogues. While they were building their boats, an Indian leader named Cacique arrived on a flotilla of barges with many soldiers who began firing volleys of arrows at these strange interlopers. The Spanish continued their work.

When the pirogues were ready, they set out for the other bank and became the first Europeans to record a crossing of the Mississippi: 'The distance was near half a league: a man standing on the shore could not be told, whether he were a man or something else, from the other side. The stream was swift, and very deep; the water, always flowing turbidly, brought along from above many trees and much timber, driven onward by its force.'

According to their accounts the river was some three miles wide. Some of the men present described the river as being wider even than the Danube. Some simply called it the Rio Grande. The name that stuck for the first century of its European existence was the Río del Espíritu Santo – the River of the Holy Spirit.

Soto had told the Indians he was immortal, but he fell ill and died. To hide his death from them, his deputy, Luis de Moscoso Alvarado, 'ordered the corpse to be taken up at night, and among the shawls that enshrouded it having cast abundance of sand, it was taken out in a canoe and committed to the middle of the stream'. And so the first European to discover the Mississippi was buried in its depths.* The remains of the party fled down the river in their primitive vessels. Their guns and crossbows were broken and they were defenceless against the Indians who harried them all the way to the sea. After nineteen days, the exhausted survivors reached the Gulf of Mexico and straggled home to bring news of their discovery to Europe.[2]

---

* Bartolomé de las Casas, the Franciscan friar and early historian of the conquistadores, wrote of Soto's death: 'Thus the most unhappy captain died as if ill-fated, without confession, and we do not doubt but that he was buried in hell.'

## LA LOUISIANE

Then there was 130 years of silence, until in 1669 the Jesuit Claude-Jean Allouez reported on his mission to the Fox River, on the western edge of Lake Michigan. The Indians there had told him that 'their river leads by a six-day voyage to the great River named Messi-Sipi'.

Though it became common to translate this Ojibwe word as 'Father of Rivers', it literally translated as 'big long river'. This 'beautiful river', the Frenchman learned, 'serves to carry the people down to the great Lake (for so they call the Sea), where they trade with Europeans who pray as we do, and use Rosaries, as well as Bells for calling to Prayers. According to the description given us, we judge them to be Spaniards.'

Intrigued, the French authorized Louis Jolliet and Jacques Marquette to descend 'the great river which they call the Michissipi'. The two men departed in May 1673, travelling in canoes down the Fox and Wisconsin Rivers to the Mississippi, then following its course south. Somewhere near the mouth of the Arkansas River, roughly 600 miles from the ocean, the men decided to return north, this time by an alternate route up the Illinois River to Lake Michigan, via a place the Indians called Checagou.[3]

They had failed to find the ocean, but their explorations had convinced them 'beyond a doubt [that] the Mississippi river discharges into the Florida or Mexican gulf'. Certain that the river Jolliet and Marquette had travelled down was the same one Soto's men had stumbled upon and then taken down to the ocean, in 1678 Louis XIV authorized a major expedition down the Mississippi.

The Sun King's chosen explorers, René-Robert Cavelier, Sieur de La Salle, and his companion Henri de Tonti, did not begin their descent until 1682 (by which time a separate French expedition had undertaken a journey north up the Mississippi, discovering the Falls of St Anthony), but once they were under way they made good time. Joining the Mississippi from the Illinois River in February, they were standing on the Gulf of Mexico by April – having travelled 1,000 miles in less than three months.

On 9 April 1682, at a ceremony just north of where the Mississippi empties into the Gulf of Mexico, La Salle erected a cross and a column bearing the French coat of arms, and buried beneath it a metal plate with an inscription in Latin claiming the length of the river for France.

He gave a speech proclaiming that the Mississippi and all the 'rivers which discharge themselves therein, from its source ... as far as its mouth at the sea' would henceforth be known as *La Louisiane*. They said the *Te Deum*, sang the royal anthem, fired off a salute and cried *Vive Le Roi!* The Mississippi watershed now belonged to France.[4]

Upon their return to Paris, Tonti and La Salle gave their reports to the King. The Louisiana they described was a rich and varied place. Upper Louisiana was notable for the 'great fertility and extent' of its plains and the 'mildness of the climate'. Tonti wrote that the lands between the mouth of the Illinois and the mouth of the Missouri 'may be said to contain the finest lands ever seen. The climate is the same as that of Paris.' Somewhere between modern Memphis, Tennessee, and the mouth of the Arkansas the landscape began to change. Winters were milder, and peach, plum and apple trees flourished. On the rivers there were immense numbers of alligators, some up to twenty feet long. Still further south was the mouth of the Red River, so named as 'it deposits a sand which makes the water as red as blood'. Here the land was less hospitable and filled with 'woods, bogs, reeds, and marshes'. By the time they had reached the sea the land was practically uninhabitable: 'The coast and banks being overflowed for more than 20 leagues above the mouth, make it inaccessible by land.'

The totality of what they had discovered was amazing. The river itself they estimated at 800 leagues long (2,400 miles) and – importantly – 'without rapids'. And because this vast watershed tapered down to a single channel, bending and weaving its way through the floodplain towards the ocean, it could be controlled from a single strategic point. 'A port or two would make us masters of the whole of this continent,' La Salle told the King. 'One single post,' he continued, 'established towards the lower part of the river, will be sufficient to protect a territory extending more than 800 leagues from north to south, and still farther from east to west, because its banks are only accessible from the sea through the mouth of the river.'

French settlement began in earnest in 1699 with the arrival of Pierre Le Moyne d'Iberville. He established settlements in Biloxi and Mobile. In 1716, Natchez was founded at the site of an ancient Indian settlement above the mouth of the Red River.

It was not until 1718 that the city that became synonymous with French empire-building in Louisiana was established. At the time, the decision to build a settlement that far downriver was controversial. The site of New Orleans did not naturally lend itself to inhabitation. Most of it was under water for much of the year. Snakes and alligators – not to mention a vast variety of disease-bearing insects – lived in the surrounding swamps. Storms, floods and hurricanes regularly terrorized the area. New Orleans was not dry ground, but neither was it a coastal city. The Mississippi entered the ocean another eighty miles downstream. Its strategic value was that it occupied a piece of wet, muddy land between the Mississippi River and the shores of Lake Pontchartrain, which was connected by a series of bayous to both the river and the Gulf of Mexico. Surrounded by water on all sides (which is why contemporaries often referred to the island or the isle of New Orleans), it commanded all the waterways in and out of the Mississippi's vast hinterland.[5]

In a few years, the French built a smart, stone settlement on a rectilinear plan, centred on a cathedral and a public square. But getting anyone to settle there was another matter. The French responded by shipping convicts to their colony, impressing Indians into labour and paying impoverished Germans to settle along the banks of the river. They also began shipping in thousands of African slaves. Within a decade 6,000 slaves had been imported to the region to do the back-breaking work of building the levees, draining the land and planting the rice that became the city's first great staple. The vital contribution of slavery convinced many whites that only black labour could make the region inhabitable. 'The lands can be drained and freed from water only by those who have negroes,' Governor Perier declared in 1731, 'since the work on levees and drainage is difficult and hard.'[6]

Even as the city rose out of the swamp, thousands died around it. Cholera, smallpox and yellow fever were endemic. Slaves, settlers and soldiers alike perished in the unforgiving environment. 'Death and disease are disrupting and suspending all operations,' one bureaucrat reported to Paris. 'The best workers are dead.' Another wrote grimly that 'the country was emptied as rapidly as it had filled'. After decades of migration, by 1746 there were still only 8,000 people in the entire region – half of them slaves – three-quarters of the whole huddled in New Orleans.[7]

While the French struggled to establish themselves as masters of the Mississippi Valley, they – and the other European powers – were becoming ever more convinced of its strategic importance. As early as

*Guillaume Delisle's 1718 map of Louisiana.*

1718, the French cartographer Guillaume Delisle produced a remarkable map of Louisiana which showed how the Mississippi and its tributaries united the entire central American land mass into a single community of waterways.

This geographical unity – and the French control of it from New Orleans – was the source of jealousy for the other Europeans (the Spanish on the Red River, the English on the Ohio) who jostled for control of portions of the Mississippi Valley. At the same time, claims were inexact and borders unclear. A flavour of the uncertainty over who controlled what was captured in the title of Daniel Coxe's *A Description of the English Province of Carolana [sic], by the Spaniards called Florida, And by the French La Louisiane* (1722). What was not in doubt was the importance of the river system at the centre of these imperial squabbles. 'The great river Meschacebe runs through the midst of this country …' Coxe told his readers, 'so that the whole country may be almost entirely visited by navigable rivers without any falls or cataracts.'[8]

The French would not control this great river system for much longer. In 1763 – the same year that St Louis was established at the mouth of the Missouri – Louis XV ceded Louisiana to the Spanish to prevent it from falling into British hands following his defeat in the Seven Years War.

The cession radically simplified the political geography of North America: the entire known continent was now split between Spain and Britain. While the British made extensive claims in what was broadly defined as Spanish *Luisiana* – most notably in the Ohio Valley – they were equivocal about settling the interior of the continent. Louisiana's new owners were similarly ambivalent. For the Spanish imperial strategists in Madrid, the principal value of Louisiana was that it provided a vast buffer protecting the empire's core asset: the gold and silver mines of Mexico. Initiatives to attract migrants and foster economic growth occurred fitfully. Most of Louisiana went on much as it had before: a string of distant posts, forts and fur-trading points, surrounded by Indians and populated almost entirely by French speakers.[9]

## 'PREGNANT WITH A HUNDRED STATES'

The Americans who arrived on the scene in the 1780s had no doubts at all about the importance of settling and exploiting the Mississippi Valley. Having negotiated hard at Paris in 1783 to win the continent west to the Mississippi, they fully intended to take command of it.

Perhaps no ruling class was ever as obsessed with rivers as the Founding Fathers. Jefferson devoted the opening pages of his *Notes on the State of Virginia* (1785) to a detailed list of the continent's waterways, writing that 'the Mississippi will be one of the principal channels of future commerce for the country'. Washington declared himself in awe of 'the vast inland navigation of these United States'. Washington's court poet, Joel Barlow, picked up the theme in his epic poem *The Columbiad* (1807): 'Here my bold Mississippi bends his way ...'

> *Strong in his march, and charged with all the fates*
> *Of regions pregnant with a hundred states,*
> *He holds in balance, ranged on either hand,*
> *Two distant oceans and their sundering land;*
> *Commands and drains the interior tracts that lie*
> *Outmeasuring Europe's total breadth of sky.*

When, in 1780, the Spanish had encouraged the Americans to make an early peace at the expense of sacrificing their claims to the Mississippi, Benjamin Franklin wrote that under no circumstances were they to entertain such an offer. 'Poor as we are, yet as I know we shall be rich, I would rather agree with them to buy at a great Price the whole of their Right on the Mississippi than sell a Drop of its Waters. – A Neighbour might as well ask me to sell my Street Door.'[10]

Obsessing over the Mississippi and its tributaries was not simply an elite concern. Every American who dreamed of moving west over the Appalachians and finding a plot of land for themselves and their family was invested in its fate. Because once they went west across the mountains they were cut off from the economy of the Atlantic seaboard. The Appalachians were a commercial barrier as well as a geographic one. The cost of shipping goods across them – even for relatively short distances – was prohibitive. When François Michaux visited the Ohio Valley in 1801, he observed that in parts of western Pennsylvania only 200 miles from Philadelphia farmers preferred to ship their goods to New Orleans, which was 2,200 miles away. In Kentucky, Michaux observed the same phenomenon. It was the same price to ship a thousand pounds of produce to New Orleans as it was to send twenty-five pounds over the mountains to Philadelphia. These were facts of life out west; they shaped every calculation. A frontiersman who 'could neither transport, sell, nor exchange anything they had', one commentator wrote, was doomed to be 'as poor as the poorest wretches of Europe'. Without roads, without towns, without postal services, there was no way to get goods to market – except the Mississippi. Access to any part of the river system meant access to a market somewhere along its banks.[11]

Consequently, Americans became experts on the Mississippi. They knew that the Missouri was navigable below the Great Falls, the Mississippi below the Falls of St Anthony, and the Ohio below the rapids at Louisville. They knew the Platte was clear and fast, the Red River salty and silty, and the Ouachita dark and labyrinthine. They knew by name the distant tributaries of the Tennessee, the Arkansas and the Wabash. They knew which rivers froze in winter, which dried up in the summer and which were blocked with brush year round.

And yet not even the Americans could comprehend the entirety of the Mississippi basin. For this was a land of some one and a quarter million square miles, whose rivers drained some 40 per cent of the entire United States, and contained more navigable waterways than the rest of the world combined.

If the Mississippi basin had not existed, America's fate might have been that of Australia or Saharan Africa or Siberia – a vast continent settled on the coasts and largely empty in the interior.

As it was, the Mississippi and its branches gave unity to places as far-flung as Milk River, Montana; Skunk Run, Pennsylvania; Whisky Run, Nebraska; Carrizo Creek, New Mexico; Poor Fork, Kentucky; and Black Bayou, Texas.

So tentacular is the Mississippi and its tributaries that they brush up against other river systems, presenting tantalizing possibilities. The Ohio, the Illinois and the Wisconsin all graze the Great Lakes on their journeys southward. The Tennessee only narrowly misses the Mobile River, which drains into the Gulf of Mexico. The Missouri comes within one hundred miles of the Columbia, which debouches into the Pacific, and within fifty miles of the Saskatchewan, which empties into Lake Winnipeg. And in central Colorado, the Arkansas, the Rio Grande and the Colorado Rivers mingle without ever quite meeting, before heading their separate ways, two coming together again in the Gulf of Mexico, the third destined for the Gulf of California. The Mississippi was not

*A hydrological map of the United States demonstrating the extent of the Mississippi River and its tributaries.*

just the key to the American land mass but a gateway to new empires beyond.

But there was one characteristic of this immense river system that Americans understood all too well. It takes a drop of water ninety days to travel the 2,340 miles from the source of the Mississippi to its mouth. This averages out at a speed of twenty-six miles per day. A frontiersman who lashed together a raft in Kentucky, or put to water in a canoe in Illinois, could probably, weather withstanding, expect to match that speed. The river could be fickle, and journey times might fluctuate, but what the Mississippi guaranteed was a destination. All the waters it encompassed, from North Dakota to West Virginia, would eventually gather in a single channel, rolling towards the sea, past the city of New Orleans.*

In the first decades of the republic's existence, however, as thousands of Americans streamed west across the Appalachians to settle the frontier, New Orleans remained stubbornly in the hands of a foreign power. Far from being a meeting place of waters, men and goods, that city on the bank of the Mississippi became a stopper, bottling up the commercial potential of the American interior.

The tensions generated by this frustration of the frontier's ambitions threatened to tear apart the young nation. If the United States government could not guarantee the frontier access to the sea, then the frontier was ripe for secession or an alliance with Spain – or some combination of the two.

The stakes could not have been higher. And nobody understood them better than Thomas Jefferson. 'There is on the globe one single spot,' he declared, 'the possessor of which is our natural & habitual enemy. It is New Orleans, through which the produce of three-eighths of our territory must pass to market, and from its fertility it will ere long yield more than half of our whole produce and contain more than half our inhabitants.'[12]

And in 1801 Jefferson became president and set out to secure that city for his country by any means necessary.

---

* Michaux calculated that in springtime, when the river flowed faster, larger boats could travel the 2,100 miles from Pittsburgh to New Orleans in forty-five to fifty days. Lighter vessels could do the same journey in twenty to twenty-five days. (Michaux, *Travels*, 76–77.)

# Thomas Jefferson Dreams of an Empire of Liberty

On the day of Thomas Jefferson's inauguration, groups of his admirers marched the streets of Washington singing songs in his honour. The last verse of one of the more popular tunes, 'Jefferson and Liberty', sketched an image of the nation's borders as the third president found them upon taking office:

> *From Georgia up to Lake Champlain,*
> *From seas to Mississippi's shore,*
> *Ye sons of freedom loud proclaim,*
> THE REIGN OF TERROR IS NO MORE.

His supporters knew their man. The tall, slight figure with a distracted air who walked from his boarding house that morning to be sworn in at the newly built Senate building in his simple black suit was obsessed with land. Jefferson believed that America's destiny lay westwards. So did his supporters. Jefferson believed that the mission of America's leaders was to expand the nation's borders. And so did his supporters. That was why they had voted for him. And in his inaugural address Jefferson did not disappoint them. He spoke of 'a rising nation, spread over a wide and fruitful land, traversing all the seas with the rich productions of their industry', and of a people 'possessing a chosen country, with room enough for our descendants to the thousandth and thousandth generation'. Yet as immense as this land was, Thomas Jefferson wanted to make it yet more immense.[1]

\* \* \*

By the time Jefferson became president, he had already occupied nearly every political office a man could aspire to hold. In his twenties he was elected to Virginia's House of Burgesses. At the age of thirty-three, he was a member of the Continental Congress and the author of the Declaration of Independence. During the Revolutionary War he was governor of Virginia. When that war ended, he spent five years in Paris as minister to France. In the 1790s, he was appointed secretary of state, serving under George Washington, and was subsequently vice president under John Adams.

It was wholly characteristic of Jefferson that he held such achievements in scant regard. When he chose the inscription for his tombstone, he mentioned none of these positions. He asked instead to be remembered only as the author of the Declaration of Independence and of Virginia's Statute for Religious Freedom, and as founder of the University of Virginia. This disregard for political glory was noted by his contemporaries. One senator who knew him well observed that Jefferson was temperamentally ill-suited for politics: 'He is very credulous – he knows little of the nature of man – very little indeed. He has travelled the tour of Europe – he has been Minister at Versailles. He has had great opportunities to know man – but he has neglected them. He is not a practical man. He has much knowledge of books, of insects, of shells – & of all that charms a virtuoso – but he knows not the human heart. He is a closet politician – but not a practical statesman.'[2]

Jefferson himself frequently expressed frustration that politics kept on interfering with his true calling – his study of science, linguistics, astronomy, geography, botany, meteorology and much else besides. Before he was elected president of the United States he had been president of the American Philosophical Society, and he seems to have considered the latter office the more august of the two.* For Jefferson was an intellectual. He listed his 'trinity of the three greatest men the world had ever produced' as Francis Bacon, Isaac Newton and John Locke. He maintained a correspondence in several languages with

---

* When he was notified of his election, Jefferson wrote in reply that this was 'the most flattering incident of my life', while also observing that the duties of the post were 'far beyond my titles. I feel no qualification for this distinguished post, but a sincere zeal for all the objects of our institution, and an ardent desire to see knowledge so disseminated to mankind, that it may at length reach even the extremes of society, beggars and kings.'

almost every major thinker of his day. His letters to Alexander von Humboldt, Thomas Paine, the Comte de Buffon, the Comte de Volney, Charles Willson Peale and Richard Price sit alongside his enormous official correspondence.

And it wasn't just intellectuals. Jefferson corresponded with Joel Barlow on the design of submarines, Eli Whitney on the construction of cotton gins and James Sylvanus McLean on steam power. He tinkered himself, receiving an honorary membership of the English Board of Agriculture and a gold medal from the Agricultural Society of Paris for inventing a new kind of plough.

By his own account, Jefferson's ruling passion was astronomy, which he studied obsessively while formally a law student at William and Mary. One of his slaves, Peter Fossett, recalled that Jefferson and James Madison would spend hours together at the telescope on the north terrace of Monticello. 'He was more a scientist than a statesman,' Fossett observed.

He was also a musician, who in his youth spent three hours a day practising the violin. 'He kept three fiddles,' another slave, Isaac Jefferson, later wrote, 'Mr Jefferson always singing when ridin' or walkin': hardly see him anywhere out doors but what he was a-singin: had a fine clear voice, sung minuets & such: fiddled in the parlor.'

Jefferson's dynamism and his roving, eccentric, brilliant mind was one of the marvels of the age. 'Even his discourse partook of his personal demeanor,' one senator said of him. 'It was loose and rambling, and yet he scattered information wherever he went, and some even brilliant sentiments sparkled from him.'

Jefferson delighted in his intellectual omnivorism. 'There is not a sprig of grass that shoots uninteresting to me,' he told his daughter Patsy, 'nor anything that moves.'[3]

Where Jefferson's intellectual interests and his political activities intersected was on the subject of land. Jefferson was a true Enlightenment radical in that he believed that mankind was capable of making totally new things – things hitherto unknown in history or nature. America was not metaphorically 'the New World': to Jefferson it was literally a departure from the rest of the known planet. He sincerely believed that America defied the laws of nature that prevailed elsewhere. In Paris he had been exposed to the ideas of Georges Cuvier, who had introduced the notion that species could go extinct. Not so, Jefferson claimed:

supposedly extinct mammoths and ground sloths still existed in the American West. He had read the work of the English clergyman Thomas Malthus, who had shown that because populations grew out of proportion to growth in agricultural productivity, population pressures would begin to exert themselves on the rapidly growing nations of Western Europe. Not so in the New World, Jefferson replied. For in America the 'immense extent of uncultivated and fertile lands enables every one, who will labor, to marry young, and to raise a family of any size'. So it went on. The establishment of the American republic required a reassessment of everything.

'We can no longer say there is nothing new under the sun,' Jefferson wrote to the English scientist Joseph Priestley. 'For this whole chapter in the history of man is new. The great extent of our Republic is new. Its sparse habitation is new. The mighty wave of public opinion which has rolled over it is new.'[4]

America's lands were to be the scene for the most astonishing innovation of all: the establishment of the American republic. From the outset, Jefferson believed that this republic was destined to expand. 'Our confederacy,' he wrote in 1786, 'must be viewed as the nest from which all America, North & South is to be peopled.' But America's expansion would be like nothing else in history for it would create a new kind of empire, an 'empire of liberty'.

His argument was simple and arresting. As America expanded westwards, new territories would be organized and given a clear path to statehood and equal political status in the Union. There would be no patchwork of dependencies, satellites and protectorates. Instead, there would be an expanding horizon of political liberty. Migrants to these new territories would buy land from the government and then settle down to farm and improve that land.

There were several happy side effects of this proposed system of settlement. First, by creating a republic of yeoman farmers, the United States would avoid the twin processes of industrialization and urbanization which Jefferson believed had poisoned Europe. 'Corruption of morals in the mass of cultivators is a phenomenon of which no age nor nation has furnished an example,' he declared in *Notes on the State of Virginia*. 'Those who labour in the earth are the chosen people of God.'

Farmers who bought their land from the United States government also solved the pressing problem of revenue. When Jefferson assumed office, America's debts were $83 million. He took the debt question very seriously. 'If the debt shall once more be swelled to a formidable size,' he told his treasury secretary, Albert Gallatin, 'its entire discharge will be despaired of, and we shall be committed to the English career of debt, corruption & rottenness, closing with revolution.'

The Jeffersonian solution to the debt problem lay in the soil of the New World. The government would pay down its debts by selling land to its citizens who ventured west to become farmers. Throughout the 1780s, even while he was in Paris, he had kept a close eye on the progress of land sales arising from the Land Ordinance, for he saw in them the path to freedom from debt. Once the debt was paid off, land sales could be used to fund the government. Jefferson hated taxation and he loathed banks – 'Banking establishments are more dangerous than standing armies,' he told one correspondent – and America's wilds would obviate the need for either. The American continent was itself a land bank, a bountiful expanse that would fund the government, produce virtuous citizen-farmers and play host to an ever-expanding empire of liberty.[5,6]

The biggest challenge to realizing the Empire of Liberty was posed by geography. None of Jefferson's grand plans could be achieved without control of the Mississippi basin. So long as the Spanish remained lodged in New Orleans, all his hopes for the republic were thwarted. As president, Jefferson became so obsessed with the Mississippi that when guests came to dinner at the presidential mansion he displayed two bottles of Mississippi River water on the table to remind them and him of the great stream that ran through the centre of the country.

### 'REASON AND EVENTS'

Those bottles of river water were also the reminder of a decade of political failure. After the 1783 Peace of Paris the Spanish had unilaterally closed the Mississippi to all American vessels. Settlers in the Ohio and Cumberland valleys found themselves trapped on the frontier, with no way to get their goods to market. At the time, many American politicians were optimistic about their prospects of reopening the river and securing Spanish recognition of their borders. Spain was an old and failing power, they reasoned, while America was a wilful young nation which in the fullness of time would secure what it was rightly owed. Thomas Jefferson held this view. It was only a matter of time, he believed, until the Spanish reversed their previous policy. 'Reason and events,' he predicted, would 'familiarize' the Spanish with the American position and encourage them to accede to it.[7]

Instead, the United States government was rocked by a series of crises in the Mississippi Valley.

In 1790 the Nootka Sound affair – a squabble between Britain and Spain over rights to a desolate stretch of coastline in the Pacific Northwest – brought the two empires to the brink of war. This set alarm bells ringing in Philadelphia, where Jefferson warned Washington that a British army was preparing to march from Canada to the northern waters of the Mississippi and then sail south to New Orleans. The aim of British policy was no less than to see that 'Louisiana & the Floridas be added to the British empire'. This was intolerable, and Jefferson declared that the United States 'ought to make ourselves parties in the *general war* expected to take place, should this be the only means of preventing' the 'calamity' of a British seizure of the Mississippi. Washington concurred, as did other influential men. This was not a matter where America could stand idly by. 'Upon the whole that navigation we must have,' wrote the Marquis de Lafayette, 'and in case the people of Louisiana wish to make a fifteenth state, who the devil can help it.'[8]

The Nootka Sound controversy was forgotten by Christmas but it had led Jefferson to think deeply about the situation in Louisiana. In a memorandum written in August 1790, Jefferson outlined America's options in the region. The Americans had to do something – else they would risk the loss of the West. 'Were we to give up half our territory rather than engage in a just war to preserve it,' Jefferson warned, 'we should not keep the other half long.' That left two options: war or diplomacy. Jefferson preferred diplomacy and suggested that Spain ought to 'cede to us all territory on our side of the Mississippi, on condition that we guarantee all her possessions on the Western waters of that river'. This would give the United States New Orleans and the Floridas, and remove forever the prospect of a 'bloody and eternal war' on its southern flank.[9]

As Jefferson's policy of negotiating with the Spanish was beginning to win converts in government, another crisis struck the Mississippi. This time it originated in Paris, where the revolution had produced a war with Spain. Zealous revolutionaries dreamt of a global war of liberation that would dissolve the empires of France's enemies. While French policy-making waxed utopian, a proposal arrived in Paris from Tennessee. 'It is in the universal interest of the people as well as the French republic to annihilate the despotism of the crowned tyrants,' the letter began, before going on to suggest that France seek the 'general emancipation' of Francophone settlers in Louisiana then labouring under 'Castille's tyrannical yoke'. The letter proposed a 'legion' of Americans, armed by France, descend the Mississippi and end Spanish rule there.

In response, the French sent Edmond-Charles Genêt across the ocean in 1793 with orders to do just that. Once ashore, Genêt began a triumphal march across the Atlantic seaboard, hosting massive rallies at which he preached revolution and recruited for an expedition to New Orleans. Soon he was in touch with George Rogers Clark, who was now a drunk in Kentucky. Before long, Clark was boasting that he had several thousand men ready to sail down the river at a moment's notice and capture New Orleans. Genêt, who believed America's leaders approved of his actions, kept them well informed of his intentions. Meanwhile, the Spanish minister in Philadelphia lodged furious complaints. In the end, Spanish and American interests converged and, following Spanish protests and a good deal of domestic alarm, Washington moved to halt Genêt's crusade. Momentum was lost. The various plots fizzled out. Clark's army never materialized. Not long afterwards, the Frenchman was recalled to Paris.[10]

Twice in three years the vision of first an English and then a French army marching across Louisiana had flared in the American imagination. But while France and Britain were the European powers the Americans feared most, Spain also proved an inventive and frustrating opponent.

The Spanish policy of blocking American expansion westwards had two prongs. The first was funnelling support to the five southern Indians tribes – the Creek, Cherokee, Choctaw, Seminole, and Chickasaw. Another was to try to win over Americans on the frontier with only tenuous loyalties to the fledgling United States. For there were plenty of Americans west of the Appalachians angry at their government's inability to secure them access to New Orleans. Some influential settlers began to believe that if the government across the mountains could not advance their commercial interests, then they should deal with those who could

– the Spanish. The focus of Spanish efforts at subversion was Kentucky, which was filled with frontiersmen bridling at government from distant Richmond. Harry Innes, a Kentucky lawyer and leading separatist, stated baldly that 'this western country will, in a few years, Revolt from the Union and endeavor to erect an Independent Government'. Innes's ally, Congressman John Brown, let the Spanish minister in Philadelphia know that if he could secure him the Mississippi, then Kentucky would 'erect herself into an independent government'. By 1789 it seemed as though the Spanish conspiracy was on the verge of success. 'This affair,' Louisiana Governor Esteban Miro wrote home to Madrid, 'progresses more rapidly than I had anticipated.'[11]

In the event it was Spanish resolve, not American unity, that broke first. By 1795 Spain felt thoroughly isolated and had come to believe that America and Britain were about to partition the Mississippi Valley at its expense. Looking to forestall that eventuality, the Spanish intimated they were willing to make a deal. The Americans sent Charles Pinckney to Madrid that summer to negotiate. What they sought was Spanish recognition of the 1783 Anglo-American treaty. This meant free navigation of the Mississippi and recognition of America's borders west to the Mississippi. Crucially, Pinckney demanded the Spanish grant the *right* of deposit at New Orleans to American traders coming down the Mississippi. This was vital as rafts cobbled together in Kentucky and Tennessee were not seaworthy, and so American produce had to be deposited onshore, stored in a warehouse and then loaded aboard ocean-going vessels for transport. Amid a flurry of concessions, the Spanish held fast on this point, granting only the *privilege* of deposit for three years, to be renewed at Spanish discretion.[12]

The Pinckney Treaty was such a stunning American diplomatic coup that for a period it looked as though the Mississippi question had been effectively resolved. Soon 500 ships a year were travelling from American settlements in the West down the river to New Orleans, breathing economic life into those regions, encouraging westward migration, lifting land prices and securing western attachments. The crisis seemed to be over: the river was open, the West was loyal and America had successfully seen off all European contenders for control of the Mississippi Valley.

\* \* \*

And then alarming rumours began to drift across the Atlantic.

While Pinckney had been negotiating in Madrid, the Spanish had been in simultaneous talks with the French. The result was a treaty that restored the Franco-Spanish alliance. In Europe, it looked as though the French were going to be able to impose a new order on the continent. That left the rest of the world open for imperial exploitation. In 1799, Napoleon seized control of the French state and pressured the Spanish to sign over Louisiana and the Floridas to France. The Spanish king clung to the Floridas but agreed at the Treaty of San Ildefonso in October 1800 to hand over the former French possessions to Napoleon. The treaty was secret but word of it soon leaked out.[13]

As Jefferson settled into office in 1801, the wildest stories were circulating across the frontier about French intentions in the region. General James Wilkinson reported: 'We have rumours here flying through the woods from Pensacola to St. Louis, and even from Madrid, that the French are to have Louisiana and the Floridas.' American diplomats were sending similar reports from Europe.

Ominously (for the Americans, at least), peace was settling over Europe. A series of treaties in 1801 climaxed with a Franco-British treaty signed at Amiens in 1802.

Yet even as Europe disarmed, there was intelligence about an immense French fleet gathering in the Lowlands.

The Americans watched uneasily. Jefferson could sense the brewing crisis but could not initiate negotiations until events came to a head.

Appropriately, the trigger was pulled at New Orleans in October 1802 when the Spanish intendant in Louisiana, Don Juan Ventura Morales, peremptorily revoked the privilege of deposit, effectively closing the Mississippi to American traders in a move that was widely interpreted as a prelude to Spain retroceding Louisiana to France.

Morales's actions electrified American public opinion.'When the navigation of the Mississippi was obstructed,' one senator later wrote, 'it seemed then as if the national pulse was about to cease.' Jefferson and his allies shot off letters to the West, promising that they would do all they could to resolve the matter once and for all.

In January 1803, Jefferson ordered his faithful lieutenant James Monroe to board a ship bound for Paris. His mission was simple: to purchase New Orleans and the Floridas. His budget was $9,375,000. 'All eyes, all hopes are now fixed on you,' Jefferson told Monroe, 'for on the event of this mission depends the future destinies of this republic.'[14]

Jefferson was wrong. The fate of Louisiana would not be decided in Paris but on the plains and plateaus of Haiti, by former slaves engaged in a desperate struggle for freedom.

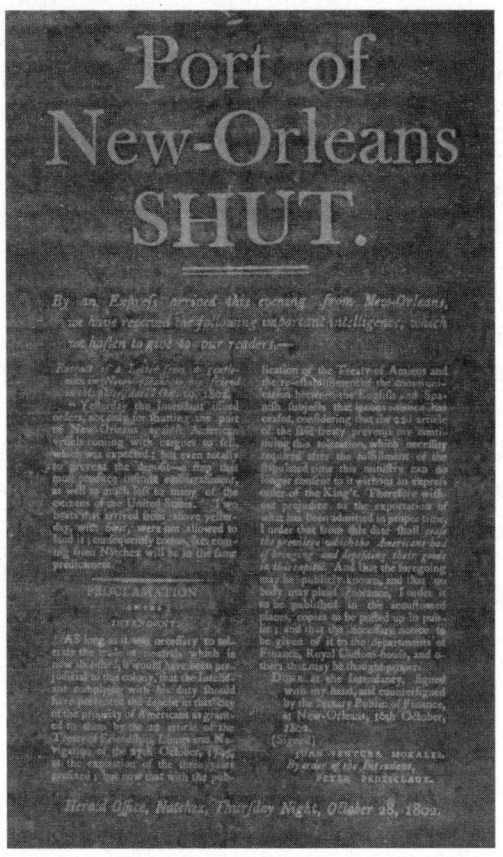

*A handbill announcing the suspension of the privilege of deposit in New Orleans in 1802.*

# This Affair of Louisiana

In July 1801, Jefferson met with Louis-André Pichon, the French representative to the United States. Relations between the two nations were only gradually recovering after a war scare in 1798–99. Even with that in the past, and the Francophile Jefferson as president, there was still tension between the two nations. Many insiders, Jefferson among them, believed that a war was imminent unless an agreement was reached on the fate of New Orleans.

But that day, Pichon and Jefferson did not dwell on these matters. Instead, they discussed events on a Caribbean island just east of Cuba, and some 700 miles from the Florida Keys.

### THE BLACK REPUBLIC

Hispaniola had been discovered by Columbus on his first voyage to the new world. After Cuba, it was the largest island in the Caribbean and, despite the harsh climate, was equally fertile. When the French arrived in the region they staked a claim to the island and, after much squabbling, the island was divided in two. The western half went to France and the eastern half to Spain. Confusingly, the two parts were given variations of the same name: Saint-Domingue and Santo Domingo.

With their portion of Hispaniola secured to them by treaty, the French embarked on the most intense experiment in plantation slavery ever conducted in the western hemisphere. French planters began importing tens of thousands of slaves from Africa each year and set them to work growing coffee, sugar and cotton. By 1790 the island's produce accounted for 40 per cent of Europe's sugar consumption and 60 per cent of its coffee. Saint-Domingue accounted for almost half of France's entire overseas trade. In the decade after the American Revolution, the colony's production doubled and more slaves arrived on the island each year to labour on the plantations. By 1789 there were 500,000 slaves on the island, 60 per cent of whom had been born across the ocean. Alongside them lived 30,000 free people of colour and 30,000 whites. An astonishing 90 per cent of the island was enslaved – a situation that was obviously untenable to those slave-owners with even the slightest imagination. As one planter commented, he and his kind 'walked on barrels of gunpowder'.[1]

In 1789 the barrels of gunpowder exploded. The French Revolution sent shockwaves through the island. The planters closed ranks in reaction to the egalitarian ideals emanating from Paris. But others took inspiration from events in France. The result was a general slave uprising in 1791. According to legend, the rebellion was initiated by a Vodou ceremony on the night of 22 August amid thunder, lightning and animal sacrifice in the Bois Caïman, in the hills overlooking Cap-Français. By November, the 10,000 slaves who had risen up in August had become 80,000. Plumes of black smoke rose from the burning plantations that studded the great plain surrounding the city, which was now packed with terrified white refugees.

Over the next decade the island descended into chaos. Political factions were formed along every possible division of race, legal status and political affiliation. Further complicating matters were invasions by the Spanish and the British.

Out of this turmoil arose Toussaint Louverture, a former slave who established himself as the pre-eminent leader on the island. Louverture was a dauntless military commander and a flexible politician. He was also an Enlightenment philosopher-statesman in the same mode as Jefferson. He drilled his soldiers in political theory, reminding them that they were 'free republican men' who lived equally under the laws of the republic, regardless of skin colour. He held secular rituals to bind together the multiracial republic he envisioned, replete with Liberty Trees, altars to the *patrie* and rallies that celebrated the achievements of the French Revolution. He even dabbled in urban planning, producing blueprints for gridded towns connected by boulevards with names like Rue Republicaine and Rue de Légalité. Louverture's charisma and idealism impressed visitors. 'There is no man more attached to the ideal of French republicanism,' one French official reported to Paris. The apogee of Louverture's enlightened statecraft was the 1801 Constitution. The preamble declared Saint-Domingue to be 'part of the French Empire, but ruled under particular laws'. Those laws included the abolition of slavery and the creation of Louverture as head of the army for life in recognition of his 'steadfastness, activity, indefatigable zeal and rare virtues'.[2]

The Constitution stopped short of declaring Saint-Domingue independent from France – but this was no consolation to First Consul Napoleon Bonaparte. To him, Louverture was a parvenu, one of the 'gilded africans' of Saint-Domingue who had ideas above their station. Napoleon wanted to restore the French empire in the Americas and replenish the state's coffers with revenues from cotton, coffee and sugar. He had a vision of a cohesive French trade bloc in the western hemisphere. Saint-Domingue would produce cash crops, Louisiana would furnish staples, and New Orleans would be the central node, the vital port at the centre of it all. His plan had two phases. In the first he would reimpose slavery on Saint-Domingue. Then, he would regain control of Louisiana from the Spanish. And it was on account of this grand plan that Pichon was sitting across from Jefferson that July day in 1801.[3]

Pichon's pitch was simple. America was a slave-owning nation. Saint-Domingue was a cauldron of black rebellion a few hundred miles offshore. Napoleon was extinguishing a potent threat. French and American interests coincided.

He was half right. The Americans had greeted the 1791 uprising with dismay. Washington recorded his concern about the 'unfortunate insurrection of the Negroes in Hispaniola'. When it became apparent that far from being a tropical jacquerie, the rebellion had catalysed a broader revolutionary movement informed by radical Enlightenment philosophy, they became even more alarmed. Madison was warned that the rebel slaves 'are free, they are military. Their habits of subordination & labor are broken ... It is impossible to be too much on our guard against the consequences of a large detachment of republican blacks from St. Domingo [being sent] to Louisiana, accompanied by the sudden emancipation of the blacks there.'[4]

But American policy towards Saint-Domingue shifted as Louverture's star rose and relations with France cooled. Far from harming American trade in the Caribbean, the chaos in Saint-Domingue was a boon to American merchants. Between 1790 and 1796, American trade with the island grew from $3.2 to $8.4 million. So valuable was the trade that when John Adams organized a general embargo of France and its possessions, a special exception was carved out – known as Toussaint's Clause – for Saint-Domingue. The Adams administration held a favourable view of Louverture himself, with Secretary of State Timothy Pickering describing him as 'a prudent and judicious man possessing the general confidence of the people of all colours'. The result was a flood of American supplies to Louverture. In a single month in 1800 he took receipt of 20,000 rifles and 60,000 pounds of gunpowder from the United States.[5]

Jefferson was characteristically equivocal in his view of events in Saint-Domingue. His curiosity was piqued by the spectacle of a black republic in the Caribbean. He was also alive to the fact that anything that weakened European influence in the Caribbean was good for the United States. At the same time, as a slave-owner he was deeply concerned that events in Saint-Domingue might 'excite an insurrection among the negroes' of the American South. He also feared that if Saint-Domingue became a pariah state run by vengeful former slaves, it could morph into a hub of Caribbean piracy, an 'American Algiers' disrupting US trade. On occasion, he let the mask slip and revealed his unvarnished opinion of the black rebels, describing Louverture and his like as 'the Cannibals of the terrible republic'.[6]

It was this version of Jefferson that Pichon met with that July day. When the Frenchman introduced the idea of a French intervention on the island, Jefferson seemed to concur. Apropos of the potential menace of former slaves to European trade, Jefferson repeated his concerns about Saint-Domingue becoming 'another Algiers in the seas of America'. When Pichon raised the issue of a French expedition to reconquer Saint-Domingue, Jefferson stated that 'nothing will be easier than to furnish your army and fleet with everything and to reduce Toussaint to starvation'. Pichon was elated. Jefferson seemed to have committed the United States to supporting and supplying the French invasion of Louverture's republic.[7]

## 'THE HELL THEY DESERVE'

A few months after Pichon's meeting, an army sailed from Brest for Saint-Domingue. Napoleon had selected his brother-in-law, General Charles Leclerc, to lead a 20,000-strong force to reclaim the island. Napoleon's instructions reflected the substance of Pichon's reports from America. Leclerc's mission, Napoleon wrote, enjoyed the support of all the colonial powers because 'the Spanish, the English, and the Americans view with equal anxiety the black republic'. Moreover, 'Jefferson has promised that from the moment that the French army arrives, every measure shall be taken to starve Toussaint and to aid the army.' That, it seemed, took care of logistical concerns. Leclerc was free to execute Napoleon's three-stage plan. In the first, he would win over the local black elite and try to lull them into a false sense of security while his army secured the island's strongpoints. Then the leadership would be arrested and deported, its supporters purged from the army and the bureaucracy, and violence would be used to break such resistance as emerged to the reimposition of French rule. 'The third period,' Napoleon wrote, 'shall be that when Toussaint, Moise, and Dessalines no longer exist' and any remaining resistance 'can be destroyed'.[8]

At the very end of December 1801, Louverture spotted the white sails of Leclerc's fleet as they glided into Samaná Bay. He understood Napoleon's intentions immediately. Watching from the mountains, he told his chief of staff, 'We shall perish. All France is come to overwhelm us.' Well aware that fighting a conventional war against Napoleon's battle-hardened forces was suicide, Louverture ordered his generals to pursue a scorched-earth policy. 'Tear up the roads with shot,' he ordered; 'throw corpses and horses into all the fountains; burn and annihilate everything, in order that those who have come to reduce us to slavery may have before their eyes the image of that hell which they deserve.'

Louverture fought heroically for several months but French bribery worked. More and more of his generals went over to Leclerc. Eventually, in May 1802 he agreed to sign a ceasefire. In June, Leclerc kidnapped Louverture and shipped him to France. By July he was in a dungeon in the Fort de Joux in the Jura mountains.[9]

With his reconquest of Saint-Domingue going to plan, Napoleon prepared for phase two: taking control of New Orleans and Louisiana.

Around the time Louverture was deported to France, Admiral Decrès gave instructions to General Claude Victor to prepare an army to ship out to New Orleans from the Dutch port of Hellevoetsluis. A new governor of French Louisiana was named, Pierre-Clément Laussat, with instructions to go to New Orleans ahead of Victor's army.

The Americans watched with rising concern. In April, Jefferson had sent instructions to his ambassador in Paris, Robert Livingston, demanding he find a solution to 'this affair of Louisiana'. In that letter he noted that 'the troops sent to St. Domingo, [are] to proceed to Louisiana after finishing their work in that island', and prayed that 'some circumstance might arise which might make the cession of' New Orleans palatable to the French. The events of that spring and summer only confirmed the urgency of the cause. New instructions to Livingston made explicit the need to open direct negotiations on the question of New Orleans.

Livingston leapt into action. That summer he wrote an essay titled 'Whether it will be advantageous to France to take possession of Louisiana?', in which he described the territory as an 'immense wilderness' and wrote that 'it is obvious that the colonization of Louisiana would be injurious to France'. He had copies printed and circulated among Napoleon's inner circle. Simultaneously, he began suggesting to the French that in exchange for America writing down certain debts owed them, the French should cede New Orleans. Foreign Minister Talleyrand loftily rebuffed the idea, telling the American 'none but spendthrifts satisfy their debts by selling their lands' – but the seed of the idea had been planted. So long as Napoleon's Saint-Domingue strategy was intact, there was no need to entertain such proposals. As the American ambassador to London observed, Victor's expedition 'will go directly to the Mississippi, unless the bad state of the affairs of St Domingo should alter its destination'.[10]

That summer the situation in Saint-Domingue began to deteriorate. After enjoying success in the early stages of his campaign, Leclerc found himself bedevilled by problems. First, there was no sign of any American aid, let alone an American attempt to starve his opponents. American merchants and bankers stonewalled all efforts by French officers to procure supplies for their men. When Pichon went directly to Madison on the matter, he obfuscated. No American support was forthcoming.

Then there was disease. As the summer set in, yellow fever began to cripple his army.[11] Not long after he dispatched Louverture to France as a prisoner, Leclerc had to send a letter to Napoleon begging for reinforcements. In six months his army had been reduced from 20,000 to 4,000 men. 'The ravages of sickness here are too great for words. Not a day passes without my being told of the death of someone whom I have cause to regret bitterly.'

What sealed Leclerc's fate was news from France that arrived on the island that August. Napoleon had restored slavery in Guadeloupe, apparently pre-empting Leclerc's victory in Saint-Domingue. Leclerc was aghast. With the news from Guadeloupe, 'the moral force I had obtained here is destroyed. I can do nothing by persuasion. I can depend only on force and I have no troops.'[12]

As summer turned to autumn, the tide turned. The black population of Saint-Domingue rose as a body to resist their return to slavery. The generals who had defected to Leclerc returned to the mountains to wage war on him. Outnumbered, Leclerc resorted to atrocities. 'Since terror is the only resource left to me,' he told Napoleon, 'I employ it.' But it did not work. 'These men die with an incredible fanaticism,' he complained. 'They laugh at death; it is the same with the women.' They fought with a ferocity and purpose of mind that could not but impress the French. Black regiments sang the Marseillaise as they charged into battle. They went to the gallows insisting they would never be slaves again. One of Leclerc's Polish regiments was so moved by their national feeling they switched sides and fought the French. In October, Leclerc wrote home that the only way to win would be to kill 'half of the blacks living on the plains'. A month later, he succumbed to yellow fever.

'Damn sugar, damn coffee, damn colonies!' Napoleon raged when he heard the news of Leclerc's death.

Donatien Rochambeau, the son of the man who had fought alongside Washington at Yorktown, was appointed to continue his bloody work. The new commander declared this was 'no longer a war. It is a fight of tigers.' He ordered hunting dogs from Jamaica to track and kill his foe. He organized mass drownings in the bay next to Le Cap. He announced he was willing to kill 30,000 blacks if it meant he could restore slavery on Saint-Domingue. 'We are pleading the case of all the planters in the New World,' he declared.[13]

## THE CONSUL'S GIFT

By January 1803 the fate of Louisiana was poised on a knife edge. In Virginia, James Monroe prepared to travel to France to make Jefferson's offer to Napoleon in person. At Brest, Pierre-Clément Laussat boarded a ship travelling in the opposite direction, to take up his position as governor of French Louisiana. In Washington, Jefferson was convinced that war with France was inevitable. In Versailles, Livingston continued to make the argument for the cession of New Orleans to America to anyone who would listen. From Saint-Domingue, Rochambeau wrote home demanding more reinforcements. In a dungeon on the Swiss border, Toussaint Louverture lay dying. In Hellevoetsluis, General Victor's fleet and army was still wintering in harbour. In New Orleans, Don Juan Ventura Morales stoutly maintained his prohibition on American navigation of the Mississippi River. In London and in Paris, governments were preparing for the collapse of the Treaty of Amiens and the resumption of a global war between the French and British empires. And in the mind of the First Consul a new grand strategy was germinating.

Napoleon's capacity to read the geopolitical chessboard was unmatched – and he knew when he was in a corner. War with England was a matter of months away. Soon every spot of French soil on the globe would be a target for the Royal Navy. As soon as war was declared, Saint-Domingue, New Orleans and every other French possession in the western hemisphere would be blockaded. Rochambeau's defeat would then be inevitable. As for Laussat, he would be stranded in Louisiana with no army and no authority. At this point, the Americans would make common cause with the British and launch an invasion of New Orleans. The alternative was risking a British invasion of Louisiana from Canada, which might mean the permanent loss of the American West. An alliance with Britain – however distasteful to Jefferson's Anglophobe sensibilities – was a matter of necessity if it prevented either French or British hegemony in the western hemisphere.*

---

* On this point, Napoleon was eerily accurate in his analysis of American intentions. In this same period Jefferson was telling his colleagues that 'the day that France takes possession of New Orleans ... we must marry ourselves to the British fleet and nation'.

What Napoleon needed was money and allies – and if not allies, then at least fewer enemies. If war meant that he would certainly lose Louisiana – even if only temporarily – then expedience dictated that he should make something of it while peace lingered. The way out of the bind was a bravura move that perhaps only a genius and a tyrant could have conceived of, let alone executed: he would sell New Orleans to the Americans, and not just New Orleans but the entirety of Louisiana. At a stroke, he would fill his treasury and keep the Americans out of the imminent conflict. In the long run, by empowering the Americans with the wealth of the Mississippi Valley and the strategic port of New Orleans, he might even succeed in creating a rival power that would contest British power in the Atlantic, and so tilt the balance of forces ever so slightly in France's favour in Europe.

On 7 April 1803, James Monroe sighted the French coast from his frigate and Toussaint Louverture died in his prison cell in the Fort de Joux. It was only on 10 April, the same day Monroe docked at Le Havre, that Napoleon revealed his plan to his advisers. By this point there was still time to pull off his grand strategic reversal: General Victor's army remained stuck in Hellevoetsluis and Louisiana had yet to be formally transferred from Spain to France. French national pride was not quite yet at stake.

At a summit at Saint-Cloud he told Admiral Decrès and finance minister Barbé-Marbois that he was intent on selling Louisiana. 'They ask of me only one town in Louisiana; but I already consider the colony as entirely lost; and it appears to me that in the hands of this growing power it will be more useful to the policy, and even to the commerce, of France than if I should attempt to keep it.' Besides, he added, 'I can scarcely say that I cede it to them, for it is not yet in our possession.'

The next day he informed Talleyrand, who was instructed to begin discussions with Livingston that evening. This he did, though the alarmed American initially turned down the offer, telling him 'that our wishes extended only to New Orleans & the Floridas'.[14] Talleyrand could not sell what he did not own – for even after several years in Paris, Livingston had yet to discover that the Floridas had not been ceded to France – but he pushed him to name a price for Louisiana, inclusive of New Orleans.

The next day, during a midnight conference with Barbé-Marbois, Livingston was once again pressured to give a number. By this time, Monroe had arrived in Paris and had found himself a latecomer to a round of extraordinary diplomatic negotiations that he was meant to have initiated.

Livingston and Monroe were in a difficult position. They were on the cusp of a major coup – winning New Orleans and the Mississippi Valley for their country. At the same time, they were fearful of spending too much and concerned about over-reaching their instructions. They considered writing to Jefferson to get clarification – but a response would be at least ten weeks away and Napoleon's mind could change in an instant.[15]

For there was considerable disagreement within Napoleon's inner circle about the proposed sale. Nobody was more vocal in their opposition than Napoleon's younger brothers, Lucien and Joseph. Joseph had learned of the sale first, and told his appalled brother of 'this incredible fantasy of selling Louisiana' and the disastrous consequences for national honour should it go through. A few days later, they confronted Napoleon in the Tuileries while the First Consul was in the bath. After some raillery, conversation turned to Louisiana. The mood quickly soured. When the two declared they would lead resistance to the sale in the Chamber of Deputies, Napoleon told them they could do as they liked, but 'I will do it without anyone's consent.' Joseph shot back that he was setting a poor example as first magistrate of the republic. To which Napoleon replied that first the retrocession of Louisiana – and now its sale – had been 'designed by me, negotiated by me, will be ratified and executed by me all alone ... by me who laughs at your opposition'. Such actions, Joseph warned, would earn them all a jail cell in French Guiana. Napoleon, quivering with rage, half rose from his bath, dripping suds and scented water, pointed at Joseph and cried, 'You are insolent!' before plunging backwards into the tub. The result, Lucien recorded in his memoirs, was *'une explosion aquatique'* that sent a wave of perfumed bathwater across the room. The valet waiting on Napoleon was so unnerved that he collapsed in shock. His fainting fit ended the contretemps, which had, in any event, done nothing to change Napoleon's mind.[16]

Livingston and Monroe had no way of knowing of the behind-the-scenes drama. Cut out of the French decision-making process and cut off from their superiors in Washington, they were plunged into hasty and indecorous negotiations to secure New Orleans before the window of opportunity slammed shut. Scarcely three weeks after Talleyrand had first floated the idea to Livingston, the essentials of the deal were agreed upon. The United States would pay $15 million dollars for French Louisiana, including New Orleans and all the forts and settlements up the length of the Mississippi and its tributaries.

On the surface, it was a triumph for the two American negotiators; in reality, the French were dictating terms. Jefferson had authorized Monroe to spend $9 million to purchase New Orleans and West Florida. He had now spent more than half as much again to buy something else entirely – something Livingston himself had described as an economically useless wasteland. Most importantly, Barbé-Marbois secured major political protections for French creoles on the verge of becoming Americans. Article III of the treaty required that 'the inhabitants of the ceded territory shall be incorporated in the Union of the United States ... as soon as possible' and afforded all the 'rights, advantages and immunities of citizens of the United States'. Taken as a whole, the treaty might well be impossible to get through Congress. It might also be unconstitutional. Yet the treaty granted the Americans only six months to ratify what was guaranteed to be a controversial transaction.[17]

Was it all that bad? The Americans had, after all, purchased some 820,000 square miles, doubling the size of their young country. Put another way: the Louisiana Purchase cost 4 cents an acre – at a time when the federal government sold lands in the public domain for a minimum of $2 per acre.

But this only became apparent after the fact. In Paris, in late April 1803, with the threat of war looming from every side, with an historic opportunity to solve their country's dominant geopolitical dilemma, and with Talleyrand and Bonaparte engaged in high-handed imperial diplomacy, none of this was obvious. The French simply would not specify what the borders of Louisiana were. When the Americans brought out maps and asked Talleyrand to point out where the limits of this vast land lay, he refused to comment. 'I do not know,' Talleyrand told Livingston when asked once again about Louisiana's boundaries. 'You must take it as you received it.' When the negotiators finally won an audience with Napoleon himself, they raised the issue – but he was no more helpful. Napoleon granted that the borders were fuzzy but also counselled that this might not be such a bad thing. 'If an obscurity did not exist,' he told the Americans, 'perhaps it would be good policy to put it there.'[18]

Despite the uncertainty, Monroe and Livingston pressed on. On 30 April, the treaty was signed. By the first week of May, the treaty was on a ship bound for New England. On 12 May, the British ambassador visited Talleyrand and requested his passport and permission to leave the French capital – the traditional prelude to a declaration of war.

The next day, Livingston and Monroe wrote a long letter to Madison defending their actions. The purchase, they wrote, amounted to 'a great stride to real and substantial independence' for their country, that would strengthen the Union, end fractious disputes with foreign powers and bring 'hundred millions of acres of the best quality' land into the public domain for the government to sell and so 'discharge the debt' incurred in buying it.

On 18 May, a state of war was declared between Britain and France. The same day, in Saint-Domingue, Louverture's successor Jean-Jacques Dessalines ripped the white out of the French *Tricolore* and ordered the new Haitian flag to be stitched out of the remaining red and blue portions.

On 30 June, news of the Louisiana purchase arrived on American soil. It did not reach Washington until the evening of 3 July – just in time to be the centrepiece for the next day's Independence Day celebrations. Jefferson was exultant. From the jaws of war he had snatched his empire of liberty. On the Trans-Appalachian frontier, news of the purchase was met with ecstasy. From Tennessee, Andrew Jackson sent the president the 'unanimous Congratulations' of the citizens of the West 'on the Joyfull event of the cession of Louisiana and New Orleans'. 'Every face wears a smile,' he wrote, 'and every heart leaps with Joy.'

That same month, news of renewed Anglo-French conflict reached the Caribbean and the Royal Navy resumed its blockade of Saint-Domingue. By winter, Rochambeau had been driven back into Cap Français. On 30 November, with the city on the brink of being overrun by Dessalines's forces, Rochambeau surrendered to the British and sailed out of the harbour. Of the 44,000 men France had poured into Saint-Domingue, 85 per cent had been killed, wounded or struck down by disease.

On 1 January 1804, Dessalines issued a declaration of independence, permanently abolished slavery and installed himself as Emperor of Haiti. Not long afterwards, the new emperor ordered the murder of all whites left on the island. This appalled the Americans, who now reversed their former policy of trade and engagement and sought to isolate and embargo the island. In 1805, Jefferson signed into law the first of several acts of Congress that limited commerce with Haiti. Jefferson also withheld diplomatic recognition of the new nation. The former slaves of Saint-Domingue, who had done so much to enable the Louisiana Purchase, were made pariahs by the Americans, and their contribution to America's historic westward expansion was soon forgotten.[19]

One man who did not forget was Alexander Hamilton. The Louisiana Purchase, he wrote, was an event of great significance to the future of the American experiment. But no one should fool themselves into thinking that it came about on account of 'any wise or vigorous measures on the part of the American government'. Rather Americans were indebted 'to the deadly climate of St. Domingo, and to the courage and obstinate resistance made by its black inhabitants'.[20]

# Committing Louisianicide

Fort Adams sat on a bluff overlooking a crook in the Mississippi River, forty-five miles south of Natchez, on the United States' southern extremity. The other side of the river was Spanish Louisiana. Originally the fort had been little more than some earthworks with an arsenal and a barracks. Over the years, as tensions on the southern border mounted, stone fortifications had been added on the heights, offering a view of Spanish manoeuvres down the river and across the other shore. In early 1803, Jefferson had ordered a general build-up at Fort Adams in preparation for a likely war with France over Louisiana. Men, artillery and supplies were floated down the river. The commanding officer, General James Wilkinson, ordered the 'extending and strengthening [of] our works at this critical pass'. Some men were sent into the swamps to cut wood; others baked bricks inside the fort. 'I hold this point to be the door to our whole western country,' Wilkinson told his civilian counterpart, William C. C. Claiborne, governor of the Mississippi Territory and the man Jefferson had tapped to be the first governor of New Orleans.[1]

By mid-November 1803, the situation at Fort Adams was bleak. Amid driving winter rains, the local planters pushed their slaves to harvest the cotton crop. Rumours about Spanish intentions were rife. Many people believed they would contest the handover of Louisiana to the Americans. Congress certainly feared they might. That October a bill had been passed empowering the president to use force, if necessary, to take New Orleans. Secretary of State Madison had written to Claiborne on Halloween advising him that 'in order to add the effect of terror to the force of arms', it would be wise to spread rumours that 'a very great force' was being prepared in Kentucky, Mississippi and Tennessee to support the invasion, should it arise. This much was true. Claiborne kept close tabs on the strength of the local militia and reckoned that even without substantial reinforcements they could expect to marshal a total of 500 men, a mixture of US soldiers and militiamen. It should be enough – but Claiborne was skittish. He was only twenty-nine years old. It took three weeks to get a message from Fort Adams to Washington. And, as he noted in his reply to Madison, 'the Eyes of all America are turned to this quarter of the Union'.[2]

This much was true. Jefferson would now depend on Claiborne and Wilkinson to close the deal Monroe and Livingston had brokered in Paris and secure New Orleans – whether Napoleon kept his word or not.

## FEAR AND TREMBLING

In a conversation with his brothers shortly after he revealed his plan to sell Louisiana, Napoleon joked darkly that he was committing 'Louisianicide'. In reality, the burden of that commission fell on Thomas Jefferson. The American president had spent money he did not have to buy a tract of land he had not wanted from a man who could not legally sell it in a transaction which was likely illegal under the terms of the Constitution. All of which meant that nothing could be taken as granted. Not a smooth transfer of power in the lower Mississippi; not ratification by the Congress; not, least of all, the easy absorption of the enormous and ill-defined territory into the American body politic.[3]

Foremost on Jefferson's mind was the constitutionality of the purchase. Jefferson had been taking advice for months on whether such an acquisition was permissible under the Constitution. The general opinion of his cabinet was summed up by Levi Lincoln, the postmaster general, who argued that the need to secure New Orleans and the free navigation of the Mississippi was 'so great, as to justify, almost any risque for their attainment'. But, on the verge of securing the empire of liberty he had dreamt about for decades, Jefferson faltered over the legal technicalities. Eventually he was overwhelmed by his cabinet. By mid-August he signalled that he was willing to let go of the idea of a constitutional amendment – but he remained unconvinced about his legal footing. 'The less we say about constitutional difficulties respecting Louisiana the better,' he concluded, a little glumly, to Madison.[4]

In this period Jefferson relied heavily on Albert Gallatin for the tricky task of negotiating the financing of the purchase. In Congress, Gallatin had represented Pennsylvania's westernmost district, a seat which ran from Lake Erie to the Virginia boundary. As a resident and former representative of the frontier, Gallatin was passionate about the Louisiana Purchase. He was a loyal Jeffersonian, but to the president, Gallatin's value lay in his masterful knowledge of the public finances. During the Adams presidency, Gallatin had caught Jefferson's eye with the publication of *A Sketch of the Finances of the United States*, a comprehensive overview of Federalist fiscal policy. Gallatin, Jefferson wrote, was 'the only man in the United States who understands, through all the labyrinths Hamilton involved it, the precise state of the Treasury'. Appointed treasury secretary, Gallatin's task was to take a butcher's knife to public spending to pay off the national debt and roll back the Hamiltonian project of creating a permanent debt and a sophisticated, English-style financial system to fund it. Such a financial system would enable the United States government to fund elaborate public policy programmes – such as purchasing new lands equivalent to 100 per cent of its existing territory. Irony of ironies, then, that the Louisiana Purchase thrust Gallatin back into the world of European high finance.[5]

Even before the treaty was signed in Paris, Napoleon's ministers had taken on the Dutch bank of Hope & Company and London's Barings' Bank to help manage the sale. Under the terms of the treaty, the bonds issued in payment for Louisiana would be redeemed in fifteen years. But Napoleon was fighting the English in the present and needed the money straight away.

The solution was to sell the American stock to the Anglo-Dutch bankers in exchange for ready cash – in effect, transferring ownership of Louisiana to a financial consortium and have the Americans pay them. The sums involved were immense. The United States was adding 20 per cent to their national debt; Barings' was purchasing bonds equivalent to 100 per cent of their partnership capital. Sir Francis Baring was open about his concerns – 'We all tremble at the magnitude of the American account' – but the Americans, the French and the bankers were now bound by a web of treaties, financial contracts and payment schedules.

Gallatin was soon deep in the weeds of international finance. Some of it was thoroughly unglamorous – he had difficulty finding a printer able to do the copper engraving for the 11,250 bond certificates he had to issue – and much of it was tedious but consequential. In the winter of 1803, Alexander Baring arrived in Washington and the two men finalized the small print.

While they were in conference, the British government woke up to the fact that a bank owned by an English baronet was funding Napoleon's war against Britain. In mid-December, the prime minister, Henry Addington, sent Alexander's father, Sir Francis, a letter stating that, given 'the avow'd purpose' of France was 'to employ all their resources with a view to their projected invasion of this Kingdom', it was improper for 'any subjects of this Country to facilitate at this time ... pecuniary arrangements as may subsist between other foreign powers, and the Government of France'.

In case Baring did not grasp the government's desire, Addington was explicit: 'I have therefore to desire that you would decline being a party to any remittances to France on account of the debt due from the United States of America in consequence of the cession of Louisiana.'

Baring ignored the prime minister's request. For the next two years, several million francs a month flowed from Barings' to the French treasury to help fund the war on Britain. The British bankers chose Jefferson and Napoleon over King and Country.[6]

## 'IT WILL PROVE A CURSE'

That summer of 1803, as the wheels of international finance began to turn, Jefferson retreated to his library in Monticello and picked over his vast collection of maps and books in order to confirm the limits and contents of the land his government had purchased. Then he wrote a sixty-page memo for Congress as an official account of what Louisiana consisted of. From his research, Jefferson gained a pretty clear idea of what the limits of the Louisiana Purchase were:

> The unquestioned bounds of Louisiana are the Iberville & Mississippi on the East, the Mexicana,* or the high lands East of it, on the West; then from the head of the Mexicana gaining the high lands which include the waters of the Mississippi, and following those highlands round the head springs of the western waters of the Mississippi to it's source.

In other words, the Louisiana Purchase was simply the western watershed of the Mississippi basin. Interestingly, however, this fair description of Louisiana's limits never made it into the report to Congress. Instead, in his memo Jefferson merely stated that Louisiana's boundaries 'are at present involved in some obscurity'. At some point that summer he must have decided to heed Napoleon's advice and insert some ambiguity into the question of Louisiana's borders.[7]

The report was otherwise a scrupulous† compilation of the best information available to the president from his desk in Monticello. He wrote at length about the laws, the native inhabitants and the geographical features of Louisiana. Despite imprecise information, he gave an overview of estimates of the total population of Louisiana which were between 60,000 and 90,000, with the majority living in Lower Louisiana, and between 8,000 and 10,000 living in New Orleans itself. Half the total population were black slaves. There were several thousand free people of colour, who enjoyed legal rights and had even formed their own militia unit. The white population was predominantly French, with some Spanish, German and Irish.[8]

The diversity of Louisiana was astounding – and concerning. A French traveller who published his reflections on Louisiana the same

---

* Mexicana is the old Spanish name for the Sabine River that is now the border between Louisiana and Texas.

† Jefferson could not resist inserting some tall tales into his 'Account'. In listing the mineral resources in Upper Louisiana, he included reference to a 'Salt Mountain ... 180 miles long, and 45 in width, composed of solid rock salt, without any trees, or even shrubs on it' that supposedly resided 1,000 miles up the Missouri River. Federalist satirists had a field day, with one newspaper speculating what other wonders awaited in Louisiana: a 'vast river of *golden eagles* ready coined', perhaps, an 'immense mountain of *solid refined sugar*', or a 'considerable lake of pure Whiskey'. (The 'golden eagles' refer to the $10 gold coin then in circulation.) (David Dzurec, 'Of Salt Mountains, Prairie Dogs, and Horned Frogs: The Louisiana Purchase and the Evolution of Federalist Satire 1803–1812', *Journal of the Early Republic*, 35/1 (2015), 79–108.)

year it was sold to the Americans provided a damning account of the inhabitants of the territory. The creoles were 'devoid of moral energy'; the Acadians were 'rude and sluggish'; the Germans had 'brutal manners, and proneness to intoxication'; the free people of colour were 'vain and insolent, perfidious and debauched, much given to lying, and great cowards. They have an inveterate hatred against the whites'; the black slaves were 'indolent, vicious and debauched'.

It was an alarming picture, and one the Americans readily accepted. Senator Fisher Ames described New Orleans as a '*Gallo-Hispano-Indian omnium gatherum* of savages and adventurers'. One of Hamilton's correspondents warned him of potential slave rebellions, noting that the 'Blacks have already been guilty of two or three insurrections within a few years back'. The French, he said, were hardly more dependable. Disgruntled locals he had met complained of having been sold by Napoleon for 'about eleven *sous* per head'. Everyone was alarmed at the prospect of absorbing an armed free black population. The ongoing conflict in Saint-Domingue loomed large. As one writer concluded, the very presence of 'free negroes and mulattoes ... goads the slaves' to insurrection and 'doomed the whites ... to the fate suffered ... in Saint Domingo [*sic*]'.[9]

All these fears came into the open when Congress met to debate the purchase in October 1803. One New England senator complained that 'Spain has not given a good title to France, [and] this treaty has given none to us'. There was 'no correct information' on 'the limits & extent of Louisiana', but every reason to believe that an 'extension of the body politic will enfeeble the circulation of its powers & energies in the extreme parts'. Moreover, the logic of the purchase posed serious questions for the legitimacy of the constitutional order. For 'Louisiana is of itself a world', and once such a 'vast wilderness' was settled, formed into states and admitted to the Union, then 'would not the influence and votes of the old states be controlled & negatived by the new?' Where would it end? 'If we can admit Louisiana, why not the British provinces, why not the terrible Republic of France itself!'[10]

Most congressmen were willing to look past such concerns, but even so they found themselves troubled by the prospect of adding non-Americans to the Union. Some were concerned with the lack of republican principles among the white population of Louisiana. 'The inhabitants of Louisiana,' said James Jackson of Georgia, 'are too ignorant to elect a legislature – they would consider jurors as a curse to them.' His colleague from Maryland agreed. 'Those people are absolutely incapable of governing themselves, of electing their rulers or appointing jurors.' The free blacks were another concern. 'A very few free negroes in Louisiana would revolutionize that country,' Jackson warned, noting with satisfaction that 'in Georgia we prohibit men from manumitting their slaves'.

For others, it was the slaves themselves who were the problem. They feared the political empowerment of the slave-owning states by granting them yet more 'negro Electors' due to the three-fifths clause in the Constitution. For John Smith of New York it was also a matter of security. 'Will you increase their number,' he asked, '& lay the necessary foundation for the horrors of another St. Domingo? If slaves are admitted there, I fear, we shall have cause to lament the acquisition of that country – it will prove a curse.'

But the southerners would hear none of it. 'Slaves must be admitted into that territory,' Jackson replied, 'it cannot be cultivated without them.' Hillhouse of Connecticut responded, 'If that country cannot be cultivated without slaves, let slaves hold it – or let it remain a wilderness forever.' Jackson was unmoved. 'You cannot prevent slavery – neither laws moral or human can do it – Men will be governed by their interest, not the law.'

Congress ultimately reached the peculiar conclusion that black slavery was key to the economic success of Louisiana, but that its white population could not be trusted with self-government. As Senator Jonathan Dayton of New Jersey put it: 'An elective government & trial by jury would be a curse of that people; but slavery is essential to their existence.' It was not a promising formula for an empire of liberty.[11]

Despite their misgivings, Congress ratified the Louisiana Purchase by a sizeable majority. And despite the illegality and the indignity of the sale, the Spanish delivered the keys to New Orleans to Pierre-Clément Laussat on a silver tray on 30 November, and the Spanish flag was lowered and the French *Tricolore* raised. And despite his fears, Claiborne found himself camped outside the city on 17 December, General Wilkinson by his side, and the only inconvenience he had suffered on the short trip downriver was when the schooner *Bilboa* he had requisitioned in Natchez became stuck on a sandbar at Point Coupee.

Laussat was governor of Louisiana for only twenty days. On 20 December, the citizens of New Orleans gathered at the Place d'Armes to watch as American forces marched to the sound of drums along the waterfront and beneath balconies crowded with wealthy creoles into the city. Laussat met with Wilkinson and Claiborne in the city hall. The Frenchman read the treaty of transfer and then the three exchanged ratifications. Laussat handed over the keys to the city, tied together with a *tricolore* ribbon. They then emerged onto the Place d'Armes and watched as the French flag began to descend over Louisiana and the Stars and Stripes began to rise. When the two flags were equal, they halted, and an artillery salute was fired from forts and batteries all over the city. A squadron of French soldiers then took possession of their flag, received the salute of the assembled Americans and marched out of the city, amid a stunned and tearful silence.

When news of the handover reached Washington, members of Congress, the president and vice president, and members of the cabinet attended a party at Stelle's Hotel. There were many rounds of toasts. 'The tempestuous sea of Liberty,' went one, 'may [it] never be calm.' 'A number of the guests drank so many toasts,' one senator recalled, 'that in the night they returned to their houses without their hats.'

Shortly afterwards, Gallatin transferred a third of the purchase stock to Barings' and made arrangements for the remainder to be forwarded on to Europe. From there, fragments of America's promise to pay for the region were sold on and scattered to vaults across the continent, where they would remain, silently waiting for redemption. In the meantime, Louisiana had become American.[12]

# Filling in the Map

On 9 March 1804, a peculiar ceremony took place in St Louis, a thousand miles upriver from New Orleans. Under the terms of the Louisiana Purchase, all the settlements along the Mississippi had to be formally transferred from the Spanish to the French, and then from the French to the Americans. After the successful handover of New Orleans, Captain Amos Stoddard was sent to St Louis with instructions to take control of the city 'in the most polite and friendly manner'. The French were unable to send a representative, so in a curious bureaucratic twist Laussat deputized Stoddard to fulfil that role as well. In his dual capacity as both the American and the French commissioner responsible for overseeing the transfer, Stoddard watched the lowering of the Spanish flag on 9 March.

According to local tradition, as Spanish rule came to an end, some French citizens approached the American and asked that the French flag be allowed to fly over Louisiana for one final time, and Stoddard, mindful of his instructions to maintain good relations with the citizenry, permitted it to do so. For a day and a night St Louis was French and then, on 10 March, the United States flag was raised, the artillery sounded a salute, the small group of Americans present cheered and the handover of Louisiana was completed.[1]

## A LITERARY PURSUIT

Watching impatiently as the Stars and Stripes rose above St Louis was a man for whom the transfer was a beginning, not an ending. A few years before, Meriwether Lewis had been a little-known officer in the United States Army. Then in 1800 the new president plucked Lewis from obscurity and invited him to be his private assistant in Washington. Lewis immediately accepted the offer. He travelled to Washington and took up residence in the President's House. Jefferson was a widower, Lewis a bachelor. They spent almost the whole time together: work, meals, long evening conversations. 'Capt. Lewis and myself are like two mice in a church,' Jefferson told his daughter Martha. Jefferson depended on Lewis in matters large and small. When each year Jefferson was obliged to give the State of the Union address (a Federalist innovation that he considered 'royal' and 'pompous'), he wrote the speech but had Lewis read it to Congress.[2]

In the summer of 1802, Jefferson read Alexander Mackenzie's *Voyages* (1801), which chronicled the Scotsman's epic 1793 overland journey from Montreal to the coast of British Columbia. Mackenzie had concluded his book with a call for the British government to invest in the exploration and settlement of the Pacific Northwest. Mackenzie's book excited and disturbed the president in equal measure. While he admired Mackenzie's feat, he was frustrated that the achievement was not an American one and was concerned by talk of British empire-building in Oregon.

Furthermore, Jefferson had been contemplating such a mission for many years. On various occasions he had approached George Rogers Clark, the French naturalist André Michaux and Captain Cook's former crewman John Ledyard, to see if they would take on the challenge. Clark was too old. Michaux was keen but then got caught up in Genêt's 1793 misadventure. Ledyard decided to try and take the long way round – via Siberia and the Bering Strait – but was arrested in Irkutsk under orders from Catherine the Great. The idea had then lain dormant for a decade. But Mackenzie had piqued his interest again. So in 1802 Jefferson proposed to Meriwether Lewis that he might do it himself. Lewis accepted.[3]

Jefferson's instructions to Lewis were famously thorough, including requests that Lewis write a vocabulary of all the Indian languages he encountered, keep detailed botanical and mineralogical notes, maintain climatic and meteorological records, and keep track of all animals and remains of animals he came across, especially those 'deemed rare or extinct'.*

At his most succinct, Jefferson told Lewis his mission was to discover 'the course and source of the [Missouri], and of the most convenient water communication from thence to the Pacific ocean'.

At this time very little was known of the origins of the Missouri. Some people, including Jefferson, believed that the Missouri might run all the way to the Pacific. If this was the case, then a voyage up the river would establish American territorial claims in the remote Northwest. America would finally be a transcontinental power, stretching, as had long been hoped, from sea to shining sea.[4]

All this had been conceived and planned before news of the Louisiana Purchase arrived in Washington on 3 July 1803.

Jefferson had initially sold the expedition to Congress as 'a literary pursuit' that would enhance America's knowledge of the lands west of the Mississippi. Lewis had left Washington in the spring, travelling to Pittsburgh via Harper's Ferry and Philadelphia. Along the way he had

---

* Jefferson was thinking of mammoths again. The president's obsession with finding bizarre natural phenomena in the far west was ridiculed in an anonymous poem about Lewis (allegedly written by John Quincy Adams) published shortly after his return to Washington:

He never with a Mammoth met,
   However you may wonder;
Nor even with a Mammoth's bone,
   Above the ground or under –
And, spite of all the pains he took
   The animal to track, sir,
He never could o'ertake the hog
   With navel on his back, sir.

And from the day his course began,
   Till even it was ended,
He never found an Indian tribe
   From Welchmen straight descended:
Nor, much as of Philosophers
   The fancies it might tickle;
To season his adventures, met
   A Mountain, sous'd in pickle.

*Monthly Anthology, and Boston Review*, 4/3 (1807), 143.

invited William Clark, a fellow army officer (and the younger brother of George Rogers Clark), to join him on the journey. While waiting for keelboats to be built in Pittsburgh, Lewis bought a Newfoundland, who he named Seaman, who was about to embark on the longest walk in canine history.

After many delays, the two men met at Louisville, Kentucky, in mid-October and headed down the Ohio to St Louis.

On 7 December, Lewis presented himself to Carlos de Hault de Lassus, the Spanish lieutenant governor for Upper Louisiana. He handed him a now-outdated letter from Thomas Jefferson in which the president requested permission for the expedition to pass through Spanish Louisiana, reassuring him that its purposes were 'merely literary'. De Lassus was not fooled and politely refused the request, telling Lewis that while he personally wished his journey 'every success', his orders 'forbad his granting me permission at this time to ascend the Missouri River'.

The Spaniard wrote to his own superiors reporting the encounter and his own suspicions about the true nature of Lewis's expedition: 'I believe that his mission has no other object than to discover the Pacific Ocean.'

Around the same time, a letter arrived from Jefferson in which he recast the purpose of the mission in light of the Louisiana Purchase. Lewis's mission, he wrote, 'since the acquisition of Louisiana, interests every body in the highest degree'. Lewis would no longer be travelling through foreign territory but would be within America's borders – indeed, his travels would help establish the extent of those borders:

> As the boundaries of interior Louisiana are the high lands inclosing all the waters which run into the Mississippi or Missouri ... it becomes interesting to fix with precision by celestial observations the longitude & latitude of the sources of these rivers, as furnishing points in the contour of our new limits. This will be attempted distinctly from your mission, which we consider as of major importance, & therefore not to be delayed or hazarded by any episodes whatever.

'Interesting' was a piece of presidential understatement. Precise celestial observations of the sources of the Missouri and its tributaries would be the basis for future territorial claims. If those waters stretched into British Canada, Spanish California or the disputed territory of the Pacific Northwest, then those would effectively be the limits of the Louisiana Purchase. The substance of Lewis's discoveries would determine the extent of the territory Livingston and Monroe had acquired in Paris.

But for now Lewis could do nothing until the handover was complete.[5]*

## ON THE BOUNDLESS MISSOURI

The expedition finally got under way on 21 May 1804. Lewis and Clark led thirty men, mostly Americans (including one enslaved man, York, owned by Clark), but with some Frenchmen recruited from St Louis, travelling on a keelboat and two pirogues.

They were not quite travelling into the unknown, but they had very little reliable information about where they were heading. Before Lewis had left Washington, Gallatin had commissioned a map for him to take up the river. It was an amalgamation of all the best knowledge about the far west at that time.

It was largely blank. Only three places were known by their exact longitude and latitude: St Louis; the Mandan villages (modern-day Bismarck, North Dakota), whose coordinates had been established by David Thompson, a British explorer and fur trader, in 1798; the mouth of the Columbia River on the Pacific coast, discovered by the American captain Robert Gray in 1792. In between lay over 3,000 miles of unmapped territory.[6]

Just because Europeans knew very little about Upper Louisiana, it did not mean it was empty. Tens of thousands of Indians lived along the route they were venturing up, mostly on the banks of the Missouri and its tributaries. This posed its own set of challenges. Indian cooperation

---

* Jefferson would later reiterate the significance of these celestial observations in a letter to Portuguese intellectual José Corrêa da Serra: 'The most important justification of it [the Lewis & Clark expedition], still due to the public depends on these astronomical observations, as from them alone can be obtained the correct geography of the country, which was the main object of the expedition' (Thomas Jefferson to José Corrêa da Serra, 20 July 1816).

and assistance would be vital for the success of the mission. At the same time, they were there to tell the Indians that they were now living on American soil.

'It will now be proper you should inform those through whose country you will pass,' Jefferson had instructed Lewis, 'that their late fathers the Spaniards have agreed to withdraw all their troops from all the waters & country of the Mississippi & Missouri, that they have surrendered to us all their subjects ... that henceforward we become their fathers and friends.'

To help soften the message, Lewis had assembled an immense amount of gifts to be distributed to Indians they encountered. These included everything from scissors and fishing hooks to kettles, beads and needles. All told, he had compiled twenty-one bundles of presents, each numbered, some waterproofed, many allocated in advance to specific tribes they expected to meet along the way. Some of these gifts were intended to communicate that the Indians were now Americans. One Omaha chief was allocated an American flag, an officer's coat and some scarlet leggings. They also carried a sackful of peace medals, struck with Jefferson's likeness, to distribute to chieftains. The average warrior might just get a certificate declaring its possessor a 'friend and ally' of the United States. These were among the least desirable items. One Omaha warrior named Big Blue Eyes was so disgusted when given such a certificate that he promptly handed it back.[7]

In late October, they arrived at the Mandan villages, some 1,600 miles from St Louis. There they built a fort and settled down for the winter. Relations with the Mandans were cordial. They were a settled tribe who held an annual market where Indians from all over the Northern Plains gathered to trade. They had been hosting English, French and Spanish fur traders for decades and easily absorbed the Americans into the rhythms of their daily lives.

Mandan friendliness took many forms – some shocking to the patrician sensibilities of Lewis and Clark. On 5 January 1805, the Americans were invited to join in the buffalo-calling ceremony, an annual ritual intended to ensure the return of the buffalo herds the Mandans depended on for meat and skins. In the Mandan belief system, younger warriors could extract the hunting prowess of their elders by sharing their wives with them. One part of the ceremony involved warriors going around and offering their wives to older, more experienced hunters. The Mandans regarded the Americans as particularly desirable in this regard, with Clark noting that 'the Indians say all white flesh is medicine'. 'We sent a man to this medicine dance last night,' he recorded in his journal. 'They gave him four girls.'

Such dalliances were not without their hazards. A few months later, Clark reported that his men were 'generally healthy except venereal complaints which is very common amongst the natives and the men catch it from them'. The men who contracted such complaints carried them to the Pacific and back.[8]*

* * *

> The ice came down in great quantities. The river rose 13 inches the last 24 hours. I observed [the] extraordinary dexterity of the Indians in jumping from one cake of ice to another, for the purpose of catching the [frozen] buffalo as they float down. Many of the cakes of ice which they pass over are not two feet Square. The plains are on fire in view of the fort on both sides of the river. It is said to be common for the Indians to burn the plains near their villages every spring for the benefit of their horses, and to induce the buffalo to come near to them.

Clark's striking description of the thawing of the Missouri in late March 1805 was written as they prepared to strike camp and begin the next, more perilous, phase of their expedition.

On 7 April, Lewis sent the keelboat and a crew of ten back to St Louis with a treasure trove of samples for Jefferson showcasing their discoveries to date. 'We were now about to penetrate a country at least two thousand miles in width,' he told the president in an accompanying letter, 'on which the foot of civilized man had never trodden.'[9]

Ahead of them the Missouri River stretched in almost a straight line back to the Rockies, where it turned south until it reached its origins at the forks of the Missouri in south-west Montana.

---

* The historian Eldon G. Chuinard notes that the captains had brought syringes, lancets and two pounds of mercury to help treat syphilis and that such treatments were effective – in the short term at least. The Mandan episode was not the last time sexually transmitted diseases afflicted the expedition. On the return journey, two men were taken ill with infections picked up during encounters with Chinook women in the Pacific Northwest.

Initially, its course ran abreast of the 49th parallel that now demarcates the American/Canadian border. In the days and weeks after their departure from the Mandan villages Lewis's geopolitical antennae were particularly sensitive. If any of the tributaries flowing in to the north bank of the Missouri had their sources deep inside Canada, then those lands drained by them would also constitute a part of the Louisiana Purchase. This would doubtless cause a confrontation with Great Britain. It was perhaps fortunate, then, that they counted only five river mouths on the north bank of the Missouri, and only three of them had their sources in Canada, none extending any great distance into the interior.[10]

Meanwhile, Lewis had more immediate problems than great-power politics. On 29 April, the party became the first Americans to see a grizzly bear. Lewis claimed that while 'the Indians may well fear this animal equipped as they generally are with their bows and arrows', they were 'by no means as formidable or dangerous' to white men armed with rifles. He soon discovered this was not the case. The bears proved capable of absorbing immense amounts of gunfire. One bear was shot five times in the lungs and still kept moving. Another was shot multiple times in the body, lungs and head before it died. The grizzlies were attracted to their hunting kills and circled their camp at night. There were enough instances of men out hunting or scouting alone being chased by bears that Lewis had to forbid solo journeys. He himself had an alarming sequence of encounters in the wild on 14 June. First a grizzly 'pitched at me, open-mouthed and [at] full speed', then a wolverine attacked him, and finally he was chased by three buffalo. 'It now seemed to me that all the beasts of the neighbourhood had made a league to destroy me,' a chastened Lewis wrote in his journal that evening. But the grizzlies remained the number-one threat. 'These bear being so hard to die rather intimidates us all,' he wrote. 'I must confess that I do not like the gentlemen and had rather fight two Indians than one bear.'[11]

On 26 May the party spotted the Rockies and Lewis admitted he 'felt a secret pleasure in finding myself so near the head of the heretofore conceived boundless Missouri'. In mid-June they reached the great falls of the Missouri and abandoned their pirogues to make the portage. Then they felled two tall firs and cut from them two large rough-hewn canoes. In these they pressed on to the forks, harried by gnats, ravaged by blisters, cut by prickly pairs and by turns frozen in the mountain waters and scorched by the high-summer heat. Finally, on 27 July, they arrived at the source of the Missouri, some 3,000 miles from St Louis. They named the three rivers that met there after Jefferson, Madison and Gallatin.*

The party turned westwards, searching for a way across the Continental Divide. The captains split up. On 12 August, Lewis hiked up a dwindling stream towards a pass. This unassuming rivulet was 'the most distant fountain of the waters of the mighty Missouri in search of which we have spent so many toilsome days and restless nights'. It narrowed to nothing and one of the men stood with a foot on either side and 'thanked his god that he had lived to bestride the mighty & heretofore deemed endless Missouri'.

'We proceeded on to the top of the dividing ridge,' Lewis wrote, 'from which I discovered immense ranges of high mountains still to the west of us with their tops partially covered with snow.' Beyond were the Bitterroot Mountains of Idaho and the Columbia River watershed. But there was no tributary of the Missouri extending to the Pacific. Meriwether Lewis had discovered the limits of the Louisiana Purchase.[12]

## JEFFERSON'S MEN

The Lewis and Clark expedition was only the most famous of several exploratory missions Jefferson authorized in order to discover the extent of the lands he had bought from Napoleon. In each case, the intention was the same: to send highly trained, highly trusted men to gather information about the West that would allow his administration 'to prepare a map of Louisiana, which in it's contour and main waters will be perfectly correct, & will give us a skeleton to be filled up with details hereafter'. This in turn would help establish American territorial claims.

Zebulon Pike was dispatched northwards to try and find the source of the Mississippi. Pike thought he discovered the source at Cass Lake,

---

* Lewis went further and named two of the Jefferson River's tributaries in the president's honour. In his journal he described the naming process: '[We] called the bold rapid and clear stream Wisdom, and the more mild and placid one which flows in from the S. E. Philanthropy, in commemoration of two of those cardinal virtues, which have so eminently marked that deservedly celebrated character through life' (Lewis's journal, 6 Aug. 1805). Even thousands of miles from Washington, Lewis was capable of great feats of sycophancy.

Minnesota,* and otherwise had a grand time waylaying a North West Company fur trader, shooting down a British flag and handing out peace medals to the local Ojibwe.

Two expeditions were sent up the Red River. The first was brief and uneventful. The second, led by Thomas Freeman and Peter Custis, departed in April 1806. The Spanish, however, caught wind of their journey, and dispatched a military force to intercept them. On 29 July, at Spanish Bluff on the Texas–Arkansas border, the party was turned back.

Meanwhile, Zebulon Pike had set out on another adventure, this time to find the source of the Arkansas River and then trek overland to the headwaters of the Red River and travel down it back to Natchitoches. It was a quixotic plan which led to Pike getting lost three times and leading his hungry and frostbitten men in circles around central Colorado in the middle of winter. Eventually, in February 1807, he was rescued (and arrested) by a Spanish force sent from Santa Fe who marched the Americans down to Chihuahua for a dressing-down from Nemesio de Salcedo, the senior Spanish officer in the region. They were then marched up through Texas, arriving back on American soil in June.

Pike had hoped to use the trip as a way of currying favour with Jefferson by sending him the kind of samples and curios that Lewis and Clark had gathered in such abundance. Sadly, he lost almost everything while in Spanish custody. One of the few things he was able to send the president was a pair of (live) grizzly bear cubs. Jefferson kept the bears in the White House for a time and then wisely† palmed them off on his friend Charles Willson Peale.[13]

---

* He hadn't, though he was very close. Lake Itasca, the actual source, was only forty miles away.

† Jefferson wrote to Anne Cary Randolph on 1 Nov. 1807: 'I have received from Capt. Pike a pair of Grisly bears brought from the head of the Arkansa, These are too dangerous & troublesome for me to keep. I shall therefore send them to Peale's Museum.' Donald Jackson quotes Peale's biographer as to what happened when the bears took up residence in Philadelphia: 'The bears, from playful cubs, grew large and fierce. They would attack anyone, man or beast, who came within their reach. A teasing monkey had arm and shoulder blade torn off by a sweep of the great claws. They met their fate when one of them, one night, broke loose from his cage and stalked into the cellar of Philosophical Hall. The Peale family was in terror, and with reason. Peale closed the cellar door and window, and in the morning entered and shot the creature. The survivor was killed in its cage and mounted with its mate' (Donald J. Jackson, *Thomas Jefferson and the Stony Mountains*, 260).

Pike's capture did provide useful information about Spanish intentions in the aftermath of the Louisiana Purchase. Having sustained a major diplomatic defeat in Paris, the Spanish were scrambling to conduct damage limitation. In Madrid, delusory ideas prevailed about the capacity of Spain to roll back American claims west of the Mississippi. As St Louis was in the act of being turned over to the United States in March 1804, an imperial council in Spain was calling for the confluence of the Missouri and the Mississippi to remain in Spanish hands. Officials on the ground were more clear-eyed about the extent of American ambitions out west. That same month an official in New Orleans wrote of the 'hasty and gigantic steps which our neighbors are taking towards the South Sea', predicting that the Americans would have a port on the Pacific 'within five years'. (His prediction was only two years off.)[14]

Jefferson's various attempts to learn more about the lands west of the Mississippi confirmed Spain's worst fears about American designs. As Salcedo noted in the summer of 1804, 'although it is almost eight months since the United States of America took possession of [Louisiana], they are maintaining themselves in the greatest inaction and are guarding a most profound silence concerning the time when they are to begin the marking of their boundaries. Meanwhile with great activity and care they are sending expeditions to the Upper Mississippi, Missouri, Arkansas and Red Rivers, in order to reconnoitre their sources and courses, examine their lands, and attract and conciliate the Indian nations to them.'

Salcedo was not wrong. In the end, the Americans followed Napoleon's advice to the letter: studiously avoiding making firm commitments on paper while feverishly establishing facts on the ground. The Louisiana Purchase would not have designated borders until 1821 – and by then it had morphed into something else entirely from what Jefferson had originally envisioned purchasing in 1803.[15]

# Everything Shifts

There was a comet in the sky in 1811 and when the citizens of Louisville, Kentucky, were awoken in the night by a deafening sound, they reckoned it might have fallen out of the heavens and crashed into the Ohio. Running from their beds to the riverbank, they encountered something no less portentous.

By the light of the full moon they saw the steamboat *New Orleans* idling at anchor across the water. Over the coming decades the steamboats would become a common sight at Louisville, but the *New Orleans* was the first on the Mississippi. That winter it travelled from Pittsburgh to New Orleans on its maiden voyage. It made the journey in almost exactly three months, a respectable time given that it was feted at every stop along the way, narrowly avoided being swept by a fire originating in its onboard kitchen and got caught in an earthquake at New Madrid, Missouri. At 148 feet in length and 371 tons in weight, it was the largest boat of any kind on the river – and the fastest as well. Sceptical old boatmen reckoned that while it would be fine travelling with the current, its bulk meant it could never make it back upstream. The *New Orleans* proved them wrong, and was soon in regular service between its namesake and Natchez, cruising against the current at a stately three miles an hour at a time when a regular craft might hope to do ten miles a day.

The *New Orleans*, like the comet emblazoned in the night sky, was the harbinger of great changes and of a new, accelerated era in the history of the Mississippi Valley.[1]

## ANNIHILATED BY STEAM

The steamboat revolution, like the Louisiana Purchase, had its genesis in Paris in 1803. In 1801 Robert Livingston, a wealthy politician from New York, was appointed as the United States' minister to France. In Paris he met Robert Fulton, an American inventor experimenting with steam-powered locomotion. Livingston became Fulton's patron and funded a series of promising experiments on the Seine. On leaving his post in 1804, Livingston returned to his home state and continued working with Fulton, this time with the Hudson as their testing ground.

But Fulton already had his eye on the biggest river of all. 'Whatever may be the fate of steamboats for the Hudson,' he wrote, 'everything is completely proved for the Mississippi, and the object is immense.' The steamboat, he predicted, 'will give a cheap and quick conveyance to the merchandise on the Mississippi, Missouri, and other great rivers, which are now laying open their treasures to the enterprise of our countrymen'. In 1809 the two men teamed up with engineer Nicholas Roosevelt and got to work building the *New Orleans*. In 1811, with the help of governor William C. C. Claiborne, they received a monopoly on commercial steam travel on the Mississippi.[2]

With the success of the *New Orleans*'s maiden voyage, the three men effected a revolution in the Mississippi Valley. A barge or keelboat took three to four months travelling upstream from New Orleans to Louisville – roughly three times the duration of a transatlantic passage. By 1815 that journey could be done in two weeks by steamboat. With improvements in design, infrastructure and personnel, that time fell to ten days in 1824, then to eight days in 1833. By 1853 the 1,350-mile journey could be completed in four days.

With faster speeds and shorter journey times came new lines. Soon towns along the Wabash, the Illinois and the Red River had access to steam power. The *General Jackson* plied the route to Nashville. The *Comet* travelled to distant Arkansas Post. The *Velocipede* visited the lead mines of Missouri. As services became more regular and routes proliferated, freight and passenger prices fell, enabling a massive increase in trade and travel throughout the Mississippi Valley. Steamboats joined together the scattered tributaries of the Mississippi in a common network of high-speed travel. 'Steam navigation colonized the West!'

one breathless American wrote in retrospect. 'It advanced the career of national colonization and national production, at least a century!'[3]

Visitors to the region exulted in the speed, convenience and luxury of steamboat travel. One traveller thought of the steamboat, with its 'splendid cabin, richly carpeted, its finishings of mahogany, its mirrors and fine furniture, its bar-room, and sliding-tables', as a 'floating hotel'. Francis Hall, a British cavalry officer, was sceptical of America, Americans and steamboats. Boarding the *Paragon*, he confessed his 'apprehension' at dining in close quarters with 150 strangers. But the service aboard and the 'general attention to quiet and decorum' left him pleasantly surprised. 'Truly, thought I, these republicans are not so barbarous.'

For most seasoned westerners, used to arduous, months-long journeys, it was the speed of steam travel that captivated them. Henry Rowe Schoolcraft, boarding the *St Louis* at Potosi, Missouri, bound for New Orleans, had his senses scrambled by the speed at which he made the journey:

> Trees, points of land, islands, every physical object on shore, we rushed by with a velocity that left but vague and indistinct impressions. We seemed floating, as it were, on the waters of chaos, where mud, trees, boats, were carried along swiftly by the current, without any additional impulse of a steam-engine, puffing itself off at every stroke of the piston. The whole voyage to New Orleans had some analogy to the recollection of a gay dream, in which objects were recollected as a long line of loosely-connected panoramic fragments.

'Distance is no longer thought of in this region,' one writer declared, 'it is almost annihilated by steam.'[4]

## SOME BETTER COUNTRY

The arrival of the steamboat heightened the contrast between old and new – and there were many old things and many ancient practices surviving in the Mississippi Valley. Far down the Red River, traveller Henry Ker found inscriptions on a cave entrance that he estimated were five hundred years old. In Upper Louisiana some of the tribes of the plains still buried their dead on wooden scaffolds. Some travellers were startled to meet Indians who had never seen or tasted bread. Others blundered into regions swept by the seasonal, semi-ritualized patterns of war that prevailed along the Missouri. Camping on an island near the mouth of the Platte River in Nebraska, John Bradbury 'observed in the night the reflection of immense fires, occasioned by burning the prairies'. These were lit by returning war parties covering the tracks of their retreat. Some encounters seemed to harken back to the age of Soto. An Irish traveller named Fortescue Cuming met a Chickasaw archer on the banks of the Mississippi near Memphis, Tennessee. 'His natural colour was entirely concealed under the bright vermillion, the white, and the blue grey, with which he was covered,' Cuming wrote. 'He was drest very fantastically in an old fashioned, large figured, high coloured calico shirt – deer skin leggins and mockesons, ornamented with a plume of beautiful heron's feathers nodding over his forehead from the back of his head.'[5]

For many Americans brought to the West for the first time by steam, the frontiersmen were no less alien than the Indians. One itinerant preacher registered his disgust at watching a French settler and his native wife sitting down to dinner in a wigwam in northern Illinois. 'For supper the husband had a terrapin, the squaw an opossum;* and we had biscuit and uncooked mackerel, which we carried with us.' Another missionary was shocked by his experiences among the Scots-Irish squatters of frontier Missouri and Arkansas. Approaching a log cabin so riddled with holes that he could see the faces of the children inside, he met an old man whose 'shock-headed appearance was as though he had slept alternately on a heap of cockleburs and ashes'. Upon meeting the whole family, he discovered 'not a particle of cloth of any kind ... about their bodies. Men and women were dressed in skins that once the wild deer claimed, but covered and saturated with grease, blood, and dirt.' Where some might have seen poverty he saw moral failing, concluding that 'a kind of half-savage life appeared to be their choice'.[6]

---

* Revulsion at frontier dining habits was a hallmark of missionary memoirs. John Mason Peck recalled with horror the food eaten by Scots-Irish squatters in Missouri: 'Venison, bear-meat, and hog-meat dressed and cooked in the most slovenly and filthy manner, with corn-bread baked in form of a pone, and when cold as hard as a brickbat, constituted their provisions.' Timothy Flint once encountered a settlement surviving on 'Bear-meat and raccoon-bacon'.

Concern for the moral condition of the frontier attracted missionaries to the region, among them Timothy Flint, a Harvard-trained Presbyterian, who travelled from Massachusetts to Missouri in 1815. Flint had a keen eye for the gritty underside of frontier society and was appalled by the universal love for fighting, duelling and drinking he observed in frontier communities. At the same time, he retained an optimism about the future. He firmly believed that 'God made the earth to be inhabited', and so viewed the spread of civilization – however haphazardly – as a fulfilment of His will. Watching a migrant hammering together their first log cabin in a wood, Flint allowed his imagination to leap forward to a time when the surrounding area would be fields of corn and wheat, when the log cabins would be replaced by brick buildings and when this humble farmer might have risen up to become an assembly member, a justice of the peace – even a judge. 'It has afforded me more pleasing reflections,' he wrote, 'to contemplate these beginnings of social toil in the wide wilderness.'[7]

Flint's confidence in this process was unsettled by what he termed 'the moving or migratory character of the western people'. 'Though they have generally good houses,' he wrote, 'they might almost as well, like the Tartars, dwell in tents. Everything shifts under your eye.'

The transitory nature of frontier society was something almost everyone remarked upon. Nobody had ever expected the frontier to expand so rapidly. At the time of the Louisiana Purchase, Jefferson had thought that it would take fifty years for the frontier to reach the new lands. Flint recalled a time only ten years before his arrival in St Louis when the Mississippi 'was to us, the "ultima Thule" – a limit almost to the range of thought'.

Yet by 1820 there were settlers pushing out into remote parts of Arkansas and Missouri. This world in motion baffled the New Englander. 'Scarcely has a family fixed itself' in one location, Flint wrote, 'than the assembled family about the winter fire begin to talk about the prevailing theme, – some country that has become the rage, as a point of immigration. They offer their farm for sale, and move away.'

Fellow missionary John Mason Peck observed the same phenomenon. The squatters he met in Missouri had come from the 'settlements', the backcountry of Tennessee, North Carolina and Kentucky. Soon they would clear out for Arkansas. Taking their place would be farmers with land rights and longer-term aspirations to settle the region. In the mid-1810s, Peck watched this second wave of settlers come in 'like an avalanche. It seemed as though Kentucky and Tennessee were breaking up and moving to the "Far West."'

Yet even these new waves of migrants always had their hopes set on somewhere better just over the horizon. Thomas Nuttall, an English botanist who went down the Ohio heading for Arkansas in 1815, recalled the 'jarring vortex of heterogeneous population' he travelled among, 'all searching for some better country, which ever lies to the west, as Eden did to the east'.[8]

Part of the mythology of the West was that this migration constituted a kind of force unto itself, guided by its own mysterious logic, and beyond the control of any earthly power. In reality, this vast movement of people was enabled by government policy dating back to the Jeffersonian era.

In the late 1790s, while in Congress, Albert Gallatin had campaigned to reform federal land policy. Under the Land Act of 1796, the minimum purchase size from a government land office remained a section, but the minimum price per acre was raised to $2. In other words, anyone wishing to purchase public lands had to have ready access to $1,280.

Under this system land sales had been very slow. Only 121,540 acres of public land were sold between 1796 and 1800. Gallatin had two aims. He wanted more Americans to be able to buy land and he wanted the federal government to have a reliable source of revenue from land sales. To this end, he supported the Land Act of 1800 that reduced the minimum purchase size to 320 acres (a half section) and extended four years of credit to purchasers.

No sooner had the Congress passed this Act than, in 1804, it passed another Land Act further reducing the minimum purchase size to 160 acres (a quarter section) and reducing the minimum price per acre to $1.64.

In 1812, a law was passed establishing a General Land Office (GLO) under the control of the Department of the Treasury. This office had complete responsibility for surveying, selling and patenting land. The GLO expanded the number of land offices it operated from four in 1800 to twenty-seven by 1817. These offices were spread across the frontier and dealt directly with settlers looking to buy land.[9]

These developments primed an explosion in migration. But they did not happen in isolation. Crucial to the success of this new land policy was an aggressive Indian policy. During his presidency, Jefferson advocated for what would later be called 'Indian removal'. He wanted to negotiate with Indians to buy their land and relocate them to lands elsewhere.

Specifically, Jefferson wanted to buy the strategically and commercially valuable lands along the rivers of the Mississippi Valley. The speed with which Jefferson executed this policy was remarkable. In November 1804, when Lewis and Clark had only just arrived at the Mandan villages, the United States signed a treaty in St Louis with Sauk and Fox Indians to buy 1.5 million acres of land in between the Mississippi, Missouri, Illinois and Wisconsin Rivers for $2,500 and a $1,000 annuity. This was the first of dozens of treaties that ultimately transferred 128 million acres – an area the size of modern Spain – to American hands. Jefferson pursued this policy with singular focus, his eye always on the long-term goal of what he referred to ominously as the 'final consolidation' of the Indians on land west of the Mississippi.[10]

Extinguishing Indian claims and reforming the land-sales process were useful only insofar as settlers could actually afford to buy land. Putting land within reach of the average settler required improving access to credit. In practice, this meant more and larger banks. Banks, of course, were anathema to Jefferson, but as treasury secretary, Gallatin had believed they were important enough to have gone head-to-head with the president on the matter. Gallatin did so again under President Madison. In 1816, Gallatin was able to win political support for the creation of a new bank, referred to as the Second Bank of the United States (SBUS). This bank had nineteen regional branches, stretching as far west as Louisville and as far south as New Orleans. The regional branches provided funding for dozens of state banks that sprouted up across the West.

By the end of the decade, Tennessee had ten banks, Ohio twenty-six, and Pennsylvania forty-one. Kentucky went from having one bank in 1817 to forty-one in 1818. All of these banks issued their own paper currency. In a short period of time, the money supply more than doubled. Everyone knew this paper money was not sound (it was colloquially referred to as 'rag' money issued by 'rag banks'; people whose wealth was based on this kind of uncertain paper money were known as 'rag earls'), but in the heady rush of economic expansion it did not matter. Peck recalled how paper money was everywhere out west, the notes of the banks 'scattered over the frontiers like the leaves of the trees by an autumnal frost'.[11]

With paper money in their hands, settlers could go down to the local land office, buy a quarter section and move to territory that had been surveyed and cleared of Indians. Thousands did so. Before the war of 1812 public land sales had averaged 350,000 acres annually. By 1815 annual land sales had tripled to 1 million acres and then tripled again to 3 million in 1819.

As hundreds of thousands of people moved into the territories, those territories became eligible for statehood. In the period between 1796 and 1816 only two new states joined the Union. Six new states joined the Union between 1816 and 1821.

Some doubted the legitimacy of a system that turned the federal government into creditor and landlord and United States citizens into debtors and land speculators. But in the flush times their voices were drowned out.

Many officials on the frontier embraced their role as land salesmen for the United States government. There was something for everyone out west, one Arkansas land office official wrote. 'The slave holder will no doubt settle in Missouri and Arkansas. The cotton planter & man who is fond of a warm climate will prefer the Red River country. The farmer who is a slave holder and who likes a cooler climate will settle in the Missouri Territory, and those people who are opposed to slavery and have no Negroes will I presume prefer the state of Illinois.'

This attitude was shared by statesmen in Washington. The popularity of western migration and the enthusiasm for forming new states proved the viability of the system of territorial aggrandizement envisioned in the Constitution, the Northwest Ordinance and the various Land Acts passed since the 1780s. The Louisiana Purchase was the great test of that system, and the early indicators suggested that the system had passed with flying colours.

'Who can limit the extent to which the federative principle may operate effectively?' Jefferson boasted. And who could doubt the wisdom of territorial expansion when that expansion would 'pay for itself' in public land sale revenues?

The frontier was tumultuous but beneath the surface chaos was a beautiful logic. Clear survey lines, symmetrical townships and neat subdivisions of sections, half sections and quarter sections were spreading out across the face of the country. Travelling in the West, Timothy Flint remarked on 'the beautiful simplicity of the limits of farms, introduced by our government, in causing the land to be all surveyed in exact squares'. 'Contemplating the hedge of verdure that will bound the squares on these smooth and fertile plains' and the many other useful improvements that lay in the future, Flint glimpsed 'the guardian genius, Liberty, hovering over the country'.[12]

## DOWN RIVER

Liberty did not hover over the plantations of the Lower Mississippi Valley. As far back as March 1802, Jefferson, informed by his advisers that the 'rich loam' of the lower Mississippi guaranteed 'abundance almost without labor', had described cotton as 'the most profitable production' in the country. Reading the pages of the *Transactions of the American Philosophical Society*, Jefferson would have doubtless noted William Dunbar's estimation that, with proper stewardship, the lands in the 'sugar latitude' around New Orleans could annually produce 'twenty five thousand hogsheads of sugar [and] twelve thousand puncheons of rum'.

By 1820 that vision of bounty was realized. The value of American cotton exports had tripled. Louisiana sugar production had soared past Dunbar's estimates. Observers were stunned by the agricultural wealth of the country. Passing through Natchez, Henry Fearon recalled the streets were 'literally crammed with cotton bales'. 'I could never have formed a conception of the amount in any other way,' another traveller wrote of the sight of cotton bales blanketing the waterside at New Orleans, 'than by seeing the immense piles of it that fill the streets, as the crop is coming in.'[13]

The rapid spread of the slave system into the Louisiana Purchase lands was made possible by government policy. The so-called 'sugar gold fields' were only profitable on account of a protective tariff. American diplomats sought good relations with Britain to keep cotton flowing to Liverpool. By 1820 American cotton accounted for 60 per cent of all British cotton imports.

All of this depended on slave labour, and the federal government used its considerable powers to prop up slavery in the Deep South.

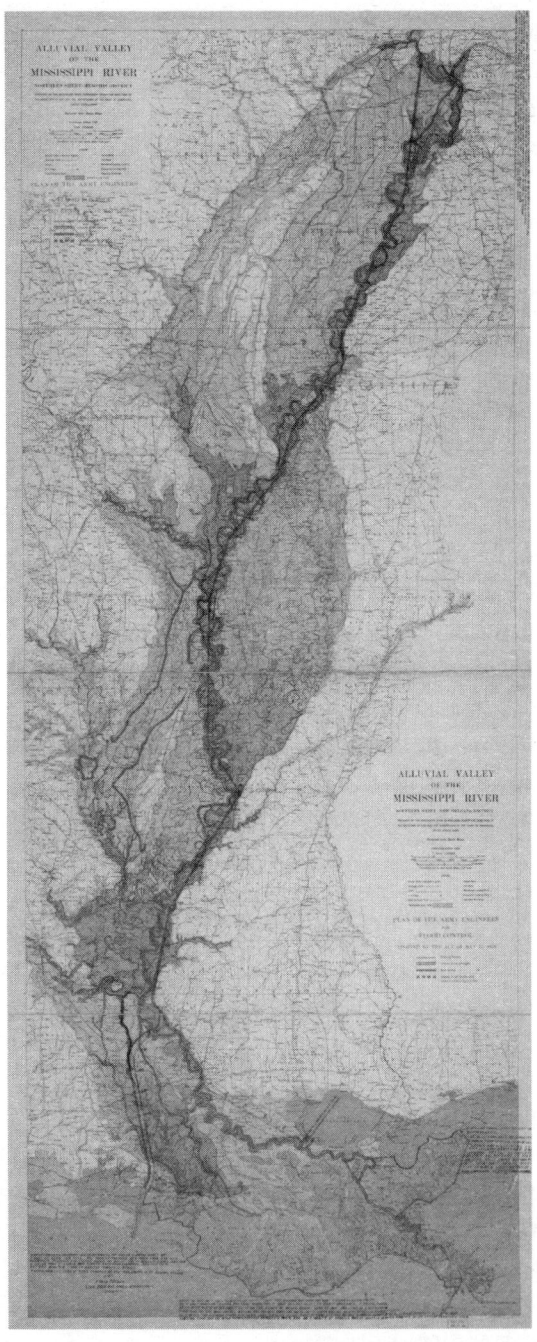

*A map of the rich alluvial floodplains of the lower Mississippi – the heartland of the southern slave system.*

Under federal law, any escaped slave who made it to a free state could be arrested and re-enslaved with the full backing of American law. If a slave made it out of the United States, government representatives would plead the case of individual slave-owners to try and obtain their deportation. When Nelson Hacket managed the near-impossible feat of escaping slavery in Arkansas by stealing his master's horse and riding to Canada, state officials sparked an international crisis by demanding the British authorities return him to slavery – which they eventually did. In extremis, the US government used its military might to enforce the slave system. When, in 1811, slaves on the sugar plantations of the German Coast murdered their masters and marched down the levee towards New Orleans, federal forces were mobilized to crush the uprising.[14]

Above all, the federal government sold the land that made the entire system possible. Surveying and selling the rich lands of the lower Mississippi had been a priority since the Jefferson administration. In 1806, Jefferson wrote of the 'extreme public importance' of selling off the lands, stating his belief that American control of Louisiana would 'never be safe until made so by its own population'. At Treasury, Gallatin's mind was on the money. In the decade after the Louisiana Purchase, Gallatin kept up a drumbeat of letters demanding the expediting of the survey and sale of the Louisiana lands. Gallatin maintained a laser focus on the long-term goal of opening up the rich alluvial lands of the Mississippi to cotton and sugar cultivation. Unsurprisingly, government surveyors soon realized that the way to please their superiors was to cater to the land needs of the swelling planter class. One reported to Gallatin that it had been brought to his attention that there were 'large portions of very valuable public lands' in the south-eastern district of the Orleans Territory and as 'the rich planters on the Mississippi are anxiously awaiting the sales of those lands', he was doing all he could to prioritize their survey and sale.[15]

The government's attempts to intensify the cultivation of the lower Mississippi were successful. That success triggered a distinctive wave of migration that was shorn of any of the residual romance and idealism that clung to the movement of white settlers into the Ohio Valley and beyond.

By 1820, some 120,000 slaves had been moved from the Chesapeake to the new lands opened up by the Louisiana Purchase. These were the vanguard of an estimated one million slaves forcibly relocated from the older slave communities of Virginia and Maryland to the new slave territories of the Southwest in the years before the Civil War.

The opening-up of the untouched soil of the lower Mississippi solved a major problem for the established planter class in those states. The once fertile flatlands of Virginia and Maryland – what Jefferson referred to wistfully as 'our old fields' – could no longer produce. Two centuries of intense tobacco cultivation had exhausted the soil.

But they still contained half a million slaves. The economics were simple: planters who found 'it difficult to subsist' in the Atlantic states could 'with the same means accumulate fortunes on the Lower Mississippi'. Even those who did not want to migrate southwards stood to benefit. As land prices went up along the Red River, the value of slaves on the James River rose as well. This created a thriving internal market for slaves. Slave traders – who the slaves referred to as 'soul drivers' – roamed the decaying plantations of the Chesapeake looking for men and women to sell on the block in New Orleans.

Their presence was an unremarkable fact of life. 'There are generally negro purchasers from Georgia passing about the state,' Jefferson noted in a letter to his son-in-law, who was pondering a move to the Mississippi Territory. Jefferson prided himself on not selling his slaves, on moral grounds – although he made some important exceptions. Slaves who ran away, resisted or otherwise proved difficult lay outside of Jefferson's sympathies. How he framed these decisions was revealing of what the genteel patricians of Virginia knew about the reality of slavery in the Southwest. Explaining why he wanted to sell Brown Colbert, Jefferson wrote that 'if he could be sold in any other quarter so distant as never more to be heard of among us, it would to the [other slaves] be as if he were put out of the way by death'. Jefferson well understood how terrifying slaves found the prospect and used it to manage his workforce.[16]

The fear of sale 'down the river' loomed over every slave cabin. 'The trader was all around,' Lewis Hayden recalled, 'the slave-pen at hand, and we did not know what time any of us might be in it.' When the time came, slaves were moved southwards by every method available. Israel Campbell was taken by flatboat from Kentucky to Mississippi. Solomon Northup was taken in the brig *Orleans* from Norfolk to New Orleans. John Brown was taken on the steamboat *Neptune* from Illinois to

Louisiana. Henry Watson was marched from Richmond through Tennessee to Natchez.

However they made the journey southwards, slaves invariably recalled it as one of the most traumatic experiences of their lives. Everything familiar was taken away from them. Family members vanished. Support networks disappeared. Even the consolations of a stable environment and a regular rhythm of life were stripped away. Disembarking at New Orleans, Solomon Northup recalled the desperate loneliness that swept over him. 'In all the crowd that thronged the wharf, there was no one who knew or cared for me. Not one. No familiar voice greeted my ears, nor was there a single face that I had ever seen … There was a feeling of utter desolation in my heart.'[17]

'Why do slaves dread so bad to go to the South – to Mississippi or Louisiana?' Lewis Clarke asked rhetorically in his memoir of slavery. 'Because they know that slaves are driven very hard there, and worked to death in a few years.'

The casino capitalism that prevailed in the Southwest exaggerated the cruelty and intensity of an already cruel and intense plantation model. Everything was built on debt. Planters borrowed to buy land, slaves and equipment. In turn, they were speculating on the general increase of asset prices. If the price of cotton soared, the price of their land and slaves soared with it. 'Buying a plantation,' one Louisiana planter admitted, is 'essentially a gambling operation.' If the debt-funded investment paid off, the planter reaped massive returns in a couple of years. But the downside risks were equally daunting. If the price of cotton crashed, the planter was in hock to the banks.

Consequently, all eyes in the cotton belt were on the latest prices from Liverpool. And everyone from the slave in the field to the planter in his mansion house felt the consequence of price shifts on the Liverpool exchange. 'When the price rises in the English market, even but half a farthing a pound,' John Brown recalled, 'the poor slaves immediately feel the effects, for they are harder driven, and the whip is kept more constantly going.' If prices collapsed, slaves – whose persons collateralized the debts of their masters – found themselves owned by creditors and auctioned off to yet another master. Sometimes their bankrupt owner would simply spirit his workforce off in the middle of the night and head for some distant corner of the cotton frontier, far from the grasp of his creditors. Either way, the slave's life swung on the hinge of uncertain market forces.[18]

The reality of the plantation South was far removed from the popular image of moonlight and magnolia. The South was not a timeless, static place. Everything was new, dynamic and in violent motion.

The stories of slaves forcibly transported southwards were mirror images of the stories of their masters' voluntary migration to the cotton frontier.

'You find the Virginian upon the Red River,' one newspaper wrote; 'you find the North Carolina man, the South Carolina man, the man from Georgia, alongside of him.'

In the slave pen at New Orleans, William Anderson found himself among men, women and children 'brought here from Kentucky, Virginia and Tennessee'.

Once they had been hustled south, slaves were sold and resold and sold again. Henry Watson was sold five times; William Anderson eight. A few, like William Wells Brown, were put to work on steamboats, and spent their days coursing up and down the Mississippi. Others were dragged from pillar to post by the vagaries of their masters' lives. Dred Scott was born in Virginia and moved first to Alabama and St Louis, where he was sold on and moved with his new master (an army doctor) successively to Illinois, Iowa, Wisconsin, St Louis again, Louisiana, Wisconsin again, St Louis once more, Florida, back to St Louis, Iowa again, and then one final time to St Louis.[19]

If the ways of slavery were many, the ways of freedom were no less various. Jacob Green rode his master's horse from Maryland to freedom in Pennsylvania. His owner tracked him down and sold him to a planter in Tennessee. Hired out to work in New Orleans, Green stole aboard a ship and hid himself beneath the cotton in the hold. Arriving in New York, he swam ashore and met a man named Grundy who arranged to have him smuggled to Canada. Before that could happen, his master reappeared and attempted to take him back to slavery. Over the next few months, Green was arrested and escaped no fewer than three times. Finally, he stowed away on a steamboat bound for Cleveland, where he evaded a slave patrol by hiding in a chimney. Eventually he made contact with members of the Underground Railroad, who disguised him as a woman and took him by railroad, steamboat and horse-drawn carriage to Toronto.[20]

John Brown relied on older techniques to escape from slavery on the banks of the Mississippi. Slavery took Brown from Virginia, to Georgia, to New Orleans. Freedom began one night when he rowed across the Mississippi into Arkansas and set out northwards. He hid by day and walked by night. He ate raw corn, potatoes, pine roots and sassafras buds. He slept under logs and kept a wide berth from the alligators lying about in the bayous. Arriving at St Louis, he made his way across the river to Illinois and pushed on to Indiana. In Terre Haute he was taken in by Quakers working on the Underground Railroad. They greeted him as a friend and an equal and as yet 'another of the travellers bound to the North Star'.[21]

# The Broom of Destruction

In the winter of 1818, the bonds issued to pay for the Louisiana Purchase began to come due.

Written on sheets of engraved paper scattered in vaults throughout Europe were terms stipulating that the United States Treasury had to start fulfilling its contractual obligations to its creditors. That meant prompt payment in gold or silver. The Treasury kept its balances at the SBUS and so William H. Crawford, the treasury secretary, notified the bank that it should prepare a disbursement of $2 million in 1818 and a further $2 million in 1819.

Initially, Crawford did not see any trouble ahead. There was 'a superabundance of revenue', he bragged to Albert Gallatin in October 1817, largely due to the sales of public lands which were 'increasing with a rapidity wholly unexampled'. The United States was 'on the brink of [an] enviable situation' in which it would have more revenue than it had liabilities. It seemed likely that they could even redeem the Louisiana bonds ahead of schedule.[1]

Crawford's hubris was soon exposed. The reality was that the SBUS struggled to retain specie reserves due to a chronic trade deficit that by 1818 had grown to $28.5 million. This too had to be paid in specie. Hard currency was being relentlessly sucked out of the country just as the United States was about to have to honour one of its most significant sovereign obligations.

The 1818 disbursement left only $2.5 million in the SBUS. Officials warned Crawford that the 1819 payment would result in bankruptcy. Crawford, aghast at the situation he found himself in, wondered whether he might be able to postpone the Louisiana payments. When he raised the issue with James Monroe, the president reminded him that 'faithfully & honestly ... paying public creditors' was the 'great object of the government' and that Crawford should proceed on that basis.[2]

The only option left was for the SBUS to curtail credit issuance and to demand payment in specie in order to replenish its reserves. The SBUS's principal business was lending to state banks, who in turn lent to other smaller financial institutions that up until then had been making payments to each other in paper money of dubious provenance. The new policy required that the SBUS demand that these paper bills be redeemed in specie. The treasury secretary knew that a demand for repayment at the centre would ripple out into every corner of the country, as overextended local banks called in loans and refused to roll over debt in order to amass specie to send back to the state banks and thence to the SBUS.

A radical curtailment of the money supply in the context of a land bubble, a trade deficit, a manufacturing depression and a commodity price dip was a recipe for economic catastrophe. In the spring of 1819, Crawford wrote another, chastened letter to Gallatin outlining the doomsday scenario. 'If the remittance of two millions of dollars to Europe during the ensuing autumn cannot be avoided,' he wrote, 'something like a general bankruptcy is greatly to be apprehended.'[3]

The second Louisiana bond payment went through on schedule, and something like a general bankruptcy is exactly what ensued. The SBUS's insistence on payment in hard currency unleashed a chain reaction of credit calls, defaults, bank runs and bankruptcies that affected the entire nation.

An Englishman named James Flint who happened to be travelling in the Mississippi Valley when the crisis struck recorded how it unfolded on the frontier. As the circulation of SBUS notes decreased from $10 million in 1818 to $3.6 million in 1820, state banks were compelled to reduce the circulation of their notes by about a third. The result was a cash drought. Flint noted that everywhere he went 'specie is almost entirely withdrawn from retail business', with regular citizens either unwilling or unable to use precious currency in everyday transactions, paralysing economic activity. Such paper money as remained in circulation was treated with great suspicion. With so many different banks, each with their own notes in circulation, it became impossible to know which to trust. The economy fragmented into microclimates of monetary trust where 'the notes current in one part, are either refused, or taken at a large discount, in another'. Wide-scale bank failure was the inevitable product of this crisis of confidence. Twenty per cent, possibly more, of all American banks failed between 1818 and 1822, with most of the failures concentrated on the frontier.[4]

All of this hit land speculators hard. By 1819, Americans who had bought land on credit from the government were in debt to the tune of $23 million. These payments also had to be paid in specie. As the money supply shrank and deflation kicked in, the relative value of individual debts grew.

Land prices now tumbled. At the Falls of the Ohio, the traditional transit point for settlers heading west, Flint noted that 'tavern-keepers observe that travellers are not nearly so numerous as they were last year'. The westward movement had ground to a halt. Demand for land evaporated. In 1818, the government had sold 3.4 million acres for $13.6 million; by 1823, public land sales had fallen to 600,000 acres. The bubble in land prices popped.

The result was a wave of foreclosures. Many people simply returned the title to their property to the land office where they had bought it the year prior. By April 1820, the governor of Ohio reckoned that 'the greater part of our mercantile citizens are in a state of bankruptcy'. And bankruptcy was no small matter when people could go to debtor's jail for sums as small as one dollar. Unsurprisingly, most people preferred to blame the banks rather than themselves – but the banks and the people were of a whole. 'The recent history of banking in these western States, is probably unrivalled,' Flint wrote. 'Such a system of knavery could only be developed in a country where avarice and credulity are prominent features of character.'[5]

## BOONE'S LICK BLUES

The crisis hit hardest at the very limit of the frontier, in one of the very first territories carved out of the Louisiana Purchase – Missouri. Missouri was the real test case for Jefferson's empire of liberty. And the territory was filling up fast. In the decade following 1810 its population increased by 235 per cent. The population of St Louis tripled and smart stone buildings sprouted up throughout the city. Most settlers headed upriver, to the long stretch of the Missouri that ran a westerly course through the centre of the territory to a region called Boone's Lick. When Lewis and Clark had travelled through it in 1804, it had been pastures filled with deer. Fifteen years later, Clark was the governor of the territory and Boone's Lick was an 'El Dorado' for western settlers looking for rich lands at low prices. Across the frontier, word had spread of Missouri's temperate climate, fertile soil and excellent transport connections. Missouri fever caught hold. Travellers on the Ohio witnessed a veritable armada of settlers heading downriver. In St Charles County, just north of St Louis, locals watched as trains of wagons trundled past, all bound for Boone's Lick.[6]

Settlers were hungry for land, but public land sales were slow in coming. Many settlers blamed Clark, who was considered overly mindful of Indian interests. In reality, Clark and other federal officials, especially representatives of the General Land Office, were bogged down in the contentious business of organizing a survey of the state. There was a mire of overlapping claims that had to be resolved before land could be sold at auction. Some dated back to the period of Spanish rule. Others arose out of military bounties granted during the War of 1812. In the winter of 1811–12, a series of earthquakes had devastated New Madrid in southern Missouri. Survivors were given grants of land elsewhere in the territory. Making matters even more complicated, in 1814 the government had passed a pre-emption act stating that anyone 'who has actually inhabited and cultivated a tract of land' within Missouri had the exclusive right to buy that land when it came to auction. The law effectively legalized squatting and hastened along an already disorderly migration into the territory.[7]

For Missouri land speculators the complexities of land-dealing was part of the fun. One traveller recorded how local speculators talked of 'land-claims, settlement-rights, preemption-rights, Spanish grants, confirmed claims, unconfirmed claims, and New Madrid claims' on every occasion. 'They were like the weather in other countries, standing and perpetual topics of conversation.' But for the surveyors it was maddening.

'The words "actually inhabited and cultivated" require a commentary,' surveyor Harry Carroll wrote sarcastically of the pre-emption law to his superior in Washington. Did 'round logs, unhewn, rolled over one another without cement, pinning, closing or covering in' constitute a habitation? Did a few 'garden seeds put into an open patch, the vegetables gathered in a few weeks, the spot then abandoned' constitute cultivation? Did 'lying out under the open sky, without the parade of a hut, fulfil the intent of the Act'? In Carroll's opinion, many of the migrants were living in the 'hunter's state' and could hardly be considered settlers at all.

Locals thought little better of the likes of Harry Carroll. Government officials were bombarded with complaints about surveyors engaged in fraud and private speculation. Doubtless many were. 'It is easy for a crafty surveyor to become a crafty land speculator,' one observer wrote to the commissioner of the GLO in Washington. The mutual suspicion with which surveyor and settler regarded one another sometimes flared into violence. One February day in 1820, Harry Carroll was shot down while out horse-riding by a migrant who had previously complained to the authorities of his alleged corruption. He died on the spot.[8]

In the face of all these difficulties, the surveys went ahead and by 1819 close to 9 million acres of Missouri land were ready to go on sale. Amid immense public excitement, the first sales began that year. Sales were brisk and prices affordable. Throughout Boone's Lick hundreds of families went to their local land office, paid for half up front, took the rest on credit and realized the Jeffersonian dream of becoming independent farmers.

'While the rest of the country was in gloom, Missouri [is] prosperous,' the St Louis *Enquirer* boasted in June. 'Its rich and beautiful prairies are rapidly taking on the aspect of cultivated fields; farms are opening, houses are being built; towns and villages are springing up in all directions ... and the whole community animated with the consciousness, that all the comforts of life lay within the reach of every industrious man.' That year, some 900,000 acres were sold for $2.4 million.[9]

In the second half of 1820, the financial crisis finally reached Missouri. It followed the same pattern as elsewhere – except its severity was exacerbated by the peculiarities of the frontier economy. In Missouri, the money supply contracted by between 80 per cent and 90 per cent. The state's two banks collapsed. Demand for land cratered. Land sales that year fell to 76,000 acres that fetched a meagre $137,000. Millions of acres of surveyed land went unsold.

Naturally, land prices fell. Citizens who had bought land on credit owed $1.5 million for assets whose value had since crashed. In a memorial sent to Congress, desperate settlers lamented that they had bought land when 'money was plenty', but now due to deflation they were 'bound for the same number of dollars' and 'pay in reality a much higher price for their lands, than they even engaged to pay'. Many went bankrupt. Advertisements for estate sales were published in local newspapers. People went to jail for debt. Tens of thousands of acres of land were seized by creditors or returned to the land office by settlers who couldn't make their payments. As hard currency vanished, the economy returned to a state of barter, with tradesmen advertising that they would accept payment in beef, pork, tobacco, lard, salt, sugar, beeswax, honey and linen – anything but worthless rag money.

'That broom of destruction, the sale of public lands, has swept off all our currency,' one Missourian wrote at the height of the crisis, 'and although the people differ in opinion on the subject, all agree that something must be done to save us from final ruin.'[10]

### LET IT COME!

While Missouri was engulfed in an economic crisis originating in Washington, Washington was engulfed in a political crisis originating in Missouri.

The people of Missouri, like all Americans, wanted equal political rights – rights which they were denied so long as Missouri remained a territory. In 1818 there was a successful campaign to submit Missouri's application to become the twenty-fourth state in the Union. The enabling act was introduced to the House of Representatives on 13 February 1819.

The very same day, Congressman James Tallmadge of New York added an amendment to the bill consisting of two parts. One would have forbidden the importation of slaves into Missouri; the other would have allowed for the gradual emancipation of all slave children born after Missouri achieved statehood.

At this point there were 10,000 slaves in Missouri, accounting for 15 per cent of the population. The epicentre of slaveholding was Boone's Lick, but even there it was rare to see the large slave workforces found in Alabama or Louisiana. The dispersed, small-scale nature of slavery in

Missouri led some apologists to idealize it. The slaves themselves knew otherwise. Former slave William Wells Brown recalled in his memoirs that 'though slavery is thought, by some, to be mild in Missouri ... yet no part of our slaveholding country is more noted for the barbarity of its inhabitants'. Brown knew of slaves flogged to death and many more regularly brutalized by their masters in an attempt to 'tame' them. Missouri statutes empowered local officials to whip slaves for minor infractions such as going for a stroll without a written permit from their master.[11]

Yet the moral dimensions of slavery were not the principal reason why Tallmadge put forward the amendment. In fact, as he noted in his speech to the House, he had not opposed Alabama joining the Union as a slave state, and he had no desire to 'intermeddle with the slaveholding states' already established. Tallmadge didn't like American slavery – which he described as 'the most cruel and debasing the world has ever witnessed' – but he respected its legal status in lands that had been part of the United States since independence. But 'all these reasons cease when we cross the banks of the Mississippi, a newly acquired territory, never contemplated in the formation of our government, not included within the compromise or mutual pledge in the adoption of our Constitution – a new territory acquired by our common fund, and ought justly to be subject to our common legislation'.

The House agreed with him and sent his amendment to the Senate, where it was narrowly voted down. Although the amendment was defeated, the question of Missouri statehood was moved into the next legislative session and Tallmadge succeeded in pushing the question of slavery's expansion into Louisiana to the fore and sparking a major national crisis.[12]

A few months later, during 4 July celebrations in Marthasville, in the heart of Boone's Lick Country, a settler gave a toast in which he made plain his thoughts on Tallmadge and his congressional ally John Taylor: '[To] Messrs. Tallmadge and Taylor – Politically insane. May the next congress appoint them a dark room, a strait waistcoat, and a thin water gruel diet.'

This was but one drop in a wave of political activity that crashed over the Missouri frontier in response to events in Washington. For 1819 was a year of protests, gatherings, editorials, memorials and resolutions in Missouri as settlers voiced their anger and dismay at the attempt by eastern congressmen to control their political institutions. As many Missourians were recent arrivals from Virginia, Kentucky and Tennessee, the issues resonated in those states as well. The emerging East/West divide was in part one of attitudes, outlooks and culture.

The context of the land boom and the subsequent crash was all important here. For what did politicians in Albany know of Marthasville, some one thousand miles distant? What conceivable reason could there be to agitate about slavery – a constitutionally protected form of economic organization – at a time of financial hardship? Were there not just as many slaves in New York as in Missouri?* What did the Northeast know about their suffering when not a single bank in New England had failed, while virtually every bank on the frontier had gone under? And was it not the federal government in Washington that had first hoarded land and then sold it on to desperate migrants on credit? And was it not the government, in connivance with the SBUS and the banking oligarchs of the East Coast, that had then pulled out the rug from beneath them, bankrupting migrant families and spiriting away their precious supplies of gold and silver to sit unused in the vast and distant vaults of vast and distant banks?

On the frontier, the individual question of slavery mattered less. Rather, slavery was part of a bundle of issues – banking, tariffs, state's rights, internal improvements – that, taken together, pointed towards a concerted attempt to accrue power in one part of the Union at the expense of the rights and liberties of those in another. One Virginia intellectual framed the debate as a struggle between independent farmers and banking interests, the latter seeking 'new usurpations of internal power over persons and property', whose overreach would 'beget a dissolution of the union'.

And while southern and western politicians were particularly prone to such apocalyptic pronunciations on the imminent collapse of the constitutional order, the Yankees could be just as fierce. 'If a dissolution

---

* There were almost exactly the same number of slaves in New York State – 10,000 – as in Missouri, according to the 1820 census. New York's path to (gradual) emancipation was one of the longest in the Union, beginning in 1799 and only ending in 1827.

of the Union must take place, let it be so!' Tallmadge told the House. 'If civil war ... must come, I can only say, let it come!'[13]

The Missouri Crisis also revealed a generational divide within America's leadership. The discussion in Jefferson's circle tended to treat the whole matter as yet another dastardly attempt by the Federalists to resurrect their moribund party. Slavery was not the real issue – political jockeying lay behind it all. President Monroe said as much to Jefferson, writing that this was a cynical attempt to create an artificial 'distinction between slave holding and non-slave holding states' in order to produce a 'perpetual excitement' that would 'marshal the States differing in that circumstance [slavery], in unceasing opposition, & hostility with each other'. Confronted with a novel constitutional crisis, these old men relived the political factionalism of the 1780s and 1790s rather than grapple with the fundamental issues at hand.[14]

For Taylor and Tallmadge were not Federalists – nor were countless others who found themselves passionately engaged in the attempt to keep slavery out of the West. Among the ascendant political generation, slavery was accepted as a serious – perhaps the most serious – political issue of the day.

This was captured in the diary of John Quincy Adams, then serving as Monroe's secretary of state. In conversation with Henry Clay, Adams recorded his shock when Clay mentioned in passing that, on account of the passions raised by the Missouri debates, 'he had not a doubt that within five years from this time the Union would be divided into three distinct confederacies'. A week later, in conversation with his cabinet colleague John C. Calhoun, he recorded another extraordinary exchange:

> I had some conversation with Calhoun on the slave question pending in Congress. He said he did not think it would produce a dissolution of the Union, but, if it should, the South would be from necessity compelled to form an alliance, offensive and defensive, with Great Britain.
> I said that would be returning to the colonial state.
> He said, yes, pretty much, but it would be forced upon them.

While visions of political collapse were not new, the explicit understanding that it was the interconnected questions of slavery and territorial expansion that would act as the twin wedges driving the Union apart was novel. The particular clarity with which all the participants suddenly grasped that fact is striking, and indicative of the power of a crisis to move the tectonic plates of politics. In a matter of months, in 1819 new attitudes crystallized which would govern the direction of American politics through to the Civil War.

Adams was not immune either. Having entered the crisis sceptical of the legal basis of Taylor and Tallmadge's arguments, he soon found his political imagination transformed. His conversation with Calhoun left him almost in a state of revelation. Calhoun spoke of dissolution – but perhaps dissolution was the necessary precursor to reconstruction.

'Slavery is the great and foul stain upon the North American Union,' Adams mused, and perhaps a 'temporary' dissolution might allow for the Union to be 'reorganized on the fundamental principle of emancipation. This object is vast in its compass, awful in its prospects, sublime and beautiful in its issue.'[15]

Even as they glimpsed new political futures, the politicians in Washington worked inside the constraints of past political decisions.

Two questions dominated the debate. The first was the Constitution's position on the rights of Congress to mould the political institutions of states seeking to join the Union. On this matter no less an authority than James Madison concluded that the relevant passages of the Constitution were 'somewhat of a ductile nature'. When combined with the similarly ambiguous question of slavery's constitutional protections, the result was a debate that allowed for every shade of legal opinion while giving primacy to none.[16]*

Then there was the Louisiana Purchase treaty of 1803. Seventeen years after Talleyrand and Napoleon had pressured Livingston and Monroe into concluding their hasty negotiations in Paris, American statesmen had to contend with the significance of Article III, which had guaranteed to Louisianans 'the enjoyment of all [the]

---

* Indeed, no definitive legal ruling on this difficult and weighty matter would be forthcoming until yet another crisis originating in Missouri hit Washington in 1857, with the infamous Supreme Court ruling in the case of *Dred Scott v. Sandford*.

rights, advantages and immunities of citizens of the United States'. The treaty had been ratified by the Senate and signed by the president. It had the force of law. The government had just brought itself to the brink of ruin by honouring the financial aspects of the treaty. Could it now ignore this obvious requirement that it safeguard all forms of constitutionally protected property – which clearly included slaves?

It was hard for the anti-slavery party to wriggle out of this one. Their opponents read out the text of the article on the House floor, letting the words speak for themselves. Taylor, like many others on his side, concluded that if the effect of the treaty was to mandate slavery in new states carved from the Louisiana Purchase, then they should repudiate it. This was a desperate suggestion. In the end, there was no alternative but to honour it. Two decades after being cobbled together in France, the Louisiana Treaty checkmated those engaged, in Tallmadge's words, in the 'great and glorious cause [of] setting bounds to slavery'.[17]

There were two crises in 1819–21. One was a financial crisis caused by debt; the other was a political crisis caused by slavery. Both were connected to the fundamental question of what to do with the lands of the Louisiana Purchase.

The resolution to the political crisis came in March 1820. The famous Missouri Compromise hammered out by Henry Clay allowed Missouri to enter the Union as a slave state but stipulated that thereafter slavery and involuntary servitude would be 'forever prohibited' in 'all that territory ceded by France to the United States, under the name of Louisiana, which lies north of thirty-six degrees and thirty minutes north latitude'.

Less famous was the solution to the financial crisis that Congress passed a month later. The Land Act of 1820 ended the practice of selling land on credit, while further reducing the minimum price to $1.25 per acre and the minimum tract size from 160 to 80 acres. The following year Congress would pass the Relief Act of 1821 to help bail out insolvent settlers. The solution to a financial bubble swollen up by wild land speculation was to reduce land prices and parcel sizes, and give relief to land speculators. This was exactly in keeping with the pattern of government policy since 1796 and would be replicated during similar crises in 1837 and 1857.[18]

*An illustration of the Missouri Compromise which banned slavery above the 36° 30' line.*

The steps taken to remedy the financial crisis were soon forgotten. But the Missouri Compromise and the 36° 30' line demarcating slavery were seared into the national debate over westward expansion.

Few people perceived the importance of this new line as well as Thomas Jefferson. By 1820, Jefferson was an old and worried man. He had been hit hard by the Panic of 1819. Like all planters, Jefferson's finances were dependent on the price his crops and his lands could collect at market. The crash of 1819 sent both tumbling. The crisis had produced 'a distress in the country of which I have never seen an equal. The solidest men can neither collect nor pay a dollar.'

Worse still, in 1818 he had co-signed for a loan for his friend Wilson Cary Nicholas, a Virginia politician and a major land speculator. In 1819 Nicholas defaulted on the joint loan and in 1820 he died, leaving his financial mess in Jefferson's hands. Jefferson never really recovered. As a short-term measure, he had his grandson Thomas co-sign Nicholas's bad debt, in exchange for a plot of land. Now if Jefferson defaulted, his grandson would be contractually obligated to honour the debt. It was a desperate move for a man who had once denounced the creation of a permanent public debt on the grounds that 'no generation [should] contract debts greater than may be paid during the course of its own existence'.

This was not the only long-held principle compromised in the attempt to appease his creditors. In the summer of 1820 he entered into negotiations with John Wayles Eppes, a relation of his dead wife Martha, to sell some of his slaves in exchange for ready cash to pay down his debts. Jefferson admitted to 'having scruples about selling negroes', but rationalized these away on the grounds that selling his human property to Eppes was 'in fact to keep them in the family'. Eppes ultimately paid Jefferson $4,000 for between ten and twenty slaves.

These measures only just kept the wolves from the door. Jefferson's position was desperate and he still had to find $1,200 per year just to cover the interest payments on Nicholas's debts. 'Our friend W. C. N. gave me the *coup de grâce*,' he told Madison, not long before his death.[19]

It was with much of his optimism already drained away that Jefferson looked upon events in the country at large. The Missouri Crisis and its resolution appalled him. The old political divisions between Federalist and Republican, he complained to Gallatin, had been replaced by 'a new one, of slave-holding, & non-slave-holding states, which, while it had a semblance of being Moral, was at the same time Geographical'.

This development filled him with fear for the future, because it pushed the question of slavery to the forefront of public life. Haunted by the slave revolution he had partially enabled in Haiti, Jefferson, in his letters from this period, described in vivid terms the slaveholding South's dilemma. 'We have the wolf by the ear,' he told one correspondent. 'And we can neither hold him, nor safely let him go.' For what would emancipation look like? Jefferson, possessed of the most capacious imagination of his age, could not imagine a world where slavery ended peacefully. 'Are our slaves to be presented with freedom and a dagger?' he asked John Adams.[20]

Equally concerning was what had triggered the debate in the first place: the incorporation of the Louisiana Purchase into the Union.

Jefferson had envisioned an empire of liberty, dozens of sturdy republics mushrooming up across the American continent, creating a rational, peaceful world, removed from the chaos and tyranny of European politics. Instead, the forces unleashed by westward migration had crashed the economy, nearly crashed the political system and might one day crash the racial order.

And Missouri was only the second state to be formed from the Louisiana Purchase. While he could not know that the last state (Oklahoma) created out of his chance bargain with Napoleon would not join the Union until 1907, it was apparent even then that the political pressures summoned up by the addition of new states from that vast extent of land would be awesome and quite possibly unmanageable.

The shadows were deepening at Monticello; Jefferson had much to ponder. In a few years he would die. The sale of his estate – including his slaves, who would be sold on the block on his plantations – would barely cover a third of the debts he had accrued in his lifetime. These, as he had long dreaded, would be passed on to his children. The country, too, was addicted to speculation and paper money and stock-jobbing – well advanced on the 'English career of debt, corruption & rottenness' that he had once assailed. His beloved Virginia was dying before his eyes, young Virginians preferring to venture out into the new lands he had helped win them, rather than staying in the Old Dominion to tend to their old fields, made sterile by the plantation system. In Congress, abolitionists quoted his words from the Declaration of Independence in order to assail an institution that had sustained him his entire life. On the frontier, debates about slavery and freedom and expansion threatened to destroy a country he had helped summon into existence. 'I envy not the present generation the glory of throwing away the fruits of their fathers' sacrifices,' he wrote at the height of the Missouri Crisis, 'and of rendering desperate the experiment which was to decide ultimately whether man is capable of self government.' To sabotage the American project, he told another, was to commit 'treason against the hopes of the world'.[21]

And yet even as he wrote these words, the government led by his protégé James Monroe was finalizing a new treaty that would further expand the nation's limits and finally accomplish the long-held dream of making the United States a transcontinental power.

# PART III

# THE FLORIDAS

There remained to Spain, Mexico and Florida; and forthwith the pressure of the stark forest riflemen began to be felt on the outskirts of these two provinces. Florida was the first to fall.

THEODORE ROOSEVELT

# A Pistol Pointed at the Heart of the Republic

When Mad Dog heard reports of a party of white men travelling through the backcountry, he knew it meant trouble. He was told it was a mixed group of Spaniards and Americans, loaded with provisions. At regular intervals they would stop, erect a platform and take measurements using special equipment. They would then record these measurements in journals and on large leaves of parchment. They had set out just south of Fort Adams on the Mississippi River and were heading eastwards, hewing to a near perfectly horizontal line, despite the swamps, bogs and bayous in their path. This told Mad Dog all he needed to know: this was a surveying party. And surveys meant trouble to come.

Mad Dog was a Creek chieftain, and in April 1798 the Creek controlled the lands the white men were trespassing on. Angered at their intrusion, he leapt into action. Andrew Ellicott, the American responsible for the survey, had sailed ahead of the main party from New Orleans to Pensacola with his Spanish counterpart. When he came ashore, a furious Mad Dog was waiting for him. The white men would appear at an appointed meeting place in the interior in a few days, Mad Dog told them, and make plain their intentions before the Creek people. As a display of his authority, he also demanded that the Spanish governor of West Florida, Vicente Folch, also attend the talks.

A week later they met at Miller's Place, an old trading post on the banks of the Conecuh River, thirty miles inland from Pensacola. Here the white men explained themselves. Yes, they were a survey party, they said, but 'the line we were tracing, was not a line of property, but of jurisdiction, a line between white people, and not intended in any way to affect the Indians'. Their sole purpose was to mark out a new international border between Spanish Florida and the United States – nothing more. Mad Dog would have easily been able to confirm that fact. It was public knowledge that Ellicott was under instructions from Jefferson to run the line marking the new Florida border as agreed under a treaty signed by American and Spanish diplomats in Madrid in 1795. Their statements satisfied the Creek chieftain. He told them that although 'many crooked talks had been sent into their country', having listened to their remarks, he had concluded that 'their talks were the same and straight', and that the Creeks would have no objection to the survey party completing their work.

Mad Dog was justly confident that they would not linger after their work was done. The place that the white men called Florida was not a desirable land. As per Pinckney's Treaty, Florida was bounded to the north by the 31st parallel, to the east by the Atlantic, to the south by the Gulf of Mexico, and to the west by the Mississippi River.[1]

During the twenty years of British rule (1763–83), this large L-shaped piece of territory had been divided in two. East Florida contained almost the entire modern state of Florida and the historic Spanish settlements at St Marks, Fernandina and St Augustine.

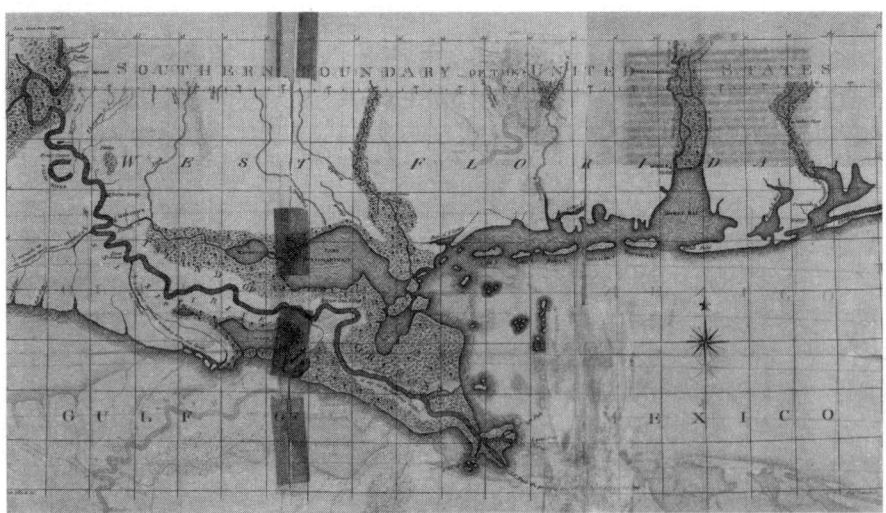

*A map of the Gulf Coast at the turn of the nineteenth century.*

West Florida was a corridor of land running from the Mississippi to the Perdido River, encompassing the old French settlements at Biloxi and Mobile, and the harbour at Pensacola, settled and developed by the Spanish in the seventeenth century.

West Florida was an awkward size – only sixty-two miles wide at its greatest extent – and was described by Ellicott as 'being low, sandy, and miserably poor, and producing little beside pitch pine'.

East Florida was practically empty. Two centuries of warfare between English and Spanish settlers had devastated the native populations. The populations of the Yamassee and Apalachee people were greatly reduced and in a state of dependency on the Spanish. Jervis Cutler, an American who left a description of the condition of the southern Indians in this period, documented the near total destruction of the smaller Florida tribes. The Pacanas, the Tunica, the Pascagoula and the Tenisaw all had thirty or fewer male members. The only significant independent Indian force were the Seminole. The landscape was as bleak as its inhabitants' fortunes. One American described it as 'low, flat, excessively poor, and badly watered; abounding in Cyprus ponds, Bay-galls, and Saw-Palmetto-flats: – fit only for the present occupants, Gofers, Salamanders, and Bull-Snakes'.

The Floridas possessed a number of other qualities that made white settlement unlikely. In his diary of his travels through the region, English naturalist William Bartram left an agonizing account of his battles with gnats, flies and mosquitoes, 'persecuting spirits, who formed a vast cloud around our caravan so thick as to obscure every distant object'. Some were as big as bumblebees. Others attacked with stings 'no less acute than a prick from a red-hot needle, or a spark of fire on the skin'. Horses suffered under their attentions, with Bartram recording that 'the head, neck and shoulders of the leading horses were continually in a gore of blood'. At night not even large fires could hold off their assault, which 'kept us awake during the long and tedious night' – although this did have the advantage that 'the alligators had no chance of taking us napping'. Another description of eighteenth-century Florida supplied a long list of lethal diseases that awaited settlers, among them 'dropsies, consumptions, hemorrhoidal and habitual fluxes, relaxed and bilious habits of body, ruptures, worm-fevers ... the leprosy, elephantiasis and body yaws'. Home remedies abounded to stave off sickness, though some of these sounded so awful ('Spaniards wear the nest of the great travelling spider sowed in a rag about their necks as a sure way to assuage a hectick fever') that many would-be immigrants sought out less deadly climes instead.

The hostility of the country to white settlers made itself felt during the 1798 surveying expedition. Folch was so ill from one of the various endemic diseases that he was unable to rise from his sickbed in Pensacola to attend the meeting at Miller's Place. In his journal, Ellicott recorded 'being blistered ... from head to feet' by poison ivy. The pain was such that several times a day he had to jump into the river to cool off 'and lay whole hours in it during the night, which was the only relief I could find'. One can only imagine what kind of impression Mad Dog took away of these white men, who seemed so ill-suited for life in tropical Florida. But it probably reinforced the belief that they would never settle in large numbers. In West Florida, they numbered fewer than 10,000, most of those on plantations on the Mississippi. In East Florida – an area that now contains over 20 million people – the population of whites and black slaves never exceeded 5,000.[2]

## THE OUTLET

The Louisiana Purchase changed everything. It magnified the strategic importance of the Floridas. This new reality was captured in a saying current at the time that Florida was 'a pistol pointed at the heart of the republic'. In this metaphor, West Florida was the barrel and East Florida was the lock, hammer and grip. The muzzle was pointed directly at New Orleans and the trigger was in the hands of whoever controlled the whole. This was why Livingston and Monroe had been tasked with securing New Orleans *and* West Florida. One was needed to ensure the security of the other. 'If we look forward to the free use of the Mississippi,' one congressional committee concluded, 'the Floridas must become a part of the United States, either by purchase or by conquest.'[3]

The protection of New Orleans was reason enough to obtain the Floridas. But in American eyes there was even more at stake. Alexander von Humboldt famously described the Caribbean as an 'American Mediterranean'. Like its European counterpart, the Caribbean was 'an interior sea with several mouths' and scattered round it were Americans,

English, French, Spanish, Danish and Dutch, as well as several million black slaves and a wide variety of indigenous peoples.

America was exposed to the Caribbean by way of the Mississippi Valley, whose produce was carried south to New Orleans and thence to the Gulf of Mexico. Here it was hostage to the peculiarities of the prevailing equinoctial current that drives in to the Caribbean from the east, through the Lesser Antilles, before hitting the coast of Honduras and heading up through the Yucatán Straits into the Gulf of Mexico. This powerful natural force drove all shipping in the Caribbean in a clockwise direction. It was particularly strong in the Gulf of Mexico, rendering it 'utterly impracticable' for shipping to leave that sea by any other means except the Straits of Florida.

These straits were perilous. One report compared them unfavourably with the entry to the Mediterranean at Gibraltar. Whereas 'the straits of Gibraltar are as a door, which a vessel may pass in a few hours, and then be out upon the broad ocean', the Straits of Florida were 450 miles long, 50 miles wide, lined with reefs, and buffeted by headwinds. It was

*A map of the Caribbean littoral in 1803.*

through this fraught passageway, as one West Indian merchant told Parliament, that Europe was 'connected with America by a chain of gold'. The entire produce of the Mississippi Valley – including the bulk of the lucrative cotton trade – had to pass through these straits. 'Hence the remark so often made by the military men,' one American report observed, 'that the mouth of the Mississippi is at these straits, and not at the Balize.'* Making matters worse, in the thousand miles between Savannah and New Orleans the United States had not 'one single fortified harbor or port of refuge', while the British and the Spanish perched like vultures on their islands surrounding the Florida Keys. Should they look to interdict American trade, then 'not a rag of American commerce could quit the Gulf'.[4]

This was not, in fact, quite true. There was a perfect harbour in the Floridas – it was just on the wrong side of the straits. The deep, naturally protected harbour at Havana was the tantalizing strategic solution that lay just beyond America's grasp. Indeed, American statesmen came to believe that, properly understood, Cuba was part of Florida and that American politicians could rectify nature's mistake by incorporating both the peninsula and the island into the Union. This view was captured in Jefferson's remark to Madison that once they possessed Florida and had Spanish consent 'to our receiving Cuba into our union … I would immediately erect a column on the Southernmost limit of Cuba & inscribe on it a Ne plus ultra as to us in that direction'. With both Florida and Cuba under their control, America would never again have to worry about their security position in the Caribbean. Once this sentiment is understood, the trajectory of the subsequent two hundred years of Cuban-American relations begins to make a lot more sense.[5]

There was one final piece to the strategic puzzle. The Gulf Coast between New Orleans and the Florida Peninsula is riddled with waterways: the Pearl, the Conecuh, the Perdido, the Pascagoula and the Apalachicola Rivers, all of which penetrate deep into the interior.

---

* The Balize was a fort at the mouth of the Mississippi. Frederick Jackson Turner would later write that the invasion of Cuba during the Spanish-American War was just another 'chapter in the long struggle of the people of that [Mississippi] Valley to hold the approaches to their great river'.

By far the most important of these is the Mobile, which enters the gulf at Mobile Bay. The Mobile has two main branches: the Alabama, which cuts diagonally across that state and into north-western Georgia, and the Tombigbee, whose tributaries have their origins in northern Alabama. In fact, the Tombigbee's tributaries come within thirty miles of the Great Bend of the Tennessee River, which dips into Alabama near Muscle Shoals before re-entering Tennessee bound for the Mississippi. This was enticing of itself. As one Tennessee politician observed in 1797, if the Americans settled Muscle Shoals and established a 'portage across from the Tennessee, to the Tombigbee', the result would be a direct route from Tennessee to Mobile and 'an outlet to commerce equal if not superior to any in the United States'.[6]

There was more. There were three great cotton-growing regions in the Deep South. One was the alluvial plains of the lower Mississippi between Natchez and Memphis. The second lay in the brown friable soil found in the limestone valleys around Muscle Shoals. The third was the famed 'Black Belt' – the crescent of loose, deep, dark loam that begins in north-east Mississippi and sweeps through central Alabama before petering out in western Georgia. If Mobile and Muscle Shoals could be connected by roads, canals and steamboats, then at a stroke two of these three great centres of cotton production could be combined into a single system capable of transporting cotton produced on the Gulf Plains to Liverpool, Hamburg, Bordeaux and anywhere else it might be sold.

This vision of an integrated cotton-producing system in the interior of Alabama and Mississippi hovered just out of reach. Sitting on top of its rich soil were tens of thousands of Indians. Chickasaw in Tennessee, Choctaw in Mississippi and Alabama, Creek in Alabama and Florida, and Cherokee in Georgia, Alabama and Tennessee. The Creek alone had a population of some 20,000, including 5,000 warriors. These were not, as some whites liked to imagine them, vagrant hunter-gatherers. The Creeks lived in a patchwork of several dozen towns and villages, practised farming alongside hunting, and were acculturating to American norms. Whatever their status, and to whatever extent they had adopted American ways, the southern Indians were intent on remaining who they were and where they were. They had observed the destruction of the tribes in neighbouring regions and, through close proximity, had come to understand the American modus operandi when it came to Indian affairs. The Americans would have liked nothing more than to magic them away from their valuable cotton lands. But the southern tribes would not go quietly.[7]

Florida, in American eyes, represented a unified system consisting of the coast, the gulf and the interior. Lasting control of any one part presupposed the control of every other part. The land of the Floridas might itself, in James Monroe's words, be worth 'comparably nothing', but as a strategic whole it was of paramount importance. The Floridas controlled the Gulf of Mexico and the Mississippi and Alabama watersheds, and so commanded the 'most fertile and productive parts of this Union, on which the navigation and commerce of the whole so essentially depend'.[8]

Mad Dog probably understood much of American strategic thinking. The Creek had been dealing with the Spaniards for centuries and were regularly briefed by Spanish officials on American intentions. Creek traders travelled around the gulf, including to Cuba, and were familiar with the political and commercial landscape of the Caribbean. They were also aware of the role that the British played in the region. During the Revolutionary War the Creek had sided with the loyalists. British merchants operating from the Bahamas – only eighty miles off the coast of Florida – maintained a presence throughout the Creek homelands. Some Creek diplomats had even travelled to London to meet with British officials. The Creek then, like many southern Indians, probably viewed their position as being strengthened by the presence of different European powers in the Floridas and the Caribbean more generally. They had been playing the Spanish, the Americans and the British against each other for some time. So long as they could keep on doing so, they ought to be able to maintain the balance of power in the Gulf Plains and – most importantly – retain their ancestral lands. That is probably how Mad Dog interpreted the 1798 episode concerning the Spanish-American survey party.

What Mad Dog could not have known was that the balance of power in the Floridas was about to be shattered. Not for the first time in American history the shock would be supplied by Napoleon Bonaparte.

# The Original Lone Star State

The fort at Baton Rouge lay at the westernmost edge of Spanish Florida. Built on a promontory overlooking the Mississippi, most of its guns were pointed across the river at American Louisiana. Inside the cypress palisade, reinforced by a rampart made of packed earth, were a parade ground, a storehouse, an arsenal and some barrack blocks that were home to two dozen Spanish soldiers. Over the complex flew the Spanish colours.

There was, however, a flaw in the fort's defences: an opening in the palisade where cows were brought in and out to supply the garrison with fresh milk. And in the early hours of 23 September 1810, a group of sixty men on horseback, obscured by thick fog, filed through the gap and took up position inside the fort.

When the alarmed Spaniards realized there had been an incursion, they ran to take up defensive positions. Their commander, Lieutenant Louis Antonio de Grand Pré, gave the order to fire. There was a crackle of ineffective musketry and then the horsemen yelled 'Hurrah for Washington' and charged into their ranks. Grand Pré took two bullets in the shoulder and was finished off by a sabre. Another Spaniard was killed and several others wounded. The invaders took no casualties. Across town the governor of the Baton Rouge District, Carlos de Hault de Lassus, was awakened by the noise and hurried from his home to investigate. Upon arrival, he was hit in the face with a rifle butt and menaced with a bayonet and pistol while he lay dazed on the ground. His house was raided and his official correspondence rifled. As dawn broke, the sun rose over a new state. The men who had brought it into being assembled in the parade ground of the fort and watched as the Spanish flag was lowered and the flag of the Republic of West Florida, a single white star on a field of blue, was lifted over Baton Rouge.[1]

It might not have looked like much, but this backcountry putsch on the periphery of the Spanish Empire was not a local affair. It was one of a series of events that marked the beginning of the end of three hundred years of Spanish rule in the Americas – and which delivered Florida into American hands.

## THE FLORIDA JUNTA

The events in Baton Rouge in September 1810 had their origins in Madrid in March 1808. That month the Spanish capital had exploded in rebellion over the kidnapping of Ferdinand VII and his replacement as King of Spain by Joseph Bonaparte, Napoleon's brother. Spain was swept by nationalistic fervour as people rose up against the French military occupation. That summer Spanish loyalists strung together a slew of victories that sent the French army reeling. In the provinces, local *juntas*, or government councils, were set up to continue the administration of Ferdinand's exiled regime. As the resistance movement gained momentum, a *cortes*, or parliament, was established. Spain, which had hitherto been a French ally, now found itself thrown into the arms of the British, who began supplying and supporting their war against Napoleon.

Then, in the late summer of 1808, Napoleon struck back. That August he launched a full-blown invasion of Spain and over the next year rolled back the Spanish armies, banished the *cortes* and suppressed the *juntas*. By 1810 Joseph Bonaparte was firmly settled on the Spanish throne.

The effective collapse of Bourbon power raised questions for Spain's colonies across the Americas. In the years leading up to the events of 1808, many Spanish Americans had chafed under rule from faraway Madrid, but there had been only sporadic (and doomed) attempts at independence. Now they had no choice but to confront the matter. They could submit to Napoleon, remain loyal to the deposed Ferdinand or go it alone.

Across the continent, independence was the common refrain. Guatemala issued a thundering proclamation denouncing the 'detestable and odious yoke' of French rule and mocking Joseph as 'that shadow of a king' to whom only 'slaves, and those who have the hearts of slaves' would subject themselves. Appended to this inflammatory declaration of Guatemala's political claims was a brief note reassuring that the author remained loyal to their 'beloved and legitimate sovereign ... Lord Ferdinand VII'. Events in Cartagena took a more radical turn, where after a perfunctory statement that they remained 'ever obedient to the authority of the old government', revolutionaries declared that 'under the influence of the purest principles of equity' they had 'altered the government to which they had till then been subject, and substituted another more congenial to their ideas'. Their compatriots in Buenos Aires agreed, declaring that 'in consequence of the decay of the national government and of the representation of the sovereign, the command of the provinces might devolve into the hands of the junta' – namely themselves. They, too, of course, also 'confirmed their fidelity, loyalty, and affection for the just cause of King Ferdinand VII'.

By September, all eyes were on Mexico, the jewel in the crown of Spanish America. From Washington the British minister wrote to London that the 'remaining provinces [of Spanish America] will be more or less influenced' by how the Mexican people reacted to the arrival of the new viceroy appointed by Joseph I. Two days after Francisco Venegas took office, that question was answered with the storied *Grito de Dolores*\* of 16 September that marked the beginning of the Hidalgo Rebellion and the decade-long struggle for Mexican independence.

But no part of the Spanish Empire went as far or as fast as Venezuela. That April a revolution in Caracas deposed the captain general of Venezuela and installed a Supreme Junta. By July a Venezuelan delegation – led by Simón Bolívar – was in London pleading for assistance and perhaps even recognition as an independent state. In a letter to the foreign secretary, Marquis Wellesley, they declared their opposition to Bonaparte and insisted on the 'sincere disposition of the people of Venezuela to preserve their relations of friendship, commerce, and amicable intercourse with the subjects of his Britannic majesty'. One

---

\* Literally 'The Cry of Dolores' – so-named for a patriotic call-to-arms given in the town of Dolores Hidalgo that was the first act in the Mexican War of Independence. Every September the Mexican president re-enacts the *grito* from a balcony in Mexico City to inaugurate Mexico's Independence Day festivities.

sceptical British civil servant noted that their somewhat contradictory aims were 'the alliance and friendship of England *even against the parent-state* – the freedom of their country from every government in Spain *but that of Ferdinand the 7th*'.[2]

It was against this backdrop of revolution cloaked in loyalty that the people of West Florida considered their own relationship with the fraying authority of Madrid. And by 1810 that authority had been fraying for some time. Following the Louisiana Purchase, it was widely assumed that West Florida would fall into the lap of the United States. From Paris, Livingston wrote to Madison that, to secure the region, all the administration had to do was 'proclaim your right and take possession'.

Jefferson made preliminary moves to do just that, but when it looked as though Spain was ready to go to war over Florida he backed down. Thwarted, Jefferson then asked Congress for $2 million to bribe the French to force Spain to surrender the province. When this too failed, a new policy was pronounced whereby West Florida was declared a lawful part of the Louisiana Purchase, but one that remained regrettably outside of the United States.

In the meantime, the western edge of West Florida became a haven for miscreants. In 1804, the Kemper brothers – Reuben, Nathan and Samuel, a trio of Virginia-born thugs who kept the severed ears of one of their enemies pickled in a jar behind the counter of the saloon they operated in Mississippi – led an abortive uprising against Spanish rule. That August the Kempers made a raid across the border and shot a constable, kidnapped a few Spanish officials and burned down some plantation buildings. They liberated some convicts, armed them and then issued a manifesto calling for the local population to 'throw off the galling yoke of tyranny and become freemen'. When this did not spark a general uprising, the brothers fled back to Mississippi.

The Spanish dismissed the Kempers and their like as 'white Indians and river pirates', but in truth they were a real threat to Spanish rule. In the years after the Kemper revolt, the province became increasingly lawless and trawled by 'roving bands of murderous American highwaymen'. Spanish officials were powerless. There were fewer than fifty troops in the entire region between the Mississippi and the Pearl River, where the majority of the population resided. There were several hundred troops in Mobile and Pensacola but no road connecting these garrisons to Baton Rouge. Furthermore, almost no Spaniards lived in the area. The population consisted of old English loyalists, some French planters and large numbers of American farmers. As the region descended into chaos, these people naturally looked elsewhere for protection. There were persistent rumours, either fanciful or wilfully exaggerated, that the French creoles were agitating for Napoleon to come and occupy the Floridas.[3] Some speculated that the Royal Navy might sweep into Pensacola and restore order. But most looked across the Mississippi to America and forward to the day when West Florida would be annexed to the United States.[4]

In the summer of 1810, as *juntas* sprouted across the Spanish Empire and the newspapers were filled with the latest news from Buenos Aires, Caracas and Madrid, the western districts of West Florida began organizing citizens' councils. Mimicking *juntas* elsewhere, these meetings often included the singing of the Spanish national anthem and noisy promises to 'promote the safety, honor, and happiness of ... the dominions of their beloved king Ferdinand the seventh'. As the summer wore on, these bodies staged elections and sent delegates to a central convention held at St John's Plains, near Baton Rouge. This body made more extravagant claims, arrogating to itself the power to 'provide for the publick safety, to create a revenue ... to create tribunals civil and criminal, and to define their own powers relating to other concerns of the government'. The Spanish administration, led by de Lassus, permitted the establishment of this convention – they were so badly outnumbered they could do little else. De Lassus went further and seemed to confer some legitimacy upon it by attending several banquets where he accepted the toasts and acclamation of the conventioneers. By September, an uneasy and unclassifiable new status quo seemed to have emerged whereby Spanish officials remained in office and Florida remained in the empire, while Anglo settlers took control of novel and largely fictitious organs of government.[5]

## 'SUBVERSIVE OF THE ORDER OF THINGS'

Behind the facade of cordiality, the West Florida borderlands were seething with intrigue. Apparently loyal settlers bombarded their countrymen in the United States with requests for annexation. Citizens sent letters to President Madison asking to be brought into the Union. The Mississippi Territory's governor, David Holmes, who had sent observers to the West Florida convention, highlighted the potential for another Haiti-style slave rebellion, warning Washington that 'a great portion of the population of West Florida consist[ed] of slaves' and that if the region fell into a 'state of Anarchy and confusion ... we shall be placed in a very unpleasant if not in a precarious situation as respects our slaves'. This was passed on to Madison – himself a slave-owner – who told Holmes to keep 'a wakeful eye to occurrences & appearances in W. Florida'.

In fact, by this point Madison had already taken the decision to foster revolution in the region. That June, governor William Claiborne was in Washington on a rare trip away from his post at New Orleans. In conference with Madison on 13 June, he must have been given explicit instructions from the president, for the very next day he wrote an extraordinary letter to his confederate William Wykoff, who lived on a plantation across the river from Baton Rouge.

Ferdinand's rule in Spain had collapsed, Claiborne wrote, and 'all hopes of successful resistance to Bonaparte were at an end'. The United States could not countenance having France as a neighbour to the south. Besides, West Florida had been sold by France as part of the Louisiana Purchase, even if the Spanish persisted in believing otherwise. The United States should just seize the province. But, he wrote,

> I am persuaded under present circumstances, it would be more pleasing that the taking possession of the country, be preceded by a request from the inhabitants.
> Can no means be devised to *obtain such request*?

Ideally, Claiborne wrote, 'the good inhabitants, the honest cultivators of the soil, will unite' and reject the folly of independence or imaginary unions with France or England, and instead adopt 'the line of conduct which honest policy points out ... Nature has decreed the union of Florida with the United States, and the welfare of the inhabitants imperiously demands it.' This of course should be enabled 'through the medium of a convention of delegates, named by the people', who would then appeal to the United States. Having outlined his plan for the active subversion of Spanish rule, Claiborne reminded Wykoff to 'consider this letter as confidential' and to 'act with all the circumspection which its nature requires'.⁶

De Lassus's own private correspondence precipitated the revolt in West Florida. The convention met over twenty times in the summer and autumn of 1810 without declaring independence. But in mid-September it learned of certain intercepted letters in which de Lassus begged his superiors for reinforcements to help him crush the convention and reimpose Spanish rule.

No sooner had these damning documents come into the possession of the Anglo conventioneers than the raid on the fort of Baton Rouge was authorized and the Lone Star flag of West Florida hoisted up. In the days that followed, a formal declaration of independence was issued and the rudiments of a republic were established. By November, the West Florida Republic had a constitution, a senate, a house of representatives and a militia. The legislature elected Fulwar Skipwith as head of the executive branch. On 26 November, Skipwith delivered a remarkable inaugural address in which he reminded his audience that 'the people of the Floridas, in common with the rest of the Spanish colonies, had consisted of but one family', but following their abandonment by Ferdinand VII, they 'were restored to the original rights and natural charter of man; that of providing for their own preservation and government'. Skipwith hedged on annexation and implied that West Florida desired to remain autonomous.

Skipwith's burgeoning interest in steering West Florida towards sovereignty was extinguished by the appearance of William Claiborne and several hundred American troops on the east bank of the Mississippi on 7 December.⁷

Claiborne carried with him copies in English, French and Spanish of a presidential decree issued by Madison on 27 October which declared that 'a crisis has at length arrived subversive of the order of things under the Spanish Authorities' and that the United States was now obliged for reasons of national security to take possession of West Florida. This statement represented the natural outcome of the administration's thinking ever since news of the 23 September putsch had arrived in Washington. The fact that West Florida was even thinking of maintaining its independence set alarm bells ringing. As Madison put it in a letter to Jefferson in October, if the United States did not take possession, there would 'be danger of its passing into the hands of a third &

dangerous party ... our occupancy of W. F. would be resented by Spain, by England, & by France, and bring on, not a triangular, but quadrangular contest.' It was to forestall just such a collision of European great powers in America's backyard that Madison issued his proclamation eight days later.[8]

Once he received news of the proclamation, Claiborne moved swiftly, sending emissaries across the Mississippi to ensure his arrival would not spark a shooting war. Once he was convinced it would not, he crossed the river at St Francisville on 8 December and was escorted by local citizens and the West Florida militia to the town centre. Claiborne watched as the Lone Star of West Florida was lowered with all due dignity and then had the United States flag raised. A few days later, the ceremony was repeated in Baton Rouge.* The Republic of West Florida's turn on the American stage was at an end. It had existed for seventy-eight days.[9]

In the first glow of victory, Claiborne was overcome with visions of sweeping through the Floridas and seizing Cuba as well. 'There is nothing I so much desire as to see the Flag of my Country wave on the Moro Castle,' he wrote to Jefferson. 'Cuba is the real Mouth of the Mississippi, and the nation possessing it, may possibly at a future day command the western Country. But let that Island be ours, and the American Union is placed beyond the reach of change.'

Talk of invading Cuba was premature. The United States was not – and did not want to be – at war with Spain. Besides, not even the bulk of West Florida was in American hands. In its short life, the West Florida Republic had only ever really encompassed the area up to the Pearl River. The Skipwith administration had enlisted Reuben Kemper (now dressed up as a colonel) to lead an army to invade the remainder of the

---

* The peaceable handover of Baton Rouge was briefly threatened by West Florida president Fulwar Skipwith's eleventh-hour discovery of the joys of executive authority. Upon learning of Claiborne's arrival, he issued a declaration condemning the American invasion and made known his intention to defend West Florida and 'with twenty men, if a greater number could not be procured, surround the flag staff and die in its defense'. In the end, he contented himself with a 'peaceful protest' when Claiborne arrived but did nothing to prevent annexation.

province.* By December, the Spanish were holed up in fortified positions in Mobile, while Kemper's ragtag band laid desultory siege to the town.

When Claiborne arrived on the scene, he dispatched a young army officer, Captain Edmund Pendleton Gaines, to call off Kemper and prevent further aggression towards Spain. Gaines arrived in Mobile with fifty men and – acting quite independently – proceeded to demand the Spanish surrender the town to the Americans. This peculiar three-way stand-off persisted until January, when it became apparent that the Spanish would not surrender Mobile. The Americans (including Kemper) then withdrew, leaving Mobile and Pensacola in Spanish hands while the rest of the province came under American rule.[10]

This incident would be historical marginalia had it not resulted in the promulgation of a new and portentous American policy. Aware that he could not peaceably secure the rest of the Floridas, but having already convinced himself and the nation of their strategic importance, Madison asked Congress to approve a new measure – the so-called No-Transfer Resolution.

The resolution declared that in 'view [of] the peculiar situation of Spain, and of her American provinces; and considering the influence which the destiny of the territory adjoining the southern border of the United States may have upon their security, tranquility, and commerce',

---

* This army marched to the tune of the newly composed 'Vive La', also known as the 'The Song of the West Floridian Army in 1810'. Its last two verses give a flavour of the West Florida Republic's self image (reproduced in Arthur, *West Florida Rebellion*, 130):

West Floriday, that lovely nation,
Free from king and tyranny,
Thru' the world shall be respected
For her true love of Liberty.

*Vive la* the new convention.
*Vive la* the rights of man.
*Vive la* West Floriday.
The new convention is the plan.

We can drink and not get drunk.
We can fight and not be slain.
We can go to Pensacola
And can be welcomed back again.

the Congress could not permit 'the said territory [Florida] to pass into the hands of any foreign power' and committed itself to the 'temporary occupation' of Florida should it ever be at risk of falling into the possession of a power other than Spain.[11]

The principal target of this new policy was Britain. The outcome of the events of 1810 was that the exiled regime of Ferdinand VII had become entirely dependent on British support. The Americans looked on with alarm, with one diplomat in Madrid warning Washington that 'G. B. is now playing a deep speculating game with the poor Spaniards'. But this new state of relations was in part the fault of the United States. Once Ferdinand's regime had been decisively routed by Napoleon, the United States took the decision to cease recognizing the Spanish ambassador to the United States. In effect, this meant that between 1810 and 1815 there was no official contact between the Spanish and American governments.[12]

The American position was understandable – Spain was in a state of upheaval and Ferdinand's claim to the throne was far from secure – but it drove the Spanish into the arms of Britain. That December, as Claiborne took possession of Baton Rouge, the unrecognized Spanish minister in Washington, Luis de Onís, wrote to his British counterpart, William Morier, requesting that as 'no regard will be paid to my representations', Britain might speak on behalf of Spain. Morier assured Onís he would, and duly wrote to Secretary of State Robert Smith describing the 'title of the United States to West Florida ... [as] manifestly doubtful' and protesting against American actions in 'wresting a province from a friendly power, and that in the time of her adversity'. He concluded this ominous note by reminding Smith that it was 'impossible to disguise the deep and lively interest which his majesty takes in every thing that relates to Spain'. Morier also wrote to London, reminding his superiors that American possession of the Floridas would allow them to 'interfere, with great advantage, in case of a rupture, with the trade in the Gulf of Mexico, and with ours in the West Indies'.[13]

Almost without anyone quite realizing it, the Florida question had shape-shifted from a Spanish-American dispute to an Anglo-American one. And Britain and the United States were about to go to war.

# Enter Jackson

When the smoke cleared on the morning of 8 January 1815, Andrew Jackson was a national hero.

Fifteen days earlier, the War of 1812 had officially ended when British and American negotiators signed a peace treaty in the Belgian city of Ghent. But neither nation's military commanders in America knew that yet.

In the first days of the new year, a British army of several thousand professional soldiers led by Major General Sir Edward Pakenham, the Duke of Wellington's brother-in-law and a veteran of the Peninsular War, supported by a Royal Navy fleet hovering offshore, had landed on the shores of Lake Borgne and marched to within five miles of New Orleans.

Awaiting them was a smaller, hodgepodge American force consisting of members of the Tennessee, Kentucky, Louisiana and New Orleans militias, along with two battalions of free men of colour, some United States Army infantry and dragoons, a few Baratarian pirates, some Choctaw scouts and sundry local adventurers, including the ubiquitous Reuben Kemper.

As the British descended on the town, Jackson lured them into a frontal attack on his heavily defended position. On a sugar plantation owned by a Frenchman named Jacques Villeré, he had established his men on a parapet overlooking a drainage canal. On his flanks were the Mississippi and impenetrable swamplands. His riflemen and artillery pieces were arrayed along the high ground overlooking the field of battle.

Dawn broke; the British engaged. As they approached, Jackson's batteries laid down a deadly fire. The British guns replied but without effect. Jackson later wrote that it was 'the unerring hand of providence [that] shielded my men from the showers of Balls, bombs & Rocketts, when every Ball & Bomb from our guns carried with them the mission of death'. Pakenham's battle plan depended on certain units bringing ladders to the line of fire so that the infantrymen could scale the parapet. But the ladder-bearers panicked under the barrage and left their loads scattered over the battlefield. Meanwhile, other units had taken up positions in the canal and waited patiently for the missing ladders to arrive. 'A dreadful fire was accordingly opened upon them,' British soldier George Robert Gleig recalled, 'and they were mowed down by hundreds, while they stood waiting for orders.'

Watching the slaughter unfold, Pakenham, who was nothing if not brave, rode up to the front line to urge his men onwards. As he came within range of the Americans, his horse was shot from beneath him. When he attempted to mount another he was shot through the spine. His aides took him from the battlefield; he died shortly afterwards.

Meanwhile, the carnage in the canal continued. 'It was in vain that the most obstinate courage was displayed,' Gleig wrote. 'They fell by the hands of men whom they absolutely did not see; for the Americans, without so much as lifting their faces above the rampart, swung their firelocks by one arm over the wall, and discharged them directly upon their heads.'

After a few hours the British retreated. A couple of days later, in the dead of night, they were evacuated by the Royal Navy. Pakenham was sent back to London in a barrel of rum, along with a dispatch reporting with admirable understatement the 'unfortunate result' of the battle that had resulted in two British generals killed and 2,000 casualties, with no tactical or strategic advantage to show for it.[1]

Only thirteen Americans had died and Jackson returned to New Orleans a conquering hero. His faithful deputy, John Coffee, a fellow Tennessean who saw action that day, wrote home to his wife describing Jackson's entry into the city:

*An illustration of the Battle of New Orleans. Note the ladders carried by the British soldiers.*

I wish you could have been here to have seen him received into Orleans, after the memorable battle. A triumphal arch, adorned with wreaths, supported by eighteen pillars (one for each state) and eighteen damsels, the fairest in the City, bearing a motto emblematic of the state she represented; all so arranged as to leave an open avenue through which the General and suite passed, and was crowned with laurels and his path strewed with flowers by the damsels. He was then conducted to the church that was spacious and richly adorned where they sung Te Deum, several hours, and the scene closed.

As the news of his victory began to percolate through the country national hysteria took hold. Washington went 'wild with delight', with crowds celebrating in the street outside the President's Mansion. In Baltimore, the respected *Niles' Weekly Register* abandoned its usual staid formatting and decorated its front page with a rampant eagle and an enormous headline:

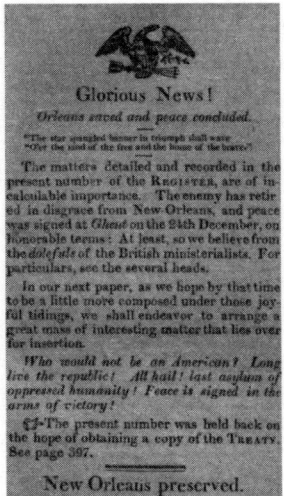

*Niles' Weekly Register celebrates the American victory.*

GLORIOUS NEWS!

Orleans saved and peace concluded.

*Who would not be an American? Long live the republic! All hail! last asylum of oppressed humanity! Peace is signed in the arms of victory!*

Jackson was flooded with grateful letters from all over the country. 'On the News of your victory,' one friend wrote, 'the Eyes of Every real American sparkled with emotions of Joy.' 'You have, my dear friend,' wrote another, 'immortalised yourself and your army.'[2]

The Battle of New Orleans was the beginning of the end of the Mississippi Question. Never again would a foreign power challenge the United States' possession of Louisiana.

It also marked the culmination of a new chapter in the struggle for Florida – a chapter whose author and protagonist was Andrew Jackson.

### 'I SHALL PAY THE DEBT'

In an age full of unlikely life stories, his was especially remarkable. Andrew Jackson was born in 1767 to recently arrived Scots-Irish migrants. After transiting through Philadelphia, his parents headed to the Carolinas, and Jackson was born somewhere in the North Carolina/South Carolina borderlands. His family were the proverbial dirt-poor backcountry settlers. His father broke his health trying to eke out a living from the soil and died shortly before Jackson was born. His mother moved the family in with some well-off relatives who ensured Jackson received a basic education. When the British army arrived in South Carolina in 1780, the Jackson boys took up arms against the British. The eldest, Hugh, died in combat in 1779. Andrew and Robert, the two youngest, joined the local militia and participated in the bitter insurgency that swept the South.

One night in 1781, Jackson was ambushed and he was taken prisoner by the Redcoats. A British officer ordered the young captive to clean his boots. Jackson refused, claiming his rights as a prisoner of war. In response, the officer beat him with his sabre, leaving a life-long scar across his hand.

The brothers were taken to a disease-ridden internment camp in Camden, where both caught smallpox. Robert died; Jackson survived – just – and after his release walked the forty-five miles home, shoeless. Not long afterwards, his mother went to look after American prisoners of war held at Charleston. There she caught cholera and died.

By the time he was fourteen, his entire immediate family had died. Jackson was to become one of the greatest haters, one of the most committed practitioners of vendetta, that America ever produced. Unsurprisingly, given the details of his childhood, his hatred was purest for the British. 'I owe to Britain a debt of retaliatory vengeance,' he told his wife, Rachel, not long before the Battle of New Orleans; 'should our forces meet I trust I shall pay the debt.'[3]

After the revolution Jackson moved to Salisbury, North Carolina, where he studied law and developed a reputation as a 'roaring, game-cocking, horse-racing, card-playing, mischievous fellow'. Now a teenager, he was six foot one, filled with energy and possessed of a towering ambition. His physical presence, his love of gambling and drink and his outsized personality all measured up to frontier ideals of manliness and marked him out as a leader of men.

The friendships he formed in this period led to his first government position. In 1788, a friend offered him the role of public prosecutor in the Western District of North Carolina (modern Tennessee). Jackson accepted and that spring crossed the Appalachians to Nashville to take up his post. The journey introduced many of the recurring themes of his adult life. En route, he fought his first duel, bought his first slave (Nancy, aged eighteen) and narrowly escaped an ambush by Indians attempting to staunch the westward flow of settlers. Above all, the journey west reaffirmed his identification with the frontier. Nashville was a small town, home to a couple of hundred people, where Indian-fighting was a fact of life. In Nashville, Jackson fell in with a political grouping clustered around William Blount, who became his first political patron, consistently promoting the young man, and helping him navigate the lucrative, risky and politically complex world of the frontier economy. Jackson soon had a thriving trade in furs, tobacco, skins, beef, cotton and horses, and was buying and selling significant numbers of slaves.

But his political fortunes were growing even faster. When Tennessee became a state in 1796, Blount selected Jackson to be the state's first and only congressman. Following Blount's impeachment, Jackson – aged thirty – took up his seat in the Senate. Jackson did not enjoy life in Philadelphia. The rhythms of the legislative process and the routines of city living were not for him. The action was on the frontier. He had 'a good mind', he wrote to a friend back home, 'to leave Congress and Congress things, turn speculator and go snacks at home with the best of them. There is a damn sight more to be got by it, depend on it.'

In 1798, he vacated his seat in Congress, returned to Tennessee and plunged himself into a world of cotton, slaves and land speculation. He also recalibrated his political ambitions. Legislating left him cold; Jackson instead sought a senior position in the Tennessee militia and in 1803 won election to the position of major general. Military rank was important to Jackson insofar as it led to military glory. And Jackson, for all his titanic energies, could not – yet – control the tides of war and peace. So Jackson tended to his farm, his land speculations and his proliferating business interests – and waited for war.[4]

When war with Britain came, in June 1812, Jackson was forty-five and impatient to get into the field. 'Do not stand to stipulate for the theatre on which you are to fight,' Jackson told the 29,000 men of the state militia. 'It is enough for a brave man to know that his country needs his services; no matter whether against the Creeks in the south, or the

Showaneese [Shawnee] in the north; whether against the blacks at Pensacola, or the British in Detroit.'*

Jackson was spoiling for a fight and didn't much care who the opponent was. But the War Office in Washington had other ideas. Jackson was left dangling for months while orders shot out all over the country for militias to muster. In December, he finally received orders to take his men to Natchez to prepare for a British invasion of Louisiana. Jackson marched south, only to arrive in Natchez and receive orders calling the whole operation off. An enraged Jackson marched his men back up the Natchez Trace to Nashville, returned to his plantation and once again waited for instructions.[5]

## THE RED STICK WAR

A conflict of a very different kind ultimately came to Jackson's rescue. In 1811, the Shawnee leader Tecumseh had visited the southern tribes in a bid to inspire a Pan-Indian movement to resist white settlement. In a speech to the Creek at Tookaubatchee on the Tallapoosa River in central Alabama, Tecumseh laid out an apocalyptic vision of his proposed conflict with the Americans:

> Let the white race perish! They seize your land; they corrupt your women; they trample on the bones of your dead! Back whence they came, upon a trail of blood, they must be driven! Back – aye, back into the great water whose accursed waves brought them to our shores! Burn their dwellings – destroy their stock – slay their wives and children, that the very breed may perish. War now! War always! War on the living! War on the dead! Dig their very corpses from their graves. The red man's land must give no shelter to a white man's bones![6]

His audience were well aware that the idea of driving 7 million Americans back into the sea was a fantasy. Some present would have been alive during the American Revolution, when the Creek sided with

---

* Jackson was referring to Britain's native allies: the Shawnee along the Great Lakes and the Creek in Florida. The 'blacks at Pensacola' refers to a group of maroons who received occasional British support.

the British. If they joined Tecumseh's crusade against the Americans, they would inevitably have to seek the aid of the British once again. In reality, the choice was between seeking accommodation with the United States or the protection of Great Britain. Choosing the British had its own set of risks. As one American representative reminded the Creek: 'When the British want war, they are your fathers, and give you arms and ammunition for blood. In time of peace, you are a set of naked, mangy dogs, not worth their notice.'[7]

For many Creek it was an appealing message all the same. Tecumseh was calling for a radical rejection of American ways and the purification of indigenous life. Many Creek were receptive to such ideas, especially as the Indians of the Mississippi Valley were living through a religious revival spearheaded by Tecumseh's brother, the prophet Tenskwatawa, that claimed authority through magic, prophecy and ritual. The followers of this new movement were called Red Sticks, after the coloured staffs they carried into battle.[8]

In early 1812, the Red Sticks began murdering white settlers. When Red Sticks killed Americans, government officials demanded the 'friendly' Creek hold their own people to account. When the Creek duly executed the men responsible, they themselves became the target of retaliation. By the time the War of 1812 began, a Creek civil war – a war within a war – had already broken out. By July 1813, Red Stick raiding parties were wreaking havoc in Creek country, burning villages, killing friendly chiefs, slaughtering livestock and destroying crops.

Then, in August, a large Red Stick party assaulted Fort Mims, a fortified plantation near Mobile garrisoned by Mississippi militiamen, where white and Creek refugees had gathered for protection. The defence of Fort Mims was careless, to say the least. On 30 August, approximately one thousand Red Sticks streamed through the open gates of the fort and began massacring the defenders.

In the aftermath, gruesome stories about what passed at Fort Mims circulated around the frontier. 'Blood and brains bespattered the whole earth,' one early chronicler claimed. 'Children were seized by the legs, and killed by batting their heads against the stockading. The women were scalped, and those who were pregnant were opened, while they were alive, and the embryo infants let out of the womb.' Accurate or not, these stories fell on receptive ears. A circular to the Tennessee militia the year before had offered up nightmarish visions of an 'infant babe of nine days old torn from the arms of its mother and beat to pieces upon the walls of the house ... children of six years of age stabbed with knives, their heads split open with Tomahawks, and others torn to pieces, and devoured alive by dogs'.

Across the South, and in Tennessee especially, regular citizens responded to news of Fort Mims by joining the militia. Davy Crockett, later of Alamo fame, left his wife and children on their little farm and headed to Winchester to volunteer. His wife begged him not to go. 'I reasoned the case with her as well as I could,' he wrote later, 'and told her, that if every man would wait till his wife got willing for him to go to war, there would be no fighting done, until we would all be killed in our own houses.' Stirred by such sentiments, the men of Tennessee prepared to go to war.[9]

News of the Fort Mims atrocity reached Andrew Jackson at an inopportune moment. That summer Jackson had acted as second in a duel involving a young officer named Billy Carroll. Billy's opponent was Jesse Benton, brother of Thomas Hart Benton, who in eight years' time would become the first United States senator from Missouri. But in 1813 the brothers Benton were hot-headed, ambitious young men looking to make a name for themselves in Tennessee. The duel ended with Billy getting shot in the thumb and Jesse across the buttocks. Thomas was out of town when the confrontation occurred and arrived back in Nashville to rumours that Jackson had humiliated his brother by accusing him of conducting himself inappropriately during the duel. In a fit of pique, Thomas issued certain threats towards Jackson; Jackson responded by declaring to all and sundry that he would thrash Benton on sight.

A few days after the Red Sticks stormed Fort Mims, Jackson, his nephew Stockley Hays and John Coffee rode into Nashville. All of them were armed. As they walked past the City Hotel they spotted the Bentons, who were also armed. 'Now, you damned rascal,' Jackson said to Thomas, drawing out a whip, 'I am going to punish you. Defend yourself.' Thomas's hand went to his pocket; Jackson, assuming he was going for his gun, drew a pistol and pursued him into the hotel. There Jesse was waiting for him, gun drawn. Shots were exchanged. John Coffee ran into the hotel after Jackson, his own gun out. Finding Thomas, he began pistol-whipping him. Thomas ran away and promptly fell down the stairs at the rear of the hotel. Now Hays entered the fray, his sword cane at the ready. Failing to run Jesse through, he took him to the ground and repeatedly stabbed him with two dirks. Jesse put his pistol to Hays's torso and pulled the trigger. The gun failed to go off. Bystanders intervened and the fight was halted. Jackson was found on the floor in a pool of blood. He had been shot four times and his left arm was shattered. He was taken, unconscious, to a bed. He bled through two mattresses before the doctors could staunch the bleeding. Jackson didn't leave that bed for three weeks.[10]

When he did, it was at the head of a column of 2,500 men eager for revenge on the Red Sticks. His arm in a sling, Jackson rode before his men as they marched from Fayetteville to Huntsville on the Tennessee River in northern Alabama. John Coffee's cavalry went ahead to scout out the enemy. All he found was empty villages. 'I burnt three towns but never saw an Indian,' he wrote home to his wife. 'I am now convinced that the Indians will never meet us in action.' By November, Jackson's army had joined up with Creek and Cherokee allies and was ready to strike. Coffee's pessimism was soon dispelled. On 3 November, Jackson's army surrounded Tallushatchee and massacred its inhabitants. 'We now shot them like dogs,' Crockett recalled of his part in the assault, and then burned down the village. The Americans killed 186 men that day and lost only five.

The next day, with the army low on supplies, Crockett and some militiamen went back to the charred village to forage for food. Beneath the ruins of a house in which some Indians had been incinerated, they found a cellar containing a stash of potatoes that 'looked like they had been stewed with fat meat'. 'Hunger compelled us to eat them, though I had a little rather not, if I could have helped it, for the oil of the Indians we had burned up on the day before had run down on them.'[11]

Six days after Tallushatchee, Jackson engaged the Red Sticks again at Talladega. This time he was up against 1,100 warriors, the 'very choice of the Creek nation'. 'They were all painted as red as scarlet,' Crockett wrote, 'and were just as naked as they were born.' Jackson lured them into a trap and another massacre ensued. Three hundred Red Sticks died; the Americans lost only fifteen men.

Jackson was just getting started. 'I am preparing supplies to enable me to carry a war of destruction through every part of the Creek nation,' he wrote a week after Talladega. 'I will shew them what kind of reliance is to be placed on these prophets & those who instigated them to this war. Long shall they remember Ft. Mims in bitterness & tears.'[12]

That December, Jackson's offensive ground to a halt. His supplies were exhausted and his troops famished. The Tennessee militiamen mutinied on more than one occasion. In one instance, Jackson turned his artillery on his own men to stop them from marching back home. In January, he was resupplied and fresh troops replaced those who had already returned to Tennessee.

Jackson rashly committed these untested men to two engagements, at Emuckfaw and Enotachopco, that very nearly ended in disaster. At Enotachopco, his men were ambushed as they crossed a creek. A massacre of the Americans was only averted by the bravery of the Cherokee cavalry, who turned the tide at the decisive moment. Coffee was injured in the engagement and Jackson's brother-in-law killed. Afterwards, Jackson gave the Cherokees orders to 'scour the country' and 'kill and destroy all warriors ... burn all houses & villages & take all women & children prisoners' while he continued to build up the main force.[13]

By March he was ready. With 4,000 men, he marched on the Red Stick stronghold at Tohopeka, also known as Horseshoe Bend. At a meander on the Tallapoosa River in central Alabama, the Red Sticks' prophets had massed the bulk of their forces and had assured them that their magic would protect them from the Americans. The settlement was particularly well defended. Protected on three sides by water, the peninsula was walled off by stout wooden breastworks. 'It is impossible to conceive a situation more eligible for defence than the one they had chosen,' Jackson acknowledged. However, the Americans had the advantage of outnumbering the Red Sticks by almost three to one. Jackson split his forces. Coffee's cavalry, along with Cherokee and Choctaw warriors, crossed the river and took up a position on the opposite bank while Jackson's infantry and artillery assaulted the breastworks.

On 27 March 1814, the artillery barrage began – initially to little effect. The Red Sticks' defences held. Then something unanticipated happened at their rear. The Cherokee and Choctaw warriors swam the river, cut loose the Red Sticks' canoes and began setting fire to their encampment. When Jackson saw smoke rising in the distance, he ordered his men to charge the breastworks. Meanwhile, Coffee began ferrying his men across the river. Caught in a pincer, and with their fortress aflame, the trapped Red Sticks fought desperately. Eventually they were beaten back to the river. Some tried to flee downstream on logs. They were easy pickings for the marksmen on the other bank. 'They would drop like turtles into the water' when shot, one soldier recalled. Many fought and died in the shallows. 'The whole margin of the river which surrounded the peninsula was strewn with the slain,' Jackson wrote. 'The Tallapoosa might truly be called a River of blood,' another soldier said, 'for the water was so stained ... it could not be used.'

The slaughter went on through the night. Red Sticks who hid in caverns beneath the riverbank had the earth collapsed on top of them. Those who hid in bunkers were smoked out and shot down. Some lay low in thick undergrowth. Torches were thrown into the brush and they were burned alive. Soldiers went house to house killing occupants. Some Tennessee men were spotted taking strips of skin from the dead Indians to use as bridles. The next day they tallied the dead, cutting the nose of each to ensure they didn't double count. Five hundred and fifty-seven Red Sticks were dead on the ground, and Coffee estimated another 300 died in the river. Jackson lost seventy men – a third of those were Indian allies. 'I feel peculiarly happy in being able to announce to you the fortunate eventuation of my expedition to the Tallapoosa,' Jackson wrote to his superiors the next day. 'The power of the Creeks is I think forever broken.'[14]

## COLONEL NICOLLS'S WAR

Two months later, news of the battle of Horseshoe Bend was related to a British officer who had appeared some two hundred miles up the Apalachicola River. Captain Hugh Pigot of HMS *Orpheus* anchored near the St Vincent Sound that May and then sent Captain George Woodbine up the Apalachicola to make contact with the Creek villages upriver.

The timing of the *Orpheus*'s arrival was significant. In October 1813, Napoleon was defeated at the Battle of Leipzig and in 1814 was forced into exile on Elba. Peace temporarily returned to Europe. But the war in America went on and the British now had more resources to devote to it. That April, Admiral Cochrane, commander of the fleet in the American theatre, issued a proclamation offering freedom to all

American slaves who made it to British lines – a provocation aimed at inciting southern slaves to marronage and perhaps even insurrection.

Woodbine's appearance far up the Apalachicola represented another prong in the British strategy: integrating the southern tribes into the British war effort. What Woodbine heard and witnessed on his journey into Florida was both alarming and encouraging. A chief named Yellow Hair told him that 'the Americans had driven a thousand warriors of the Creek nation from their towns and obliged them to take shelter in the marshes near Pensacola with little or no provisions'. Yellow Hair begged him for 'twenty-five to thirty head of cattle to prevent them from starving'. Woodbine gave them what little he had: barrels of cornflour, tobacco, a few dozen blankets, a small quantity of pistols, flints and ammunition. He also appointed some permanent agents to stay among them, drew up a list of friendly tribes in the region and drafted a simple but detailed map of the Apalachicola River for his superiors to examine.

Most importantly, Woodbine transcribed a letter from the Creek chiefs addressed directly to George III and his ministers. In it the chiefs thanked Woodbine and Pigot for their aid and said they hoped that 'our ever beloved Father and King would shortly hear of our chastening these wicked and rebellious Americans'. 'We have always been in our hearts Englishmen,' the letter went on, 'and never shall any nation [among] us forget the love we bear for our father King George and the British nation.' The Creek then proceeded to give detailed and actionable advice on how to conduct the war on the Americans in the southern theatre – advice which Woodbine seems to have copied wholesale into his own report. This remarkable document was then signed with a cross by each chief and sent back across the ocean to London.[15]

The letter arrived during a summer of strategizing in Westminster. The Creek emerged as a viable partner at a time when the Spanish had proved that they were not. In April 1813, General James Wilkinson had appeared in Mobile Bay with 800 men and five gunboats. Wilkinson carried with him an act of Congress, signed by Madison, authorizing him to take possession of Mobile to prevent it falling into British hands. Here was the No-Transfer Resolution in action, enforced at gunpoint. The Spanish officer surrendered without firing a shot. Spain and the United States were still at peace – or rather not technically at war – but such legal niceties were increasingly irrelevant.

With the Americans now in Mobile, Pensacola remained the only settlement in West Florida from which the British could stage their proposed invasion of the Lower Mississippi Valley, through an assault on either New Orleans or Baton Rouge by way of Mobile. The British hoped that, with the Royal Navy dominant on the seas and the army on land supported by Indians and runaway slaves, they would be able to cut off the Mississippi, break the American will to fight and force them to accept terms.[16]

British officials were doubly receptive to the Creek letter on account of public opinion, which was firmly behind the Native Americans. A pamphlet circulated in London that referred to 'our faithful Indian allies' who were being systematically robbed of their lands. Another document stated that the Americans considered the Indians 'as an inferior and unprotected class of beings, and act accordingly'. Indigenous peoples were 'objects of deadly democratic hate ... the views of the American government, seem long to have pointed at a systematic plan for *exterminating the Indians*'. This was pursued by 'the burning of Indian villages and corn-fields, and driving Indians from their hunting grounds'. 'To aim at starving or expatriating a whole people,' the author concluded, 'is surely more heinous than killing a few individuals.' British policy should not limit itself to winning the war, but ought to establish Britain as '*the avowed guarantor and protector*' of Indian rights and Indian territory.[17]

Some indication that Whitehall shared these sentiments was provided when the British announced their choice of commander. Edward Nicolls was in his early thirties when he was promoted to lieutenant colonel in the Royal Marines and put in charge of Britain's war in the Florida borderlands. Nicolls arrived in Apalachicola in August with some regular marine officers and NCOs, but the bulk of his forces were regulars in the Corps of Colonial Marines, an outfit whose members were all former slaves. Nicolls was expected to supplement this force with additional runaways and to train and arm the Creek. He would use this hybrid force to clear the way for Cochrane's fleet to land Pakenham's army.

His was not a conventional British force. But then Nicolls was not a conventional officer. Singularly courageous, during his colourful career Nicolls reckoned he had fought in 'upwards of a hundred engagements', in the course of which he had broken his left leg, badly wounded his right leg, 'been shot through the body and the right arm, his head severely cut with a sabre, and bayonetted in the chest whilst fighting hand to hand with the enemy, he also totally lost his sight of his right eye by a wound from a grape shot [sic]'. What truly set him apart was his convictions. A committed abolitionist, Nicolls was convinced of the fundamental equality of whites, blacks and Indians. He refused, for instance, to use the term 'savage', for 'their conduct entitles them to a better epithet', and became a vocal and determined advocate for the rights of the Creek to persist as 'a free and independent nation'.

Crucially, Nicolls had the resources to act on his principles. He arrived in Apalachicola with two artillery pieces, 2,000 stands of arms and 1,000 swords, as well as barrels of gunpowder, uniforms and other materiel to aid the war effort. He bore with him a proclamation issued by Cochrane in July addressed to the 'great and illustrious Chiefs of the Indian nations', which declared that King George would 'not suffer his Indian children to be made slaves of by his rebellious subjects' and that Britain and the Indians now had 'common cause' against the United States.

Nicolls relocated to Pensacola and converted the nominally Spanish town into a British fortress. Indians flocked to his standard. So too did the black population, drawn by his abolitionist rhetoric. In an address given on the main square, Nicolls told his white troops that they were part of a liberating force faced with the 'glorious prospect' of emancipating southern slaves. Turning his attentions to black audience members, Nicolls declared they had the opportunity to help 'unrivet the chains of thousands of your colour now living in bonds', and to turn the tables on their former masters and 'teach them and the world to respect you'. Forty fugitive slaves enlisted on the spot. An additional 300 black runaways subsequently arrived in Mobile looking to join his army. Finally, Nicolls announced his intentions to the Americans themselves, issuing a proclamation declaring that 'the American usurpation in this country must be abolished, and the lawful owners of the soil put in possession'.

The American nightmare of a combined British, black and Indian force, operating from Spanish Florida, had been realized.[18]

\* \* \*

The same week that Nicolls arrived in Florida, Andrew Jackson signed a treaty ending the Red Stick War. At Fort Jackson, a newly built military base twenty miles west of Horseshoe Bend, Jackson assembled the Creek leaders and imposed upon them a punitive treaty that ceded to the United States some 23 million acres of land in central Alabama and southern Georgia, equivalent to three-fifths of the present state of Alabama and one-fifth of Georgia. This vast L-shaped tract gave the United States control of the bulk of the navigable rivers and almost all the lands bordering on Spanish Florida.

Gallingly, the proposed signatories of the treaty were almost uniformly 'friendly' Creek. When Jackson made clear his demands, the chiefs were stunned. 'We thought to destroy those Red Sticks and save their lands,' one pleaded. 'It was the land I wanted to save. You say you fought for it, I wanted to save that land. Friends and brothers, White Brothers – you have fought for us – our warriors were with you, you fought and spilled your blood together.'

Jackson was unmoved. The United States needed the land, he explained, for reasons of national security. The territory 'must be taken from your whole nation, in such a manner as to destroy the communication with our enemies everywhere'. In other words, the Indians had to be cooped up in the interior, far from the mouths of rivers where they could meet with troublesome foreign powers.

Jackson was in a strong negotiating position. The war had destroyed the fragile Creek economy and famine stalked the land. 'Could you only see the misery and wretchedness of those creatures perishing from want of food,' Jackson wrote home to his wife, 'and Picking up the grains of corn scattered from the mouths of the horses and trodden in the earth – I know your humanity would feel for them.'

The starving Creek signed. Only one of the signatories was a Red Stick.

In his private correspondence Jackson made clear the true significance of the Treaty of Fort Jackson. He had delivered into the public domain the heart of the Black Belt and the waterways that connected Muscle Shoals to the sea. The day after the treaty he boasted to John Coffee that he had secured 'to the U.S. a free settlement from Georgia to Mobile', including 'in my opinion the best unsettled country in America'. 'I have no doubt, so soon as congress meets, a law will be passed, directing these lines to be run, the country sectioned &

prepared for sale – on which event, I hope you will be appointed surveyor.'[19]

Having defeated his allies, Jackson turned his attentions southwards to Nicolls at Pensacola. Jackson had long been agitating for a broader campaign aimed at conquering Florida. 'I hope the government will permit us to traverse the Southern coast,' he had written eighteen months prior, 'and aid in planting the American eagles on the ramparts of Mobile, Pensacola and Fort St. Augustine ... British influence in East Florida must be destroyed, or we have the whole Southern tribe of Indians to fight and insurrections to quell in all the Southern States.'

Back then a British-backed Indian revolt had been hypothetical; now it was all too real. Jackson had been receiving good intelligence about goings-on in Florida. The appearance of the *Orpheus*, the travels of Captains Pigot and Woodbine, the arrival of Nicolls, the establishment of the British at Pensacola – all of this was known to him. The most prominent surviving Red Stick leader – Hidlis Hadjo, who had participated in the attack on Fort Mims – was said to be 'living in a handsome suit of apartments' at Pensacola courtesy of the British, and remained in command of three hundred warriors.

'Does the law of nations, or the policy of the republic, forbid us to go there and bayonet these villains?' one scandalized American demanded. Neither set of laws concerned Jackson. Nor did his lack of orders from Washington.[20] He answered to what he saw as the dictates of circumstance. In mid-August, Claiborne wrote to him in a panic from New Orleans, informing him that there were Indians at Pensacola 'in English uniform and doing duty in the Garrison. Would to God, you had orders to take Pensacola!' Jackson's reply was simple: 'The Country must and shall be defended.'[21]

On 22 August, Jackson arrived in Mobile to take charge of the defence. The British at Pensacola were only fifty miles away; they could appear at any moment. If the British established themselves at Mobile, they could effectively undo all of Jackson's victories inland by blocking all traffic coming down the Alabama and Tombigbee Rivers. Worse yet, they would then be within striking distance of the Pearl River, which guarded the approaches to New Orleans. Alternatively, they could go by land and water to Baton Rouge and bisect the Mississippi there. In Mobile, Jackson sent Major William Lawrence and 160 men to repair Fort Bowyer, a dilapidated outpost on the lip of a sand spit guarding

Mobile Bay. The action was timely. On 14 September, Nicolls's marines attacked and were repulsed. The next day four Royal Navy vessels tried to enter the bay and were also fought off. The British limped back to Pensacola.[22]

That town now had Jackson's full attention. Over the summer, Jackson had initiated a characteristically provocative correspondence with the Spanish commander, Mateo González Manrique, in which he warned that if Spain permitted Pensacola to become a haven for British and Indian forces, Jackson would hold him culpable and would seek retribution on the basis of 'An Eye for an Eye, Toothe for Toothe, and Scalp for Scalp'. The failed assault on Mobile confirmed that Pensacola was indeed a staging point for attacks on the United States. In late October, Jackson linked up with Coffee and marched with an army of 4,000 men on Pensacola. He still had no authorization for invading a foreign power – and he well knew it. 'I act without the orders of the government,' he wrote to Washington from the campaign trail, '[yet] I feel a confidence that I shall stand Justified to my government for having undertaken the expedition.'

On 6 November 1814, his army converged on the town. Massively outnumbered, the Spanish commander surrendered after token resistance. Nicolls evacuated his army, including several hundred Indian soldiers, to frigates waiting offshore. As they left, the British destroyed the fortifications guarding the bay. Having defended Mobile and neutralized Pensacola, Jackson returned the town to the Spanish and turned his attentions to New Orleans, where glory awaited him on the cane fields of the Villeré plantation.[23]

# Two Trips to London

In mid-August 1815, Colonel Nicolls returned to London on an extraordinary mission.

Nicolls had not been impressed by the peace treaty signed at Ghent. That had been a purely bilateral affair that ignored the variety of participants in the recent war. No Native Americans had participated in the negotiations. In theory, British diplomats represented the interests of their indigenous allies as well as those of the Crown. In practice, the British allowed themselves to be satisfied with a single clause concerning their Indian allies. Article IX stated that the United States would 'restore to such Tribes or Nations … all the possessions, rights, and privileges' which they had possessed prior to the outbreak of war. The position of Britain's black allies was even more parlous. The very first article of the treaty declared that all property confiscated during the war including 'any slaves' would be 'restored without delay'.

When the terms of the treaty became known to the British commanders in the Gulf of Mexico, diplomatic theory rapidly met post-conflict reality. Complexities that could be glossed over in Ghent were impossible to dodge in Florida. For one thing, the Indians were not bound by the terms of the treaty; they were expected to reach their own separate understandings with the United States. Moreover, slaves that had been granted freedom upon reaching British lines – and who in many cases had served in the British army – could not simply be re-enslaved. Admiral Cochrane tried his best to make the facts on the ground match the spirit of the treaty. He suggested that the Indians make peace with the Americans and look forward to a future where 'they will grow rich and being free from war become populous, so as to be able to defend themselves from all future encroachments of the United States'. How they were to do this when their lands had been seized was not clear. As for the several hundred former slaves now under British protection, Cochrane suggested rather lamely that British officers 'endeavour to persuade [them] to go back with their former masters'.[1]

Nicolls was having none of it. In the months after the peace, he took upon himself the task of seeing that some kind of justice was done to Britain's erstwhile black and Indian allies. He was able to get some former slaves to safety in Bermuda, but several hundred remained in Florida. Nicolls established them in a British fort on Prospect Bluff, some thirty miles up the Apalachicola River, and began systematically arming them with all the leftover guns, munitions and artillery pieces from the war. By the end of the year it was known across the South that heavily armed, British-trained black soldiers had a stronghold in Spanish Florida and had offered a sanctuary to 'fugitive slaves from all the Southern Section of the union'.

Nicolls also began moving among the Creek, trying to formulate a lasting post-war settlement. He felt strongly on this point. 'These poor people ... have sacrificed everything for us,' he wrote to one British diplomat, and 'from the very hostile and rancorous hatred of the [Americans] bordering on the Indians, I am led to think that the 9th article of the treaty of peace will not be carried into effect'. What Nicolls proposed was a lasting compact between the Creek and the British. A permanent British presence at the mouths of the rivers along the Florida coast would support and supply the independent Creek communities inland. This aligned with Creek aspirations. At a meeting with Nicolls in March, Creek leaders stated openly that the British departure would be the 'signal for our destruction'. 'Secure for us the mouths of the rivers Apalachicola, Alabama, and St Marys,' they asked, or else 'we shall be totally ruined.' 'We have fought and bled for [the British] against the Americans,' they reminded him, which had only served to make the Americans 'more bitter enemies' of the Creek nation. They had already been 'driven to the desert lands of the sea from the fertile fields of our forefathers' and faced famine. The British had to help.[2]

Nicolls's superiors wanted to extricate themselves from the region completely. That summer he was ordered to cease all operations in

Florida and return to Britain. Blacks and Indians alike would have to navigate the peace without British support.

But Nicolls still had a card to play. He returned to London in the company of the Red Stick prophet Hidlis Hadjo, who he introduced as a Creek king come to England to negotiate a treaty with the British. Whitehall was aghast. Nicolls had acted under no authority but his own, and his piece of independent diplomacy threatened the recent peace with the United States. Nicolls was unrepentant, writing to Lord Bathurst (secretary of state for war and the colonies) that Hadjo had always 'behaved with greatest gallantry and humanity' and that he 'should consider myself as guilty of the strongest ingratitude to men with whom I have fought and bled in my country's cause' if he did not advocate for their interests.[3]

What followed was a long silence as British officialdom digested this unwelcome development. In the event, Hadjo waited a year at Nicolls's home in Eltham before he received an audience with Bathurst. What passed between the two men is not clear, but it rapidly became apparent that a treaty was off the cards. Soon, Nicolls was haggling with Bathurst's clerk, trying to secure gifts of farm equipment and money for the Creek leader to take back to Florida. Ultimately, Hadjo was sent on his way with twelve spades, twelve pickaxes, six scythes, twenty-four hoes and sundry other implements, as well as £100 from the Crown and the honorary rank of brigadier general in the British army. It was a small reward for close to eighteen months in Britain. Hadjo finally departed for the Bahamas in December 1816 and arrived home in Florida in June 1817.

Behind the scenes, Bathurst was furious. In one report he complained that 'major Nicolls' conduct in bringing Hidlis Hadjo to their country had been productive of great inconvenience and expense and was entirely unauthorized'. The brittle tone of the correspondence between Bathurst and Nicolls spoke volumes about Whitehall's displeasure. The message was clear: there would be no such unscheduled visits in the future.[4]

## A GLASSY CALM

Hadjo's reception in London contrasted with the welcome offered to another American visitor to the city that year. John Quincy Adams arrived in London from Ghent, where he had been one of three American negotiators. Now he had been appointed the United States' minister to Britain. Adams reached Dover on 24 May 1815. Four days later, he met with the foreign secretary, Viscount Castlereagh. Within a fortnight, he had been formally presented to the Prince Regent. The British were keen to mend fences with the Americans.

Adams arrived at a fortuitous moment. Following Napoleon's final defeat at Waterloo that June, Europe was at peace and Europe's statesmen were resolved to prolong the lifetime of that peace as far as they could. Castlereagh declared that 'the avowed and true policy of Great Britain is ... to secure ... a long interval of repose'. Within a year of Napoleon's banishment the continent was at rest. 'The world of Europe is in a glassy calm,' Adams wrote to his father in the beginning of 1816. 'Not a breath of wind or a ripple of water moving.'

Amid this new-found tranquillity, Adams got to work representing the interests of his country. A good deal of his correspondence from this period concerned the fate of slaves freed by the British during the war. Among his papers were 'a list of seven hundred and two slaves taken in the state of Georgia', their names recorded in neat columns across several pages of manuscript. Another document called for the 'restitution of the slaves' owned by one Raleigh W. Downman. The petition stated that Downman had suffered the loss of eleven slaves worth a total of $4,260 after a Royal Navy schooner had appeared near his plantation on the Rappahannock River in Virginia in 1814. The age and value of each slave at the time of their seizure was recorded. The youngest, Cyrus, was three months old and worth $80.[5]

To their credit, the British would not return anyone emancipated during the course of the war.[6] But on all other matters Castlereagh was keen to reach an understanding. Of particular interest to Adams was the fate of Florida. In a long and wide-ranging meeting between the two men in Castlereagh's library, the foreign secretary went out of his way to reassure Adams that Britain had no desire to further involve itself in Florida. Any notion that Britain had 'any little, trickish policy of thrusting ourselves in, there between you and Spain' was simply journalistic invention. 'We have no desire to add an inch of ground to our territories in any part of the world.' (Castlereagh could not resist the follow-up jibe – aimed, no doubt, at Jackson – that this British passivity was in contrast to the American 'system of encroachment upon your neighbours'.) As for Spain, 'Great-Britain has done every thing for Spain – We have saved, we have delivered her – We have restored her Government to her', but now could do no more, especially not in Florida.[7]

How much of all this Adams took at face value and how much he considered as customary diplomatic blandishments is not clear. Castlereagh, however, was being largely transparent about British intentions in Florida. Their indifference to Hidlis Hadjo and Edward Nicolls – who, as the two men spoke, were cooling their heels in Eltham – was proof that the British had turned their backs on their Indian allies.

The Spanish were faring little better. They were outraged at Nicolls's behaviour in Pensacola – where he had, among other slights to Spanish honour, liberated some Spanish-owned slaves – and were concerned by British policy towards South America. A few weeks before his meeting with Adams, Castlereagh had received a letter from the Spanish ambassador in London accusing British representatives in South America of 'tacitly recognizing the government of the rebel colonies of Spain, and in favouring them openly in their insurrection against the legitimate authorities of his majesty'.

In fact, the twin betrayals of the Spanish and the Indians in Florida were bound up in the same cold-hearted commercial logic of British foreign policy. Commerce was king in the Foreign Office. The markets of the Americas, the prime minister declared, 'furnish the best prospect for British produce and manufactures', and so those markets had to be opened and kept open for British firms to exploit.

Of paramount importance was the British textile trade, which was dependent on American cotton grown in the South and transported from New Orleans through the Straits of Florida to market at Liverpool. In the decade after the Treaty of Ghent, British consumption of cotton would double to 423,000 bales. To satisfy that demand, even more American land would have to come under the plantation system.

And as Adams and Castlereagh chatted in London, Andrew Jackson was overseeing the transfer of millions of acres of prime cotton-growing soil to southern slave-owners.[8]

# Alabama Fever

Jackson did not forget Florida when the war ended. In fact, his new-found celebrity meant he was given responsibilities that bound his personal reputation and future political fortunes to outcomes along the Gulf Coast and its hinterland.

After hostilities ended, Jackson accepted command of the United States' army's southern division, commanding all forces south of the Ohio River. He was also tasked with building a military road connecting Nashville to New Orleans, running through Choctaw lands in Mississippi and Alabama. This road, once completed, would – in conjunction with the Federal Road running from Milledgeville, Georgia, to Mobile, Alabama,[1] and the road Jackson's army had built through east-central Alabama during the Red Stick War – effectively enclose the Creek heartlands with routes along which white settlers and their slaves could enter the rich prairie lands of the Gulf Plains.[2]

In Jackson's mind there was no division between the strategic interests of the United States and his cherished goal of handing over Indian land to white planters – nor did he conceal his thinking from his superiors or anyone else.

During the war – before the Treaty of Fort Jackson, before the Battle of New Orleans, when it was far from clear that the United States was going to secure a favourable peace – he had written to the secretary of war outlining his vision. With the Creek cession, the United States would have 20 million acres of 'first-rate land' connecting two axes of settlement: Georgia in the east to the Mississippi in the west, and Tennessee in the north to Mobile in the south. 'This country, populated, becomes an effective defence to the southwestern frontier,' he concluded, therefore 'the line should be run without delay, and the land offered for sale.' He went on to suggest that it would be 'good policy to give each able-bodied man who would settle upon this land half a section, at $2 per acre, payable in two years, with interest. This measure would insure the security of this frontier, and make citizens of the soldiers who effected its conquest.'

Writing to a Nashville friend, he was more blunt. It was not enough to banish the Creek. 'Now is the time ... to extinguish the Cherokee and Chickasaw' claims and replace all the Indians in the South with 'a hardy race that would defend it' – namely, white frontiersmen accustomed to Indian-fighting. Men like Jackson. It was a vision of ethnic cleansing that would become known by the euphemism 'removal'. For Jackson it was just good policy. 'Our national security requires it,' he wrote. 'Now is the time to obtain it and it ought and must be had.'[3]

Not long after the Battle of New Orleans, while John Coffee was already running the boundaries for the Creek cession imposed at Fort Jackson, Jackson heard alarming news. Article IX of the Treaty of Ghent required the restoration of all lands to their 1811 condition. This annulled the Treaty of Fort Jackson, which had seized a vast portion of the Creek nation. In June 1815, the Madison administration reluctantly accepted it would have to abide by the treaty and sent a letter to Jackson informing him of the decision. To make matters even worse, some months later the administration signed a treaty with the Cherokees that transferred over to them 4 million acres of ceded Creek land due south of the Great Bend of the Tennessee River. It looked as though Jackson's work was going to be undone by politicians in Washington.[4]

Jackson made his views clear. On the question of Article IX he was adamant. The Treaty of Fort Jackson had ended the Red Stick War, a conflict distinct from the War of 1812. Whatever was agreed at Ghent did not apply to the Creek cession. If the British wanted to enforce it, they could attempt to do so; Andrew Jackson would not. The Cherokee question led him to unleash his most violent rhetoric on the secretary of war. 'The western people are loud in their complaints against' the treaty, Jackson wrote, and they feared that the 'security for which they fought & bled is taken from them, & the Country gained at the expense of some of the best blood of their Land' was being taken from them 'and bestowed on a nation of Indians whose hatchet and scalping knife has left many an orphan & many a parent without a child'. The Creek cession had been won with their 'valor' – would white settlers now be removed from it to give homes to 'the murderers of their wives & children'? Were that to happen, Jackson hinted darkly, 'your forebodings will be something like mine that evil may result'. It was a thinly veiled threat, directed at a man who by rights could have fired him for insubordination.[5]

But the political winds blew ever in Jackson's favour. London was more interested in securing American cotton than it was in the rights of its former Creek allies. Washington was wary of the political backlash from the westerners if it were seen to favour Cherokee interests over those of white settlers. Article IX was quietly forgotten about.

As for the Cherokee question, the administration agreed to settle it, and all other outstanding issues with the Indian tribes, through a new round of treaty negotiations – negotiations that Jackson would dominate. In September 1816, the Cherokee – who not long before had been roundly praised for their 'daring intrepid & preserving bravery' during the Red Stick War – signed a treaty that delivered the lands they had only recently won along the Tennessee and Tombigbee Rivers to the Americans. The Cherokee had possessed them for six months.

A few days later, Jackson imposed a similar treaty on the Chickasaw which saw them surrender 6 million acres of south-western Tennessee and north-western Alabama. Both treaties were secured through abundant bribery that even Jackson found distasteful.

A month later, John Coffee concluded a treaty with the Choctaw that acquired a small but strategically important tract at Muscle Shoals.

The three treaties, combined with the Treaty of Fort Jackson, delivered the best cotton-growing land in Alabama into the public domain, total control of the Mobile River and its tributaries to the United States army, and near-total sovereignty over the Florida borderlands. The Indians had been cut off from the ocean; the interior was now open for white settlement.

Jackson was triumphant. 'The whole southern country from Kentucky and Tennessee to Mobile,' he wrote to Washington, 'has been opened by the late treaties.' The dream of connecting the Tennessee River to Mobile was now complete. The strategic position of the United States in the Gulf Plains was indomitable. All that remained was to people the land with Americans.[6]

## SOMETHING LIKE A MANIA

In December 1817, Anne Royall, a writer and journalist from Baltimore, travelled from Kentucky through Tennessee to Huntsville, Alabama, the cotton boom town on the Great Bend of the Tennessee River. On the final leg of the journey she fell in with two Tennesseans heading the same way. Conversation turned to Andrew Jackson and opinions diverged:

> 'By G—d, I suppose, you think General Jackson is a G—d almighty about here.'
> 'By G—d, sir, I think he is next to him,' said the Huntsville man; 'and none but a d—d fool would have made the remark.'
> Now thought I, they will fight.
> 'You, nor no other man, Sir, shall speak disrespectfully of General Jackson, in my presence.'
> This spirited reply, rather cooled the little gentleman's ire.

There could be no doubt about it: Royall was entering Jackson country.

As they approached the outskirts of Huntsville, Royall glimpsed the cotton fields for the first time. The picking season for cotton lasts from August to January, and by the time Royall arrived in Alabama the fields were largely picked over. Even without their distinctive snowy bolls, the immense size of the cotton fields – Royall reckoned some of them at between 400 and 500 acres – was a spectacle in itself. 'Fancy is inadequate to conceive a prospect more grand,' she wrote. 'Although the land is level, you cannot see the end of the fields either way. To a stranger, coming suddenly amongst these fields, it has the appearance of magic.'

Shortly afterwards, she entered Huntsville itself. The town had come a long way since 1811, when it had become the first incorporated town in the future state of Alabama. So too had surrounding Madison County, whose population had grown ninefold to 10,000 by the time Royall arrived. Huntsville, the county seat, was home to 1,200 people, mostly migrants from Georgia and the Carolinas who were pursuing the cotton frontier as it barrelled south-westwards. With its stone buildings – a courthouse, a brick market house, some lawyers' offices and a bank (but no church – services were held in the courthouse) – Huntsville offered at least the veneer of permanence amid the frenzy of migration. 'The citizens are gay, polite, and hospitable, and live in great splendor,' Royall reported. In the parlour of her hotel she found all of southern society represented: 'the sweet girl, the grave matron, the sparkling belle, the conceited fop, the modest young gentleman, veteran soldier, and a sociable old planter. They were all talking and laughing about ... planting cotton.'

From her bedroom window she had a view over a neighbouring plantation where the last of the fields were being picked over by a few dozen slaves. 'They face about to every point. Some are erect, and others stooping, and all their hands move very fast,' she wrote. 'It appears an endless business.'

In town, Royall met John Coffee, who she knew only by reputation. He was not the forbidding soldier she expected. In fact, she was rather taken with him, reporting that 'his face is round and full, and features handsome. His complexion is ruddy though sunburnt. His hair and eyes black, and a soft serenity diffuses his countenance. His hair is carelessly thrown one side, in front, and displays one of the finest foreheads in nature – high, smooth, and retreating,' Royall wrote. 'He is as mild as the dew drop.' He struck her as a placid, deliberate man. 'All these Tennesseeans are mild and gentle.'[7]

John Coffee was putting on a masterful performance of composure for the visiting writer. For in the period that Royall met him he was a very busy man indeed. In March 1817, Coffee had been appointed – as Jackson had promised – surveyor-general of the northern district of Alabama. This was among the most coveted positions in the United States government. Only Jackson's energetic lobbying ensured that Coffee was the final choice.[8]

It was no sinecure. All eyes were on Alabama. Large-scale land sales in the territory[9] had already begun in 1817 – land offices in St Stephens and Milledgeville shifted $1.5 million worth of land that year – but the smart money had its eyes on the prime cotton-growing lands on the banks of the Great Bend of the Tennessee River which came under Coffee's jurisdiction. Expectations were high. Even before Coffee's appointment was confirmed, the state was flooded with migrants. Many were well-heeled planters doing their due diligence before making large purchases in the region. Most were humbler sorts, frontiersmen from the Carolinas, Georgia and Tennessee who had sold everything and moved to Alabama in pursuit of a dream.

The government kept a close eye on developments as it hoped to fill the Treasury with the proceeds from land sales. Reports from Huntsville raised their hopes. 'Great numbers of people in this country are desirous to buy lands there,' one official wrote to the GLO from Huntsville, 'and many gentlemen from the eastern states (very considerable capitalists too) have arrived in this country and have hired their negroes.' He forecast that when those lands were offered they 'would sell generally as high, and perhaps higher than any lands in the United States ever sold'.

Coffee's instructions from Washington could not have been clearer. 'The President expects that every exertion will be made ... to bring the public lands in that district as early as possible into the market.'[10]

Coffee's team began work in May. The initial goal was to survey fifty townships on the north bank of the Tennessee River and fifty on the south bank, a total of 2.3 million acres. The work was expensive – Coffee estimated it cost $30,000 to survey a hundred townships – and difficult. Surveyors faced every possible challenge in the backcountry. Disease was rampant and at times Coffee had to suspend work as his clerks were too sick to perform their duties. Obtaining basic supplies was difficult. In Alabama, the massive inflow of people into a region with almost no settlements and few roads had led to an explosion in the price of staples. Then there were fears of confrontations with Indians or squatters (the authorities didn't tend to distinguish between the two; Edmund Gaines referred collectively to 'our red and white people of the woods') which might lead to violence. A man seeking to make a career in this field had to possess the 'bodily strength and constitution sufficient to undergo the privations and rough fatigues of a deputy surveyor in the wilderness', one GLO official wrote. Such men weren't even particularly well paid. What motivated them? A hint appeared in an unassuming advertisement posted in the Huntsville *Republican* in January 1818, when the first land auctions were imminent. 'We the undersigned,' it read,

> lately deputy surveyors in the country north of the Tennessee river, which is about to be offered for sale ... having had free use of the field notes of the office and having been enabled to obtain a general as well as particular knowledge of the whole, have now opened an office ... where any one of us will always be found

ready to give any information to people wishing to purchase to an advantage ... Those persons wishing to purchase to a great advantage and who have not had a good knowledge of the country, would do well to give us a call.

It transpired that Coffee had signed off on this piece of naked corruption, on the agreement that they would kick up half of what they took to him.[11]

When sales began in February they surpassed all expectations. In a few weeks $2.5 million worth of land was sold off. By June, the team of clerks working from the Huntsville land office had sold 406,000 acres for $3.1 million – a 15,744 per cent increase on the year prior. More importantly, the average price paid per acre more than tripled from $2 to $7.7. 'Never did lands sell better in the United States,' one official wrote to Washington. 'There appears to prevail something like a land mania,' wrote another, 'and I am told there will be an immense emigration from the east.' The sales continued in the summer and then on deep into the winter. All told, 973,361 acres – or an area 150 per cent the size of Luxembourg – was sold for $7.2 million that year in Huntsville. And this was just the beginning. Coffee's team had plans to survey and bring to market a further 5.5 million acres. Simultaneously, hundreds of thousands of acres of Alabama land were being prepared for sale at land offices in St Stephens, Milledgeville and Cahaba.[12]

It might seem peculiar that land prices kept soaring higher and higher when it was apparent that there was clearly no shortage of land to go round in Alabama. But peculiar dynamics were at work in Alabama in this period. There were two reasons people paid premium prices for land. The first was cotton. The cotton trade had bounced back stronger than ever after the peace was signed. Between 1810 and 1820 American cotton exports more than doubled and came to account for a third of all US exports. This avalanche of cotton descended on the textile mills of north-west England, which were expanding at as fast a rate as cotton could be produced. As production took off in the years after Ghent, the price of raw cotton went vertical, ultimately peaking at 33 cents per pound. Cotton culture was a productivity game, with planters trying to maximize yield. One of the few variables they could control was soil quality. Prime cotton-growing lands offered the opportunity to produce outsized yields per acre at a time when cotton prices were at historic highs. Consequently, planters were willing to pay top prices for those lands, lands which happened to be in Alabama.[13]

In tandem with this phenomenon of uniquely high cotton prices was the opening-up of Alabama to settlement after the various treaties Jackson had hammered out since 1814. The population of Alabama grew twelvefold between 1810 and 1820. (This included a 1,400 per cent increase in the slave population.) Travellers reported seeing great caravans of people, produce and livestock travelling down the Federal Road into the territory. All of these people needed homes to live in and communities to join. Property development schemes formed that also drove up land prices. John Coffee participated in two such schemes. The first, the aptly named community of Cottonport, was a disappointment. The second, which founded the town of Florence near Muscle Shoals, was a great success. Under the auspices of the Cypress Land Company, a group of Tennesseans including Coffee invested $85,000 to purchase 5,515 acres of Alabama land. They then laid out a town of 415 lots, which they marketed as destined to 'become the New York of the south'. The scheme was a hit, with Andrew Jackson, James Madison and other notables all buying lots. The value of Cypress Land Company stock increased tenfold.[14]

After a certain point, land prices in Alabama slipped the surly bonds of economic logic and entered a different realm altogether. As word spread across the country about the land bonanza in Alabama, a regional happening turned into a national obsession. The collective madness that enveloped the country on the subject of Alabama lands became the New World equivalent of Tulip mania or the South Sea Bubble, and the prototype of subsequent American speculative bubbles. People sold everything and moved to Alabama. Stories of young men who had gone to Alabama and turned into millionaires almost overnight triggered contagious emigration. One North Carolinian wrote that 'the *Alabama Fever* rages here with great violence and has *carried off* vast numbers of our citizens'. Virginians feared that their state might become depopulated as a consequence of mass migration to the southern frontier.

Observers were in awe of what was unfolding at the Alabama land sales. In most states, $15 an acre was considered a high price for land –

in Alabama it got you nothing. The Huntsville *Republican* printed an advert for a lost land certificate that revealed its owners had paid $31 per acre. Along the banks of the Great Bend land sold for $53 per acre. One of Coffee's partners in the Cypress Land Company wrote to Jackson reporting on auctions where 'good lands' sold for anything between $24 and $78 an acre. A newspaper in Alexandria, Louisiana, reported that a squatter in Alabama had bought land at the unheard-of price of $107 per acre.[15]

These dizzying numbers drew hordes of ambitious young men to the Alabama land offices. John Campbell, who arrived from Virginia in 1817, marvelled that a place which 'ten years ago belonged to the Cherokee' had been transformed into one where planters were 'clearing between four and five hundred dollars a hand'. 'There has not been a single instance of any person settling in this country ... who had not become wealthy in a few years,' he wrote home. 'I am determined to turn all of my energies toward the acquisition of wealth for some time to come.'

Convinced that prices would rise in the future at the same rate they had in the past, such men laid out immense sums for cotton lands. They were helped along by the seventy new banks that had sprung up in neighbouring Kentucky and Tennessee in the years after the war (as well as Huntsville's own Planters & Merchants Bank) that supplied dubious paper money and the government's own credit scheme, which required buyers to put down only one-fortieth of the asking price on the day of purchase.

The financial subtleties of land speculation consumed the state. A visitor to Huntsville, one satirist wrote, was 'certain to catch the price of cotton, the fall or rise of exchange, Land Office Money or goods for sale, bills, post and shaving note drafts, specie, par and below par ... which are re-echoed from one corner of the public square to the other'. 'Extravaganza was the order of the day,' another observer wrote. 'The mania of speculation was epidemic.'

Trapped at the heart of the maelstrom were GLO clerks whose offices were packed with aggressive men scrutinizing maps and arguing over the relative merits of tracts. The atmosphere at auctions was rancorous. Every species of collusion, intimidation and fraud was used to secure land at below-market prices. The surveyor-general in the southern half of the state warned of 'intruders who threaten with assassination, any person who will dare to bid for the lands' they sought and complained that large and unruly crowds at auctions 'grossly insulted' the land office officials in charge of proceedings.[16]

In this chaotic manner, $16 million worth of Alabama land was sold between 1816 and 1820. In 1818, at the height of the bubble, 60 per cent of all public land revenues came from Alabama alone. Almost all of this was purchased on government credit, with the consequence that of the total land debt of $22 million, $10 million was incurred by land sales in Alabama, a place that had existed for only three years and which had fewer than 130,000 residents, half of whom were slaves.[17]

John Coffee was delighted. As a government servant, he was gratified with the speedy and lucrative sale of the public lands. As a disciple of Jackson, he was glad to see the Indians dispelled and white settlers installed. Above all, as a land speculator himself, he relished the high drama of the scramble for Alabama. In a triumphant letter to Jackson, he described the clash of various land-speculation companies at

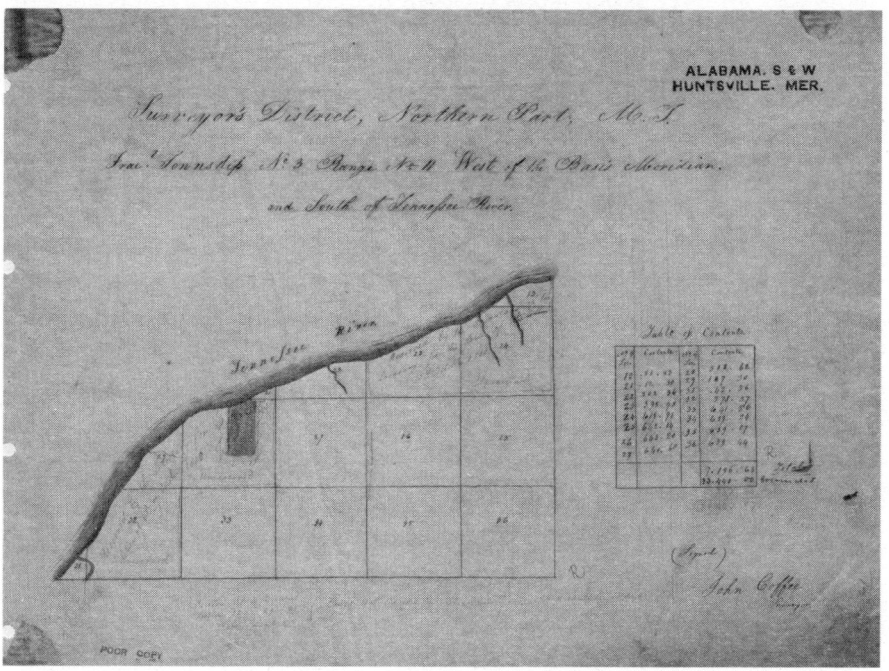

*Andrew Jackson's piece of the Scramble for Alabama. Parcels of land along the Tennessee River were highly sought after.*

auctions as though he were narrating an episode from the Red Stick War:

> The company that was forming when you passed here, have been very much chagrined. they have been lashed through every sale when they bid for good land, and if they got it, it was at a very high price, the sharp shooters have cut them side and edge, and still have the means of keeping up the fire, the company has been formed of men from Virginia, Kentucky, Georgia, and Madison County, not one Tennessean is in it, indeed the scheme when it was understood, was thought so illiberal, that we have joined forces against it, and have been thereby able to defeat their plans.

Jackson also made some purchases in this period. But by this stage he had transcended the low scrabble for land. When he bid for lands at Huntsville during the November auctions, the speculators present paid him the highest possible compliment they knew of. In a session in which plots sold for over $50 an acre, Jackson bought his prime tract along the Tennessee River at the minimum price of $2 per acre. Whether out of fear, awe or respect, no one would bid against the general.[18]

# Jackson Redux

In Alabama, Anne Royall also met Andrew Jackson. She was in her room when she heard his name shouted in the street outside. 'Running to my window, I saw him walking slowly up the hill, between two gentlemen, his aides. He was dressed in a blue frock coat, with epaulettes, a common hat with a black cockade, and a sword by his side. He is very tall and slender.' That evening he paid a visit to her hotel and Royall had the chance to study him up close. 'His person is finely shaped, and his features not handsome, but strikingly bold and determined. He is very easy and affable in his manners, and loves a jest … He appears to be about 50 years of age. There is a great deal of dignity about him. He related many hardships endured by his men, in the army, but never breathed a word of his own. His language is pure and fluent, and he has the appearance of having kept the best company.'[1]

Jackson was a southern gentleman to a fault and was always courtly and well-mannered around women. The impression he made that evening, however, appears in stark contrast to the tone of a circular he had issued to the Tennessee militia one week prior:

> The Seminole Indians have raised the war hatchet. They have stained our land with the blood of our Citizens; their war spirit must be put down; and they taught to know that their safety depends upon the friendship and protection of the United States … Your General who led you to victory on the plains of Talledega, Emuckfau, and Tohopeka, asks you to accompany him

to the heart of the Seminole Towns, and there aid in giving peace and safety to the Southern Frontier.[2]

It was January 1818, and Jackson was returning to Florida.

## 'PROSTITUTED SOIL'

In 1817, two crises had unfolded in East Florida. The first was occasioned by the arrival on Amelia Island, a coastal island of only eighteen square miles on the Georgia border, of a Scottish adventurer named Gregor MacGregor. MacGregor was a former British officer who had travelled to South America to join the cause of independence. In Venezuela, he had served as a cavalry officer under Francisco de Miranda and became friendly with Simón Bolívar, later marrying one of his cousins. MacGregor won some celebrated victories in the Venezuelan army but fell afoul of infighting among the revolutionaries and by 1817 was sidelined.

It was in this period of restless inactivity that the idea of seizing one of the ports in Spanish Florida was suggested to him. Such a port, he was told, would become 'a rendezvous for all adventurers who might feel disposed to espouse the cause of Independence'. Florida was perfectly situated between the United States and the major harbours of Mexico and the Caribbean rim. It was the ideal staging ground for fresh campaigns against the Spanish Empire. That summer, MacGregor headed to Philadelphia and then made his way down the coast, fundraising for his expedition as he went, ultimately receiving $160,000 from well-wishers in New York, Charleston and Savannah.

On 29 June, he arrived at Amelia Island with his army of 150 soldiers of fortune. 'I shall sleep either in hell or Amelia tonight,' he told his men. They stormed the town of Fernandina, encountering no resistance from the Spanish garrison. The next day he issued a proclamation introducing himself as 'brigadier-general of the army of the United Provinces of New Granada and Venezuela, and general-in-chief of the armies for the two Floridas'. His arrival marked the day that Amelia's inhabitants became 'instruments in the commencement of a national emancipation'. First they would work for the liberation 'of the Floridas from tyranny ... Then I shall hope to lead you to the continent of South America to gather fresh laurels in freedom's cause.' He declared the establishment of the Republic of the Floridas and raised its flag – a green cross of St George on a field of white – over Fernandina.

The Monroe administration looked on in disbelief. MacGregor had demonstrated the disastrously feeble position of the Spanish. In a single day, he had taken control of an island that, while tiny, contained 40 per cent of the population of East Florida. More alarming still, not only was MacGregor British, but among his retinue was George Woodbine, the Royal Marines officer who had fought alongside Nicolls in the War of 1812. It looked as though the Floridas were once again exposed to a British invasion.

Then things got stranger. In September, Woodbine and MacGregor travelled to Jamaica and the Bahamas, to raise money and recruits for the next phase of their war of liberation. In their absence, another adventurer, a Frenchman named Louis-Michel Aury, sailed into Fernandina and annexed the island to the Republic of Mexico. For the next four months the Mexican flag flew over north Florida.[3]

Meanwhile, on the other side of East Florida, a different sort of trouble was brewing along the banks of the Apalachicola River. In 1816, Jackson had sent a force to destroy the settlement of freed slaves at Prospect Bluff. General Edmund Gaines built a fort – Fort Scott – upriver inside the Georgia line and that July descended on Prospect Bluff with gunboats. A lucky shot in the initial bombardment struck the fort's arsenal, killing 270 of the 350 defenders in an instant.[4] The survivors fled deeper into East Florida, where they mingled with other fugitives.

This region was home to a group of Indians the Americans referred to as Seminoles. Like the other southern Indians, the Seminoles spoke a Muskogee language, but otherwise they were *sui generis*, less a defined grouping than a hybrid community formed by the remnants of the decimated Florida tribes. Among their number were runaway slaves and their descendants.

Since the Red Stick War, the Seminole homelands had also become a haven for survivors of Jackson's campaigns in Alabama, among them Hidlis Hadjo.

Also present was a Scottish trader named Alexander Arbuthnot, who acted as a go-between for the Red Stick exiles and the British authorities in the Bahamas, who the Indians hoped might yet intervene on their behalf. Another Englishman in the region was Robert Ambrister, a former Royal Marines officer who had served under Nicolls in the War of 1812. These men kept the flame of Nicolls's idealism alive in the Florida borderlands, moving among the scattered settlements along the Suwanee, the Apalachicola and around Lake Miccosukee, reminding the Indians of their rights under the Treaty of Ghent.

All the while, Americans were arriving to settle lands obtained under the terms of the Treaty of Fort Jackson. These lands still contained Red Stick tribes and bordered Seminole settlements. Conflict was inevitable, with both whites and Indians accusing the others of wrongdoing. In February 1817, tensions boiled over. That month, a group of Seminole warriors broke into the Garrett family home on the St Mary's River in southern Georgia. Identifying a kettle they believed belonged to a murdered Indian, they proceeded to shoot, stab and scalp Mrs Garrett and her two infant sons. The house was looted and set aflame, before the intruders fled back into Spanish territory. The Garrett slaying outraged the South and the government sent General Gaines to the region.

Gaines was authorized to clear Indians off the Creek cession. In November, he went to evict some Red Sticks from the settlement of Fowltown on the Flint River, just east of Fort Scott. There, his troops were met by a Seminole force. A skirmish broke out; men died on both sides. The Americans returned in force and razed Fowltown. The Indians fled into Seminole territory. A week later they struck back, ambushing an American flotilla led by Lieutenant Richard W. Scott heading up the Apalachicola to resupply Fort Scott. The American boats carried women and children, as well as a group of hospitalized soldiers. Attacked at close range by Indian riflemen in the undergrowth, the Americans were quickly overwhelmed. Fifty died and, according to lurid accounts sent back to Washington, the Indians dispatched the women, children and invalid soldiers by dashing their brains out on the side of their boats.[5]

The borderland violence along the Apalachicola and the bizarre goings-on in Amelia Island were distinct events. Nevertheless, in American minds they were intimately connected. They were evidence in support of the administration's basic thesis that the Spanish had lost control of the Floridas and had therefore lost right of possession. As Monroe later told Congress, the 'inability of Spain to fulfil her engagements and to sustain her authority in the Floridas' had led that region 'to be perverted by foreign adventurers and savages' hostile to the United States. One congressman went further, describing Florida as 'prostituted soil' that had been violated by every one of America's enemies.[6]

## THE AVENGING ROD

In the winter of 1817, the administration acted. Publicly invoking the No-Transfer Resolution for the first time,* Monroe dispatched Gaines to seize Amelia Island. By New Year's Day, the Stars and Stripes flew over Fernandina.

At the same time, he put Jackson in charge of quelling the nascent Indian War in East Florida. That would turn out to be a much more prolonged and controversial business.

Jackson's subsequent actions generated such an uproar and had such profound consequences that the nature of his instructions from Monroe are worth considering in some detail.

Over the course of December, Monroe and Secretary of War John C. Calhoun had sent a series of instructions to their commanders in the South that reflected a growing interest in events in East Florida and gave their generals greater latitude to intervene as they saw fit to protect the national interest. What was not in doubt was that the United States had the right to intervene in Spanish Florida. The administration argued that, under existing treaties, the Spanish were obliged to maintain order among the indigenous tribes. If they failed to do so – as it now seemed they had – then the United States was permitted to impose order on them. Convinced the law was on their side, Monroe and Calhoun gave their commanders instruction to conduct 'offensive operations' and mete out 'exemplary punishment' to America's enemies.[7]

Jackson's instructions, however, contained an important caveat:

---

* See Monroe's Special Message of 13 Jan. 1818. The No-Transfer Resolution had been secret since its promulgation in 1811. News that it was official policy of the United States government produced shock and resentment. The *Edinburgh Monthly Review* fumed that the resolution 'breathes as much of the profligate spirit of encroachment, and disregard to the rights of territory, as any thing that ever proceeded from the French cabinet during the tyranny of Buonaparte ... Let such things be sanctioned, and there is an end to the rights of nation.' (*Edinburgh Monthly Review*, ii, July–December 1819, 320–21).

> It is the wish of the President, that you consider yourself at liberty to march across the Florida line, and to attack them within its limits, should it be found necessary, *unless they should shelter themselves under a Spanish fort. In the last event you will immediately notify this department.*⁸

In other words, the United States Army should invade Spanish territory but should not engage the Spaniards who resided there.

Jackson immediately detected an inconsistency here. On a practical level, it seemed absurd to give the Indians such an easy means of escaping justice. After all, it was inevitable that they would take refuge in Spanish forts – they had done so during the War of 1812. More importantly, the United States now had the chance to act decisively to end the charade of Spanish rule in Florida and to complete the conquest of the Gulf Coast. Surely they should seize the moment?

Jackson replied that complying 'with the last clause of your order' would lead to a catastrophe. Allowing the Indians safe harbour in Spanish forts would make a swift campaign impossible and give their enemies – including the hated British – time to rally and encircle the American force. 'What may not be the result?' he asked. 'Defeat and massacre ... The arms of the United States must be carried to any point within the limits of East Florida, where an enemy is permitted and protected, or disgrace attends ... Let it be signified to me through any channel ... that the possession of the Floridas would be desirable to the United States and in sixty days it will be accomplished.'⁹

Monroe received this letter but made a show of not reading it in full. He handed it to Calhoun, who made no comment. The letter was filed away and (allegedly) forgotten about. Jackson did not receive a reply for six months – by which time the war was over.¹⁰*

What was going on? The innocent explanation was that Monroe was simply negligent in his duties. Aged sixty in 1818, Monroe was a dilatory and indecisive old man, fearful of conflict. Contemporaries viewed him

---

\* Jackson's biographer Robert Remini notes that although Monroe did not reply to this letter, Calhoun continued his correspondence with Jackson, including a 6 February letter that instructed him to use '*all the measures* which you have adopted to terminate the rupture with the Indians ... and the confidence reposed in your skill and promptitude assures us that peace will be restored on such conditions as will make it honourable and permanent'.

as someone who had earned the right to be president more through seniority than merit. As the bearer of the Jeffersonian flame that Jefferson had passed on to Madison and Madison to him, Monroe's colleagues spoke of him in kindly rather than reverent tones. Jefferson once remarked of Monroe that 'he was a man whose soul might be turned inside out without discovering a blemish to the world'. As president, he presided over a cabinet brimming with ambitious young men. Monroe – with his old-fashioned manners and his clothes and haircut unchanged since the revolutionary era – was out of place among this new breed of American statesmen. John Quincy Adams, his secretary of state, complained to his diary that the president 'puts off every thing for a future time'. Monroe's equivocations drove his treasury secretary, William Crawford, almost to treason. A conversation over the army budget in the President's Mansion ended with Crawford calling the president an 'infernal scoundrel' and menacing him with his cane. The navy secretary happened to be in the room and recalled that 'Mr. Monroe seized the tongs and ordered him instantly to leave the room or he would chastise him, and he rang the bell for the servant'. Crawford remained in his post but never set foot in the building for the remainder of Monroe's presidency.[11]

Yet Monroe was no naif. His genial ambiguity concealed a far more complex set of motives and a far deeper understanding of events than he made plain. In this respect, he was a true Jeffersonian – Jefferson himself having hidden his ambition behind a facade of avuncular eccentricity and his *realpolitik* behind a smokescreen of high-flown rhetoric.

When it came to Florida, Monroe was as motivated as anyone to secure it for the United States. It was he who had tried and failed to secure it in Paris in 1803 and then failed again on a subsequent trip to Europe in 1806, and had won only chunks of it as secretary of state during the War of 1812. During his tenure at the State Department, the British ambassador had noted Monroe's slippery 'double language' and complained of the American position on Florida that 'to judge what they mean by what they say is utterly impracticable'. Monroe, like so many who occupy positions of high power, had one eye on the history books. He was keen to ensure that his own record was spotless and that nobody could ever accuse him of having compromised the sanctity of the Constitution. At the same time, certain things had to be done – the acquisition of Florida among them. Just as Jefferson had made free use of the wholly unscrupulous General Wilkinson to advance American interests on the frontier, so too did Monroe deploy Jackson in Florida.

His subsequent behaviour supports this thesis. Monroe consistently flip-flopped on the significance of Jackson's actions in Florida in 1818, publicly sighing over his bullheaded general while privately acknowledging his utility as a tool of American expansionism. Damningly, after the whole scandal blew up, Monroe went into damage-limitation mode and wrote to Jackson suggesting they might collaborate on doctoring their correspondence to 'invalidate' certain objections that had arisen in the aftermath of Jackson's rampage. Jackson refused to alter a word.[12]

Jackson arrived at Fort Scott on 9 March. On 15 March he crossed into Spanish Florida and occupied Prospect Bluff, building Fort Gadsden on the site of the destroyed maroon stronghold.

To Jackson, Florida was 'the dark scene of Spanish and British machinations, and the *primum mobile* of Indian carnage and massacre'. It had to be subdued.

Having joined up with the rest of his force and some Creek allies, Jackson had an army some 4,200 strong and set his sights on destroying every enemy of the United States he could find, be they Indian, black, British or Spanish.

First his army headed for Lake Miccosukee, destroying every settlement they passed through along the way. At their destination, they found 'more than fifty fresh scalps ... and in the centre of the public square, the old Red Stick's standard, a red pole was erected, crowned with scalps, recognised by the hair, as torn from the heads of the unfortunate companions of [Lieutenant Richard W.] Scott'.

Jackson then learned that some Indians had fled to St Marks, so he marched on the Spanish settlement, seizing it on 7 April and raising the American flag. In St Marks, he also discovered the Scottish trader Arbuthnot, who he promptly took prisoner.

But there were bigger prizes in the area. Nearby, one of his men ran up a British flag, and two Indians, thinking the British had come, approached them. It was Hidlis Hadjo and another Red Stick leader, named Himollemico. Jackson ordered the two men summarily executed without a trial. Hidlis Hadjo – the Red Stick warrior who had seen London, stood as an equal before King George's ministers and carried on his person a commission as a general in the British army – was hanged on 8 April.

Jackson now turned his attentions east, to the black and Seminole settlements along the Econfina and Suwanee Rivers. Before they headed into battle, Jackson reminded his men 'to recollect we war with savages who have without mercy torn the locks from the head of the aged matron down to the infant babe. These are the wretches who should feel the avenging rod.'

During the course of this campaign, he burned down 300 villages. He also captured Robert Ambrister and remanded him in custody along with Arbuthnot.

His work done, he wheeled back and returned to St Marks, where he organized a court martial of Ambrister and Arbuthnot. After a two-day trial, the court sentenced both men to death, but later showed mercy on Ambrister and repealed the sentence. Jackson overruled the court and ordered both men killed.

On 29 April, Ambrister was shot and the seventy-year-old Arbuthnot hanged from the yardarm of his ship, the *Chance*.

'I hope the execution of these Two unprincipled villains will prove an awful example to the world,' Jackson wrote to Calhoun, 'and convince the Government of Great Britain as well as her subjects that certain, if slow retribution awaits those unchristian wretches who by false promises delude & excite a Indian tribe to all the horrid deeds of savage war.'

Jackson marched back to Fort Gadsden and was about to declare victory when, on 5 May, he was informed that the Indians had now gathered in Pensacola, the seat of Spanish government.

Without a second thought, Jackson marched westwards, arriving at the gates of Pensacola on 24 May. He confidently predicted that his army would be 'hailed as deliverers' by a Spanish population in 'cruel bondage' to a hostile Indian population. Governor Masot quickly disabused him of that notion and protested that 'the greater part of [the Indians] were women and children ... [and] these few unarmed and miserable men were not hostile to the United States'.

Jackson had no time for such details. He stormed the town, shipped the Spanish off to Havana, raised the American flag and established a garrison and the rudiments of military government. For good measure, he sent two companies to 'scour the country between the Mobile and Apalachicola rivers, exterminating every hostile party who dare resist, or will not surrender and remove with their families above the 31st Degree of latitude'.

He considered the conquest of Florida almost complete. In a letter to Calhoun, he asked for the 5th infantry and a 22-gun brig to seize St Augustine. 'Add another Regt. and one Frigate and I will insure you Cuba in a few days.'

For now he had to rest. His health had been broken by the campaign. He was emaciated and coughing blood. He began the journey home. By 2 June, Jackson was in the United States, reporting to his wife on his achievements:

> My Love, I reached here on last evening, on my return march with the Tennessee Troops, for Nashville having, I trust, put an end to Indian hostilities for the future. The Just Vengeance of heaven having visited and punished with death, the exciters of the Indian war, and horrid massacre of our innocent women & children on the Southern frontier. I have destroyed the Babylon of the South, the hot bed of the Indian war & depredations on our frontier, by taking St Marks & Pensacola – which is now garrisoned by our Troops, and the American flag waving on their ramparts, we have Suffered privation but we have met them like Soldiers ... Kiss my Two little Andrews for me present me affectionately to all friends, & believe me to be your affectionate Husband.

He had been in Florida less than three months, in which time he had conquered two Spanish towns, murdered two Creek chieftains, executed two British citizens and burned to the ground the homes of hundreds of black and Indian families.

Only three Americans died in battle during the campaign.

By some estimates, sixty enemy 'combatants' were killed by American forces. Unknown others had been driven into the Florida wilderness.

So ended the First Seminole War. One disgusted contemporary referred to Jackson's expedition as the 'Seminole Indian hunt, which has been dignified with the name of war'. A Virginia congressman was even more direct in his assessment:

Sir, had not the God I worship, a God of mercy as well as truth, taught me to forgive mine enemies, did he, as the Great Spirit whom the Seminole adores, allow me to indulge revenge; were I an Indian, I would swear eternal hatred to your race.[13]

# Giant Steps

Summer in Washington was and remains a gruelling affair, and the summer of 1818 was no different.

Some days that July, John Quincy Adams watched his thermometer rise above ninety degrees and remain there through the night. 'There was not a spot in the house where I could stand or sit ten minutes in quiet,' he recorded in his diary, 'and I sauntered about the house from room to room like a ghost in Tartary, almost naked and without finding rest for the sole of my foot.'

There was more besides the torpor to keep Adams up at night. As the heat intensified in May, Jackson's dispatches had arrived at intervals in the city, each one bringing fresh revelations from his rampage through Florida. Sensing danger, in late May President Monroe had fled the city for his Albemarle farm. Luis de Onís, the Spanish ambassador, began peppering Adams with letters from his summer retreat in Pennsylvania and then announced his intention to return to the city to lodge a formal complaint.

The final bombshell did not land until 7 July, when news broke that Jackson had seized Pensacola and raised the American flag above sovereign Spanish territory. The same night, Adams was woken in his sleep by a servant, sent by Onís, demanding an immediate meeting. The next day, the French ambassador came to his house in a state of great agitation, speaking of events of Florida 'in a very grave tone; shaking his head and saying it was a very disagreeable affair'.

As the significance of what Jackson had done began to sink in, panic took hold at the highest levels of government. It seemed as though in a matter of weeks Jackson had managed to involve the United States in a war with both Spain and the United Kingdom.

The news had reached Europe, where it created an uproar. Albert Gallatin, then serving as minister to France, reported from Paris that the cost of insurance on American shipping had shot up in anticipation of a conflict.

In London, Castlereagh later told the American ambassador, 'Such was the temper of parliament, and the feeling of the country' when the executions of Ambrister and Arbuthnot became public knowledge 'that war might have been produced by holding up a finger'.[1]

Monroe did not return to Washington until 14 July, but when he did so he was quickly immersed in the scandal. Reflecting the intensity of the crisis, his cabinet met four times that week. There were a number of complaints against Jackson; among them that he had violated the Constitution, broken international law and disobeyed direct orders from the president.

That he might have entangled his country in a global war was a problem of a different magnitude altogether.

The cabinet was unified in its condemnation. They advised the president to distance himself from the rogue general and initiate a formal investigation into his actions. None was more insistent or more violent in their condemnation than Secretary of War Calhoun, who was personally affronted (and perhaps personally exposed) by Jackson's insubordination.

There was, however, one man in the cabinet who defended Jackson and did so firmly, persistently and brilliantly: Secretary of State John Quincy Adams.[2]

## THE MAN FROM BRAINTREE

The period from the Battle of New Orleans to the end of Monroe's presidency is remembered as the Era of Good Feelings, when the country enjoyed a decade of political consensus, national unity and public confidence.

There was perhaps no better illustration of this sense of common purpose than a man as different from Andrew Jackson as John Quincy Adams coming to the general's political rescue in the scorching summer of 1818.

Adams's background was as illustrious as Jackson's was obscure. In his family tree was Saer de Quincy, a Norman noble who signed the Magna Carta at Runnymede in 1215. More immediately, Adams was the son of President John Adams and a relative of the revolutionary hero Samuel Adams. His family were New England puritans through and through. Both his grandfathers were clergymen; his father and his grandfather were Harvard graduates.

Far from being crushed by the weight of his forefathers' achievements, Adams set out to exceed them on every count. Not only did he attend Harvard, but he graduated in two years and ended up serving on its Board of Overseers.

Not only did he throw himself into public service, but he occupied his first government role – as secretary to Francis Dana, the first American minister to Russia – at the age of only fourteen. He was appointed ambassador to Netherlands at twenty-seven and would also serve as ambassador to Prussia, Russia and England, and as a negotiator at Ghent. In between stints overseas he served as a senator for Massachusetts for five years, during which time he committed what one observer called 'political patricide' by splitting from the Federalists – the party his father had led – over the issue of the Louisiana Purchase, which he enthusiastically supported.

Not only did he, like his father, practise law, but he was offered a seat on the Supreme Court by Madison, though he turned it down – to his father's horror – to pursue other avenues of advancement.

Not only did he, through all his wanderings, maintain the mores of his New England heritage, but he became the very embodiment of the prim, fanatically hard-working Yankee. In the opulent court of Tsar Alexander, he successfully negotiated an exemption from the dress requirements on the grounds that they could not be reconciled with either Protestant sobriety or republican thrift. In Washington, his working day began at four with an hour-long swim in the Potomac, nude except for some thick goggles and a cap. He usually attended church in the morning and spent his evenings in prayer and reflection. In between, he regularly worked twelve-hour days and still found time to serve as vice president of the American Bible Society and president of the American Academy of Arts and Sciences.

On the side, he was an omnivorous reader and composed verse of some accomplishment. 'Could I have chosen my own genius and condition,' he once wrote, 'I should have made myself a great poet.' Yet he remained one of the great stylists of his age, with no less an authority than Jefferson praising his 'pointed pen'. He poured his literary efforts into his journal, which he faithfully kept for seventy-one years, producing in the process the greatest document of his age or any age. Nowhere was Adams more at home than on the page, levelling someone with his quill. His acid takedowns of contemporaries (such as his passing remark on the 'ravenous imbecility' of a Tennessee congressman) make for enjoyable reading, but they offer a glimpse of an ineffably superior, unlikeable man. Even his friends found him hard work. 'Mr. Adams [is] very civil but has a disagreeable manner,' wrote one. 'He is from New England, a "Yankee."'[3]

What set Adams apart from his contemporaries was the sheer amount of time he had spent abroad. By the time he was summoned to Washington in 1817, to serve as Monroe's secretary of state, he had spent twenty-two of his fifty years overseas. He had met virtually every major European statesman of his day and experienced first-hand more historical drama than most people would experience in several lifetimes. Within a three-year period, he was in St Petersburg when Napoleon burned down Moscow, in Paris during the Hundred Days and in London when news arrived of Wellington's victory at Waterloo.

According to popular prejudice, such a long period abroad ought to have corrupted Adams's pure American republicanism. In fact the opposite was the case. In London, Paris and St Petersburg, Adams had seen how American diplomats were humiliated by the older powers of Europe. While transiting through Scandinavia in 1809, he had come across several hundred American merchant seamen who had been seized by Danish privateers and were stranded in a strange country without so much as a consul to plead their case. Most poignantly, when he arrived in Berlin in 1797, he was questioned 'at the gates by a dapper lieutenant, who did not know until one of his private soldiers explained to him, who the United States of America were'.[4]

While many Americans wallowed in self-satisfaction, Adams had been abroad and had experienced the parlous position of America in the world. Outrage at the mistreatment of his country and his countrymen fuelled his nationalism. For Adams, the struggle for America's recognition in international affairs was not a matter of abstract symbolism, but one of desperate importance.

In a telling episode during the negotiations at Ghent, Adams refused to sign the final treaty over the seemingly insignificant issue of the *alternat*, the custom whereby in the duplicates of treaties the precedence of names was reversed to ensure symbolic equality between signatory nations.* Up till then, Anglo-American diplomatic agreements had not followed the custom of the *alternat*. When he saw the wording of the treaty, Adams made a stand on principle, to the dismay of his fellow negotiators, Henry Clay and Albert Gallatin. Clay claimed the *alternat* was 'a matter of no consequence' and that republican America should not care for Old World 'punctilios', to which Adams replied it was precisely because it was 'a point to which all the European Powers always adhered' that the United States should insist on it. Gallatin complained that Adams's stubbornness would 'throw the whole business into confusion', to which a furious Adams replied:

> Mr Gallatin, you and Mr Clay may do as you please; but I will not sign the Treaty, without the alternative [*alternat*], observed throughout.
> Now don't fly off in this manner, said Mr Gallatin.
> Indeed Sir, said I; I will not sign the Treaty in any other form.

Adams got his way, and the treaty (and every subsequent treaty) with Britain followed the convention he had fought for at Ghent. It was a small, hard-won victory for America's recognition as an equal player in the game of international diplomacy.[5]

It was this insistence that America had to assert itself in the world that gave Adams common cause with Jackson in 1818. Using all his powers of persuasion in successive cabinet meetings that July, he convinced Monroe to view Jackson's actions as an opportunity for the final settling of the Florida question. In so doing, Adams cited precedent from every conceivable legal authority – but this was window-dressing. Legal or not, Jackson's incursion had made facts on

---

\* For instance, if a line in one copy of the treaty read 'an agreement between Great Britain and the United States', the same line in the duplicate would read 'an agreement between the United States and Great Britain'. In other words, the order of precedence alternates – hence the French *alternat*.

the ground that his government had to either support or condemn. As the general said in his own inimitable style: 'Damn Grotius! Damn Pufendorf! Damn Vattel! This is a mere matter between Jim Monroe and myself.'*

Indeed it was. If Monroe disavowed Jackson, he was by implication disavowing the United States' right to ensure the security of its southern frontier. Jackson had made explicit through force what was implicit in the administration's diplomacy, namely the centrality of Florida to the United States' strategic interests. The fortunes of the two men were now bound together.[6]

Monroe capitulated to the force of Adams's arguments. With regard to Jackson, he limited himself to sending the general a carefully worded letter chiding him for 'transcending' his orders and requesting the end of military action in Florida and the restoration of Spanish authority in Pensacola and St Marks.

In the meantime, he gave his secretary of state permission to try and bring negotiations with the Spanish to a satisfactory conclusion.[7]

Ever since Ferdinand VII's restoration in 1814, the United States and Spain had been involved in fitful negotiations to regularize relations. The principal points of discussion were the establishment of a western limit to the Louisiana Purchase (in doubt as the Spanish had never recognized its legality), the attitude of the United States towards Spain's rebellious colonies in Latin America, outstanding spoliation claims made by American merchants against Spain, and the Florida question.

Negotiations had been hamstrung by the selection of Onís to represent the Spanish Crown. Onís had never forgiven the Americans for refusing to recognize him as the legitimate representative of Spain during the years that Joseph Bonaparte ruled from Madrid. This anger found expression in a letter in which he fantasized that the English would invade Louisiana, partition the United States and render it a 'nullity' in world affairs. This letter fell into the hands of Venezuelan revolutionaries, who shared it with the Americans. Thereafter, Onís was *persona non grata*. It was only in 1817 that the Americans finally

---

* One congressman who knew both men quipped: 'Jackson made law, Adams quoted it.'

and grudgingly accepted him as the Spanish representative in Washington. For his part, Adams disliked the man, describing him as 'cold, calculating, wily ... proud because he is a Spaniard, but supple and cunning'.[8]

Irrespective of their mutual antipathy, both sides needed a deal. The United States wanted Florida before anyone else – the British foremost in their minds – laid claim to it. Spain wanted to neutralize the United States, so they could focus their energies on rolling back the tide of revolution sweeping through their Latin American possessions. The sticking point was on how to reach a deal. The Spanish pushed for mediation through a third party; the Americans insisted on a bilateral agreement. If Spain could convince the great powers of Europe to agree to mediation, American policy would be thrown into disarray. Once more the fate of Florida hinged on decisions made in Europe.

In England, public revulsion at the summary execution of Arbuthnot and Ambrister was captured in a satirical cartoon by George Cruikshank. Titled 'American Justice', it depicted Jackson as a deranged pirate, with daggers stuffed between his belt and blood-stained britches. A skeletal army stands behind him as he receives a piece of paper with 'the government of the Floridas' written on it from a mad-eyed James Monroe, who sits on a throne beneath a pair of crossed and bloody knives with 'Indian Blood' and 'English Blood' written above them. A speech bubble captures Monroe's instructions to his general: 'Where e'er you catch the English String 'em up like Herrings! – Go, Rob the Indians! Seize their Country! Sell 'em for Slaves!' In the background, we see Arbuthnot and

*George Cruikshank's cartoon 'American Justice' lampooned Monroe's policy in Florida.*

Ambrister in heaven, appealing for justice from Britannia, while an angry British lion glares at Jackson.[9]

Cruikshank's cartoon reflected the outrage of the British press over goings-on in Florida. But in 1819 Britain was not a democracy and the men who managed Britain's foreign affairs prided themselves on their indifference to public sentiment. In the Commons, Earl Bathurst observed that both Arbuthnot and Ambrister had been in Florida in a private capacity, which therefore 'exempted the government of this country from the necessity of embarking in a demand of reparation, which must have led to a war if persisted in'. And in the summer of 1818, an Anglo-American war was the furthest thing from British minds. Nothing – not even the murder of two British subjects – would disturb Castlereagh's policy of repose.[10]

Peaceable, profitable relations with America were the carrot. The stick, in Castlereagh's mind, was the united front America's leadership displayed to the world. That November, Adams sent a long and impassioned account of how he viewed Jackson's actions in Florida to the American minister in Spain. The letter was published well before it reached Madrid and was aimed at a domestic audience. It was remarkable for its appeal to sentiment and its vivid accounts of Indian violence in the Florida borderlands – Adams even recounted lurid stories of women and infants having their brains dashed out on the sides of boats by Indian soldiers. Adams referred to the Indian and Black inhabitants of East Florida as 'banditti', 'savages', 'outlaws' and 'malefactors', and accused Arbuthnot and Ambrister of having whipped up a 'savage, servile, exterminating war against the United States'. Perhaps most strikingly for a man who that year was immersed in two separate negotiations over the placement of international borderlines, he described the Spanish-American border in Florida as an 'imaginary line' of little consequence. Adams ensured that this language was repeated in Monroe's State of the Union address the same month. But this was not Adams's language – it was cribbed from Jackson's own dispatches from Florida. John Quincy Adams, Harvard graduate and man of letters, who had never seen a cotton field, much less a mangrove swamp, aped the language of the southern frontier to advance American policy.[11]

\* \* \*

It worked. Castlereagh was impressed by American cohesion and ultimately realistic about the fate of Florida. Might made right. The inability of Spain to protect itself spoke volumes. 'Spain is weak. You are strong,' he told the American ambassador.

And Britain would rather wed itself to strength than to weakness. Castlereagh's patience with Ferdinand and his ministers was at an end. Britain would no longer backstop Spanish blundering in Florida or anywhere else. By 1818, it was clear that the Spanish had no more cards to play. That November, Onís was sent orders to strike a deal with Washington.[12]

By January 1819, the broad outlines of a treaty were agreed upon. Spain would cede the Floridas in their entirety, in exchange for the United States forgiving $5 million worth of spoliation claims. The United States renounced all claims to Texas, and promised not to recognize any of the new South American republics.

All that remained was the matter of the western border of the Louisiana Purchase. In the South, there was little doubt about the United States' priorities. Huddled together over a map on 3 February, Jackson gave Adams his blessing for a compromise on the Sabine River as the new Spanish-American border – what is today the state line between Texas and Louisiana.

'The possession of the Floridas was of so great importance to the Southern frontier of the United States, and so essential even to their safety,' Jackson said, that the surrender of an American claim to Texas was worthwhile so long as the United States secured control of 'the Mouths of the Florida Rivers'.

Adams and Onís hammered out a line that went due north from the mouth of the Sabine until it hit the Red River. Then it followed that river until 100 degrees west longitude, where it broke northwards until it struck the Arkansas River, which it followed to its source.

The border ought to have followed the Rocky Mountains north to the Canadian border. The Continental Divide – as Lewis and Clark had proven in 1805 – was indubitably the limit of the Louisiana Purchase. But Adams had grander ideas.

On 15 February, 'after a long and violent struggle', Onís agreed to a line that ran due west along the 42nd parallel across the Rockies to the Pacific. At a stroke, and acting quite independently, Adams had won for the first time recognition that the United States was a transcontinental power encompassing the Atlantic and Pacific oceans.

On 22 February, the two diplomats signed and sealed the treaty. Two days later it was ratified in the United States Senate. America had a new border that moved by stages from the Gulf of Mexico to the shores of the Pacific Northwest, the so-called 'Step Boundary'.

Adams was triumphant. 'The acknowledgment of a definite line of boundary to the South Sea, forms a great Epocha [*sic*] in our History,' he wrote in his diary. 'The first proposal of it in this Negotiation was my own ... I first introduced it ... I record the first assertion of this claim for the United States as my own; because it is known to be mine, perhaps only to the members of the present Administration; and may perhaps never be known to the public.' In fact, the treaty went down in history as both the Adams–Onís Treaty and the Transcontinental Treaty. Adams's contribution was not forgotten.[13]

Monroe claimed his share of the glory as well. In a triumphant swing through the South that summer, he soaked in the acclaim of the crowds for his muscular defence of American interests. In Huntsville in June,

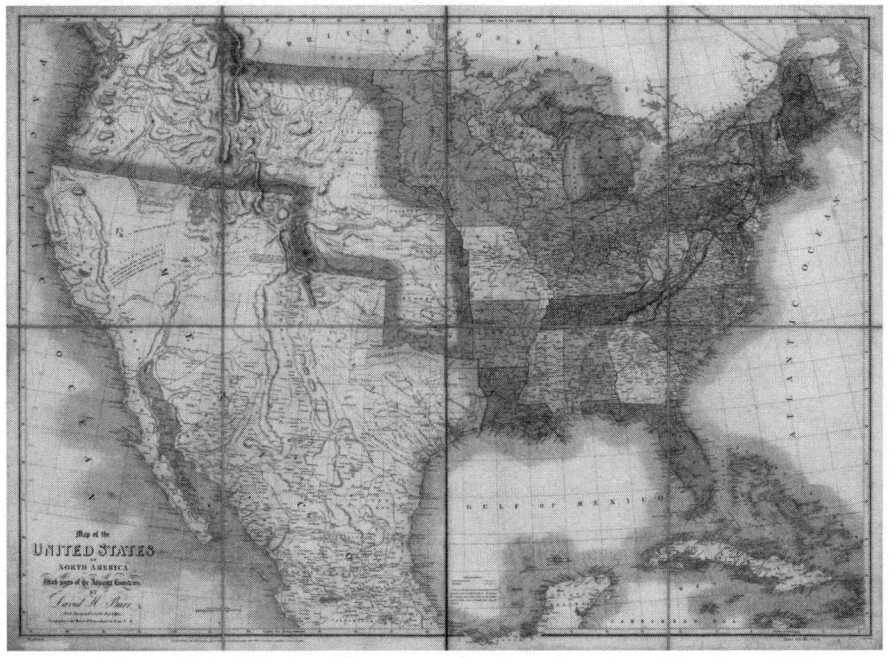

*A map of the 'Step Boundary' produced by the Adams-Onís treaty.*

Monroe banqueted with local grandees. As was custom, rounds of toasts followed the meal. They raised their glasses to the president, to Andrew Jackson, to John Coffee, to the heroes of the Battle of New Orleans, to the men of the West and to 'The Late Treaty with Spain – It finishes the work begun by the acquisition of Louisiana'. The Huntsville *Republican* praised the treaty in fulsome terms: 'It rounds off our southern possessions and forever precludes foreign emissaries from stirring up Indians to war and Negroes to rebellion, whilst it gives to the Southern country important outlets to the sea ... It is [a treaty] that fully comes up to the expectations of the great body of the American people.'[14]

## A COURSE THROUGH THE OCEAN OF TIME

The Spanish took two years to ratify the treaty and it was not until 17 July 1821 that the formal handover ceremony was conducted in Pensacola. Monroe had asked Jackson to be the first governor of the new territory of Florida and he had accepted. Fittingly enough, then, it was Jackson who took possession of the town that day, finally making legal what he had long sought to do extra-legally. At ten that morning, Colonel José Callava, the governor of Pensacola handed over the keys, documents and archives of the town to Jackson and then the two men watched the lowering of the Spanish flag and the raising of the American one as the band played 'The Star-Spangled Banner'. A ship offshore fired a salute. Three hundred years of Spanish rule in Florida was at an end.[15]

While the transfer of Florida was a relief, the passage of two years had done little to calm American anxieties about the broader strategic picture in the Gulf of Mexico and beyond.

Even as its authority collapsed, Spain remained a thorn in America's side. In 1820, Spanish troops at Cadiz, bound for South America to put down the ongoing wars of independence, mutinied. The revolution that followed imposed a liberal constitution on Ferdinand VII. For a period it looked as though Madrid might tack towards a policy of accommodation with its colonies. But Ferdinand remained immune to reason. Behind the liberals' backs, he plotted with the French to restore his absolute rule at home and abroad. In 1822, he stage-managed a French invasion of Spain in 1823 that toppled the liberals. Soon alarming rumours circulated in Washington that 12,000 French soldiers were preparing to depart for South America – and who could tell what visions of American empire might resurface in French minds once they disembarked there.[16]

Threats were proliferating on other fronts as well. In September 1821, Tsar Alexander issued a decree claiming for Russia exclusive control of the Pacific Northwest coastline as far south as 45° 50' north latitude (essentially everything north of California) and excluding Americans from its waters. This was a shocking development and seemed to be a prelude to greater Russian involvement all along the Pacific Rim.[17]

Meanwhile, British commercial penetration in South America continued apace. A visitor to Chile in 1821 recorded that Chileans were clothed and fed by English merchants, read English newspapers, used English technologies and followed English fashions. British vessels dominated the coastal trade between Concepción and Copiapó. Bernardo O'Higgins, the 'Supreme Director' of the revolutionary Chilean state, had been educated in London and had hired a former Royal Navy admiral, Thomas Cochrane, to run the Chilean navy. In London, British banks raised a series of high-profile loans to fund the nascent states of Chile, Peru, Argentina and Colombia,* all with an end of drawing South America into economic dependency on the United Kingdom.† Without firing a shot, it seemed as though the English had established a sphere of influence in America's backyard.[18]

All of this disturbed America's leaders. In his diary, John Quincy Adams sketched out the doomsday scenario:

---

* In 1822 Gregor MacGregor, the Scotsman who had briefly occupied Amelia Island in 1817, got in on the action. He set himself up as 'Cacique' of the fictional central American kingdom of Poyais (his Vice-Cacique was former Royal Marine George Woodbine) and raised a loan of £200,000 on the London money markets. The flag of the Kingdom of Poyais was a green St George's cross on a field of white – the same that had flown above his short-lived Republic of the Floridas. When settlers arrived in Poyais and discovered it did not exist, a scandal erupted and MacGregor fled to France.

† 'Americans were keenly aware and highly critical of Britain's informal imperialism throughout the period between 1815 and 1860. From Argentina, for example, Acting Chargé d'Affaires John M. Forbes wrote that "England derives from this Country and Chile all the advantages of colonial dependence without the responsibility or expence of Civil or Military administration"' (Kinley J. Brauer, 'The United States and British Imperial Expansion, 1815–60', *Diplomatic History*, 12/1 (1988), 19–37).

> If then the Holy Allies, should subdue Spanish America, however they might at first set up the Standard of Spain, the ultimate result of their undertaking would be to recolonize them partitioned out among themselves – Russia might take California, Peru, Chile – France, Mexico where we know she has been intriguing to get a Monarchy under a Prince of the House of Bourbon, as well as at Buenos Ayres – And Great Britain as her last resort, if she could not resist this course of things would take at least the Island of Cuba, for her share of the scramble. Then what would be our situation. England holding Cuba – France, Mexico.[19]

Then, unexpectedly, in the summer of 1823 the English came to the rescue. That August, George Canning, the new British foreign secretary, made a remarkable offer to Richard Rush, the American ambassador in London. Ever since the Congress of Aix-la-Chapelle in 1818, the British had soured on the quintuple alliance forged following Napoleon's defeat. Under the auspices of the peculiar conservative utopianism of Tsar Alexander and the rabid reactionary spirit of Metternich and others, the congress system established at the Congress of Vienna had morphed into something intolerable to Whitehall. In a statement of Britain's foreign policy principles, the Foreign Office castigated the congress system as having transformed itself from a body with the limited aim of securing peace in Europe into a 'Union for the Government of the World' that had arrogated to itself the right of 'Superintendence of the Internal Affairs of other States'. Britain desired a policy of non-intervention, not one of endless meddling. The final rupture came at the Congress of Verona in 1822, where the Duke of Wellington, representing Britain, stormed out, telling the other attendees: 'We stand alone and we do so by choice.'

Thereafter, England's rupture with Spain was complete. Canning moved to recognize the independence of Latin America and so end more than a decade of equivocation. It was in this context that he approached Rush and suggested that the English and the Americans might put forward a joint statement declaring the irreversible fact of South American independence, their disavowal of any imperial designs on that continent and their opposition to any attempt by a European power to reimpose colonial rule on that continent. Rush communicated this extraordinary proposal to Adams and Monroe, setting the stage for a climactic statement of the United States' own foreign policy principles.[20]

Monroe informed his inner circle of Castlereagh's offer and canvassed opinion on how he should respond.

Few doubted the significance of the proposal. Jefferson described it as 'the most momentous which has ever been offered to my contemplation since that of independence ... this sets our compass, and points the course which we are to steer thro' the ocean of time'. At stake was not just the future of American policy and the Anglo-American relationship, but also the political complexion of the entire western hemisphere.

At home, public support for the South American independence movements was reaching its apogee. The leaders of the revolutionary struggle were celebrities to regular Americans. There were two hundred children christened Bolivar, twelve states had towns named after him – even Andrew Jackson's prize colt stud was named after the Venezuelan hero. At Fourth of July banquets and other civic occasions, toasts were regularly drunk to the cause of independence. At the dinner Monroe attended in Huntsville in 1819, a glass was raised to 'the friends of freedom in South America – struggling as we have done, may they become as we are'.

Among the political class, those who hearkened back to the days of America's revolutionary glory projected their republican ideals onto the politics of South American independence. Henry Clay emerged as the most enthusiastic exponent of the cause, rhapsodizing over 'glorious spectacle of eighteen millions of people, struggling to burst their chains and to be free', and insisting that 'the independence ... of Spanish America [was] an interest of primary consideration' to the United States.

Support went beyond mere rhetoric. Privateers and volunteer brigades were outfitted in New York, Baltimore and New Orleans. There was an embarrassing incident in 1816 when it emerged that the United States military was supplying gunpowder from its own arsenals to Venezuelan rebels.

Of course, there was also money at stake. Americans fantasized about the day when the 'indolence' of Spanish rule was thrown off and the riches of South America were 'laid open to the industry and enterprize of the more active part of mankind'. Monroe had already dispatched commercial agents across the Caribbean and the continent. Now, with the cession of Florida accomplished, the United States should proceed with recognition and take the spoils of independence.[21]

Everyone Monroe consulted said he should accept Canning's offer – everyone except John Quincy Adams. The secretary of state was, like many New Englanders, less enthusiastic about the South American cause. As his friend (and fellow Yankee) Edward Everett put it, 'we have no concern with South America; we have no sympathy ... Not all the treaties we could make, nor the money we could lend them, would transform their Pueyrredons and their Artigases, into Adamses or Franklins, or their Bolivars into Washingtons.' (In a private letter to his brother, Adams was even more damning, writing that to compare the revolutionary heroes of Latin America with Cervantes's Sancho Panza was to do 'injustice to the wisdom and moderation of the sagacious Squire of the valiant Knight of La Mancha'.)*

From a foreign policy perspective, Adams was suspicious of the interventionism espoused by Clay and others. He believed it was subversive of republican principles. It was not the role of American foreign policy to go 'abroad, in search of monsters to destroy'. As Monroe's secretary of state, he had presided over the president's policy of recognizing the independence of the new states – starting with Colombia in 1821 – but insisted this was done in the spirit of realism. Adams's policy was not so far off Canning's one of non-intervention. But native pride forbade Adams from following Britain when it came to relations in America's own backyard. He had no intention of letting the United States become the 'cockboat [sailing] in the wake of the British man-of-war'. The United States, Adams declared, ought to hew to an independent policy and declare its own interests in South America, unencumbered by association with another country.[22]

* * *

---

* His scepticism was shared by his father, who on one occasion declared that the project of Venezuelan independence planned by Francisco de Miranda was 'as visionary, though far less innocent, than that of his countryman Gonzalez, of an excursion to the Moon in a car drawn by geese trained and disciplined for the purpose' (John Adams to James Lloyd, 27 Mar. 1815).

Adams, once more, won the day. The result was the Monroe Doctrine, proclaimed before Congress on 2 December 1823, which declared it 'a principle in which the rights and interests of the United States are involved, that the American continents, by the free and independent condition which they have assumed and maintain, are henceforth not to be considered as subjects for future colonization by any European powers'.

The debate continues to this day as to whether the Monroe Doctrine was a statement of Pan-American idealism or a naked assertion of the United States' hegemony in the western hemisphere.

If the latter, then it was not a particularly convincing one. In 1822, an emissary of a group of Cuban politicians and planters arrived in Washington asking the United States to annex their island. Cuba – which Americans had dreamt of possessing for decades – was within their grasp. Yet after much discussion it was decided that the United States could not risk antagonizing Britain, and so a reluctant Monroe refused the offer. Despite the bluster, the United States still had to tread lightly in its own backyard.[23]

What is not in doubt is that the Monroe Doctrine arose out of the struggle for Florida. It was an extension of the No-Transfer Resolution to the entire western hemisphere.

A secret policy born of the murky contest for the West Florida borderlands became the inspiration for the most influential statement of American foreign policy interests.

And even though the Monroe Doctrine was not enforceable in 1823, it reflected a new-found geopolitical confidence following America's annexation of the Floridas. With control of the Straits of Florida and the greater part of the Gulf Coast, America could now project power southwards as never before.

Although America did not begin consistently asserting its supremacy in this region for another couple of decades, that it would be able to do so at all was the product of a decade of warfare and diplomacy focused on bringing Florida into the Union.

And once America began to involve itself in the Caribbean and South America, it did so with zeal. It has been conventional, especially during the Cold War, to understand the troubled relationship between the United States and its neighbours as rooted in ideological differences. This is not the case. As the American ambassador to Panama observed in 1980, 'What we see in Central America today would not be much different if Fidel Castro and the Soviet Union did not exist.' It was the geopolitical revolution accomplished by the acquisition of Florida that made possible all that followed. The origins of the United States' grim record of overt and clandestine involvement in Cuba, Chile, Brazil, Mexico, Bolivia, Grenada, Costa Rica, Colombia, Ecuador, Nicaragua, Jamaica, Honduras, Panama, Paraguay, Guatemala, Haiti, the Dominican Republic and Venezuela lie in the struggle for Florida. And the methods the United States used to secure Florida – the dirty wars, the coups, the illegal invasions, the political subversion – were later rolled out across the rest of the hemisphere.[24]

In 1823, all this lay in the future. Adams viewed the United States' victory as being essentially tactical. He had steered its policy between the Scylla of British influence* and the Charybdis of utopian internationalism.

Indeed, Adams believed that he – more than the president – had delivered every major policy victory of the Monroe administration. 'Of the Public History of Mr Monroe's Administration,' he boasted to his wife, 'all that will be worth telling to Posterity hitherto has been transacted through the Department of State – The Treaties with Great-Britain, with Spain, with France and with Russia, and the whole course of policy with regard to South America ... The acquisition of Florida, and the extension of the territories of the Union to the Pacific Ocean ... the formal admission of our right to border upon the South-Sea ... has been first obtained, I might confidently say by me.'

He had justifiably high hopes for his chances in the 1824 presidential election. His opponent for the highest office would be Andrew Jackson.[25]

---

* Adams had accurately forecast that there was no cost in turning down the British offer. Canning went ahead with recognizing the South American republics and bragged to the Commons that he had 'called the New World into existence to redress the balance of the Old'. Moreover, he believed he had put the new republics firmly into the British camp: 'Spanish America is free, and if we do not mismanage our affairs sadly, she is English.'

# The Widower

On the morning of 4 March 1829, Andrew Jackson stood on the East Portico of the Capitol Building and faced the 20,000-strong crowd who had come to watch him assume the presidency.

It was not a happy day for Jackson. He believed he ought to have taken office four years before. Jackson had won the most electoral college seats in 1824, but not enough to get a clear majority. The election had gone to the House, where Henry Clay engineered a victory for John Quincy Adams, in exchange for becoming his secretary of state. Jackson damned Clay as 'the Judas of the West' and told his supporters the Republic had been sold out. He retreated to Tennessee.

In 1828, he ran again, in a notoriously dirty contest against the incumbent Adams. The election became a referendum on Jackson's conduct during his wars in the Florida borderlands.

Jackson had always known how he was perceived in Washington. At times, he made light of it, joking how people expected to meet him with 'a Tomahawk in one hand, and a scalping knife in the other'.

But the election of 1828 went beyond that. Adams's supporters published handbills with black coffins representing each extrajudicial killing committed during Jackson's various campaigns. They included two apiece for Ambrister and Arbuthnot, and Hidlis Hadjo and Himollemico. The accompanying text recounted the massacres at Tallushatchee, Talladega and Horseshoe Bend, and claimed that Jackson had breakfasted on dead Indians.

The Grand Guignol was for the masses. The political elite focused on Jackson's high-handed manner during his various rampages through the Floridas. During a hearing on the Seminole War, Clay had warned that Jackson was the man on the white horse that augured the end of the Republic. 'Beware how you give a fatal sanction ... to military insubordination,' he told the House. 'Remember that Greece had her Alexander, Rome her Caesar, England her Cromwell, France her Bonaparte.' Jackson – who as a child had been whipped by a British officer's sabre during the Revolutionary War – was now described as 'monarchical' and dubbed 'King Andrew'.

All of this grated. But what he found unforgivable were the smears made against his wife, Rachel. 'I have made many sacrifices for the good of my country,' Jackson complained to John Coffee, 'but the present, being placed in a situation that I cannot act, and punish those slanderers, not only of me, but Mrs. J. is a sacrifice too great to be well endured.' Only days after he won the election by a landslide, Rachel died. Jackson believed his enemies had killed her.

He was still in mourning when he looked over the crowd that March day. Dressed all in black, hatless in reverence to the people, he still had a bullet in his chest from an 1806 duel, and another in his arm from his barroom brawl with Thomas and Jesse Benton; he was gaunt, sickly and heartbroken. Only days before, rumours had circulated that he had died of the ill health that had plagued him for years. But Jackson would give his enemies no such satisfaction. John Quincy Adams had gossiped in his diary about Jackson's rumoured death; when he arrived in Washington very much alive, Adams refused to come to the inauguration. Jackson stood before the American public – his public – as the anguished, wrathful, solitary and singular man he had always been, and proceeded to give one of the shortest inaugural addresses in American history.[1]

## GIVE, GIVE, GIVE!!

As Jackson stood on the steps of the Capitol, between 50,000 and 60,000 southern Indians still lived on some 100 million acres of land, amounting to one-tenth of Georgia, one-sixth of Alabama and half each of Mississippi and Florida.

In his speech, Jackson made a passing reference to this fact, a single line in which he promised 'to observe toward the Indian tribes within our limits a just and liberal policy'.

This was either understatement or deception. For after twenty years, the Gulf Plains were still neither secure from foreign influence nor safe for white settlers. This was an affront both to Jackson's strategic vision and his inaugural promise that the government be 'administered for the good of the people, and ... regulated by their will'. The people wanted land. Jackson would give it to them.[2]

Jackson made his real Indian policy plain at the State of the Union address that December. In his speech, he noted that hitherto the stated aim of United States policy was to 'civilize' the Indians. This policy had failed as the Indians had 'retained their savage habits'. Now, surrounded by whites and incapable of adapting to new conditions, they faced extinction. 'The fate of the Mohegan, the Narragansett, and the Delaware,' Jackson told Congress, 'is fast over-taking the Choctaw, the Cherokee, and the Creek.' To avoid this outcome, Jackson proposed a new policy, 'removal', whereby Indians would sign over their existing lands to the United States government in exchange for new lands west of the Mississippi, in modern-day Arkansas and Oklahoma. The government would assist by organizing and funding their voyage west, and even compensate them for any improvements they left behind.

Removal was not Jackson's invention. In his proposed constitutional amendment to enable the Louisiana Purchase, Jefferson had suggested a similar solution. In the administrations of James Monroe and John Quincy Adams, removal had been openly discussed.

But Jackson had been obsessing over removal for much longer and had far more experience of native peoples than any of his predecessors.

In July 1817, Jackson had negotiated a treaty with the Cherokee which stated that the United States would match 'acre for acre' all Cherokee land surrendered to the east of the Mississippi with corresponding lands to the west. Each Cherokee warrior would receive a rifle, a blanket and either a brass kettle or a beaver trap as 'full compensation for the improvements which they may leave'. The United States also agreed 'to furnish flat bottomed boats and provisions' for the journey west.

Jackson was overjoyed when the Cherokee signed. In a letter to John Coffee, he claimed that though the land at stake was 'unimportant', the 'principle established by the treaty' was vital. Jackson genuinely viewed it as a win-win. He had secured 'the permanent happiness of the Cherokee nation' in Arkansas and had turned their former lands into the 'peaceful abode for the honest citizen protected by our laws'.

Ever since that treaty, groups of Indians had been travelling west under similar terms, demonstrating to Jackson that removal was a viable policy.[3]

Those Indians who remained on their ancestral lands – which was the vast majority – were sceptical. One Creek leader told a British naval officer that 'the Americans ... wished to get rid of them, and had offered them other lands beyond the Mississippi, but of such barren land that it would be impossible for them to subsist there'. Others rightly asked what guarantees they would have that those new lands would not in turn be taken from them. After all, the southern tribes were living on far less land than they had done only a generation before. White hunger for land was the one constant in all their dealings with Americans. There seemed no reason why their appetite would be satiated at the banks of the Mississippi. Nor was it obvious why they should move at all. Their current tribal lands were secured by treaties. The United States government had recognized their possession. Far from living a 'wandering life', most southern Indians were sedentary agriculturists. Why would they consent to losing all they owned and being herded to a strange and distant land? Jackson did not dispute this. In his address to Congress, he had insisted that 'this emigration should be voluntary, for it would be as cruel as unjust to compel the aborigines to abandon the graves of their fathers'. However, as he well knew, circumstances had conspired to ensure that this decision would be forced upon them.[4]

On 28 May 1830 the Indian Removal Act became law. Its passage through Congress was a hard-won victory for the Jackson administration. Northern evangelicals in the Senate unleashed a devastating rhetorical cannonade on the policy. Theodore Frelinghuysen, senator for New Jersey and former president of the American Board of Commissioners for Foreign Missions, provided a damning survey of American policy towards the Indians:

> As the tide of our population rolled on, we have added purchase to purchase. The confiding Indian listened to our professions of friendship. We called him brother, and he believed us. Millions after millions he has yielded to our importunity, until we have acquired more than can be cultivated in centuries, and yet we

crave more. We have crowded the tribes upon a few miserable acres on our southern frontier: it is all that is left to them of their once boundless forests, and still, like the horse leech, our insatiable cupidity cries, give, give, give!![5]

Slave state votes in the Senate ensured a majority for removal. It was much closer in the House, where amid numerous defections it squeezed by with a majority of only five votes. Among those who voted against the policy was Davy Crockett, congressman for Tennessee and veteran of the Red Stick War. When his party handlers told him to vote for it, he responded that 'I believed it was a wicked, unjust measure, and that I should go against it, let the cost to myself be what it might.' His vote did indeed cost him his seat at the next election, and soon he was on his way to Texas.[6]

Having won the vote, the administration now had to go out and negotiate voluntary treaties with each of the southern tribes. Jackson had good reason to be confident about the prospects for these negotiations.

A month after his election, and a few days before Rachel died, the Georgia legislature passed a measure extending the laws of the state over the Indians within its limits. Over the next year Alabama, Mississippi and Tennessee followed suit. At first glance, it might not be obvious why this step was such a calamity for the Indians. After all, the United States was a union of states and everyone had to abide by state as well as federal law. But one need only reflect on how state law was used in the Jim Crow era to immiserate the black population to get an inkling of the disaster this represented.

In fact, one of Jackson's correspondents made the exact same parallel, observing to the president that by those new laws Indians could 'be treated as free persons of Colour' and 'that point alone [ought to] fetch the whole nation to reflection'.

The states made every effort to introduce laws that made life impossible for Indians. Indian tribal administrations were dissolved, their assemblies banned, their ranks abolished. They would be punished for attempting to establish and enforce their own laws and were simultaneously forbidden to vote, bring suit or testify in white courts. Indians could face imprisonment for discussing or organizing resistance to land cessions or to removal, yet were also subject to state taxes and militia duty, and could be sued for debt. Indians were denied all the basic rights of citizenship while being burdened with all its responsibilities. In effect, they were reduced to the status of a subject people wholly dependent on the mercy of the surrounding white population.

'Under the administration of [Georgia] law,' one white anti-removal activist wrote, 'a white man might rob or murder a Cherokee, in the presence of many Indians, and descendants of Indians; and yet the offence could not be proved ... He is exposed to the greatest evils of slavery, without any of its alleviations ... How long could a Cherokee live under such treatment as this?'[7]

It was a Kafkaesque situation, by equal measures cruel and absurd – and Americans well knew it. Some proponents of removal seemed to exult in the fact that, once exposed to the reality of living under American laws, the Indians would gladly flee westwards. 'Take from them their own code of laws, and reduce them to plain citizenship,' Coffee told Jackson, 'and they will soon determine to move.'[8]

Jackson himself took no delight in the Indians' dilemma but was more than happy to use the states' decision as leverage over them. It was to save the Indians 'from the mercenary influence of white men' and to ensure they were forever 'undisturbed by the local authority of the states' that he insisted they go west. It was a refrain he repeated in letter after letter and speech after speech.

'Remove west of the Mississippi,' the president wrote to a Choctaw leader. 'There you can be happy – there you will have a home, you and your children for ever, free from the interposition, or interruption which now assails you – and which must continue to assail you, whilst you reside among your white brothers. Go then to the west, where happiness and peace await you. There the state laws cannot molest or disturb you.'

But when his enticements met with resistance, he reminded them that the state laws were coming for them whether they made a deal with him or not. And Jackson would not be spurned twice. When the Creek and Cherokee refused to meet to discuss removal in the summer of 1830, Jackson issued a dire warning. 'When they find that they cannot live under the laws of Alabama, they must find, at their own expense, & by their own means, a country, & a home.' Refusal to negotiate now 'will lead to the destruction of the poor ignorant Indians. It must be so, I have used all the persuasive means in my power; I have exonerated the national character from all imputation, and now leave the poor deluded Creeks & Cherokees to their fate, and their annihilation.'[9]

The Indians knew Jackson. They knew his history, his temper and his methods. They knew he was not bluffing. The white men of Georgia, Alabama and Mississippi were certainly not bluffing – they were already swarming over Indian lands.

Some Indians went west before state laws were extended over their lands. Others held out long enough to experience the pain and indignity of life under them. Along the way, many tribal leaders succumbed to the mixture of bribes and threats held out to them during marathon negotiations with Coffee and John Eaton, the secretary of war.

In any event, they signed. The Choctaw signed in 1830; the Chickasaw, Creek and Seminole in 1832.

Each experience of removal was unique; all were poorly organized and needlessly cruel. The Choctaw, who left first, went in several waves. Those who went in the winter of 1831–32 died in vast numbers due to the severe cold. Those who went in the summers of 1832 and 1833 were caught up in a cholera epidemic and died in even greater numbers. Twenty per cent of the Choctaw population died during the traumatic journey westwards.

Alexis de Tocqueville witnessed one Choctaw party crossing the icy Mississippi in the winter of 1831. 'The Indians had brought their families with them and hauled along the wounded, the sick, newborn babies, and old men on the verge of death,' he wrote. 'They had neither tents nor wagons, simply a few provisions and arms. I saw them embark to cross the wide river and that solemn spectacle will never be erased from my memory. Not a sob or complaint could be heard from this assembled crowd; they stood silent.'

The mirror image of Indian despair was white jubilation. When the citizens of Mississippi learned that the Choctaw had signed the treaty surrendering their lands, they held a celebratory banquet in Natchez where a toast was given in honour of Andrew Jackson: 'He found our territory occupied by a few wandering Indians. He will leave it to the cultivation of thousands of grateful freemen.'[10]

Thirty years later, 72 per cent of the population of surrounding Adams County were enslaved.

## 'WE WERE THEN YOUR FRIENDS'

By 1833, only the Cherokee had not signed. Alone among the southern tribes, they chose a strategy of coordinated resistance to removal.

The Cherokee were well positioned to go down such a path. Settled in north-west Georgia, they had been living near whites for decades. During the Monroe administration, a great effort had been made to establish missionary schools among them to guide the tribe towards assimilation with the white majority. One consequence of this was that northern evangelicals, educators and philanthropists who operated and funded these schools developed close relationships with the Cherokee.

Significantly, insofar as the civilizing policy was pursued in good faith, it succeeded in its own terms among the Cherokee. By the time Jackson became president, the Cherokee were thriving. An 1826 census of tribal property revealed the tribe owned 1,560 slaves, 2,942 ploughs and close to 100,000 livestock, and operated dozens of sawmills, grist mills, blacksmiths and cotton gins, as well as eighteen schools.

Their capital at New Echota was a bustling backcountry settlement that published the *Cherokee Phoenix*, a bilingual newspaper catering to a population that was 90 per cent literate. These markers of cultural development were central to a new Cherokee identity. 'We are ... on the improve,' boasted John Ridge – himself educated in a mission school – in a letter to Albert Gallatin. The new generation of Cherokee were 'of fine habits, temperate & genteel in their deportment' and were engaged in 'effecting the civilization of man'.

Cherokee notables adopted the ways of frontier businessmen like Andrew Jackson. John Ross was only one-eighth Indian and the rest Scots-Irish; according to some accounts he had blond hair and blue eyes. As a young man, he had ridden with the Cherokee cavalry during the campaigns climaxing with the battle at Horseshoe Bend; as an adult, Ross owned nineteen slaves, a 300-acre plantation and a lucrative ferry operation. He held the federally appointed position of postmaster and lived on a $6,000 farm on the Coosa River.[11]

Tangible evidence of Cherokee progress made not a jot of difference to American policy. Far from softening attitudes, Cherokee advancement hardened American resolve. As they took steps to develop themselves along American lines, they had created institutions that threatened to endure as alternatives and points of resistance to federal and state institutions. It transpired that the United States feared Cherokee civilization more than Cherokee savagery, precisely because they feared that it might succeed. Tellingly, the proximate cause of Georgia's decision to extend state law over Indian lands was the promulgation of a Cherokee constitution in July 1827. The Cherokee bid for independence and autonomy had to be smothered in its cradle.[12]

Familiarity with American ways meant that the Cherokee could mount a sophisticated and sustained campaign of resistance to removal. John Ridge and Elias Boudinot went on lecture tours of the Northeast, where they drew massive crowds who were surprised by how American these Cherokee seemed in their dress, manners and speech. The result was an outpouring of support for the Cherokee. Associations formed across the North to express solidarity with their plight and revulsion at the administration's actions. A group of pious women from Maine petitioned Congress on their behalf. A New York committee in aid of the Cherokee nation was established on Wall Street. Literary figures like Ralph Waldo Emerson wrote to the president begging for an end to the policy of removal.

The tribe also mounted a legal challenge to the constitutionality of Georgia's actions, taking on two-time attorney general (and 1832 presidential candidate) William Wirt as their counsel. John Ross relocated to Washington, where he helped manage their legal affairs but also became the main Cherokee interlocutor with the administration, systematically rebutting the arguments they put forward in defence of their policy of removal.

Ross also opened a correspondence with Jackson in which he pleaded the Cherokee case directly to the president. In one letter, sent in the spring of 1834, Ross appealed to Jackson as a fellow veteran of the long-ago wars in the Alabama heartlands:

> Twenty years have now elapsed since we participated with you in the toils and dangers of war, and obtained a victory over the unfortunate and deluded red foe at Tehopekah, on the memorable 27th March 1814, that portentous day was shrouded by a cloud of darkness, besprinkled with the awful streaks of blood and death. It is in the hour of such times alone that the heart of man can be truly tested and correctly judged.

We were then your friends – and the conduct of man is an index to his disposition. Now in these days of profound peace, why should the gallant soldiers who in time of war walked hand in hand thro' blood and carnage, be not still friends? We answer, that we are yet your friends. And we love our people, our country, and the homes of the childhood of our departed sires.[13]

The results were impressive. The Supreme Court handed down two rulings that vindicated the Cherokee position. Ross was able to get an audience with Jackson in the White House. The public tumult over the treatment of the Cherokees reached a fever pitch. One activist recalled how in those years 'the pulpit thundered, the press groaned, and an almost universal cry of indignation was heard throughout the land'.[14]

And yet nothing could prevent removal. In the end, Ridge and Boudinot blinked first and, without the support of the vast majority of the tribe, signed a treaty at New Echota in 1835 capitulating to Jackson.

Ross led the vast majority of the Cherokee in continued resistance: 15,665 Cherokee – 96 per cent of the population – signed a memorial presented to Congress repudiating the treaty. Ross remained indefatigable in his assertion of Cherokee rights, even as his world collapsed around him. His own house was confiscated by the state of Georgia and raffled off in a lottery. He came home one day to find a stranger taking possession of his property.

Then, in the summer of 1838, he returned from a trip to Washington to learn that the worst had at last happened. In late May, soldiers had burst into Cherokee homes in the early hours of the morning, forced their occupants to leave at gunpoint, with only the clothes on their backs, and had marched them under armed guard to transit camps where they would await deportation to the West.

In a stunned letter to his people, Ross reflected that 'when the strong arm of power is raised against the weak and defenseless, the force of argument must fail'. 'Our nation,' he continued, 'have been besieged by a powerful army' that had now rendered them 'homeless and outcasts' in their own lands. All that remained was to take 'a passing view of the houses and farms we once inhabited and cultivated and the places in which we happily worshipped almighty god' and to steel themselves for the journey ahead.

That winter, his people went west along the Trail of Tears. Between a fifth and a quarter of the Cherokee died on it, among them Ross's wife.[15]

Concurrent with the expulsion of Indians westwards was the transfer of their lands to white men. Inevitably, the two processes were intimately linked. In a bid to reduce costs, the Jackson administration privatized the removal process, allowing entrepreneurs to take on the immense and complex task of transporting an entire nation to faraway Arkansas. In some instances, the speculators who were engaged in large-scale land fraud were the very same people who profited from the business of deporting Indians westwards. James C. Watson, for example, was a leading light in both the Columbus Land Company, a land-speculation business, and the Alabama Emigrating Company, which facilitated removal. During the chaos of the removal years, mercurial men like Watson made money every which way.[16]

The presence of large numbers of well-organized and completely unscrupulous land speculators in the region as the agonizing process of removal progressed ensured that it would be anarchic, violent and maximally cruel.

Under the terms of the various removal treaties, there was usually some provision that allowed for Indian families to remain on a given portion of land (usually a half or quarter section) if they wished. On paper, this seemed like a reasonable concession to Indian requests. In reality, those families who sought to remain were beset on all sides.

The Creek cession was a case in a point. A great number of Creeks attempted to use the provisions of their removal treaty to remain on some portion of their ancestral lands. That treaty provided that any Creek could at any time sell their allotted lands and go westwards. Situated as they were on top of prime Black Belt soil, the Creek lands were soon under siege by land speculators. Some were harassed until they gave in and sold at cut-price rates. A Creek man named Tefulgar was convinced to sell his plot for $510 by speculators who soon after sold it for $5,000. In many cases, naked fraud was used. With the local courts and land offices in the hands of their cronies, speculators began hiring so-called 'land-lookers', Indians who for a fee would impersonate the actual Creek owners of certain lands and go to court and testify that they wanted to transfer land to whichever crew of speculators had bribed them. This left the real owners twice dispossessed, as they now had lands in neither Alabama nor Arkansas. Creek leaders informed Jackson that their lands were being 'stolen from us by bad white men and bad Indians', but nothing came of their pleas for aid.[17]

By the mid-1830s, the atmosphere in Creek country was apocalyptic. Native peoples were being defrauded in every possible manner. Speculators clashed with each other and with United States Army forces who tried to retain order. The sheer aggressiveness of the speculators stunned the officers in charge. 'I would prefer to fight all the Indian warriors in the Creek nation [than] to have any agency in settling the difficulties between the land speculators of this country,' General Jesup wrote. Into this carnival of fraud, backcountry violence and bureaucratic cowardice arrived Josiah Nott, a scientific racist obsessed with cranial measurements, who began digging up Creek graves to add their skulls to his private collection.

When some of the Creek at length took up arms in resistance – the Second Creek War of 1836–37 – they were crushed and the remainder of the nation deported in shackles to Arkansas. Jacob Rhett Motte, an army surgeon who was involved in the expulsion of the Creek insurgents, described how many hanged themselves the night before their departure. He recalled watching one manacled Creek try to slit his own throat with a blunt knife while being marched west. A Creek leader named Opothle Yoholo concluded that the events of these years 'portended the gradual declension and final extinction of the Creeks ... they were doomed to destruction; that Almighty God had so decreed it.'

Not all people in the Creek country were so gloomy. In these years James C. Watson took control of 201,600 acres of Creek land at 75 cents per acre. A subsequent investigation into the goings-on in the Creek cession concluded that 'a greater mass of corruption, perhaps, has never been congregated in any part of the world, than has been engendered by the Creek treaty'.[18]

All of this occurred in tandem with the government-sanctioned sale of public lands through the General Land Office.

It cannot be repeated enough that the stated goal of federal land policy was to ensure that public lands were purchased and occupied by 'actual settlers' and not land speculators.

In the Gulf Plains, the exact opposite occurred. The Choctaw cession was the exemplary case. These lands included the most coveted cotton-growing soils in the country – the rich alluvial plains of the Yazoo Delta between Memphis and Vicksburg. The Choctaw removal treaty was signed in March 1832. Not long afterwards, John Coffee was appointed to survey the land and prepare it for sale. In December 1833, Andrew Jackson issued a presidential proclamation declaring that sales would begin in four weeks. Over the next six years, 10 million acres of Mississippi land – an area the size of Denmark – was sold off at auctions that drew the attention of the entire country. A traveller passing through Natchez in 1836 reported that 'the people here are run mad with speculation. They do business in ... a kind of phrenzy.'[19]

The outcome of these sales was the accumulation of land in the hands of a small number of men. A survey of GLO sales in Issaquena County in the heart of the Yazoo Delta shows that the same few names were responsible for the vast majority of land transactions. By 1860 Stephen Duncan had nine different plantations in this region. Wade Hampton owned 350 slaves in Issaquena alone – one portion of a slave empire that stretched from South Carolina to the Mississippi River. By the Civil War, 92 per cent of Issaquena County's population was enslaved, a figure that spoke not just to the immense human suffering of the slave system but also to the incredible concentration of capital, labour and land in the hands of the planter elite.

Across the Gulf Plains, the same pattern was replicated. Individual settlers were outbid by organized and well-capitalized groups of speculators who drew on funds not just in Charleston and Savannah but from across the North. By 1841, twenty people owned a third of the land in Pontotoc County, in the north-western tip of the Black Belt. By one estimate, 87 per cent of the Creek cession went to purchasers of 2,000 acres or more.

The concentration of landownership in the hands of groups who expected immediate and lucrative returns on their investment necessarily meant the intensification of the plantation system. Those slaves who managed to escape recalled the unrelenting brutality of plantation life on the former Indian lands. 'In Alabama,' Henry Gowens recalled, 'it was whip, whip, continually, old and young ... It seemed as if the whipping had to be done.' 'I have ridden hundreds of miles in Alabama,' Philip Younger wrote from freedom in Canada, 'and have heard the whip going, all along from farm to farm, while they were weighing out cotton.' 'There was so much whipping in Alabama,' George Johnson remembered, 'one man there, on another farm, was tied up and received five hundred and fifty lashes for striking the overseer.'

While speculators, financiers and slave traders collaborated to concentrate enslaved blacks on prime lands, most whites were forced to the margins. White settlers without political and financial connections took up residence on marginal lands in pine woods, in hill country and wherever else was spurned by the cotton magnates and land-speculation companies. One visitor to these regions described them as 'rude, illiterate, and independent' and 'as wild as the Indians they had supplanted'. Yet even on these unwanted lands, prices were still too high for the very poorest. 'Land here is high,' one would-be settler reported home to North Carolina, 'no chance for a poor man to get land.'[20]

## THE FIRE NEXT TIME

The system of public land sales reached its zenith during Jackson's presidency. Between 1829 and 1837, 50 million acres were sold through land offices. Twice as much land was sold during Jackson's two terms as had been sold during the entire history of the public land system up to that point. The public land system brought $60 million into the national coffers during his presidency. In 1836, land sales brought in an historic high of $25 million, which accounted for 50 per cent of all government revenue – an unprecedented figure.[21]

The irony was that Jackson would have preferred to abolish the land office system and make the public lands more readily available to humbler sorts, and yet instead he permitted it to reach its apotheosis while he sat in office.

Why? The answer was the tariff. Following the War of 1812 the United States was saddled with an enormous debt – some $127 million. In an attempt to reduce the debt load in 1816, a tariff on imported goods was passed. The tariff was a revenue measure for the nation as a whole, but it also served as a protective measure for manufacturing interests in the north of the country who faced fierce competition from British imports. During the Era of Good Feelings, the political class rallied around a nationalist consensus that held the tariff was a policy that benefited everyone.

But in the mid-1820s that consensus fell apart. A new generation of politicians from South Carolina began arguing that the tariff was a tyrannical imposition. They claimed that a tariff fell hardest on the South, making it effectively a colonial appendage of the North. 'We stand towards the United States in the relation of Ireland to England,' one South Carolina senator claimed. 'The fruits of our labors are drawn from us to enrich other and more favored sections of the union.'

There was no greater convert to this doctrine than John C. Calhoun. Calhoun had voted for the tariff of 1816, but by 1828 – when he was elected vice president under Jackson – his politics had radically changed. Previously a nationalist, he was reborn a strident defender of southern interests. Just after the 1828 election, Calhoun anonymously published a pamphlet in which he decried the tariff as 'unconstitutional, unequal and oppressive'. Then he went a step further. The tariff issue, he claimed, was not about the tariff. It was about the powers of the federal government versus those of the states. If the federal government could impose a tariff that was loathed by the southern states, what else might it do? The answer to Calhoun was simple: it would try and abolish slavery. 'Those who now make war on our gains,' he warned, 'would then make it on our labour.'[22]

Jackson did not know that the man standing next to him on inauguration day* had written these incendiary remarks, but he did know how serious an issue the tariff was. Shortly before he took office, he let it be known that the 'leading objects of his administration would be to quiet the public mind in regard to the tariff, [and] to pay the public debt'. If the debt could be paid off, then the tariff could be reduced and the outlandish claims of the South Carolina firebrands would be discredited.

---

* By 1830, however, it had become apparent that his vice president was subverting his administration. Rather than confront the issue head-on, which could have been explosive, Jackson manufactured a personal feud out of Calhoun's behaviour during the First Seminole War. Then, in his capacity as secretary of war, Calhoun had advised Monroe to discipline Jackson for exceeding his orders. After Monroe let Jackson off, Calhoun tried to conceal his involvement in the matter. Jackson probably knew what Calhoun had done but chose to ignore it for political reasons. Now, over a decade later, he began to ask Calhoun what his position had been all those years before. Calhoun was well aware what Jackson was up to but ultimately chose to publish the relevant correspondence in February 1831. Jackson now had his pretext for going to war with Calhoun. 'A man who could secretly make the attempt ... to destroy me, and that under the strongest professions of friendship,' he said, 'is base enough to do anything.' Calhoun resigned the vice-presidency in 1832 and returned to the Senate, where he became the chief spokesman for nullification in Washington.

But before that could happen, Calhoun and his followers precipitated a full-blown crisis.

Calhoun developed and publicized the doctrine of nullification, a theory that claimed the states could nullify federal laws they believed to be unconstitutional – like the tariff.

What if the federal government tried to force a state to observe a law that it had previously nullified? In that case, the South Carolinians argued, the state would naturally secede from the Union.

The logic was now clear for all to see: nullification would lead to secession, which would lead to civil war.

Following Jackson's re-election in 1832, it seemed as though South Carolina was on the verge of secession. Large and tumultuous public meetings were held in Charleston, where the tariff was castigated and nullification espoused. South Carolina politicians began stockpiling swords, rifles and powder. Jackson's point man in Charleston, Joel Poinsett, informed him that local militia leaders 'drill and exercise their men without intermission' in preparation for the coming confrontation with the federal government.

'Woe to those nullifiers who shed the first blood,' Jackson warned. 'The Union shall be preserved.'

But Jackson knew that he had to take the sting out of the nullifiers' claims. He did so by promising to reduce the tariff at the earliest possible date. And that date was drawing closer due to the money flowing into the Treasury from the sale of Indian lands in the Gulf Plains.

In 1833, Henry Clay steered a compromise through Congress that reduced the tariff and silenced the nullifiers. On 1 January 1835, the United States paid off its national debt for the only time in its history.

A week later, a party was held in Washington to celebrate the payment of the national debt and observe the twentieth anniversary of the Battle of New Orleans. It was an event rich in symbolism and irony. The war that had propelled Jackson to the presidency had also created the debt crisis that had rocked the Union. The sale of the Indian territories Jackson had secured that day had now been used to wash away the debt and extinguish the flames of secession. The man who had saved the nation militarily from the British now saved them fiscally from civil war.[23]

\* \* \*

Jackson's titanic attempt to resolve the contradictions in the American system was both a success and a failure. The nullifiers were held at bay; there was no civil war in 1833. Jackson preserved the Union for another thirty years. But Jackson's presidency had a radicalizing effect. The lesson many Americans drew from his tenure was that the federal government would pay any price, bear any burden, to ensure the flourishing of the slave system.

Indian removal was a case study in government support for the slave system. Removal took eight years, seventy treaties and $68 million to secure control of 100 million acres of land for southern slave-owners.

The campaign to prevent removal, although it failed, had a galvanizing effect on northern opinion. The methods of the anti-removal campaigners were copied by a new generation of abolitionists who drew a straight line between removal and slavery.

When William Lloyd Garrison established *The Liberator* in 1831, he gestured to the centrality of removal to the slave system in the masthead, which showed a slave being sold on the block while Indian treaties lay in the dust beneath him. 'We are perfectly convinced,' Garrison told his readers, 'that ALMIGHTY WISDOM AND JUSTICE, will shortly scourge this country by sword, pestilence or famine, or some other awful judgment for our criminal and inhuman conduct towards the Indian and the African.'

Even those centrist politicians who rejected abolitionism came to accept its fundamental claim: that the Jackson presidency had exposed that the United States government was run by and for slaveholders. Henry Clay – the great compromiser – declared that Americans had become the 'slave of slaves'. John Quincy Adams concluded in his diary that under Jackson 'the overseer ascendency is complete'.

In the 1840s, this phenomenon of state capture by a slaveholding minority would become known as the 'slave power'. Northerners who spoke of the pernicious influence of the slave power looked back to the Jacksonian era to explain how this dynamic worked and who it served. They recalled that 'Florida was purchased in the interest of slavery, and received into the Union as a Slave State'; that the 'National Government assisted in expelling the red man from seven or eight States of the South ... so that the white man could enter with his [slaves]'; that the government had engaged in several 'disgraceful Florida wars at the bidding of the slave-catchers of Georgia and South Carolina'. They came to believe that American expansion was dictated by the whims of slave power.

And in the 1840s, the United States would begin to expand again and on an even greater scale.[24]

## CODA

In 1835, the Second Seminole War broke out. It lasted seven years and occupied the attention of four presidents. By 1840, the American army had the initiative and Seminole leaders began to surrender.

One of the last to lay down his arms was Coacoochee, also known as Wild Cat. In March 1841, he came to negotiate terms with Colonel William J. Worth at his camp in Tampa Bay. Forty-three years before, Mad Dog had dealt haughtily with the Europeans who had strayed into Florida. Now, in a speech to Worth, Coacoochee acknowledged the hopelessness of continued resistance to white encroachment.

> The land I was upon I loved, my body is made of its sands; the Great Spirit gave me legs to walk over it; hands to aid myself; eyes to see its ponds, rivers, forests, and game; then a head with which I think. The sun, which is warm and bright as my feelings are now, shines to warm us and bring forth our crops, and the moon brings back the spirits of our warriors, our fathers, wives, and children. The white man comes; he grows pale and sick, why cannot we live here in peace? I have said I am the enemy to the white man. I could live in peace with him, but they first steal our cattle and horses, cheat us, and take our lands. The white men are as thick as the leaves in the hammock; they come upon us thicker every year.

A few months later, the US military transported Coacoochee west in chains.[25]

# PART IV

# THE OREGON COUNTRY

The nation that possesses Oregon will not only control the navigation of the Pacific, the trade of the Pacific and Sandwich Islands, but the trade of China itself.

ALEXANDER DUNCAN, 1845

# Consider the Otter

*Enhydra lutris*, or the North American sea otter, is a beautiful animal. Living along the immense arc of coastline connecting the Bering Strait to California, it is peculiarly adapted to life in the cold, turbulent waters of the North Pacific. Their powerful sense of smell and large lungs make them excellent hunters, expert at scouring the ocean floor. Once they have caught their prey, their long, nimble forepaws can prise open their catch and scrape out meat and tissue. Their hind paws, by contrast, are broader and stubbier – almost like bear claws – but flare like seal flippers when they swim, allowing them to move with speed and grace. Unlike freshwater otters, sea otters are large and bulky, growing to five feet and weighing up to one hundred pounds. Their size does not make them any less athletic. Full-grown sea otters can jump several metres out of the water and cruise in a leaping motion across the surface of the ocean. But the most remarkable thing about the sea otter is its fur. Infants are brown all over. Adults have yellow-white heads, snow-capped tails and a rich glossy fur everywhere else – black tips shading to silvery roots. This fur is the densest of any mammal in the world, with up to a million fibres per square inch, keeping them warm in the freezing water. While their habitat is hostile to humans, sea otters relish life at sea. They spend most of their lives on large fog-bound beds of kelp that float a few miles offshore. Chronically social, they love to play together and groom one another, and even hold paws while sleeping on their backs so they do not drift apart. They are also doting parents. When the mother floats on her back, her child will sleep on her chest, and when their young are distressed, the mothers will hold them lovingly and stroke them while making a low wailing sound, leading some native peoples to believe that they are singing to their young to quieten them, or perhaps to lullaby them to sleep.

Today the sea otter is indelibly associated with the Pacific Northwest. It has become something of a global icon, famous for its inquisitive, shaggy-dog face, its maritime sunbathing and its use of rocks to crack open clams. But when eighteenth-century Americans thought of *Enhydra lutris*, they made different associations. When they thought of the sea otter, they did not think of a sleek, charming, playful mustelid. They thought of China.[1]

## FLOWERY FLAG DEVILS IN THE CELESTIAL KINGDOM

In the 1730s, an Italian jesuit missionary named Giuseppe Castiglione painted a portrait of the Qianlong Emperor, who ruled China from 1736 to 1796. Castiglione depicted him dressed in a golden robe, sitting on a golden throne, set against a golden wall. His robe is adorned with lions, his throne carved with dragons, and the exquisite carpet on the floor brilliantly patterned in red, green, blue and yet more gold. Qianlong sports a scarlet hat trimmed with sable black fur, the same thick, luxurious fur that trims his cape, his collar and the sleeves and hem of his robe. The emperor's face is impassive: seemingly indifferent to the evidence of his own majesty. Castiglione's portrait became the representative image of how eighteenth-century Europeans viewed China: glamorous, remote and fabulously wealthy.

This was certainly still the dominant view of China by the time of the American Revolution. In *The Wealth of Nations* (published in 1776), Adam Smith wrote that 'China has been long one of the richest, that is, one of the most fertile, best cultivated, most industrious and most populous countries in the world.' If Western pride could not quite acknowledge China as a peer, it readily allowed that China was an advanced civilization in its own right. The newly independent Americans wholeheartedly agreed. China, in the minds of the revolutionary generation, was the model of a great power set apart from the intrigues of Old Europe. Jefferson dreamed of the United States standing 'with respect to Europe precisely on the footing of China'.[2]

To the mass of ordinary Americans, China was associated with tea. In the 1760s, the colonies had become addicted to tea, importing millions of pounds of it each year. Officially, all tea had to be imported from Britain. But in order to escape British taxes, smuggling from other countries became widespread. In 1767, Whitehall struck back in the form of the Townshend Acts, which raised an import duty on tea in the colonies. The Acts resulted in a major crisis over the question of London's powers to impose taxes on the colonies. Then in 1773, Parliament passed the Tea Act, which granted the East India Company a monopoly on tea importation into the colonies. This produced another crisis, this time concerning the right of American merchants to conduct their business free from government interference. Tea was now enmeshed in the core issues of the revolution: free trade, the taxation power and America's relationship to Britain. The symbolic significance of tea was enshrined forever on the night of 16 December 1773, when 340 chests of Chinese tea owned by the East India Company were dumped in Boston Harbor, sparking a crisis that produced the Declaration of Independence three years later. The American Revolution, of course, was about more than just tea. But for the revolutionary generation, drinking tea was about more than just consumption. When one New England merchant declared that 'the inhabitants of America must have Tea', he was tacitly saying that they must also have liberty, commerce and independence from Britain.[3]

All of which accounts for the slightly delirious atmosphere in February 1784 as the *Empress of China* prepared to embark on the newly independent United States' first trade mission to China. As the 360-ton barque lay at anchor off Manhattan, the press projected onto it all the hopes of the young republic. One newspaper declared that the ship and its forty-man crew were 'the first instruments, in the hands of Providence, who have undertaken to extend the commerce of the United States of America to that distant and to us unexplored country'. These hopes were shared by the ship's supercargo, the patriotic Samuel Shaw, who believed the young nation had 'a character to establish among the great powers of the earth'. He now bore responsibility for establishing that character. When they lifted anchor on 22 February and sailed down the East River towards the Atlantic, the *Empress of China* was joined by the *Edward*, sailing for London with the definitive articles of peace approved by the Continental Congress. Ten years prior, the Boston Tea Party had helped spark the revolutionary conflagration;

now Shaw, a Boston native, sailed for China to buy tea free of British taxes. Borne along by these hopes, the *Empress of China* sailed past Manhattan, where, with crowds thronging the pier, the naval battery fired a thirteen-gun salute in her honour, one for each state, and was greeted by a twelve-gun salvo in reply. The drama and romance of the moment was captured by poet Philip Freneau in an ode, 'On the First American Ship that Explored the Route to China and the East-Indies, after the Revolution':

> *She spreads her wings to meet the Sun,*
> *Those golden regions to explore*
> *Where George forbade to sail before.*
>
> *To that old track no more confined,*
> *By Britain's jealous court assigned,*
> *She round the stormy cape shall sail*
> *And, eastward, catch the odorous gale.*
>
> *To countries placed in burning climes*
> *And islands of remotest times*
> *She now her eager course explores,*
> *And soon shall greet Chinesian shores.*
>
> *From thence their fragrant teas to bring*
> *Without the leave of Britain's king.*

The voyage out was uneventful. After crossing the Atlantic, the *Empress of China* headed south to round the Cape of Good Hope. In mid-July they glimpsed Java and soon after passed through the Sunda Strait. By mid-August they were at Macao, readying for their journey up the Pearl River past Whampoa to Canton, where they docked on 30 August.

It now fell to Shaw to navigate the byzantine system of trade that then prevailed under the name of the Canton System. Under this regime, trade with China was not organized in accordance with international treaties, as was the norm in Europe, but permitted by the sufferance of the emperor, handled by an oligopoly of Hong merchants and conducted according to a set of protocols invented by Chinese officialdom. Inbound vessels had to pay a series of tolls and customs duties;

acquire the services of a pilot, a compradore and a translator; rent out a factory inside the quarter assigned to foreigners; and otherwise scrupulously observe the rituals that accompanied the arrival of a foreign ship in the Celestial Kingdom.* This system was very far from the American ideal of free trade and was intended, inter alia, to remind foreigners of their subordinate position in the eyes of their hosts. The system was degrading to European sensibilities. One Frenchman complained that 'there is not a cup of tea drank in Europe which has not been productive of humiliation to those who purchased it at Canton'.

Shaw took these rituals in his stride. The Chinese 'were very indulgent towards us', he noted, though it took some time for them to comprehend the difference between the Americans and the British. Once they had, 'they styled us the *New People*', Shaw wrote with evident pride. In time, the Chinese would come to associate the Americans with their Star-Spangled Banner; thereafter, Americans were referred to as 'flowery flag devils'.[4]

The *Empress of China* lingered at Canton for four months while she filled her hold with porcelain, nankeens and 800 chests of tea. On 28 December, she headed home, arriving back in New York on 10 May 1785, after a total of 443 days at sea. The ship's return, and the safe passage of its precious cargo, drew praise from the press. Shaw was triumphant. 'To every Lover of his Country,' he boasted in a letter to John Jay, 'it must be a pleasing reflection that a communication is thus happily opened between us and the Eastern Extreme of the Globe.' The cargo of the *Empress of China* went on sale and Shaw was rewarded for his efforts with the post of consul at Canton, the first American to hold that position. In no time at all, more ships had set out for Canton and a permanent channel of trade with China was opened, inaugurating a new era in the fortunes of the new republic.[5]

There was just one problem. Once the *Empress of China* unloaded its cargo of tea, chinaware and textiles on the wharfs of New York, its sponsors reckoned on a profit of 30 per cent on $120,000 ventured. This was

---

* One of the more peculiar customs involved a day reserved for the displaying of 'sing-songs' – wind-up clocks, musical boxes and other automata – on the deck of the ship. The Hoppo, or chief customs official, would solemnly inspect each and then select his favourites, which would be 'gifted' to him by the ship's supercargo.

respectable, but hardly profitable enough to justify all the hazards of a long and dangerous voyage. The problem, as every European trading power knew, was that while Americans wanted Chinese goods, the Chinese did not want American goods. Consequently, the Chinese demanded payment in gold and silver – something anathema to the mercantilist theories of the day. Moreover, it was difficult in practice for American merchants to acquire a large amount of specie and then safely transport it halfway around the world. If the China trade was to generate profits commensurate with the risks it entailed, some object of exchange other than hard currency would have to be found. As it turned out, the solution lay hidden in Castiglione's portrait of Qianlong, in the rich fur trimming of the emperor's robe.[6]

### THE GOLDEN ROUND

In February 1788, Captain James Cook departed Hawaii for the Northwest Coast of America. Although Cook was then on his third circumnavigation of the world, this was his first visit to America. Indeed, he would be the first English-speaking sailor to visit the Pacific Northwest since Francis Drake and the *Golden Hind* landed at the place they called New Albion in 1579. Although Cook and his crew knew that land awaited them, they felt as though they were sailing into the unknown. The ocean was empty, save for the odd piece of driftwood. 'If we had not known that the continent of North America was not far distant,' one sailor wrote, 'we might, from the few signs of the vicinity of land hitherto met with, have concluded, that there was none within some thousand leagues of us.'

On 6 March they glimpsed land. The coast was broken up by bays and inlets separated by rocky promontories. The face of the country was a series of rolling hills and valleys, thickly forested. As they sailed south, they saw the coastline of the modern states of Washington and Oregon. Here the view was more spectacular, one crewman recalled, 'being full of high mountains, whose summits were covered with snow', while the lands closer to the shore formed 'one vast forest'. When the wind turned, they sailed for Vancouver Island. Here, adrift among whales, seals and sea lions, the sense that they had strayed far from the known world was stronger than ever. 'We were now so far advanced to the Northward and Eastward,' one crewman noted in his journal, 'as to have reached that void space in our maps, which is marked as a country unknown.'[7]

If the coast was unknown to Europeans, it was home to a number of native peoples. From the ocean, Cook's men could see the smoke rising from fires in the bays along the shore. No sooner had they sighted land, than throngs of curious locals appeared alongside them in canoes, 'their faces [painted] all over with horizontal and perpendicular stripes of black, yellow, and red'. It rapidly became apparent that these were not the first white men they had encountered. Through sign language, they indicated that Cook should come ashore to trade. Many showcased their wares from their canoes. 'The articles which they offered to sale were skins of various animals,' Cook noted, 'in particular, of the sea otters.' They also knew what they wanted in return. The sailors gladly traded for pelts. But as they did so, they could only speculate as to who had begun this trade with the native peoples.[8]

The mystery was solved as they sailed north towards the Bering Strait. In October they stopped at the island of Unalaska, where they met some Russian furriers. Cook invited the men into his cabin. When he laid out his charts, they pointed out the areas along the coast known to them. In subsequent visits to their ramshackle trading post, Cook came to understand their purpose in being there. 'Their great object is the sea beaver or otter. I never heard them inquire after any other animal.' He noted that 'The fur of these animals, as mentioned in the Russian accounts, is certainly softer and finer than that of any others we know of; and therefore the discovery of this part of the continent of North America, where so valuable an article of commerce may be met with, cannot be a matter of indifference.'[9]

At the end of October, Cook set sail for Hawaii, where on 14 February 1779 he was murdered at Kealakekua Bay. James King took charge and sailed for Canton. There the crew made a marvellous discovery. They had paid little regard to the furs they had purchased along the American coast. Sailors used them as blankets or makeshift linings; some plugged holes with them. But they discovered that in China they were luxury items. An individual sea otter pelt could fetch as much as $120. The crew were so excited by this lucrative business that they demanded that King return to the Northwest Coast at once, so they could repeat the trade. When King insisted they return to England, the crew nearly mutinied. Discipline was restored and King took his men back home, returning to England in the autumn of 1780 after four and a half years at sea.

Cook did not live to see it, but his final voyage had discovered one of the known world's last great untapped trade routes. It was common knowledge that Russia traded beaver furs with China. That trade was one of the wonders of eighteenth-century commerce. Those beaver furs were supplied by Britain's Hudson's Bay Company (HBC) through a supply chain that spanned the globe. Cree or Assiniboine trappers operating in the remotest parts of central Canada caught beaver and then paddled in canoes to designated trading posts, where they traded their pelts with HBC furriers. These furs were collected in bundles and sent to Montreal, where they were gathered in warehouses and shipped across the Atlantic. In Europe, the furs were sold off at international markets held in London, Leipzig and Frankfurt. Here they were purchased in quantities by Russian merchants, who sent them to Moscow, and then taken by horse, carriage and sled over the Urals, across Siberia and then south past Lake Baikal to Kiakhta, a trading post on what is now the Mongolian border. From Kiakhta, baggage trains took the furs to market in China's coastal metropolises, where they were used to make hats, gowns and mufflers. The patchwork of relationships and trade routes that conveyed Canadian beaver skins to Chinese consumers was so improbable, and on such a vast scale, that Adam Smith took it as an exemplar of the possibilities opened up by global commerce.[10]

What Cook's expedition had discovered was *another* Russian fur trade which had hitherto been secret. In the Chinese market, sea otter fur was valued above all others. According to Chinese sumptuary laws, only the highest-ranking subjects of the empire enjoyed the right to wear it. Long-serving bureaucrats and loyal soldiers were personally gifted sea otter pelts by the emperor. For centuries, emperors had trimmed their capes and lined the cuffs and hems of their gowns with the fur of the sea otter. Since Vitus Bering had crossed from Kamchatka onto the Aleutian Islands in the 1740s, Russian merchants had been quietly supplying Chinese high society with sea otter furs. With the arrival of Captain King and his crew in Canton in 1779, the secret was out.[11]

News of the discovery broke in the United States first. Among Cook's crew was John Ledyard, a native of Groton, Connecticut, who signed on to Cook's expedition in July 1776, unaware that the Declaration of

Independence had been issued the week before. After the expedition ended, he deserted and returned to the United States. In 1783, he published his memoir of the voyage, in which he recounted the 'astonishing profits' available in the maritime fur trade. Ledyard tried to organize a mission back to the Oregon coastline. It was he who proposed the idea of sending the Empress of China to Canton. His original plan was to send her via the Pacific Northwest, but ultimately the expedition's sponsors settled for a simpler, smaller-scale voyage.

Ledyard's revelations did, however, inspire a group of Boston merchants to send the *Columbia* and the *Lady Washington*, under the command of Captains Robert Gray and John Kendrick, back to the North Pacific in September 1787. Almost exactly a year later, the two ships arrived at Nootka Sound and began plying the coast for furs. Everywhere they anchored they were crowded by locals looking to trade, and they had little difficulty converting their cargo of goods into peltry. On one occasion they took $8,000 worth of sea otter skins in exchange for a box of chisels. At the end of the year, Gray sailed for China, via Hawaii, arriving in Canton in February 1790, where he exchanged his supply of furs for 336 chests of tea. By August 1790, Gray was back in Boston, having become at once the first American sailor to circumnavigate the globe, the first to visit Hawaii and the first to trade American sea otter skins for Chinese tea. Not one to rest on his laurels, six weeks later Gray boarded the *Columbia* and sailed once more for Oregon.[12]

After safely returning the *Columbia* to Boston in July 1793, Gray never sailed to the Pacific Northwest again. But in his wake came a steady stream of imitators. By the end of the century, dozens of American vessels were visiting the Oregon coast each year, takings tens of thousands of sea otter pelts with them when they sailed onwards to Canton. The maritime fur trade accounted for only a small part of the United States' blossoming trade with China, but it took the lion's share of the glory, the glamour and the profits. Seamen who endured the arduous multi-year voyage could typically expect to reap profits of 300–500 per cent, an enterprise so lucrative it became known as the 'golden round'. By 1800, the Pacific teemed with American shipping, making the United States second only to Britain in the number of vessels it sent to Canton. In the process, a commercial corridor was forged that bound the fortunes of the Atlantic seaboard with the great Chinese merchant houses on the Pearl River.[13]

Yet even as this commerce grew, Oregon itself remained a mystery. One sailor spoke for many when he described the 'dark anticipations' that coursed through him upon glimpsing 'the snow-clad mountains of the Northwest Coast ... No cultivated fields, no towns, hamlets, or cottages enliven the prospect to a sailor as he views the land after a long voyage ... It is one vast wilderness and unbroken solitude.'[14]

## BY LAND

The mystery of Oregon was unravelled in stages, beginning with the arrival of Lewis and Clark in 1805. Fur, China and the Pacific Northwest were threaded into the mission of the Corps of Discovery. As described above, Jefferson had taken inspiration for the trek to the sea from the memoirs of the Scottish explorer Alexander Mackenzie published in 1801, which described his 1793 overland journey from Montreal to the Pacific. Mackenzie ended his book with a summons to British empire-building on the Oregon coast which would result in British dominance of the continental fur trade, the maritime fur trade 'and the markets of the four quarters of the globe'. Jefferson's instructions to Meriwether Lewis were framed in opposition to Mackenzie's ambitions. The Corps of Discovery should find a water route across the continent, and along the way survey the fur trade, all with the end of warding off British influence in those distant quarters. Lewis and Clark were scrupulous in following Jefferson's commands. Along the length of the Missouri, they monitored the state of beaver populations and scoured the country for signs of intruding British furriers. But upon arriving at the foothills of the Rockies, they found themselves plunged into a whole new arena in the struggle to dominate the North American fur industry.[15]

In late August 1805, the Corps crossed the Continental Divide and entered Oregon. The first native peoples they met were so remote from the coast that they had never seen Europeans before. But as Lewis and Clark moved westwards, they discovered tributaries of the Columbia River and then, in early October, paddled their canoes onto the Columbia itself. At once, signs of British influence multiplied. Along the thickly settled banks of the Columbia they encountered British-made rifles, Indians wearing European clothes and 'one half white child' among a group of Wasco-Wishram Indians living east of The Dalles. Continuing down the river, they recorded meeting on 1 November a Chinook man who bragged about his ability in dealing with European traders. 'Those people are high with what they have to sell,' Clark noted, 'and say the white people below give them great prices for what they sell to them.' On 4 November, with Mount Hood visible in the distance, one member of the expedition described meeting an Indian that 'could talk & speak some words [of] English such as cursing and blackguard'. They were now very close to their destination. On 7 November, they glimpsed the ocean. 'Great joy in camp [as] we are in view of the ocean,' Clark wrote, 'this great Pacific Ocean which we been so long anxious to see, and the roaring or noise made by the waves breaking on the rocky shores ... may be heard distinctly.' But it wasn't until 15 November that the Corps stood at Point Ellice and watched the 'immense swells' of the Pacific Ocean where the full force of the mighty Columbia River joined the sea. On 3 December, Clark, in imitation of Mackenzie, left his own inscription on a rock near the ocean: 'William Clark December 3rd 1805. By land from the U. States in 1804 & 1805.'[16]

The Corps erected a small fort, Fort Clatsop, in a bay off the main channel, and spent three damp, cold months at the mouth of the Columbia, with little to do apart from scout for sea otter skins. Trade came readily enough. Chinook traders were soon coming in numbers to Fort Clatsop. In February, Lewis wrote a long account of the sea otter, judging it 'as large as a common mastiff dog' with stubby legs and 'broad, large and webbed' feet. Lewis's prose purpled when it came to the subject of the otter's fur. 'The colour is a uniform dark brown and when in good order and season perfectly black and glossy,' he wrote. 'It is the richest and I think the most delicious fur in the world.'[17]

The winter at Fort Clatsop afforded time to reflect on the geography of Oregon. The lands immediately westward of the Continental Divide were unforgiving; one of the Corps described them as a 'horrible mountainous desert'. Even outside of winter, this was a dry, barren place. This held true even on the easterly waters of the Columbia, and the landscape did not change until past The Dalles, when the Cascade Mountains reared up and the terrain became green, wet and thickly forested. Oregon was effectively divided by the Cascades into two zones: humid, mountainous lowlands to the west; arid highlands to the east. Through both flowed the single unifying feature: the Columbia River. Although they had only explored a portion of it, the captains had gained an appreciation of the river's significance. Sprawled across Oregon, Washington, Idaho and British Columbia (as well as portions of Montana, Wyoming, Nevada and Utah), draining 220,000 square miles of territory, and extending 1,240 miles from its headwaters in Canada to its mouth at Grays Harbor, where it discharges 150 billion gallons of water a day into the Pacific with force enough to create some of the most turbulent nautical conditions on the planet, the Columbia River basin was a universe unto itself.

Jefferson had tasked them with finding a water route connecting the upper Missouri to the Pacific. On that count their discoveries had not been encouraging. The president's dream of a 'single, direct water communication' between the Atlantic and the Pacific entailed a 2,600-mile journey up the Missouri, a 340-mile portage over the Rockies to a navigable tributary of the Columbia, followed by a 640-mile journey in hand-made canoes to the ocean. Yet Lewis convinced himself that this overland route to Oregon was commercially viable. As he put it in a letter to Jefferson: 'We view this passage across the Continent as affording immense advantages to the fur trade.' Lewis went on to sketch an ambitious scheme for a new transcontinental trade route that would

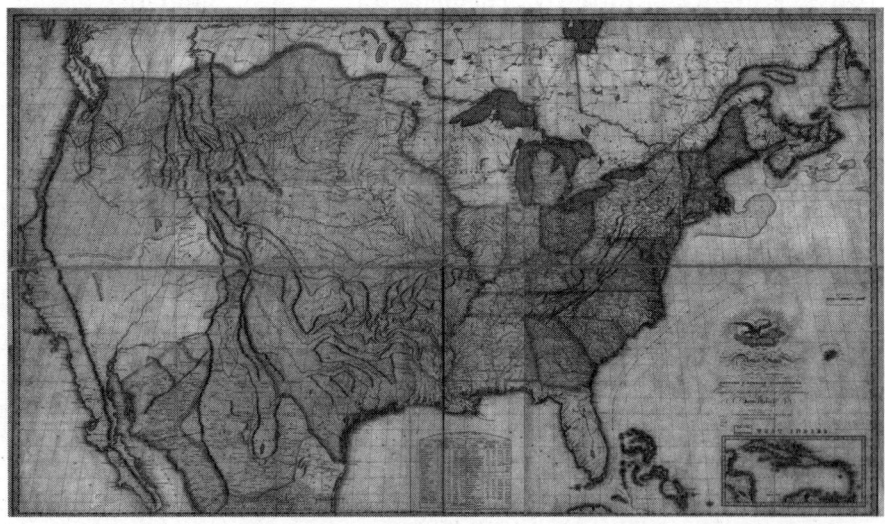

*This 1816 map captures the size of the Oregon Country and its distance from the settled part of the United States.*

connect China with the Atlantic seaboard via Oregon, the Rockies and the Missouri River. The crux of the trade would be the sea otter, and to illustrate his point, Lewis sent along with his letter several sea otter skins for the president to examine.[18]

Lewis advocated for this ambitious scheme as he believed that he would be the man to profit from it. In the years after his return from Oregon, Lewis busied himself with attempts to organize a new fur company operating along the lines imagined in his letter to Jefferson. All his efforts failed. Lewis had neither the temperament nor the commercial experience to build a business of this scale. His endeavours came to an end in October 1809, when Meriwether Lewis died in mysterious circumstances in a tavern in rural Tennessee.[19] But the dream of building a fur empire in the Pacific Northwest survived his death, and the mantle of effecting it passed on to a man who had the resources and the will to build what Lewis could not.

That man was John Jacob Astor.

## ASTORIA

Before there was John D. Rockefeller, before there was J. P. Morgan, before there was Andrew Carnegie and Cornelius Vanderbilt, before there was Gould and Frick and Stanford and Mellon and every other American plutocrat, there was John Jacob Astor. Born in the small town of Walldorf in Baden-Württemberg, Astor emigrated to the United States in 1783 at the age of twenty. Originally he came to America to expand his brother's trade in musical instruments, but he quickly moved into the fur trade. First he focused on simply importing Canadian furs for resale in New York. Then he began to grow his domestic network, building a web of connections in Albany, the Great Lakes and Detroit. The indefatigable Astor worked the trade relentlessly – endlessly travelling, endlessly networking, endlessly accumulating and reinvesting profits – with the consequence that by the turn of the century he was a millionaire – the first dollar millionaire in American history – and had built the cornerstone of a fortune that would make him the fourth-richest American who ever lived.[20]

Astor had fine-tuned political antennae and was (despite his thick German accent, poor personal manners[21] and questionable patriotism) excellent at cultivating powerful men. He thoroughly charmed Jefferson and the two men traded favours over the course of his two presidential terms. Astor was well placed, then, to exploit the revelations produced by the Lewis and Clark expedition. In the aftermath of the Corps's return, Astor began to plot out his most ambitious scheme yet and one that would require both vast financial resources and high-level political cover. He proposed to create a new corporate organization, the American Fur Company, that would exploit the commercial possibilities opened up by the Corps of Discovery's expedition west. His plan was to build a chain of posts up the Missouri and over the Rockies all the way to the mouth of the Columbia, where he would erect a permanent trading house that would ship furs directly to Canton. His aim was nothing less than to 'place the monopoly of the fur trade of the world in the hands of this country, and ... extend its dominion over a most interesting part ... of the North American continent'. Astor was aiming not just at trade but at colonization. His scheme enjoyed support at the very highest levels. What Astor hoped to build was nothing less, as Jefferson put it, than 'the germ of a great, free and independent empire' in the Pacific Northwest.[22]

Captain Gray's expedition was funded by a consortium of Boston merchants. Lewis and Clark had travelled west with the full faith and credit of the United States government behind them. Astor's plan was to replicate both journeys at once and at his own expense. The scale of the project was vast. Astor invested $500,000 up front to pay for men and supplies to travel simultaneously by sea around Cape Horn and by land across the Rockies. A hundred men were hired for the purpose, the majority of them lured away from employment at the North West Company. Most were British citizens: a mix of Scotsmen, French Canadians and Métis. There were few Americans.

On 6 September 1810, the *Tonquin* left Manhattan for the Pacific Northwest with thirty-four men aboard. Arriving in Hawaii in February, where twelve native men were recruited to the expedition, it sighted Cape Disappointment on 22 March. The *Tonquin* now faced the formidable task of crossing the treacherous bar that lay across the mouth of the Columbia. 'The aspect of the coast was wild and dangerous,' one crewman wrote, and 'the waves were too high for any boat to live in.' Nonetheless the captain, Jonathan Thorn, sent out a boat to test the waters. When the first mate objected that the sea was too rough, Thorn delivered a stinging rebuke: 'Mr. Fox, if you are afraid of water, you should have remained at Boston.' The rest of the crew tried to intervene on their behalf but to no avail. The men of the *Tonquin* watched as the little boat rowed into the heaving seas and vanished. Unbowed, Thorn sent another two boats out to test the waters, with similar results. Eight men died that evening on the Columbia Bar. Later that night, the *Tonquin* made its own turbulent passage across the bar and the next day the crew awoke in the calm of Baker Bay.[23]

Now ashore, command of the expedition passed to Duncan McDougall, who selected a spot fifteen miles up the south bank of the river for their settlement named, in honour of their sponsor, Fort Astoria. In sight of the 'wild confusion' of the Columbia Bar and enclosed by an 'impervious and magnificent forest', the site of Fort Astoria, Alexander Ross wrote, 'might challenge the whole continent to produce a spot of equal extent presenting more difficulties to the settler'.

McDougall took up the challenge, and beating back 'the impervious and magnificent forest' became the work of all Astorians, clerks and trappers alike. Each man was given an axe and a rifle and sent into the forest. It was back-breaking work for which Astor's men were ill-trained. The men soon learned that felling huge trees in a thick forest required forethought. Trees felled in the wrong way became tangled in the canopy. Even once a tree was toppled, it had to be hauled away – which still left the complex work of removing and destroying the roots. Astorians experimented with blowing up stumps with gunpowder, which inevitably led to more carnage, one man losing his hand in an explosion. After weeks of this dangerous and difficult work, Ross reckoned that they had cleared less than an acre of land. 'There is an art in felling a tree,' he mused in his memoirs, 'but unfortunately none of us had learned that art.' It wasn't until mid-May that the foundations were laid for the first building in the new complex. In the meantime, the Astorians ate roots and boiled fish and lived in cloth tents surrounded by hostile Indians.[24]

While Astoria was being hacked out of the wilderness, a series of unsettling events occurred. On 5 June, the *Tonquin* sailed along the coast to pursue the sea otter trade. Ten days later, it stopped in the Clayoquot Sound near Vancouver Island and began trading with local tribes. Captain Thorn proved ill-suited for the interminable rounds of haggling. At length, he lost his temper and slapped one of the tribal elders around the face with a rolled-up sea otter skin. Thorn tried to sail away but was persuaded to stay a day longer so they could resume trading. The next day, the natives returned to trade, having to all appearances forgotten the fracas. But once aboard, they took out hidden knives and massacred the crew. When the killing was over, a large group assembled on the deck to celebrate their victory. However, one of the *Tonquin*'s crew had escaped and hidden in the magazine. Hearing the festivities above, the crewman set fire to the ship's store of gunpowder and the resulting detonation, in the words of one eyewitness, sent 'arms, legs and heads flying in all directions'. The blast killed everyone and destroyed the *Tonquin* so completely that its wreck was never found.[25]

It was many months until the exact fate of the *Tonquin* was known at Astoria. In the meantime, the mystery of its disappearance was complemented by some unnerving arrivals at the fort. In mid-July, David Thompson of the North West Company unexpectedly appeared in a canoe at the mouth of the Columbia. Thompson told McDougall and the other partners that the North West Company had penetrated the Columbia River Valley from the north and established fur-trading outposts along the river. This meant the Astorians would now be in direct competition for furs with the Canadians, ending any hope that Astor would enjoy a monopoly on furs in the Pacific Northwest.

Then for several months beginning in January 1812, groups of skeletal people arrived at the fort, whose 'emaciated, downcast looks and tattered garments ... all bespoke their extreme sufferings during a long and severe winter'. These were the survivors of the overland party led by Wilson Price Hunt. Their journey west had begun in Montreal in July 1810 and took them first to Mackinac Island, the great fur-trading hub on Lake Huron, where Hunt hoped to recruit more men.* Leaving

---

\* Ross left an excellent account of Hunt's doomed attempts to recruit on Mackinac: 'The Montreal men are expert canoe-men, the Mackinac men expert bottle-men ... Canadians in general drink, and sometimes even to excess ... but to see drunkenness and debauchery, with all their concomitant vices, carried on systematically, it is necessary to see Mackinac. Here Hunt ... in vain sought recruits, at least such as would suit their purpose; for in the morning they were found drinking, at noon drunk, in the evening dead drunk, and in the night seldom sober. Hogarth's drunkards in Gin Lane and Beer Alley were nothing compared to the drunkards of Mackinac at this time. Every nook and corner in the whole island swarmed, at all hours of the day and night, with motley groups of uproarious tipplers and whisky-hunters. Mackinac at this time resembled a great bedlam, the frantic inmates running to and fro in wild forgetfulness.'

Mackinac in early August, they headed for Green Bay on Lake Michigan, then took the Fox and Wisconsin Rivers to the Mississippi, arriving in St Louis in September. After wintering in north-west Missouri, the journey proper got under way in April 1811. Hunt's original plan had been to follow the route of Lewis and Clark. However, as they made their way up the Missouri, they learned that hostile Blackfoot Indians blocked their path higher up the river. To avoid this danger, Hunt decided to march overland across South Dakota and Wyoming, cross the Continental Divide into southern Idaho and paddle down the Snake River to the Columbia. This gambit proved disastrous and led to unbelievable hardship and at least one allegation of cannibalism. The last stragglers did not make it to the mouth of the Columbia until May. Roughly half of the expedition had died, disappeared or deserted since they left the Missouri 2,000 miles and 340 days before.[26]

If an ill sign had hovered over the Astoria venture from the outset, exactly what fate it portended finally became clear in June 1812, when war broke out between the United States and Great Britain. The War of 1812 sealed the fate of Astor's great project. The British knew this was their opportunity to claim Oregon. 'The territorial possession of the countries bordering on the Columbia,' one North West Company partner told a British minister, 'and finally the whole north-west coast of the continent of America, will depend upon the measures to be adopted by His Majesty's government on the present occasion.' The British government responded by providing Royal Navy protection for their company's resupply ship, the *Isaac Tod*, which left Plymouth in March 1813. Once the North West Company men learnt of the *Isaac Tod*'s departure, they paddled down the Columbia and made the Astorians an offer. They should sell their fort, furs and supplies to the North West Company and those that wished could be absorbed into their employ. The alternative was to wait for a Royal Navy schooner to arrive at the Columbia and reduce their little outpost to smoking ruins. It made no small difference to the tenor of the negotiations that almost all of the Astorians were British nationals and former North West Company employees, with little interest in dying under the American flag for a German fur tycoon.

In October 1813 the deal was struck. Astoria and everything in it was sold for $44,000. As promised, HMS *Raccoon* appeared on 12 December, captained by William Black. Mooring at Astoria at night, Black came ashore, enjoyed the fort's hospitality and then, in a theatrical flourish after dinner, smashed a bottle of Madeira on the flagpole and took possession in the name of King George. When the next morning Captain Black finally saw the full extent of Astoria by daylight – a few weather-beaten buildings, a wooden palisade, a vegetable garden, some pigs – he burst into laughter. 'What, is this the fort I have heard so much of? Great God, I could batter it down with a four-pounder in two hours!' Black took comfort in the fact he had at least ensured that the Pacific Northwest was henceforth 'the property of the [British] empire'. Black sailed away shortly afterwards, leaving the Union Jack flying over Astoria, now renamed Fort George.[27]

The fate of the Pacific Northwest was decided that December evening in 1813 when Captain William Black of HMS *Raccoon* drunkenly smashed a bottle of Madeira on the flagpole of Fort Astoria. Black's moment of bravado had serious consequences. Astoria had been sold by the Pacific Fur Company to the North West Company in a transaction between two private entities. At the time of the *Raccoon*'s arrival, Astoria was not in any meaningful sense United States territory. By seizing it for Britain as part of the spoils of war, Black transformed its legal status. At Ghent in 1814 the negotiators agreed that all territories taken during the war should be returned to their pre-war status. Once the peace treaty was signed, the Americans insisted that Astoria was covered by this provision. After several years of back-and-forth over the matter, the British conceded the point. It was too late for Astor to rescue his investment – let alone revive his dream of a fur empire on the Pacific – and he wisely began to ease himself out of the fur business and into his storied investments in Manhattan real estate. But Astor's loss was his adopted country's profit. His gamble on the Pacific Northwest made possible the day in August 1819 when Captain James Biddle of the USS *Ontario* sailed up the Columbia to formally assert the United States' claim. Biddle's presence was purely symbolic, as Fort George remained under the control of its lawful owners, the British North West Company. But in so far as international law was concerned, the United States had confirmed a territorial claim that had been recognized in an international treaty with Britain.[28]

\* \* \*

These obscure transactions along an obscure stretch of the Pacific coastline had world-historical consequences. Since the birth of the United States, there had been Americans who dreamed of extending their nation to the shores of the Pacific. The recognition of Astoria as American territory, combined with the claims established by Gray, Lewis and Clark, meant that the best chances of America becoming a transcontinental power lay in the Pacific Northwest. And once the United States extended to the Pacific, it would become a Pacific power with permanent interests in Asia. Oregon was the United States' window onto Asia. Its fur trade was the key that would unlock the wealth of China. These primordial facts were forgotten as the decades passed and America's commercial ties to Asia thickened and American strategic commitments across the Pacific Rim multiplied. They seem quaint today besides the titanic struggle between China and the United States for global supremacy. The fact remains that the roots of the great-power conflict that will likely define this century can be traced back to the contest over the rivers, harbours and mustelids of the Pacific Northwest. When pondering the origins of the Sino-American showdown in the twenty-first century, we could do worse than to remember Oregon – and consider the otter.

# The Shape of a Problem

In his diary for 27 January 1821, Secretary of State John Quincy Adams described a testy encounter with Stratford Canning, Britain's ambassador in Washington. The cause of the irritation was Oregon and the two nations' claims there. The men exchanged barbs as they tried to pin down the other's exact aims in the Pacific Northwest. The two continued to wrangle until finally Adams coolly reprimanded Canning for 'cavilling with us about territory, on this North-American Continent'. Canning leapt at the bait. Was the secretary of state suggesting that the United States questioned Britain's right to any territory at all on the continent? Did he doubt Britain's claims to the Athabasca Country? To Rupert's Land? To Quebec? 'No, said I,' came the magisterial response; 'there the boundary is marked, and we have no disposition to encroach upon it – Keep what is yours, but leave the rest of this Continent to us.'[1]

As Adams well knew, the two men were meeting in the middle of a period when the matter of what was whose in the Pacific Northwest was rapidly being settled. In 1819, Adams had negotiated the Transcontinental Treaty that had – on the map at least – taken America's border to the Pacific for the first time. In reality, the treaty was slightly more nuanced. Under the terms of the treaty, Spain ceded to the United States all its claims above the 42nd parallel north, and those claims were tendentious and dated back to the explorations of the conquistadores. The Americans interpreted them as extending to the 56th parallel. However, in 1824 the United States retreated slightly from this claim as part of a diplomatic settlement with Tsar Alexander I of Russia. Under the terms of the Russo-American Treaty of 1824, Russia ceded to the United States all their territorial claims south of parallel 54° 40' north, acquiring in exchange for recognition of everything north of that line as Russian territory.

To American eyes, the result of these diplomatic initiatives was rather pleasing. The Louisiana Purchase had taken American territory to the Rockies. Treaties with Russia and Spain had extinguished foreign claims in a swathe of territory encompassing nearly a thousand miles of coastline. The actions of Gray, Lewis and Clark and the Astorians had established American claims by discovery and settlement inside a rectangle of land demarcated by the 42nd parallel to the south, the 54th parallel to the north, the Rockies to the east and the Pacific Ocean to the west. The Americans referred to this rectangle of land – which now contains the states of Washington, Oregon and Idaho, as well as the province of British Columbia – as the Oregon country. Technically, it ought to have been called the Columbia country, as the whole region was drained by the Columbia River. But by whatever name, the Americans considered it theirs.

The Americans, however, could not brush off the claims of the British Empire. Instead, over the course of endless rounds of negotiations in the years after the Treaty of Ghent, the two countries reached a new modus vivendi. In 1818, they signed a convention that solidified the Canadian border at the 49th parallel, from the Lake of the Woods to the Rocky Mountains, ending the Anglo-American territorial disputes that arose out of the Louisiana Purchase. That left the border west of the Rockies. The Americans proposed extending the 49th parallel to the Pacific. The British proposed that the border should run along the 49th parallel to the Columbia River and then follow its channel to the ocean, leaving the northern bank to the British and the southern bank to the Americans. Both sides balked. The result was a mutually dissatisfying stopgap measure. The two countries agreed to a period of 'joint occupation' whereby 'the country on the north-west coast of America claimed by either nation, shall, without prejudice to the claims of either, be opened for a limited time for the purposes of trade to the inhabitants of both'.

Joint occupation was a misnomer. Neither country would occupy Oregon in any strict sense. Rather, it would be left open as an arena for commercial exploitation. Initially, this period would last ten years, but with no permanent solution forthcoming, it was subsequently agreed that joint occupation would be extended indefinitely, but could be terminated by either party with one year's notice. This territorial dispute became known the Oregon Question. In the grand scheme of things it was a trifle, concerned with a triangle of land upwards of the Columbia River's north bank containing nothing besides beavers, bears and pine trees. But the Oregon Question came to encompass issues much more significant than the mere land involved.[2]

## THE VIEW FROM THE NORTH

Not long after the Treaty of Ghent was signed, an English traveller named Francis Hall disembarked in Manhattan for a tour of the United States and Canada. Hall was a military man and the War of 1812 was fresh in the memory. Yet Hall encountered no ill will, indeed he was taken with the verve and spirit of the Americans. Americans were plainly dressed and plain-spoken. A culture of equality was evident: at taverns magistrates supped with shopkeepers, and everyone conversed with one another irrespective of wealth or rank. Men even shared their beds with strangers if the inn was full. In Poughkeepsie he admired the tidy, spacious wooden houses, with their generous windows and raised verandahs. In America the average farmer could live in dignity and some measure of style, which was only their due, 'for they are industrious and enterprising'.[3]

After cruising in a steamboat up the Hudson, he went by cart and carriage to Whitehall, and then took a sleigh across a frozen Lake Champlain into Canada. The change was striking. 'Nothing could be more Siberian than the aspect of the Canadian frontier: a narrow road, choked with snow, led through a wood, in which, patches were occasionally cleared, on either side, to admit the construction of a few log-huts, round which a brood of ragged children, a starved pig, and a few half-broken rustic implements.' This part of Canada – Lower Canada – was predominantly French, and felt not just foreign but archaic. French peasants wore the red or blue caps of medieval villeins. Crucifixes and miniature shrines lined the side of the road. The average French Canadian was superstitious, ignorant and poorly fed compared to his American counterpart. Unlike the enterprising Yankees, the Canadians preferred to 'endure an evil rather than overcome it'.[4]

The comparison with the United States was stark. 'On one side, there is America, with "millions on millions" of acres beyond what her population can fill up, on the other, England, contending for, and expending her best blood and treasure in defence of, a country, one half of which is little better than a barren waste of snows, and the other, a wild forest.' The verdict was reinforced by his subsequent journey south back into New York and then on to Pennsylvania, Maryland, Virginia and the Carolinas. America's 'national genius', Hall concluded, resided in its pioneer spirit. 'However rugged the path', the American frontiersman, 'with his axe on his shoulder, his family and stock in a light wagon', plunged onwards into the continent, 'into forests, which have never heard the woodman's stroke', and 'gradually converts the lonely wilderness into a flourishing farm'. This westward drive, Hall predicted, 'will finally know no limit but the Pacific'.[5]

Hall's book was read with interest in London. For some in Westminster, Hall's account proved that Canada was simply not worth the cost of its defence. But for others, Canada had a mystique that went beyond imperial budgeting. The greatest British hero of the eighteenth century was General James Wolfe, whose death at the moment of his victory at the Battle of the Plains of Abraham in 1759 led to the British conquest of French Canada. Wolfe became the prototypical martyr of empire, lionized in poetry* and venerated in engravings, oils and statuary for decades after his death. It was to his memory that William Huskisson appealed in a famous speech in the Commons objecting to the notion that Canada should be severed from Britain. That province was not 'a matter of pounds, shillings and pence', he told the House. 'Canada is bound to us by the recollections of honourable valour, both naval and military. It is a trophy too glorious to part with ... Canada cannot but be maintained by every means within our power. We are bound, if we wish to bear untarnished our honour, to give Canada protection to the last extremity.'[6]

And nobody harboured any doubts that protection would be required, for it had already been called upon twice since Wolfe's death:

---

* Wolfe is mentioned in the first stanza of 'The Maple Leaf Forever', Canada's unofficial national anthem: 'In days of yore, from Britain's shore,/Wolfe, the dauntless hero, came/And planted firm Britannia's flag/On Canada's fair domain.'

by American campaigns in 1776 and again in 1812. Both these ventures were consonant with a firm and oft-stated conviction that Canada was properly part of the United States. The Articles of the Confederation had explicitly stated that Canada belonged inside the Union. Presidents Washington, Jefferson and Madison had all said the same. Even the relatively Anglophile John Quincy Adams insisted that 'the whole Continent of North-America' was 'destined by Divine Providence to be peopled by one *Nation* – speaking one language – professing one general System of religious and political principles'. The British knew the Americans hankered after Canada but could do little about it. As one British statesman put it to Adams: 'The United States can never be in danger of invasion from Canada ... But Canada must always be in the most imminent danger of invasion from the United States.'[7]

If Britain's grasp on eastern Canada was slender, its hold on the Pacific Northwest was almost nil. Nonetheless, national honour and the national interest kept Britain involved there.

Honour, because its shores had been explored by British seamen and its interior by British adventurers. The strength of the claims that both had established had led the British to reject the American offer in the 1820s to draw the border along the 49th parallel. Explaining that decision to the prime minister, Lord Liverpool, in 1826, George Canning, the foreign secretary, wrote that when he even considered the idea of 'abandoning the whole N.W. Coast of America to the Yankees ... I feel the shame of such a statement burning upon my face by anticipation.'

Interest, because the British had one great strategic asset in the region: the Hudson's Bay Company. First incorporated in 1670, the HBC was vastly expanded in 1821 after the British state merged it with the North West Company. This enlarged enterprise was a corporate leviathan that controlled some 3 million square miles, or a third of the continent. The HBC did not exist to promote settlement.[8] It existed to collect furs to sell on the international market. From Canning's perspective, the HBC's stewardship of the Pacific Northwest was useful so long as it generated revenues for London and perpetuated a British claim in Oregon. Canning also understood the value of the HBC's produce in China, and viewed Oregon as a conduit to the wealth of Asia. To Lord Liverpool, he noted that within a decade the East India Company's monopoly on the China trade would expire and the HBC would be able to start shipping furs 'direct across the Pacific' to Canton. Surrendering Britain's claims to the mouth of the Columbia would be unforgivable if it meant forgoing the 'advantage of an immense direct intercourse' between China and Oregon.[9]

All that hinged on the continuing supply of furs in Oregon and the continuing demand for them in China. If either faltered, the justification for a British outpost in the Pacific Northwest would evaporate. Besides, the political winds in England were in the sails of liberal free traders, not seventeenth-century monopolists. Supporting the archaic and unfashionable HBC only made sense if it was profitable. But Britain's interest in the Columbia River Valley would expire the day the last beaver was trapped in its waters. On that day, monopoly would capitulate to free trade and honour would submit to realism. The question was when that day would come.[10]

## THE VIEW FROM THE SOUTH

John Floyd was an unlikely spokesman for Oregon. A doctor turned politician, Floyd represented a backcountry Virginia district in Congress. He had scant connections to the Pacific Northwest. He was friends with William Clark and a cousin of Michael Floyd, who had travelled west with the Corps of Discovery – and had the unenviable distinction of being the sole member not to return with it. In Washington, he boarded at Brown's Hotel, along with two senior members of Astor's American Fur Company. Also living at Brown's was his son-in-law, the newly elected Senator Thomas Hart Benton, who was busy carving out a reputation as the tribune of the West. Perhaps he felt an emotional connection to Oregon through the unfortunate death of his cousin. Perhaps Clark or Benton had impressed upon him its importance to the country. Perhaps around the fire at Brown's he had heard talk of the riches of the fur trade in the Columbia Valley.

In reality, even his contemporaries struggled to understand what animated Floyd's obsession with the distant, drizzly land that he had never visited. If his motivations were obscure, then his temperament was well suited to the vainglorious task of bringing Oregon into the Union. 'Floyd is a man, having in the main honest intentions,' John Quincy Adams wrote, 'but with an intellect somewhat obfuscated …

eager for distinction, and forming gigantic projects upon crude and half-digested information.' If Adams believed such a set of traits disqualified a man from taking an interest in the fragile geopolitics of the Pacific Northwest, he was wrong. Floyd was the first in a long line of American visionaries, fantasists and fools who grappled with the Oregon Question.[11]

In December 1820, Floyd called for the creation of a congressional body to 'inquire into the situation of the settlements upon the Pacific Ocean and the expediency of occupying the Columbia River', and subsequently chaired the committee authorized to do so. The following January, the committee issued a report summarizing the result of its investigations. The casual reader of the report would have no inkling that its principal author personally knew men who had suffered every hardship, including death, in their journeys to and from the Oregon Country.

The Oregon of Floyd's imagination was miraculously close to the settled portions of the United States. One merely had to travel up the 'smooth and deep [Missouri] river', traverse a convenient 'portage of only two hundred miles', before arriving at 'another river, equally smooth, deep, and certain, running to the great Western Ocean'. 'Thus are those two great oceans separated by a single portage of two hundred miles!' Floyd marvelled. 'The practicability of a speedy, safe and easy communication with the Pacific, is no longer a matter of doubt or conjecture.' Moreover, there were several openings in the Rockies 'so smooth and open' that a wagon could pass through. And once Floyd's imagined traveller was smoothly across the Continental Divide (Floyd believed the journey from St Louis to Astoria could be done in eighty-three days), a land of bounty awaited. Oregon had the best timber, the best grass, the best horses, the best furs, the best harbours and the best whales producing the best oil: 'far preferable to that taken on any other coast, being clear and transparent as rock water'.

Floyd also stressed the strategic significance of the Pacific Northwest. American merchants had $8 million invested in the Pacific yet no safe port for their fleets to shelter in. Floyd grasped the significance of Oregon's beavers and and sea otters in the lucrative China trade. Oregon's 'position in regard to China' alone made it valuable to the United States. And China was just the beginning. From their eyrie on the Pacific Northwest, the United States would be in a position to dominate the trade of the Pacific and with it the world. 'How vast and incomprehensibly rich must be that country,' Floyd wrote, that supplied 'the whole globe with all the busy imagination of man can desire, for his ease, comfort, and enjoyment.'[12]

The result of this high-flown oratory was a series of bills that went before Congress in the 1820s. They differed in their specifics but conformed in their generalities. Floyd proposed that a fort should be built at the mouth of the Columbia and a series of posts constructed up the Missouri to the foothills of the Rockies. The United States should take possession of the Pacific Northwest, organize it as the Oregon Territory, extinguish the Indian title to the land and offer free land to settlers wishing to move there. All but one of Floyd's bills failed to win a majority (and that lone success was quickly smothered in the Senate), but the debates kept the Oregon Question alive in Congress in the years that it otherwise lay dormant in the American imagination.

Floyd was not without his critics. Some observed that it was simply impractical to administer a region on the other side of the continent separated from the settled states by the Rocky Mountains, the Great Plains and the Missouri River. One congressman noted that if Oregon became a state, an elected representative covering thirty miles a day would take 306 days to get to Washington and back. Subtracting Sundays, they would have two weeks to spend in Washington between their epic journeys to and from their district. 'A young, able-bodied Senator might travel from Oregon to Washington and back once a year,' he observed, 'but he could do nothing else.'

And of course if Floyd's bill was ever passed, it would immediately trigger a confrontation with Britain. Establishing a military post at the mouth of the Columbia would violate the spirit if not the letter of joint occupation. Declaring sovereignty and parcelling up the land for settlers would trample on the treaty of 1818 and constitute a direct challenge to British power. The stated policy of the United States government was to try to 'prevent all collision' with Britain over Oregon. With the wounds of the War of 1812 still healing, few in Congress challenged the wisdom of that course – especially as reports had filtered back to Washington that the lands in Oregon were unsuitable for agriculture. Should the United States 'risk the chance of a long and sanguinary war, for the sake of making an experiment in the hemlock forests of the Columbia coasts?'

asked Missouri Representative Edward Bates. 'Was it worth paying for? Was it worth fighting for? Was it, in fact, hardly worth caring for?'[13]

The favoured policy was one of procrastination. Many reasoned that just as Louisiana and Florida had ultimately fallen into the lap of the United States, so too would Oregon. Antagonizing Great Britain would be needlessly expensive and would at best bring forward by a few years an event that was preordained. 'My opinion is that the country must necessarily be settled by the United States,' Albert Gallatin told Henry Clay in 1827, 'and ultimately fall into their hands, provided the natural course of events is not prevented, and merely by suffering them to take their course.' The same sentiment was expressed by a young congressman named James Polk of Tennessee in explaining his decision to vote against Floyd's bill: 'By delay we can lose nothing. By action now we may hazard much.'[14]

Procrastination was certainly John Quincy Adams's favoured policy. Adams viewed Floyd's proposals with derision, describing his report as 'a tissue of errors in fact and abortive reasoning, of invidious reflections and rude invectives. There was nothing could purify it but the fire.' Having spent so much time first as ambassador to London, then as secretary of state and ultimately as president presiding over a rapprochement with Britain, he was in no hurry to destroy all that hard work for Oregon, which he believed was destined to become American. 'That the United States should form establishments there with views of absolute territorial right and inland communication is not only to be expected, but is pointed out by the finger of Nature,' he wrote, adding that 'there cannot be a doubt that' a territory would be established in Oregon 'in the course of a very few years'.[15]

Adams's interest in Oregon was shaped by his Yankee pedigree. He was a New Englander, a firm supporter of the maritime interest and a friend of many of those in the China trade. Adams understood Britain's Oregon policy as part of a broader strategy of preventing any challenge to its dominance in Asia and so perpetuating Britain's 'unlimited commercial ascendency' across the globe. Keeping the United States out of the Columbia Valley was one move in a larger commercial and geopolitical chess game. The British, as one of his correspondents wrote, sought 'entire and supreme control all over the Pacific'. Adams agreed. A strong policy in Oregon was required to prevent Britain from monopolizing the trade of Asia.

Viewed from Boston and Canton, the Oregon Question took on immense significance. 'The present condition of the Northwest coast of this continent,' Adams wrote in 1823, is 'becoming from day to day more important', bound up as it was 'with the boundary relations between us and the British North American dominions; with the fur trade; the fisheries in the Pacific Ocean; the commerce with the Sandwich Islands and China'. Far from being a backwater, the Pacific Northwest was filled with commercial opportunity and fraught with geopolitical peril.

The problem in the 1820s was that the United States had very little purchase in the region. American vessels dominated the coastal trade, but the number of itinerant trappers in the interior was in the dozens. And American frontiersmen had shown no interest in settling a country where even fur hunters feared to tread. Joint occupation seemed to have been an ambiguous victory for the British, protecting British mercantile interests while forcing them neither to cede nor defend their territorial claims. The ambivalence of the arrangement mirrored the fluidity of British policy but ran counter to the long-term interests of the United States that ultimately required access to the Pacific coast. So long as Oregon remained a sanctuary for the HBC's trappers, British interests were served and American ambitions frustrated.[16]

## THE VIEW FROM THE GROUND

The actual conditions prevailing inside the contested triangle of land in the Pacific Northwest were largely unknown to outsiders. That changed when George Simpson appeared at Fort George in November 1824. Born in obscure circumstances in Dingwall, Ross-shire, George Simpson arrived in Canada in 1820, thirty-two and a rising star in the HBC administration. By decade's end he had become the head of the HBC's operations in-country, a position he would hold unchallenged until the Civil War. Of Napoleonic stature and with kingly pretensions, Simpson ruled the HBC's vast domain with essentially vice-regal authority. But in 1824 Simpson was a corporate manager on a mission. In these years he was found storming around the HBC demesne in his canoe or snowshoes, bringing with him his gospel of 'economy'. Bloat and lassitude were the foes of the HBC and, by extension, of George Simpson. He fought them with crusading energy. Everything could be done cheaper, faster and by fewer people. Simpson led by example, working at a rate that few could compute. 'The toils of business are to me a pleasure,' he once wrote. This was the George Simpson of 24 August 1824 – evangelist of thrift, avatar of the Protestant work ethic – when he set off from the HBC's headquarters at York Factory to make his first visit to the Pacific Northwest.[17]

True to his nature, Simpson crossed the continent on the York Express (the name given to the series of rivers, lakes and portages that connected York Factory, on the Arctic Ocean, with its outposts on the Columbia) in record time. In 1824, the fastest any man had traversed the 2,500 miles of the Express was in 104 days. Simpson did it in 84. This was a new record but it brought no satisfaction. As he had pushed his men across the continent, permitting them a maximum of six hours' sleep a night, Simpson had stopped at various HBC posts to examine accounts, interview employees and, on several occasions, relieve under-performers of their jobs. He arrived on the Pacific convinced that gross mismanagement was rife. At Fort George he put the men on notice. Hitherto, they had been consuming so many expensive imported European goods that 'they may be said to have been eating Gold'. This when they were surrounded by a country filled with game and a river abounding with salmon. 'I have therefore given intimation,' Simpson wrote with barely concealed relish, 'that they had better Hoard the European provisions and Luxuries they have got now in Store as their future supplies will be very scanty.' Belt-tightening was accompanied by a radical overhaul of operations. Poorly performing outposts were shuttered and the number of full-time employees was halved to eighty-two.[18]

At the same time, Simpson glimpsed profitability once his reforms came into effect. London might be wavering, but Simpson insisted that the Columbia District had a future. 'The Trade of this Coast and its interior Country is unquestionably worth contending for,' he wrote. The prize, he understood, was China. Simpson sketched out a proposal that would unite the Columbia fur trade with commercial opportunities in China, Russian Alaska, Mexican California and the freshly independent republics along South America's Pacific flank. It was a plan for British commercial dominance of the entire Pacific Rim, orchestrated from the HBC's perch at the mouth of the Columbia.[19]

This was, of course, the American nightmare, and Simpson was equally attuned to the Anglo-American dimension of the HBC's operations in Oregon. He was aware that Whitehall ultimately sought to partition the region along the line of the Columbia River. This would essentially cede the south-eastern portion of Oregon (known as the Snake Country) to the Americans. He was equally aware that American furriers were the advance guard of the settler army. If they could be warded off, the resolution of the Oregon Question could be deferred for years, perhaps decades. Accordingly, Simpson made two important decisions. First, he decided to close down Fort George, on the south bank of the Columbia, and move operations to Fort Vancouver, on the north bank, opposite the mouth of the Willamette River. This would bring the HBC's base in the Columbia District closer to the forts upriver, as well as to the richer agricultural lands in the Willamette Valley. He further directed that the focus of immediate trapping efforts should be in the Snake Country, noting that 'the country is a rich preserve of Beaver and which for political reasons we should endeavour to destroy as fast as possible'. Those 'political reasons' were the deterrence of American trappers and, behind them, American settlers.[20]

On 19 March 1825, Simpson recorded in his diary the ceremonial opening of Fort Vancouver. At dawn, in the presence 'of the Gentlemen, Servants, Chiefs & Indians I Baptised it by breaking a Bottle of Rum on the Flag Staff and repeating the following words in a loud voice, "In behalf of the Honourable Hudson's Bay Company I hereby name this Establishment Fort Vancouver God Save King George the 4th" with three cheers. Gave a couple of Drams to the people and Indians on the occasion. The object of naming it after that distinguished navigator is to identify our claim to the Soil and Trade with his discovery of the River and Coast on behalf of Great Britain. ... At 9 o'clock A.M. took leave ... embarked and continued our Voyage.' By the end of April, Simpson was back across the Continental Divide.[21]

Simpson left the Columbia District in the capable hands of John McLoughlin, a tall, powerfully built veteran of the fur trade. 'He is such a figure as I should not like to meet on a dark night in one of the by-lanes in the neighbourhood of London,' Simpson once wrote of the chief factor; 'his beard would do honour to the chin of a Grizzly Bear.' Unlike Simpson, McLoughlin was based permanently at Fort Vancouver and for twenty-five years was the HBC's man on the ground in the Pacific Northwest. But he was still a manager, not a *voyageur*. The actual burden of implementing Simpson's new regime fell on men like Philip

Skene Ogden. The Canadian-born son of American loyalists, Ogden had been in the fur trade since he was a teenager, working for the American Fur Company and the North West Company, before becoming an HBC employee after the 1821 merger. By the time Simpson appeared in the country, Ogden was a twenty-year veteran of the fur trade. Described as a 'humorous, honest, eccentric, law-defying' adventurer, Ogden prided himself on his ruthlessness and reliability. Ogden could be depended upon for the harshest duties McLoughlin had in mind – service in the most remote, and most geopolitically sensitive, region in the Pacific Northwest, the Snake Country.[22]

Roughly corresponding to the valley of the Snake River, the Snake Country had gained a fearsome reputation. In the early 1820s, the HBC had sent a fur-trading expedition there under the command of Finan McDonald which had produced 4,000 beaver skins, a war with the Piegan and six dead trappers. McDonald swore off going again. 'I got safe home from the Snake Country thank [God],' he said afterwards, 'and when that country will see me again the Beaver will have gold skin.'

Now Simpson wanted the country cleared out of beaver entirely, to fend off American encroachments. Ogden was the man chosen for the job. The annual expeditions to the Snake Country that Ogden organized in the latter half of the 1820s generated hardship on such a scale it is hard to believe that men willingly sought employment in them. Watching his team sleep one March night in the open air 'in pouring rain and without blankets', Ogden marvelled at their hardiness. 'A convict at Botany Bay is a gentleman at care compared to my trappers.' The position of the native peoples they moved among was equally dire. Ogden recalled entering an Indian home to discover that they ate ants and locusts to stay alive through the winter. Sometimes not even insects were forthcoming. An old woman told Ogden that one winter she had eaten two of her children after they died of starvation to avoid the same fate herself. To these people the fur traders represented a lifeline. Ogden regularly exchanged a hot meal for information on Blackfeet raiding parties or the activities of rival American furriers. Native families could trade beaver skins for European goods. For men, employment in a fur expedition could mean comparative prosperity. Eagerness to please their employers might account for the astonishing behaviour of one native guide when he detected a grizzly bear in the forest. 'The Indian requested the loan of a small axe with bow and arrows. Stripping himself naked, he rushed on the bear but paid dearly for his rashness. I do not suppose he will recover. He was injured in the head and lost one eye which was literally torn out. The bear remained in the bushes.'[23]

Even amid this desperate struggle for survival, politics was never far away. A few weeks after Simpson left Fort Vancouver in April 1825, Ogden set out for the Snake Country. By late May, he had strayed into northern Utah, dipping below the 42nd parallel. One day, while they were camped waiting for some trappers to return, a party of Americans marched out of the forest 'with Colours flying', set up a camp nearby '& lost no time in informing all hands in Camp that they were in the United States Territories & were all free indebted or engaged & to add to this they would pay Cash for their Beaver'. Some of Ogden's men deserted, taking their cargo of beaver skins with them. Many more considered following their example.

The next day an American named Gardner came into camp and confronted Ogden. 'He questioned me as follows: Do you know in whose Country you are? to which I made answer that I did not as it was not determined between Great Britain [and] America to whom it belonged, to which he made answer that it was that it had been ceded to the latter & as I had no license to trap or trade to return from whence I came.' Ogden stood firm. Gardner withdrew but not long afterwards, one of his party tried to steal some of their horses and drew a pistol when Ogden intervened. The following day, the scene was repeated. This time Gardner threatened William Kittson, Ogden's deputy, when he tried to prevent the theft of a horse and some beaver skins. 'Gardner immediately turns to me,' Kittson wrote, 'saying Sir I think you speak too bravely you better take care or I will soon settle your business. Well says I you seem to look for Blood do your worse and make it a point of dispute between our two Governments.' This was no idle remark, as neither Washington nor London wanted bickering trappers to spark an international incident. The HBC had handed down strict instructions to Ogden to avoid violent confrontations in Oregon. The encounter did not escalate, and the two parties soon went their separate ways. In the end, roughly a dozen HBC men defected to the Americans, among them an Iroquois named Frasier Sasanare, who Kittson noted 'took nothing with him but his riding horse. Left wife and furs behind.'[24]

For twenty years, this was the face of joint occupation: rival bands of European fur traders posturing in remote corners of Oregon. Simpson's policy in the Snake Country worked. By the mid-1830s, the region was trapped out and had become a fur desert. American furriers retreated to the eastern side of the Rockies and contented themselves with hunting on the upper Missouri and its tributaries. McLoughlin's men were reassigned to other parts of Oregon where they could hunt beaver without any fear of American competition. In fact, in this period there were basically no Americans in Oregon. The interior was British. Americans continued to dominate the coastal otter trade but had no need or desire to challenge British dominance in the Columbia River Valley.

Out of an unsatisfying diplomatic compromise a surprisingly stable accommodation had emerged – and might have endured so long as the fur trade remained the only reason to care about Oregon. But change was coming to Oregon, by land and by sea.

# Into the Pacific

The Congreve rocket occupies a special place in American history. During the War of 1812, Congreve rockets were used by the British during the bombardment of Baltimore, an event that inspired the composition of 'The Star-Spangled Banner', whose fifth line ('And the Rockets' red glare, the Bombs bursting in air') commemorates American courage in standing up to the newfangled technology of the British invaders.

Twenty-five years later, on 24 July 1842, the Congreve rocket made another mark on American history. This time the Americans were firing, rather than being fired at – and the setting was not the Chesapeake Bay but the tiny island of Malolo in Fiji in the South Pacific. That day Lieutenant Charles Wilkes, commander of the United States Exploring Expedition (U.S. Ex. Ex.), ordered the bombardment of the fortified town of Sualib on Malolo, to avenge the murder of two American sailors the day prior. When his Congreve rockets crashed into Sualib, they exploded among the thatched roofs and began a fire that soon swelled into an inferno. 'A scene of confusion ensued that baffles description,' Wilkes later wrote. 'The shouts of men were intermingled with the cries and shrieks of the women and children, the roaring of the fire, the bursting of the bamboos, and an occasional volley of musketry.' The heat was so intense, the Americans temporarily withdrew, 'until the conflagration should have exhausted its fury'. When they returned, they found Sualib's inhabitants either dead or vanished. From Sualib they marched on Arro, the only other settlement on the island, systematically destroying the neat gardens of yams, bananas and cocoa trees they found along the way. Arro was razed without resistance, its inhabitants either killed at Sualib or already having fled into the bush.[1]

The next day, Wilkes gathered his men on a hilltop on the southern part of the island and waited for a peace delegation to arrive. Around four that afternoon, 'the sound of distant wailings was heard, which gradually drew nearer and nearer'. A train of natives was seen approaching the hill. When they arrived, they paused reverentially and then, at Wilkes's signal, fell to their hands and knees and began crawling upwards, 'occasionally stopping to utter piteous moans and wailings'. Through a translator, they begged for peace while Wilkes sat in stony silence. Wilkes then berated them as 'cannibals', 'a nest of pirates' and a 'ruthless and murderous race'. 'I told them they might consider themselves fortunate that we did not exterminate them.' But he was willing to end the conflict so long as they promised never to harm a white man again. This they swore to uphold. Shortly afterwards, the U.S. Ex. Ex. sailed off, leaving in their wake the charred remains of Sualib and Arro. Malolo would long remember the Americans' visit. In Wilkes's mammoth four-volume, 2,000-page account of the U.S. Ex. Ex.'s voyage, he devoted ten pages to their time on the island.[2]

The events of 23–25 July 1842 have sunk into obscurity. Many people have heard about Wounded Knee and the Trail of Tears; nobody speaks of Malolo. Yet what happened in Fiji that month was part of an historical process no less significant than the conquest and settlement of North America – and intimately linked to it. The dramatic arrival of American naval power in the remote Pacific in the 1840s, exemplified by the explosion of American rocketry over Sualib, marked a new epoch in world history in which the destinies of Asia and America became conjoined and contested across the vast expanse of the Pacific Ocean.

## SEA CUCUMBERS, SANDALWOOD AND SPERMACETI

The Pacific Ocean measures 9,000 miles across, containing within it 30,000 islands spread over 68 million square miles of water, constituting roughly a third of the world's surface. It was a field of endeavour as grand as the continental West, and it was in much the same spirit that American sailors voyaged onto what Herman Melville called the 'watery prairies' of the high seas. In 1815, these were not regions unknown: American ships had been visiting them for half a century. But in the following years, the steady trickle of American shipping into the Pacific turned into a deluge that would transform America, Asia and the peoples that lived in and around the ocean between.

Peace launched this invasion of the Pacific. The Treaty of Ghent put an end to the Anglo-American conflict in the western hemisphere. The Congress of Vienna removed the Napoleonic threat to the global order. American vessels could now travel round Cape Horn without fear. The collapse of the Spanish Empire in the same period opened up South America's Pacific ports, which hitherto had been sealed off by Spain's mercantilist policies. The ports of Valparaíso, Coquimbo, Callao, Paita and many more beckoned. Yankee merchants responded with enthusiasm. But once at harbour, they inevitably looked westwards to the island chains beyond, where new markets and new resources lay along the sea lanes to Asia.[3]

Many of the American vessels that sailed into the Pacific ultimately had their eyes set on China and Chinese tea – but the terms of the China trade had changed. After reaching its zenith in 1805, the sea otter trade began to decline. By 1825, the old hunting grounds along the Oregon coast were exhausted. *Enhydra lutris* had been hunted to the verge of extinction; the glory days of the trade were over. However, the demand for Chinese tea remained as strong as ever – and the Pacific was full of goods for the ravenous Chinese market.

For a period it seemed that each decade produced a new commodity for American merchants to pluck from the ocean and sell in Canton. In the 1780s it was seal skins, which took captains sailing principally from coastal Connecticut to rocky outcrops along a crescent stretching from the Falklands round Cape Horn to Chile, and later pushed them on to Tasmania and Antarctica. In the first twenty years of the trade, it is estimated that some 2.5 million seal skins were shipped to Canton, the product of a methodical butchery that one seal hunter described as 'a system of extermination'. The inevitable result was that by 1830 the seal populations were devastated and could no longer yield sufficient quantities for the Canton market.[4]

Well before then, another promising new product had been discovered. Around the turn of the century, Yankee merchants began shipping huge quantities of fragrant sandalwood to China, where it was burned in shrines and temples across the country. In the early days, the profits were vast – one Boston vessel purchased sandalwood worth

$20,000 in Canton in exchange for $50 of goods – and the scale of the extraction commensurately intensive. On Hawaii, one of the first places where large sandalwood groves were discovered, the local monarchs conscripted tens of thousands of their subjects as lumberjacks and sent them into the interior. At the peak of the Hawaiian sandalwood trade in 1821, 4 million pounds were sent to China in a single year. Thereafter the trade fell precipitously, with the ancient forests destroyed. By then American ships had discovered new stocks in Melanesia, the Marquesas, the New Hebrides and especially Fiji, which for a period was referred to as the Sandalwood Islands in honour of its position in the trade.[5]

Ships visiting these far-flung atolls and islets in search of sandalwood stumbled across another item that was in high demand in China: bêche-de-mer, more commonly known as sea cucumber. Unprepossessing in appearance and in odour – one British naturalist described them as 'looking like sausages which have been rolled in mud and then thrown up the chimney' – they were highly prized in China for their restorative powers and their place in traditional Chinese cuisine. In the same bays they harvested them, American captains discovered other products that could find a market in China: mother-of-pearl and tortoise shells, shark fins and abalone, the nests of swiftlets (the principal ingredient in bird's nest soup), and coral moss. (The last was memorably described by one American sailor as 'exceedingly unpalatable to European or American tastes. In both smell and taste, when served up on the table, it is like a vessel's bilge water, immediately creating nausea, and an aversion to it.') By the 1830s, American vessels in the Pacific were like magpies, darting between islands to fill up their holds with an array of goods that had nothing in common save a common market in China. Thus could Herman Melville write in *Omoo* (1847) of his time 'cruising over the tranquil Pacific; touching here and there, as caprice suggested, and collecting romantic articles of commerce; – beach-de-mer, the pearl-oyster, arrow-root, ambergris, sandal-wood, cocoa-nut oil, and edible birdsnests'.[6]

Not all of the new commercial possibilities centred on China. Merchants from Salem, Massachusetts, came to monopolize the American trade in Indonesian spices, at one point purchasing seven-eighths of all the pepper produced on Sumatra. Boston captains mined a profitable trade in the Philippines, purchasing rice and sugar in exchange for a range of American and European textiles: bobbin lace and quilling, flowered muslins, chintz and checked ginghams. The Boston firm of Bryant and Sturgis dominated the lucrative California tallow and hide trade that thrived between 1820 and 1850. Half a million hides were sent to Massachusetts, the raw materials for the burgeoning shoemaking industry, and also turned into bridles, harnesses, trunks, suitcases, gloves, aprons and drum-skins. The majority of trade taking place outside the China circuit was banal. Americans shipped glass, needles and gravestones to Tahiti; blankets, umbrellas and shoes to Hawaii; crockery, molasses and calico to California. One observant visitor to Santiago, Chile, noticed that the doors and window frames of newly built houses had been made in, and shipped from, New England.[7]

Far and away the most important of these trades was the one made famous by Herman Melville in *Moby-Dick*. In the decades following the War of 1812 the whaling business entered its golden age. Prior to 1815, few American whalers had strayed into the Pacific. Then, in 1818, an American vessel discovered new fisheries off the coast of Chile and Peru. The next year the first whaling crews visited Hawaii. In 1820, a Nantucket ship discovered an immense population of sperm whales near Japan. Over the following decades American ships would open up new hunting grounds in Australia, New Zealand, Kodiak, Kamchatka and the Okhotsk Sea. By the time Melville composed his literary monument to American whaling, he could justly write that American whalers had penetrated 'into the remotest secret drawers and lockers of the world'.

The whaling frenzy, however, was whipped up by economic causes, not wanderlust. Whale products were used everywhere. Whale oil burned in street lamps and was used as an industrial lubricant in textile factories. Ambergris was a vital ingredient in perfume. Whalebones were used in the construction of corsets, combs and skirt hoops. Spermaceti, the waxy white substance found in the head cavity of the sperm whale, was used in the manufacture of candles and soap.

This abundance of commercial opportunity led to an explosion in whaling. Between 1815 and 1820, the number of whalers from Nantucket alone grew from twenty-five to ninety. By 1846, the United States had a total whaling fleet of 735 ships – out of a total global fleet of 900 whalers. At the peak of American whaling in 1853, this armada would kill 8,000 whales, producing 103,000 barrels of sperm oil and 260,000 barrels of whale oil, in a business that brought in $11 million each season.

Could the whale 'long endure so wide a chase, and so remorseless a havoc', Melville asked in *Moby-Dick*. In time, it was proved that it could not. But in contrast to the rapid destruction of the sea otter populations and the sandalwood groves, the whaling population held out for decades against the onslaught. The relative resilience of the whale meant that there was almost half a century for the industry to mature, and the American presence in the Pacific to mature with it. American whalers touched on every single port between Cape Horn and the Strait of Malacca. They practically took over the commercial activities of the Hawaiian harbours of Oahu and Lahaina, which no less an authority than the HBC's George Simpson declared had been 'intended by Providence to be a common centre for the whaling-grounds'. As the number of American whalers grew, the accents of New Bedford and Nantucket became commonplace across the Pacific. A whole generation of New Englanders went to sea. How many could say with Ishmael that 'a whale-ship was my Yale College and my Harvard' is not clear. But it is quite plausible that the total population of American whaling men extended into the hundreds of thousands in these years, adding to the legion of Americans who went to sea after 1815 and, as Melville wrote, 'overran and conquered the watery world' of the Pacific.[8]

By the end of the 1830s, there was a permanent population of Americans in the Pacific: shopkeepers in Valparaíso, ranchers in California, missionaries in Hawaii, sealers on nameless Antarctic rocks, and whalers everywhere. Many relished the freedom and anonymity of a roving life, far from home. But many more felt abandoned by their country and their government. Richard Henry Dana worked the California tallow and hide trade on the brig *Pilgrim* in the mid-1830s. Remarking on his feelings when he reflected on his position as the humblest sort of sailor in the American merchant navy, Dana wrote that 'beside the length of the voyage, and the hard and exposed life, we were in the remote parts of the earth, on an almost desert coast, in a country where there is neither law nor gospel, and where sailors are at their captain's mercy, there being no American consul, or any one to whom a complaint could be made'. Far in advance of the flag, Americans had furthered the interests of their country. Would their country protect theirs?[9]

## WINDOWS ON THE PACIFIC

Unsurprisingly it was a Yankee, John Adams, who was among the first to grasp the implications of America's growing naval presence across the globe. Writing in 1813, Adams noted that the rise of American naval power marked 'a grand era in the History of the World. The consequences of it, will be greater than any of us can foresee.' What Adams understood was that while land powers have parochial interests, sea powers have global interests. The American West was a continental empire that the United States would in time subdue. But by going to sea, the United States made itself a part of what William Seward called 'the contest for the ultimate empire of the ocean'. No longer would the United States have the luxury of worrying purely about local matters – it would have to participate fully in international politics. Washington, the soldier, had warned his fellow Americans against foreign entanglements; Adams, the maritime lawyer, looked upon his country's expanding web of naval interests and came to a very different conclusion: 'We shall interfere everywhere.'[10]

Inevitably it was the Northeast, the heartland of America's shipping trade, that took up the task of lobbying on behalf of America's sprawling maritime interests. Along an arc of coastline from the Battery to Passamaquoddy Bay, this region had been enriched by America's triumphant arrival in the Pacific. Manhattan and Boston had taken the lion's share of the spoils, but across the Yankee seaboard numerous towns had grown rich on the profits of the Pacific trade. Sag Harbor and Greenport in Long Island. Bridgeport and New London in Connecticut. Bristol and Providence in Rhode Island. Beverly, Barnstaple and Braintree in Massachusetts. Portsmouth in New Hampshire. Gloucester, Bath and Wicasset in Maine. Meditating on the opulent houses and immaculately maintained lawns of the whaling capital of New Bedford, Melville's Ishmael reflects that 'all these brave houses and flowery gardens came from the Atlantic, Pacific, and Indian Oceans. One and all, they were harpooned and dragged up hither from the bottom of the sea.'

From these coastal outposts the fruits of the trade flowed into the hinterland such that, from his desk at Concord, Ralph Waldo Emerson could write in 1837 that 'I listen by night, I gaze by day at the endless procession of wagons loaded with the wealth of all regions of England

and China, of Turkey, of the Indies, which from Boston creep by my gate to all the towns of New Hampshire and Vermont.' But the interior benefited as suppliers of the fleet, not simply as consumers of their cargo. The growth in commerce led to a shipbuilding boom that created hundreds of jobs along the Mystic and the Merrimac, the Kennebec and the Penobscot Rivers. Yankee fleets were reliable consumers of cordage, staves, flour, vinegar, tar, corn, rum, pickled pork and much more besides. The activities of the merchant marine spurred New England's economic development. The importation of hides supplied the region's shoe factories. Local textile mills used spermaceti as a softening agent and whale oil as a lubricant. The finished products of both industries found a ready market in the Pacific. Standing in San Diego harbour in the mid-1830s, Richard Henry Dana watched the *Pilgrim* unload 'boots and shoes from Lynn, calicoes and cotton from Lowell' and could not help but note the irony that the local *Californios* were buying shoes made from their own hides 'which have been carried twice round Cape Horn' for the tidy sum of four dollars a pair.[11]

The ultimate beneficiaries of all this activity – the financiers, the ship-owners, the heads of the great mercantile houses – were in awe at their own success. Within forty years of Captain Gray's pioneering voyage to China, they had built a network of offices and outposts that connected Boston with Canton via Chile, Peru, California, the Philippines and Hawaii. They had put hundreds of ships to sea and thousands of hands to work. The capital of New York and New England, the wealth of its most influential men, was now on the ocean. Yet the scale of the accomplishment also filled them with anxiety. They had extended themselves into an arena far beyond the gaze of the federal government and were vulnerable to attack from pirates, indigenous peoples and hostile European powers. 'The people are anxious; it is natural,' Massachusetts congressman Edward Everett wrote in 1834. 'There is a vast property afloat; our merchants have connexions with every accessible port on the habitable globe.' The complaints of the maritime interests were legion, but above all they complained about the lack of a safe harbour in the Pacific.[12]

These entreaties could not be entirely dismissed as special pleading. From an economic perspective the maritime trade was benefiting the entire Union, not just the Northeast. At its height, the whaling business was estimated to be the fourth-largest industry in the United States. The

China trade, while small, provided the nation's entire supply of tea. The employment and consumption generated by the merchant navy benefited Americans across the country. Moreover, national honour and national pride was on the line. From a standing start, the United States had built one of the largest fleets in the world. In a matter of decades, they had risen to become the second carrier in the Pacific – second to the centuries-old naval might of Great Britain. In the process, these ships and their sailors had established America as a player in the Pacific, where they contended not just with Britain but with Russia and France as well, and had forged enduring connections in Java, Japan, China, the Philippines and Hawaii. The government could not ignore so large and so profitable an agglomeration of interests.

The United States Navy emerged as the arm of government most vocal in calling for greater commitment in the Pacific. In its annual reports to Congress, the Navy Department kept track of America's escalating involvement in the Pacific. As early as 1827, the report noted that in the previous year 'five millions of American property and 2,000 seamen were in the single port of Honolulu' and called for greater naval commitment in the region. By 1835, the navy was openly calling for the establishment of 'a post to which our vessels may resort [on the Pacific]'. The theme was picked up in the 1842 report which noted that 'the people of various countries are rapidly forming settlements all along the shores of the Pacific, from the Columbia River to the Gulf of California … with the countenance and support of their respective Governments. In the meantime, we are doing literally nothing for our own interests in that quarter.' The navy had done what it could in previous decades, creating the Pacific Squadron in 1818 and the East Indies Squadron in 1835, which by 1842 contained a quarter of the entire fleet. Now the navy was asking for more: more ships, and a Pacific port to harbour them in.[13]

In 1841 these ideas won an advocate in the President's Mansion. The 1840 election saw the incumbent Martin Van Buren lose to the Whig candidate William Henry Harrison. On 4 March 1841, Harrison was sworn in as president and then delivered the longest inaugural address in presidential history. The sixty-eight-year-old Harrison gave the interminable speech outside in the cold, wearing neither hat nor overcoat, not even a pair of gloves. A month later he was dead of pneumonia.

These were the circumstances that propelled his vice president, John Tyler, to the highest office in the land. It was the first time that a sitting president had died and uncertainty surrounded the terms of Tyler's succession. Not the least of the concerns was the character of Tyler himself. Born in Virginia in 1790 to a wealthy, slave-owning family, Tyler was a blue-blooded patrician, an ardent believer in states' rights and small government, and a guilt-free slaveholder. He was not a Whig. Tyler had been a Jeffersonian Democrat all his life but had left the party in protest at Jackson's authoritarian style. The Whigs welcomed him into the party not for his views but for his standing in the South, where they struggled to win votes. He was added to the presidential ticket in 1840 in a standard bid to balance out the ticket, nothing more. Unsurprisingly, upon Harrison's death many Whigs were uncomfortable with having him occupy the presidency. They had won the election for Harrison and Whiggery – not for Tyler and southern rights. They dubbed Tyler 'his accidency' and regarded him with suspicion shading into odium. Tyler was unmoved by their opinions and unbothered by the fact that only freak chance had made him president. Tyler was proud, independent-minded and contemptuous of the niceties of democratic politics. He had long sought higher office and now he had achieved it. He intended to wield power as he wished.

What few could have predicted was that this scion of the Virginia Tidewater elite would prove to be an enthusiastic proponent of navalism. Tyler's father had been room-mates with Jefferson when the two studied law at Williamsburg, and the two families remained close. John Tyler considered himself the rightful heir to the Sage of Monticello, the relay runner to whom the baton of true Jeffersonianism had been passed as the United States sprinted towards mid-century. In this spirit, Tyler never ceased believing that the vast territorial extent of the United States was proof of the genius of the American political order. 'My imagination has led me to look into the distant future,' he declared in an 1832 speech, 'and there to contemplate the greatness of free America. I have beheld her walking on the waves of the mighty deep, carrying along with her tidings of great joy to distant nations.'

It was in this tradition that, as president, Tyler looked to continue expanding the Union. His focus was on Texas, but Oregon also figured in his plans. In extending American rule beyond the Rockies, he would prove that Jefferson's vision remained in rude health and that 'the influence of our political system is destined to be as actively and as beneficially felt on the distant shores of the Pacific as it is now on those of the Atlantic Ocean'.

Consequently Tyler embraced the quest for a Pacific harbour, or what his secretary of state, Daniel Webster, called 'windows on the Pacific'. Ideally, Webster wanted San Francisco ('that beautiful bay … capable of accommodating the whole naval power of the world') and he hatched a complex plan for tripartite negotiations with Britain and Mexico to that end. These never transpired – not least as Britain had no interest in playing midwife to an American empire. Tyler might have let the United States' hopes for a Pacific outlet reside in the mouth of the Columbia River, but then, in June 1842, Charles Wilkes and the U.S. Ex. Ex. returned to the United States after nearly four years at sea.[14]

Securing congressional funding for the U.S. Ex. Ex. was the signal victory of the navalist lobby in the 1830s. The actual aims of the expedition were as various as the justifications made for its existence. Rarely has a government venture had so many subplots and ancillary projects – including among them the discovery of a new continent* – encompassed in its remit. Rarer still that its many goals should have been fulfilled, albeit over hundreds of days and thousands of miles.

At its heart, however, the U.S. Ex. Ex. was a surveying expedition. American captains had long complained of their poor charts and American patriots bristled at their dependence on British mapmakers. A thorough survey of the Pacific's shores, islands, shoals and sea lanes would go some way towards satisfying the merchant marine and soothing American pride. Charles Wilkes had been chosen as its commander chiefly for his gifts as a nautical surveyor, and the Ex. Ex. was manned by artists, geologists, botanists, mineralogists, linguists and conchologists who would supplement the business of chart-making with rich written reports describing the landscape and seascape of the Pacific

---

* Wilkes staked a claim to the discovery of Antarctica. The claim is disputed, in part because there is a technical distinction between the discovery of the continental mass of Antarctica and the exploration of the mass of seaborne ice that surrounds it – navigators were often unsure about which they had disembarked upon – but also because of a mass of rival claims dating to some decades prior. What Wilkes did do for the first time was survey 1,500 miles of the Antarctic coast, now known as Wilkes Land.

Rim. To this mammoth task the navy committed six ships and more than 500 sailors.[15]

Surveying the Pacific was a tedious business ('God grant [an end to this expedition],' one member of the U.S. Ex. Ex. confided in his journal, 'for I am wearied to death with the never ending graph work'), except for when it produced violent affrays with indigenous people, as at Malolo. Wilkes took the work seriously and, as a naval man, regarded it as essential to the nation's maritime interests. Under Wilkes's command, the Ex. Ex. surveyed 280 islands, producing 241 charts – many of which were still in use during World War II. Alongside this, the expedition's scientists produced nineteen volumes of reports and atlases, and brought back to the United States 4,000 zoological specimens, 1,100 birds, 50,000 plants, 5,000 cultural objects, as well as corals, minerals, seeds and even skeletons, not to mention a wealth of hydrological, meteorological, astronomical and oceanographic data. For his contributions to the natural sciences, Wilkes would later receive a Founder's Medal from the Royal Geographical Society in London – substantially more recognition* than he ever received from his own country.[16]

Of all the places Wilkes surveyed, none was more sensitive than Oregon. Gathering precise information about the state of Oregon's shorelines and waterways was one of the central aims of the Ex. Ex. Wilkes spent three months there during the spring and summer of 1841, his ships fanning out to explore different portions of the coast and interior. In this time his men surveyed 800 miles of Oregon's shoreline and 100 miles of the Columbia River. Wilkes spent considerable time ashore and was impressed with what he saw of the HBC operation, and pleasantly surprised by the courtesy extended to him by John McLoughlin,

---

* Wilkes's reputation in the United States was marred by his behaviour while at sea. Nicknamed the 'Stormy Petrel', Wilkes was both a martinet (infamously he reintroduced the archaic and cruel practice of 'flogging around the fleet') and an emotionally volatile man prone to fainting fits and bouts of hysterical weeping. His men loathed him. 'Wilkes merits hanging,' one sailor wrote, 'only that he deserved impaling, long, long ago.' He also drew widespread criticism from within the navy for promoting himself to the rank of captain while leading the U.S. Ex. Ex. and adding to his uniform 'an immense pair of Epaulettes'. His actions led to a public outcry, resulting in a formal investigation into his leadership which overshadowed the genuine accomplishments of the expedition. One of Herman Melville's cousins served as an officer under Wilkes, and Melville later drew upon aspects of Wilkes's character when inventing Ahab.

who provided him with boats, horses and guides to aid in his surveying trips. McLoughlin even donated an ox for the Americans' Fourth of July feast. Displays of goodwill could not conceal the geopolitical tensions in the region. Both Wilkes and McLoughlin knew they trod on disputed land. Wilkes was in Oregon as an agent of his government and a commissioned officer in its armed forces. What he reported back to Washington would have a decisive impact on how the Oregon Question was resolved. Indeed, Wilkes began writing his report on Oregon shortly after the U.S. Ex. Ex. departed the Pacific Northwest in August 1841. It was finished by the time the expedition docked in New York in June 1842.

Wilkes's confidential report on Oregon had three important implications for Tyler's search for a Pacific harbour. First, Wilkes destroyed forever the notion that the mouth of the Columbia River could be a suitable port for American shipping. 'Mere description can give but little idea of the terrors of the bar of the Columbia,' Wilkes wrote of the entrance to the Columbia; 'all who have seen it have spoken of the wilderness of the ocean, and the incessant roar of the waters, representing it as one of the most fearful sights that can possibly meet the eye of the sailor.' So violent was the mouth of the Columbia that the Ex. Ex. lost one of its own vessels, the *Peacock*, in its waters.[17]

Thankfully, Wilkes had discovered the perfect substitute. One hundred miles north of the Columbia was the Strait of Juan de Fuca, a broad channel connecting the Salish Sea to the Pacific Ocean. Along the northern shore of the channel is Vancouver Island; its southern bank is the northern coast of the Olympic Peninsula. If ships enter the Salish Sea and head north they will rejoin the Pacific via the Strait of Georgia. Should they turn south they enter Puget Sound, a system of waterways and inlets remarkable for their depth, tranquillity and extent. Puget Sound had been visited many times before, but it had never been subject to a rigorous survey. Upon the conclusion of his survey, Wilkes declared that 'nothing can exceed the beauty of these waters, and their safety ... I venture nothing in saying, there is no country in the world that possesses water equal to these.' Wilkes had visited the harbour at San Francisco, which he considered one of the finest in the world, but happily allowed that Puget Sound was its equal. The construction of port facilities on Puget Sound would turn it into a strategic asset worthy of 'a great maritime nation'.[18]

As important as these conclusions was the simple fact that Wilkes had gone about his task with precision and diligence. Wilkes's report, and the groundbreaking 1844 map of Oregon that was subsequently produced, dispelled decades of conjecture and fancy. He had brought the resources and the prestige of the United States government to bear on a subject that had long been the domain of traders, trappers and adventurers. In quite literally putting Oregon on the map, Wilkes made it possible for serious people to discuss it with facts, charts and data at their disposal. As one early historian put it, Wilkes's survey of Oregon was 'not only true but bore a great nation's stamp of authenticity. These shores, which hitherto were little more than myths in the world's mind, were now clothed in reality.'[19]

In clothing Oregon with reality, Wilkes also transformed the terms of the Oregon Question. If the mouth of the Columbia was not a suitable harbour and Puget Sound could not be surrendered, then Britain's proposed division of the Oregon Country along the course of the Columbia River had to be resisted at all costs.

The effect on United States policy was felt immediately. A few months after Wilkes's report landed in Washington, Webster wrote to the United States ambassador in London, Edward Everett, instructing

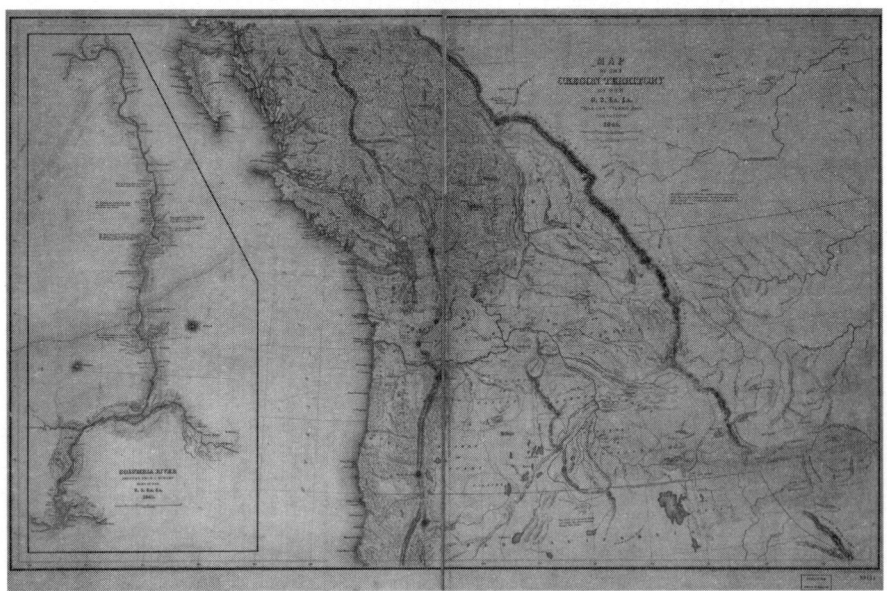

*Wilkes's map of Oregon.*

him to reject the British notion of using the Columbia as a border, even though 'at first blush the Columbia River might seem to present itself as a convenient line of division'. 'If we should consent to be limited by the river on the north,' Webster went on, 'we shall not have one tolerable harbor on the coast.' The United States was now committed to a border that began at 'the entrance of the Straits of St. Juan de Fuca' and would 'give us a harbor at the southwest corner of these inland waters'.

Webster's position became the norm among the maritime interest and their spokesmen. Puget Sound, one New York congressman declared, 'is the key to the Pacific. It will command the trade of the isles of the Pacific, of the East, and of China.' The New England commercial community also spoke up in support of securing Puget Sound. In 1845, William Sturgis, a major figure in Boston commercial circles, delivered an influential speech on Oregon. Puget Sound, he said, was the perfect harbour: 'easy of access, safe, and navigable at all seasons and in any weather'. As far as New England was concerned it was all that was at stake in Oregon. Sturgis declared his indifference to the 'dreary deserts' of eastern Oregon and remarked it would be a 'lesser evil' if the 'unoccupied portion of the Oregon Territory should sink into' the earth and so end what he viewed as a frivolous dispute between Britain and America over worthless land. Sturgis's remarks accurately reflected a significant portion of elite opinion. As far as America's admirals, merchants and captains were concerned, the Oregon Question was a maritime question coupled to the United States' burgeoning interests across the Pacific Rim.

Yet mere months after the publication of Wilkes's report, these assumptions would be upturned and the pursuit of a Pacific harbour would be overtaken by events on land. The cause of Oregon was about to be reclaimed by the pioneers of the West and reconnected to the mission of continental settlement.[20]

# Oregon Fever

As the grass thickened on the prairie in the late spring of 1843, word spread across the frontier for the emigrants to assemble. By the second week of May, hundreds of them had descended on the small town of Independence, Missouri, just west of St Louis. By day, they swarmed the town. From the streets rose the clamour of blacksmiths mending wagons and shodding mules and oxen. Grocers and dry-goods stores were packed with men haggling over the price of salt, coffee, vinegar and other staples. Saddlers, bridle-makers and coopers did a roaring trade. In the evening, the emigrants retired to their camps on the edge of town, where their horses and livestock – somewhere between 3,000 and 5,000 of them – had been put out to graze.

They were, by their own lights, a mixed bunch from all over the Trans-Mississippi frontier: Illinois, Iowa, Arkansas, the western counties of Kentucky, Tennessee and Missouri. Most were strangers to all but their own family. The men were the lean, yellow-faced patriarchs of hard-pressed frontier households. The women were raw-skinned and wore bonnets or held ragged parasols to shelter from the sun. Their children went barefoot and wore broadcloth or baggy brown homespun clothes and in the evening slept in rows in the wagon beds. These people had sold everything they possessed and bet it on a wagon and a new life out west.

Scattered among the mass of plain farmers were other frontier types. There were ambitious local grandees positioning themselves to be leaders of the new communities waiting to be formed across the plains. There were wifeless young men with bowie knives on their belts who talked large, chewed copious amounts of tobacco and left a trail of yellow-brown spittle in their wake. There were a handful of trappers and missionaries and old mountain men who knew the routes out west. At night they gathered round fires. Some played the fiddle and some read their Bibles, and all spoke of what might await them on the prairies and beyond.

They knew, whether they admitted it around the campfire or not, that much of the country thought them insane. Horace Greeley, one of the most famous newspapermen in the country, had told his readers that their journey was madness, that 90 per cent of these emigrants would die, that it was 'palpable homicide to tempt or send women and children' into the wilderness.

Nevertheless, on 20 May the emigrants moved to the official jumping-off spot at Fitzhugh's Mill, twelve miles west of Independence, and held a meeting to organize the leadership of the wagon train and plan its order of march. To shore up morale, long speeches were given. Speakers appealed to pride, patriotism and greed. They were bound for a country, one said, 'where the soil yielded the richest return for the slightest amount of cultivation, where the trees were loaded with perennial fruit, and where ... salmon and other fish crowded the streams, and where the principal labor of the settler would be confined to keeping their gardens free from the inroads of buffalo, elk, deer, and wild turkeys'. And by virtue of prospering, they would ensure their country prospered too. Their descendants, he said, 'would honor us for placing the fairest portion of our land under the dominion of the Stars and Stripes'. Two days later, they assembled in formation on the easternmost edge of the Great Plains, 900 people in a hundred wagons with thousands of livestock corralled before them by mounted outriders. As day broke, they trundled onto the prairie with the sun at their backs. Some had written their destination on their wagon covers: FOR OREGON.[1]

## THE SUMMONS

In 1835, there were twenty-six Americans living in the entire Pacific Northwest. The main barrier to settlement was the Rocky Mountains. Although knowledge of the far west had been steadily increasing since the Lewis and Clark expedition, the general belief was that the Rockies were impassable except by foot or on horseback. So long as the overland route to Oregon could not be completed by wagon, there was no prospect of establishing permanent communities.

That belief was exploded in 1824 when a group of fur traders, including the legendary explorer Jedediah Smith, heading west through the mountains discovered the South Pass. Its importance was not missed. In a letter to the secretary of war written in 1830, Smith trumpeted the South Pass and pointed out its obvious advantages as a means of enabling westward expansion. 'This is the first time that wagons ever went to the Rocky Mountains,' he wrote, 'and the ease and safety with which it was done prove the facility of communicating overland with the Pacific Ocean.' Smith's achievement was hailed by boosters of western expansion. In a few years, one predicted, 'a trip to the Pacific, by way of the Rocky Mountains, will be no more of an undertaking than was a journey from the Atlantic cities to Missouri twenty years ago'.[2]

The South Pass provided the means; Hall Jackson Kelley provided the motive. New Hampshire-born and Middlebury-educated, by the late 1820s Kelley was based in Boston, where he had been first a schoolmaster, then a surveyor and finally a failed investor in a textile mill. But Kelley knew he was marked for a higher calling. 'In my youth the Lord Jesus revealed to me in visions the lonely, laborious and eventful life I was to live,' he later wrote, 'and gave at the time of the visions, and afterwards, unmistakable signs that the revelations were by Him.' In 1817, the divine word came to him that he should 'promote the propagation of Christianity in the dark and cruel places about the shores of the Pacific'. Kelley founded the American Society for Encouraging the Settlement of the Oregon Territory and toured New England touting the project of colonization. By the end of the decade, his name was being mentioned in connection with Oregon in congressional debates. By 1831, Kelley was putting together a minutely detailed plan for the mass migration of several thousand carefully chosen people to Oregon. It was a mission, he believed, that was 'planned by Providence, made easy by nature, and urged and encouraged by the persuasive motives of philanthropy'.[3]

One can imagine Kelley's excitement when, in 1831, four Nez Perce Indians arrived in St Louis seeking religious instruction for the tribes west of the Rockies. The exact details of their request are unclear. Communication was hampered by a lack of interpreters, and all four died within months of arrival. Nevertheless, news of their visit electrified American evangelicals. 'Who will respond to the call from beyond the Rocky mountains?' asked one Christian newspaper. 'All we want is the men. Who will go? Who?' Not, it transpired, Hall Jackson Kelley. His own schemes were weighed down by their own ambition, and a growing number of potential backers were put off by his manic manner.

Instead, two Methodist missionaries from New England, Jason and Daniel Lee, stepped forward. Jason emerges from Hubert Howe Bancroft's early history of Oregon as physically impressive ('tall, and powerfully built ... rather massive jaws; eyes of superlative spiritualistic blue, high, retreating forehead ... and withal a stomach like that of an ostrich, which would digest anything') but wanting intelligence.[4] His nephew Daniel was cut from much the same cloth: 'a man in stature, but a child in mind and manners'. But Oregon required brawn, not brains. In April 1834, the Lees joined a party of fur trappers heading westwards to Oregon. By September, they had crossed the mountains and were busy establishing a mission in the Willamette Valley. They also became regular guests at Fort Vancouver, where they served a diverse congregation of Indians, Scots, Métis, Hawaiians, Frenchmen and three Japanese shipwreck survivors who had washed ashore near Cape Flattery earlier that year. Later they established another mission up the river at The Dalles, where missionaries preached on a stony outcrop which still stands in the city centre, known as Pulpit Rock.[5]

A few years later, the Lees were joined by two Presbyterian missionaries, Henry Spalding and Marcus Whitman, and their wives. Eliza and Narcissa were both resilient, resourceful women who dealt with the hardships of the frontier stoically. Marcus was a natural outdoorsman, described by one acquaintance as 'a man of strong sterling character and lots of push'. Henry was bookish and accident-prone. On the boat to Council Bluffs, a cow kicked him overboard. Despite Henry's attempts to wriggle his way out of the mission (citing his wife's health, which was indeed very poor), the party pressed on, securing a place in a caravan of furriers heading to the Rockies. On 3 July, their wagon entered the South Pass. They celebrated Independence Day with a religious service on the Continental Divide. Standing 'upon the summit of those sky-built mountains', Spalding wrote, '[we] commended and consecrated our mission, to be commenced somewhere in the yet far-off West'. Eliza Spalding also celebrated the occasion of an historic first: she and Narcissa Whitman had become the first European women to cross the Rockies.

In September they arrived at their destination. With the help of John McLoughlin, they were soon established. The Whitmans went among the Cayuse in the Walla Walla Valley, where they built a mission complex. The Spaldings preached to the Nez Perce in their territory along the Clearwater River, north-east of the Whitman Mission. Spalding organized the importation of a printing press from missionaries in Hawaii, learnt Sahaptin and began printing religious tracts in the Nez Perce language, the first texts published in the Oregon Country.[6]

Reinforcements sent from the East swelled the number of missions and missionaries in Oregon, and by 1840 the American population had grown to 150. It was a minuscule number, far smaller than the number of HBC employees in the region, but it represented a toehold of American influence and a beacon of American ambition. All the missionaries became enthusiastic supporters of the Oregon cause. 'It does not concern me so much what is to become of any particular set of Indians,' Whitman stated in a letter home; 'our greatest work is to be to aid the white settlement of this country.' Lee, Spalding and Kelley made similar statements. All of them published books, wrote letters and delivered lectures calling for Oregon to be integrated into the Union. These joined a growing literature on Oregon that emerged over the course of the decade. Americans read accounts of Oregon from the missionaries alongside those of figures like Nathaniel Wyeth, William Slacum, Thomas Jefferson Farnham and John C. Frémont, as well as that of Wilkes and the U.S. Ex. Ex. These narratives produced a fascination with Oregon among the public at large which by the early 1840s had turned into a social and political phenomenon.[7]

Marcus Whitman had the chance to witness this first-hand. In 1842 the Presbyterian missions were at risk of being closed down due to feuding between Spalding and another missionary. Desperate to continue their work, Whitman travelled east in October to petition the board in person. Whitman arrived in Boston in March 1843, having made the winter journey in record time (his travelling companion claimed 'this was the only time I ever knew him to travel on Sunday') and exhibiting visible signs of frostbite. Whitman convinced his superiors to continue the mission and prepared to head back to the Walla Walla Valley.

His timing could scarcely have been better. He arrived back in the United States as public obsession with Oregon approached its peak. Up and down the country, emigrant societies were being formed, petitions were being drafted and public meetings were being held. The Oregon issue was discussed in great detail and with immense passion in Congress, where bills for the immediate annexation and settlement of the region were debated.

Upon his arrival in Independence, Missouri, in May 1843, Whitman found himself in the midst of the vast wagon train preparing to head west. Here was the living manifestation of the political mania sweeping the country. 'Just now Oregon is the pioneer's land of promise,' one Iowa newspaper wrote that spring. 'The Oregon fever has broken out, and is now raging like any other contagion.'

> *Oregon.*—The Oregon fever is raging in almost every part of the Union. Companies are forming at the East, and in several parts of Ohio, which, added to those of Illinois, Iowa and Missouri, will make a pretty formidable army. The larger portion of these will probably join the companies at Fort Independence, Missouri, and proceed together across the mountains. It would be reasonable to suppose that there will be at least five thousand Americans west of the Rocky Mountains by next autumn.

*Newspapers reported on – and helped spread – Oregon fever in the early 1840s.*

This migration, later remembered as the Great Migration of 1843, represented a massive escalation in American commitments in Oregon. If it succeeded, the American population of the territory would double overnight. Whitman's arrival at Independence strained coincidence: it seemed providential. Here was a man who had done the journey, had lived in the region for seven years and was a man of God besides.

The emigrants pressed him for information at every turn. His advice never varied. 'Travel, *travel*, travel – nothing else will take you to the end of your journey; nothing is wise that does not help you along, nothing is good for you that causes a moment's delay.' Looking back on his contribution in a letter to his father-in-law, Whitman was less folksy. 'As I hold the settlement of this country by Americans, rather than by English colonists, most important, I am happy to have been the means of landing so large an immigration on the shores of the Columbia with their wagons, families and stock, all in safety.'

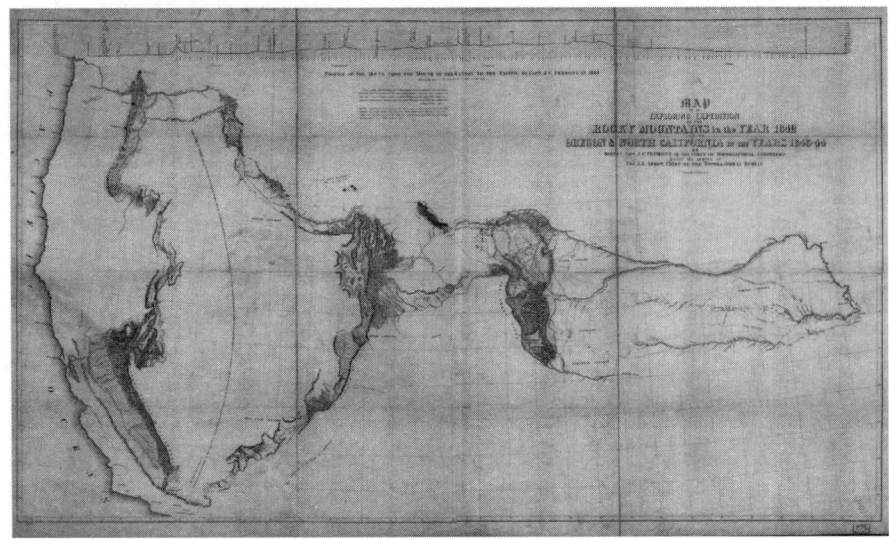

*A map of John C. Frémont's journey along the Oregon Trail.*

It was easy, in retrospect, to see the workings of God in this epochal westward movement. But for the average emigrant staring out into the prairies that spring, all was uncertainty. Whitman might have appeared as a Moses, but that only heightened the sense that they were venturing into a cruel, vast and hazardous wilderness. Ahead of them lay months of hardship and the 2,000 miles of the Oregon Trail.[8]

## THE TRAIL

A journey down the Oregon Trail could not be improvised. It required precise organization and provisioning. The traditional jump-off points were at Independence and St Joseph in Missouri, and Council Bluffs in Iowa. Emigrants usually aimed to arrive at or near these places towards the end of April, in time for a late-May or early-June departure. Timing was critical. If the caravans left too early, the grass on the prairies would not be thick enough to sustain their horses and livestock. If the caravans left too late, the emigrants risked becoming stranded in the mountains and highlands of eastern Oregon in winter. A wagon train that left Independence on 1 June could expect to be at Fort Vancouver in mid-October, a journey of around four months – assuming nothing went wrong.

Careful preparation was the best defence against misadventure. Emigrants needed a wagon drawn by either oxen or mules. This would carry their supplies across the mountains – and they would need a lot of supplies. One handbook recommended that for a journey of 110 days, an adult migrant should take 150 pounds of flour, 25 pounds each of bacon and sugar, 15 pounds of coffee, as well as significant quantities of vinegar, beans, salt and 'antiscorbutics' – usually dried fruit, canned vegetables and wild onions – to guard against scurvy. Just the basics amounted to an immense quantity of food (a party of 150 emigrants was carrying with them six or seven tonnes of flour alone) and did not include the cows that migrants herded along before them on the plains as a ready supply of fresh beef.

Provisioning went beyond food. Emigrants needed two pairs of good boots, feet wraps, puttees, thick flannel shirts, socks, underwear, several blankets, a pillow, a groundcloth, a tent for every five men, cutlery, a kettle, plates, pots and pans, four pounds of soap, two toothbrushes, a knife, a whetstone, a spade or hatchet, spare buttons, an awl, sewing needles, pins, thread, beeswax, a supply of opium, quinine and blue mass, a comb, four handkerchiefs, an overcoat and a hat. This did not even take into account what was required to keep a wagon in working order. 'Every set of six wagons should have a tongue, coupling pole, king-bolt, and pair of hounds extra,' one guidebook advised. 'Every set of six mule wagons should be furnished with five pairs of hames, two double trees, four whipple-trees, and two pairs of lead bars extra.' The total investment in a wagon, draught animals, livestock and supplies typically came to $1,000.

Such a commitment was only viable because most emigrants travelled as families. Jessy Thornton recalled that his 1847 wagon train consisted of 130 men, 65 women and 125 children spread out over 72 wagons. The presence of so many women and children gave the Oregon Trail a more domestic character. There was, however, still a need for single men in the caravans, who were useful as hunters, scouts and guards. When John Minto set off down the trail in 1844, he had only been living in the United States for four years after emigrating from Newcastle aged eighteen. Arriving at St Joseph, he found a man with space in his wagon and provisions to share if he would help 'get my family and effects to Oregon'. Minto accepted.[9]

Once families had gathered and provisioned, they assembled with the rest of the caravan and held a constitutional convention which created a 'government' that lasted for the duration of the journey westwards. The details varied. One train leaving Iowa in 1843 had a constitution with seven articles outlining a division of powers between a legislative, executive and 'military authority'.* Almost all wagon trains had a hierarchy of colonels, captains, sergeants and corporals who were elected by the emigrants and endowed with certain powers and responsibilities. They were usually advised by a council of a dozen or so elders who presided over meetings and tribunals along the route. These preparatory rituals were essential to the identity and the mythos of the Oregon emigrants. The creation of para-governmental institutions to organize and sustain their community along the trail was both a practical measure and a reconsecration of the American ideal. It announced a commitment to a civilizational principle and an embodied intention to bring that principle intact to Oregon. One emigrant described his wagon train as an 'infant republic' which everyone assumed would mature into an adult state beyond the Rockies.[10]

Once they were on the plains, however, the wagon train took on a paramilitary character. For all the idealism inherent in creating self-governing, self-regulated communities, the real reason for travelling in caravans was self-defence. The native peoples who lived on the plains between the Missouri and the Rockies were feared across the United States. 'The Sioux, Arapahoes, Cheyennes, Utes, Snakes, Blackfeet, and Kiowa,' the emigrant's handbook intoned, were 'marauding and erratic savages' who had made 'war the business and pastime of their lives'. Everyone assumed that the Plains tribes would be the principal threat to wagons heading west. The emigrants came armed accordingly. Minto arrived at St Joseph with 'a nice new rifle ... five pounds of powder, twenty-five pounds of lead, one dozen boxes of percussion shots caps, five pounds of shot ... also, I bought two pocketknives, two sheath knives, a hatchet to answer for a tomahawk, and an axe.' Thornton recorded that the 130 men in his wagon train had 104 pistols, 155 guns, 1,672 pounds of lead and 1,100 pounds of powder between them. The

---

* This wagon train actually formed a society for the purpose of emigration which raised a joint stock fund, kept journals of its proceedings and published news of its activities in local newspapers. Its by-laws created courts for the arbitration of disputes that might arise along the trail and forbade the admission of black or mixed-race people to the society, nor any 'person of intemperate or immoral habits or principles'.

men in William Kelly's wagon each had 'a revolver, a sword, and bowie-knife; the mounted men having besides a pair of holster-pistols and a rifle slung from the horn of their saddles, over and above which there were several double and single-shot guns and rifles suspended in the wagons ... where they would be easily accessible in case of attack'. Some emigrant societies stipulated that men had to bring certain quantities of munitions. The daily routine of the wagon trains was essentially martial. In the morning, the emigrants would be woken before dawn by a rifle shot that substituted for an alarm clock. Once they set out on the plains, the mounted men divided up into outriders, scouts and a rearguard, all heavily armed. The main group was organized into a column that could be quickly formed into a defensible position if attacked. Each evening witnessed the defining ritual of the journey west when the wagons formed themselves into a circle, the wheels of each interlocking with those before and behind, and a length of chain would be run through the spokes binding the whole together. The tired travellers would then light a fire, share a meal and post watchmen to look out for Indians while the rest slept.[11]

The attacks never came. Before 1849, lethal encounters between emigrants and native peoples were vanishingly rare. Overall, the Oregon Trail had a mortality rate of around 6 per cent. Emigrants died of disease and exposure; they drowned in river crossings; children were thrown off wagons and crushed or trampled; men were killed in shooting accidents; some died of old age or in childbirth and some murdered each other in personal vendettas. Very few were killed by the Plains tribes.

The real danger the emigrants faced was attrition. This was a silent and invisible enemy that was strengthened by the emigrants' own zeal and aided by accident and happenstance. Survival on the Oregon Trail was a matter of vigilance and self-control. Above all, emigrants had to tend to the well-being of their draught animals. If they drove them too hard, or overburdened them with supplies, they would die of exhaustion and their owners would be stranded hundreds if not thousands of miles from the nearest settlement. Mules and oxen needed to be well fed, well shod and well watered. Resting them periodically was far wiser than impetuously driving them onwards. Yet even with the best care, these animals were still vulnerable. They could be scattered by storms and cyclones, stolen or stampeded by Indian raiders, lost fording rivers, felled by disease or poisoned by bad water. There were even accounts of oxen being struck by lightning. Most commonly, however, they were gradually ground down by long days and insubstantial forage. Humans were as vulnerable as their livestock to bad luck and freak occurrences. A broken axle. A wagon stuck in quicksand. Five days lost attempting to cross a high river. A week spent recuperating from sickness. Delays ate into limited provisions and drew out the expedition into the lethal winter months. The art of successfully traversing the Oregon Trail lay in exercising restraint in working livestock forward while reducing the number of delays that held a wagon back. Every emigrant needed good discipline and good luck.[12]

After the initial excitement of departure wore off, the emigrants settled into the routine of the wagon train. The first phase of the journey was the easiest, along a well-worn overland route to the Platte River. The landscape was featureless: no trees, no scrub or vegetation; just green, gently undulating prairie. The plains here were largely empty of game, though this was of little concern as their supplies were fresh. There were, however, Pawnee Indians, often the first native peoples any of them had ever seen. The first sighting of native peoples always generated fear as well as fascination; they soon learnt that the Pawnee had little interest in them.

This part of the journey was uneventful. Groups of scouts were sent ahead to look for game and an appropriate bivouac for the night. Women knitted in the wagons as they trundled westwards. In the evening, men griped about their leaders while the children played. As days passed by without incident, over a landscape devoid of animal or vegetable, tedium became the dominant note of their westward odyssey. 'The journey was somewhat monotonous,' Francis Parkman wrote of this stage of the trail. 'One day we rode on for hours, without seeing a tree or a bush; before, behind, and on either side, stretched the vast expanse, rolling in a succession of graceful swells, covered with the unbroken carpet of fresh green grass.'[13]

The first obstacle of any note was the Kansas River, which most migrants crossed with the help of ferrymen. The crossings of the Black Vermillion, Little Blue and Big Blue Rivers were comparatively easy, and within a month of departure the caravans reached their first major landmark: the Platte River.

From the bluffs overlooking Grand Island, the emigrants had the opportunity of surveying the Platte Valley in all its barren majesty. They had now entered Nebraska and the land here was perfectly flat and sandier than in Kansas. From any point of elevation they could see for miles, the clear air making distant objects seem deceptively close. They also noted that the vastness of the plain produced strange sonic effects. Sound dissipated eerily fast, swallowed up by the flatlands. Through this empty landscape wound the broad Platte, a silver ribbon unravelling across the green prairie. 'It was right welcome; strange too, and striking to the imagination,' Parkman said of his first glimpse of the river. 'For league after league a plain as level as a frozen lake was outspread beneath us; here and there the Platte, divided into a dozen threadlike sluices, was traversing it.' The Platte was an unerring guide to the South Pass. Although it had numerous streams, its main channel headed north-west in a near straight line to the mountains. If the wagons hewed to its course, they would reach the Continental Divide.[14]

The plains around the Platte were home to the buffalo, the symbol of the western plains. 'No adequate conception can be formed of the immensity of the numerous herds, which here abound,' one emigrant guide wrote. 'The entire plains and prairies are densely covered, and completely blackened with them, as far as the most acute vision extends.' The buffalo provided a supply of game and their droppings were a passable substitute for firewood, given the lack of timber. Parties of men were dispatched to collect the precious stuff. 'You would laugh I know to see me going along with a bag on my back gathering Buffalo dung to cook with,' one emigrant wrote home, 'but we have to do it. The darn stuff burns fine in a stove.' The warmth was needed. The plains were wet and cold even in the summer and especially at night. 'Suffered very much from a very hard, cold rain,' James Nesmith recorded in his journal for 21 June 1843. 'Waded a slough and camped on the river bank among some willows. Lay in wet blankets on the wet sand. Extremely cold.'[15]

Near the headwaters of the Platte, the landscape began to change again. The soil became sandier; the landscape drier and dustier. A series of stone monuments rose out of the land: Courthouse Rock, Chimney Rock, Scott's Bluff. They were impressive in their own right and a welcome relief from the relentlessly horizontal landscape of Nebraska. These landmarks also signalled their entry into the region the emigrants had long regarded with fear and trepidation: what was popularly known as the Great American Desert. The region round there struck Virgil Pringle as 'perfectly sterile'. 'The wind blew very severe,' he wrote, 'and moved the sand in clouds all day.' Migrants noted pools of alkaline water on the plains along the North Platte that were deadly for livestock. Parkman described the whole as 'a long narrow sandy plain, reaching like an outstretched belt nearly to the Rocky Mountains'.[16]

Before leaving the Platte, the wagon trains reached Fort Laramie, a fur-trading outpost owned by the American Fur Company. This was the last opportunity to resupply before they went over the Continental Divide, and emigrants took the chance to assess their position. Many began to dump superfluous material. Emigrants noted the wide range of refuse found along the trail around the fort: stoves, wagon wheels, axle-trees, anvils, bellows, chisels, axes, spades, ploughs.

The local Sioux also camped near the fort and regularly sought to extract 'gifts' from the wagon trains, leading to tense encounters. Sarah Royce recalled her wagon train 'moving between long, but not very compact rows of half naked redskins ... revolvers, knives, hatchets, glittered in their belts; rifles and guns bristled on their shoulders'. Many regarded the Sioux's demands as a form of blackmail. The Sioux, of course, were simply adhering to a pattern of tribute and ritual bribery which had defined their relations with the Americans ever since Lewis and Clark appeared up the Missouri. Moreover, there was a real cost to them in the migration, felt in the reduction in their game supply and the spread of disease along the trail. Francis Parkman, who was more sensitive than most to the position of native peoples along the overland routes, observed near Fort Laramie 'a group of stately figures, their white buffalo robes thrown over their shoulders, gazing coldly upon' his wagon train's evening camp. Inhabiting their minds for an instant, Parkman saw the emigrants not as the Americans did – as brave pioneers – but as a portent of disaster, a 'slow, heavy procession' of invaders into the Sioux homelands 'whom they and their descendants, in the space of a century, are to sweep from the face of the earth'.[17]

After Fort Laramie they left the Platte and crossed a 'country of barren, rolling plains' to the Sweetwater, whose source lay at the eastern approaches of the South Pass. There were two more landmarks here: Independence Rock, the great granite pebble into which pioneers carved their names, and Devil's Gate, a narrow gorge carved out of the rock by the path of the river.

Beyond lay the South Pass, the gateway to the Pacific. Its appearance was contrary to what many emigrants expected. 'It will be seen that it in no manner resembles the places to which the term [pass] is commonly applied,' Frémont wrote. 'Nothing of the gorge-like character and winding ascents of the Allegheny passes in America; nothing of the Great St. Bernard and Simplon passes in Europe.' Instead, the pass was 'a sandy plain, one hundred and twenty miles long' which ascended almost imperceptibly to around 7,000 feet, 'and the traveler, without being reminded of any change by toilsome ascents, suddenly finds himself on the waters which flow to the Pacific ocean'.[18]

By now it was late July. The emigrants had travelled a thousand miles since Independence and had 1,200 miles to go until they reached the Willamette Valley. Crossing the South Pass was a major accomplishment. But any joy in attaining it was tempered by the harshness of the landscape. If the South Pass was the gateway to the Pacific Northwest, then their first impression was of a 'sandy, extremely sterile' land without water or grass, what Pringle described as 'high, broken and desert country'. By this stage many of the travellers were sick – Minto noted that so many of his party were ill when they reached the South Pass there weren't men to stand guard at night – and all were worn down by the hardships of the trail. Almost every party would have sustained a death or heard of one in a neighbouring caravan; they had all travelled down a path punctuated by freshly dug graves. Supplies were starting to dissipate just as the landscape was growing less forgiving. Water had vanished and with it game, timber and pasturage. They had entered what geographers call 'Arid America', a region so dry that the moisture would be scoured from their wagons, making axles brittle and shrinking the spokes in their wheels.

Disillusionment set in among pioneers a thousand miles from home and over a thousand from their destination – a destination whose virtues they were beginning to doubt. 'Crossed the Divide,' Nesmith wrote in his diary on 7 August. 'We now consider ourselves in Oregon Territory, and we consider this part of it a poor sample of the El Dorado.' Whatever they had endured to this point, the worst of the trail was yet to come. Looking back on his journey westwards in 1847, Hezekiah Packingham judged the second half far more trying than the first. 'My trip was pleasant till I got to the South Pass,' he wrote to his brother. 'After the country was rugged, bad, bad roads.'[19]

With the Rockies behind them, the emigrants crossed the Green River, a tributary of the Colorado, and travelled north-west up the Bear River Valley. The terrain there was as alien as they would encounter anywhere along the trail. They travelled across bone-dry plains and wound their way through defiles and gorges studded with greasewood and sage. Nesmith noted the volcanic character of the country around the Bear, describing 'stones which lay about large sinks in the ground, [that] have the appearance of melted clay, and ring like earthenware'. Their route passed through Soda Springs, an area famous for its geysers. One emigrant memorably described the springs 'bubbling, and foaming, and sending up from their clear depths ... a continual discharge of gas and steam, as though they were sunken cauldrons of boiling water'. The surrounding land he noted was 'a sterile, flinty waste ... worthless for agricultural purposes'. There were trout in the streams for food but no timber, only thick sage scrub, which the emigrants had to clear to make a path for their wagons, and then burn to warm themselves in the evening. Although it was August, the altitude meant that the nights could be bitterly cold.[20]

Breaking out of this strange region, they were greeted by a welcome sight. The Portneuf River is a small, unnavigable stream lined by scrub in the highlands of south-eastern Idaho. It is also a branch of the Snake River, which flows into the Columbia and hence into the Pacific. This was the first time the emigrants had struck a tributary of the Columbia. For many this was the moment when they considered themselves in the Oregon Country proper. One wrote that upon seeing the Portneuf 'every head was uncovered, and a cheer rang back into the gorge to the ears of our companions ... It is impossible to describe the enthusiasm which this event created in our party. Each wagon as it arrived at the point unfolding to the view the region which had been the object of our dearest hopes and the occasion of our weary travel, set up a cheer.' One of their number scrambled up to a ledge with a bugle and began urging the wagons on with patriotic tunes.

Nearby was Fort Hall, an HBC post. The commander, Alexander Grant, was usually on hand to provide a strong dose of realism to the emigrants. Typically, he advised them to dump their wagons, load up on supplies and make for the Columbia on horseback. Up until 1843, most emigrants had in fact abandoned their wagons at this juncture, but starting from that year a wagon route was hacked out of the sage and underbrush.* Still, with oxen teams weakening and provisions starting to dwindle, many emigrants took the opportunity to abandon more of their possessions. Most were now singularly focused on ensuring they didn't starve en route to Oregon. Minto left Fort Hall with these words of advice ringing in his ears: 'Boys, you are going through a hard country. You have guns and ammunition. Take my advice: anything you see as big as a blackbird, kill it and eat it.' Fort Hall was the last outpost before they made the Columbia. Between it and the Willamette Valley, Minto wrote, lay 'six hundred miles of hungry land'.[21]

The trail now followed a long northwesterly arc over several tributaries of the Snake – the Boise, Malheur and Burnt Rivers – through what Frémont described as 'a melancholy and strange-looking country – one of fracture, and violence, and fire'. It could at times feel fiercely empty. For many years the main landmark emigrants fixed their path to was the Lone Tree: a solitary fir or ponderosa in an otherwise arid valley. In 1843, an emigrant cut it down for firewood. Generally the colour of the country was gloomy: grey scrub, brown grass, black volcanic rock. Game was scarce and wolves were plenty. Near Salmon Falls were large encampments of Shoshone, who were eager to trade. Frémont was offered dried salmon roe, fresh fish, flapjacks made of pressed choke-cherries and service berries. Nearby, women gathered camas roots and foraged for grasshoppers, crickets and lizards. 'We are encamped immediately on the river bank,' Frémont wrote, 'and with the salmon jumping up out of the water, and Indians paddling about in boats made of rushes, or laughing around the fires, the camp to-night has quite a lively appearance.'[22]

They were approaching the western limit of the Snake Country. The trail ahead traversed the Powder River into the Grande Ronde Valley and then over the Blue Mountains, crossing what is now the Oregon–

---

* One emigrant related a conversation which he heard between a fellow traveller and Alexander Grant. The former asked the latter whether he thought the emigrants could take their wagons through to the Columbia. Grant replied: 'Mr. Cave, it's no use my answering your question. It's just about a year since a lot of people came here just as you have done and asked me the same question. I told them "No; that we found it very difficult to pass the narrow trails with our pack ponies." They went on, just as you will do; just as if I had not spoken a word, and the next I heard of them they were at Fort Walla Walla. You —— Yankees will do anything you like.'

Idaho border. By the Grande Ronde, the landscape became green and lush once more, lifting the spirits of emigrants now marching on one or two meals a day. The rich grass restored the strength of jaded draught animals. Arriving on the western foothills of the Blue Mountains, they sighted the twin peaks of Mount Hood and Mount Adams on the horizon as they entered the Umatilla Valley and then followed it to the Walla Walla.

Waiting for them was the Whitman Station, a welcome sight for exhausted wagon trains. 'I was never more pleased to see a house or white people in my life,' Medorem Crawford wrote. The Whitmans had a mill and supplied the grateful emigrants with fresh flour. Now only a few days march from the Columbia, the emigrants studied the country closely. Some were doubtful. 'The prospect is dreary,' Nesmith concluded. 'If this is a fair specimen of Oregon, it falls far below the conceptions which I formed of the country.' Most emigrants were less pessimistic. Pressing on to the main channel of the Columbia, they rejoiced in their successful passage of the trail. 'There was something inspiring and animating in beholding this [river],' one wrote. 'We could scarce persuade ourselves that our journey had arrived at its termination. We were full of hope, and as it was understood that we had but one more difficult part of the road to surmount, we moved forward with redoubled energy.'[23]

The final stretch was indeed among the most challenging. For many years the wagon road connecting the upper Columbia with The Dalles was almost impassable, and so emigrants had to lash their wagons onto rafts and float them down the river. Emigrants who did so without taking on the help of a local pilot often suffered terribly in the Columbia's fast and dangerous waters. Many capsized, losing their possessions in the current, and often their lives as well. After The Dalles they could rejoin the overland route across the Cascades to Fort Vancouver, where they were invariably received by John McLoughlin.

It was commonly accepted among the emigrants that the HBC was a despotic and malevolent entity intent on harming American settlers in Oregon. Many emigrants were surprised to find McLoughlin welcoming and generous with food and credit. McLoughlin went far beyond his duties to ensure that American pioneers made the final stage of the journey safely, often organizing rescue parties and sending rafts and boats upriver to smooth the emigrants' passage down. 'He is courteous, intelligent and companionable,' one emigrant wrote, 'and a more kind, hospitable and liberal gentleman, the world never saw.' At Fort Vancouver, John Minto was delighted to receive 'an excellent English dinner of roast beef and vegetables'.[24]

With the regular arrival of the pioneer parties each October, these first winter months in the Columbia Valley were filled with anxiety. Arriving parties brought tales of hardship down the trail behind them. Much of the suffering was caused either by misadventures on the Columbia or by becoming stranded in the final mountain ranges on the approaches to Willamette Valley. Minto recalled coming across beleaguered families all along the trail near The Dalles in December. They were all in 'dire straits for food'. 'I saw one man, the father of four children, lying on his back upon a rock, taking the rain in his face, seemingly having given up all thought of manly struggle.'

Alarmed by such reports, starting from 1844, many emigrants took the Applegate cut-off, an alternative route that circumvented the Snake River Valley and approached the Willamette from the south. Virgil Pringle took this route and by the end of October found his party in a desperate state. Writing from the South Umpqua River on 21 October, he recorded 'a series of hardships, break-downs' and of 'being constantly wet and labouring hard' with 'very little to eat, the provisions being exhausted in the whole company'. By 8 November, they were marching on empty stomachs and started slaughtering their remaining cattle for food. One woman in their party died only one week before they finally reached the Willamette.

They fared better than some. In the winter of 1846, Thomas Holt set out from his home in the Willamette Valley as part of a group sent to help stragglers along the Applegate cut-off. Only days out from the settlements along the Willamette, he found whole families of emigrants trapped in snowdrifts, their oxen crippled or dead, the children 'crying for bread'. In one valley 'we met 8 wagons and as many families, all out of provisions'. The mountains were littered with the carcasses of oxen and mules. Some families had simply retreated into their wagons to try and brave out the winter. On Boxing Day, in deep snow, Holt found a family on the Elk River who had had 'nothing to eat for four days, but a little tallow boiled in water'. Such cases dramatically illustrated the perils produced by miscalculations made months before and thousands of miles up the trail.[25]

Even for those who made it safely to the Willamette Valley the completion of the Oregon Trail amounted to trading one set of challenges for another. They had arrived in a primitive frontier community in the heart of winter having lost most their possessions and a good deal of their strength along the way. Pringle noted that his reception in Salem was generous, 'but our living is poor ... and we nothing but labor to give'. Another put the successful emigrant's predicament in starker terms. They were 'more than two thousand miles from the land that gave us birth; with no promise of support or protection from our government; exposed to the inclemencies of a dreary rainy season, of about five months, of almost incessant rain, hail, sleet and snow; without houses, without a sufficiency of clothing, or provision; entirely destitute of the means of agriculture; and surrounded with innumerable savages'.

All the high-flown rhetoric of piercing the wilderness to bring the light of civilization to the dark forests of the Pacific Northwest now collided with the reality of a bare-knuckle struggle for survival in a hostile environment.

There was, however, no turning back. James Nesmith arrived at the falls of the Willamette on 27 October. The next day he made the final entry in his journal: 'Saturday, October 28. – Went to work.'[26]

# The Pioneers and the Politicians

'On the Platte one may sometimes see the shattered wrecks of ancient claw-footed tables, well waxed and rubbed, or massive bureaus of carved oak,' Francis Parkman wrote in his account of the Oregon Trail. 'These, many of them no doubt the relics of ancestral prosperity in the colonial time, must have encountered strange vicissitudes. Imported, perhaps, originally from England; then, with the declining fortunes of their owners, borne across the Alleghenies to the remote wilderness of Ohio or Kentucky; then to Illinois or Missouri; and now at last fondly stowed away in the family wagon for the interminable journey to Oregon.'

Parkman was not unique in situating the emigrants' epic trek across the plains within a romantic narrative. In previous generations, migration to a new frontier had been a reflex action, undertaken when the opportunity arose or when opportunity ran out. The frontier was a practical option, not a mythic place. By the 1840s that had changed. From the outset, the Oregon Trail attracted to itself an outsized amount of glamour, theatrics and self-mythologizing. John Minto was inspired to go to Oregon after reading James Fenimore Cooper's *The Pioneers* (1823) on his voyage across the Atlantic. When he arrived at St Joseph, he whirled his cap around his head and declared to the gathered crowd: 'Boys, here is a fellow that goes to Oregon, or dies in a sand bank.' Such grandstanding was common. One of the early westbound parties marched out of Peoria holding a banner that read 'Oregon or the Grave'. Pioneers decorated their wagon covers with eagles, lions and motivational slogans: 'Patience and Perseverance', 'Never say die', 'Westward the tide of Oregon rolls'. This bravado was amplified in the press and in published accounts, and rubbed off on poets and dreamers across the country. 'Eastward I go only by force, but westward I go free,' Henry David Thoreau wrote. 'I must walk toward Oregon ... that way the nation is moving.'

There was a gulf between presentation and reality – as those who watched the migration realized. In reality, the emigrants' motives were far less romantic. Francis Parkman, who trained his Harvard-educated eye on the plain folk he met along the trail, concluded that the emigrants were straightforward people, not men of destiny. And they had no thought of travelling to Oregon 'or indeed anywhere, from any other motive than gain'.[1]

## THE ULTRAS

What they hoped to gain was land. The proximate cause of the outbreak of Oregon Fever in the spring of 1843 was the passage of a bill in the Senate. The bill's champion was Lewis Linn, a Missouri Democrat. In 1837, Linn had discovered the Oregon cause and made it his own. The next year he chaired a committee that published a report on the disputed region. The same year he put forward the first of many Oregon bills. Linn would submit an Oregon bill for the Senate's consideration every year until he died in October 1843. They were for the most part variants on Floyd's 1821 proposal, but Linn added a new feature. He wanted to give a section of land to each white adult male who settled in Oregon. Every year the bill failed in the Senate. Then, in February 1843, it squeaked through by two votes and was sent to the House, where it was voted down.

The news of Linn's triumph in the Senate electrified the frontier. On his way up the Missouri, Minto recorded that the men he met 'could talk of nothing but Oregon'. Upon arrival in the migrant camps he was quickly informed by Colonel Simmons 'of the probable reward in land that those who reached Oregon would be given by national grant'. The same month, Jesse Applegate wrote to his brother advising him to immediately head to Missouri to join a wagon train. 'If you are going to Oregon by all means go this spring,' he said, 'for if Linn's Bill pass next year every man and every man's neighbour will move in that direction.' Peter Burnett remembered his calculation exactly. He was heavily in debt after a failed business endeavour when he heard of 'a bill pending in Congress, introduced in the Senate by Dr. Linn ... which proposed to donate to each immigrant six hundred and forty acres of land'. Burnett did his sums and figured that 'if Dr. Linn's bill should pass, the land would ultimately enable me to pay up'. By 17 May, he was at Independence.[2]

The failure of Linn's measure in the House did not deter them. Many believed, as one emigrant put it, that at some point in the near future the law 'or a law like it, will pass, and I am going to Oregon anyhow'. After all, this was not the only land act Linn was associated with. His fellow Missouri senator, Thomas Hart Benton, had spent years campaigning to make western land accessible to settlers. Benton championed a federal pre-emption act which essentially legalized squatting. Linn enthusiastically supported Benton's proposal. In a speech endorsing it, he declared that the settlement of the earth was a 'scriptural injunction'. He paid no heed to claims that the beneficiaries of the act were 'squatters' and 'land-stealers', for 'this was a nation of land stealers from the beginning'. Besides, 'the movement of the people would be onward', and no government would ever dare 'send an army to destroy the "squatters"'. The bill passed and was signed into law by President Tyler in September 1841.[3]

The Preemption Act was a significant precursor to Linn's Oregon bill. It enshrined in law a principle that Linn now sought to extend beyond the Rockies. It was an audacious move on Linn's part. It was one thing to legalize squatting in the United States – quite another to encourage it in a disputed region several thousand miles from Washington that was not even part of the national domain. Linn was luring settlers across the Oregon Trail with the promise of land, in the near certainty that the arrival of large numbers of American settlers would precipitate a collision with the British.

That the Senate would pass such a rash measure was testament to the influence of a coterie of Democratic politicians in the upper chamber. They hailed from the Northwest: Lewis Cass of Michigan, Sidney Breese and Stephen Douglas of Illinois, Edward Hannegan of Indiana, William Allen of Ohio (nicknamed the 'Ohio fog horn'), and Lewis Linn and Thomas Hart Benton of Missouri. They were known variously as the Progressive Democracy and the Oregon ultras, and they were associated with one of the most famous slogans in American political history: 'Fifty-four Forty or Fight!'

Linn and his colleagues sincerely believed that the United States had unchallenged title to the entirety of the territory between 42 degrees latitude (the northern limit of Mexico as per the Adams–Onís treaty) and 54° 40' latitude (the southern limit of Russian Alaska as per the St Petersburg Convention of 1824). In their view, the so-called Oregon Question was a canard and talk of settling at the 49th parallel was tantamount to treason. The United States had discovered, explored and settled the Pacific Northwest. Oregon was theirs. Only the spinelessness of American diplomats had permitted the British to insinuate themselves into the territory, and only pettifogging Anglophile politicians had given any colour of legitimacy to British claims west of the Rockies.

They developed a narrative whereby America had won Oregon and then lost it at the negotiating table. They were therefore not asking for Oregon to be occupied, but *reoccupied*. They sought the return of territory that had always been theirs. This was irredentism, not mere expansionism, and it bloated the ultras with the righteousness of their cause. 'We are all for Oregon, the whole of Oregon, and nothing else,' William Allen told the Senate in a characteristic outburst, 'and if it must be obtained at the mouth of the cannon or point of the bayonet we are ready and willing for it at any time, the sooner the better.'[4]

The ultras were inspired by more than lines on maps. Oregon was the point of political union for their two great passions: ardent expansionism and bitter Anglophobia. In a decade which saw a great deal of outlandish expansionist rhetoric, the ultras were the undisputed champions of jingoistic bombast. One of their number told Congress that he wanted the United States to expand such that he 'would live to hear the sound from the Speaker's chair, "the gentleman from Texas." He wanted them also to hear "the gentleman from Oregon." He would even go further, and have "the gentleman from Nova Scotia," "the gentleman from Canada," "the gentleman from Cuba," "the gentleman from Mexico," ay, even "the gentleman from Patagonia."' The extent of their ambitions was gleefully mocked in the press. One cartoon depicted Lewis Cass as a war engine emitting shot and gas and calling for the annexation of New Mexico, California, Chihuahua, Mexico, Peru, Yucatán and Cuba. Their congressional colleagues, however, could not afford to laugh off their territorial demands. After all, they were United States senators whose words were reprinted around the nation and the world. John C. Calhoun was bitterly critical of Cass, describing him as 'of the progressive democracy in the worst sense of that phrase ... With General Cass "progress" means Territorial acquisition by fair means or foul indifferently.' Cass was not a special case but representative 'of the worst elements in the country – North western ignorance and vulgarity, popular violence and ambition ... under his guidance ... we shall be launched into an endless career of ambition and insolence; and be involved in wars of plunder with every friendly power that owns an inch of tempting soil in our neighbourhood.'[5]

Although they cast their rhetorical net wide, the ultras' true target was Canada and their real enemy was Britain. Britain was 'haughty, grasping, unjust', 'the pharisee of nations', 'their hereditary enemy, the enemy of all free governments'. Their loathing was informed by substantive complaints. The Midwest bordered Canada and felt itself peculiarly vulnerable to British meddling. Dating back to the revolution, the people of the old Northwest Territory accused the British (not

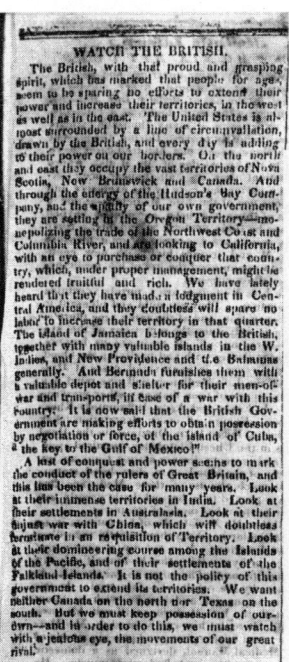

*This article promotes the idea that the British were seeking to encircle the United States, a belief widely held among Americans eager to seize Oregon.*

without basis) of funding Indian resistance to American settlers, climaxing in Tecumseh's campaigns in the 1810s. This history heightened their sense of Britain's malevolent proximity. They believed the conquest of Canada was the only way to end the threat.* All of these concerns were superimposed onto the Oregon Question. Many argued that if Britain held Oregon, it would stir up Indian resistance from the Columbia Valley to the Great Plains. Others observed that dividing Oregon along the 49th parallel left America's isolated Pacific possessions vulnerable to surprise attacks from the north. In both cases the ultras were transplanting old, local anxieties to the new frontier beyond the Rockies.[6]

Commercial grievances mingled with security concerns. The South had grown rich off cotton exports to Liverpool; New England and New York had profited from the transatlantic trade with Britain. But the Midwest raised wheat – and wheat was barred from the English market by the protective Corn Laws. Furthermore, the states along the upper Mississippi were the natural entrepôts for the trade in furs that stretched across the Rockies. Ever since the Louisiana Purchase, westerners had seen their states as the gateway to the riches of the far west. Beyond that lay the Pacific coast and the riches of Asia. The distances might have been immense, but the opportunity felt nearby. And yet when they looked west, they found Britain barring their way again, this time in the form of the sharp-elbowed, avowedly monopolistic HBC.

This sense that they were hemmed in on all sides and excluded from the global economy gave rise to a larger, more conspiratorial, claim that the United States was in a titanic struggle with the British Empire for control over global trade. The ultras imagined Oregon as the final link

---

* British travellers were startled at how casually the Americans discussed seizing Canada. Sarah Mytton Maury, who visited at the height of Oregon Fever, reported that all along the border there were groups of armed men who talked openly 'of invading Canada' and apparently enjoyed the sanction of the authorities. While visiting Congress, she recorded a remarkable comment made by Charles Jared Ingersoll, an influential Pennsylvania Democrat: 'I received a letter from Mr. Smith, the Attorney General of the Canadas, dated Montreal, in the middle of January, 1845; the snow was then fifteen feet deep at Quebec. Ingersoll was present when I received the letter, and I read it aloud to him, as the most suitable person to give a reply. "When," said Mr. Smith, "when are the Americans coming to take Canada?" "Whenever it's thawed," carelessly returned the Chairman of Foreign Relations, taking up his hat and gloves to go away, as if for the purpose.'

in a vast chain of British commercial domination. If Britain secured the mouth of the Columbia and access to the Strait of Juan de Fuca, one ultra claimed, 'the cross of St. George would float in triumph over every island in the Pacific. It is not so much a few acres of land that Great Britain wants, as it is a monopoly of the furs of the Northwest, the pearls and gold of Panama and Choco, minerals of Peru, hides of California, the whale fisheries, and, in fine, the whole trade of China, the Pacific islands, and the western shore of Mexico and Central America.' The contest for Oregon was existential. If the United States surrendered Oregon, it sacrificed its prosperity. And if it triumphed in Oregon, it would be in a position to end British commercial primacy. 'It is an inch of ground upon which we can place a fulcrum,' one Indiana congressman explained, 'giving us the lever by which to overturn the world of British commerce.'[7]

While the ultras loved to harp on these themes, there was another matter guiding their thinking. One so insidious and so divisive that they dared not name it: slavery. In theory, slavery had nothing to do with Oregon. The climate and landscape of the Pacific Northwest made plantation slavery impossible. From a political perspective, it lay well above the Missouri Compromise line. That was the theory. In practice, slavery shaped many of the unspoken political assumptions of the Oregon crusade. With the exception of the Missouri delegation, the ultras hailed from free states. But as Democrats they were in a coalition with the southern slaveholders. Jackson had forged this coalition by insisting that this glaring difference between the West and the South did not matter. Slavery was peripheral to politics. Neither southern Democrats or northern Democrats should talk about it. Only detested radicals – abolitionists in the North, nullifiers in the South – dared politicize slavery, and they did so because they hated that which the Jacksonians loved most: the Union.

The problem was that the midwestern electorate did care about slavery. A common feature of memoirs of the Oregon Trail was the encounter with slavery in St Louis as pioneers headed to the jumping-off points. Often this was the first time they had witnessed its practice. They were appalled at what they saw. Myron Eells shared a steamboat with slave traders and their coffles on the way to Missouri. 'People on the boat talk about buying and selling slaves with as much freedom as farmers talk of selling cattle, in the New England states,' he wrote in his diary. The sight of men and women treated as chattel moved him 'to indignation on account of the wretchedness of slavery'. Even William Kelly, whose journal contained none of the moral concern of Eells's, was disgusted by what he saw in St Louis. 'Slavery in the abstract and in theory is a sinful, hideous, and abominable institution,' he concluded. Most midwesterners' views were closer to Kelly's than Eells's. They saw no contradiction in loathing slavery and also loathing black Americans. As Jesse Applegate put it, 'Many of those people [Oregon pioneers] hated slavery, but a much larger number of them hated free negroes worse even than slaves.'

Slavery was seen as a threat to the dignity of white labour. It also degraded the integrity of the democratic system. While most white northerners hated abolitionists, they were sensitive to their accusations that the planters of the South used pliant northern politicians as tools for the advancement of their sectional interests. In the 1840s, this allegation was made against men like Cass and Benton who lent their voices to the chorus of Democrats calling for the annexation of Texas – a territory destined to join the Union as a slave state. Abolitionists taunted northern Democrats for 'whoring after Texas' on behalf of southern slaveholders. The charge stuck because many would-be emigrants felt they could never prosper in a country where slavery was legal. It was jarring to see their representatives calling for the addition of territory which they could never call home.

John Minto reported hearing conversations of this kind. On the steamer to St Louis, he listened to some 'fascinating descriptions of life in Texas' from a young Texan aboard. When he expressed interest in possibly migrating there, he was warned off: '"No, stranger; don't you go to Texas. They have slaves there, and you could not hold your tongue on that subject, and that is dangerous there."' At Independence, he heard some other emigrants discussing why they wanted to move west. 'I am not satisfied here,' Robert Morrison said. 'Unless a man keeps niggers (and I won't) he has no even chance; he cannot compete with the man that does ... I'm going to Oregon, where there'll be no slaves, and we'll all start even.'[8]

The ultras responded to this kind of sentiment by pairing their calls for future slave states with calls for future free states. They could then defend themselves – and by extension their constituents – from accusations of kowtowing to the planter elite by claiming that they were in favour of all territorial expansion: slave *and* free. They could even claim to be taking the high ground: to be putting the Union above sectional squabbles and the greatness of a rising nation beyond the seditious ravings of a few political malcontents. This kind of bargain – northern votes for southern votes, freedom for slavery, Oregon for Texas – was tolerable so long as it held.[9]

## RIFLES BEYOND THE ROCKIES

The ultras' calculations amounted to nothing without action. At the time of Wilkes's visit to Oregon, the 150 Americans resident there were heavily outnumbered by 800 HBC employees and their dependants. Linn's proposal to give land to settlers who travelled to the Columbia Valley was an explicit attempt to turn the demographics in the United States' favour. This was not a secret. Linn told the Senate his aim was 'to encourage emigration' by means of land grants. 'Without these encouragements [of land] there would be no emigration of our citizens, and England would be left to occupy the whole country.' Benton agreed. 'Nobody would go there without the inducement of land,' he said. 'I go now for vindicating our rights on the Columbia,' he roared; 'this bill, and making these grants of land ... will soon place the thirty or forty thousand rifles beyond the Rocky Mountains, which will be our effective negotiators.' The Oregon pioneers were not just plucky settlers traversing the plains in their Pennsylvania wagons; they were the shock troops of American empire.[10]

To a greater or lesser degree, almost all the emigrants understood the politics of the Oregon Question and how they were being deployed within it. 'Fifty-four Forty' was written in large letters on the side of the train that served Independence, and slogans like '54-40 or Fight' and 'Oregon, the Whole or None' on the side of wagons heading west. One pioneer claimed that the only two books that settlers took west were the Bible and Linn's 1838 report on Oregon. Once in Oregon, settlements were named after politicians who championed their cause – Linnton was the name of one of the first towns built at the mouth of the Willamette – and John Minto claimed to have met children named after Floyd, Benton and Linn. In their memoirs and letters, they often referred to Benton's remark about the United States needing rifles beyond the Rockies.

The emigrants had brought a lot of weaponry along the Oregon Trail and expected to use it against the British as well as the Indians. They understood that they were moving into a geopolitical hotspot. In 1842, some months before Oregon Fever broke out, the English-born Minto was confronted by an American asking "'which side I would take in case I went to Oregon and war arose between the Britain and United States governments for dominion over the country." With rising indignation at the doubt implied, I replied: "The United States, of course!" and was let down with the exclamation: "That's loyal, my friend."'

Once he reached the Columbia in the autumn of 1843, Minto quickly observed signs of open hostility towards the British in the region. On one occasion, McLoughlin sent a boat upriver to help a party of emigrants descend safely to their destination. When one of the emigrants joked that the boat was a bribe from the HBC to the leader of their wagon train, the man snapped that he would take McLoughlin's charity, but if he dared make demands of him, he would 'have no hesitation in knocking their stockade [Fort Vancouver] down about their ears'. When one British officer asked Jesse Applegate 'if he believed his neighbours would fight for the possession of Oregon', Applegate replied: 'Fight, Lieutenant, yes; they would not only fight you Britishers, but their own commanders also if they did not command to suit them.'[11]

Far from just being foot soldiers in the politicians' campaign, the settlers developed a symbiotic relationship with the ultras. The most important way they did so was through petitions. Almost every year from 1838 to 1846, a petition would be composed, signed and sent to Washington, where it would be delivered to a friendly politician and submitted to Congress. These documents were quoted in congressional debates and reprinted in newspapers, helping shape the narrative emerging around Oregon and stiffen the spines of Oregon's tribunes in the House and Senate. The petitions demonstrated a remarkably sophisticated grasp of geopolitics. One addressed to Linn noted Oregon's 'happy position for trade with China, India, and the western coasts of America'. Another directly alluded to the fact that settlers were acting as unaccredited agents of American foreign policy who by virtue of their 'local situation, [were] prepared to hold in check the avarice of a foreign power, and to establish and maintain American interests generally'. This dovetailed with Myron Eells's claim that the settlers were a political 'nucleus', 'an entering wedge which the Hudson's Bay Company could not get rid of'.

The emigrants also used petitions to win the sympathy of the American public. They developed a compelling narrative in which they had trekked across the continent to advance their country's fortunes and had now been abandoned by their government. There was a grain of truth to this. Joint occupation had been ambiguous from the start and

> ARRIVAL FROM OREGON. We were most agreeably surprised yesterday by a call from Dr. Whitman from Oregon, a member of the American Presbyterian Mission in that Territory. A slight glance at him when he entered our office, would have convinced any one that he had seen all the hardships of a life in the wilderness. He was dressed in an old cap that appeared to have seen some ten years' service, faded and nearly destitute of fur; a vest whose natural color had long since fled, and a shirt—we could not see that he had any—an overcoat every thread of which could be easily seen, buckskin pants, &c.—the roughest man that we have seen this many a day—*too poor, in fact, to get any better wardrobe!* The Doctor is one of those daring and good men who went to Oregon some years ago, to teach the Indians religion, agriculture, letters, &c. A noble pioneer do we judge him to be—a man fitted to be a chief in rearing a moral empire among the wild men of the wilderness. We did not learn what success the worthy man had in leading the Indians to embrace the Christian faith, but he very modestly remarked that many of them had begun to cultivate the earth and raise cattle.
>
> He brings information that the settlers on the Williamette are doing well; that the Americans are building a town at the falls of the Williamette; that a Mr Moor, of Mr Farnham's party, some sixty years of age, was occupying one side of the falls, in the hope that Government would make him wealthy by the passage of a pre-emption law; that the old man Blair, another member of the same party, was living comfortably a short distance above, as all who have read Mr F.'s travels will know he deserves to do. Dr. W. left Oregon six months ago; ascended the banks of Snake or Laptin River to Fort Hall, and was piloted thence to Sante Fe, by the way of the Soda Springs, Brown's Hole Colorado of the West, the Wina, and waters of the del Norte. From Santa Fe he came thro' the Indians that have been removed from the States to Missouri. The Doctor's track among the mountains lay along the western side of the Anabuac range; and he remarks that there is considerable good land in that region.
>
> We give the hardy and self-denying man a hearty welcome to his native land. We are sorry to say that his first reception, on arriving in our city, was but slightly calculated to give him a favorable impression of the morals of his kinsmen. He fell into the hands of our vampire cabmen, who, in connection with a keeper of a tavern house in West street, three or four doors from the corner near the Battery, fleeced him out of two of the last few dollars which the poor man had.—*N. Y. Tribune.*

*A report on the situation of American settlers in Oregon. Accounts like these kept the cause of Oregon alive back east.*

tacitly assumed that settlement would not occur within Oregon's limits. American citizens were moving into a legal grey zone. In Oregon there were no courts or judges, no military posts or militias, no statehouses or assemblies. In Thomas Jefferson Farnham's petition to Congress he noted that everywhere he went in Oregon he heard the same complaints: 'Why are we left without protection in this domain? Why are foreigners permitted to domineer over American citizens?' 'Unless we can have laws to govern us that will be respected and obeyed,' another lamented, 'our situation will be a deplorable one. Where the highest court of appeal is the rifle, safety in life and property can not be depended on.' Many petitions stressed that the Oregon emigrants were not lawless frontiersmen, but law-abiding, God-fearing families who sought to reproduce the ordered societies they had left behind. The absence of governance undermined that mission.[12]

Even as they pleaded powerlessness, the settlers took dramatic steps to claim the political initiative. In the spring of 1843, they met at Champoeg in the Willamette Valley and formed a provisional government. The significance of this body grew with the tide of emigration. The arrival of 900 settlers that winter, and a further 4,500 in 1844 and 1845, transformed the balance of power in Oregon. The American settlers now heavily outnumbered the HBC. The provisional government declared itself the sovereign authority in the region and, incredibly, the HBC seemed to acquiesce to their power grab. One of the government's first actions was to legalize pre-emption claims. This led to the practice of 'claim-jumping', with settlers marking out land claims in the expectation of annexation by the United States. In March 1845, some settlers crossed over to the north bank of the Columbia and began establishing claims in the immediate vicinity of Fort Vancouver. McLoughlin ordered all signs of settlement destroyed, but within days they had reappeared.

It was an ominous development. For decades there had been an informal understanding that Americans would stay below the Columbia. The willingness of the settlers to flout that convention signalled a major escalation. It was the presumption rather than the hostility of the newly arrived Americans that rankled. Upon arriving at Fort Vancouver, one emigrant wandered aboard an HBC ship. When he was confronted on deck by the captain, the following exchange transpired. 'Where do you come from and why do you come here?' asked the captain. 'We come from Missouri, across the Rocky Mountains; we've come to settle in Oregon and rule this country,' came the reply. The captain stared at him silently for a period and then said: 'Well, young man, I have sailed in every quarter of the globe, and have seen most of the peoples upon it; but a more uncouth, and, at the same time, bolder set of men than you Americans I have never seen.'

Incidents like these were reported to George Simpson, who in turn relayed the deteriorating situation in the Oregon Country to his superiors in London. He left little doubt as to where the situation was heading. 'The proceedings in Congress and other reports in the public prints, which find their way to the Willamette by every opportunity, seem to influence the minds of the great body of the most ignorant settlers against us, who look upon us as intruders,' he wrote. 'And if they were not overawed in some degree by the semblance of law ... there would be no salvation, either for the lives or property of British subjects.' The HBC, he went on, 'is looked upon with much jealous rancour and hostility, leading to serious apprehensions on the minds' of employees. Nobody could tell when the tensions would spill over into violence. Everyone understood that violence in Oregon could easily spark a war between Britain and the United States. Oregon Fever had precipitated the Oregon Crisis.[13]

# Careering Towards Compromise

On the night of 29 December 1837, a group of men boarded seven boats, pushed off the riverbank at Chippawa and slipped into the main channel of the Niagara River. Earlier that day, a Royal Navy officer named Andrew Drew and a militia colonel named Allan MacNab had put the word out for 'a few fellows with cutlasses who would follow [them] to the Devil'. Fifty-six men responded to the call and they set out onto the river that night to raise hell. Chippawa, Ontario, sat directly across from Niagara Falls, New York. The river that ran between them was the Canadian-American border. Some time after midnight, Drew and his boats entered American territory. Their destination was Schlosser's Landing, where a small steamboat named the *Caroline* was moored. The oarsmen paddled silently. The raiders clutched their assorted weapons: pistols, cutlasses, muskets, boarding pikes. Aboard the *Caroline*, most of the crew were asleep. The nightwatchman did not see them until they were yards away. When he glimpsed them pulling up out of the night, he cried over his shoulder, 'Turn up, boys, the enemy are coming!' Within moments, the Canadians were swarming the *Caroline* 'with muskets, swords, and cutlasses'. The American crew staggered out of bed to find themselves being menaced by heavily armed men as gunfire rang out on deck. Amid the melee, Captain Drew was seen driving three prisoners ahead of him off the boat, hurried along with the occasional slap from the flat of his sword. The men followed his lead and soon the crew of the *Caroline* had been hustled ashore.

The attack was over almost as suddenly as it had begun. One American lay dying on the riverbank. The rest looked on as the

Canadians got back into their boats. Before they rowed away into the night, two of them went aboard the *Caroline*, lit a fire and then lashed the little steamer to one of their own craft. They sailed back towards Chippawa with the *Caroline* towed in their wake. The fire they had kindled in her cabin grew into a blaze that lit up the water's surface and was visible all along the shore. Once they reached the centre of the river, they cut her loose and the flaming American ship was carried by the current towards the thundering roar of the Niagara Falls. Cheers went up from the Canadian side as the *Caroline* disintegrated in the foaming waters and her burning remnants disappeared over the waterfall and into the United States.[1]

## THE CRISIS OF ANGLO-AMERICAN RELATIONS

History conjures up its own metaphors. There was no better metaphor for the state of Anglo-American relations in these years than a flaming wreck hurtling towards a precipice. In this period, confrontations between the two countries came one after the other without relief.

The origins of the *Caroline* affair lay in the Rebellions of 1837–38, an uprising in Canada that enjoyed warm support in the United States. The *Caroline* – manned by American partisans of the rebel cause – was a highly visible expression of those cross-border sympathies, and its destruction produced war fever across the Great Lakes and the New York borderland. In central Buffalo, soldiers paraded, old artillery pieces were wheeled out and volunteers took oaths to defend the country to the last. One journalist from the New York *Herald* saw these outpourings and concluded that 'surely war with England was unavoidable'. Many in Washington felt the same way. President Tyler delivered a special message describing the incident as 'a hostile though temporary invasion of our territory, producing the strongest feelings of resentment on the part of our citizens'. Tyler did not want war over the *Caroline* and nor did the British foreign secretary, Lord Palmerston. While the embarrassed British authorities tried to explain away the reckless actions of the border garrisons, Tyler sent General Winfield Scott to the border to help reduce tensions on the American side.[2]

This crisis was defused, but others rolled in, one on top of the other like waves on a flood tide. There was the McLeod Affair in 1840, involving a Canadian sheriff who got drunk in a New York bar, boasted of his involvement in the assault on the *Caroline* and was arrested and tried for murder, triggering a geopolitical crisis that Palmerston declared could 'produce war'.

There was a border dispute over the Maine boundary (dating back to 1783 and the deficiencies of the Mitchell map that Adams, Jay and Franklin used to draw the nation's original borders) which in the late 1830s produced the Aroostook War between bands of Canadian and American lumberjacks along the St Croix River. On this occasion, the British ambassador warned Palmerston that 'the whole northern frontier of the United States is in an inflammable condition, and would cheerfully respond to a call of their government' for war with Britain, should these skirmishes escalate.

These fears did not arise, but no sooner were they laid to rest than another crisis flared up. This one originated in tropical latitudes and involved the brig *Creole*, which was seized by slaves and redirected to the Bahamas – British territory. This time the South cried for war with Britain.

As if a dispute over Oregon, riverine raiding across the Niagara, warring lumberjacks and a slave uprising on the high seas were not enough, there was one final snarl in Anglo-American relations. In 1837, the United States experienced a major financial crisis that led to a wave of defaults on British loans. 'At the time that the great commercial distress took place,' one British traveller in the country reported, 'the abuse of England was beyond all bounds; and in a public meeting of democrats at Philadelphia, the first resolution passed was "that they did not owe England one farthing," and this is the general outcry of the lower orders ... This country [Britain] has now *fifty-five millions sterling* invested in American securities ... and the *majority* [of Americans] consider that a war will sponge out this debt.'[3]

By the winter of 1841, both sides recognized that a diplomatic intervention was needed to prevent a general breakdown in relations between the two countries. That year also offered an opening for good-faith diplomacy. In August, the Melbourne government collapsed and the bellicose Palmerston left the Foreign Office. His replacement was the doveish Lord Aberdeen, put in office by the equally pacific Sir Robert Peel. Their overtures found a welcome reception in the United States, and in December 1841 Aberdeen appointed a special representative to travel to Washington to resolve the various differences between the United States and Great Britain.

Alexander Baring, Lord Ashburton, was an inspired choice for the role. A scion of the Baring financial dynasty and an urbane, worldly gentleman of sixty-two, he had four decades of experience in American affairs, dating back to his walk-on role on the sidelines of the Louisiana Purchase. His wife Anne Louisa was the daughter of an American senator from Pennsylvania. He even owned a million acres of land in Maine. Furthermore, he had a direct connection with Secretary of State Daniel Webster, who had served as a legal adviser at Baring's. Even without this commonality, Ashburton and Webster made a fine pair. Webster represented Anglophile Massachusetts, a state whose interests dovetailed with Britain's. Webster's reputation for statesmanship had spread across the Atlantic, where he was admired and respected by the British elite. Aberdeen knew that Webster was by some distance the friendliest secretary of state he could expect to treat with. He had high hopes for Ashburton's mission – hopes which were soon borne out.

The resulting Webster–Ashburton Treaty of August 1842 resolved the Maine border dispute, and some other outstanding issues, but demonstrated the limits of diplomacy in periods of extreme political agitation. The Democrats attacked the treaty as the handiwork of a corrupt and obsequious Webster, who had sold out his own country to an aristocratic hireling of the British Crown. Andrew Jackson called the treaty 'not only disgraceful, but humiliating to our national character and humbling us in dust and ashes'. Thomas Hart Benton declared they should 'mark all the new boundary of Maine with black stones, and veil with black the state'. Lewis Cass – then serving as American ambassador to France – resigned in protest at the treaty and returned home to Michigan, where he was appointed to the Senate.

It was not just the Jacksonians who felt cheated. Maine was a New England cause and many Yankees who were otherwise tepid on territorial issues felt passionately about this one. They observed that it was southern votes – shepherded by John C. Calhoun* – that had helped

---

* Calhoun's leading role in the treaty's ratification caught the attention and the bile of John Quincy Adams's pen. 'Calhoun is the High Priest of Moloch – The embodied Spirit of Slavery,' he wrote in his diary. 'There is a temperance in his manner obviously aiming to conciliate the Northern political sopranos who abhor slavery, and help to forge fetters for the Slave.'

secure the treaty's ratification. The South was heavily invested in keeping the cotton flowing to Liverpool; the surrender of a few acres of pine forest was a small price to pay to keep that trade open. Once again, the South had scored a victory at the North's expense.

The ultras preferred to blame Yankees and Whigs* for the treaty, rather than the southerners and Democrats. Webster's sacrifice of Maine hardened their resolve to bring all of Oregon into the Union. To their mind, the Webster–Ashburton Treaty – far from reducing tensions – raised the stakes in Oregon.[4]

The treaty's reception in Britain was little better. Palmerston led the charge from the opposition bench, describing the treaty as a 'needless, gratuitous, and imbecile surrender'. In private he raged that the brokering of such a 'disgraceful and disadvantageous arrangement with the Americans' could hardly 'be otherwise when we sent a half Yankee to conduct our negotiation'. His sentiments were echoed in the popular press. The British had always viewed the Americans suspiciously; the events of the 1840s brought them into even lower disrepute. There was an edge of anxiety, as well. In 1840, the population of America overtook England's for the first time. The Americans spoke freely of surpassing their old colonial master, and their explosive growth lent credence to that conviction. When Palmerston warned his countrymen that 'with such cunning Fellows as these Yankees it never answers to give way', they were primed to listen. 'Their System of Encroachments is founded very much on Bully,' Palmerston continued. 'They will give way when in the wrong, if they are firmly and perseveringly pressed.' The accounts of British travellers reinforced this idea. Frederick Marryat reported that the Americans were possessed of a 'deep irreconcilable hatred' of Britain and relished the chance to seize 'upon the Canadas and our other transatlantic possessions'. 'They want to whip the whole world,'

---

* Daniel Webster once mocked this tendency (on this occasion expressed by Thomas Hart Benton) in a Senate speech: 'Mr. Benton of the Western Country, it is said, has an unwarranted (any is unwarranted) prejudice against the Eastern region. We wonder he welcomes the diurnal visits of the Sun, considering that it rises in the East.'

he warned.* The time had come, it seemed, for Britain to stand up to America's bullying.

The irony was that just at that moment Britain was doing a bit of bullying of its own – in China.⁵

## THE CANTON CONNECTION

In the 1830s, the British Parliament decided to abolish the East India Company's monopoly on the trade with China, a measure that had been debated on and off for years. The EIC's era of unchallenged commercial supremacy in Canton came to an end on 22 March 1834, when the *Sarah* set sail from Whampoa bound for London, carrying tea owned by Jardine, Matheson, & Co. The voyage of the *Sarah* represented a gamble on free trade – a gamble inspired by the immense success of Americans in the China trade. 'Let any merchant look back at the quickness and certainty of the Americans, in all their [East] Indian transactions,' one British advocate of reform wrote admiringly, 'and then let him pronounce whether a trade, carried on in such a manner as ours, can thrive.' Advocates of laissez-faire argued that whatever would be lost in ending the EIC monopoly would be recovered by the gains from unleashing the energies of free trade and private enterprise. China was a market of 300 million hungering for the fruits of British industry; Britain was poised to profit from this untapped market. 'If we could add but one inch to the shirt of every Chinese,' one British textile manufacturer said, 'we could keep the mills of Manchester running for ever.'⁶

By the end of the decade, these hopes had been dashed. The liberalization of the China trade had not brought about the promised revolution. While British exports of Chinese tea did increase somewhat, Chinese imports of British goods remained low. In order to keep their

---

* Marryat blamed the press for stirring up popular Anglophobia: 'Whenever it is requisite to throw a tub to the whale, the press is immediately full of abuse; everything is attributed to England, and the machinations of England; she is, by their accounts, here, there, and everywhere, plotting mischief and injury, from the Gulf of Florida to the Rocky Mountains. If we are to believe the democratic press, England is the cause of everything offensive to the majority – if money is scarce, it is England that has occasioned it – if credit is bad, it is England – if eggs are not fresh or beef is tough, it is, it must be, England.'

trade balance with China in a surplus, British merchants became ever more dependent on the one good the Chinese did want: opium. Between 1818 and 1831, illicit opium imports into China had increased from 4,000 chests a year to 20,000. After 1834, they rose even further, approaching 40,000 chests by the end of the decade. While British opium smugglers built fortunes on the contraband trade, British officials chafed against the Chinese refusal to embrace European trading principles. The Canton System was restrictive and arbitrary, they argued, and was stacked against British merchants. They believed access to more Chinese ports on terms defined by bilateral treaties would better serve British interests.[7]

The Chinese were unmoved by British complaints. The mandarins of the Celestial Empire held foreigners and their manufactures in contempt. The British were 'outside barbarians' who were permitted to purchase tea and other goods 'as a signal mark of favour' from the emperor. Their griping could be disregarded. But in the 1830s, the Daoguang Emperor made a decision that put the Qing Dynasty on a collision course with the British Empire: he initiated a nationwide crackdown on the opium trade. In March 1839, his campaign came to Canton. Foreign merchants were forced to hand over their supplies of the drug, and in April 1839, 20,000 chests of opium owned by British merchants, worth £2 million, were destroyed. Afterwards, the merchants were asked to sign an agreement promising never to trade in the drug again. The British emissary refused and relocated to Hong Kong where his forces began skirmishing with the Chinese fleet.

In these disputes lay the origins of the First Opium War, which is something of a misnomer as drugs were the pretext for the war, not its root cause. The British waged war on China between 1839 and 1842 to establish the China trade on terms 'equally advantageous and honourable' – terms defined by London, of course. To make the terms of trade palatable to British sensibilities, Palmerston sent twenty-two warships, twenty-seven transport vessels, and 3,600 troops to China. This expedition proceeded to engage in some of the most one-sided military campaigns of the nineteenth century (in one encounter in January 1841, the British killed 280 Chinese troops and wounded 462, destroyed eleven war junks, and took 173 guns at the cost of thirty-eight wounded and none dead) and blasted their way up to the gates of the imperial capital at Nanking before the Chinese capitulated and accepted terms.

The Treaty of Nanking, signed aboard HMS *Cornwallis* at anchor in the Yangtze in August 1842, made no mention of opium. The Chinese simply agreed to open up their ports to the British merchants and to conform to a European pattern of commercial relations. They also paid Britain $21 million in reparations and ceded the island of Hong Kong.

*An article giving an American perspective on the outcome of the Opium War.*

Few doubted the significance of the treaty. Several thousand soldiers sent from the other side of the planet had prostrated the Chinese state in a matter of months. Rarely has a trade treaty been so indicative of national weakness and so productive of national shame. Returning to Canton in November 1842, the American missionary Peter Parker observed evidence of a 'new order of things' in the downcast expressions of the populace. 'I was particularly struck with the changed aspect of affairs on my arrival in Canton. The haughty demeanour of the people as I passed along the streets was far less apparent than when I left. They appeared like a humbled nation.' British sea power had forced free trade on the Qing Dynasty. The Canton System was over; the Century of Humiliation was at hand.[8]

The Opium War was closely followed in the United States. Reactions to the British campaigns were mixed. For many Americans, a war waged over the right to traffic opium was final proof of British wickedness. Those more closely involved in the China trade, however, took a loftier view. If in the past Americans had looked admiringly on the Chinese, by 1842 familiarity had bred contempt. They could not comprehend China's refusal to progress in tandem with the West. Some commentators viewed the British campaign as equivalent to the American endeavour to spread civilization to the frontier. 'It is another movement of the Anglo-Saxon spirit in the remote east,' judged one New York journalist, 'against the barriers of semi-barbarians and a half-civilized race who have been stationary for twenty centuries or more.' In a provocative speech, John Quincy Adams frankly declared that the war was a positive occurrence, as it corrected the 'enormous outrage' of China's 'anti-commercial' policy which he believed, along with many other high-minded Americans, violated both 'the rights of human nature, and ... the rights of nations'.[9]

Whatever view they took on the rights and wrongs of the war itself, all informed observers understood that the Treaty of Nanking transformed the United States' position in the region. Britain had forced open the door to China; the United States was eager to follow them through it. By 1842, President Tyler was telling his confidants that 'he had his eye fixed upon China, and would avail himself of any favourable opportunity to commence negotiations with the Celestial Empire'. News of the British treaty gave him his opening; Tyler moved quickly. On 30 December 1842, he delivered a special message to Congress requesting it to fund a special mission to China to extract a comparable treaty for the United States. Congress obliged.[10]

The man chosen to broker the United States' first official treaty with China was a product of the New England seaboard. Caleb Cushing's father was a shipping magnate from Newburyport, Massachusetts. His cousin John Perkins Cushing was a giant of the China trade, who by 1830 had made enough money smuggling opium to retire to his 200-acre

Belmont estate, where he was waited on by Chinese servants he had brought back with him from Canton. Once described as 'brilliant and cold as an icicle. A man of splendid intellect ... but of unbounded ambition,' Caleb Cushing was something of a prodigy at Harvard and his obvious talents (and his inherited wealth) smoothed his way into politics. Unusually for Massachusetts, Cushing was a Democrat, and his politics were more aligned with the Midwest ultras than with Boston whiggery. His contrariness even extended to supporting the widely hated president, John Tyler. For his part, Tyler valued Cushing's perspectives on the emerging maritime contest in the Pacific. Cushing also had the confidence of Tyler's perennially impecunious secretary of state, Daniel Webster, who he occasionally lent money to. Cushing's knowledge of Asia, his strident nationalism and his connections in the President's Mansion all made him a natural choice to lead the mission to China.[11]

Cushing departed Washington in July 1843 in a flotilla of four navy vessels with a combined total of 200 guns. The gunships were a not-so-subtle message from Tyler to the Chinese. The president wanted 'to keep before the eyes of the Chinese the high character, importance, and power of the United States'. Cushing was outfitted in the uniform of a major general, complete with gilt buttons on his blue coat, a gold stripe on his white pantaloons and a white plume in his hat. He also brought with him proofs of the United States' technological prowess, among them a set of charts, a pair of six-shooting pistols, some rifles, a model of a war steamer, a daguerreotype apparatus, the *Encyclopaedia Americana*, a telescope, a spy-glass, a thermometer and 'some useful articles made of India rubber'.

While flaunting the United States' strength, he was also told to remind the Chinese of 'the remoteness of the United States from China, and still more, the fact that they have no colonial possessions in her neighbourhood'. In his personal letter to the emperor, Tyler expressed his hopes for a commercial treaty. 'The Chinese love to trade with our people,' he wrote, 'but if the Chinese and the Americans will trade, there should be rules ... Let it be just. Let there be no unfair advantage on either side. Let the people trade not only at Canton, but also at Amoy, Ningpo, Shanghai, Fu-chow, and all such other places as may offer profitable exchanges both to China and to the United States.' This letter was among his luggage when Cushing arrived at the mouth of the Pearl River in February 1844. By the end of June, he was engaged in negotiations with Chinese officials. On 3 July 1844, the Treaty of Wanghia was signed in Kun Iam Temple in Macao, granting to the United States all of the perquisites won by Britain the previous summer. Almost exactly sixty years after the *Empress of China* sailed into Whampoa, the United States had finally secured regular access to the Chinese market.[12]

Cushing did not view the opening of China in isolation. He saw it as part of a broader contest between Britain and the United States for access to the riches of Asia and the Pacific Rim. An inveterate Anglophobe – he had called for war with Britain during the Aroostook War and again during the *Caroline* crisis – Cushing saw Britain's actions in China as a prelude to similar campaigns against Japan, Hawaii and ultimately Oregon. 'If the British Empire should accomplish this further object,' Cushing warned, it would 'have a complete belt of fortresses environing the globe, to the immense future peril, not only of our territorial possessions, but of all our vast commerce on the Pacific'. In the aftermath of the treaties of Nanking and Wanghia, the struggle for Oregon had taken on a new aspect. If the United States wanted to capitalize on the new order of things in China, it would have to secure a permanent presence on the Pacific Ocean – it would have to take Oregon.[13]

Cushing was not alone in connecting the Opium War to Oregon. The ultras viewed Britain's campaign in China as vindication of their worst fears. The British Empire seemed bent on global domination. William Allen painted a picture of England 'gorged with possessions, both continental and insular, overrun, almost overloaded with subjects of all castes, colors, and condition', weighed down with commitments from Argentina to India and yet still capable of scattering 'dismay and death' along China's coasts – all for the sake of opium sales. John Wentworth of Illinois agreed. 'Under the pretence of Christianizing the world, she is robbing every feeble nation of its territory. Whilst pretending to convert the Chinese, she makes a market for her opium ... Under the guise of philanthropy she strives to enslave the world. This nation will endeavor to rob us of Oregon.'[14]

These ideas filtered into the mainstream. 'There is an obvious connexion between the Chinese war, the Sandwich Island affair,* and

---

* A reference to the Paulet affair, when a British naval officer, Captain George Paulet, seized control of Hawaii for five months in 1843.

[Britain's] palpably unwarrantable and contumacious attitude in reference to Oregon,' observed one American writer. 'If she maintains her position in Oregon, a rail-road to the Pacific and a line of steamers via the Sandwich Islands to China, will throw into her lap all the European ... commerce with the eastern and southern coast of Asia.' Even those less inclined to conspiracies theories wondered if the United States ought not to be more proactive in its response to developments in Asia. 'Can we not participate more intimately in the eastern trade than we yet have done?' asked the *Southern Quarterly Review*. 'May not our commerce, to the opening ports of China, for example, rival if not surpass that of any people on the earth?' To many observers, it seemed only reasonable that the United States should claim one spot on the Pacific for itself. Britain had Singapore, Australia, New Zealand and now Hong Kong. Surely the United States could claim Oregon. This was certainly the view of Tyler, who also connected British manoeuvres across the Pacific with events in Oregon. Watching England's machinations across the Pacific Rim in 1843, Tyler concluded that 'we should lose no time in opening a negotiation relative to the Oregon'.[15]

The issue was whether he would still be in office to effect such a negotiation. For, by the time news of the Treaty of Wanghia reached Washington, the city was immersed in the presidential election of 1844 – one in which the Oregon Question played a leading role.

## A LINE TO THE STRAITS

The ultras' signal achievement was to make Oregon – All Oregon, Fifty-four Forty – a central plank of the Democratic Party platform in the 1844 election. Reflecting the increasingly sectional nature of the politics of territorial expansion, Oregon was presented as a counterweight to Texas: a gift for the Midwest in exchange for their support for the extension of slavery south-westwards. After James Knox Polk of Tennessee was nominated as the Democrats' candidate, he ran promising the 'reannexation of Texas and the reoccupation of Oregon'. Polk won and used his inaugural address to reaffirm his campaign commitment. 'Our title to the country of the Oregon is "clear and unquestionable,"' he said, 'and already are our people preparing to perfect that title by occupying it with their wives and children ... To us belongs the duty of protecting them.' Polk would not be another caretaker of an issue that had bedevilled four administrations. He would obtain Oregon and extend the Union to the shores of the Pacific.[16]

Events spiralled rapidly. After Britain peremptorily rejected a compromise offer in the summer of 1845, Polk publicly recommitted to the All Oregon position in a fiery State of the Union address. In language taken straight out of the harangues of Hannegan and Cass, he denied the legitimacy of 'British pretensions ... to any portion of the Oregon Territory'. He had made the compromise offer out of deference to the policy of his predecessors. Its 'extraordinary' rejection by Britain relieved the United States of all responsibility for what followed. 'All attempts at compromise having failed,' Polk declared ominously, 'it becomes the duty of Congress to consider what measures it may be proper to adopt for the security and protection of our citizens now inhabiting or who may hereafter inhabit Oregon.'[17]

Privately, Polk expressed more moderate views than the ultras obliged him to make in public. On one occasion, he told his cabinet that he doubted that 'the judgment of the civilized world would be in our favor in a war waged for a comparatively worthless territory north of 49'. Still, he needed the ultras' support – for now.

Peel was in a similar predicament. Palmerston was bellowing for war from the opposite side of the aisle and the press followed his lead. The time was not yet right to broach a compromise. Tempers had to run hot before they could cool. Peel, like Polk, judged it prudent to escalate in order to de-escalate.[18]

From the outside, however, it looked as though war was inevitable. 'If our rights shall be invaded,' Peel told a cheering Parliament, 'we are resolved – and we are prepared – to maintain them.' *The Times* warned that 'Oregon will never be wrested from the British Crown, to which it belongs, but by war.' Peel ordered the navy to reinforce the Pacific and sent ships to visit British outposts on Vancouver Island and up the Columbia. The British presence on the Great Lakes was bulked up. All this was in addition to the shoring-up of frontier defences in the wake of the *Caroline* affair and the Aroostook War.

And this was done under the supposedly conciliatory policy of Aberdeen and Peel. Palmerston hovered in the background. His declared policy was war over Oregon. Nobody doubted his sincerity. Nor did anybody doubt that the Americans were willing to go to the brink. In these months, the unbridled rhetoric of the ultras filled newspaper columns on both sides of the Atlantic. Theirs was not the stuff of calibrated diplomatic language. They frankly welcomed war. 'War with us would but be a signal for the loss of Canada,' John Wentworth declared. 'The star-spangled banner would wave in triumph over Abraham's heights, and shouts of victory ring over the graves of Wolfe and Montgomery. There would be no stopping to organize armies on this side; but, at the first signal of war, our indignant citizens would pour upon Canada from Maine to Michigan, and overrun the country like a tornado.' 'Oregon – every foot or not an inch,' Edward Hannegan proclaimed; '54 degrees and forty minutes or *delenda est Britannia*.' This rhetoric was read in London. Samples of it made their way into the innermost circles of the British establishment. At a diplomatic dinner in London hosted by Aberdeen, Gansevoort Melville, brother of Herman and secretary of the American delegation, shocked the table with an impromptu speech on the Oregon Question. 'I was one who helped to place Mr. Polk where he now is,' he said, 'and I know that he will not *dare* to recede from 54.40!' This kind of statement fuelled the belief among informed observers that a conflict was imminent. 'Go to war about the snow peaks and desolate regions of Oregon!' lamented one British banker. 'I should as soon think of getting into a contest about the navigation of the Arctic Sea.'[19]

As 1845 turned to 1846, the diplomatic winds began to shift. Developments in the Oregon Country helped ease the situation. Midway through 1845, the HBC withdrew from Fort Vancouver and relocated its main depot to Fort Victoria, on the tip of Vancouver Island. In his communications to John McLoughlin, George Simpson made plain his reasoning. 'From what we know of the character of the people proceeding to settle west of the mountains,' he wrote, 'I think we cannot be too much on our guard against lawless aggression.' Simpson had no interest in subjecting his fur-trading empire to the 'infant government' the settlers had established in the country, whose edicts were enforced by 'the Bowie knife, Revolving Pistol and Rifle' – all implements that at some point could be turned on HBC employees and property. McLoughlin had reluctantly come to the same conclusion. In his final communication as chief factor of Fort Vancouver, written that November, McLoughlin laid out his position. The settlers, he noted, were 'desperate and reckless characters ... the outcasts of society who have sought a refuge in the wilds of Oregon'. Their encroachments on company property augured a crisis which would lead to a dishonourable capitulation or armed contest the HBC would surely lose. It was a striking admission. The mighty Hudson's Bay Company had been driven out[20] of its own territory by a few thousand backcountry settlers.[21]

This humiliating withdrawal was welcomed in London, where it harmonized with the Peel ministry's animating policy goal: free trade. Peel's stated aim was to repeal the Corn Laws and dismantle the remnants of Britain's protectionist system. It was a momentous move, but one whose time, Peel believed, had come. But repealing the Corn Laws was also a revolutionary step. So revolutionary that when Peel proposed it, his government collapsed. The Whigs, led by John Russell, tried to make a ministry but when Russell appointed Palmerston to the Foreign Office, the stock markets crashed on the expectation that Palmerston would start new wars. Russell's government crashed with it. After a short stint in opposition, Peel and Aberdeen returned to office in December 1845.

These developments in Westminster worked subtly on the Oregon Question. Peel's own vulnerability enhanced his negotiating position with the Americans. Palmerston was not a distant prospect but a looming threat. Polk would much rather negotiate with Aberdeen. The likelihood of an end to the Corn Laws also shaped Britain's Oregon policy. Peel and Aberdeen believed that opening up the British market to American grains would mollify 'the warriors of the western states' and allow Polk to climb down from Fifty-four Forty with his dignity and his political coalition alike intact. 'The admission of maize,' mused the prime minister, 'will I believe go far to promote the settlement of Oregon.'

Against this broader canvas, Peel could frame the coming Oregon deal as reflective of the larger triumph of laissez-faire. The HBC's retreat from its Columbia base symbolized the demise of protectionism. The future belonged to free trade, not to crown monopolies.[22]

That winter, Peel worked assiduously to win the establishment to his way of thinking. By January, the first green shoots of change were appearing, and by the end of spring, the transformation of received wisdom on the Oregon Question was complete. The betrayal of the HBC was a small price to pay for peace and prosperity. The fur men took a different view. 'All is ended in giving the Americans all they possibly wished for or required,' Peter Skene Ogden later wrote. 'Truly may we say, "put not your trust in Prime Ministers."'[23]

Across the Atlantic, James Polk was preparing for a betrayal of his own. His manoeuvrings on Oregon were camouflaged by a concurrent showdown with Mexico triggered by the annexation of Texas. In the same months that British opinion turned doveish on Oregon, American opinion had turned hawkish on Mexico. American and Mexican forces clashed on the border in April 1846, leading to a declaration of war in May. The advent of war with Mexico overshadowed the Oregon dispute. It also made the prospect of war with Britain look foolhardy: the United States barely had a large enough military to fight a war on one front, let alone two.

As war broke out in Mexico, new voices found their way into the debate over Oregon. From New England came the voice of commercial reason. Peace petitions from the ports and harbours of the Atlantic seaboard flooded into the offices of Yankee congressmen. One after another, these representatives went before Congress and detailed the destruction to American shipping and American whaling if the United States went to war with Britain. The entire value of Oregon to the United States, they argued, lay in Puget Sound. They had no need of the country north of the 49th parallel. Robert Winthrop of Massachusetts reminded the House that it was Boston's Captain Robert Gray who had explored the Columbia and Boston's merchants who had exploited the Pacific Northwest's commercial potential. 'The Oregon question,' he said, 'is emphatically a Massachusetts question.' The country should take the counsel of New England on the matter and ignore the ravings of the Midwest ultras.[24]

New England found an unexpected ally at its side when John C. Calhoun returned to Washington in January. Calhoun, for all his other failings, was a genuine believer in laissez-faire.* He had come back from South Carolina to protect both. Calhoun represented a bloc of southern congressmen who were indifferent to Oregon and baffled by the emotions it roused. They cared about cotton and slavery. 'I don't [care] a fig about *any* of Oregon,' the influential Georgia Whig Robert Toombs said. 'The country is too large now, and I don't want a foot of Oregon or

---

* When Sarah Mytton Maury asked him what the future looked like, Calhoun replied: 'Peace and Free Trade.'

an acre of any other country, especially without niggers.' The southerners preferred to take as small a portion of Oregon as possible and do so without a ruinous war with Britain.

Their logic was twofold. First, preserve the cotton trade. Second, preserve the domestic political balance of power. All Oregon meant several more states without slavery, which meant a dozen more senators and congressmen opposed to the Peculiar Institution. 'The slavery question did not apply [in Oregon],' one Georgia politician wrote, 'but to us it involved the question of power' in Congress. Many of these men were Whigs and were not beholden to either Polk or the ultras. But even those who were Democrats rationalized their defection from the All Oregon cause as an act of statesmanship, to save the country from a war with Britain. For his part, Toombs believed that Polk had never wanted Fifty-four Forty. 'He is playing a low grog-shop politician's trick, nothing more. He would be as much surprised and astonished and frightened at getting into war with England as if the Devil were to rise up before him at his bidding.' Polk's promises to the ultras had committed him to an outcome he knew he could not procure. His secret wish, Toombs believed, was 'to be forced by the British Whigs and Southern Calhoun men to compromise'. Calhoun was happy to oblige. As winter turned to spring, he went to work in Congress. When he arrived in January, he later boasted, 'It was dangerous to whisper 49.' By May, he had won round a majority of Washington to compromise. It was a remarkable turnaround, made possible by an unlikely coalition. 'The chivalry of the West goes hot and strong for 54–40,' the New York *Herald* wrote that April, 'while the ardent South, and the calculating East, coalesce, for once, on this point, and quietly and temperately call for 49.'[25]

The spirit of compromise was far advanced by the time the ultras realized that their position was imperilled. In March, a North Carolina senator known to be a confidant of Polk let slip in a debate with Hannegan that Polk was ready to compromise. Hannegan exploded: 'If they speak the language of James K. Polk, James K. Polk has spoken words of falsehood, and with the tongue of a serpent.' That week Polk was visited by Allen, Benton, Cass and Hannegan – all pleading with him to clarify his position on Oregon. Polk simply said that he stood by his remarks on the subject made in his State of the Union address – which upon rereading many found alarmingly supple.

Polk, who was not running for re-election, comforted himself with the notion that their clamour was generated by personal ambition, not the national interest. 'Too many Democratic Senators have been more concerned about the Presidential election in '48, than they have been about settling Oregon either at 49° or 54° 40',' he wrote in his diary; 'and for the sake of the country I deeply deplore it.'

The fate of the ultras was almost sealed. Their voters were fixated on Texas. Their president was speaking in riddles. Their southern allies had allied against them with New England. They were adrift. 'The rampant patriots in Congress,' one English correspondent wrote mockingly, 'who threw themselves upon their war-horses and charged upon St. George with the certainty of the American people following them, have to their confusion found themselves riding all alone in their glory, whilst the nation has either forgotten them in their profound contempt or made merry at their ludicrous pranks.'[26]

The endgame was swift. In May 1846, Peel pushed Corn Law repeal through the Commons, and Aberdeen presented a modified version of Polk's July proposal to the American ambassador. It placed the border exactly where he had drawn it previously. The only addition was a clause allowing free navigation of the Columbia for the HBC. When the treaty arrived in Washington, Polk claimed that he found the offer distasteful but was duty-bound to seek the advice of the Senate and that he would abide by their counsel. Polk knew the sentiment of the Senate. As Toombs predicted, the Calhoun men and their New England allies delivered the president the compromise he had publicly disavowed and secretly sought. The ultras raged. They declared treason in the Senate chamber. William Allen resigned his chair of the Foreign Affairs Committee. He tried to engineer a general resignation among Democrats, but failed and went alone. Even some of the old ultra warriors defected in the final days of the Oregon Question, among them Thomas Hart Benton, who had been championing the cause for twenty-five years. On 18 June, the Senate approved the treaty 41–14. Polk barely mentioned the event in his diary.

The treaty then went to Britain, where on 25 June the Duke of Wellington forced the repeal of the Corn Laws through the House of Lords. Shortly afterwards, Peel's ministry collapsed. One of his final acts as prime minister was to settle the Oregon Question and with it the last major point of contention between the two countries. The global economic order had shifted decisively towards free trade. That shift carried with it Oregon into the United States.

In the final telling, the Oregon Treaty added 285,000 square miles to the United States, constituting the states of Oregon, Washington and Idaho, as well as portions of Montana and Wyoming. 'We shall have then a country, bounded at the North latitude by 49 degrees, to the Pacific – and the South on the same ocean by 32 degrees,' one newspaper wrote, 'and the western and eastern boundaries, being what Nature intended them, the Pacific, with China in the outline, and the Atlantic with Europe in the background.'

The Pacific dimension to the Oregon Treaty was all-important. The great British geographer Halford Mackinder later wrote that the moment the United States secured a Pacific port, the country ceased to be an Atlantic power facing Europe and became a Pacific power facing Asia. Because the United States acquired California and its harbours at San Francisco and San Diego only two years later, the significance of the Oregon settlement of 1846 is often overlooked. But in 1846 people could not know that California was soon to join the Union.* Oregon was responsible for the United States' historic pivot to Asia. It is because of Oregon that President Barack Obama could declare in 2011 that 'the United States has been, and always will be, a Pacific nation'. And it is in Oregon's historic connection with China through the fur trade that we can trace a thread of historical continuity between the two countries from 1776 to the present that comprehends the coming of the American Revolution and the opening-up of the Celestial Empire, the Oregon Trail and the Opium Wars, the ascendance of American power and the advent of the Century of Humiliation.[27]

---

\* Although, even as the Oregon Question was being settled, many felt that the annexation of California was not far off. Arriving in Boston in February 1846, Alexander Mackay remembered his carriage drawing up outside 'the United States Hotel, an enormous pile of red brick ... having a large wing on one side called Texas, and one in process of completion, on the other, to be called Oregon. The next addition made will, doubtless, be California.'

# PART V

# TEXAS, CALIFORNIA AND THE SOUTHWEST

To us it was an empire and of incalculable value; but it might have been obtained by other means.

ULYSSES S. GRANT, 1885

# The Runaway Scrape

In the spring of 1836, General Edmund Pendleton Gaines was dispatched from New Orleans to monitor a crisis unfolding on the United States' southern border. By the end of April, Gaines was standing on the border which, as stipulated by the Adams–Onís Treaty of 1819, lay at the Sabine River, on the western edge of the state of Louisiana.

This was normally an obscure, unprepossessing part of the United States. One traveller described the Sabine as 'a sluggish, muddy, narrow stream', remarkable only because it had been arbitrarily selected as the dividing line between two nations. But that spring of 1836, the area was filled with desperate people. Hundreds of recently arrived families were living in improvised lean-tos in the forests by the river. A measles epidemic had broken out and dozens lay dying without any hope of receiving medical assistance. And they were the lucky ones.[1]

The opposite bank of the Sabine was crowded with refugees waiting to cross into the United States. Identical scenes were playing out at rivers further inland. The Mexican province of Coahuila y Tejas that bordered the United States had a long coastline riven with waterways. Beyond the Sabine lay the Trinity, the Brazos, the Colorado, the Guadalupe, the San Antonio and the Nueces.

Six months prior, the largely American settlers who lived along and between those rivers had declared their independence and proclaimed themselves citizens of the Republic of Texas. In response, Mexican general Antonio López de Santa Anna had crossed the Rio Grande in January and prepared to lay siege to San Antonio. Texan soldiers led by William Barret Travis ignored orders to abandon their positions and retreated into an old Spanish mission named the Alamo. By late February, some 200 Texan soldiers prepared to defend the Alamo against Santa Anna's 1,500-strong army. On 6 March, the Mexicans overwhelmed the Alamo's defences. Only women, children and the handful of black slaves were spared. The Alamo's defenders were killed to the last man. A few weeks later, Santa Anna ordered the massacre of some 400 Texan soldiers who had surrendered near Goliad. In due course, these events would be mythologized and the Alamo would become the 'Thermopylae of Texas'. But in the short term, they destroyed the bulk of the Texan fighting force, leaving only a rump army led by Sam Houston reeling towards the American border. With the Texan army in retreat and the rampaging Mexican army declaring that their motto was 'Extermination to the Sabine or death', the mass of Texan civilians took flight.[2]

So began the 'Runaway Scrape', the near biblical exodus of Anglo-American settlers out of Texas. News of the Alamo and the Goliad massacres spread from settlement to settlement, sowing panic and terror. In some communities, news of the Mexican invasion arrived in the morning and the area was abandoned by midday. On the sugar and cotton plantations, the evacuations were often more orderly. Wagons were carefully loaded with provisions and cattle and horses were corralled together. When the time came to leave, whites settled into the wagons and joined the columns of refugees on the road; their black slaves trudged behind on foot. But many Texans lived in tiny hamlets or on family ranches. The men were away fighting and the women were left to confront the crisis on their own. Many simply fled. Survivors never forgot the eerie scenes that met them in such places. Mary Baylor remembered passing by houses 'with all the doors open. The tables had been set, all of the victuals on the table' – but the inhabitants had gone.[3]

All Texas, it seemed, had upped sticks and hit the road. Among them were many of the young state's leaders. While the drama at the Alamo unfolded, a convention held in Washington-on-the-Brazos had approved a declaration of independence* and a constitution, and elected

---

* The Texas declaration of independence was written in one night and was approved unanimously the next morning, after only one hour of debate. The man who wrote it, George Campbell Childress, had been living in Texas for less than three months.

a provisional president, before fleeing northwards to escape the Mexican army. But the bulk of the people that crowded the roads were women, children and slaves. 'As far as the eye could see, extended backward and forward,' one man later wrote, 'was an indiscriminate mass of human beings, walking, riding, and on every kind of vehicle.' It was unseasonably wet and cold, and this shivering mass walked down churned-up dirt roads that had become 'long quagmires of bottomless mud'. Measles, whooping cough and other diseases swept through the columns, and eyewitnesses recalled seeing mothers lying by the side of the road, dying, their children in their arms. But fear drove most onwards. Rumours spread that Santa Anna intended to march on New Orleans,* that the Comanche were readying for an assault, that the Mexican army were going to rape every white woman they found. Anne Fagan Teal recalled a horseman riding past the column shouting, 'Run, run for your lives: Mexicans and Indians are coming, burning and killing as they come.'4

This terrified mass of humanity fled northwards, pausing to cross rivers swollen by the spring thaw. There were traumatic scenes as makeshift ferries disintegrated in the swift water, alligators attacked men fording rivers and sickly children died in their mothers' arms. For those who survived, the final stage of this odyssey was the so-called 'Sabine Chute', the last stretch of land between the Neches and the American border. It was a pitiful sight. 'The road from Nacogdoches to the Sabine,' one eye-witness wrote, 'is one unbroken line of women and children, on foot, with nothing but their clothes on their back.'5

This was what Gaines saw on the Sabine in late April 1836. But even amid the chaos, Gaines glimpsed the bigger picture and understood what was truly at stake. 'The affairs of this infant republic [Texas],' he wrote to the secretary of war from his camp on the southern border, 'are

---

* The American press widely repeated reports that Santa Anna intended to 'unfurl the banner of Mexico from the walls of the Capitol of the United States' (Memphis *Enquirer*, Apr. 12 1836). The American representative in Mexico City, Anthony Butler, claimed that Santa Anna had told the French and British ministers: 'I mean to run that line [the Mexican-American border] at the Mouth of my Cannon, and after the line is established ... I will march to the capital and lay Washington City in Ashes, as it has already been done once.' (Quoted in Bill Walraven and Marjorie K. Walraven, 'The "Sabine Chute": The U.S. Army and the Texas Revolution', *Southwestern Historical Quarterly*, 107/4 (2004), 572–601.)

*An 1837 map of Texas. Arkansas and Louisiana lie to the north and east. To the south are the Mexican states of Chihuahua, Coahuila, and Tamaulipas.*

assuming an aspect not only of deepest interest to its inhabitants of the present moment, and of the million and tens of millions destined in the present century to enjoy its fertile soil and salubrious atmosphere, but an aspect of incalculable importance to our beloved country.'[6]

## *TEJANOS* INTO TEXANS

The history of the United States' interest in Texas began with a shipwreck, a mutiny and a murder. In 1684, the French explorer La Salle landed in Texas after trying and failing to locate the mouth of the Mississippi. After his flagship, *La Belle*, became stranded on a mudbank on the Texan coast, La Salle spent several years making increasingly desperate attempts to find the Mississippi. But he was hopelessly lost and his men knew it. Eventually they rebelled and murdered him. They were in turn massacred by Karankawa Indians. From these inauspicious beginnings was birthed a French claim to Texas that would linger unpressed for over a century.[7]

Thomas Jefferson revived the claim following the Louisiana Purchase, asserting that the United States now had title to Texas by right of discovery on account of La Salle's disastrous turn there 120 years prior. Soon American cartographers were carefully marking the site of La Salle's landing on maps as part of a broader diplomatic campaign to assert the United States' claim. The Spanish responded aggressively to American manoeuvring in the Southwest. Convinced that the United States was about to invade their northern frontier, Spain went to the brink of war in 1806, with a Spanish army confronting an American force led by General James Wilkinson on the Sabine. The crisis passed, and eventually the United States formally renounced claims to Texas as part of the Adams–Onís Treaty.[8]

In 1821, Mexico declared its independence from Spain. The new nation retained the old Spanish suspicion of its northern neighbour. 'The haughtiness of these Republicans does not permit them to look upon us as equals but as inferiors,' warned Mexico's first minister to Washington in 1822. 'Their conceit extends itself in my opinion to believe that their capital will be that of all Americas.' Mexican fears were duly confirmed when John Quincy Adams sanctioned two initiatives to try and purchase Texas. Andrew Jackson made another attempt in 1835, this time seeking to buy parts of California as well. All of these overtures were rebuffed.[9]

Even as it refused to sell Texas, the Mexican government made the fateful decision to allow American settlers into the province. The opening-up of Texas to foreign colonists began in the dying days of Spanish rule, with the arrival of Moses Austin in Mexico City. Austin had made a fortune in Missouri speculating in mining, banking and land, before losing it all in the Panic of 1819. After a brief stint in a St Louis prison for debt, he headed south to rebuild his fortunes on the Mexican frontier. After many months of negotiation, Austin made a deal with the authorities. He would find families who wished to settle in Texas and bring them to the province. Each family he brought would be given land; for his services, Austin would receive a grant of land and a small fee for each family he settled. Moses died in 1821, but his work was continued by his son Stephen. By 1825, Stephen Austin reported that he had settled 2,000 people (among them 400 slaves) in the Brazos Valley. Seeking to expand on this success, that year the state of Coahuila y Tejas passed a colonization law whereby licensed agents (*empresarios*) were allowed to promote and organize the migration of colonists into the province.[10]

By 1830, some 15,000 settlers had arrived in Texas. The Mexican administration understood from the beginning that the colonization law was a Faustian bargain. They wanted white settlers to spur economic development but feared internal subversion. These fears were proved accurate when an official named Manuel de Mier y Terán was sent to report on the state of the province in 1828. Terán was appalled at what he found. As he travelled north from San Antonio, any sign that he was still in Mexico vanished. Everyone was American. Some were rich planters, others criminals and squatters, many simply the kind of hardy farmers found on every frontier. Terán judged them a 'shrewd and unruly' lot. Ominously, they were insistent on the subject of their rights. 'Honorable and dishonorable alike traveled with their political constitutions in their pockets,' he wrote, 'demanding the privileges, authority, and officers which such a constitution grants.' Discontent and disloyalty was widespread and an uprising in Texas, he worried, 'could throw the whole nation into revolution'. Terán's report made waves in Mexico City. The foreign minister, Lucas Alamán, concluded that the pattern of behaviour in Texas closely resembled that in Florida, and that it would end in much the same way: with a Texan revolt supported by the United States that seized the province from Mexico. 'Where others send invading armies,' Alamán warned, the Americans 'send their colonists'.

In 1830, Mexico passed a law banning all further American migration into Texas.[11]

\* \* \*

The law of 1830 did nothing to prevent the fulfilment of Alamán's prophecy. Settlers continued to stream into the country illegally. By 1834, the population of Texas had increased to over 30,000, with more arriving each month. The coming crisis was clear for all to see. 'The Anglo-Americans have penetrated independently into that province,' Alexis de Tocqueville wrote, 'buying lands and taking over industry, rapidly supplanting the original population. One can see that if Mexico does not hasten to put a stop to this development, Texas will soon be lost to them.'[12]

The breaking point came in 1835. That year Santa Anna became president of Mexico and scrapped the liberal, federalist constitution of 1824, replacing it with a more conservative constitution that concentrated power in Mexico City. The move was unpopular throughout the country and triggered protests and uprisings in many states. It was against this backdrop that the Texans launched their own revolution, claiming to be inspired by loyalty to the 1824 constitution. It was indeed a rerun of the West Florida revolt of 1810: a secessionist settler rebellion disguised as an act of fidelity to an older, purer form of government.

After the first shots were fired at Gonzales on 2 October 1835, Texas was swept with war fever. The fledgling state organized an army and a navy, issued letters of marque and reprisal to privateers in the Gulf of Mexico, and sent out summons for a constitutional convention. Envoys were dispatched to the United States to whip up public support and broach the subject of Texas joining the Union. Volunteers were soon crowding into ships at New Orleans. Charity events were hosted across the country to raise money for the Texas army. Some states sent boots and blankets; others rifles, artillery pieces and ammunition. The ladies of Newport, Kentucky, donated a flag depicting Lady Liberty holding a sword with a banner reading 'Liberty or Death' draped across it.*
American newspapers closely followed the Texans' early victories. The clamour went up for immediate annexation. 'Let the independence of Texas be recognized by the United States,' declared the Richmond *Enquirer*. 'Let it become a member of our Federal Government. Let its boundaries be extended to the Rio Grande, and to California and the Pacific Ocean.'

---

* This flag now hangs behind the speaker's podium in the Texas capitol building.

With annexation beckoning, speculators began drooling over the prospect of Texas lands rocketing in value. 'Let me advise you to come on with all the money you can command & invest in Texas lands,' one speculator told a friend on 5 January 1836. 'The lands are the richest on the face of the globe and the titles indisputable, no one can possibly lose who will embark in the speculation.'[13]

Six weeks later a Mexican army crossed the Rio Grande.

## SAN JACINTO

Following the massacres at Goliad and the Alamo, the fate of Texas lay in the hands of two men: Antonio López de Santa Anna and Sam Houston.

For Santa Anna, the Texas campaign was something of a homecoming. In 1813 he had been a young lieutenant in an expedition sent to Texas to crush an American filibustering expedition. For the nineteen-year-old Santa Anna, it was an introduction to the ruthless ways of Spanish soldiering. It also introduced him to a province some 700 miles from Mexico City that very few people ever visited. Santa Anna incorporated his knowledge of the frontier into his budding political brand.

For this was a young man on the make. Born into comfortable circumstances in Veracruz in 1794, Santa Anna joined the army two months before the Mexican War of Independence broke out and his formative years were shaped by the upheaval of that decade-long struggle. He made Veracruz his power base and eventually accumulated a 500,000-acre estate on the road between his home town and Mexico City.

In the decades following independence, he demonstrated remarkable ability in navigating the chaos of Mexican politics – Mexico had fifty governments in the first thirty years of independence – and establishing himself among the *caudillos*, the tough-nosed military men who held the balance of power in the country. Santa Anna became the most notorious of them all, participating in multiple revolts and claiming the presidency on six different occasions over the course of his long and colourful career.

Santa Anna had only contempt for democracy. He sought to rule by overawing the people with spectacle and, failing that, dominating them with military force. When he crossed the Rio Grande in 1836, riding a black stallion with a lavishly embroidered saddle and solid gold stirrups, he had just crushed an uprising in Zacatecas and was confident that he could bring Texas to heel as well.

Given his background, he was an easy figure for the American press to demonize. To newspaper readers he was a 'blood thirsty monster', 'that fiend in human shape', a tyrant with 'a lurking devil in his look'. The truth was less dramatic. Joe – one of the slaves Santa Anna spared at the Alamo – described him as 'a lightly built, slender man, rather tall – sharp, but handsome and animated features, dressed very plainly, somewhat like a Methodist preacher'.[14]

The man who stood in his way was almost a caricature of an American frontiersman. One 1836 profile described Sam Houston as the 'Washington of Texas', over six feet tall with 'a commanding appearance' and sporting buckskin trousers. Houston was a protégé of Andrew Jackson, having served with him as a volunteer during the Red Stick War. At the Battle of Horseshoe Bend, Houston took an arrow to the groin while leading a charge on the breastwork. Refusing a direct order to withdraw, Houston fought on and took an additional two bullets to the arm and shoulder. His bravery caught the attention of Jackson, who took him under his wing. Houston joined the Tennessee militia and became a congressman in 1823, then governor in 1827. Houston's promising career collapsed in 1829 after his marriage to Eliza Allen failed after eleven weeks. Houston's reaction was to quit the governorship and then the state, travelling in disguise to Arkansas, where he adopted Cherokee ways and began to drink heavily.

Then, in 1832, Jackson suggested Houston might go to Texas and report on the state of affairs there. Houston crossed illegally into Mexico that December and was soon caught up in the political turmoil that culminated in 1835 with open rebellion against Mexico.[15]

The fate of that rebellion seemed in grave doubt as March turned to April and Houston kept on retreating, with Santa Anna close behind. Houston's army continued falling back, until after five weeks they had arrived at the last river before the American border. Santa Anna had left his other generals behind and had forced his army of 1,400 men on in dogged pursuit.

On 18 April, Houston learned that Santa Anna's force was on the west bank of the San Jacinto River, near Galveston Bay. On 21 April, he made his move. Santa Anna's forces were camped in a wood, with a small lake to their rear and the San Jacinto bending around their flanks. They had erected a breastwork and the exhausted men were resting after a long march when the Texans struck. Houston softened up the breastwork with fire from two artillery pieces donated by sympathetic women in the United States. Then, according to one account, 'Houston sounded aloud the word CHARGE; and every Texan promptly responded by shouting ALAMO! ALAMO!! in voices that resembled the Indian war whoop, and struck the terror of vengeance into the souls of the butchering enemy.' Once the Texans crossed the fortifications, the Mexican line broke and a massacre ensued. 'Boys, you know how to take prisoners,' one Texan captain said; 'take them with the butt of your guns ... remember the Alamo ... and knock their brains out!' One soldier named Jimmie Curtice had lost his son-in-law at the Alamo and was observed caving in the skulls of fleeing Mexican soldiers, shouting 'Alamo!' each time he hit home. Many Mexicans were forced into the water, where they were shot down by the dozen. Houston, whose ankle had been shattered by a bullet, rode around the battlefield trying to end the killing, but it was nightfall before the Texans began taking prisoners. Some 630 Mexicans were killed and a further 700 captured. The Texans lost nine men.

The next morning, Santa Anna was found hiding in a pine thicket, wearing a linen shirt, some 'sharp pointed shoes' and a large diamond shirt stud, with doubloons stuffed in his belt. He was led to Houston, who was lying in agony on a stretcher in the middle of a field covered in 'dead men, dead horses, guns, bayonets, swords, drums, trumpets ... the chaos of a routed army'. Santa Anna congratulated Houston on his victory and reminded him that 'it now remains for him to be generous to the vanquished'. 'You should have remembered that at the Alamo,' Houston replied.[16]

The totality of the victory thrilled Texas. Dilue Harris was at Liberty on the Trinity River when she met some young men shouting, 'Turn back! The Texas army has whipped the Mexican army and the Mexican army are prisoners. No danger! No danger! Turn back!' The news was met with jubilation in the United States, where the public had followed events in Texas with growing anxiety.

Yet the decisiveness of the military victory concealed the indecisiveness of the political outcome. A few weeks after the Battle of San Jacinto,

Houston extracted a treaty from Santa Anna which recognized Texas's independence and its borders from the Sabine to the Rio Grande. However, Santa Anna could not personally make such commitments – only the Mexican Congress could, and they naturally refused to ratify. Consequently, even though Mexico withdrew its forces north of the Rio Grande, it still formally considered Texas an integral part of its territory.

Moreover, Jackson shocked everyone by refusing to countenance annexing Texas. At first, he even refused to recognize Texan independence, telling Congress that the United States should 'stand aloof' from the conflict. On the very last day of his presidency, Jackson changed his mind and granted recognition. His calculations in 1836 were, in part, informed by a genuine respect for the United States' official policy of neutrality. It was also an election year and Jackson hoped to avoid scuppering the chances of his chosen successor, Martin Van Buren.

For the Whig opposition had already seized on the issue of Texas. Events there, one author claimed, 'originated in a settled design, among the slaveholders of this country ... to wrest the large and valuable territory of Texas from the Mexican Republic, in order to re-establish the SYSTEM OF SLAVERY; to open a vast and profitable SLAVE MARKET therein; and, ultimately, to annex it to the United States.' As Whig grandees like John Quincy Adams began agitating against such a move, Jackson judged it politically prudent to postpone a decision on the matter.

On acceding to the presidency, Van Buren followed his example. Texas did not join the American Union but instead remained a sovereign state. Although many Texans wanted to be a part of the United States, they were happy, after the trauma of the Runaway Scrape, to face the tribulations of independence. 'It was a terrible baptism, that of the Lone Star republic,' wrote one witness to those turbulent months, 'but, we had triumphed and it was to the future that our eyes were now turned.'[17]

# Marching Alone

In June 1836, Dilue Harris's brother went on a trip with some friends to visit Texas's new capital city, Houston, recently founded only twenty-five miles from the San Jacinto battlefield. 'After being absent some time they said that it was hard work to find the city in the pine woods; and that, when they did, it consisted of one dugout canoe, a bottle gourd of whisky and a surveyor's chain and compass, and was inhabited by four men with an ordinary camping outfit.' The 'city' of Houston, it turned out, was still in a state of nature. The boys came back with stories of mosquitoes 'as large as grasshoppers' and panthers in the woods. One of them went for a swim in a bayou, 'but in a few minutes the water was alive with alligators'. Houston, much like the Republic of Texas, was still a work in progress.[1]

### LONE STAR WAXING

Texans were good at progress. In the aftermath of independence, residents watched in wonder as Houston began to develop at speed. In March 1837, the first court session of the Republic of Texas was held there in the shade of a pine tree, with the jury sitting on a log. A year later, a courthouse and a jail had been built, as well as a schoolhouse and some government buildings. A Presbyterian preacher began to give regular services in the Hall of Representatives, ending years of frontier godlessness. Steamboats started to ply regular routes up Texas's rivers, providing commercial connections to New Orleans. Cotton gins and sawmills were set up. Texas executed its first two men, the murderers

James Jones and John Quick, before a crowd of more than 2,000 Houstonians in January 1838.[2]

The pace of change was driven by mass immigration into the young republic. In 1836, the non-Indian population was around 40,000, including about 4,000 slaves. By 1845, the population had tripled to 120,000. 'Such has been the emigration to this country,' wrote one newspaper, 'that almost every city, town, or village, from Maine to Florida, and from the "Bay State" to Oregon, has furnished its quota to the population of Texas.' The roads from Louisiana were crammed with wagons, and settlements mushroomed along the banks of Texas's rivers. A French diplomat posted to Texas was in awe at the rate of growth. Only twenty months before, he noted in 1839, Houston had barely existed. Now it was flourishing. The Texans had achieved in three years what the Spanish had not done in the three centuries since Cortés landed at Veracruz. On a trip to the coast, he saw the explosive growth of Galveston, the port that was coming to dominate Texas's cotton trade. 'Only two years ago this magnificent country ... was but a vast wilderness,' he marvelled. 'Today there are towns everywhere ... everywhere they are digging, building, improving ports and roads, clearing rivers. It is impossible not to recognize immediately a country in the midst of rapid progress and destined to a great future ... What a race! What can the Mexicans do against men of this kidney!'[3]

*An article reporting sceptically on emigration to Texas.*

Ambition and avarice combined to destabilize Texas's development. Land speculation remained the perennial threat to steady economic growth or even basic governance. No sooner had a capital been built at Houston than the congress gathered to discuss relocating it elsewhere. 'The land speculators wanted to move the seat of government,' one Texas resident recalled, but 'no two members could agree. Some wanted to locate it at San Antonio, others at the head of the Colorado, or at Brazoria, Nacogdoches, or San Saba – every man was for himself.' Every land speculator had their own pet project and hoped that they could finagle the legislature into moving the capital to their favoured location. As Texas was larger than France, there was no shortage of space – and so no shortage of schemes.

In Texas, however, land speculators had to face very different realities from those in the United States. Texas had almost no state capacity. There was no US Army coming to police the frontiers. There was no government expenditure to improve the navigation of the rivers or to build roads and bridges. And the Texas frontier was a desolate and dangerous place. San Antonio – which one speculator claimed would one day be 'the Manchester of Texas' – was dominated by the Comanche, who extracted tribute in exchange for peace. When the fragile understanding between the Comanche and the Texans broke down, violence ensued. In March 1840, some Texans killed members of a visiting Comanche delegation and the city turned into a war zone. Vicious fighting left the main square and commercial streets strewn with dead. One local man named Captain Matt 'Old Paint' Caldwell was caught in hand-to-hand fighting near the courthouse and 'when the fight began, he wrenched a gun from an Indian and killed him with it, and beat another to death with the butt end of the gun. He was shot through the right leg, wounded as he thought by the first volley of the soldiers. After breaking the gun, he then fought with rocks, with his back to the Court House wall.' Caldwell later found the bullet he'd been shot with lodged in his blood-filled boots. Several dozen Comanche died in this episode, along with seven Texans.[4]

## G.T.T.

To many American observers, the very idea that you would move your national capital on the whim of land speculators – the very notion, in fact, that you would attempt to establish an administrative centre in the Comancheria, or in the dusty hills of West Texas, or far up clogged and unnavigable branches of the Brazos – was absurd. To them the entire enterprise of Texas was absurd. It had incompletely divorced from Mexico, only to be rebuffed by the United States. Now it was betwixt and between, a parody of a state. Texas, as it appeared in the northern press, was a fantasia of crime, disorder and dysfunction. 'We talk of Texas as a nest of rogues,' remarked one Massachusetts newspaper, 'and the people as runaway villains and gallows birds from the United States.' Indeed, Texas had an unenviable reputation for being the favoured refuge of Americans of every stripe. One Mississippian observed in the 1830s that large numbers of poor whites were leaving for Texas, some 'running from wives, some from debts, and some from the rope'.[5]

The phenomenon of indigent and bankrupt Americans fleeing south of the border soon had an acronym: G.T.T. – Gone to Texas. The newspapers were filled with men who had G.T.T.: Vicksburg bankers;* St Louis treasury officials;† pension managers in Wheeling, West Virginia; a town treasurer from Turner, Maine; a pair of Manhattan stockbrokers. One Baltimore satirist reported the case of a woman 'who has had fourteen husbands, all of whom have gone to Texas'. 'Texas is the land of promise and safety to all those whose regard for their necks induces them to leave the law behind them,' declared one northern writer. 'The veriest scoundrel and criminal on this side of the Sabine, becomes a patriot and hero on the other.'[6]

*An article reporting on the phenomenon of 'G.T.T.'.*

---

\* 'If all the men in Mississippi who have been engaged in banking during the last three years, for the purpose of making large fortunes with a dollar capital, were now to close banks and turn out *highwaymen*, we have no doubt but the change would have a tendency to elevate the tone of public morals' (*Houston Telegraph*, 10 July 1839).

† There was a rash of sub-treasurers discovered to have been engaged in fraud during the Van Buren administration, leading the *Haverhill Gazette* to write that 'Every sub-treasurer who runs away with the people's money rids the country of another Van Buren office-holder, and generally adds an enterprising citizen to the growing republic of Texas' (*Haverhill Gazette*, MA, 18 Jan. 1839).

However low their reputation north of the border, the mass of Texans remained stubbornly convinced that annexation by the United States figured in their destiny. The vast majority were born in America, had family in America and believed that bonds of language, commerce and republicanism bound the two nations together. Sooner or later, they reasoned, sympathy would prevail over calculation and Texas would be absorbed into the Union.

They had reason to be hopeful. Most Americans reciprocated the affections felt by Texans towards the United States. They viewed Texas as little different from what Missouri or Ohio had been to previous generations – the new frontier, the next chapter in the republic's advance across the continent – and felt it natural to extend the blessings of republican government to Texans, just as they had to Ohioans and Missourians.

But for this to come to pass would require action by the president and ratification by Congress. Jackson had not taken action; neither had Van Buren. Harrison's term in office was perfunctory and Tyler was too bogged down in domestic politics to pay the matter any mind. Even if the issue had come before the Senate, it would have required a two-thirds majority to succeed, and it was not obvious it could reach that threshold. Many northern politicians were under pressure from abolitionists to oppose annexation. Aside from their disdain for Texas's anarchic situation, they feared that the entire movement to annex Texas was a plot hatched by southern slave-owners to draw into the Union an enormous new domain suitable for the expansion of the slave system.

### LONE STAR FOREVER

The rub for the Texans (and the irony for the abolitionists) was that the slave-owning elite had a different plan altogether.

The first inkling of their real ambition came in a December 1836 letter from William Wharton to Stephen Austin, written aboard a steamboat near Maysville, Kentucky. Wharton had been appointed the first Texan minister to the United States and was travelling along the Ohio to take up his post in Washington. Wharton had gauged sentiment towards Texas as he travelled through the country and now warned Austin that southern support for Texas was more complicated than it first appeared. 'Both friends and foes bitterly oppose' Texas joining the Union, he wrote. Their foes were the abolitionists bent on resisting the 'extension of slavery'. This much was expected. But talking to slave-owners across the South, Wharton discovered that they *also* opposed annexation. They believed that the southern states were 'oppressed by high tariffs and other northern measures', and would soon 'be driven to nullification, secession' and perhaps even civil war. Their advice to Wharton was that 'we should go on as we have commenced conquering and to conquer and never pause until we had annexed all or the best portion of Mexico to Texas, thereby establishing an independent government that would rival this in extent, resources, and population.'[7]

Wharton was dismissive of these schemes, stating that Texans were 'farmers and planters from the middle walks of life', born in the United States and fond of its institutions. But Texas was not run by people 'from the middle walks of life' – Texas was under the control of the planter elite. The constitution gave explicit protection to slavery. Not only was Congress forbidden to 'pass laws for the emancipation of slaves', individual slave-owners could not emancipate their own slaves without congressional approval. The organs of government established by the Texas constitution were dominated by slave-owners. Shortly after independence, one French diplomat wrote that the promise of fresh soil for cotton culture had attracted the 'rich planters of Mississippi, Alabama, Georgia, Tennessee, and the Carolinas ... [who] are moving in masses to Texas with their slaves'. These men soon took over the political system. One survey of the Texas congress found that

*A redback – in this case a three dollar bill – printed by the Republic of Texas. Note the cotton plant in bloom on the left-hand side.*

all but one of its members had emigrated to Texas from a slave state in the United States – the vast majority coming from the Deep South. Within a few years of independence, Texas's biggest settlement was the port of Galveston, which handled millions of pounds of cotton each year. Steamships, barques and riverboats crowded its harbour, brimming with cotton and bound for New Orleans and Liverpool. Cotton accounted for over 90 per cent of the republic's exports and was its only reliable source of foreign currency. So central was the crop to Texas's fortunes that its own currency – the notoriously unstable 'redback' – featured an engraving of a cotton plant in full bloom.[8]

Mirabeau Buonaparte Lamar embodied the views and interests of the Texan planter elite. A Georgia-born journalist, politico and poet of small renown, Lamar illegally migrated to Texas in 1835. There he threw himself into the revolutionary cause and led the cavalry at San Jacinto. Lamar served as Texas's first vice president and succeeded Sam Houston as president in December 1838.* Accounts of Lamar vary. To many contemporaries he was a romantic figure. One newspaper gushed that he was 'a Georgian of considerable distinction … his liberality, talent, bravery and bearing have raised him to the head of the state … he is a man of honor and character, and no renegade or adventurer.' A French diplomat was less generous, describing Lamar as 'small, ugly, awkward, ordinary. Unbelievable efforts are needed to get him to say even a few words, and then his diction is slow and labored. There is only one way to bring him out of his deep lethargy, and that is to make some allusion to a war with Mexico. Immediately his face lights up, his eyes flash, and he speaks enthusiastically in quick, short syllables, rapidly and confidently, about his plans for campaign and conquest.'[9]

Lamar was deeply involved in the various secessionist schemes hatched in the southern states. While still in Georgia, he was part of a faction of nullifiers that supported Calhoun and South Carolina in their confrontation with Andrew Jackson over the tariff. While Houston was a convinced Jacksonian who placed union above section, Lamar was part of a new generation of southern radicals who placed loyalty to the

---

\* According to the Texan constitution, the first president was to serve a single two-year term. Thereafter, presidents held office for three years and could not run for re-election in consecutive terms.

slave-owning South above any obligation to the United States. Lamar held Jackson in contempt and regarded his actions during the Nullification Crisis as a prelude to a broader assault on southern liberties.* Lamar's nullifier pedigree was well known and informed his vision for a permanently independent Texas. In his inaugural address, Lamar declared that 'the annexation of Texas to the American Union' would be 'the grave of all [Texas's] hopes of happiness and greatness' and a betrayal of the 'blood of our martyred heroes'. The United States, he believed, was accelerating towards an 'awful catastrophe' due to the conflict over slavery. It was better if Texas steered clear of that 'devouring vortex' and hewed to its own course.[10]

But in the secret councils of the southern plantocracy, Texan independence was a means to an even greater end. With its strong constitutional protections of slavery and its vast frontier stretching – potentially – to the Pacific, Texas was not just a rival to the United States, but an alternative. 'If then infatuated Fanaticks ever drive us to a separation,' wrote one Missouri planter to Lamar, 'I look to Texas as a Country to fall back upon.' By remaining independent, wrote a Georgian correspondent, 'you will be silently building up a rock of salvation & a pillar of strength for the South on which we may stand & take refuge when driven to separation by the abolition of the North.'

Texas was the lifeboat the seceding southern states would one day pile into. Better, then, that it should be large and stable. Its pro-slavery constitution was a good start. But Texas should also seek to expand further. 'The greater part of Mexico, must & will be wielded by Texas,' wrote future Texan president Anson Jones to Lamar. 'A great Republic ... must someday spread its branches far & wide over the South & South Western portions of this continent. Of this coming republican Empire, Texas is only the Nucleus ... The centre of a great Planet that is to form and take its station among the constellations of Nations.' This was

---

* Lamar gave his verdict on Jackson during an 1835 speech in Montgomery, Alabama, shortly before his emigration to Texas: 'Who is Andrew Jackson? Let me not attempt to describe his character – to draw him in his proper colors, the foulest language is too fair. Who can do justice to Caligula & Nero? and who can portray the man who combines all that is revolting in the one with the disgusting ferocity of the other? As an individual, a rebrobate; as a military man, a murderer; and as a public functionary, the alternate flatterer & base betrayer of all principles and all parties' (*MBL Papers*, i, 197).

Texas's brilliant future should it choose independence over annexation. 'Texas, has laid open before her a path – a highway – that if properly pursued must lead her onward to glory & fame,' Jones concluded. 'Let her for the present march alone.'[11]

Lamar's administration was an attempt to put these dreams into practice: to build a model slave state, a prototype for the Confederate States of America. It was not a success. One of Lamar's few unambiguous policy victories was his enactment of a Texas version of Indian removal, which, with great violence and at great expense, expelled indigenous peoples from the eastern half of Texas.

Lamar then turned to the project of territorial expansion. In the minds of his friends and advisers, Texas could grow to encompass California, Oregon, several of the northerly Mexican provinces, perhaps even Russian Alaska. But all roads west ran through New Mexico. First, they would have to take Santa Fe. The result was a botched invasion of the Mexican province in 1841 whose only achievement was to revive the slumbering conflict between Mexico and Texas.

Since 1836, Mexico had been too bankrupt and too busy with its own internal upheavals to focus on the Lone Star State. In 1838, Mexico also had to fend off a foreign intervention when France blockaded and bombarded Veracruz. The Pastry War, as it came to be known,* was an ignominious episode which left Veracruz in ruins and ended in Mexico paying off the French. It also had the consequence of rehabilitating Santa Anna, a native son of Veracruz, who hastened to his home town in 1838 to organize its defence. Badly wounded during the shelling, he lost his right leg below the thigh. But Santa Anna's heroics banished the memory of San Jacinto and restored him to the presidency. He now presented himself as the staunch defender of Mexico's injured national honour. A large bronze statue was built of him in Mexico City facing north to Texas. In 1842, his martyred leg was disinterred, brought to the capital by carriage and buried with full military honours. His regime was heavy on martial bombast and dominated by generals who were only too eager to respond in kind to Lamar's invasion of New Mexico.

* The 'war' began after Mexico refused to compensate French merchants who made claims against the government for damaged or destroyed property. Many of the claims were specious or inflated. The name of the conflict derived from the fact that of the $600,000 in claims against the Mexican government, a tenth were made by a single pastry chef for the loss of business valued at $1,000.

In March 1842, and then again that September, a Mexican army crossed the Rio Grande and occupied San Antonio before withdrawing. On the second occasion, the Texan army beat the Mexicans back and then followed the retreating force south of the Rio Grande. There were skirmishes and massacres on both sides of the unofficial border. The conflict even spread to the Gulf, with the Texan and Mexican navies clashing at Campeche in 1843. Seven years after the Alamo, Texas and Mexico were once again on the brink of another devastating war.[12]

## LONE STAR WANING

Lamar funded his military adventures with debt and paper money. During his administration, the public revenue doubled, while the public debt more than tripled, the money supply increased sixfold and the redback plummeted to less than a fifth of its nominal value. Inside Texas chaos reigned. The citizenry was assailed by Indian tribes and Mexican armies. The state could not pay its public servants or operate a postal service. Not only did Lamar fail to abolish the tariff, but Texan cotton merchants had to pay the three-cent duty when sending their cotton to the United States. Worse still, the cotton price experienced a steady decline in the early 1840s, ending the stream of migrants into Texas. As immigration slowed to a trickle, the demand for land dried up. The entire fiscal basis of the Texan state – that it would fund the government by selling public lands – evaporated.

Lamar left office in December 1841. The Texan electorate replaced him with Sam Houston, hoping the hero of San Jacinto could right the ship of state. 'Old Sam H.,' observed one Texan, 'with all his faults appears to be the only man for Texas – He is still unsteady, intemperate, but drunk in a ditch is worth a thousand of Lamar.'[13]

Houston recognized that so long as Texas remained at war with Mexico, apart from the United States and adrift of Europe, it was not a viable state. His personal preference was for annexation to the United States. But Houston was a realist and knew that annexation had been rejected by the United States before and could be rejected again. Accordingly, he prepared a back-up plan.

Texas would seek rapprochement with France and Britain, and use their influence to end the war with Mexico. In tandem, Texas would try to secure full diplomatic recognition and a trade deal that would open up those markets to Texan cotton. Houston knew that any deal brokered with the Europeans would be contingent on Texas forswearing future absorption into the United States. This was a bargain he was willing to make, reckoning that fear of losing Texas – and with it, perhaps, New Mexico and California – to European influence would force the annexation issue in Washington. It was a conscious gamble on Houston's part. Texas had to risk losing annexation in order to win the United States around to it. It was risky politics but brilliant psychology.* Henceforth, as Houston put it, Texas would be 'more coy than forward' in its courtship of the Union.[14]

Houston played his hand expertly. Upon taking office, he extended an annexation proposal to the United States. He then began clearing house. He made treaties with the various Indian tribes. He vetoed further spending on military affairs, withdrew the fleet from Mexico's coastline and sought peace with Mexico. When that was spurned, he unilaterally declared an armistice. At the same time, he began to engage Europe. In October 1842, he issued an appeal to Britain and France calling for their 'direct interference' in Texas's affairs. The British were keen. Once negotiations got under way in London, Houston instructed his representative in Washington to withdraw the annexation offer.[15]

Lonely men make easy marks, and in 1843 President John Tyler was a very lonely man. His wife Letitia had died the previous September. In 1841, his entire cabinet had resigned in protest at his policies, leaving only Secretary of State Daniel Webster in office. At length, Webster also resigned, leaving office in May 1843. Tyler's administration was moribund; his political career seemed finished. But Tyler was a seasoned politician and, despite his desolate position, remained convinced that he could find a way of winning the looming presidential election. Henry Clay was the nominee presumptive for the Whigs; Martin Van Buren the same for the Democrats. Both men were anti-annexation. Tyler reckoned he could claim the annexationist banner and ride with it to an electoral victory in 1844.

---

* As Houston put it on another occasion: 'If we evince too much anxiety it will be regarded as importunity, and the voice of supplication seldom commands, in such cases, great respect.'

But Tyler was moved by reasons of state as well as by mere ambition for office. Wandering in the political wilderness, he had come under the influence of a coterie of southern politicians with strong views on the Texas question. These men believed that Texas was the last great cotton-growing region in the world, and that if the United States controlled Texas, it would control global cotton production. The logical corollary of this position was that Britain would seek to wrest control of this monopoly from the United States by attacking the institution that undergirded it: slavery. Southerners in Tyler's circle came to believe that Texas would be the arena for a confrontation between Britain and America, abolition and slavery.

It was in this context that Secretary of State Abel Upshur wrote an anxious letter to Calhoun in August 1843 stating that the British threat made Texas's continuing independence 'fatal to the Union, and ruinous to the whole country'. Upshur asked Calhoun to rally the South behind annexation. A few weeks later, Tyler authorized Upshur to reopen annexation negotiations with Texas.

At the same time, Tyler deployed another administration proxy, Mississippi senator Robert J. Walker, to approach Andrew Jackson to see if the old hero would lend his prestige to the annexationist cause. Jackson grasped the danger immediately. 'The present golden moment to obtain Texas must not be lost,' he told Walker, or Texas would 'be thrown into the arms of England and be forever lost to the United States'. In a sign of the growing unity of purpose between the former president and Tyler administration, Jackson's nephew, Andrew Jackson Donelson, was dispatched to Austin to serve as chargé d'affaires at the American mission.

As the slave-owning men at the summit of American politics scrambled to effect annexation, Houston remained in conference with the Mexican, British and French governments. As 1843 gave way to 1844, the Texas question was finally at issue.[16]

# Fortuna in a Frolic

The Tyler administration's hope for a speedy and favourable resolution to the Texas question blew up one glorious February afternoon in 1844. That day, the 28th, the USS *Princeton*, a state-of-the-art modern warship, went for a cruise along the Potomac. Aboard were the president, the cabinet, various senators and congressmen, the cream of Washington society and the ship's captain, the brash and ambitious Robert F. Stockton. 'The day was passed in the very height of hilarity and joy', according to one account, accompanied by several ceremonial firings of the ship's immense gun, known ironically as 'the Peacemaker' on account of its great size. Many of the guests then moved to the cabin for a lavish meal. At dinner, the widowed John Tyler devoted his attentions to Julia Gardiner, a beautiful New York heiress. As the *Princeton* approached Mount Vernon, Secretary of the Navy Thomas Walker Gilmer declared they ought to fire the Peacemaker once more to toast the memory of George Washington and led a party including Abel Upshur back to the deck to observe the gun in action. When the gun fired, it malfunctioned and the breech exploded, sending a large fragment ricocheting into the gathered grandees. Seven men, including Upshur, Gilmer, Julia Gardiner's father and one of Tyler's slaves, died instantly. Thomas Hart Benton and Captain Stockton, who were standing directly next to the gun, miraculously survived uninjured. When the smoke cleared, the deck of the *Princeton* was a scene of carnage filled with dead politicians, wounded sailors, and other stunned and staggered observers.[1] Tyler's courting of Julia Gardiner below deck quite possibly saved his life. The two married a few months later.

*An illustration of the explosion of the 'Peacemaker' aboard the USS* Princeton *in February 1844.*

But the explosion on the USS *Princeton* had calamitous consequences for the intended union of Texas and the United States.[2]

Up to that point, the administration's Texas campaign had been advancing smoothly. A wide range of trusted and prominent men publicly came out in support of annexation. Chief among them was Andrew Jackson, who wrote repeatedly on the subject, framing it in terms of national defence. For Jackson, the Texas question was the second coming of the Florida question. If they let the British gain a beachhead in Texas, they would 'raise a servile war, take New Orleans, arouse the Indians on our west to war, and ... throw the whole west into flames'. The notion that Texas was a new front in the long war against Britain was picked up and amplified by newspapers aligned with the administration.[3]

Another intervention came from Robert J. Walker, the Mississippi senator. Walker was a transplant from Pennsylvania and hence well positioned to sell a southern problem to a northern audience. In a widely circulated pamphlet, Walker argued that the North should embrace annexation because it solved the problem of slavery. In Walker's view, the North and South were united in their common interest in the perpetuation of slavery due to the economic benefits it brought to both. However, should the slaves ever be freed, the free blacks would flee to neighbouring free states, with the result that the North would be 'inundated' with 'paupers, beggars, thieves, assassins, and desperadoes'. In support of this claim, Walker referenced spurious data 'proving' that the 'dreadful condition' of free blacks in the North was already 'much worse' than that of slaves in the South and would become worse still if joined by large numbers of newly emancipated slaves.* 'Much, if not all of this great evil, will be prevented by the reannexation of Texas,' Walker wrote, because 'as slavery advanced in Texas, it would recede from the States bordering on the free States of the North and West; and thus they would be released from actual contact with what they consider an evil'. This idea, later known as the 'safety-valve' theory, might seem bizarre but was taken seriously at the time. It provided anti-abolition *and* anti-slavery northern democrats a reason to support the acquisition of a large chunk of slave territory in the South.[4]

The public campaign promoting annexation was important but not sufficient. Annexation was a diplomatic process that had to be negotiated between the administration and Texas and then ratified by the United States Senate. The Senate was notoriously indifferent to the currents of public opinion, believing its role was to stand above the maelstrom of mass politics. The Texans were baffled by the barrage of conflicting opinions on the annexation question they observed in the American press. It would require patience, art and equanimity to extract a treaty from the Texans and then shepherd that treaty through the Senate. It required someone who could handle big-picture diplomatic questions as well as the minutiae of congressional haggling and who could manage the vain, neurotic and complex personalities involved in both. Above all, it required a public servant who would set aside all ambition and focus their energies on the task of securing Texas for the Union. In 1843–44 that person was Secretary of State Abel Upshur, who

---

* The 1840 census gathered data on rates of insanity, blindness and other disabilities which seemed to suggest that free blacks in the North suffered from these problems at a far higher rate than enslaved blacks in the South. This data was construed by pro-slavery advocates as proof that slavery was a benign institution and that blacks suffered in a state of freedom. The census data was filled with errors and was debunked at the time. Much of the data was prima facie absurd. For instance, it was alleged that of the black population of Worcester, Massachusetts, 133 of 151 were insane.

had emerged as the indispensable man on the annexation question. And now Upshur was dead.⁵

## CALHOUN AT STATE

Tyler replaced him with a man of very different cast: John C. Calhoun. Like Tyler, Calhoun had been in the political wilderness since the Nullification Crisis. Despised by the Jacksonians, and despising them in turn, Calhoun had drifted so far from the Democratic fold as to come nearly into the orbit of the Whigs. But no party could contain a man as singular and radical as Calhoun. Instead, he retreated to South Carolina, a state whose politics he dominated and where he retained a Senate seat for over fifteen years. South Carolina's aristocratic political organization aggravated Calhoun's natural preference for the abstract over the concrete. Spared direct contact with the electorate – the state's two senators were appointed by the legislature – Calhoun devoted his time to admiring the pristine political theories of his own invention. With age he developed a gaunt face, harrowing eyes and a head of hair that shot upwards out of its roots as though electrified, and this fearsome appearance, combined with his relentless, monomaniacal theorizing, gave him the air of a deranged Old Testament prophet. The English travel writer Harriet Martineau spent time with Calhoun in the mid-1830s and described him as a 'cast-iron man, who looks as if he had never been born and never could be extinguished', who would speak for hours in 'his close, rapid, theoretical, illustrated talk'. 'I know of no man who lives in such utter intellectual solitude,' she wrote. 'I never saw any one who so completely gave me the idea of possession.'* Massachusetts

---

\* Others who encountered Calhoun left similarly striking descriptions of the man. Mary Coffee noted he looked like 'his Satanic Majesty when he gets into one of his violent passions ... with clenched fists, teeth grinning from ear to ear, and his great white eyes'. Henry Clay, describing a meeting with Calhoun during the Nullification Crisis, recalled him as 'careworn, with furrowed brow, haggard and intensely gazing, looking as if he were dissecting the last abstraction which sprung from the metaphysician's brain, and muttering to himself, in half-uttered tones, "This is indeed a real crisis."' John Quincy Adams was less impressed: 'Mr. Calhoun's friendships and enmities are regulated exclusively by his interests. His opinions are the sport of every popular blast, and his career as a statesman has been marked by a series of the most flagrant inconsistencies ... Calhoun veers round in his politics, to be always before the wind, and makes his intellect the pander to his will.'

Senator Daniel Webster once described Calhoun in two words: 'always severe'.[6]

By 1844, Calhoun had transformed into an American Lenin: he observed profound contradictions within the Union and was convinced that only radical action by a political vanguard could save the country. The contradiction lay between the limited powers the Constitution bestowed on the government and the limitless prerogatives claimed by the democratic system developed since its ratification. In Calhoun's view, democracy meant simply the rule of a 'numerical majority'. By contrast, the Constitution preserved certain rights for political minorities. This conflict between democratic majorities and constitutional minorities would end with the majority effecting 'the subversion of the Constitution' and finally by 'openly and boldly' choosing to 'annul' the Constitution and its restrictions on democratic rule. Government by the 'numerical majority' would thus lead 'in all cases' to 'absolute government' – to tyranny.

When Calhoun wrote of political minorities he was referring to southern slaveholders. In his lifetime, the position of the South had undergone a radical reversal. In 1790, Virginia was the largest state, North Carolina was the third-largest state behind Pennsylvania, and Maryland was only just smaller than New York. This demographic equality was reflected in rough parity between North and South in the Senate and in the House of Representatives. By 1840, the three largest states – New York, Pennsylvania and Ohio – held together a larger population than that of the seven largest southern states combined. Maryland was smaller than Maine. Driving these trends was immigration, which quadrupled in the 1830s and doubled again in the 1840s. The vast majority of new arrivals settled in the North, with the consequence that by 1860 the population of the North would be 50 per cent larger than the South – and a third of the South's population were black slaves. Calhoun would not live to see it, but the writing was on the wall in 1844. While the sectional balance held in the Senate, the North was producing significant majorities in the House. Among the delegations sent by northern states were not just the odd abolitionist, but scores of moderate anti-slavery congressmen. And the Union was still only twenty-six states strong. When Calhoun looked west, he saw a long line of free territories waiting for admission into the Union. The South had Florida. Even if Texas could be annexed, it would not be the

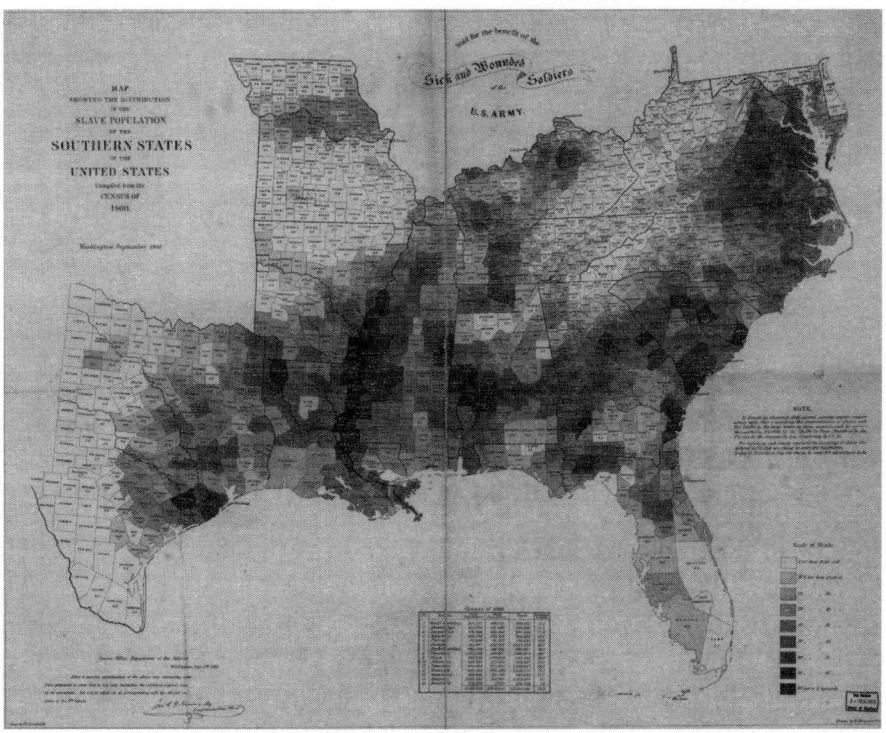

*An 1860 map showing the extent of slavery in the American South. Darker shading indicates a higher enslaved population.*

*next* slave state but quite probably the *last* slave state to join the United States.⁷

What was to be done? Calhoun's tactics pre-empted the Leninist doctrine of 'the worse, the better'. The South should not keep its head down and hope the abolitionist storm blew over. That would just give time for the ranks of the numerical majority to swell. Instead, an elite of southern political combatants should press the issue at every turn. Not only would they fight real threats to slavery – proposed restrictions on the slave trade in Washington D.C. or northern non-compliance with the Fugitive Slave Act, for instance – they had to make *everything* about slavery. By scratching the political itch of slavery, by publicly and loudly pointing out the grave contradiction in the American system, they would rally the South in defence of its rights and awaken the North to the very real risk of civil war if there was not some radical intervention. In Calhoun's mind, the United States would be saved the day he was elected president with a mandate to make the constitutional reforms necessary to preserve the Union. Thus Calhoun's theorizing served to resolve the greatest contradiction of all: the disjuncture between his contempt for American democracy and his ambition for the presidency.

So long as he remained in the Senate, Calhoun could do little harm. But elevated to secretary of state by Upshur's sudden death, he was gifted a platform for political mischief.

What Calhoun did next was among the most irresponsible actions ever committed by a senior American diplomat. Upon succeeding Upshur, Calhoun found among his correspondence a letter from the British foreign secretary, Lord Aberdeen, explaining British policy in Texas. In the letter, Aberdeen explicitly denied that Britain sought to 'abolitionize' Texas, but concluded with a broad statement that Britain hoped for the 'general abolition of slavery throughout the world' at some distant time in the future. Upon this throwaway line, Calhoun 'erected a superstructure of alarm', to borrow from Benton's droll account of the affair, and proceeded to dash out a long letter to the British minister in Washington, Richard Pakenham.

The Pakenham Letter, as it came to be known, was a monument of recklessness. Calhoun not only accused the British of conspiring to foment abolition and slave revolt within the United States, but went on to defend the institution of slavery at some length. Rehashing the same outlandish claims made by Walker, Calhoun asserted that whereas data proved that under a condition of freedom black Americans 'have been invariably sunk into vice and pauperism', under a condition of slavery 'they have improved greatly in every respect'. 'What is called slavery is in reality a political institution,' Calhoun concluded, that benefited black and white, and was 'essential to the peace, safety, and prosperity of those states of the Union in which it exists'.[8]

Negotiations with Texas closed on 12 April 1844 with a signed treaty of annexation. On 22 April, Tyler sent the treaty to the Senate for ratification. Calhoun included the Pakenham Letter among the supplementary documents that accompanied the treaty. The result was a firestorm. Senators justly regarded the letter as a provocation designed to link the annexation of Texas with a raft of fringe ideas about the benevolence of slavery. The national interest was being subordinated to the narrow interests of the southern slaveholding elite. Equally galling was Calhoun's parading of the United States' dirty laundry on the international stage. Britain forcefully denied Calhoun's allegations and expressed frustration with being so obviously drawn into American domestic politics. Even Texan officials denied that Britain was seeking to end slavery in their country.

Then there was the fact that the letter itself was just bizarre. 'It must have been a strange despatch for a British minister to receive,' Benton wrote, 'an argument in favor of slavery propagandism – supported by comparative statements taken from the United States census, between the numbers of deaf, dumb, blind, idiotic, insane, criminal, and paupers among the free and the slave negroes … It must have been complete mystification to Lord Aberdeen.'

It was a new low for the Tyler administration and a new departure in Calhoun's career. A man who had been a congressman, a senator, secretary of war, secretary of state and vice president (twice) was now reduced to throwing ideological incendiaries in the halls of power.

'What can be more sad than for a man to serve under John Tyler?' one correspondent asked Martin Van Buren. 'What, unless it to be found an argument in defence of slavery on fictitious statistics, and address it to a British minister!'[9]

The annexation treaty went down in defeat in early June, 35–16.

## A PLEDGED MAN

Andrew Jackson was disgusted but not surprised by Calhoun's actions. The moment he read the Pakenham Letter, Jackson knew that the annexation treaty was dead. Jackson was intimately familiar with Calhoun's wrecking tactics. To Jackson and his inner circle, the Texas imbroglio was a rerun of the Nullification Crisis. 'From the day that you stifled his first demon attempt,' wrote one adviser, the newspaperman Francis Blair, 'this natural conspirator has been brooding over his abominable design.' Calhoun's ultimate plan, Blair believed, was to trigger an apocalyptic showdown over slavery using Texas as the pretext. Jackson did not disagree, but was more focused on finding a practical resolution to the Texas question. Entrusting their hopes to the shipwrecked Tyler administration had always been a risky proposition. If they wanted to ensure annexation, they would have to get the right man – their man – into the President's Mansion.[10]

The election of 1844 was now only six months away and was shaping up to be an unusual contest. Alongside the Whigs and Democrats, the Tyler administration was preparing to run its own campaign, which would invariably tend to split the Democratic vote. Also in the mix was another third party – the tiny abolitionist Liberty Party. The Liberty Party's members were as alienated from conventional party politics as Calhoun and the southern radicals. Most of its members would ordinarily be associated with the Whigs, but abolitionists despised Henry Clay, the Whig nominee presumptive, who they considered 'a gambler, debauchee, professed and practiced duellist, slaveholder, and advocate for slavery'. They were also outraged by the annexation question, and were implacably opposed to letting 'slave-cursed Texas' into the Union.[11]

Not many people cared what abolitionists thought of Texas – but they cared a great deal about Martin Van Buren and Henry Clay's position on the subject. By a quirk of fate, both men published their views on annexation on 27 April, the same day the Pakenham Letter appeared in the press. Clay's statement, known as the Raleigh Letter, was dashed off in North Carolina as Clay made his way home to Kentucky after what he judged a successful trip through the South to shore up his support ahead of the Whig convention in Baltimore in May.

In the letter Clay declared his support for Texas one day joining the Union and said that the United States ought to resort to arms, if necessary, to prevent a third power taking control of it. However, he opposed immediate annexation for a simple reason: 'Annexation and war with Mexico are identical.' Texas was at war with Mexico. If Texas joined the United States, then the United States would inherit that war. 'I regard all wars as great calamities, to be avoided,' Clay wrote. 'I certainly am not willing to involve this country in a foreign war for the object of acquiring Texas.'

Van Buren's letter reached much the same conclusion: there was no prospect of annexation so long as Mexico and Texas remained at war.

As either Clay or Van Buren would be president by year end, the question now seemed settled: Texas would not be joining the Union.[12]

Jackson read the Raleigh Letter first and was exultant. 'Clay's letter killed him,' he told Blair, and Clay was now a 'dead political duck'. Then Jackson read Van Buren's letter and despaired. 'I write under a vertigo, great pain in head and body,' Jackson wrote, 'and fearful that the letters of my dear friends[13] ... have afforded the means for their political destruction.' But it was not in Jackson's nature, although he was seventy-seven and could scarcely rise from his sickbed, to despair for too long. The old embers still burned inside him; Texas had stirred them to a new flame. 'I am for the annexation regardless of all consequences,' he declared, and almost as soon as he read Van Buren's letter he knew that he would have to set aside his friendship for him in service to the higher cause of continental expansion. 'However we may be attached to men, we cannot abandon principle,' he told Blair, and their task now was to find a 'pledged man in favour of Texas' to be the Democratic candidate. In fact, Jackson already had a pledged man in mind. A few days later he summoned James Knox Polk for an audience at the Hermitage.[14]

On paper, Polk and Jackson had a great deal in common. They were both raised in Scots-Irish families on the Carolina frontier. They had both moved to Tennessee as young men. They had both made their money in slaves and land. They both had happy, childless marriages to devout Presbyterians. For all that, they were completely different men. Polk was born in 1795, the first of ten children of a wealthy planter and land speculator. A sickly child, Polk grew up to be a slight, unprepossessing man with very little physical presence. He was intelligent, however, and attended the University of North Carolina, where he received a degree in mathematics and Classics. After graduating, he trained as a lawyer in Nashville and was soon involved in local Democratic Party politics.

'A narrow, secretive, lumpish, and colorless man', as one historian has described him, Polk had few natural talents as a politician. In an age that valued oratory and in a state that valued backcountry smarts and frontier grit, Polk was never going to be an instant success. But Polk was methodical, hard-working and persistent. He also knew who to please. Most junior politicians start out as the disciple to a senior politician of an older generation. Most in time transcend that initial apprenticeship. Polk's tutelage to Andrew Jackson was of a different magnitude altogether.

Jackson had two great protégés: James Polk and Sam Houston. Houston was a rolling stone and soon left Tennessee for Texas. Polk, by contrast, offered himself up to Jackson like a medieval knight-errant surrendering his will to his feudal liege. He dedicated himself to Jackson's political causes. He married his wife, Sarah, at Jackson's suggestion. He selected his home for its proximity to the Hermitage. After Polk was elected to the House of Representatives in 1825, he proved his loyalty to the Jacksonian cause in Congress. During the Bank War, Polk helped lead congressional Democrats in their assault on the Bank of the United States, and for his loyalty he was awarded first the chair of the Ways and Means Committee and then the Speakership of the House. With Jackson's blessing, in 1839 Polk returned to Tennessee to serve as governor. But in 1841, Polk lost his seat to his Whig opponent James C. Jones, known as Lean Jimmy. In 1843, Polk lost to Lean Jimmy again. By the spring of 1844, he was forty-seven, jobless and without clear prospects.[15]

When Polk arrived at the Hermitage on 12 May 1844, he had no notion at all of promoting himself as a candidate for the presidency. The vice-presidency seemed a more promising option – an unpopular office, shunned by the ambitious, that would give him a way back into public life after a pair of humiliating electoral defeats. Polk was startled to discover that Jackson had very different plans for him. 'The candidate for the first office should be an annexation man, and from the Southwest,' Jackson told him, and that candidate was James Knox Polk. 'I have never aspired so high,' Polk replied, and privately wrote that 'the attempt to place me in the first position would be utterly abortive'. Jackson, however, was insistent. The alternative was to allow Van Buren to take the nomination and lose the general election to the hated Henry Clay, who had been anointed at the Whig convention two weeks prior. Besides, Polk did not have to do anything – merely assent to surrogates putting forward his name at the Democratic convention as a potential compromise candidate. He reluctantly granted permission.

'The recent explosion at Washington, and the incurable split in the party ... puts a new face on things,' Polk wrote to his confederate Cave Johnson. 'Fortuna is in a frolic.' But he remained realistic. 'After all however, I think it probable that my chief hope will be for the second office.'[16]

The Democratic convention (also held in Baltimore) was only two weeks away and events unfolded rapidly. In an age before systematic opinion polling, it was near impossible to judge the true state of public sentiment. Jackson, of course, laid claim to special powers of insight into the aspirations of the American electorate. His conviction was that 'the Texas question is the all-absorbing one ... and swallows up all others' – but it was a conviction arrived at by instinct, not by data.

Nevertheless, the Van Buren team began to worry that Jackson was right. 'There is a political conflagration raging throughout the whole south-west,' one adviser wrote. 'The Breeders of mules and horses and hogs cry out let us have Texas right or wrong, whether or no.' Jackson's public interventions on the Texas question had whipped up the electorate. Animal spirits ran rampant in the American political pysche. 'Partiality for Jackson and a rabid desire to get more land brought the whole mass to a decision at once in favor of Old Hickory's positive views,' observed Amos Kendall, the architect of the Jacksonian party system. 'The Texas artillery was just ready to let loose upon Mr. Clay,' he wrote, but Van Buren's letter had ensured that he would now 'receive the shot[s] which were intended for him'.[17]

The Van Burenites still believed that sheer momentum could win them the candidacy in the early rounds of voting in Baltimore. But at the last moment they were thwarted by the appearance at the convention of Mississippi senator Robert J. Walker. 'Walker is a man of the mole policy,' complained one Van Buren man: 'he works underground and in the dark.' In Baltimore, Walker burrowed deep inside the convention's bureaucratic architecture and, through an astute piece of administrative manoeuvring, had the convention rules changed to require a two-thirds majority for the victorious candidate.

Walker's intervention was decisive. In the first round of voting, Van Buren won a plurality of the votes – but not two-thirds. As voting continued, he began to bleed votes to his closest rival, Michigan senator Lewis Cass. By the seventh round of voting, the convention seemed hopelessly deadlocked between Van Buren and Cass.

At this point Polk's surrogates – Gideon Pillow, a Nashville lawyer, and George Bancroft, a Massachusetts historian and politico – began to tout Polk as a compromise candidate. Polk, who hadn't even been on the ballot in the first seven rounds of voting, won a clutch of votes in the eighth round, and then was unanimously elected Democratic candidate for president in the ninth.

He was presented to the party and the country as 'Young Hickory',[18] the heir to Andrew Jackson. 'He is one of Jackson's Colts,' enthused one newspaper, 'and of the true breed and mettle. He will sweep the country with an enthusiasm inferior only to that excited by [Jackson] himself.'

This was wishful thinking. Polk was unknown to the electorate at large. What mattered, though, was not the man but what he represented. The Democratic convention issued a political platform that called for 'the re-annexation of Texas at the earliest practicable period'. Polk went before the nation as a pledged Texas man and turned the election of 1844 into a referendum on continental expansion.[19]

## THE GREAT NATION OF FUTURITY

Shortly after the Baltimore convention, the *National Intelligencer* ran a short piece entitled 'The Scene at the Telegraph' that described the moment when Washington learned the identity of the Democratic Party candidate for president. A 'crowd of expectant Democrats' had gathered at the north door of the Capitol building and waited as, inside, a telegraph machine, connected by a wire that ran all the way to Baltimore, tapped out the names of the states that had voted for Polk.

'When, at length, the wonder-working Telegraph proclaimed the final nomination, it was heard by all the faithful with speechless amazement.' That 'all the chiefs' of the party – Calhoun, Cass, Van Buren and others – had been 'thrown aside, overslaughed, for one of the subalterns of the party – one not before spoken of or thought of – was a result hardly credible'.

Whig newspapers all over the country echoed this incredulous reaction. 'James K. Polk, a man never before thought of for the presidency by any one of the millions of the people in the United States ... has been nominated,' wrote the *Berkshire County Whig*. 'We do not remember, just at this moment, whether we have heard anything more preposterous or not.' Some reacted with amusement, many more with disdain. The Whigs had nominated Henry Clay, one of the most accomplished statesmen the country had produced since independence. The Democrats had put up an obscure ex-congressman who was little more than 'General Jackson's chief cook and bottle-washer'. The mocking question went up across the country: 'Who is James K. Polk?'[20]

It was the wrong question to ask the electorate in 1844. The most striking aspect of the scene at the Capitol described in the *National Intelligencer* was not the announcement of Polk's candidacy but *how* that announcement was made: by the 'wonder-working Telegraph'. Samuel Morse's first thirty-six-mile telegraph line was laid between

Washington and Baltimore in the month of the Democratic Party convention and sent its famous inaugural message – WHAT HATH GOD WROUGHT – a few days before voting began to determine the 1844 nominee. The 1844 convention was thus the first in American history to be followed in something like real time, with news, rumours and gossip from the convention arriving almost instantaneously in Washington. 'Information is communicated with lightning speed,' one newspaper marvelled. 'Locomotives go at a snail's pace compared to it.' Another report calculated that the telegraph travelled at a speed of 288,000 miles per second.[21]

Polk may have been a bland, stolid, humourless man, but he was associated in the public mind with the forces of acceleration in American life symbolized in May 1844 by the 'lightning speed' with which the electric telegraph reported news of his nomination. This was just the latest technology that had upturned American life. Every American eligible to vote in 1844 had seen the country transformed around them by successive waves of innovation. First had come the steamboats, with their proliferating routes opening up America's waterways. Then it had been the turn of the canals, which had reached their apotheosis with the monumental Erie Canal, completed in 1825. Only two years later the nation's first commercial railway, the Baltimore and Ohio, opened for business. By 1839, there were several thousand miles of track laid; that number would triple in the 1840s.

Now it was the turn of the telegraph to change the texture and the pace of American life. Of course, these new technologies were not unique to the United States, but they did seem uniquely suited to solving some of the key challenges faced by a large, sparsely populated country. 'By the agency of steam operating upon the boat, the railroad car, and the press, combined with that great American intervention – the greatest of the age and of the world – the magnetic telegraph,' Senator Sidney Breese of Illinois declared, the United States would become 'more compact, and in more constant and harmonious intercourse' than ever before. Technological innovations seemed to accrete and work in combination with each other for the benefit of the United States.

And by compressing time and space, technology made itself the handmaid of American expansionism. Journalist John O'Sullivan observed that the United States was already 'organized under that admirable federative principle which can govern equally a continent or a county', and now that it was fitted with 'a vast skeleton framework of railroads, and an infinitely ramified nervous system of magnetic telegraphs', it could 'over spread' the entire North American continent. Soon the long journeys and the long waits for information of the very recent past would be banished forever. Soon, O'Sullivan wrote, senators and congressmen from the Pacific Coast would travel to Washington 'within less time than a few years ago was devoted to a similar journey by those from Ohio', while the telegraph would enable newspapermen in San Francisco and Astoria 'to set up in type the first half of the President's inaugural before the echoes of the latter half shall have died away beneath the lofty porch of the Capitol'.[22]

There was not yet a name in 1844 for this mystical conviction that continental expansion combined with technological innovation had brought the United States to the verge of world-historical greatness. The phrase 'manifest destiny' would not be coined for another year. Much of the language and the bombast was little different from that of Jefferson's time, but with a gloss of technophilia, and proclaimed in the portentous tone of revival-tent millenarianism. Yet it was felt more widely than it ever had been in Jefferson's day. Americans had matured into imperialism. Territorial aggrandizement was now the norm, not the exception.

Travelling in the United States in the 1830s, Harriet Martineau 'was told in triumph of the rapid sales of land; of the glorious additions which had been made by the acquisition of Louisiana and Florida, and of the probable gain of Texas. Land was spoken of as the unfailing resource … the great wealth of the nation; the grand security of every man in it.' The nation's destiny was entwined with individual destinies. Continentalism dovetailed with personal enrichment and self-actualization. 'The possession of land is the aim of all action … and the cure for all social evils, among men in the United States,' Martineau wrote. 'If a man is disappointed in politics or love, he goes and buys land. If he disgraces himself, he betakes himself to a lot in the west.'

The mass of Americans, then, had selfish reasons to buy into the starry-eyed rhetoric of the era. But it was not just the 'breeders of mules and horses and hogs' who cheered on expansionism. Writers, journalists and intellectuals all threw their weight behind the enlargement of the United States. 'Railroad iron is a magician's rod, in its power to evoke the sleeping energies of land and water,' Ralph Waldo Emerson declared in a lecture given in February 1844. But it was just one tool among many given to the United States by Providence to open up the interior to settlement: 'The bountiful continent is ours, state on state, and territory on territory, to the waves of the Pacific sea.' Walt Whitman concurred: 'The daring, burrowing energies of the Nation will never rest till the whole of this northern section of the Great West World is circled in the mighty Republic.' And it would not stop there. The whole globe was spread out before Americans and soon they would feel 'equally at home, on any "unappropriated" part' of the map. 'We Americans are the peculiar, chosen people – the Israel of our time,' Herman Melville announced. 'God has predestinated, mankind expects, great things from our race; and great things we feel in our souls. The rest of the nations must soon be in our rear. We are the pioneers of the world; the advance-guard, sent on through the wilderness of untried things, to break a new path in the New World that is ours.' The United States, John O'Sullivan wrote, was 'destined to be the great nation of futurity'.[23]

The Whigs were unmoved by, and even a little scornful of, these sentiments. They could not grasp that Texas was an electorally decisive political issue. Campaigning in his first congressional race in Illinois, Abraham Lincoln ignored the issue altogether. 'I never was much interested in the Texas question,' he later acknowledged. In the mind of the Whig leadership, territory was the last thing the United States needed more of. 'We have a Republic, gentlemen, of vast extent and unequalled natural advantages,' Daniel Webster told Whigs in Worcester County, Massachusetts. 'Instead of aiming to enlarge its boundaries, let us seek, rather, to strengthen its union, to draw out its resources, to maintain and improve its institutions ... You have a Sparta, embellish it!'

Clay signalled his indifference to the territorial issue by choosing as his running mate New Jersey senator Theodore Frelinghuysen, the great moralist who had led the opposition to Indian removal – not a man who would win him votes in the South and the West. Clay thought he simply did not need Texas to win. After all, he was Henry Clay, 'the Star of the West', a Kentucky slaveholder with dozens of slaves working on his Ashland plantation: surely he of all people understood the South and the West. In Clay's view, the winning Whig formula was sound economics: internal improvements, banks and the tariff. But, as Emerson observed, 'Banks and tariffs ... are flat and dull.' Americans wanted romance. 'America is a poem in our eyes,' Emerson wrote; 'its ample geography dazzles the imagination.' And Americans wanted to be dazzled – not lectured about economic policy.[24]

Clay was wide of the mark. Texas had taken hold of the public imagination in places far distant from the Rio Grande. In 1842, Charles Dickens found himself in an inn in Carondolet, Missouri. 'The landlord was a dry, tough, hard-faced old fellow ...' he wrote,

> He had all his life been restless and locomotive, with an irresistible desire for change; and was still the son of his old self: for if he had nothing to keep him at home, he said ... he would clean up his musket, and be off to Texas to-morrow morning. He was one of the very many descendants of Cain proper to this continent, who seem destined from their birth to serve as pioneers in the great human army; who gladly go on from year to year extending its outposts, and leaving home after home behind them.

A Whig operative in Illinois provided a more jaundiced, but no less revealing, analysis of why Texas resonated in his state. 'The old pioneers want it because they always want some place to drift to – lawyers want it because they think a great field for litigation will be opened, and law business is now at a low ebb in this state – and speculators want it because their business has been pretty much at a stand[still], in the State for a good long while.' 'Polk & Texas, that's the thing,' complained one Mississippi Whig, 'it goes like wild-fire with the folks as can't read, nor don't git no papers.'[25]

As the campaign progressed through the summer, more and more reports like these found their way to Whig and Democratic leaders. The Democrats were exultant. 'From all quarters reports are gratifying,' Jackson gloated in a letter to Polk. 'Let the Texan question be kept up.' Jackson helped consolidate Polk's position through another judicious intervention. Over the summer he negotiated John Tyler's departure from the contest. That August, Tyler dropped out of the race, leaving his voters to Polk.

With the Democratic vote no longer split, and the Whigs having badly misjudged public enthusiasm for Texas, Clay now felt compelled to take drastic action. Looking to modify the position taken in the

Raleigh Letter, Clay issued another public statement in which he declared he was not opposed to annexation under certain conditions. When it was pointed out that Mexico had already stated it would consider annexation an act of war, Clay issued yet another letter which seemed to walk back the first. The result was a nonsensical policy that alienated the abolitionist wing of his own party and won him no new votes. It also revived allegations of trimming that had dogged him throughout his career. Henry Clay, one newspaper jeered, was 'for or against annexation according as he may catch a few votes'. The problem was that it was true. Clay spoke too much, politicked too much and appeared much too slippery. All the while, Polk silently amassed momentum.[26]

The election was close. Polk won the popular vote by only 40,000 votes. The Democrats made a clean sweep of the Deep South, took most of the Midwest and won several states on the North Atlantic seaboard. The Whigs took the Upper South, New England and Ohio. Polk's 170–105 victory in the electoral college concealed how tight the election had been. In nine states the margin of victory was less than 5 per cent. In Tennessee, Clay won by a mere 123 votes. Given the evenly divided electorate, the abolitionist Liberty Party effectively played the role of kingmaker to slave-owner James Polk. If only a third of the 15,812 votes cast for the Liberty Party in New York had gone instead to Clay he would have won the state's thirty-six electoral college votes and with it the election. As it was, the Empire State went to the Democrats and sent Polk to Washington as the United States' eleventh president, and, at forty-nine years old, its youngest to date. The 1844 election, arguably among the most important elections of the nineteenth century, was decided by the votes of a few thousand disaffected New Yorkers on the political fringe. As Lincoln observed in 1845, if the 'whig abolitionists of New York had voted with us last fall, Mr. Clay would now be president, whig principles in the ascendent, and Texas not annexed'. In fairness to Liberty Party voters, Clay had done nothing to court them and a great deal to antagonize them. Equally, a Polk victory in November 1844 should not *ipso facto* have led to immediate annexation.

That it did was due to John Tyler. Having watched his earlier annexation treaty go down in failure, President Tyler now claimed that the 1844 election was effectively a referendum on Texas, and Polk's victory a mandate for annexation. Tyler adjusted his legislative strategy by opting to achieve annexation through a congressional resolution, which required a bare majority, rather than a ratified treaty, which required a two-thirds majority. In late January, the Democrat-controlled House passed such a resolution. Polk arrived in Washington just as the debate had moved to the Senate, where greater resistance was expected.

Here Polk made his first, fateful intervention. In order to get a resolution through the Senate, Thomas Hart Benton had suggested that Congress should pass a general bill for annexation that empowered a five-man presidential commission to negotiate the exact terms with Texas. Polk's contribution, according to Benton, came in the form of secret assurances that he would force the Texans to accept the Nueces, not the Rio Grande, as the southern border, and in so doing offer Mexico an avenue to avoid war with the United States over Texas. This promise won the votes of a handful of senators, and the resolution passed 27–25. On 2 March 1845, the entire package was finally sent through Congress, and on 3 March, Tyler's last day in office, the president gave his signature to annexation and sent a dispatch rider to Texas with the resolution in his saddlebag. The next morning, James Polk was sworn in on the steps of the Capitol.[27]

Benton had surrendered Congress's prerogatives over the exact language of annexation as a gesture of respect and goodwill to the

A cartoon celebrating the 'marriage' of Texas into the union of states.

incoming president. In part he may have believed – like many in Washington – that Polk was a weak, inexperienced man, who veteran politicians could manipulate. Equally, in an age of honour, Benton assumed that Polk would never deceive a room full of United States senators and would be beholden to his guarantees concerning Texas's southern boundary. But Polk had not come to Washington to be the proxy for powerful insiders. Nor did he put honour above expediency. As one of his aides once remarked, 'His secretiveness was large, and few men could better keep their own secrets.' Polk's secret purpose was to begin his administration with a free hand on the Texas issue, even if that meant bending the truth about his intended negotiating position.

In reality, he had no intention of compromising on the Rio Grande border. By the time Benton discovered the truth, it was too late and the United States and Mexico were on a collision course. 'Thus was Texas incorporated into the Union,' Benton later wrote: 'by a deception, and by deluding five senators out of their votes. It was not a barren fraud, but one prolific of evil, and pregnant with bloody fruit.'[28]

# From Intrigue to War

The passage of an annexation resolution by the United States Congress did not constitute annexation. It amounted to an *offer* of annexation that the Republic of Texas could refuse, accept or renegotiate. Accordingly, in the spring and summer of 1845 the action shifted to Texas, where a convention on annexation was to meet, with great symbolism, on 4 July.

Polk was keen to put the matter to rest for good and urged the Texans to embrace annexation, if only to secure the protection of the United States military. 'Let the Convention pass this general Resolution, on the 4th of July,' he wrote to the American chargé, Andrew Jackson Donelson, '[and] we will protect them against their Mexican enemies.'

To Donelson, Polk also expressed private, sentimental reasons for wanting to smoothly expedite annexation. Andrew Jackson lay dying at the Hermitage and Polk wanted to gift him Texas before his great mentor passed on. 'I hope he may live to see the last earthly object of his wishes consummated,' Polk wrote, 'the annexation of Texas to our Union, and what would be still more consoling to the closing hours of his life, to shake by the hand his old friend Houston as the Senator elect from the new State of Texas.'

Events would not move fast enough for that. On 6 June, Jackson wrote the final letter of his life, a brief note to Polk offering his thoughts on his cabinet. On 8 June he died. Sam Houston arrived two hours after his death, in time to shake his hand but not in time enough to find it warm. Houston wept over Jackson's corpse before turning to Sam Houston Jr, just turned two years old. 'My son,' he said, 'try to remember that you have looked on the face of Andrew Jackson.' On 23 June, the Texan congress ratified the United States' annexation resolution. On 4 July, the convention unanimously approved annexation.[1]

The Mexican response was predictable. Even before news of annexation arrived, the Mexican congress passed a law to raise volunteers. In its aftermath, war fever broke out. 'Extermination and death will be the cry of the valiant regulars and the citizen soldiery, marching enthusiastically to conquer Texas,' claimed one newspaper. General Arista, in command of 3,000 men at Matamoros on the Rio Grande, said simply that 'the time to fight has come'. An additional 8–10,000 men were gathered at San Luis Potosí ready to march on the Rio Grande. The Mexican press kept up a steady stream of bile aimed at the Americans. The summer and autumn of 1845 were filled with invasion scares as the American press reported on Mexican movements along the border.

In response, Polk moved to secure Texas. The fleet was sent into the Gulf of Mexico to loiter near Tampico and Veracruz. American forces under General Zachary Taylor were moved from Natchitoches to Corpus Christi along the Nueces River, 200 miles north of the Rio Grande. By the end of the summer, 3,500 American soldiers were in Texas, roughly half of the entire United States Army.

Despite concerns of a Mexican invasion, the American newspapers were exultant. 'Texas is now ours,' John O'Sullivan proclaimed, and there was no power on earth capable of 'limiting our greatness and checking the fulfilment of our manifest destiny to overspread the continent allotted by Providence for the free development of our yearly multiplying millions'. Texas, O'Sullivan noted (and as many Mexicans had long feared), was not the end point of American territorial aspirations but the doorway to fresh acquisitions on the American continent. The *New York Morning News* stated the issue plainly: 'Who's the next customer, California or Canada?'[2]

Polk wanted California, not Canada. Specifically, Polk wanted the great natural harbour of San Francisco. To Polk's mind, Texas was Tyler's achievement. California would be his legacy.

But there were also political considerations. Texas entered the Union in December 1845 as a slave state. Polk was a Texas man; he was also a slave-owner. When he moved into the President's Mansion, his wife fired the staff and replaced them with their slaves from Tennessee, who she installed in the cellar. But unlike Calhoun and the southern radicals, he did not define himself by his status as a slaveholder.

Polk followed the path that Jackson trod, which viewed slavery as an unfortunate but inescapable (and immensely lucrative) aspect of American life that enjoyed ironclad constitutional protections. Jackson had not shut his eyes to the political dangers posed by the slavery question; rather, he believed the correct strategy was to isolate the radicals at either end of the spectrum (abolitionists and Calhounites, respectively) and gather the great body of Americans in the middle around what mattered most: the Union. The role of the prudent American statesman, then, was to ensure the centre held by maintaining sectional equipoise. Jackson had observed as far back as 1836 that Texas would upset the sectional balance. His solution was to try and secure California as a fillip for the northern shipping interests.

Polk inherited this policy and in 1845 was in a position to effect it. This is in some ways the most important factor in explaining the coming war, and certainly the most overlooked. It runs counter to the great myth about the conflict: namely, that it was waged to extend slavery. In fact, from Polk's point of view, the exact opposite was the case. San Francisco would be a gift to the merchants and sailors of New England – the crucible of abolitionist agitation – and as the greater part of California lay above the Missouri Compromise line, it would be free territory by default.[3]

## POLK'S PLAN

Polk had a plan to secure California at the negotiation table. As crisis succeeded crisis along the United States' southern and western border, Polk resurrected an old dispute with Mexico and put it at the centre of his administration's diplomacy.

The point at stake was the issue of claims made by American merchants against the Mexican government. Since independence in the 1820s, Americans conducting business in Mexico had complained of various wrongs committed against them and had sought financial compensation from the state. The American government had taken up the issue and for twenty years had raised it with successive Mexican regimes. Not long after Polk took office, diplomatic relations with Mexico broke off with the departure of ambassador Juan Almonte from

Washington in protest at the annexation of Texas, ending further discussion of the claims issue.

To Polk, the breakdown of US–Mexico relations presented an opportunity to broker a far-reaching deal that would reset affairs between the two nations. Destined to be neighbours, they would have to get past the current breach and find a new modus vivendi. The claims dispute was part of a bundle of issues that included boundaries, Texas and trade. Given that Mexico did not have the money to resolve the claims issue with cash, it made sense to resolve the issue with land – of which they had a great deal. In Polk's mind it was an elegant, just and eminently reasonable proposal: the cession of California and New Mexico would indemnify the claims of American merchants.[4]

Polk was a small-minded, self-righteous man, totally certain of his moral rectitude. Girded with the claims issue, he felt secure in the knowledge that his policy towards Mexico derived from legitimate grievances and he proceeded in his punctilious and parochial way to try and secure the justice American honour required. Polk believed that if he showed no sign of weakness and continued to press his case, the men in charge in Mexico City would see reason.

To this end, in November 1845 he sent John Slidell, an experienced and respected politician who spoke Spanish, to Mexico City with an offer. If Mexico was willing to accept the fact of Texas annexation with the Rio Grande as its border and cede New Mexico and Alta California, then he was willing to pay up to $40 million and have the American Treasury assume the claims. Representatives of the Mexican government refused even to meet with Slidell, who lingered several months in Mexico before heading home in early spring. In a letter to Polk, Slidell sincerely apologized for the failure of his mission and concluded that in light of it 'a war would probably be the best mode of settling our affairs with Mexico'.[5]

Slidell's letter arrived just as Polk received much the same advice from a very different source. In February 1846, a man named Colonel Atocha called on Polk at the President's Mansion. Atocha had come from Havana, where he was part of the retinue of the exiled Santa Anna. According to Atocha, Santa Anna disapproved of the course of Mexican policy and desired peace with the United States. He went on to offer his advice on how best to deal with Mexico. Polk's tepid shows of force on the border were not enough – he ought to send the army to the Rio

Grande and have the navy blockade Veracruz. Only with a 'strong force ready to strike on their coasts and border' would the Mexican government 'feel their danger' and submit to American terms. It was remarkable advice coming from a man who had lost his leg defending Veracruz from a French punitive expedition.

Polk did not offer much in the way of commentary on Atocha's advice in his diary, but it doubtless aligned neatly with Slidell's gloomy message and his own preconceptions about conniving Mexican generals. It certainly must have reinforced the wisdom of his decision to order Zachary Taylor to advance to the Rio Grande a few weeks earlier.

Yet even this decision – which is often regarded as to the Mexican-American War what the Gulf of Tonkin incident was to the Vietnam War – was a carefully modulated escalation. Taylor's force was a great deal smaller than the opposing Mexican army and at the far extent of its supply lines. Both Whigs and Democrats chastised Polk for sending *too small* a force. Furthermore, even as he began piling on military pressure, Polk continued to cling to the belief that diplomacy would win the day. It was not until early April, when he learned definitively that the Slidell mission had failed, that Polk abandoned all hope of a diplomatic solution. Polk chose war only after a strategy of diplomacy coupled with calibrated escalation had failed. His predicament seems to owe more to miscalculation than to Machiavellianism. Benton's remark that 'it is impossible to conceive of an administration less warlike, or more intriguing, than that of Mr. Polk' seems to touch on an important truth of his presidency. Young Hickory was a sheep in wolf's clothing. He had neither Jackson's bark nor Jackson's bite – which had the effect of discrediting both his diplomatic initiatives and his martial posturing. Having intrigued for a dishonourable peace, Polk blundered into a calamitous war.[6]

## ANSWERED WITH WAR

But Polk did not operate in a vacuum. Mexico's actions are regularly glossed over in accounts of the war. Typically, historians speak of Mexico as 'goaded' into war by the crafty Americans. Yet this image of Polk as matador and Mexico as bull gives too much credit to the president and too little to his southern neighbour. This framing is normally deployed to explain away two awkward facts. First, that Mexico declared war on the United States almost three weeks before Congress responded in kind. Second, that the first shots of the war were fired by Mexican soldiers. In reality, the facts speak eloquently to Mexican intentions. Mexico believed it was engaging in a just war, a necessary war and a winnable war.

Mexico's position in 1846 was strikingly similar to that of the newly independent United States in 1812, when it embarked on a war with a larger northern neighbour over obscure points of policy that drenched its northern borderlands in blood, resulted in a devastating blockade of its ports and led to a series of amphibious landings along its vulnerable coastline that climaxed with a foreign army marching on its capital and burning it to the ground. 'Who are we? and for what are we going to fight?' Andrew Jackson had asked the Tennessee militia on the eve of that war. To which he replied, 'We are going to fight for the reestablishment of our national character ... to seek some indemnity for past injuries, [and] some security against future aggressions.'

Much the same reasoning guided Mexican actions in 1846. Less than twenty-five years after independence, it faced the same questions and provided the same answers. Mexico did not want to be the kind of country that could be bullied and partitioned by a powerful neighbour without any sign of resistance or protest. Moreover, some reasoned that if Mexico's woes since independence were attributable to a lack of national feeling, then war might bind the nation anew. 'Nations determine their history only in the most dangerous crises,' one pamphleteer observed, 'and such a crisis ... has arrived.'

Familiarity with American methods stiffened Mexican resolve. Mexico was heir to Spain's humiliation in Florida. No sooner had Florida been secured than American attentions moved westwards to Texas, New Mexico and California. By 1846 Texas had been annexed, American traders dominated Santa Fe (where they sold arms to Comanche war parties raiding northern Mexico), Mormons had settled along the approaches to California, explorer John C. Frémont, who the Mexicans correctly judged to be an American agent, was on manoeuvres in Sacramento, while yet more Americans were established in Oregon and an American squadron loitered off the Pacific coast.

This sense of encirclement explains why Mexico was in no mood to negotiate. Even the offer of $40 million only heightened the sense that the American offer was essentially *plata o plomo*. After all, recent history had shown that the Americans would never be satisfied. If Mexico ceded New Mexico and California, they would demand Tamaulipas and Coahuila next. The Native American experience loomed large. They had pursued a policy of negotiated withdrawal with disastrous consequences. Indeed, the Mexicans were close observers of American racial dynamics and judged that yielding to American encroachment would effectively acknowledge the 'superiority of the Anglo-Saxon race' and legitimize American contempt for Mexico's religion, culture and racial make-up. Some even feared that if the United States was allowed to dominate Mexico, then the day would not be far off when Mexicans would be 'sold as beasts' since 'their colour was not as white as that of their conquerors'. In a sense, Mexico was moved by a mirror image of American Manifest Destiny – where further territorial losses would only confirm the failure of their national experiment, begun just twenty years earlier, which would in turn condemn them to a subordinate position inside the American caste system.[7]

Besides, the Mexican leadership did not view the war as unwinnable. Even though Mexico's population was half of the United States, even though its commerce was a sixth of its neighbour's, even though its industrial capacity was a fraction of the size, and even though the Mexican economy was throttled by debt – despite all this and many other weaknesses, they did not believe war with the United States was suicidal. Of the four major political factions in Mexico in 1846, only one advocated for further negotiations.

The pro-war majority were not delusional. Many sincerely believed they would be able to fight and win a defensive war on their northern frontier. The Mexican army was larger than the American army and included a number of well-trained and highly motivated units, whose professionalism the coming war would vindicate. Furthermore, Mexican soldiers would be fighting on their home terrain and could draw upon the support of the population. By contrast, the Mexicans judged that the smaller American army, used largely for civil-engineering projects and Indian wars, would struggle to wage war in the deserts of northern Mexico. They took heart from the Americans' poor performance in 1812 and their even more woeful conduct during the Second Seminole War. Mexican leaders thought it inconceivable that the United States could invade and conquer the entire country – as did most foreign observers.[8]

\* \* \*

It was against this backdrop that Slidell arrived in Mexico looking to by turns threaten and buy off the Mexican leadership. When President José Joaquín de Herrera learned that Slidell had landed in Veracruz, he warned one American official that 'his appearance in the capital at this time might prove destruction to the government, and thus defeat the whole affair. You know the opposition are calling us traitors for entering into this arrangement with you.' Although Herrera tried to save his administration by refusing to meet with Slidell, within a month he had been replaced by Mariano Paredes in a coup.

As a sign of his intentions, Paredes appointed the hawkish Juan Almonte, lately ambassador to the United States, to his cabinet as minister of war. Inevitably, Paredes also refused to meet with Slidell, closing the door on Polk's diplomatic initiative. In his war message on 23 April, Paredes traced the conflict back to 'the ancient injuries and the attacks' which Mexico had endured since 1836, but focused on the appearance of Taylor in the Nueces Strip, American incursions in California and the presence of their fleet in the Gulf and in the Pacific.

'So many and such bitter outrages can be tolerated no longer,' he declared, 'and I have commanded the general-in-chief of the division of our northern frontier to attack the army which is attacking us; to answer with war the enemy who makes war upon us.'[9]

Two days later, the first shots of the conflict were fired on the banks of the Rio Grande.

# The Mexican Polka

Zachary Taylor spent March 1846 marching his 3,000-man force from their camp on the Nueces River to the Rio Grande. Their journey through the Nueces Strip – the patch of land that the Mexican and American governments were threatening war over – was uninspiring. 'The one hundred and seventy miles between Corpus Christi and [the Rio Grande] was the most miserable desert, without wood or water, that I ever saw,' Lieutenant George Meade wrote in a jaundiced letter home, 'and perfectly unfit for the habitation of man.'

On 28 March, the Americans arrived at the banks of the Rio Grande and erected a stockade they christened Fort Brown. Across the river they could see the Mexican town of Matamoros, and in the evening could even talk with the ladies taking a stroll on the opposite bank. In Matamoros, General Arista had 2,000 men but neither boats to ship them across the river nor orders to do so.

And so nothing happened until 11 April, when General Pedro de Ampudia entered Matamoros with reinforcements and clear instructions to engage the Americans. Across the river the American soldiers could hear the bells tolling and the guns firing a salute to celebrate Ampudia's arrival. They knew, too, of Ampudia's fearsome reputation*

---

* In 1844, Ampudia had ruthlessly put down a filibustering expedition led by Don Francisco Sentmanat, shooting thirty-eight of fifty-three prisoners. Following his execution, Ampudia had Sentmanat's body left on display for twelve hours before having his head removed, boiled in oil and then left on permanent display in the town square of San Juan Batista. This incident was commemorated in America in the popular song 'Uncle Sam and Mexico': 'Since Texas cut off Sant Anna's peg,/We'll Amputate Ampudia's leg,/An' so his carcass de air shan't spoil,/We'll boil it in his own hot oil.'

and understood that the uneasy peace on the banks of the Rio Grande was about to come to an end.[1]

Realizing Ampudia's arrival meant war, on 15 April Taylor ordered the United States Navy to blockade the mouth of the Rio Grande at Point Isabel, to prevent Mexican resupply. Ampudia responded by issuing an ultimatum demanding the blockade be lifted; Taylor demurred. The action practically guaranteed conflict as neither army could survive more than a few weeks without fresh supplies and both had orders not to back down.

In late April, Taylor left a rump force at Fort Brown and moved the bulk of his army to Point Isabel to protect his supply lines.

In the final fragile days of peace there was an eerie increase in American deaths and disappearances, and widespread rumours of Mexican incursions upriver. On 23 April, Paredes issued his declaration of war.

Two days later a small American cavalry outfit led by Captain Seth Thornton patrolling on the northern bank of the Rio Grande was surprised by a Mexican force twenty times its size. Fourteen Americans were killed and the remainder taken prisoner. When news of the engagement reached Fort Brown, the Americans were 'electrified'. 'War has commenced,' one American wrote simply in his diary. Ampudia gave orders to bombard the Americans across from Matamoros. At Point Isabel, Taylor wrote to the governors of Texas and Louisiana, asking them to call up the militia, and then wheeled around to come to the relief of his men. On 3 May, the Mexican batteries in Matamoros opened up on the Americans at Fort Brown. The Americans replied in kind and the British consul, Francis Gifford, recorded an 'abundance of red hot shot' landing in the city. Gifford told London that he raised the Union Jack to try and signal the presence of neutrals. 'Nevertheless my house was completely riddled with balls, eight of which were lodged in it, without taking account of the many which passed entirely through. My flag was twice shot through ... All is in great confusion, as you may easily believe.'[2]

## 'WAR EXISTS'

If ever there was an opportunity for the Mexican army to prove their mettle against the interloping army of Zachary Taylor and the grasping administration of James Polk it was on 8 May 1846. Taylor was in a desert, thousands of miles from home and heavily outnumbered by a Mexican force certain of their cause and eager to repel the Yankee invader. At Palo Alto, the two armies met in perfect formation on open ground and engaged in an artillery duel. When the Mexicans fired, the Americans took cover and suffered light casualties. Taylor's guns then responded in kind, laying down 'a perfect storm of iron' on Arista's men. The Mexican infantry remained in close formation as the American artillery opened up. 'They stood like statues,' one soldier wrote, while the Americans 'tore complete lanes right through' their lines. When the Mexican cavalry ventured into the field, they were annihilated. The artillery fire was so intense the main Mexican force never even engaged. The Mexicans retired at nightfall, leaving their positions strewn with dead. Nine Americans had died against more than a hundred Mexicans.[3]

The next day Taylor pressed his advantage, encircling Arista at Resaca de la Palma. Following withering fire from the American guns, the Mexican lines broke under an American bayonet charge. Arista's army fled pell-mell towards the Rio Grande, pursued by the Americans. American infantry and cavalry overran the Mexican rear, rampaging through field kitchens and past campfires. Over a hundred were killed in what one officer described gleefully as 'a total rout of the Grand Mexican Army that was going to eat us up'. The Americans captured the entire Mexican supply train, seven artillery pieces, as well as one general, two colonels, a clutch of officers and over a hundred prisoners. Watching from the other side of the river, Gifford concluded that Arista's army had been 'destroyed, or is so scattered and horror stricken, that I consider its reorganization a matter of absolute impossibility'. A week later Taylor entered Matamoros and raised the American flag over the city.[4]

If the mission of Taylor's army was to defend the southern border and chastise the Mexican army, then it looked in mid-May 1846 as though that mission had been accomplished. Some officers concluded that the war was now over. 'We have whipped them in the open plain,' wrote Meade, 'and we have done so in the bushes, and I now believe the war will soon be ended.'⁵

For Polk, however, the purpose of a showdown with Mexico was not to assert American sovereignty over Texas – it was to obtain an alibi for the conquest of California. Consequently, when, on the evening of Saturday, 9 May, a dispatch rider brought news of the outbreak of hostilities, Polk did not hesitate. Within an hour, Polk had assembled the cabinet to inform them of the news. They unanimously approved his decision to request a declaration of war from Congress.

On Monday, 11 May, his war message went to Congress. He repeated the importance of achieving justice for America's 'much-injured and long-suffering' merchants in Mexico, but the most memorable line referred to recent events along the contested border. 'Mexico has passed the boundary of the United States, has invaded our territory and shed American blood upon the American soil,' the president said. 'War exists, and ... exists by the act of Mexico herself.'

The United States could thus claim to be acting in self-defence. More to the point, Zachary Taylor was now stranded in hostile territory facing a much larger army. Would Congress abandon him to his fate? 'We are called upon by every consideration of duty and patriotism to vindicate with decision the honor, the rights, and the interests of our country.'

Using various procedural tricks, Polk's congressional allies limited the amount of time allocated for debating the war resolution. Many congressmen took seriously the Constitution's requirement that only Congress could make war and balked at Polk's claim that war already existed. Some stated flatly that they did not believe the Rio Grande was America's southern border and that the Mexicans were justly defending their territory from foreign invasion. At the same time, it was politically impossible for even ardent critics of the administration to do nothing while American soldiers were fighting for their lives.⁶

The debate over the war was short and messy; the outcome was decisive. The House approved the resolution, with only fourteen representatives dissenting. In the Senate, the bill passed 42–2. On 13 May, a formal declaration of war was issued.

'Never was so momentous a measure adopted, with so much precipitancy; so little thought; or forced through by such objectionable means.' So wrote Calhoun, who provided one of the two Senate votes against the war. But his dissenting voice was lost in the clamour and in the end counted for little. Polk had his war.

If anyone doubted what the implications of that war would be for the territorial integrity of Mexico, the president removed all doubt in a darkly comic exchange with Secretary of State James Buchanan that evening when the cabinet gathered to discuss how to communicate America's position to other nations. Buchanan's draft message contained a paragraph claiming that the United States did not desire 'to dismember Mexico or to make conquests' and specifically disavowed any ambitions to acquire 'California or New Mexico'. Polk curtly reminded Buchanan that 'though we had not gone to war for conquest',

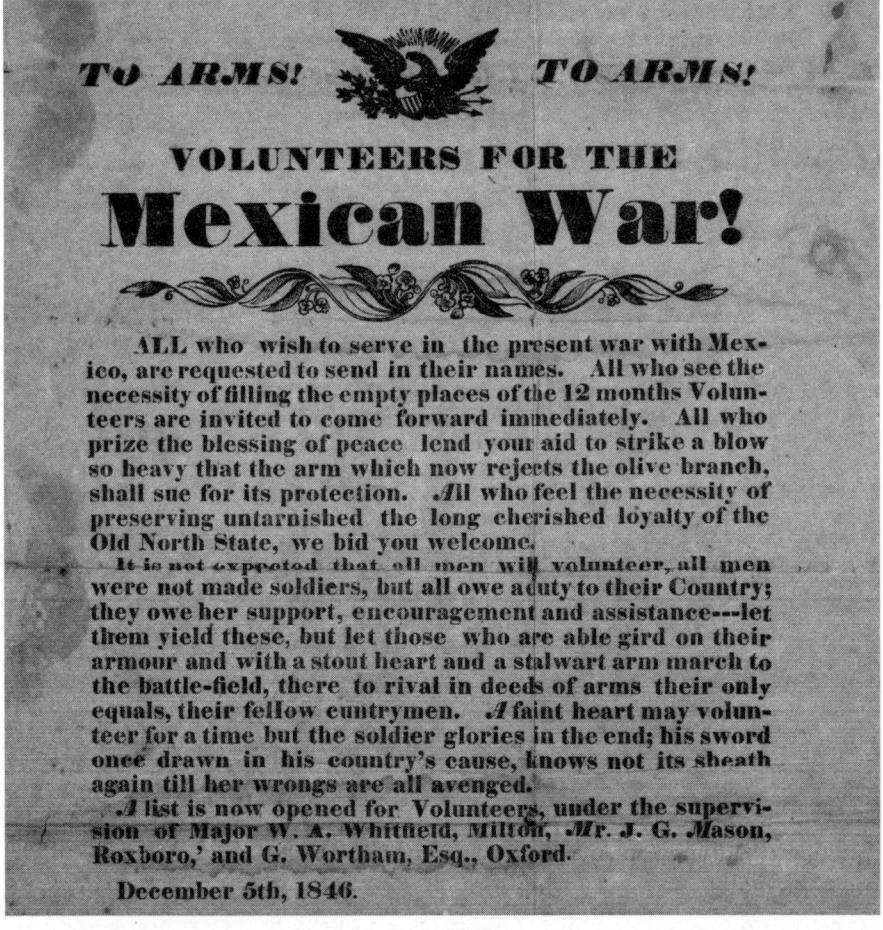

*Recruiting for the Mexican-American War.*

making peace would require California and New Mexico 'to indemnify our claimants on Mexico, and to defray the expenses of the war'. Aghast, Buchanan replied that such claims would draw France and England into the war on Mexico's side. Their views were irrelevant, Polk said, citing the Monroe Doctrine. Buchanan pressed the issue, claiming the great powers of Europe would never permit the United States to take California unopposed. Put out by Buchanan's cluelessness and insubordination, Polk bridled, and in a rare but characteristically pious outburst proclaimed that he was willing to wage war with 'all the Powers of Christendom' and 'fight until the last man among us fell in the conflict' to preserve America's independent policy. Other cabinet members came to Polk's aid – but Buchanan stood his ground, arguing with them all for some two hours. At length, Polk lost his temper, marched to his writing table and wrote the message himself. Presenting his version to Buchanan, he insisted the existing paragraphs be substituted for his own. Buchanan did not reply but silently left the room with both copies in his hands. 'I was much astonished at the views expressed by Mr. Buchanan,' Polk told his diary afterwards.

This was but one among many astonishing scenes observed that summer of 1846 as the United States mobilized for war with Mexico.[7]

## THE GREAT FIGHTING PARTY

Congress provided for the raising of 50,000 volunteers, with quotas assigned to individual states. After the narrow election of 1844 and the rancorous public debate over Texas, Mexico and western expansion, the public response to the call for volunteers to fight in Polk's war would effectively be a referendum on the administration's policy. The president and his allies had long claimed that they were acting in response to public pressure for action against Mexico. Now they had to ask the electorate to risk life and limb in a war – the first foreign war in the United States' history – and find out whether this sentiment was real or illusory.

The response was overwhelming. In towns and cities across the country, news of war was met with ecstatic public meetings where, amid parading, speechifying and heavy drinking, men offered themselves as volunteers in the war against Mexico. In New Orleans, before news of hostilities had even reached Washington, one thousand men had volunteered. 'We live, move, breathe ... in an atmosphere of enthusiasm, ardor, and excitement,' one Louisiana journalist recorded. 'We see nothing but volunteers marching, flags flying, and men mustering for service; and nothing do we hear but the blast of the war-bugle, the roll of the kettle drum, and the shrill note of the spirit-stirring fife.'

'People here are all in a state of delirium,' Herman Melville reported from upstate New York. 'A military ardor pervades all ranks – Militia Colonels wax red in their coat facings – and 'prentice boys are running off to the wars by scores. – Nothing is talked of but the "Halls of the Montezumas."'

In Chicago, an abolitionist watched with disgust as volunteers toured the grog shops in the company of a military band; similar scenes were observed throughout the Midwest as news of the war spread across the region. 'There seems to be but one party now,' one man wrote to Polk from Tennessee, '& that is the great fighting party.'[8]

The rank and file joined for money, adventure and (after it was introduced in 1847) a warrant convertible into 160 acres (a quarter section) of public lands – their own slice of Manifest Destiny. This was, indeed, what one historian has dubbed an 'Army of Manifest Destiny', and a good deal of the men who marched off to war had been influenced by the rhetoric of territorial expansion. William H. Prescott's *The History of the Conquest of Mexico* was a bestseller in the mid-1840s and volunteers destined for Mexico imagined themselves as latter-day conquistadores bound for a contemporary El Dorado. Samuel Chamberlain recalled how, shipping down the Mississippi with his regiment, 'my mind wandered in bright dreams of glory and renown in that region of romance, the land of Cortés and Montezuma'.

The officers who led them were no less motivated – believing that a stint in a victorious campaign would boost their chances of securing high office. Thomas Hart Benton wrote damningly of politicians hoping to use 'gunpowder popularity' as their 'passport to the presidency'* and Polk's army was full of political talent. Senators Franklin Pierce and Caleb Cushing† both enlisted. Dozens of former and sitting congress-

---

\* The war did in fact produce three presidents – Zachary Taylor, Franklin Pierce and Ulysses S. Grant – as well as a Confederate president, Jefferson Davis.

† One wag later wrote of Cushing's time in service that 'as a General in the Mexican war the only laurel he won was tumbling down and breaking his leg while walking with a lady in the street of some Mexican city, perhaps Jalapa'.

men joined the army. Many were Democrats – Jefferson Davis of Mississippi, Archibald Yell of Arkansas, Thomas L. Hamer of Ohio – but not all. Illinois sent both John J. Hardin, a Whig and an associate of Abraham Lincoln, and James Shields, a Democratic politician who had once challenged Lincoln to a duel. Kentucky produced a remarkable bipartisan contingent which included Democratic congressman William Orlando Butler, Whig congressman (and committed abolitionist) Cassius Marcellus Clay and, most remarkable of all, Henry Clay Jr, the son of Henry Clay. Most well-placed politicians secured enlistments as majors or colonels. Commissions for captains and lieutenants were also up for grabs, but in the spirit of Jacksonian Democracy, those positions were elected by the rank and file. Inevitably, there was a great deal of crossover between local politics and the scrabble for position within state regiments. One witness to mobilization in the Midwest observed that among the rabble of volunteers were many a 'village statesman, pregnant with undeveloped greatness, and anxious to enlarge the sphere of their influence by a military accouchement'. In Alton, Illinois, Samuel Chamberlain recorded his experience of military democracy at an election for officers held in a ten-pin alley:

> A staff officer of Governor Ford called the meeting to order, when a large red-faced man mounted the bar and delivered the following speech.
> 'Fellow citizens! I am Peter Goff, the Butcher of Middletown! I am! I am the man that shot that sneaking, white livered Yankee abolitionist s—n of a b—h, Lovejoy! I did! I want to be your Captain, I do; and I will serve the yellow bellied Mexicans the same. I will! I have treated you to fifty dollars worth of whiskey, I have, and when elected Captain I will spend fifty more, I will!'
> It is needless to state he was elected almost unanimously.

Captain Goff sparked a mutiny a week later after he assaulted three of his men during a drunken spree. The mutineers were later reconciled by an apologetic speech and a barrel of whiskey. A week later, they were bound for Mexico.[9]

All through the latter half of 1846 and into 1847 this rowdy mass of soldiery mobilized for war. The theatre of operations was huge.

Washington was 1,800 miles from Matamoros and 2,400 miles from San Francisco. Mexico City and Veracruz both lay some 2,500 miles away. Recruits assembling in the Midwest or along the north-east seaboard faced an epic journey south. Regiments departing from Boston, Baltimore or New York had to travel by boat down the Atlantic coast and around the Florida Keys, a long journey on dangerous waters. Volunteers from the South and West travelled by steamer down the Mississippi, a journey of a week or two, depending on their point of origin. Wherever they came from, the destination was the same. New Orleans was the great staging point of the war, and the levee was soon piled high with equipment and supplies. The volunteers themselves camped on the Chalmette battlefield, where thirty years before Jackson had defeated the British, and waited for transport to Mexico.[10]

Those destined for the far western theatre faced an even lengthier journey to the battlefront. Polk had ordered General Stephen Kearny to march on Santa Fe and then proceed overland to California. But beyond Missouri there were no steamers, no railways, not even any roads. Armies marched on trails that had only been established in recent decades and through terrain hostile to human existence.

Robert Whitworth, an English teenager recently arrived from Liverpool, marched with the Mormon Battalion all the way from Fort Leavenworth, Kansas, to San Diego, California, a distance of nearly 2,000 miles, in six months. Whitworth's diary is a testament to the hardships of soldiering. The men regularly walked thirty miles a day without water. The commanding officer died of sickness and the quartermaster was cashiered for fraud. When supplies ran low, rations were halved. The men became so hungry that a beaver stew was considered a rare treat. Traipsing through the Arizona desert, Whitworth met an Indian merchant and traded his last shirt for corn. All the while, Whitworth sceptically appraised the country they were suffering through and for. 'This country,' he wrote damningly of New Mexico, 'is little better than a large sand bar.' A few weeks later, now somewhere in the Sonora Desert, he declared, 'The country here is so poor and miserable that it was named Purgatory by the men, but some insisted that it was a Hotter place than that.'[11]

Yet out west the victories came as easily as they had during Taylor's opening forays on the Rio Grande. In mid-August, Kearny took Santa Fe 'without firing a gun or spilling a drop of blood', as he boasted in a letter to Polk, ending at a stroke almost 350 years of Spanish-speaking rule.

In September, Kearny set out to seize California with a force of 500 dragoons. On account of the harsh conditions they faced ahead, Kearny ordered the dragoons to ride mules rather than horses. His army of mule-mounted conquistadores was only a few days out of Santa Fe when they ran into Kit Carson, the famous mountain man of the West. Carson came from California with marvellous news: the entire province had already fallen into American possession.

Mexican rule in California had begun to unravel on 14 June, several weeks *before* news of the war reached the region, when a band of Americans under the leadership of John C. Frémont seized power in Sonoma, raised the famous Bear Flag, and proclaimed the existence of the California Republic, now better remembered as the Bear Flag Republic.

The Bear Flag revolt (reminiscent in so many ways of the West Florida rebellion of 1810) was soon overwhelmed by news of war between Mexico and America. On 7 July, Commodore Sloat sailed into Monterey and three days later the US Navy took control of San Francisco. Frémont appeared in San Diego in late July and raised the American flag over that town.

In the meantime, the *Princeton* had arrived in the region and Commodore Stockton had assumed command of the Pacific squadron. Under his leadership, Los Angeles was occupied on 13 August.

Stockton and Frémont joined forces and the bulk of the Bear Flag rebels were absorbed into the American forces. The 7,000-strong Mexican population were virtually powerless in the absence of the Mexican military and could do nothing to resist. On 17 August, Stockton issued a proclamation declaring that 'the Territory of California now belongs to the United States' and until further notice would be governed by martial law under his authority as commander-in-chief, a title he had awarded himself.

Stockton was soon giving free rein to his burgeoning megalomania. In a letter to Polk on 26 August, he congratulated himself and his men for having 'secured by their toil and daring this beautiful empire'. California, he assured the president, was safe in his hands. 'My word is at present the law of the land. My power is more than regal. The haughty Mexican Cavalier shakes hands with me with pleasure, and the beautiful women look to me with joy and gladness, as their friend and benefactor. In short all of power and luxury is spread before me, through the mysterious workings of a beneficent Providence. No man could or ought to desire more of power and respect.'[12],[13]

A month later, the Mexican population of Los Angeles staged an uprising against American rule. Resistance continued to flare up sporadically in California and New Mexico over the next year, but without Mexican military assistance it was doomed to fail. The Mexican north-west was lost forever. As summer turned to autumn, the focus of the war shifted permanently to the central and north-eastern departments of Mexico.

## BUENA VISTA

Taylor's spectacular victories in May had failed to bring Mexico to terms. Instead, every indicator suggested that Mexico was preparing to fight a long war. Accordingly, in July Taylor received orders to take Monterrey, the largest city in northern Mexico. In late September, Monterrey fell to the Americans after a vicious battle in which Mexican and American forces fought from street to street and house to house. Taylor paused at Monterrey for two months to rest his men and refresh his supplies. In November he occupied Saltillo, a short distance south, without a fight. There his army halted.

The stage was now set for what was very nearly the great American catastrophe of the war. The American strategy at the outbreak of hostilities was to occupy northern Mexico and hold it ransom until the Mexicans made peace. By the end of 1846, it was clear that this strategy had failed. But from the very beginning another, more daring, plan had been held in reserve: if they would not see reason, the Americans would seize Veracruz and march an army into Mexico City. There, in the very heart of the country, they would impose terms on the defeated Mexicans.

By January 1847, Polk had begun making preparations for this shift in strategy. He reassigned Taylor's best men to General Winfield Scott, leaving Taylor with a mixed force of volunteers from Kentucky, Arkansas, Mississippi, Indiana and Illinois. The decision was not unreasonable, but, as ever with Polk, it was poisoned by his politicking. Polk was jealous of Taylor's popularity at home and feared that the Whig general would run for president in 1848. Shifting the focus to Scott and Mexico City would help deflate Taylor's reputation and sidetrack his presidential ambitions. It was not lost on Taylor's many supporters, especially those in the army, that the president had first used Taylor to bait the Mexicans in the Nueces Strip and had now abandoned him deep inside hostile territory with a rump force of untested recruits. It looked to some as though he was trying to get Taylor killed.[14]

To make matters worse, one of Polk's more egregious errors in judgement now came back to bite him. Over the summer, Polk gave orders to the navy that if Santa Anna tried to sail back to Mexico, the blockade should be lifted to allow him through. Polk, still under the influence of the Atocha intrigue, believed that if Santa Anna returned to Mexico, he would force the government to the negotiating table. In mid-August, Santa Anna duly landed in Veracruz and a month later made a triumphant entrance into Mexico City. There he presented himself as the saviour of his country and decamped to the garrison town of San Luis Potosí to prepare for a campaign against the American invaders. 'The United States were deceived in believing that I would be capable of betraying my mother country,' he crowed. 'Before such a thing could happen, I would rather be burnt on a pyre and that my ashes were spread in such a way that not one atom was left.' From San Luis Potosí, Santa Anna and his 20,000-strong army were in striking distance of Taylor and his 5,000 men at Saltillo.[15]

In mid-February, Santa Anna made his move. Taylor knew his intentions and withdrew to a small town named Buena Vista, at the head of a narrow mountain pass known as La Angostura. The road there was bounded by a ravine on one side and a deep barranca on the other. The surrounding land was broken up by gullies and gulches and cleft by spurs and arroyos. The irregular terrain offered Taylor's vastly outnumbered force its only hope of surviving the coming onslaught.

By 20 February, Santa Anna, having forced his men on a gruelling 300-mile march through the freezing desert, finally had Taylor in his sights. Enlisting a German surgeon as an envoy, he sent him through the lines with a message. Taylor's position was hopeless. He should surrender now or be wiped out. 'Tell Santa Anna to go to hell!' Taylor said, turning to his chief of staff. 'Major Bliss, put that in Spanish, and send it back by this d—d Dutchman.'

Santa Anna did not ask twice. Although his men were exhausted, although he had sustained several thousand losses on the march alone, the general was determined to push his men into battle at the first opportunity.

On the morning of the 23rd, the Americans woke up to a terrifying sight. 'I doubt if the "Sun of Austerlitz" shone on a more brilliant spectacle than the Mexican army displayed before us,' Samuel Chamberlain recalled. 'Twenty thousand men clad in new uniforms, belts as white as snow, brasses and arms burnished until they glittered like gold and silver.' The Americans watched as the Mexican army celebrated Mass and then moved into position. Once the priests had withdrawn, the Mexican batteries opened up and the battle began.

Fighting on terrain of Taylor's choosing, the Mexicans' only hope was to storm the American artillery batteries and then overwhelm their infantry with their superior numbers. The tactic very nearly worked when early in the day a Mexican assault pierced the lines of the Second Indiana volunteers. The 'regiment broke and fled like deer', according to Chamberlain, obliging the regiments beside them to withdraw to avoid being outflanked. The American artillery began firing double shots of canister, topped up with loose stones, at point-blank range into the ranks of the approaching Mexicans. 'But though horrid lanes were cut through the hostile columns,' Chamberlain recalled, 'they still advanced.' Mexican infantry and cavalry sensed blood and swarmed towards the Americans. One eyewitness recalled that the landscape was totally hidden beneath the many thousands of Mexican soldiers, their weapons glistening in the sun.

At the decisive moment, Taylor appeared among his men, turned to his son-in-law, the congressman Jefferson Davis, and ordered Davis's Mississippi volunteers into the breach. 'Steady boys!' Taylor shouted as the Mississippi men headed into battle. 'Steady for the honor of Old Mississippi!'

After a brisk, lethal fusillade, the Mississippians threw down their rifles, took out their bowie knives and with a roar charged the oncoming Mexicans. All along the line, other American regiments followed their lead. The counter-attack succeeded, stabilizing the American lines and halting the Mexican advance.

The rest of the battle played out in the same way: the Mexicans would advance up to the barrels of the American artillery, and then be beaten back by bayonet charges. Officers led by example and many died in close-quarter fighting. Jefferson Davis survived but Congressmen

Archibald Yell and John Hardin were not so lucky. Henry Clay Jr was also killed during one of the final engagements of the day.

American élan was impressive and proved decisive. When the Mexicans retired at dusk, they had sustained some 3,000 casualties. The Americans lost one-fifth of that amount, despite being outnumbered four to one.[16]

Taylor's men went to sleep that night expecting to re-enter the fray the following morning. But when dawn broke, the Mexicans had left the field. Santa Anna judged the Americans sufficiently bloodied and his men too exhausted.

Besides, he had to return urgently to Mexico City to prepare its defence against the imminent invasion of General Winfield Scott.

*Newspaper reporting on the battle of Buena Vista.*

## VERACRUZ

Mexico City was some 280 miles inland from coastal Veracruz. Cortés had founded Veracruz in 1519, using it as his base for his assault on Tenochtitlan in the heart of the fabled Valley of Mexico.

Three hundred years later, the Americans were attempting the same feat, although their advance was aided considerably by the National Highway, one of Mexico's very few paved roads, which wound through the highlands surrounding Jalapa to connect the capital to the sea. Scott's plan was simple: seize Veracruz, march down the highway and conquer Mexico City.

Over the winter of 1846–47 the US Navy had secured the approaches to Veracruz, bombarding Tabasco and occupying the key port of Tampico. Despite valiant resistance by the Mexican army and navy, the Americans were indomitable. Mexico's fate looked bleak.

At Tampico, an American officer attending the flag-raising ceremony in the central plaza overheard the comment of an elderly Mexican man. 'That flag has been my ruin. I came from Spain, and I was then young, and was sent into Louisiana; that flag came and I then went into Florida; in a few years the same flag came, and I then came to this place expecting never to be disturbed by it again. But there it is – the same flag, the same people.'

However hackneyed allusions to Cortés and Montezuma might sound now, at the time they seemed to capture an essential truth derived from decades of unhindered American expansion. The United States was rampant; Mexico was on the verge of being overrun.[17]

Stories of Cortés and the conquistadores must have crossed the minds of the inhabitants of Veracruz when a forest of white sails appeared offshore in early March 1847. The view from aboard Scott's flotilla was no less evocative. The walled city of Veracruz, made wealthy from its historic monopoly on Mexico's colonial exports, most famously Aztec gold, was guarded by the formidable citadel of San Juan de Ulúa and dominated by the snow-capped peak of Pico de Orizaba, the tallest mountain in the country.

On 9 March, waves of American landing craft began to converge on the beaches flanking the city. In a matter of days, the Americans had landed 8,600 soldiers. By 22 March, the city was surrounded by the

American guns. Scott asked commander Juan Morales to surrender; Morales refused. The Americans took the decision to focus their fire on the city of Veracruz itself and largely ignore the citadel, which housed the actual fighting force of the Mexican army.* Consequently, when the Americans began their bombardment that afternoon, everyone present knew they were firing on defenceless civilians. They opened fire nevertheless. Americans outside the walls watched as first Veracruz was obscured by the smoke of the guns and then by the smoke of the fires that swept the pummelled city. The damage wrought by the expert American gunners was awful. Journalist William C. Tobey watched an artillery shell 'hit a large dome and pass through it. Another struck a light spire on a public building and shivered it to atoms.' Shells exploded over the rooftops while mortar rounds slammed indiscriminately into the compact residential neighbourhoods. Walls were ripped open; furniture hurled into the streets. A family was eating dinner when a round slammed into their building, killing them all. One reporter watched from the safety of the American lines as fire swept through the city, illuminating the domes and spires of the skyline, and silhouetting the forms of 'families moving about on the tops of the houses in the utmost consternation and apparent despair'. 'The shells seem to have done great execution,' one American officer noted in his journal. 'The crashing, rumbling report which they make as they fall through the roofs of the buildings, bursting and scattering death and destruction around is truly terrible.' If they could see

---

* In his official report to London, the British consul in Veracruz, who stayed in the city through the siege, commented unfavourably on American methods. 'Not a shot was fired on the castle,' he noted; 'the tide of destruction appears to have been directed exclusively on the buildings and the wretched occupiers.' He went on to observe that hundreds of civilians sought shelter at the French, Spanish and British consulates and subsequently died when these buildings were not spared by the bombardment. He accused Scott of a 'disregard for the courtesies of civilised war' and ended his report with a damning (and evocative) summary of American behaviour: 'It is impossible to close this paper without adverting to the strange mode of warfare adopted by the American commanders. With a force three times greater than necessary required to storm the town, and twice such as required to attack the castle, they never attempted it, but intrenched within their covered way, much in the same manner as they were posted behind cotton bags at New Orleans in 1814, they preferred destroying a fine city unnecessarily.' The consul neglected to mention in his report that his own daughter, aged fourteen, had died in the bombardment. (FO 205/19, report of 29 Mar. 1847; Anderson, *Artillery Officer*, 104.)

the destruction of the city, one journalist told his readers, 'you would all turn Quakers'.

After three and a half days and the firing of over 6,000 rounds, Morales gave in and surrendered the city. On 29 March, the American flag was lifted above Veracruz. One artilleryman noted in his diary that 'upon entering the City … all feelings of pride were gone when I witnessed the awful evidences of the deadly work of our destructive shells.' The city was in ruins; its inhabitants in a state of shock. This was an 'unfortunate war', he concluded. 'I think that killing people is a very poor way of settling national grievances.'[18]

## TO THE HALLS OF THE MONTEZUMAS

Santa Anna had calculated that losing Veracruz might have a strategic advantage. The city sat on the dry lowlands that from April through the summer months were swept with seasonal diseases, among them yellow fever. If his army could bar entry to the interior, disease might cripple Scott's army and end the invasion. Santa Anna parked his army at a heavily fortified mountain pass on the road to Jalapa and waited for the Americans.

But scarcely two weeks after the occupation of Veracruz, a young captain named Robert E. Lee scouted a route around the main Mexican force that allowed the Americans to outflank their opponent. At Cerro Gordo on 18 April, the Americans surprised Santa Anna and routed his army. The Mexicans lost 1,000 men dead and 3,000 captured. Five generals surrendered, as well as a large number of Mexican guns and munitions. Santa Anna only narrowly escaped and had to abandon his personal carriage, which contained $30,000 in gold and his prosthetic leg. (The leg was taken back home as a trophy by some Illinois volunteers. It remains in Illinois to this day.)

By May, the Americans had ascended into the safety of the highlands and occupied the city of Jalapa. If ever the war fulfilled its romantic promise, it was amid the orange groves and coffee fields of Jalapa. The army spent three blissful months there while Scott consolidated his supply lines and awaited fresh soldiers. His men attended bullfights and fandangos, where they mixed freely with the locals. Some of the soldiers eyed the local women; some were drawn to other features of the region. 'Until we reached Jalapa we saw very little to interest the land speculator,' one soldier wrote. But there, amid the cool mountain valleys whose 'deep rich soil' supported farms that would be the envy of any man along the Ohio or Mississippi Rivers, the average American soldier could finally imagine himself not just as an invader but as a potential settler.

The journalist James Freaner, who travelled with Scott's army, recalled the peculiar complacency of the Americans at Jalapa. There they were, an army of not more than 8,000 men, in 'the heart of a thickly peopled country, occupying their principal coast city, two of the largest forts on the North American continent ... two cities in the interior ... and are now within ninety miles of the capital, which contains upwards of 200,000 human beings'. And yet the men were relaxed and confident, 'and whilst they wait for the climactic battles they are at ease at balls and dances, playing billiards and going bowling, larking in shooting galleries, and taking long promenades'.

In August, not long before Scott began his final assault on Mexico City, Freaner rode out to Cholula to see the Great Pyramid there that had featured in the accounts of Cortés and Bernal Díaz del Castillo. History felt nearby and Freaner could not help but reflect that once it was the turn of the conquistadores, 'and now the Anglo-Saxon race looked forth from the same spot – but how great the moral change! ... Spain fallen from her high estate ... and a nation not dreamed of in the time of her glory, following in the footsteps of Cortés, to the Imperial City of the Aztecs.'

In early September, the assault on Mexico City began. The Mexican army fought with great courage and for the first time the Americans began to take heavy losses. But although it was slowed at the battles of Molino del Rey and Chapultepec, the American juggernaut could not be stopped. Mexican resistance collapsed under American cannonades.

Despite popular enthusiasm for a defence of the city, on the night of 14 September, Santa Anna withdrew his forces, abandoning the capital to the Americans.

The next day General Winfield Scott, in full dress uniform, cantered into the Zócalo with a bodyguard of dragoons. The Stars and Stripes were lifted over the Halls of Montezuma and in the National Palace a portrait of Agustín de Iturbide was replaced by one of George Washington.

Freaner could not quite believe the scale of the American accomplishment. 'We have invaded a country of 7,000,000 inhabitants, capturing its capital, containing 200,000 souls, and defended by 30,000 troops of the line, well-paid and equipped. This has been effected by an army not exceeding 15,000 men.'

It felt like something out of the chronicles of the Spanish conquest, and yet it had happened in 1847, before his very eyes.

The Americans around him were exultant. 'I am at last in Mexico,' one officer boasted, 'the great city of Montezuma, of Cortés, of the Spanish viceroys, of Mexican pride and of American conquest.'[19]

# The Ordeal of Peace

George Bancroft – the man who had helped swing the Baltimore convention to Polk – was American ambassador to the United Kingdom during the war. From his house at 90 Eaton Square, Bancroft followed the events of 1847 with growing excitement. As news of American victories in Mexico began to reach London in rapid succession, Bancroft wrote letters to the president keeping him abreast of British reactions to the triumphant march of Scott's army.

In May, he sent an ecstatic account of how London received word of the American capture of Veracruz:

> The last news from the United States was too great, too important, & too manifest to permit of being concealed or undervalued. 'You are the Lords of Mexico!' said Lord Ashburton to me. 'How could you take the castle of Vera Cruz so soon?' said Lord Grey, one of the secretaries of state; 'You have been entirely successful' said Lord Clarendon; 'I hope your sacrifice will lead to a peace.'
>
> And even Lord Palmerston, who, more than any of them, has one system of politics for England and quite a different one for other countries, spoke to me in the very warmest language of … the immense superiority of the Anglo-Saxon race as displayed in our great number of victories over the Mexicans. The newspapers indulge a good deal in splenetic remarks; but they are of no meaning; & England is even preparing to hear of our negotiating for half, or two-thirds, or even the whole of Mexico.

American conquest, far from alienating European opinion, had won it over. 'Those friendly to America desire to see our rule extended very far,' Bancroft noted in June, and many now expected that the United States would dominate the entire Pacific.

In November, with Mexico City occupied by Scott's army, Bancroft wrote to congratulate Polk 'on the great & miraculous success of our arms in Mexico'. 'The valor of our soldiers in Mexico has raised our character throughout Europe,' he told the president. 'England wishes us peace & has ... no serious objections to our getting good terms. It is becoming a fashion, rather, to expect the absorption of all Mexico.'

The great diplomatic fear at the war's outset was that it would trigger European intervention. This had not materialized. Europe had stood aside while the United States invaded Mexico.

The war years represented a watershed in transatlantic relations. Europe teetered on the edge of revolution and Ireland was in the grip of famine.* The United States was wealthier, more confident, more powerful than ever.

From Eaton Square the war had looked easy. Bancroft had no reason to doubt that an advantageous peace would swiftly follow.[1]

## 'A GIANT WHIPPING A CRIPPLE'

The view from the President's Mansion was less favourable. Polk had wanted a short, cheap war. He had got a long, expensive one, and even with the conquest of their capital, the Mexican government showed no interest in coming to terms.

As the war stretched out interminably, support for it fell. The irony for Polk was that the same forces that propelled him to the White House also helped sap support for his war. The spread of the telegraph meant that news could travel from New Orleans to Washington in three days. The war also coincided with the advent of cheap newspapers printed by steam power – the penny press – which put tabloid journalism in the

---

* Polk sent aid to Ireland to help alleviate the effects of the famine. Many U.S. commentators saw this as a sign of American power: it could rescue Old Europe while waging war with Mexico. 'The events of this war will live in the history of our country and our race,' Jefferson Davis told Congress, 'affording ... proof of the resources of such a government as ours, wholly unembarrassed in the midst of war, conquering one nation and feeding another!'

hands of regular Americans. As a consequence, Americans were practically deluged by reports from the front lines.[2]

The problem for the administration was that the news was not all good. The American press had no compunction about accurately reporting American atrocities inside Mexico. The massacre at Agua Nueva, where Arkansas volunteers murdered unarmed Mexicans in a cave, was widely reported in the United States. Similarly, the bombardment of civilians at Veracruz became a scandal at home.* Journalists also reported on the discontent felt by regular soldiers. Although American combat deaths were low – fewer than 1,500 – there were over 10,000 deaths from disease. Nothing more readily punctured the romantic fantasies of volunteers in the Army of Manifest Destiny than watching their comrades die of cholera.

Among the officer corps, the war produced an outburst of rage and disillusionment. 'Our militia & volunteers,' Winfield Scott told the secretary of war, 'have committed atrocities – horrors – in Mexico, sufficient to make Heaven weep, & every American, of Christian morals, blush for his country. Murder, robbery and rape of mothers and daughters in the presence of tied up males of the families have been common all along the Rio Grande.' In a letter home, Zachary Taylor frankly stated that nothing would please him more than learning of President Polk's death. *'Dulce et decorum est pro patria mori* is an exploded maxim,' Henry Clay Jr wrote bitterly in his journal, a few months before his death at Buena Vista.[3]

Uncensored, first-hand accounts of the grim realities of the campaigning in Mexico helped give rise to America's first anti-war movement. 'Let us not attempt to deceive ourselves,' Charles T. Porter wrote. 'The lust of conquest has begun to rage among us. It is called "making room for the Anglo-Saxon race," "working out our manifest destiny" and "enlarging the area of freedom." It has assumed the garb of noblest humanity ... but it is the spirit of conquest still.'

---

* Among Polk's correspondence is a letter signed by 'The Devil' which warned the president that 'hell will be prolonged 15,000 years longer than eternally to ride you on red-hot wheelbarrows' for his crimes in Mexico. An enclosed medal was struck 'For all the widowhood and orphanage, homes desolated, husbands murdered – and for the murder of the 2,000 defenseless women and children at the siege of Vera Cruz'. The anonymous author also included a fake $25 bill 'to defray your expenses to hell' (Anonymous to JKP, 19 Apr. 1847, in Polk, *Collected Letters*).

Porter, like many anti-war voices, feared the moral consequences of the war and considered its conduct 'disgraceful to a Christian people'. The American Peace Society helped inspire and coordinate a pacifist campaign against the continuation of the war. 'If from Maine to Texas, from the Atlantic to the Rocky Mountains,' the society noted in its journal, the *Advocate of Peace*, the people 'would with one voice demand peace on terms of justice to both parties, the sword would be sheathed at once'. Thus every American who did not publicly and proactively try to end the war was morally responsible for the carnage it wrought.

Jane Swisshelm, an impassioned twenty-one-year-old from Pennsylvania, took this principle to heart. She believed America's war on Mexico was 'a giant whipping a cripple', and that every man involved in it was culpable for 'the whole list of crimes' it produced.

Pacifist agitation against the war produced one of the most famous essays in American history. Henry David Thoreau refused to pay his poll taxes in protest at the war, and for his troubles spent a night in Concord jail. In *Civil Disobedience*, Thoreau reflected on the nature of the relationship between citizen and state in light of the evils he saw abroad in his own country. 'This people must cease to hold slaves, and to make war on Mexico,' he concluded, 'though it cost them their existence as a people.'

The connection Thoreau made between the Mexican war and slavery was common in abolitionist and anti-slavery circles. 'A vast territory (now free) is to be forced from Mexico by the horrors of war,' thundered one abolitionist newspaper, 'and united to this country for Slavery to grow and fatten upon forever.' In a speech in December 1846, the Ohio abolitionist Joshua Giddings drew a line all the way back to Texas, whose annexation was 'beyond all doubt' effected 'for the extension of slavery'. 'This war has resulted from the annexation; so that the millions of money we have squandered, and the thousands of lives which we have sacrificed in this war, are the consequence of our endeavors to extend slavery.'[4]

## WHIG UNITY

Opposition to the war became Whig orthodoxy on 13 November 1847, when Henry Clay gave a much-anticipated speech on the war in Lexington, Kentucky. Clay, still grieving his son, began dramatically:

'The day is dark and gloomy, unsettled and uncertain, like the condition of our country, in regard to the unnatural war with Mexico.' The war, he maintained, was a consequence of a reckless expansionism. 'If we had not Texas, we should have no war.'

But now the war was upon them, the Whigs had to have a policy. Clay's policy was simple: 'We do not want the mines, the mountains, the morasses, and the sterile lands of Mexico. To her the loss of them would be humiliating, and be a perpetual source of regret and mortification. To us they might prove a fatal acquisition, producing distractions, dissensions.' San Francisco, he granted, might be useful 'in respect to our commercial and navigating interests'. 'But it should form no motive in the prosecution of the war, which I would not continue a solitary hour for the sake of that harbor.'

In the audience was Abraham Lincoln, recently elected to Congress. Lincoln worshipped Clay and, inspired by his speech, went to Washington in an anti-war fervour. In his 'Spot Resolutions', Lincoln famously attacked Polk's foundational claim for the war – namely that American blood had been spilled on *American* soil. In a companion speech in January 1848, Lincoln attacked the president himself. 'I more than suspect already that he is deeply conscious of being in the wrong,' Lincoln told the House; 'that he feels the blood of this war, like the blood of Abel, is crying to heaven against him.'

Similar criticisms were made by the big beasts of the Whig party. Daniel Webster called the war unnecessary, unjustifiable and unconstitutional. Thomas Corwin described the war as 'treason to the Union' and 'a crime of such infernal hue, that every other in the catalogue of iniquity, when compared with it, whitens into virtue'. The union of moderate Whigs with anti-slavery firebrands was not always amicable (Theodore Parker, a Massachusetts abolitionist, responded to the news of Henry Clay Jr's death with a sermon in which he said the Mexican who had killed him 'fought for his country, her altars and her homes', while Clay 'fell inglorious and disgraced, a willing murderer, in that war so treacherous and so cruel') but it was ultimately coherent. However it was arrived at, Whig opposition to the war consolidated around a simple demand: 'No territory by conquest.'[5]

## DEMOCRATIC DIVIDES

The Whigs' position was a vote-winner. They won enough seats in elections in 1846 and 1847 to secure control of the House. For Polk, it presented a serious threat to his territorial ambitions. If the House was the bellwether for the presidency, then the Whigs might win in 1848 and be in a position to undo his conquests. New Mexico and California could be lost forever.

In addition to a resurgent Whig party, Polk was battling discord in his own party. Whereas the Whigs were unified around the principle of 'no territory by conquest', the Democrats were divided on the question of how much of Mexico to take.

Within the cabinet virtually every feasible option was proposed and debated. The hawks, like Robert J. Walker, wanted everything east of the Sierra Madres inclusive of Tampico, as well as Baja California. The moderates wanted to forgo territorial aggrandizement and focus on securing a swift and equitable peace. Even among the moderates, however, there was an expectation that California and much of New Mexico would end up in American hands. Polk was characteristically ambiguous, happy to flirt with large-scale conquest, but also indicating he would accept a more modest cession.

Outside of the cabinet, even grander schemes were afoot. With Scott in Mexico City, the Mexican government in disarray and the two countries still in a formal state of war, some now argued that the United States should seize the entirety of Mexico. In the Senate and in the press, advocates of the 'all Mexico' movement openly discussed the 'extinction' of Mexico nationhood as an accomplished fact. What remained was the United States' responsibility to both its fallen neighbour and its providential mission in the world.

Jane McManus Storms, a war correspondent with Scott's army, arrived at this position from essentially humanitarian grounds. Her revulsion at Mexico's backwardness led her to believe that the mass of Mexicans were 'more than ready to receive an American government'. The United States had to 'act with firmness and liberality' and bring Mexico inside the Union and bring the blessings of the constitutional order to Mexico's 'long-suffering and hardly-treated working classes'. The New York *Sun* concurred: 'To *liberate* and *ennoble* – not to *enslave* and *debase* – is our mission,' it wrote. 'Our victories will give liberty, safety, and prosperity to the vanquished.' These lofty claims – so redolent of the neoconservative nation-building rhetoric of the early twenty-first century – were given a patina of legitimacy by the fact that a delegation of prominent local citizens approached Scott in Mexico City and asked him to annex the nation to the United States.

But, as ever, darker motives informed these grand claims. In a speech at Tammany Hall in January 1848, Senator Sam Houston of Texas gave his views. At question was not Providence nor the well-being of the Mexican people. What was at stake was land. 'You may escape the small pox, but you can never escape the contagion of land-loving,' he told the crowd. 'There is not an American upon earth but what loves land.' It had been that way since Jamestown and Plymouth Rock, Houston said, and it was still that way now. 'From the first moment' on the continent, Americans had been 'trading with the Indians, and cheating them out of their lands', and everyone alive in 1848 was the heir to that tradition. 'Now the Mexicans are no better than Indians, and I see no reason why we should not go on in the same course now, and take their land.' And everyone knew what had happened to the Indians as a consequence of that process. As the 'tide of emigration' swept over a conquered Mexico, one New York journalist wrote, the fate of the Mexican people would be 'similar to that of the Indians of this country – the race, before a century rolls over us, will become extinct'.[6]

Loose talk of major territorial acquisitions did not have to damage the unity of the Democratic party. Most Democrats believed that expansion was a good thing for the country.

What poisoned the debate within the party was a legislative provision put forward by an obscure freshman congressman from Pennsylvania named David Wilmot. On 8 August 1846, during a debate over an appropriations bill related to the war, Wilmot proposed a rider that would forever afterwards be known as the Wilmot Proviso.

The proviso was only one sentence long. It demanded 'as an express and fundamental condition to the acquisition of any territory from the Republic of Mexico' that 'neither slavery nor involuntary servitude shall ever exist in any part of said territory'.

Thomas Hart Benton wrote in his memoirs that this single line of legislative prose 'became a Gorgon's head – a chimera dire – a watchword of party, and the synonym of civil war and the dissolution of the Union'.

He was not exaggerating. The Wilmot Proviso was dynamite strapped to the foundations of the constitutional order. It threatened every major assumption that had held the Union together since the controversy over Missouri statehood.

All Mexican territory, except northern California, lay below the Missouri Compromise line of 36° 30' which meant in theory slavery was permitted within it. The proviso challenged that assumption. Moreover, Wilmot had chosen his words carefully. The language he used was taken from the Northwest Ordinance of 1787 in which Congress had excluded slavery from the Northwest Territory. By referencing that language, Wilmot gestured towards the most perilous constitutional issue of the day: whether Congress had the power to outlaw slavery *in a territory*. According to Wilmot, Congress had that power as evidenced in the Northwest Ordinance. That was not a view shared in the South.

But the most devastating aspect of the proviso was the political allegiance of the man who proposed it: David Wilmot was a northern Democrat. He wasn't a Whig or an abolitionist – he belonged to the party of Jackson. 'I make no war upon the South nor upon slavery in the South,' Wilmot told the House. 'I have no squeamish sensitiveness upon the subject of slavery, nor morbid sympathy for the slave. I plead the cause of the rights of white freemen.'

Neither he nor his allies were against the war or against territorial expansion. His aim was simply to 'preserve the future homes of his children, on the distant shores of the Pacific, from the degradation and dishonor of negro servitude'. What Wilmot and his allies were articulating was a nascent political ideology advanced under the banner of the Free Soil Movement. Free Soil advocates opposed both slavery and abolitionism. They rejected racial equality as an aspiration while also rejecting slavery as a form of social and economic organization. They were not, however, opposed to expansion.* Free Soilers like Wilmot wanted land – but they wanted it free from the taint of slavery.

---

* Indeed, one reason so many northern Democrats threw their support behind the proviso was because of their outrage that southern votes had supported the Oregon compromise in 1846 and so denied northern Democrats the Oregon country up to 54° 40'. The proviso was, in some respects, revenge in the Southwest for southern betrayal in the Northwest.

By raising the issue of slavery, Wilmot violated a major taboo within the Democratic party. Slavery was off the table. Only agitators and disunionists discussed the matter. Only by ignoring slavery could northern Democrats and southern Democrats constitute a national party that won votes in both sections. The Wilmot Proviso buried that compact. The House voted on the measure twice during the war, and each time northern Whigs joined northern Democrats to secure its passage.[7]

## CALHOUN VINDICATED

Each time the Wilmot Proviso passed the House, it was blocked in the Senate by southern votes. Senator Bagby of Alabama spoke for southern slaveholders when he declared he could 'never consent that territory, acquired by common blood and common treasure, shall be open and free for the citizens of one portion of the Union, with their property, while the citizens of another portion of the Union and their property are to be excluded from it'.

The South had supplied two-thirds of the fighting men in Mexico, and many Americans considered the war an essentially southern affair. Mississippi's attitudes were typical. When the conflict broke out, the governor of Mississippi told Polk that 'we look upon the War with Mexico as peculiarly our own'. When the state was asked to levy 900 infantrymen, one Mississippian wrote to Polk complaining of 'the smallness of the call for Volunteers from the State', as local men were 'panting to enter the service & defend the Territory acquired by annexation'. During the war, Mississippi volunteers had fought bravely at Monterrey and Saltillo, and Jefferson Davis's charge at Buena Vista had arguably saved Taylor's army from annihilation.

In 1847 Mississippi sent Jefferson Davis – now a national figure on account of his heroics – to represent the state in the Senate. Davis was appalled at the Wilmot Proviso, seeing it as proof of 'that spirit of hostility to the South, that thirst for political dominion' that typified northern attitudes. But Davis was in fact relatively conciliatory in his politics – far more conciliatory than the main beneficiary of the Wilmot Proviso controversy, South Carolina senator John C. Calhoun.

Calhoun emerged from the war completely vindicated. It was he who had warned that 'the South shall do all the fighting and pay all the expense, and [the North are] to have all the conquered territory'. And it was he who had warned that bringing conquered territory into the Union would subvert the very nature of the American experiment. ('Mexico is to us the forbidden fruit,' he wrote in February 1847; 'the penalty of eating it would be to subject our institutions to political death.') Characteristically, Calhoun advanced a position that alienated nearly everyone. He poured scorn on 'All Mexico' Democrats, describing the notion that 'it is the mission of this country to spread civil and religious liberty over all the globe, and especially over this continent' as 'a sad delusion'. But Calhoun's anti-imperialism was grounded in racial thinking. The constitutional order had to be preserved for the people worthy of it. 'Nor have we ever incorporated into the Union any but the Caucasian race,' he told the Senate. 'Ours is the Government of the white man.'

Yet while Calhoun was simply contemptuous of the 'All Mexico' party, he was positively gleeful at the introduction of the Wilmot Proviso. At a stroke, northern Democrats had justified all his direst warnings about the threat posed by the 'numerical majority'. Although Calhoun did not even want any territory from the war, he understood the land hunger among southerners and their belief that the Wilmot Proviso was a northern scheme to cheat them of the spoils of war. If Calhoun could not rally the South around such a manifestly unjust measure, then that alone might 'prove that we either have not the sense or spirit to defend ourselves and our institutions'.

He still had to try. The freshman congressman from Pennsylvania had gifted Calhoun the opening he had been searching for since the Nullification Crisis. The South now had a unique opportunity to turn the tables on the North. 'I am of the impression,' Calhoun wrote, 'that if the South acts as it ought, the Wilmot Proviso, instead of proving to be the means of successfully assailing us and our peculiar institution, may be made the occasion of successfully asserting our equality and rights, by enabling us to *force* the issue on the North.'

The Wilmot Proviso was the hill Calhoun would die on.[8]

## TRIST'S PEACE

All the while, the war had not ended. Mexican guerrillas harried occupying forces in the north and laid siege to the road connecting Veracruz to the interior. Inside Mexico City, there was violence between disgruntled locals and their American occupiers. It was an intolerable situation.

The government continued to haemorrhage money on a war that its leaders were desperate to end. In the absence of a negotiated solution, the only alternative would be a massive escalation – some people now spoke of the American army occupying the entire country – which would enrage the public, destroy the Democratic party and deliver the presidency to the Whigs.

All eyes, then, were on Polk's diplomatic representative. Embedded in Scott's army as he marched from Veracruz to Mexico City was a forty-six-year-old diplomat named Nicholas Trist. Trist was from a prominent Virginia family and had married Thomas Jefferson's granddaughter. After attending West Point, he had become the elderly Jefferson's secretary and later served as secretary to Andrew Jackson. Jackson appointed Trist consul to Havana, where he remained until 1845, when Polk appointed Trist chief clerk in the State Department. Trist was not expecting to be sent to Mexico, but when Polk was casting around for a suitable envoy a consensus soon gathered around the Virginian, who had the triple benefit of being a southerner, a slaveowner and an experienced diplomat who spoke Spanish. It was not in Polk's nature to show much interest in his inferiors. For the most part, the president surrounded himself with yes-men and viewed government employees as extensions of his will. He noted in his correspondence that Trist was 'able and decent' but did not probe much deeper into the character of the man he had chosen to end the war he had begun.

This was a grave oversight. Trist was a proud, independent character who had served far more illustrious statesmen than James Polk. As a young man, he had been deeply influenced by Jefferson's revulsion at war and his insistence that the United States use non-military means to secure its foreign-policy goals. He still retained those beliefs in 1847, when he was given responsibility for brokering peace.

Trist despised Polk's war on Mexico; he was intent on ending it.[9]

The final farce of the war played out in Mexico City in the winter of 1847–48 as Trist began to negotiate with a rotating cast of Mexican politicians while Polk watched on from Washington in mounting horror. Between rounds of negotiations, Trist wrote a series of long letters to the president in which he lectured Polk about the finer points of diplomacy.

Privately, Trist agonized over his situation. 'What is my line of duty to my government and my country, in this extraordinary position in which I find myself?' Trist had no desire to extract concessions – territorial or otherwise – from a nation he felt had been terrorized by his own.

From Polk's perspective, Trist's private sentiments were irrelevant. He wasn't even meant to be negotiating. The Mexicans had lost the war. An American army was camped in their capital. Trist had with him peace terms prepared by the cabinet. His job was to get the Mexicans to sign them and come home. The final straw came in October when Trist forwarded to Washington a Mexican proposal that would draw the Texan border at the Nueces. Polk was beside himself when he received the note. As Buchanan observed in a tense letter to Trist, in conceding the Rio Grande border the United States would be simultaneously conceding the very basis of Polk's May 1846 war message. It would set the clock back to 1836 and make nonsense of every expansionist aspiration expressed since. Trist had clearly misunderstood his mission; the cabinet unanimously voted to recall him from Mexico.[10]

When, at length, news of his dismissal reached Mexico City, Trist was involved in promising negotations with José Manuel de la Peña y Peña, a moderate who earnestly wanted an end to the war. Trist decided that the prerogatives of peace took precedence over the demands of the executive. He unilaterally declared he would stay in place to continue the negotiations even though his own government had stripped him of his powers.

In this unprecedented position, Trist succeeded in negotiating a settlement. Under the Treaty of Guadalupe Hidalgo, signed outside Mexico City on 2 February 1848, Mexico recognized Texas's border at the Rio Grande, and ceded to the United States New Mexico and Alta California. Mexico lost 55 per cent of its territory and 100,000 of its citizens; the United States gained some 525,000 square miles. In exchange, the United States paid $15 million for New Mexico and California and assumed responsibility for $3.25 million in claims made against the Mexican government by its citizens.

When the treaty arrived in Washington seventeen days later, Polk was mortified but powerless to do other than forward it to the Senate for ratification. The acerbic Whig diarist Philip Hone memorably described the treaty as 'negotiated by an unauthorized agent, with an unacknowledged government, submitted by an accidental President to a dissatisfied Senate'. It was a fitting end, in Hone's view, for a war originated by 'corrupt demagogues', conducted with 'reckless extravagance' and now brought to an end by the 'strong desire of a majority of the Senate to get rid of a present evil, and avoid the future disastrous consequences of a protracted war'.

The fourteen votes against ratification came from a mixture of anti-war Whigs who wanted no territory and 'All Mexico' Democrats who wanted more. Thomas Hart Benton, who voted with the majority for ratification, could not help but note the delicious irony of how Polk's war ended: 'The treaty was a singular conclusion of the war. Undertaken to get indemnity for claims, the United States paid those claims herself.' Some estimates had the total expense of the Mexican war to the American Treasury as in excess of $100 million. In the final reckoning, the United States spent $100 million to win the right to purchase California and New Mexico for $15 million – and still picked up the tab for the claims that triggered the war in the first place.[11]

The Senate's deliberation over this unappetizing fare was enlivened by a moment of high drama on 21 February, when John Quincy Adams collapsed at his desk in the House. The news was relayed to the neighbouring chamber, where discussion of the treaty was adjourned for the day as a sign of respect. The former president was moved to the Speaker's rooms, where he died two days later. Adams faced eternity with his native Yankee stoicism. 'This is the end of the earth,' he declared shortly before his death, 'but I am composed.'

The country he left behind was far from composed. Adams's political trajectory was symptomatic of the crisis the country faced in 1848. As a young man, he had defected to the Jeffersonians to vote for the Louisiana Purchase. As secretary of state, he had staunchly supported Jackson's border wars in Florida and then expanded the borders of the United States to the Pacific with the Transcontinental Treaty. Adams's politics had begun to shift with the Missouri Compromise. By the 1830s, he was the most vocal anti-slavery voice in the House and one of the first to speak out against the annexation of Texas. His vote in the House (one of only fourteen) against the war in 1846 was complemented by Calhoun's vote (one of only two) against it in the Senate.

That the two men should have met at the tips of the political horseshoe at this crucial juncture was a testament to the unsettled state of the American body politic.

Calhoun had once been a nationalist and had served with Adams in Monroe's cabinet. In the years since, Adams had drifted towards abolitionism while Calhoun drifted towards southern radicalism. One can only speculate as to whether, when he heard the news of Adams's collapse in the neighbouring chamber, Calhoun recalled the two men's conversation at the height of the Missouri Crisis when they had mulled the possibility of secession and civil war as a consequence of slavery's expansion.

Twenty-five years later, the country was faced with another massive territorial acquisition and with the attendant political strife that they had foreseen. Calhoun was ready to support the treaty but was clear-eyed about the consequences for the Union. 'The slave question will soon come up, and be the subject of deep agitation,' he predicted on the day Adams died. 'The South will be in the crisis of its fate. If it yields now, all will be lost.'[12]

On 10 March, the Senate ratified the treaty. In June, American soldiers began to withdraw from Mexico City. General William J. Worth brought back with him from Mexico a large three-quarter-length portrait of Cortés that he gifted to Sarah Polk. The portrait was clearly to her husband's liking. When he left office in March 1849, James Polk went back to his plantation house in Columbia, Tennessee, hung the portrait of Cortés prominently over the main stairwell and, three months later, caught cholera and died.

## POLK'S AMERICA

James Polk was arguably the United States' first mediocre president. At the time of his election, he had achieved nothing of note. He hadn't fought in a war. He hadn't given an influential speech or written a notable book. He had no political following, precious few legislative accomplishments and nothing in the way of charisma. Yet in the first thousand days of his presidency, Polk annexed Texas, favourably resolved the Oregon crisis and conquered over half of Mexico.

Polk added more territory to the Union than any president, including Jefferson. Among his haul were the states of Washington, Oregon, California, Utah, Nevada, Colorado, Idaho, Arizona, New Mexico and Texas, as well as slivers of Montana, Wyoming, Oklahoma and Kansas.

In total, James Polk brought 1.2 million square miles of land into the Union, or roughly a third of the modern continental United States.

By a conservative estimate, the territory he acquired now contains a third of the United States' population and a third of its GDP. Polk's America is the America of Hollywood and Silicon Valley and Las Vegas. It is the America of Roswell, Area 51 and the Manhattan Project. It is the America of Yosemite and Death Valley and the Grand Canyon. It is the America of Texas oil and Texas beef, Arizona copper and New Mexico silver, the California redwood and the Idaho potato. It is the America of Amazon, Microsoft and Nike.

And by securing American control of 1,300 miles of Pacific coastline, including strategic ports at San Francisco, San Diego, Los Angeles and Puget Sound, Polk guaranteed the United States' influence in Asia, setting up America's confrontation with Japan in the twentieth century and China in the twenty-first. In the long view of history, Polk's single term was the most consequential presidency of the nineteenth century.[13]

In the short term, however, the fallout from Polk's tenure was catastrophic. The bitter partisanship of the war years, the introduction of the Wilmot Proviso and the southern backlash to it all suggested an imminent constitutional crisis over the westward expansion of slavery. The date of that crisis would be decided by the speed with which the lands of the Mexican cession were populated. At first, it seemed as though the new territory out west would not be settled for a generation – plenty of time, perhaps, to resolve amicably the momentous problems facing the Union.

There would be no such reprieve. For on 5 December 1848, only a few months before he left office, Polk made a startling announcement: gold had been discovered in California.

# Gold Fever

John Sutter was a wanderer, one of the many descendants of Cain that Charles Dickens had encountered in his travels across the United States.

Born Johann August Sutter in Baden in 1803, he spent his early years bouncing around Switzerland working various jobs. Along the way he married and had five children, but by his early thirties Sutter was bankrupt. At risk of being thrown in debtors' jail, in 1834 he fled Switzerland, changed his name to John and travelled to New York. In the United States, he continued to rove. He travelled to St Louis, Santa Fe and Kansas. In 1838 he joined a group of missionaries heading up the Oregon Trail. Next he secured passage to Hawaii, where he set himself up as a merchant. He prepared and provisioned the brig *Clementine* destined for Sitka, Alaska, to trade with Russian colonists. Sutter and a crew of Hawaiians followed the *Clementine* to Alaska in the spring of 1839, and from there sailed down to Alta California, arriving in San Francisco in July 1839.

In California, he styled himself 'Captain Sutter' and was soon working the Mexican governor, offering to set up a colony of migrants loyal to Mexico that would resist American encroachment. His appeals found favour and he acquired a grant of 48,400 acres of land on the Sacramento River. In honour of his homeland, he called his colony Nueva Helvetia. The Americans in the region referred to it simply as Sutter's Fort. Sutter proved an adept frontier entrepreneur. By the late 1840s, he had a farm, large herds of horses, mules, cattle and sheep, a grist mill, a dozen skilled artisans in his employ, and operated a store, saloon and a rooming house. He also skilfully navigated the treacherous politics of the region.

When the *Californios* rebelled against the Mexicans, Sutter lent them his support. And when the Americans arrived in 1846, he lifted the Stars and Stripes over Nueva Helvetia.

By late 1847, the war in California was over and Sutter had his mind set on his next business venture: he wanted to build a sawmill. He identified a suitable location at Coloma, forty-five miles north-east of his fort, and hired an old associate named James Marshall to oversee the project. As luck would have it, the Mexican-American War had discharged dozens of young men in California who were looking for work. Sutter and Marshall hired eight good-natured, teetotal Mormons recently demobilized from Kearny's Army of the West, and by autumn work at Coloma was proceeding apace.

By 1 January, the mill frame was erected and a fortnight later the brush dam was complete. Now Marshall's attention turned to the problem of the tail-race. Water-powered mills all have a head-race, the channel that directs water towards the wheel, and a tail-race, the channel that leads water away from the wheel. Tail-races need to get the water away from the wheel efficiently to prevent the build-up of water around the mill. Marshall's tail-race was too narrow. In the second half of January, Marshall began work widening the tail-race. In the daytime, the channel had to be dry so his men could work. But in the night, he let water run through the channel to help flush out the loosened earth.

On the morning of 24 January 1848, Marshall shut off the flow of water and walked down the tail-race to inspect his work.

Near the end of the tail-race, close to its junction with the south fork of the American River, Marshall saw something glittering in the water in the bed of the channel. Marshall stooped to pick it up and inspected it in his hands. 'I was entirely alone at the time,' he later wrote.

> I picked up one or two pieces and examined them attentively; and having some general knowledge of minerals, I could not call to mind more than two which in any way resembled this – sulphuret of iron, very bright and brittle; and gold, bright, yet malleable; I then tried it between two rocks, and found that it could be beaten into a different shape, but not broken. I then collected four or five pieces and went up to Mr. Scott (who was working at the carpenter's bench making the mill wheel) with the pieces in my hand and said, 'I have found it.'

'What is it?' inquired Scott.
'Gold,' I answered.
'Oh! no,' returned Scott, 'that can't be.'
I replied positively, – 'I know it to be nothing else.'

A few days later, Marshall travelled to Sutter's Fort to apprise his employer of the news. Sequestered in Sutter's study, the two men conducted a series of tests to establish whether Marshall's find was gold. They seemed to suggest it was. Sutter travelled to Coloma to inspect the tail-race himself. The Mormon workers had begun to believe that Marshall was right. Several of them had begun scouting for gold themselves and had found gold flakes lying on the surface of the ground all over Coloma. Sutter appealed to his men to keep the find secret for six weeks while they finished his mill. But, despite his pleas, word began to leak out. Workers running errands and gossips at Sutter's Fort were soon spreading marvellous tales: men working with nothing more than a pocket knife could pick out gold from exposed seams on the riverbank; another group collected a pint of gold in an afternoon – without even needing to dig. By early March, employees at Sutter's Fort were abandoning their work and heading to the diggings around Coloma.[1]

By April, the news had arrived in the settlements along the coast. There, too, it met with doubt at first. But by the end of May, all doubt had vanished. Chester Smith Lyman, a Yale-trained clergyman practising as a surveyor in San Francisco, wrote in his journal on 27 May that there was 'a great gold fever raging' in the town. Friends had started to vanish. His employees had downed tools and disappeared. His pastor preached to empty pews. The two local newspapers ceased operations after the editors, typesetters and much of their readership headed to Coloma. People of every kind and every description simply stopped what they were doing and left for the goldfields. 'Half San Francisco has already gone,' Lyman wrote dolefully. 'My business here has come to a dead halt & no hands can be had at all.'

Unable to resist the pull of the goldfields (and without much reason to stay in a ghost town), Lyman travelled up the Sacramento River in early June and eleven days later had arrived at the diggings. As his excitement rose, his journal became more telegraphic. 'Camp crowded. Get $16 to 25 a day, people washing all along the river, ferry 1 mile up. Saw many acquaintances.' Soon he was digging himself and finding

*A map of the California gold fields produced in the summer of 1849.*

gold. After a matter of weeks, Lyman was making so much money that it began to distort his entire understanding of time. When he paused for a few hours to repair a broken saddle, he noted in his diary that 'the mending of the saddle cost about $100, ie, I should probably have collected that amount of gold while mending it'. On 19 August, he recorded his progress as a wildcat miner. 'Since I came to the mines 2 months ago I have collected about 86oz of gold or not far from $1380, at $16 the oz. This is better than I could have done surveying.'[2]

## MASON'S CADDY

California produced dozens of stories like Chester Lyman's as news of the gold discovery spread. The scenes at San Francisco were repeated at Sonoma, San José, Santa Cruz, Los Angeles and San Diego as successive communities caught gold fever. Eventually, the news reached Monterey, the headquarters of the American military command, where officers soon discovered that military discipline was no match for the siren call of gold. Enlisted men ran off by the score to the goldfields. Captain Joseph L. Folsom joked to a friend that each morning he woke up expecting to find himself 'the only person left in the town'. 'Nothing but the introduction of lunatic asylums can effect a cure of the present ills of the body politic,' he wrote, 'at least until hunger drives all the visionary fools from the gold "diggins."'

At length, the army sent Colonel Richard Barnes Mason to investigate. Mason arrived at the diggings in July. In his report, he noted that long before his arrival in Coloma he saw the effect of the gold rush. Towns were abandoned; crops stood unharvested in the fields. There was an eerie silence across much of the territory – except at the site of the gold discoveries. By this point, teams of miners were working the length of the American River, many taking in an average of $25 per man per day. In some places, men had pulled tens of thousands of dollars' worth of gold out of the ground in a matter of days. Mason worried about the legality of this kind of uncontrolled mining on government lands but judged it unwise to interfere. Whatever the legal status of the gold rush, it was clear to Mason that the energies it had unleashed had transformed the territory. 'The discovery of these vast deposits of gold has entirely changed the character of Upper California,' he concluded. 'Its people ... have all gone to the mines, or are on their way thither. Labourers of every trade have left their work-benches, and tradesmen their shops; sailors desert their ships as fast as they arrive on the coast.' There was a fairy-tale quality to the ease with which money could be had. 'No capital is required to obtain this gold, as the labouring man wants nothing but his pick and shovel and tin pan, with which to dig and wash the gravel.' To confirm the veracity of his claims, Mason included in his dispatch a tea caddy filled with 200 ounces of California gold.[3]

Mason's report was sent to Washington but even as he was writing, news of the gold discoveries had reached the wider world. By the end of the summer, it had reached American settlers in Oregon and Mormons in nearby Salt Lake, and had jumped across the newly established border to Sonora, Mexico. Soon thousands of men from these regions were trooping towards California. As California was plugged into a commercial network that spanned the Pacific, the news quickly travelled across the ocean. Like an earthquake with its epicentre at Coloma, the news rippled out across the Pacific Rim. In late June the story broke in Hawaii. In August the news reached Chile. In October gold fever broke out in Peru. In November it was New Zealand's turn, followed by Australia the next month. Around this time the news found its way to China. In all those countries men immediately set about forming companies, outfitting ships and preparing to set sail for California.[4]

News of the gold rush only began to filter into the East Coast press in the late summer of 1848. At this point the stories of fantastic gold discoveries were just that – unconfirmed and incredible stories.

But if California was a golden mirage shimmering on the Pacific coast, then it flickered and vanished on 23 November 1848 when Mason's report and sample arrived in New Orleans. Around the same time, another copy of his report arrived in Washington and a navy vessel from California arrived with additional confirmation of the discovery of gold. Any notion that reports of gold were fictitious were dispelled and the hard fact of the opportunity at hand presented itself to the American public.

At once the news spread by telegraph across the eastern seaboard and mining companies began forming in Boston, Baltimore, New York and New Orleans.

Mason's report made an impression on President Polk (who was surely gratified by Mason's observation that 'there is more gold in the country drained by the Sacramento and San Joaquin Rivers than will pay the cost of the present war with Mexico a hundred times over') then writing his final State of the Union address.

On 5 December, Polk submitted his speech to Congress. Not usually known for his excitability, Polk used the speech as an occasion to promote the news of the gold discovery as 'of such an extraordinary character as would scarcely command belief were they not corroborated' by trusted sources. Noting that almost the entire population of

California had already descended on the mining regions, Polk went on to whip up gold fever further by claiming that 'the explorations already made warrant the belief that the supply is very large and that gold is found at various places in an extensive district of country'. To support his claims, Polk submitted to Congress several documents from California, including Mason's report. A few days later the tea caddy full of gold was put on public display at the War Department.

Interest in California, which was already trending up, went vertical. Men were said to go 'California mad': thinking, speaking and dreaming exclusively of the goldfields.* The penny press fed the frenzy. 'The Eldorado of the old Spaniards is discovered at last,' claimed the New York *Herald*. 'Now have the dreams of Cortez and Pizarro become realized,' agreed the Lincoln *Courier*. 'Who is not tempted to exclaim after reading this,' asked the Newark *Morning Eagle*. 'What ho! for California!'[5]

## THE ARGONAUTS

We know them as 'forty-niners'. Contemporaries called them 'Argonauts', and they converged on California from every part of the United States. Many came overland, on the winding trail from Missouri. The rest chose between two sea routes. Some went the long way round via Cape Horn, a journey of some 15,000 miles. The rest sailed to the Gulf of Mexico, trekked across the isthmus and then secured passage on a boat bound to San Francisco.

Each option had its merits, each its challenges. Going overland was the perfect compromise on expense and time. The journey took three months and cost as little as $200. Many Argonauts also thrilled to the romance of the overland route. Just as their grandparents had ridden

---

* As it was predominantly men who went 'California mad', one concerned Rhode Island preacher published a sermon titled 'The Duties of Females in Reference to the California Gold Excitement' in which he warned that they lived in an 'age of excitement and revolution' that saw men running off to a 'golden tomb' in California. The proper role of women amid this madness, he claimed, was to 'vaccinate the souls [of their children] against this gold mania sooner than you do their bodies for small pox'. 'The New England primer,' he went on, 'is worth more than all the gold mines of California, and would weigh more in the balances of the Almighty than all the gold-diggers on the banks of the Sacramento.'

their Conestoga wagons into the Ohio Valley two generations prior, so too would they forge a path across the continent to California. As gold-mining parties formed across the old trans-Appalachian frontier, they were celebrated for keeping this pioneer spirit alive. Before they left home, groups of Argonauts attended celebratory church services, participated in public parades and were lauded in speeches. The business of getting to California had been made easier by the experience of Oregon Fever six years prior. The California trail was a variant on the Oregon Trail. Argonauts gathered at Independence, Missouri, and hewed to the same path as far as Fort Hall in Idaho, where they turned south* and followed the Humboldt River across the deserts of Nevada, before ascending into the Sierra Nevada, beyond which lay the goldfields.[6]

By comparison, sailing around the tip of South America was the lowest risk of all. While it was certainly the most expensive option – tickets could cost up to $800 – it guaranteed direct passage to San Francisco and had the added advantage of allowing Argonauts to stow large quantities of goods in the hold, ready for sale in California. Travelling across the tropics and around the famously turbulent waters at Cape Horn could be stomach-turning (one Argonaut recalled his fellow passengers' 'long and loud and spontaneous roars of vomiting' during a particularly violent storm), but the main challenge was boredom on a journey that could take anywhere between four and eight months.[7]

Patience was in short supply among those rushing for the goldfields. So, in a bid to cut the travel time, an alternative route developed. Ships would sail from ports on the eastern seaboard to either Panama or Nicaragua. Passengers would then disembark and make their way across the isthmus to the Pacific coast and then try and secure passage aboard a boat to San Francisco. If all went to plan, the travel time could be as little as six weeks. However, this route came with considerable uncertainty. Although passage *to* the isthmus was guaranteed, passage *from* it was not. Many hundreds of Americans found themselves stranded in

---

* Reflecting the different character of the two migrations, contemporaries joked that at the fork in the trail there was a pile of gold-bearing quartz indicating the way to California and then a simple written sign pointing to Oregon. 'Those who could read,' went the punchline, 'took the trail to Oregon.'

Panama City, stewing in a tropical climate they were wholly unadapted to, waiting for a boat to take them north. Many ended up paying hundreds of dollars to secure a spot aboard overcrowded boats. Not a few died of tropical disease a long way from home and without ever having seen a flake of gold.[8]

Henry Hunter Peters was one of those who made it to the diggings. A well-educated northern merchant who scrupulously recorded his impressions of the gold rush in several smart, slim leather-bound journals, Peters was sent west by his employers to find commercial opportunities in California. Arriving in San Francisco Bay on Sunday, 14 April 1849, Peters succumbed to the same mania as everyone else and decided to go and see the goldfields for himself. Along with some others, he headed to Mormon Island, a diggings just south-west of Coloma. En route he encountered miners along the rivers who claimed they were making eight to ten dollars a day. The work, however, was unremitting. With the coming of spring, the mountain ice had melted and the banks of the rivers in the goldfields were swollen. Men stood in freezing water for hours digging for a few flakes of gold. After four days, Peters's party arrived at their chosen diggings and he finally got to witness the process of gold mining first-hand. 'After working a couple of hours and getting the water and mud from the hole they got to the rich gravel and stone in which the gold lays, this layer was about six inches thick, from ten buckets they took an ounce of gold, I took from three buckets ... $1.50.' Peters realized, like so many other astute men, that the real money was to be made back in San Francisco.[9]

### AMONG THE SCOUNDREL ELITE

Well-situated men like Peters could afford to treat the goldfields as a curiosity to be engaged with or ignored as the fancy took them. The government – in California and in Washington – had no such luxury.

It soon became clear that a new society was being born in the goldfields. Out in the wilderness of eastern California, people from all over the world had formed makeshift communities, governed by makeshift laws, while they tore up the landscape in their hunt for gold.

Army officers in the region sent reports to Washington describing the bizarre scenes they encountered in the goldfields. At Wood's Creek, a tributary of the Tuolumne River, they observed 'some fifty men of all nations languages and color ... busily engaged, in the bed of the creek'. Elsewhere they discovered a large tent town where 'drinking and gambling [were] the steady occupation, and mining the occasional amusement' of its 2,000 inhabitants, almost all from Sonora. The officers noted that the Sonorans had also built a large enclosure, where they held bullfights on Sundays. In Calaveras, near Sacramento, they met some Miwok Indians panning for gold in a 'pristine state of nudity'. At another site they came across 600 Hawaiians living and mining in a camp, while on a road nearby, a train of 1,500 wagons carrying 5,000 Argonauts was trundling towards Mormon Island, at the tail-end of a 2,000-mile journey from Missouri.

The miners were like termites, infesting every ravine, gully and arroyo in the territory. 'The sounds of the crowbar and pick, as they shake or shiver the rock, are echoed from a thousand cliffs,' wrote Reverend Walter Colton, in his winsome memoir of the goldfields.* The miners slept among wolves and grizzly bears and seemed to fear neither, so long as they were close to the diggings. 'If you want to find men prepared to storm the burning threshold of the infernal prison,' Colton wrote, 'go among gold-diggers.'

This ungoverned mass of miners lived in transient mining camps whose names eloquently captured the texture of life in the goldfields. Some were ethnically descriptive – Chinese Camp, French Corral, Portuguese Flat; others offered a glimpse of the turbulent realities of mining life – Poker Flat, Hell's Delight, Git-Up-And-Git, Skunk Gulch, Dry Diggings, Red Dog, Grub Gulch, Rough and Ready, Fiddle Town, Condemned Bar.

'The scene of my first mining exploits, was a village rejoicing in the suggestive appellation of Hangtown,' one man recalled. 'It received its name ... from the number of malefactors who had there expiated their

---

* Colton left an unforgettable account of a chance encounter with some miners on a winding trail somewhere in the backcountry: 'A more forlorn looking group never knocked at the gate of a pauper asylum. They were most of them dismounted, with rags fastened round their blistered feet, and with clubs in their hands, with which they were trying to force on their skeleton animals. They inquired for bread and meat: we had but little of either, but shared it with them. They took from one of their packs a large bag of gold, and began to shell out a pound or two in payment. We told them they were welcome; still they seemed anxious to pay, and we were obliged to be positive in our refusal. This company, as I afterwards ascertained, had with them over a hundred thousand dollars in grain gold.'

crimes at the hands of Judge Lynch.' That Argonaut believed that lynching was an appropriate way of policing the goldfields. 'There were in California the elite of the most desperate and consummate scoundrels from every part of the world,' he explained, who would have gladly taken advantage of 'the unsettled state of the country ... to practise their villainy'.[10]

Lynching was a symptom of a pattern of lawlessness that threatened to overwhelm the territory. As Argonauts continued to pour into the country the atmosphere in the goldfields soured. Many immigrants completed punishing journeys only to discover the best claims were staked out and once-rich veins were spent. Shattered dreams of instant wealth made them considerably less tolerant of the diversity of the goldfields. While some contemporaries marvelled at the cosmopolitan make-up of the mining camps, many if not most of the new arrivals brought their racial prejudices with them from the United States. California gold was part of the spoils of Manifest Destiny; they did not intend to share it with foreigners of every colour and hue.

'The gold-mines were preserved by nature for Americans only,' one Argonaut wrote in a letter to a newspaper. 'I ask of them who have left their homes, their comforts, their wives and children, and other dear relatives, if they would be willing to share all the hopes with the millions that might be shipped from the four quarters of the globe. I will answer for them and say no. We will share our interest in the gold-mines with none but American citizens.'

Perhaps no group drew the ire of American miners like the Mexicans – or 'greasers' as they were known. Among the Argonauts were hundreds of veterans of the Mexican-American War who were outraged to discover that some of the best diggings in California were worked by the losers of the recent conflict. For their part, many Mexicans considered California an integral part of their own country stolen from them by the United States. Tension between the two groups sometimes broke out into organized violence. On one occasion, 150 American veterans assaulted the Mexican-dominated mining camp of Sonora, wearing their old uniforms and flying their former regimental colours. One witness described their operation as an 'engine of terror' designed to expel the Mexicans from the diggings. Killing became an essential part of the gold rush. One Argonaut informed his mother in a letter home that the standard California experience was 'to shoot three Indians, hang two greasers, kill a grizzly bear, and dig a seven pound lump of gold'. The murder rate skyrocketed. Gold-rush California had a murder rate of 200 per 100,000. By comparison, the murder rate in the most violent counties in the United States today rarely exceeds 60 per 100,000. Even at the time, few frontier states ever recorded murder rates in excess of 100 per 100,000. California was uniquely violent; its entry into the United States was marked by a baptism of blood.[11]

It was soon widely accepted in Washington that California had tipped into a state of anarchy. Frenzied migration into the region had increased its population to just under 100,000 people, making California not just larger than any other territory but larger than two of the Union's thirty states. Hitherto governed by the ad hoc civilian authority established during the war by General Kearny, it now seemed to be both good governance and best constitutional practice to organize California into either a territory or a state. And this prospect resurrected the issue that everyone feared most: the Wilmot Proviso.

# Trying Conclusions

Before Polk left office, there had been attempts to divide the Mexican cession into some combination of states and territories. These had gone nowhere. The issue was passed on to Polk's successor, who, as he had feared, was a Whig and a war hero.

The Whig nomination of Zachary Taylor as candidate was the triumph of calculation over principle. Having steadfastly opposed the war, they hoped to convert Taylor's gunpowder popularity into a Whig presidency. Having steadfastly opposed the expansion of slavery and the influence of slave-owners in government, they chose a Louisiana slave-owner who held scores of men and women in bondage on his Mississippi plantation.[1] Once again, the anti-slavery wing of the Whig party had been scorned.

On this occasion, at least, cynicism paid off. Taylor won a decisive victory and performed strongly across the country. He did particularly well in the South, winning eight states and losing Virginia, Alabama and Mississippi by tiny margins.

This did not mean that southern hardliners were complacent. Even before Taylor took office, a group of congressional representatives from the slave states issued a protest outlining southern grievances with the North. But with Taylor in the President's Mansion, it failed to resonate with moderate southerners. Most southern Whigs and a good number of southern Democrats refused to sign it. Georgia Whig Alexander Stephens spoke for many in the South when he said they felt 'secure under General Taylor'.[2]

Taylor, however, was not what he seemed. After a lifetime in the army, he had spent time outside the South and had developed a distaste for southern radicalism and some sympathy for the anti-slavery, Free Soil position. His nationalist, northern-inflected politics was reflected in his cabinet, which contained only one representative of the orthodox southern position on slavery. Moreover, the éminence grise of the Taylor administration was William H. Seward, the newly elected Whig senator for New York and a committed Free Soiler.

Taylor himself paid little attention to politics. Having assumed the presidency with practically no political experience, the old general seemed to believe that integrity, straight-talking and attachment to principle would suffice to see him through his term. But what Taylor thought of as forthrightness, experienced politicians interpreted as naivety. 'He is an honest, plain, unpretending old man,' one Washington veteran wrote, 'but about as fit to be president as any New England farmer.'

The wisdom of this verdict was demonstrated in his handling of the infinitely delicate question of slavery in the territories. Taylor treated it like he would a Mexican position: with a frontal assault. He advocated for circumventing the territorial question by simply admitting California and New Mexico as states. In the spring of 1849, he quietly sent envoys to both encouraging them to form constitutional conventions. In theory, such a move had no bearing on the slavery question; in practice, it did. Secretary of State John Clayton bragged to a colleague that both territories would soon 'be admitted free and Whig'.[3]

With Taylor's encouragement, California held a constitutional convention in September 1849. California proved firmly anti-slavery. The conventioneers intoned that it would 'degrade white labor' if slavery was introduced. Like Wilmot, they were at pains to stress that a rejection of slavery was not the same as sympathy for the plight of the slave. Many called for a prohibition on slavery *and* a prohibition on free blacks living inside the state. 'I look upon slavery as one of the worst evils,' one delegate told the convention, 'but I consider a free negro population a greater evil still.' In October, the convention unanimously ratified a constitution with an explicit prohibition on slavery and sent it back to Washington for congressional approval.

In early December, Zachary Taylor used his State of the Union address to call for California's prompt admission as a state, and predicted that New Mexico should follow suit 'at no very distant period'. He offered his sincere hope that while considering both applications,

Congress would 'abstain from the introduction of those exciting topics of a sectional character which have hitherto produced painful apprehensions in the public mind'.[4]

## AT THE PRECIPICE

The South exploded. Legislatures in slave states had already passed ordinances declaring that passage of the Wilmot Proviso was just cause for secession. As the entry of California with an anti-slavery constitution was simply 'the Wilmot Proviso in another form', the moment for resistance had come.

Once again, Calhoun and the southern radicals were vindicated. Aghast at their apparent betrayal by Taylor, southern Whigs fell in behind the same men they had spurned a few months prior. 'If, by your legislation, you seek to drive us from the territories of California and New Mexico,' Georgia Whig Robert Toombs thundered, '*I am for disunion.*' Jefferson Davis declared that the prospect of California entering the Union as a free state had 'obliterated' all existing political divisions in the South. The choice faced by all southerners was simple: 'Whether they will sink below the condition to which they were born, or maintain it by forcible resistance.'[5]

The North was no less convinced of its position. Every northern legislature except one passed resolutions supporting the Wilmot Proviso. Many legislatures passed resolutions denouncing aspects of the slave system, including the slave trade in the District of Columbia. Some northern states had passed laws designed to frustrate attempts by southern slave-owners to retrieve fugitive slaves. These were no longer simply Whiggish positions. In the summer of 1849, the Democratic party of Massachusetts issued a statement declaring, 'We are opposed to slavery in every form and colour, and in favor of freedom and free soil wherever man lives.'

For many northerners the entire debate over California was nonsensical. Even those who could tolerate the existence of slavery south of the Mason–Dixon Line could not imagine how a southerner could object to a constitutional convention in faraway California democratically deciding to prohibit slavery in a region where slavery had never existed.

These arguments resonated with Taylor, who responded to southern rage by digging in his heels. The southerners in Congress (his son-in-law Jefferson Davis among them), he stated, were 'intolerant and revolutionary'. He would not be blackmailed by them. 'If the Union is to go down,' he said, 'I will go down with it.'[6]

Taylor did not have the political sensitivity or the legislative know-how to resolve the crisis he had helped precipitate. Into the vacuum stepped Henry Clay. The old Kentucky senator – the man who had stitched together compromises in 1820 and 1833 – came to the rescue, facing the crisis, as one newspaperman put it, 'with as much calmness and composure as General Taylor did the Mexicans at Buena Vista'.

On 29 January 1850, he put forward a batch of proposals designed to resolve a number of outstanding issues between North and South. The package was carefully balanced between each section. Both would benefit; both would make concessions. In a major speech in defence of his compromise given in early February, Clay declared he had never seen Congress 'so oppressed, so appalled, and so anxious'. He appealed to his fellow senators 'to repress the ardor of these passions, to look to their country, to its interests, to listen to the voice of reason'. There was still room for accommodation. He mocked the southern radicals' dreams of an independent slave-owning confederation and warned them that 'war and dissolution of the Union are identical and inevitable'. He pleaded with the North to reject the Wilmot Proviso, arguing that as slavery would never flourish in the arid landscape of New Mexico and Utah, such a measure was entirely unnecessary and unduly provocative. Finally, he appealed to both North and South 'to pause, solemnly to pause at the edge of the precipice, before the fearful and dangerous leap is taken into the yawning abyss below'.[7]

Clay's offer of a grand bargain to save the Union triggered a series of responses in the Senate that were landmarks in American oratory.

John C. Calhoun went first. Appearing before a packed Senate on 4 March, the ailing Calhoun briefly appeared at the rostrum to note that, as he was too ill to give his speech, Robert Mason of Virginia would do so on his behalf. Wrapped in a black cloak, gaunt and physically exhausted – though his eyes shimmered with intellectual fervour – Calhoun sat perfectly still while his words resounded around the Senate chamber. 'How can the Union be preserved?' he asked. How indeed, when the North sought 'control of the entire government'. The problem, Calhoun claimed, as he had always claimed, was one of political arithmetic. More free states meant more free senators and a growing abolitionist majority in Congress. Therefore Calhoun counselled for no compromise on California, New Mexico or anywhere else. In fact, California was 'the test question. If you admit her under all the difficulties that oppose her admission, you compel us to infer that you intend to exclude us from the whole of the acquired Territories ... We should be blind not to perceive in that case that your real objects are power and aggrandisement, and infatuated, not to act accordingly.'

Three days later, Daniel Webster delivered his much-anticipated speech. In the past, Webster had clashed and collaborated with both Clay and Calhoun. It was not obvious who he would side with now. To the joy of unionists, Webster stoutly supported Clay's measures and buttressed his reasoning. Like Clay, Webster argued that the Wilmot Proviso was unnecessary as slavery was 'excluded from these territories' by 'the law of nature, of physical geography', and it was not Congress's place 'to reaffirm an ordinance of Nature, nor to reenact the will of God'. Like Clay, Webster demanded that the South cease harping on disunion. 'There can be no such thing as a peaceable secession,' he told the Senate. 'Peaceable secession is an utter impossibility ... I would rather hear of natural blasts and mildews, war, pestilence, and famine, than to hear gentlemen talk of secession.' Like Clay, Webster ended with appeal to both sides to 'come out into the light of day; let us enjoy the fresh air of Liberty and Union'.

Webster's encomium to the Union triggered unionist rallies across the country. Before the end of the month, 120,000 copies of his speech had been printed. The euphoria that attended his oration overshadowed the speech William Seward gave the following Monday. Seward had little of Webster's charisma and exhibited none of his rhetorical flair. But it was no less important a statement of northern principles. 'I am opposed to any such compromise,' Seward told the Senate, 'in any and all the forms in which it has been proposed.' There was no virtue in compromising with slavery and no merit in submitting to southern threats. At some point, the constitutional niceties of the territorial question had to be rejected in favour of sound moral reasoning. Slavery was an evil. Slavery was the enemy of progress. Slavery was doomed to extinction. It was obscene to suggest that slavery should be brought to the Pacific coast in order to appease the slave-owners of the Deep South. 'There is a higher law than the Constitution,' Seward said, and that law compelled Seward to 'vote for the admission of California directly, without conditions, without qualifications, and without compromise'.[8]

Congress and the country rallied to the unionist middle ground and in the short term Calhoun and Seward's speeches had little impact on the shape of the debate. But whereas Clay and Webster offered a glorious rerun of the unionist rhetoric of the past, Calhoun and Seward offered a terrifying glimpse of the partisan rhetoric of the near future. The thrust of Calhoun's increasingly Pharisaical reasoning was to save the Constitution by destroying the constitutional order. Seward simply disavowed the Constitution altogether if it collided with insuperable moral commitments. The justifications offered by each justified the radicalism of the other.

Seward's speech vindicated the wildest fears of every southern politician. When, in a display of collegial goodwill, Mississippi senator Foote declared he was on good terms with all his colleagues, Calhoun snapped, 'I am not. I will not be on good terms with those who wish to cut my throat. The honorable Senator [Seward] from New York justifies the North in treachery. I am not the man to hold social intercourse with such as these.'

### 'TO THE MEASURE'

Calhoun would not have to mingle with Seward much longer. John C. Calhoun died of tuberculosis on 31 March 1850. His funeral was held in the Senate chamber on 3 April. The tables were pushed aside to make space for the assembled officialdom of the federal government. First the Senate entered, then the House; then the Supreme Court processed down the aisle; after them came the Diplomatic Corps dressed in black. Finally, the president entered and took a seat by the vice president, presiding over the service in his role as president of the Senate. At twelve thirty, the chaplain entered at the head of the coffin borne by six pall-bearers: Henry Clay of Kentucky, Daniel Webster of Massachusetts, Lewis Cass of Michigan, Willie Mangum of North Carolina, John Berrien of Georgia and William King of Alabama. The corpse of the great South Carolina nullifier was carried by men from every section and from each party. It was a conscious display of unionism in honour of a man who had done more than any other to loosen the bonds of the

Union. Certainly the Union had not been on Calhoun's mind in his final hour. According to southern lore, his final words were: 'The South, the South, God knows what will become of her!' In a companion legend, Calhoun made a deathbed prophecy predicting that the Union would dissolve within three presidential terms, or sometime around 1860.[9]

As spring turned to summer in 1850, it looked as though civil war might be breaking out a great deal sooner. The problem was Zachary Taylor. The old soldier believed that as president he was head of the Whig party and was infuriated at Clay and Webster's presumption in leading a legislative initiative that not only did not have his blessing but ran counter to his wishes. Taylor stubbornly withheld his support for Clay's omnibus compromise bill and continued to advocate for his own solution. The president carried a significant portion of the Whig press with him, creating a breach in the unionist ranks.

At the same time as he frustrated the search for a solution, Taylor continued to antagonize the South. When a southern delegation informed him that certain southern states might resist the collection of federal taxes in protest at northern aggression, Taylor replied that if they did so, he would blockade every southern port and personally lead an army to crush the rebels. This only encouraged southern representatives to use every available tool to stop the compromise bill.

Taylor's intransigence surprised even his northern allies. 'I think the P. as willing to try conclusions with them,' Seward wrote to a friend, 'as General Jackson was with the Nullifiers.'

The atmosphere in Congress was more rancorous than it had been during that earlier crisis. One informed observer estimated that a third of the House were coming to work armed. In mid-April, violence invaded the staid and hallowed Senate chamber. After months of antagonism, the diminutive Mississippi senator Henry Foote successfully provoked Senator Benton into a physical confrontation. Foote, according to the official report, 'indulged in personalities' and Benton lurched across the room to assault him. Foote pulled out a pistol and aimed it at the Missouri senator. Benton – nothing if not theatrical – ripped open his coat and shirt and displayed his bared chest to his colleagues. 'I am not armed,' he cried. 'I have no pistols. I disdain to carry arms. Let him fire! Stand out of the way and let the assassin fire!' In the ensuing melee, a colleague disarmed Foote and locked his gun in a desk.[10]

Emotions reached a new pitch in late June with the arrival in Washington of news from Santa Fe. In accordance with Taylor's wishes, a New Mexico convention had met in May to write a state constitution. In June the convention ratified an anti-slavery constitution. A few weeks later, they chose a House representative and two senators. By early July, the New Mexico congressional delegation were on their way to Washington.

But news of the Santa Fe convention had preceded them and sparked a firestorm. Apoplectic Texans called for a 'military promenade' on Santa Fe. The legislature obliged by calling a special session to consider military mobilization. Public rallies were held in South Carolina, Alabama and elsewhere in support of Texas. Mississippi offered to send 5,000 men to aid in the march on Santa Fe.

President Taylor was no less assertive, ordering the federal garrison at Santa Fe to violently resist Texan aggression. On 1 July, a group of southern Whigs, including Stephens and Toombs, went to discuss the issue with Taylor at the President's Mansion. Taylor was adamant. Disunion was treason, he told Stephens. If the South acted rashly, 'I will hang you with less reluctance than I hanged spies and deserters in Mexico.' Stephens went home and wrote a public letter to the leading Whig newspaper warning that 'the first federal gun that shall be fired against the people of Texas' would be the signal for the entire South to 'rally to the rescue'.

Across Washington, all the talk was of impending civil war. On the evening of 3 July, Taylor sat down to compose a national address on the Texas–New Mexico imbroglio.

The unfinished speech was still on his desk the next morning when he went to the Washington Monument to attend the Fourth of July festivities. The sixty-five-year-old Taylor sat in the scorching sun while Senator Foote gave a verbose oration. Afterwards, according to Varina Davis, the president enjoyed a 'hearty dinner of cherries' and ice cream.

The next day he developed a fever. Over the weekend, Taylor's condition continued to decline. By the beginning of the following week, it was obvious the president was dying.

'In the midst of it all,' Varina wrote, 'the cabinet ministers came in with their heads bowed, and one after the other took his hand and kissed it.' The president's last words were uttered to Jefferson Davis, his son-in-law and Varina's husband. 'He suddenly spoke,' Varina wrote, 'and said, "Apply the constitution to the measure, Sir, regardless of the consequences."'

On 9 July Taylor died. Taylor had survived service in the War of 1812, the Black Hawk War, the Second Seminole War and the Mexican-American War, only to succumb to southern logorrhoea and the high summer heat of the District of Columbia.

The greater irony was that the old soldier's death probably saved the Union. 'If general Taylor had lived,' Daniel Webster later observed, 'we should have had a civil war.'[11]

As Vice President Millard Fillmore entered the President's Mansion, a new leader emerged in Congress.

In late July, Clay's omnibus compromise bill died of exhaustion in the Senate. Clay left the chamber in disgust, effectively ending his search for compromise. Into Clay's shoes stepped Stephen Douglas, the young, ambitious senator from Illinois. Fillmore and Douglas were a far better partnership than Taylor and Clay. Both were northern men with southern sympathies who hoped to further their careers by brokering a grand bargain to save the Union. Through July, August and September, Fillmore and Douglas worked in cooperation with moderates in the House and Senate to steer each part of Clay's original compromise package through Congress.

The strategy worked – but at an immense cost. By permitting the North to abstain from supporting pro-southern legislation, and vice versa, Douglas essentially stripped Clay's compromise of all its symbolic weight. Each plank of the Compromise of 1850 passed by means of rigid sectional voting, with northern Democrats and southern Whigs defecting or abstaining to provide the necessary majorities. Far from building bridges between North and South, the compromise exposed the cleavages that divided the country. Douglas's methods hollowed out the substance of compromise. Each side felt that it had conceded too much and had been conceded too little.

The fate of the Mexico cession was a case in point. Amid fierce southern resistance, New Mexico and Utah were organized into territories and California was admitted as a free state. Diehard southern slaveholders resisted the admission of California to the bitter end. Sitting in the Senate as the measure was discussed, Jefferson Davis fantasized about snatching up the California bill and 'tearing it to pieces'. When, at length, the southerners were outvoted in Congress, Davis was among a group of ten southerners who signed a solemn protest against the bill. The admission of California, they wrote, proved that the 'exclusion of slavery from the territory of the United States' was now 'an object so high and important' in the eyes of the North 'as to justify a disregard ... of the Constitution itself. Against this conclusion we must now and forever protest.' The principle of freedom in the territories, they wrote, was not only 'destructive of the safety and liberty' of the South, but 'fatal to the peace and *equality* of the states ... and must lead, if persisted in, to the dissolution of the confederacy'.

On 9 September 1850, California joined the Union as a free state. A decade later, every single surviving signatory of that protest supported secession and joined the Confederate States of America.[12]

# Mesilla, USA

In the spring of 1851, while the United States were celebrating a compromise that had staved off secession and civil war, the citizens of Mesilla were celebrating a compromise of a different kind. Mesilla was a new settlement established after the Treaty of Guadalupe Hidalgo by Mexican citizens fleeing their old homes that were now on the American side of the border.

Then the surveyors came. The surveying of the 2,000-mile Mexican-American border was an epic task completed over several years by hundreds of men. It proceeded from west to east and it was not until late 1850 that the American survey team arrived. The citizens of Mesilla watched nervously as the survey's astronomers traipsed across the desert trying to calculate the exact latitude and longitude. In the end, they compromised and decided to run the southern boundary along 32° 22' north latitude, such that the line ran between Doña Ana, in the American territory of New Mexico, and Mesilla, in the Mexican state of Chihuahua. 'When it was known the boundary determined by the commissioners included them in Mexico,' one newspaper reported, the citizens of Mesilla 'hailed the event with salvos of cannon, and every kind of rejoicing'.[1]

But the people of Mesilla rejoiced prematurely. Their home in an obscure patch of the Chihuahuan Desert was about to get dragged into the sectional dispute over slavery, freedom and the fate of the Mexican cession.

## AN IRON MISSISSIPPI

In the 1850s, 30,000 miles of railroad were laid in the United States, over two-thirds of it in the North. Lines were built across the Appalachians, connecting the Ohio Valley with Philadelphia and New York. Beyond the mountains, they joined up with a dense network of railroads built in Ohio, Illinois, Michigan and Indiana. As early as 1853 the state of Iowa, which had joined the Union in 1846, had three railways operating inside its territory. Texas, which had joined the Union a year earlier, had none. The South struggled for years to build a line connecting Vicksburg with Montgomery, a distance of less than 300 miles. While the North planned, financed and built railroads at a vigorous rate, the South seemed incapable – both technically and temperamentally – of building an efficient, interconnected and well-maintained system of railways. For northern observers, the South's inability to build railways was a symbol of all that was wrong with the southern economy. Slavery had deadened everything. The South seemed impervious to improvement by the forces of modern technology and industry. Progress halted at the Mason–Dixon Line. 'Slavery is no scholar, no improver,' complained Walt Whitman. 'It does not love the whistle of the railroad; it does not love the newspaper, the mail-bag, a college, a book or a preacher ... it does not increase the white population; it does not improve the soil; everything goes to decay.'[2]

Within the South there were those who worried about their failure to industrialize. They brooded over the failure of the South to follow the North's lead into the new high-productivity, high-profit industries thrown up in the wake of the Industrial Revolution. Their fears were articulated by the most influential of the South's modernizers, the publisher James De Bow. His journal, *De Bow's Review*, was the *Economist* of the antebellum plantocracy – essential reading for the forward-thinking slave-owner. In its pages he expounded on the need for the South to modernize. By embracing industrialization and urbanization, the region would be afforded new dignity. 'Build up your cities and towns,' he exhorted his readers; 'it will educate your people; it will give you rank, wealth, and importance; it will break the shackles of your dependence upon others, and give influence and prosperity beyond example.'

De Bow was particularly enthusiastic about railroads. 'The wondrous element of steam,' he wrote, had 'diminished labour, destroyed space ... and created a new world.' De Bow wanted to lead the South into that new world to prevent the North from sidelining the South forever.

For the system of railroads constructed in the North represented a complete restructuring of the American economy. Previously, the general direction of economic travel was along a North–South axis corresponding to the flow of the Mississippi River. The railroad challenged that. Trains travelled along an East–West axis, connecting the Midwest to the Atlantic. Not only was the primacy of New Orleans upset – so too were the entire set of economic assumptions that underpinned the broad alliance of interests between the South and the West.

Hitherto the South and the West were almost synonymous. The election of 1844 was a case in point: both Clay and Polk were slave-owners hailing from western states. Even those western states where slavery did not exist – Ohio, Indiana and Illinois – were friendly to southern interests. In the Jacksonian era, these states had reliably delivered large numbers of votes to pro-slavery Democrats.

By the 1850s the situation had begun to shift. Slavery was in decline in the border states, with slavery increasingly concentrated in the Deep South. Mass immigration from Europe into the Midwest had eroded pro-southern sympathies. Now cheap rail connections to the East Coast created an alternative to shipping goods downriver to New Orleans. From a southern perspective, the West risked being northernized. To De Bow the proper response was to build railroads connecting the South and West, integrating the regions' economies and renewing their historical alliance. The day was not far off, De Bow believed, when the South would be moving soldiers and not cotton along its railway system. When that day came the South would need western support. 'The South must sympathize with the West, or be alone,' he warned.[3]

These motives informed southern contributions to the national debate over the construction of a transcontinental railroad. This transcontinental line would be the crowning technological achievement of the United States. It would also be the ultimate expression of the new East–West economic axis that the railroads had forged. For that very reason, the debate over where the line should run was especially rancorous. At a series of conventions in the 1850s, the southern elite threw their considerable influence behind the most southern route – from New Orleans, through Texas and along the 32nd parallel to southern California. Securing this route became an obsession for a certain kind of southerner. Building the southern route would not just be a triumph of southern engineering – it would redeem the claims of southern civilization. It would be an expression of southern confidence and a test of southern resolve.

'We may be told that it is visionary, because it is two thousand miles long,' one conventioneer said in an impassioned speech. 'Sir, it is not visionary ... Suppose that in 1830, a man had told you that in two days time a man from Charleston might plant his feet upon the Father of Waters, you would have put him in a madhouse ... Suppose a man had told you that ... a man might leave the city of Washington on a Friday night, and take his dinner in Charleston on Sunday, you would have branded him as a maniac ... When I think of these things, I am almost willing to believe anything, even if it were as visionary as any miracle recorded in the "Arabian Nights." We can build it. We only want the will to build it.'[4]

There was just one problem: Mesilla.

## ANOTHER PIECE FROM THE BODY

The task of advising the government on possible routes for the transcontinental railroad belonged with the War Department. And from 1852 to 1856 the secretary of war was Jefferson Davis, a partisan of the southern route for the transcontinental line. Studying maps and examining survey reports, Davis realized that it had a crucial advantage.

The Continental Divide was the most forbidding barrier to construction wherever one drew the line across the country. But in southern New Mexico the mountains thin and the elevation drops. A War Department survey, commissioned by Davis, observed that the elevation here did not 'exceed 4,600 feet, the lowest yet determined between the parallels thirty-two and forty-nine'. Moreover, the region was well connected to both the Rio Grande and the Gila River Valley, making construction and supply far easier. Davis was delighted – as were his southern allies. So inviting was this route through the Continental Divide that for its supporters the real barrier was less geographical and more political. Both the pass across the divide and its easterly approaches 'between Frontera ... and Mesilla' were inside Mexican territory. For the dream of the southern railroad to be realized, more land would have to taken from Mexico.[5]

The 1852 election returned the Democrats to the presidency under the leadership of Franklin Pierce. Although Pierce was from New Hampshire and was one of the few antebellum presidents not to own slaves, he firmly defended the southern orthodoxy on slavery. A proud veteran of the Mexican-American War, he was an enthusiast of continued American expansion in Cuba, Mexico and the Caribbean littoral. With an expansionist back in the presidency and dependable allies in the cabinet, the southerners seized the chance to try and secure the land needed to build their railroad.

As luck would have it, the compromise over the placing of the border near Mesilla had given them their opening. The boundary had to be ratified by the United States Senate. The Senate rejected it – because it surrendered the land needed for the railway – and so cast the entire status of the border into doubt. In response, Pierce triggered an article of the Treaty of Guadalupe Hidalgo that called for disputes between the two countries to be settled through negotiation. Pierce used the reopening of the boundary discussion to try and extract yet more land from Mexico. In his instructions to his envoy, James Gadsden, Pierce outlined a menu of five land cessions. At its greatest extent, he was willing to pay $50 million for chunks of Tamaulipas, Nuevo León, Coahuila, Chihuahua, Sonora and all of Baja California, a total of 120,000 square miles. At the very least, he was willing to pay $10 million to secure the Mesilla Valley and the southern section of Arizona.[6]

Gadsden arrived in Mexico City in the autumn of 1853, a few months after Santa Anna assumed the presidency for the eleventh time. Santa Anna was still trying to rehabilitate his reputation following the Mexican-American War and was in no mood to make territorial concessions.

Gadsden blundered ahead all the same, rattling his sabre while dangling money before his Mexican counterparts. Gadsden warned Santa Anna that 'a repetition of Texas history in the six border states' of Mexico was inevitable and that the government ought to pre-empt it by accepting Pierce's maximalist offer that would provide the two countries with a 'natural territorial boundary ... [of] Mountain and Desert outlines'. Thereafter the United States' territorial appetites would be satiated in perpetuity and the two countries would enjoy eternal peace.

Santa Anna replied that the United States, 'with knife in hand, was attempting to cut another piece from the body it had just mutilated'. His administration stood fast and that winter whittled away at Gadsden's proposal until all that remained was a 28,000-square-mile strip of land in southern New Mexico and Arizona fit for building a railroad and little else. For this the Americans would pay $10 million.[7]

Gadsden sheepishly sent his treaty to Washington, where it was submitted to the Senate. There was a short-lived attempt to promote the many virtues of this unloved patch of land, but few were convinced. 'We happen to live within a league or so of this lovely, picturesque, and God-favored land,' one Texas newspaper wrote, and 'we unhesitatingly pronounce the whole country as not being worth a *Fanega* of *Frijoles*'.

In the Senate, Thomas Hart Benton declared the lands in question to be 'so utterly desolate, desert, and God-forsaken, that ... a wolf could not make his living upon it'. The treaty was ultimately ratified, 33–12, against a backdrop of general public indifference.

Among the partisans in the North and South, the Gadsden Purchase, the country's final territorial acquisition in the contiguous United States, was the occasion for another round of sectional recriminations.

The South crowed that this was just the beginning of a new round of expansion. 'We shall soon have the Mesilla Valley,' claimed a Democrat newspaper, 'and directly Cuba, and by and by all Mexico, and eventually Canada, and finally the whole North American continent.'

Among abolitionists and Free Soilers, the purchase was met with varying degrees of anger and despair. One New Hampshire paper calculated that when the Gadsden Purchase was added to the tally of territorial acquisitions since 1787, the United States would have acquired 2 million square miles of land, but only a quarter of that had 'been secured to freedom'. 'Three-fourths of the whole have been yielded up to slavery.' 'Free men of the North!' the paper asked. 'How long will you be the willing serfs of an oligarchy that despises you, curses the country, imbrutes humanity and defies God!'[8]

The reaction in Mexico was uniformly negative. Santa Anna benefited in the short term, pocketing $700,000 of the purchase price, but his sacrifice of yet more land to their hated northern neighbour contributed to the downfall of his administration. He was overthrown in a revolution in 1854 and went into exile for the last time in August 1855. He would not return to Mexico until 1874, by then a sickly old man. He died in poverty in Mexico City in 1876, aged eighty-two. An obituary in the Mexican press described him as 'a relic of another epoch, our generation remembered him for the misfortunes he brought upon the republic'. Another newspaper ran the news of his death under the headline 'El Hombre Fatal'. 'This man appeared among us like a curse, precisely when there was not a cloud on the horizon for our country ... This man alone turned all our hopes into a nightmare.'[9]

Largely forgotten were the citizens of Mesilla, who against their wishes found themselves living once more inside the United States. They were present when, on 16 November 1854, the final sovereign transfer of territory in the contiguous United States occurred in the town plaza. Ranks of Mexican and American soldiers lined the square as General John Garland and General Angel Trias – both veterans of the Mexican-American War – finalized the transfer. At the appointed moment, Garland gave the signal and 'the stars and stripes were hoisted on a cotton tree and saluted by two 12lb. howitzers'.[10]

## THE ENDS OF THE LINE

The southern railroad was not completed until 1878, by which point its original purpose had been abrogated by the Civil War. In fact, no transcontinental railroad was built at all in the 1850s. The unquestioned merit of building a railroad to connect the country's coasts was subordinated to the increasingly violent sectional quarrel over the expansion of slavery into the territories. Politics became zero-sum. Northerners did all they could to prevent the construction of a southern route. Southerners did all they could to frustrate plans to build a northern one. Neither cared if the country suffered, so long as their opponents did not benefit.

The bitter partisan politics of those years resurrected the career of Abraham Lincoln, who won the 1860 election, a victory that marked the triumph of the new structure of American politics where the West and the North united against the South. Lincoln – Kentucky-born but Illinois-made – represented this shift. And Lincoln, the railway lawyer, had helped along its realization. The president-elect left his home town in Springfield, Illinois, for Washington, D.C. on 11 February.

Famously, Lincoln arrived in Washington in the dead of night as a security precaution against a rumoured assassination attempt. Adding to the gloom, slavery was still legal in the district and the great dome of the Capitol was still incomplete. The ongoing building work at the Capitol has often been read as the great symbol of the challenge Lincoln faced: to form a more perfect Union, to mend a house divided.

More prosaically, the dome was being rebuilt and enlarged as part of an attempt to make the building fit for purpose. The chamber of the House of Representatives was originally designed in 1807 to accommodate 145 representatives from seventeen states. By 1857 (when work on an expanded chamber was completed) it was crammed with 240 representatives from thirty-one states.

The problems of the Capitol Building, much like the problems faced by Lincoln, were downstream of the United States' epic territorial expansion since independence. Lincoln alluded directly to this fact shortly after arriving in Washington. By that point, seven southern states had seceded from the Union and several others were considering joining them. Various compromise schemes had been put forward, most of which would have effectively annulled the democratic outcome of the recent presidential election. Lincoln rejected them all, declaring that there was 'but one compromise which would really settle the slavery question, and that would be a prohibition against acquiring any more territory'.

In his inaugural address he made a similar point: 'One section of our country believes slavery is right, and ought to be extended, while the other believes it is wrong, and ought not to be extended. This is the only substantial dispute.' Slavery per se was not the concern. Its extension was the problem. The United States' expansion had aggravated an issue that might not otherwise have registered. The result was secession and civil war.[11]

Jefferson Davis set out for his inauguration as president of the Confederate States of America on 11 February, the very same day Lincoln began his journey from Springfield. Davis's plantation outside Vicksburg was only 300 miles from the Confederate capital at Montgomery. But to get there he had to take a steamboat to Jackson,

Mississippi, then a train via Chattanooga, Tennessee, and Atlanta, Georgia, before arriving 850 miles, four states and five days later in Montgomery, Alabama.

It was a stark illustration of the problems the Confederacy faced – but in those months the South was more focused on the past than the future. The seceding states walked backwards into the war, their eyes fixed on the past. About half of the Confederate states wrote formal documents listing their reasons for secession. Every single one directly referenced the question of slavery in the territories. 'We had acquired a large territory by successful war with Mexico,' the Georgia legislature declared. 'We had shed our blood and paid our money for its acquisition.' Now Lincoln and the Republicans would 'deprive us of an equal enjoyment of the common Territories of the Republic'.

All the seceding states dwelt on the milestones that had led to the secession crisis: the Northwest Ordinance, the framing of the Constitution, the Louisiana Purchase, the Missouri Compromise, the War with Mexico, the Wilmot Proviso. The crisis was bred of the United States' expansion.

In Texas, Governor Sam Houston tried his best to retell this narrative as proof of the United States' greatness. He, too, looked backwards, taking his audience back 'forty-seven years ago, [when] I enlisted, a mere boy, to sustain the National flag and in defense of a harassed frontier' during the War of 1812. Since then he had watched the Union grow. 'I have seen it extend from the wilds of Tennessee ... across the Mississippi, achieve the annexation of Texas, scaling the Rocky Mountains in its onward march, sweeping the valleys of California, and laying its pioneer footsteps in the waves of the Pacific ... Power, wealth, expansion, victory, have followed in its path ... Is not this worth perpetuating? Will you exchange this for all the hazards, the anarchy and carnage of civil war?'

The Texas legislature replied on 2 February 1861 with a document outlining their reasons for secession. 'The controlling majority of the Federal Government,' it wrote, waxing Calhounian, had used its powers 'to exclude the citizens of the Southern States ... from all the immense territory owned in common by all the States on the Pacific Ocean, for the avowed purpose of acquiring sufficient power in the common government to use it as a means of destroying the institutions of Texas and her sister slaveholding States.'[12]

The Confederate constitution that Jefferson Davis swore to uphold was designed to seal up the anti-slavery holes in the United States Constitution. Slavery was explicitly named and explicitly defended. The mistakes of the past were rectified. But in one respect, the Confederate constitution looked forward to the future. Article IV included the clause 'The Confederate States may acquire new territory ... [and may] form States to be admitted into the Confederacy.' The dreams of southern expansion had not died. Indeed, the Confederacy's most ardent supporters held high hopes for its future expansion. 'Our young Confederacy has brilliant prospects ahead,' wrote one Georgia newspaper ten days after Jefferson Davis's inauguration. 'Expansion, too will be its birthright ... We will absorb Central America and the contiguous States of Mexico ... When these golden visions become realities ... the proudest nations of the earth [will] come to woo and worship at the shrine of our imperial Confederacy.'[13]

The first step towards an imperial Confederacy was taken on 16 March, when a convention met in Mesilla and voted unanimously for secession. By June, one unionist was reporting that the region was 'now as much in the possession of the enemy as Charleston is'. In late July a Confederate force led by Texan John R. Baylor defeated a Union force at the First Battle of Mesilla. On 1 August, Baylor declared the creation of the Confederate Territory of Arizona, consisting of the southern half of the modern states of New Mexico and Arizona, with Mesilla as its capital. A few weeks later, an officer at nearby Fort Fauntleroy sent a frantic letter to the secretary of war in Washington. 'The Texas rebels and Arizona cut-throats, like the ancient Goths and Vandals, are at the very gates' of California, he warned. Their capture of Mesilla was the first stage of a wider plan of conquest.

As wild as the idea sounded, it accurately reflected some of the more ambitious plans of the Confederacy. Confederate generals in Arizona argued that the best way to circumvent the Union blockade on the Atlantic Coast was to seize access to the Pacific. Mesilla ought to be the staging post for an ambitious assault across the Continental Divide into California. 'As soon as the Confederate Army should occupy the Territory of New Mexico,' one officer wrote, 'an army of advance would be organized and "on to San Francisco" would be the watchword.' For much of 1861, it looked as though the Union's far-western frontier was in real danger.[14]

The Confederacy's dreams of territory stretching to the Pacific were a recapitulation of the Republic of Texas's dreams of two decades before – and they faced the same problem. To get to California, they would have to go through Santa Fe. In early 1862, General Sibley and 2,500 Texans marched out of Mesilla bound for northern New Mexico. They took Albuquerque on 2 March and reached Santa Fe on 13 March. Simultaneously, a smaller force led by Captain Sherod Hunter probed westwards along the Gila Valley and came within eighty miles of California.

The endeavour collapsed on 28 March, when the entire Confederate supply train was destroyed at the Battle of Glorieta Pass and Sibley was obliged to retreat to Mesilla. His chaotic and destructive march back to Confederate lines alienated much of the population and led to the Second Battle of Mesilla, which saw pro-Union guerrillas expel Confederate regulars from the city. A few days later, Mesilla was occupied by a Union force sent from southern California, ending Confederate rule in the region.

Thereafter the hopes of Confederate expansion went into sharp decline and the Confederate Territory of Arizona continued to exist only in the minds of a few fantasists. It persisted on paper, however, until 2 June 1865, when the last of the Confederate armies, the Army of the Trans-Mississippi, surrendered in Galveston, Texas. Seventeen days later, the last of the Confederacy's slaves were emancipated on 19 June 1865, now remembered as Juneteenth.

There are few traces today of the Confederates' turn in Mesilla. There is a plaque on the town square, but it is lost among the notices drawing attention to other aspects of Mesilla's history: Billy the Kid, the Butterfield Overland Trail, a sign honouring the servicemen and women of the town, another commemorating the oldest brick building in the state. Amid all this history, the Gadsden Purchase gets pride of place. In the thirties, a bandstand was built on the plaza to commemorate the transaction. The flags of Mexico and the United States grace its facade, with '54' written in large black letters between them.

Less publicized is another painting on the bandstand's rear. It shows the city seal of Mesilla: a shield in the red and yellow of imperial Spain, a dove and a cross in the top half and a hefty wooden mallet in the bottom. Beneath is written the old city motto in the Spanish of those who founded it in 1850: 'A DIOS ROGANDO Y CON EL MAZO DANDO'. It is a slightly ambiguous phrase that could be parsed in any number of ways. But, translated into vernacular American, it makes for a fitting epitaph to the story of American empire in the Southwest: 'Trust in God and Pass the Ammunition'.

# PART VI

# ALASKA

Today, two great nations of the earth seem to be advancing toward the same destination from different starting points: the Russians and the Anglo-Americans ... The point of departure is different, their paths are diverse but each of them seems destined by some secret providential design to hold in their hands the fate of half the world at some date in the future.

ALEXIS DE TOCQUEVILLE, 1835

# Young Russia Greets Young America

In September 1863, New York City was a troubled place. That July, New York regiments were thrown into battle at Gettysburg, resulting in thousands dead and wounded. The scale of the losses was only just sinking in when draft riots broke out in Lower Manhattan. Over the course of three days, hundreds of people were killed and beaten as gangs brawled in the streets and mobs burned down buildings across the city. In August, attention shifted to Europe and a war scare involving Britain and Russia. For more than two years Americans had watched with trepidation as Britain mulled intervention in the American Civil War on the side of the Confederacy. How might a new war in Europe rebound on American affairs? The answer was unclear. In the meantime, the killing continued. In September, the Union and Confederate armies clashed in Tennessee. At Chickamauga, more men died than in any other battle of the war save Gettysburg. News of the engagement was reaching the city when surprise visitors appeared in New York Harbor: a Russian squadron led by Admiral Lisovski aboard the flagship *Alexander Nevski*.

And for almost two months New Yorkers set aside their worries and threw a massive party for their Russian guests.

Festivities began on 1 October, when a reception committee took the steamer *Andrews* out into the bay to meet the Russian ships at anchor. The *Andrews* bore with it a band which played popular tunes as it cut out from Manhattan. As the boat approached the visiting ships, it took up the Russian national anthem, 'God Save the Tsar!', and ran up the white and blue ensign of the Imperial Russian Navy. Sailors swarmed the rigging of the Russian vessels and began cheering loudly as the

Americans drew near. As the *Andrews* came alongside the 4,500-ton Russian flagship, the crew of the *Nevski* raised the Stars and Stripes and a band struck up 'Yankee Doodle'. The reception committee were brought aboard on sixteen-man gigs and given a tour of the vessel by Admiral Lisovski. The Americans were gushing in their praise of Russian seamanship. The ship was so well made, one witness reported, that it might have been manufactured in America. The *Nevski*'s fifty-one guns had in fact been cast in Pittsburgh, much to the Americans' satisfaction. And although the crew were largely made up of peasants from the Russian interior, they impressed their hosts with their professionalism. 'The instant you step foot over the gangways of these ships,' one reporter wrote, 'it becomes evident that they are in the hands of men who understand how to keep a ship in the most thorough order. The decks are as white as holy-stones and sand can make them, the paint work spotless, the brass and other bright work shining as if they were cleaned every five minutes; rigging neatly coiled down on deck or on the belaying pins ... in fact, every thing looks "ship-shape and Bristol fashion" just as a sailor likes to see it.'

Once the inspection was over, Lisovski ordered a twenty-one-gun salute that thundered over the water as the band once again took up 'Yankee Doodle'. The Americans then invited the Russian sailors ashore at the foot of 23rd Street. After more formalities, the Americans led their guests in a procession through the city. First came the Russian officers in their gold-laced hats and gleaming gold and silver epaulettes. In their wake came the better part of 3,000 regular sailors in white smocks and caps. They marched through streets choked with fascinated onlookers crowding sidewalks, leaning out of every window and peering down from the rooftops. American and Russian colours decked out every major building. Tiffany & Co. on 550 Broadway displayed an immense Russian flag and 'ran two huge blue stripes of bunting, which, against the white marble facade, gave to the latter the semblance of another monster Muscovite ensign'.

The intensity of the greeting impressed everyone who witnessed it and seemed to augur a new epoch in Russo-American relations. That was certainly reflected in an exchange between Admiral Lisovski and Mayor George Opdyke recorded for posterity by eager newsmen. 'Young Russia greets Young America, and bids her live,' Lisovski said. 'We are indeed friends,' Opdyke replied. 'We greet you accordingly.'[1]

Over the next weeks, the Russians were feted around town. Russian sailors posed for photographs and took a steamer up to Niagara Falls. Russian officers were treated to an exhausting schedule of receptions, parties and galas and were visited by endless delegations of grandees and out-of-state visitors. The climax came on 5 November, with a massive ball and banquet at the Academy of Music. For the occasion the organizers procured 12,000 oysters, 10,000 chickens, 2,000 salmon and more than 3,000 bottles of wine.

After dinner, in a hall decorated with huge portraits of Washington, Lincoln, Alexander II and Peter the Great, Russian officers took to the ballroom floor with the women of Manhattan high society. 'These Slavic heroes are not the largest of the human race,' an attending journalist wrote, and as the officers took up their dance partners they were soon lost from sight 'in the embrace of grand nebulous masses of muslin and crinoline'. The party continued long into the night. 'It was undoubtedly the greatest ball ever given in this country,' one newspaper concluded.

Nor was it the final word in American hospitality. A few weeks later, the squadron moved down the coast to the Potomac and the cycle of festivities began again in Washington. President Lincoln was ill and could not attend upon the Russian visitors, so he sent his secretary of state, William Seward, to greet them. But Lincoln and his cabinet had already been upstaged by the president's wife, Mary Todd Lincoln, who had previously gone aboard the frigate *Osliaba* and raised a toast to 'the health of the Emperor of Russia'. A gesture which the New York *Herald* claimed would 'be heard with joy in the icy North and the steppes of Asia'. 'We are aware that her action was contrary to all the rules of European etiquette,' the *Herald* wrote, 'but it was in strict accordance with the spirit of our people.'

This gesture, and many others like it, did indeed make an impression on European observers. According to one Paris newspaper, 'the enthusiastic reception, the kind of popular ovation' extended by the United States to Russia, was proof that 'Russian and American affairs necessarily react upon each other and produce a mutual independence and sympathy between the two nations ... the interests of America and Russia thus become identical'.[2]

## THE SAXON AND THE COSSACK

If in 1863 Russia and the United States met each other as friends, then it was a friendship that had sprung from unpromising beginnings.

In 1781 Francis Dana, the first American envoy sent to Russia, arrived in St Petersburg in late summer, hoping to secure recognition for his country. For the next two years, Dana was ignored by Catherine the Great, who was too busy conquering Crimea to bother with the American's representations. Dana returned home in the spring of 1783, having failed to secure an audience with the tsarina and with an unfavourable impression of his host. 'This nation is far from being civilized,' his secretary (a teenage John Quincy Adams) wrote of Russia. 'Their customs, their dress, and even their amusements, are yet gross and barbarous.' The embassy's failure produced a long lull in diplomatic relations. It would be thirty years before Adams returned to St Petersburg as the first accredited American minister, and half a century until the countries signed their first trade agreement. Apart from a few intrepid merchants who made their way from Boston to the Baltic Sea, there was little intercourse between the two nations.[3]

During this same period, Russia was consolidating its presence in North America. Russians had first arrived on the continent in 1741 when Vitus Bering crossed the strait from Kamchatka. Since then the Russians had continued to make their way across the Aleutian Islands in pursuit of furs. In the same period that the Americans were fighting for independence, the Russians were nibbling at the western edges of Canada. Settlements took root on Kodiak Island in 1795 and in Sitka in 1799. Soon St Petersburg began to exert more control over the freewheeling Russian furriers. In 1799 the various fur enterprises were consolidated into the Russian-American Company (RAC).

This new focus on its far-eastern frontier drew Russia into the jostling among the great powers in the Pacific. In 1789 Russia found itself party to the Nootka Sound Crisis. In the first decade of the nineteenth century, RAC officials began to probe into British Columbia and Oregon, and in 1812 Russian officials established a colony at Fort Ross in California, bringing Russian interests to the door of Mexico. An RAC employee named Georg Anton Schäffer tried to seize Hawaii in 1815 in an abortive attempt to stake out a Russian claim in the central Pacific.

While Russia felt its way down the coasts of California, American sailors began appearing in Russian harbours north of Oregon in pursuit of sea otters. The presence of the Americans provided a lifeline for Russians living in the remote Northwest who were able to procure from them supplies not forthcoming from St Petersburg. It had proved near impossible to raise crops and keep livestock that far north. The soil was stony and the climate wet. Birds and mice ate through fields of barley, wheat and peas – which in any case were so deprived of sunlight that they never ripened. Desperate RAC officials tried to grow cabbages, lettuces and cucumbers in glasshouses, but to no avail. When they raised chickens and pigs, the flesh tasted of the fish they were fed. If the climate did not allow for agriculture, the average RAC employee was not cut out for farming. Alcoholism was rife among the furriers. Word of their dissolute habits made it back to St Petersburg, where the RAC's demesne was referred to as the 'drunk republic'. It was fortunate, then, that the RAC was peripheral to Russia's interests. In 1819 there were only 391 Russians in the tsar's North American domains. What St Petersburg really cared about was the fate of Kamchatka, Manchuria and the Amur River basin. The real function of Russia's various schemes in the eastern Pacific was to create an outer perimeter around the core of Russian interests in north-east Asia.[4]

Following the Adams–Onís Treaty, the United States found itself with a toehold on the Pacific and renewed interest in the Russian presence there. After some diplomatic false starts, a convention was signed in 1824 that was followed in 1832 by a commercial treaty covering all bilateral trade, negotiated by a young James Buchanan.

These treaties signalled a new era in Russo-American relations. Over the next few decades, Russia and the United States discovered each other. Diplomatic relations were limited to commonplace matters, handled by a small but dedicated corps of professionals who rejoiced in names like Churchill Caldom Cambreleng and Baron Diderick Tuyll van Serooskerken.

The real effect of renewed relations was felt economically. American merchants began working a profitable trade in tea, coffee, rice and sugar, returning home with holds full of Russian iron, hemp, linen and flax. Of more lasting consequence was the influence of American industrial entrepreneurs. In 1840, John H. Brown built the 2,500-ton steam frigate *Kamchatka* for Tsar Nicholas I, the largest vessel ever built in an

American shipyard at the time, and the first of many state-of-the-art ships built by the Americans for the Imperial Russian Navy. Two years later, Nicholas welcomed a delegation of American engineers to St Petersburg. They were in Russia to build the first commercial railway line in the country, connecting Moscow with St Petersburg. A native of Indiana, George Washington Whistler, oversaw the project while his son, James Abbott McNeill Whistler, took drawing lessons at the St Petersburg Academy of Fine Arts.* Along with Whistler came employees of the firm Harrison, Eastwick and Winans, who were commissioned by Nicholas to build hundreds of locomotives at the state foundry. Joseph Harrison of the same firm built the Annunciation Bridge, the first permanent iron bridge across the Neva. Another American, Charles Robinson, was the first person to install a telegraph system in Russia. Dozens of other businessmen sought their fortunes in Russia in these years, hawking guns, setting up textile factories and drilling for oil in the Sea of Asov. All this in addition to the vast numbers of brokers, merchants and financiers engaged in the cotton trade. By the eve of the Civil War, the single largest article of Russo-American trade was cotton, with the American South providing 92 per cent of Russia's total raw cotton imports.[5]

As relations between the two countries deepened, Americans began to develop a better understanding of Russia. It was not all positive. Andrew Jackson declared that relations between 'a growing absolute monarchy and a thriving democratic government' would necessarily be 'naturally antagonistic' and would result in war. This sentiment was echoed by Commodore Matthew Perry, who saw in the rapid expansion of the two countries a prelude to a gigantic showdown between 'the Saxon and the Cossack' whose outcome would determine 'the freedom or the slavery of the world'. Anti-slavery Americans saw in Russian serfdom a mirror image of the bondage they loathed in their own country. The total lack of political, social and cultural freedoms in Russia did not escape American notice. When Russia intervened in Central Europe during the revolutions of 1848, there was a spasm of anti-Russian senti-

---

* George Whistler's enduring contribution to Russia was in the selection of a five-foot gauge for Russia's railways, four inches narrower than the global norm. To this day, international passengers travelling to and from Russia by train have to wait for several hours at the border while the bogies are replaced.

ment in the United States. Exiles fleeing the Russian-backed crackdown on the liberal uprisings became celebrities in America. When the Hungarian revolutionary Lajos Kossuth visited Washington in 1852, Senator William Seward visited him daily, fawned over him at dinners and condemned Russian actions, declaring that America could not afford to be 'indifferent to similar acts of national injustice, oppression, and usurpation' on the part of the Russian government.[6]

Improbably, however, many Americans developed a favourable view of Russia. Both were young nations, both were sprawling continental nations and both were nations with rapidly expanding frontiers. The old powers of Europe were stagnant; Russia and the United States were bracingly dynamic. There was not a little wishful thinking involved in this claim (one American diplomat who served in Russia noted acidly that 'a short journey in the tsar's dominions is a grand curative for such predilections'), but it was widely believed. 'Russia and the United States are the two young, growing, giant nations of the world,' one English writer claimed, 'the Leviathans of the land.' In addition, they were both nations in which territorial expansion was linked to a providential national mission. Happily, these dual expansions did not overlap with one another and hence could be romanticized rather than fretted over. 'You are the only power that has never been jealous of the progress we have made as a nation in accomplishing what we call our manifest destiny,' James Buchanan once observed to the Russian ambassador. 'You also have your own manifest destiny and far from colliding with you with hostility and jealousy, we applaud your expansion and the extension of your power.'[7]

Real or imagined affinity aside, events at mid-century pushed the two countries closer together. The first was the arrival of the United States as a Pacific power. The Oregon Treaty and the Treaty of Guadalupe Hidalgo brought Americans to the doorstep of Russian America. The RAC had vacated its California possessions in 1841 with the sale of Fort Ross to John Sutter, but the Russians had a ringside seat to the dramatic arrival of the Argonauts in 1849. The rapid settlement of the far west brought new opportunities for Russo-American trade in the region. One of the most successful of these was the American Russian Commercial Company that, over the course of the 1850s, imported tens of thousands of tons of Alaskan ice into the bars and saloons of San Francisco. However, most of the trade went in the other direction, and by the end of the decade the Russian outposts in the Northwest were almost entirely dependent on American merchants for their supply.

The arrival of America on the Pacific coast might have been the occasion for a confrontation. Instead, the outbreak of the Crimean War in 1853 helped deepen relations. America supplied arms, medical assistance and engineering know-how to support the Russian war effort, and for a brief period it seemed as though America might find itself dragged into the war on the Russian side. This did not transpire. However, the Crimean War poisoned Russian attitudes towards Great Britain for a generation and inspired its diplomats to search for participants in an anti-British bloc. America was an obvious partner and Anglophobic overtures found a welcome reception in Washington. 'Russia and the United States are natural allies,' one American diplomat told a Russian counterpart, 'and the day will come when they will act together ... in counteracting the arrogant and insolent interference of Great Britain in the affairs of other nations.'[8]

The Crimean War led to a re-evaluation of Russia's position in North America. In a largely forgotten episode, a French and British fleet laid siege to the Russian fort at Petropavlovsk in Kamchatka for five days in September 1854. It proved to be one of a handful of occasions during the war when Russia's eastern territories were endangered, but it was a reminder of the near impossibility of protecting Russia's far-flung possessions.

And while Russia's far east was vulnerable, Russian North America was indefensible. So exposed were the tsar's lands there that during the war a scheme was floated to sell the RAC to Americans on a temporary basis to ward off a potential British invasion. The plan – an echo of the sale of Astoria to the North West Company during the War of 1812 – never came to fruition. Nor did the British ever venture across the Bering Strait. But it planted the idea of selling Russian North America to the United States in the minds of both American and Russian decision-makers. For the Americans, it conjured up the tantalizing prospect of yet more territory. For the Russians, it seemed to solve a number of problems at a stroke. In the first place, the depleted post-war imperial treasury would receive an influx of American gold. This was no small thing, given that in the event of war the colonies there would be lost anyway. It was better to sell an asset for a gain than to lose it for nothing.

And who threatened Russian North America? Perhaps Britain might menace it again, but the more likely candidate was the United States. The Russian ambassador to Washington, the suave and popular Eduard de Stoeckl, was terrified that some unforeseen sequence of events could trigger a stampede of settlers into the region. At one point, Stoeckl feared Mormons might relocate there. Following the Fraser River Gold Rush in 1858, when hordes of American miners descended on British Columbia, Stoeckl began to dread that the discovery of gold in Russian territory might trigger a similar deluge. The how mattered less than the why. Stoeckl took Manifest Destiny seriously. 'Anyone who has lived in North America,' he told his superiors, 'cannot fail to understand instinctively that this principle [Manifest Destiny] is entering more and more into the blood of the people and that new generations are sucking it in with their mother's milk.' Resisting America's westward march was futile, Stoeckl believed, and pointless when Russia had so much land already. It was better, he reasoned, to sell off what could not be defended and remove an obstacle to friendship with a natural ally in the struggle against Britain.[9]

Stoeckl's views found champions in St Petersburg, and in the dying days of Buchanan's presidency he was authorized to initiate negotiations for the sale of Russia's American possessions. These plans were overwhelmed by the tumult of the 1860 election, the ensuing secession crisis and the outbreak of the American Civil War. Stoeckl would have to wait seven years for another opportunity to arise. In fact, the opportunity may have never arisen were it not for the fact that the American secretary of state was by then William Henry Seward.

### THE LAST CONTINENTALIST

The first century of American political history produced a group of politicians whose influence was undiminished by the fact they never held the presidency. To this group belongs William Henry Seward, the veteran New York politico who narrowly lost the Republican candidacy to Abraham Lincoln in 1860 but went on to serve as secretary of state for eight years, becoming one of a handful of men to complete two terms as the United States' top diplomat. This achievement capped a three-decade career in politics that saw him rise from state senator to governor to the United States Senate in a period when New York was by far the largest and most influential state in national politics, and at a time when national politics were wracked by the sectional crisis that broke parties and made careers – among them his own.

Seward was born in Florida, New York, in 1801 to a wealthy family. After a charmed childhood, he studied law and entered politics. Seward adored politics. Over the course of his career he ran for office as a candidate for three different political parties and held as many views on each of the major issues of the day. Versatile, resilient and gifted as a writer and orator, Seward loved the theatre of retail politics as much as the substance of policy. In an era of backslapping conviviality and genial cronyism Seward thrived. One of his protégés remembered 'a slouching, slender figure; a head like a wise macaw; a beaked nose; shaggy eyebrows; unorderly hair and clothes; hoarse voice; offhand manner; free talk, and perpetual cigar'. From his mansion in Auburn, Seward organized New York's politics and his ascent within it at lavish parties where he spent money he did not always have on quantities of champagne, oysters and Cuban tobacco. When he was not at home, Seward was on the road, stumping for allies, fostering connections across the state and promoting himself as a national figure.

Travel was one of Seward's great passions. At a time when it was not unusual for leading politicians to have never gone abroad, Seward was exceptionally well-travelled. Aside from his periodic domestic tours, Seward took the time to visit Britain and Europe in 1833, Canada and Labrador in 1857, and Europe and the Middle East in 1859.

Much like his hero John Quincy Adams, Seward's time abroad exaggerated rather than diluted his patriotism. 'It is not until one visits old, oppressed, suffering Europe,' he once said, 'that he can appreciate his own government ... that he realizes the fearful responsibility of the American people to the nations of the whole earth.'

Seward's travels also intensified what was perhaps his core conviction, namely his belief in the virtue, the beneficence and the inevitability of the spread of civilization. For Seward preferred the works of man to the works of nature, and scenes of modernity to the sights of the past. Approaching London up the Thames after months of travelling across Europe and the Levant, Seward noted the 'strong and cheerful contrast to the countries where we have been. No Indian wigwam, no heathen temple, no mosque, no Catholic or Greek cathedral, no fortification, no grotesque costumes, no half-clad or naked savages, Arabs, serfs, fellahs, or coolies – only on shore a universal manufacture, and on the water merchant vessels, bearing the world's exchanges.' It was vistas like these that fired Seward's enthusiasm for grand pronunciations on the destiny of mankind. 'Our race,' he once told the New York legislature, 'is ordained to reach, on this continent, a higher standard of social perfection than it has ever yet attained, and that hence will proceed the spirit that shall renovate the world.'[10]

Seward was catapulted to the first rank of national politicians by his opposition to what he considered the antithesis of progress: slavery. Between his 'Higher Law' speech during the crisis over California's admission to the Union in March 1850 and the attack on Fort Sumter in April 1861, Seward was at the centre of what he named the 'irrepressible conflict' over slavery. Seward considered slavery a moral pollutant, a blight that choked off industry, a source of stagnation and decay. As the contest over slavery was intimately linked to the politics of territorial expansion, Seward spent much of the 1850s challenging the spread of slavery in Kansas, in Nebraska, in New Mexico and in California. During the debates over the Mexican cession, he argued forcefully against the All Mexico lobby. From the Senate floor he attacked southern filibusters who sought to claim Cuba, Nicaragua and other choice parts of the Caribbean rim for slavery. 'I want no enlargement of territory,' he said. 'I would not give one human life for all the continent that remains to be annexed.'[11]

This kind of intervention and Seward's reputation as primarily an anti-slavery figure have obscured his contribution as a continentalist. For few men were more fanatical in their desire to expand the United States. Whenever he spoke out against aggrandizement, it was almost always in the context of slavery and usually came heavily qualified. Seward insisted that the pursuit of new lands to add to the Union should 'be made with justice, honor, and humanity'. He hated wars of conquest, in the main because he believed they were unnecessary. To his colleagues who agitated for All Mexico he said simply that they ought to wait a decade. It was a certainty, Seward claimed, that in time Mexico would come to the United States and 'implore you to give her rest, and peace, and safety, by admitting her to your confederacy'. A policy of 'masterly inactivity' could be pursued on territorial matters, Seward argued, because Fate had ordained that all the lands they desired would one day be theirs. 'I would not seize with haste and force the fruit, which ripening in time, will fall of itself into our hands.' And Seward had no doubt that time would come. 'Our population is destined to roll its resistless waves to the icy barriers of the north, and to encounter oriental civilization on the shores of the Pacific. The monarchs of Europe are to have no rest while they have a colony remaining on this continent. France has already sold out. Spain has sold out. We shall see how long before England inclines to follow their example.'[12]

What, then, were the United States' true limits? The answer varied depending on Seward's mood. At various times, he considered schemes to obtain parts or all of Mexico, Haiti, Panama,* the Dominican Republic, Greenland, Iceland, Canada and titbits of rock and coral in the Atlantic and Pacific Oceans. On one occasion, he mused over potential acquisitions in China and India. On another, he became tangentially involved in a project to settle the Amur River with American settlers. In a remarkable speech given during the 1860 election, Seward guyed America's neighbours, encouraging them to build up their countries, for they were only 'building excellent states to be hereafter admitted into the American Union'.

As a rule Seward, following Jefferson, was interested primarily in the western hemisphere, which might conservatively encompass 'the whole continent of North America', but might also encompass South America to Cape Horn. But Seward's temperament was not suited to restraint. He delighted in reveries of American expansion. If the country grew as he hoped, he once told a friend, then it would be necessary to relocate the capital from Washington to somewhere further west, perhaps to California, perhaps to Mexico.

These remarks and others like them convinced his contemporaries that Seward was 'almost crazy on the subject of territorial acquisition'. The senator from New York would 'buy up the whole hemisphere from the glaciers of Greenland to the volcanoes of Tierra del Fuego,' one newspaper editorialized, 'if he only lives long enough and the credit of

---

* Seward couched his demand for Panama in typically melodramatic terms: 'We are Americans. We are charged with responsibilities of establishing on the American continent a higher condition of civilization and freedom than has ever before been attained in any part of the world. We all acknowledge and feel this responsibility. The destiny which we wish to realize as Americans is set plainly before us, and distinctly within our reach; but that destiny can only be attained by the execution of the Darien ship canal.'

*A cartoon satirising Seward's hunger for new territorial acquisitions.*

the nation holds out.' Seward was unperturbed. 'We see only the rising of the sun of empire,' he declared; 'only the fair seeds and beginnings of a great nation.'[13]

There was, however, a discernible principle guiding Seward's mania for territorial acquisition, one tied to his great love of progress. Seward believed that confident and rising civilizations engaged in commerce, and that power and influence in global affairs was determined by the share of commerce any one country controlled. And commerce wanted connections: an expanding network of commercial nodes and vertices. Railroads, canals, sea lanes, turnpikes, telegraph lines, ports, harbours and entrepôts. Invariably, Seward framed his territorial acquisitiveness in terms of securing trade routes and commercial choke points. But he never shied from the logical implications of this quest. Like other contemporary boosters of American commercial hegemony, Seward claimed that the United States' world-historical role was to break the old trade routes that united Europe and Asia across the Silk Roads and to reroute global commerce through North America. This was necessarily a challenge to Great Britain, who ruled the waves and commanded global trade. Seward embraced the challenge. Although he was in awe of Britain's achievement – on one occasion he described the world as one 'great commercial system ramified by a thousand nerves projecting from the one head at London' – he believed that the United States was the fated successor to British rule. 'A thousand years ago, King Alfred was laying the foundations of empire for Young England,' he once said, 'as we are now doing for Young America.'

And there could only be one dominant commercial empire. In many respects, Seward's views were of a piece with those expressed by the 'ultras' on the Oregon Question and were tinged by the same Anglophobia. Seward, after all, was from a state with a substantial border with Canada and he had played a key role during the McLeod Affair and the other Anglo-American crises of the 1840s. In Seward's mind, the toppling of British commercial supremacy would be the ultimate vindication of the American project. Hastening its arrival was at the heart of his drive for territory. Accordingly, he looked south – to the Caribbean, to Central America and to the approaches to the Isthmus of Panama – but more often westwards, to the Pacific. The contest for commercial primacy, he insisted, would be determined 'not on the American lakes, nor on the Atlantic coast, nor on the Caribbean sea, nor on the Mediterranean, nor on the Baltic, nor on the Atlantic ocean, but on the Pacific ocean, and its islands and continents'.[14]

The great irony of Seward's career was that once he became secretary of state and was in a position to steer American expansion, he very nearly failed to acquire any territory for the Union. His first five years in office were spent treading the tightrope walk of Civil War diplomacy. Saving the Union meant shelving plans for expansion. In the aftermath of the Confederacy's collapse and Lincoln's assassination, there was no money and little appetite for new territorial acquisitions. Seward ploughed ahead anyway but met with failure. Attempts to buy harbours in Formosa and Haiti were rebuffed. Proposals to buy Greenland and Iceland went nowhere, as did his projected purchase of British Columbia. Other projects involving Honduras, Hawaii, Fiji, Puerto Rico and Cuba met similar fates. Seward managed to bring a deal to purchase the Danish Virgin Islands – all 136 square miles of them – before the Senate, but his opponents spiked the treaty.[15] In the end, Seward only transacted on two new pieces of territory. The first was the tiny Pacific atoll of Midway, famous for the pivotal naval battle between the United States and Japan fought there in 1942 and nothing else. The second was Alaska.[16]

# Winning Walrussia

For much of his career, William Seward did not think much of Russian affairs or show any particular interest in Russia's American possessions.

One of the very few direct references he ever made to Alaska came during a campaign stop in St Paul, Minnesota, during the 1860 election, where he entertained the audience with speculative talk of annexing Russian America. 'Standing here and looking far off into the northwest,' he said, 'I see the Russian as he busily occupies himself in establishing seaports, and towns, and fortifications, on the verge of this continent, as the outposts of St. Petersburg, and I can say, "Go on and build up your outposts all along the coast, up even to the Arctic Ocean – they will yet become the outposts of my own country."'

Such statements were not designed to curry favour with the Romanov court. Seward likely believed that Russian affairs would be peripheral to his career – and that doubtless would have been the case, had it not been for the outbreak of the Civil War.[1]

Seward spent the Civil War trying to fend off the possibility of European intervention. The nightmare scenario was that Britain or France (or both) would force a peace deal that left the Confederacy intact, or involve themselves militarily on the side of the Confederacy. Their motivations for doing so were straightforward: cotton. In Lancashire alone, hundreds of thousands of workers lost their jobs as a consequence of the 'cotton famine' produced by the Union blockade of the South. The merchants, brokers and financiers of London and Liverpool almost universally supported the Confederacy. Prime

Minister Palmerston flirted with recognition, and his representatives in Washington were constantly pressuring Seward to do something to alleviate the plight of British manufacturing. A similar dynamic played out in France, the German states and everywhere else in Europe where industry was dependent on American cotton.[2]

Russia also relied heavily on American cotton for its nascent textile industry. Yet from the outset it showed solidarity with the Union cause. Early on in the war, Russia had offered to mediate between North and South. When that effort failed, the tsar pledged total support for the Union. 'This Union has been fruitful,' Foreign Minister Alexander Gorchakov wrote in a letter to Seward. 'It has exhibited to the world the spectacle of prosperity without example in the annals of history ... This Union is not simply, in our eyes, an element essential to the universal *political* equilibrium. It constitutes ... a natural community of interests and of sympathies.'

These sentiments were manna from heaven for the State Department. At the moment of the United States' greatest crisis, its diplomats were overjoyed to have the support of one of the great powers of Europe. The war years saw a flourishing of Russo-American friendship, of which the 1863 visit of the Imperial Navy to New York was but the most eye-catching example. American statesmen began to believe that Russia might emerge as the United States' chief ally against British meddling, reviving talk of a united front against London that had been circulating since the Crimean War.

Some of Seward's ambassadors went further, insisting on seeing in Tsarist Russia a nation on a parallel trajectory to the United States. Was Alexander II not seeking to end serfdom much as Lincoln sought to abolish slavery? Were the two vast and largely rural nations not moving in lockstep towards greater levels of industrialization and urbanization? 'Alexander is making speedy progress towards liberalism,' the American ambassador wrote breathlessly from Moscow. 'He increases the freedom of the press – the freedom of discussion in the senate; and the spread of schools; of telegraphs and railroads, and internal steamers – and places the enslaved millions in a new stage of progress.'

Seward was grateful for Russian support, praising the 'prudent, just and friendly course' of Russian policy and declaring that Russia 'has our friendship, in every case, in preference to any other European power'.

It was, however, on the plane of realpolitik rather than friendship that Seward reciprocated the tsar's support. In 1863 the Poles, subjects of the Russian Empire, attempted to slough off tsarist rule. Their uprising lasted eighteen months and caught the imagination of liberal Europe. France took the lead in organizing support for them and in April 1863 the French foreign minister asked Seward that the United States join France, England and Austria in issuing a declaration to Tsar Alexander II on the Polish question. Privately Seward praised the 'gallant' Poles and their bid for national self-determination. Publicly, however, he could not criticize one of the United States' few reliable allies. Fifteen years before, he had hailed Kossuth and damned Russian absolutism. Now, at the height of the Civil War – in which thousands of Polish-Americans were fighting – Seward chose power over principle. 'This is a request to which we can never accede,' he replied. Russia appreciated Seward's complicity. Gorchakov had Seward's letter widely published as proof that Russia enjoyed the moral support of the American republic.[3]

If the war years brought Seward into closer contact with the Russian diplomatic corps, then the years immediately afterwards drew his attention to the Russian far east. The conduit for this flourishing interest in the obscure eastern territories of the tsar's empire was a fellow New Yorker named Perry McDonough Collins.

A classic product of mid-century America, Collins had gone to California during the Gold Rush years and subsequently became involved in the American Russian Commercial Company. Through that enterprise, he came to believe that America's next frontier lay across the Pacific in the Amur River Valley. A convincing salesman, Collins had himself appointed United States Commercial Agent for the Amur River in 1856 and embarked on an epic journey from St Petersburg to Kamchatka that made him, inter alia, the first foreigner to descend the Amur to its mouth. Collins's explorations convinced him that the region was an untapped source of commercial wealth for the United States. The key to exploiting this wealth was a telegraph line.

In the 1850s there was considerable excitement about the proposed transatlantic telegraph. Collins sought to challenge that scheme with a different route: one that would run from St Petersburg, across Siberia to the Amur River, then up to and across the Bering Strait, before descending through Sitka, Vancouver, Astoria and at last to San Francisco, having covered a distance of 14,000 miles.* The line would be a Russo-American partnership, with each country building their portion, before eventually joining up at the Bering Strait.

Collins pitched the idea to Seward, tempting him with the prospect of 'five to ten millions of people' clamouring for 'the products of our shops and looms, our engines, machinery and implements'. Seward immediately grasped the significance of the scheme, not just in its commercial potential, but as a means of disintermediating Britain and putting the United States at the centre of global commerce. Seward championed Collins's cause in Congress, and in July 1864 a bill was passed allocating funds to the project. By October workmen from Western Union had begun work on the American portion of the line. By the end of 1865, the wire was strung across British Columbia and a small army of Russian labourers was in Siberia working towards the Bering Strait. 'We know no such word as fail,' Collins told a meeting in New York in December 1866. In Asia the 'slumbering millions of the human race await our magnetic touch', and there 'commerce in vast proportions will be made quick and soon grow to man's estate, by the life-giving principle of the telegraph. Half the population of the whole world will be tributary to us as we pass through Asia to Europe; our network of wires radiating from the grand trunk line will penetrate the great cities and marts of commerce, bringing to us the daily wants, ideas and commerce of the heretofore Eastern world.'[4]

These sentiments could have hardly been more aligned with Seward's own. Sadly for both men, the Collins line was not to be. His scheme collapsed eight months later, on 27 July 1866, when the SS *Great Eastern* arrived at Heart's Content in Newfoundland dragging behind it Cyrus Field's telegraph cable. Britain and the United States were now

---

\* Collins later conceived of two additional branch lines of the main telegraph. One would continue from San Francisco down the Pacific coast of Mexico, Central and South America and then loop around Tierra del Fuego and complete the circuit by travelling the extent of the Atlantic coast as well. He also entered negotiations for a Chinese branch that would veer off from the Amur and head south to Macao via Peking, Nanking, Shanghai, Ningpo and Amoy. These negotiations were scotched when the Chinese expressed fears that the electric lines would 'interrupt the "fung-shue" or streams of good luck passing over the country'. But Collins persisted and eventually the Chinese granted permission. Collins claimed that if all three lines were built then it would 'bring the commerce of the whole world upon the "Russian Extension Line"'.

connected across the Atlantic. The need for an alternative line across Siberia vanished.

Work on the Collins line lasted for another few months before finally coming to a halt on 24 March 1867 – just as William Seward was closing in on a deal to buy Alaska.[5]

## THE TWO-HUNDRED-THOUSAND-DOLLAR TELEGRAM

In April 1866, an assassin tried to murder Tsar Alexander II in St Petersburg. This was the first time in Russian history that a Romanov tsar had been the victim of an assassination attempt, and though it failed, it profoundly traumatized the regime.

It also served to strengthen Russo-American relations at a crucial moment. Almost exactly a year before, Abraham Lincoln had been assassinated at Ford's Theatre in Washington. Memories of their own national trauma intensified American reactions to the attempt on Alexander's life. Congress drew up a joint resolution that expressed horror at the attempt and relief at the tsar's survival, and took the occasion to celebrate the tsar's various achievements, including the emancipation of the serfs. President Johnson then appointed Gustavus Vasa Fox, the assistant secretary of the navy, to travel across the Atlantic to deliver the resolution to the tsar in person. Fox arrived in St Petersburg in August and travelled to the Peterhof, where he read out the message to the tsar with great solemnity. The tsar replied in kind, expressing his joy 'at the friendly relations existing between Russia and the United States' and his conviction that 'the national fraternity would be perpetual'.

Afterwards, the American delegation was treated to dinner, music and a tour of the vast grounds. While exploring the Peterhof's gardens, the Americans came across an oak tree that their guide told them had been grown 'from an acorn taken from the tree that shades the tomb of Washington'. 'Our officers surrounded the young tree with a feeling akin to religious sentiment,' one member of the American delegation wrote. 'Each reverently plucked a leaf from its branches to carry home with him, to testify how profound is the homage paid in Russia to the memory of the great founder of our republic.'[6]

Shortly after Fox's visit, Eduard de Stoeckl returned home to St Petersburg for one of his periodic meetings with his superiors. Talk turned to Russian America. Everyone agreed that the colony had become a burden on the empire. Sitka was an embarrassing backwater ('Of all the dirty and wretched places that I have ever seen,' George Simpson wrote of it, 'Sitka is pre-eminently the most wretched and most dirty'), the dingy headquarters of a fur trade in terminal decline. The Russian-American Company paid out a minuscule dividend of one ruble twenty-five kopecks in 1866. It owed vast sums to the Russian government and consumed vast sums in imperial spending on its defence. When the company's charter expired that year, it was not renewed. A hundred and twenty years of Russian fur trading in the American Northwest sputtered out ingloriously.

At the same time as the economic basis for Russian colonization vanished, events in Asia removed the strategic need for a continued Russian presence. Following the Second Opium War in 1860, the Qing Empire signed the Convention of Peking with Russia, France and Britain. The Russian portion of the treaty handed the tsar control of 400,000 square miles of Outer Manchuria, and with it control of the Amur River, Kamchatka and a long stretch of shoreline along the Sea of Japan. Russia had now secured control of its far east. There was no longer any use for an outer chain of Pacific colonies to act as a buffer around the hitherto imperilled core – especially when the last remaining of those colonies, Russian America, was burdensome, bankrupt and one gold strike away from being swamped by American adventurers.[7]

Stoeckl encouraged this view. He repeated his fears of a Mormon invasion or a hypothetical Alaskan Gold Rush and stressed the very real – and to Russia very dangerous – spirit of Manifest Destiny that animated American policy. 'Our role is to dominate the East,' he told Gorchakov. 'The one of the United States is to exercise an absolute control over the American continent.' It would be better to reach a cordial arrangement now than risk a future confrontation. 'In the march of progress that destiny has bequeathed to Russia and the United States,' Stoeckl continued, 'the two nations will advance without their paths being blocked, without exciting any jealousies, without their interests conflicting.' His position was a variation of the more chauvinist view expressed by Grand Duke Constantine: 'Russia must endeavour as far as possible to become stronger in her centre, in those fundamentally Russian regions which constitute her main power in population and in faith.' Russia's American periphery had exhausted its utility and could now be sold off to win American friendship, spite the British in Canada and pay down imperial debts. In March 1867, Stoeckl returned to Washington with instructions to accept no less than $5 million in gold for the sale of Russian America.[8]

Whether or not Seward knew about these developments is not clear. It is quite possible that word of Russia's willingness to sell was in the wind; it is equally possible that Seward's rabid desire for territorial expansion ensured that the possibility of acquisition remained foremost in his mind.

The norms of nineteenth-century diplomacy, however, prevented either man from acting impetuously. Fortunately for Seward, an opening had presented itself. The legislature of the Washington Territory had sent a memorial to President Johnson asking him to secure them access to fisheries in Russian America. This request gave Seward his entrée. When Stoeckl called on Seward on Monday, 11 March, as was customary after a long absence, the two men discussed outstanding official business. Seward raised the Washington memorial. Stoeckl demurred, saying that Russia could not grant access to American fishermen. Seward then hazarded a question: would the tsar consider selling the whole territory and be rid of the burden once for all? Stoeckl replied that the tsar was willing and ready to do so.

Seward went off to obtain presidential permission. This was secured at a cabinet meeting the next day. On Thursday, 14 March, Seward and Stoeckl met again and began discussing prices, with Seward venturing $5.5 million and Stoeckl holding out for more. With growing excitement, Seward went back to the cabinet and secured an agreement on general terms and permission to offer as much as $7 million for Alaska and the Aleutian Islands. Armed with cabinet approval, Seward flung himself into two weeks of top-secret negotiations with Stoeckl, the two men discussing every possible issue of interest between their two nations as they edged their way towards a deal. On 25 March, the two men agreed on a final price of $7.2 million. Seward was so impatient to transact that he insisted that Stoeckl wire St Petersburg with the terms immediately to expedite the sale.

Given the exorbitant cost of using the transatlantic line, Stoeckl asked the Americans to cover the cost. This was a wise decision. A few months later, the State Department received a bill for $10,000 for this single telegram, equivalent to over $200,000 today.

It was costly but effective. Within days, St Petersburg had assented to the deal and on the evening of 29 March 1867, Stoeckl went to Seward's home to deliver the news. Seward was playing whist with his family when Stoeckl was announced. 'I have a dispatch, Mr Seward,' Stoeckl said, 'from my Government by cable. The Emperor gives his consent to the cession. Tomorrow, if you like, I will come to the department, and we can enter upon the treaty.' 'Why wait till tomorrow, Mr Stoeckl?' Seward replied. 'Let us make the treaty tonight.' 'But your department is closed. You have no clerks, and my secretaries are scattered about the town,' Stoeckl said. 'Never mind that,' said Seward, 'if you can muster your legation together before midnight, you will find me awaiting you at the department, which will be open and ready for business.'

Seward had good reason for haste as Congress was about to adjourn for several months and he could not risk losing this opportunity.

That night, the candles in the State Department burned until daybreak as clerks and diplomats scrambled to get the treaty language prepared. By four o'clock on Saturday morning, Seward and Stoeckl had both signed the sale of Russian America to the United States. It was then to the Capitol, where senators preparing to end the session were surprised to hear of a message from the president and stunned to learn it contained a purchase of Russian America. 'I thought we were going to have another hack at Andy Johnson today,' one senator was heard to say to another, 'but it looks now as if we were going to vote for the biggest and most unheard of thing the Administration has done yet.'[9]

Six hours after the treaty had been signed, and two hours before the session was to close, the Senate agreed to hold a special session starting on 1 April to consider the transaction.

Seward now looked to Senator Charles Sumner of Massachusetts, chair of the Committee on Foreign Relations, to shepherd the treaty through the Senate. Sumner had made his name as a convinced abolitionist and he heartily loathed President Johnson, who he viewed as overly sympathetic to the defeated Confederacy. Sumner was not inclined to give Johnson a political victory. Nor was the committee he chaired convinced of the purchase's merits. 'Must have been whiskey not champagne that made this treaty,' quipped one member.

But Sumner was able to lay aside one enmity to pursue another. He had never forgiven Britain for aiding and abetting the Confederacy during the Civil War. He saw the purchase of Russian America as a way of diminishing British influence in the Pacific and of encircling north-western Canada with United States' territory.

Sumner ably supported the cause of ratification in the Senate. He dwelt on the importance of Alaska's almost 7,000 miles of coastline to American fishermen and whalers. Like Seward, he argued that the acquisition would further American penetration into Asia and capture a greater share of 'those ancient realms of fabulous wealth'. 'To unite the east of Asia with the west of America is the aspiration of commerce,' he declared, and that was reason enough to support a measure that would add to 'the unity, power, and grandeur of the Republic'.

Glancing back at the revolution, Sumner noted that as important as 'the extension of dominion is the extension of republican institutions'. In adding Russian America to the United States, they were acting in harmony with their revolutionary forebears who 'overthrew the kingly power' a century before. By peacefully removing the Tsar's colours from remote shores of the Northwest, their generation was continuing the project of the founders. 'By it we dismiss one more monarch from this continent,' Sumner told the Senate. 'One by one they have retired; first France; then Spain; then France again; and now Russia; all giving way to that absorbing unity which is declared in the national motto, *E pluribus Unum*.'[10]

On 9 April, the Senate voted 37–2 in favour of ratification. The next day Americans learned that their government had paid $7.2 million for 586,412 square miles, or roughly half a cent an acre for an area twice the size of Texas, three times the size of California and nine times the size of New England. The last, the most unforeseen and the strangest of the United States' continental expansions was complete.

Perhaps the most unusual aspect of the affair was that there was no name for this mammoth new addition to the Union. The treaty language simply referred to it as the 'Russian Possessions in North America'. This was a gift to the newspapers, who had a fine time suggesting possible names for the new territory. Sitka, Yukon, Unalaska, Behring and Aleutia were all mooted. More colourful were Norland, Polario, Frigidia, Behringia. Others offered names as ludicrous as they judged Seward's purchase of an icy, empty waste: Johnson's Polar Bear Garden, Seward's Icebox, Walrussia. One wit suggested Johnsonia, Damlongwayoff and Eversofaroff, and even dreamt up a coat of arms featuring an 'iceberg illuminated with the rays of the aurora borealis, a walrus rampant, and the Universal Yankee sitting on a barrel of whale oil, whittling the north pole with a jack-knife'. Eventually Seward ended the ribaldry by christening the territory with the name it still bears: Alaska.[11]

The Alaska Purchase was the largest single territorial acquisition since the Louisiana Purchase, larger even than the vast Mexico cession. Both those earlier expansions had taken years of wrangling to finalize. Alaska, by contrast, entered the Union swiftly and with little discussion or ceremony. On 18 October 1867, only seven months after Seward and Stoeckl had first discussed the possibility of a sale, a small group of Russian and American officials gathered round a flagpole in Sitka. The tsar was represented by the head of the Russian-American Company, Prince Dmitry Petrovich Maksutov; the United States by Major General Lovell H. Rousseau. There were no theatrics, no long speeches, no unusual occurrences at the moment of the United States' final continental addition. Russian and American battleships in the bay exchanged salutes as the imperial colours were lowered. An American flag was produced and raised to another salute. Then the Russian commissioner stepped forward and said, 'General Rousseau, by authority from His Majesty the Emperor of Russia, I transfer to the United States, the Territory of Alaska.' Rousseau accepted the transfer, the ceremony ended and Alaska became American.[12]

### THE VIEW FROM SITKA

Seward retired from public life in March 1869 and in June he decided to do what he always did when he had the opportunity: he went travelling. He set out west from Auburn, heading by train to Niagara, Detroit, Chicago, before crossing the Mississippi and travelling to Council Bluffs, Iowa. The line west followed the course of the Platte through Nebraska, but they halted at Fort Kearny in the middle of the night due to rumours of hostile Indians ahead. Journeying onwards, they entered Wyoming and that evening stopped at Cheyenne, where a delegation met Seward with a brass band and rounds of speeches. The next day their journey continued. At Salt Lake City, Seward met the Mormon leader Brigham Young, who in a previous life had been a carpenter in Auburn and had built Seward's fireplace. In Sacramento, Seward visited the ruins of Fort Sutter, the Chinese quarter, the vineyards and a cocoonery for silkworms. The party transferred to the steamboat *Yosemite* and travelled downriver, reaching San Francisco on 2 July, where Seward was treated to an ecstatic reception. 'The popular enthusiasm was irrepressible,' one witness wrote. 'It found voice in salvos of artillery, the turnout of military companies, pyrotechnic displays, the unfurling of flags to the breeze, the plaudits of excited multitudes ... the streets were thronged with people anxious to catch a glimpse of the man who had done so much to glorify and aggrandize his country.' Seward was obliged to present himself to the adoring crowd from his hotel balcony and was mobbed by visitors the next day. That week he was feted by the city at banquets and balls paid for by local business magnates. After the celebrations had died down, Seward expressed a wish to visit Alaska.[13]

A wealthy admirer arranged for him to use the steamer *Active*, and on 13 July Seward's party cast off, passed through the Golden Gate and headed up the coast. A week later, they entered the Strait of Juan de Fuca, where they paused to tour Puget Sound. Boarding the *Active* again, they continued north through the Strait of Georgia, crossed Queen Charlotte Sound and entered the Hecate Strait. For a week they journeyed through an archipelago of islands, sometimes pressed around by an impenetrable forest of firs and spruce, at others alone on open expanses of water as clear and calm as a Swiss lake. One morning the passengers came on deck to discover that the captain had got lost. Fortunately, several Chinook-speaking Indians were in the neighbourhood. Within a few hours they had put them back on course. In gratitude, Seward distributed some gifts among them: a cravat, an old frock coat, a pair of pantaloons. The recipient of the last 'regarded them with satisfaction, but with evident doubt as to the way they were to be worn. Finally he tied them round his neck in a huge knot like a cravat – and joined in the burst of merriment from the deck above.' They continued on and on 30 July steamed into Sitka, where the Stars and Stripes snapped in the breeze over Castle Hill.[14]

Sitka was as ramshackle as ever, little changed since the days of Russian rule. Colourful, red-roofed houses crowded around an Orthodox church with an onion dome that gleamed at all hours of the day in these summer months when the sun never set. In town, Tinglits mixed with soldiers, lumberjacks, fishermen 'and traders and travellers clad in the latest style of Montgomery Street, San Francisco'. It was a

Saturday and Seward was surprised to hear the church bells toll for the Sunday service. Upon inquiring, he learned that the Russians kept time with St Petersburg and so were twenty-four hours ahead of Western Standard Time. Conforming to local custom, Seward attended the Orthodox service and the next day worshipped at the Lutheran church that followed the American calendar.

The next week was spent exploring the coastline to the north, visiting local fur-trading enterprises, dropping in on Orthodox prelates and admiring the totem poles in every Indian village. They were with some Chilkat Indians on 7 August when a solar eclipse was due to occur. The Americans busied themselves with taking astronomical measurements and fiddling with telescopes while the Chilkat looked on in bemusement. Afterwards they approached Seward and asked for an illustration of how eclipses occurred. Seward did his best, using a cabin lamp for the sun, an orange for the earth, and an apple for the moon.

> When he had finished, he inquired if the chiefs had understood his explanation? After conference, as before, the reply came back: 'The chiefs have understood much, though not all, the great Tyee has told them. They understand him as saying that the eclipse was produced by the Great Spirit, and not by man. Since he says so, they will believe it. They have noticed, however, that the Great Spirit generally does whatever the "Boston men" want him to.'

They returned to Sitka. Before he departed for California, Seward gave a speech. He congratulated the new Alaskans for breaking this latest frontier and propounded on the bright future that lay ahead for the territory. Alaska was more beautiful than 'the Alps, the Apennines, the Alleghenies, or the Rocky Mountains', he declared, and filled with resources enough to draw immigrants from across Europe and the United States. The whole world, he predicted, would soon be dependent on Alaska's bounty. This development, he noted in passing, would wipe out the local tribes who here, as elsewhere, 'merely serve the turn until civilized white men come'. In Seward's mind, this was all part of the great cycle of improvement.

Within the period of my own recollection, I have seen twenty new States added to the eighteen which before that time constituted the American Union, and I now see, besides Alaska, ten Territories in a forward condition of preparation for entering into the same great political family. I have seen in my own time not only the first electric telegraph, but even the first railroad and the first steamboat invented by man. And even on this present voyage of mine, I have fallen in with the first steamboat, still afloat, that thirty-five years ago lighted her fires on the Pacific ocean. These, citizens of Sitka, are the guaranties, not only that Alaska has a future, but that that future has already begun.[15]

The next day, Seward obtained some souvenirs, among them a bald eagle that he had stuffed and sent back to Auburn, and then steamed back to California to continue his travels.

The bright future Seward had predicted for Alaska had not arrived by the time that he died in 1872. In fact, it did not arrive in the lifetime of any American alive at the time of its purchase. As late as 1940, Alaska had fewer than 100,000 inhabitants. Its slow growth meant that Alaska had to wait until 1959 to enter the Union and was, and will likely remain, the last territory ever to attain statehood.

This reflects Alaska's singular career within the United States. The sale of Russian America was the final and the most extravagantly eccentric episode in the country's westward expansion. It was not obvious at the time, but Seward's purchase was the last great feat of eighteenth-century diplomacy. A handful of men in Washington and St Petersburg coolly brokered the sale of an immense chunk of the earth's surface without a trace of sentimentality and with negligible democratic input. Three years later, Otto von Bismarck would unite Germany and usher in the age of nationalism and mass democratic politics. In this new world it was impossible for diplomats to haggle over sovereign territory with scant regard for public opinion. Even Tsarist Russia was transformed by this revolution. In 1867 there had been no domestic opposition within Russia to the sale; within two decades, Russian nationalists would be loudly bemoaning the transaction. Some still do.

Ironically, in the same period many Americans came to question the merit of buying Russian America. The Alaska Purchase became known as 'Seward's Folly', and whenever politicians wanted to mock some new scheme for territorial aggrandizement they would point to the Alaska Purchase for proof of the foolishness of acquiring territory for territory's sake. If Alaska was destined to be the last of America's great continental acquisitions, it wasn't just because Canada and Mexico weren't selling, but also because Americans weren't buying. In the 1870s, America began belatedly to urbanize and industrialize, smallholdings were swallowed up by commercial farms and ambitious young people looked to the cities for adventure, not the frontier. Increasingly, the rich tradition of American pioneering was celebrated in word more than deed. The market for public lands dried up. Fewer people believed their fortunes lay out west; almost nobody believed they resided in Alaska.

At the same time, a technological and economic revolution upturned the calculations of American statesmen. Railroads, canals and liners – and later aeroplanes, destroyers and aircraft carriers – changed geopolitics. As Seward had foreseen, power was now concentrated in key choke points. It was no longer necessary to control swathes of empty land to project power. Mastery of the globe could be managed through a web of harbours, military bases and coaling posts connected by telegrams, shipping lanes and credit lines. This was a transition from continentalism to pointillism that made the Alaska Purchase look less like a geopolitical masterstroke and more like a *folie de grandeur*.

The sale of Russian America was the product of two trends that were on the verge of exhaustion. Alaska was brought into the Union on the last wave of a historical tide that was about to recede forever.[16]

It is not surprising, then, that for all its size, Alaska looms so small in the American imagination. Aloof from so many of the forces that powered the creation of the Lower Forty-Eight, it has ploughed its own furrow. Alaska has all of the ten tallest mountains in the United States but none of its major cities. It is the United States' greatest natural reserve and is also home to the largest oilfield on the continent. It is the state with the largest native population and the only state which pays people – via the Alaska Permanent Fund – to live there. It was the last state to practise homesteading and the only part of the continental United States to be occupied during World War II, when the Imperial Japanese Army occupied some of the Aleutian Islands – an extraordinary event that has left no impression on popular memory of the war.

Seward's contemporaries would not have been surprised to learn that Alaska would remain stubbornly at the periphery of the United States. Even in their own time it was apparent that, Seward's wild predictions aside, Alaska would stand apart from the main currents of American life. In the years after the purchase, there were so few white Americans living there that the army withdrew entirely and the territory was left unorganized, unexplored and largely forgotten. At one point there was talk of turning the region into a penal colony – an American Siberia. Almost as an afterthought, in 1884 Congress enacted the Organic Act that provided for courts and judges to operate in the territory for the first time, a mere seventeen years after it had become sovereign American territory. For the average American, Alaska had little resonance. It was not until 1896 and the discovery of gold in the Klondike River, on the Canadian borderlands, that Americans became aware of the region. The Alaskan Gold Rush sent tens of thousands into the last great American wilderness in the final years of the nineteenth century. Among them was a hotel manager and brothelkeeper from Kallstadt in Bavaria named Frederick Trump.

CONCLUSION

# The Scramble for America

> America was bred in a cabin: this is not a reproach; for the origin is most honourable: but as she has exchanged her hovel of unhewn logs for a framed building, and that again for a mansion of brick, some of her cabin habits have been unconsciously retained.
>
> MORRIS BIRKBECK

Who lives where is the primordial political question. In the century after independence, the United States answered that question decisively. In 1776 both the republic and its territorial limits were little more than aspirations. By 1867 it dominated the North American continent, commanded both the Atlantic and the Pacific oceans, had nearly unchallenged primacy in the western hemisphere and was positioned for global hegemony in the twentieth century.

America's territorial expansion was so rapid and so complete that it appeared unchallengeable and consequently inevitable. It is not surprising that Americans attributed their seemingly irresistible western expansion to Providence. While this book has largely steered clear of Manifest Destiny as an explanation of American aggrandizement, its fundamental thesis merits discussion. In our telling, American continentalism was fitful, contentious and contingent. Far from being bestowed on the United States by God or Fate, the republic's western lands were won over the course of a century of hard-nosed diplomacy, war and threats of war, bribery, purchase, bluster and deceit. Manifest

Destiny was a powerful device for evading the gritty reality of how the continental United States came into being. However, in its serene confidence in the inevitability of the westward march of American power, it compels the question: how could it have been any different?

## CROSSROADS AND COUNTERFACTUALS

In hindsight, we can identify four moments when American expansion could have been checked. The first is the least interesting. The Alaska Purchase was the result of pure happenstance. It is easy to imagine any number of scenarios in which Russia never made the offer and America never sought it. But the stakes were and remain low. Had Alaska remained Russian, the outcome would have been a frostier Cold War, perhaps, but the fate of a single polar province would not have had world-historical significance.

By contrast, the Louisiana Purchase was the decisive moment in America's expansion and arguably the most significant moment of the nineteenth century. It was also a case study in historical contingency. A remarkably disparate array of forces and personalities came together in the spring of 1803 to conclude the sale. Any number of them could have individually or in combination worked to derail the deal. And yet the Louisiana Purchase was the product more of calculation than caprice. Napoleon knew that control of the Mississippi Valley was a core, non-negotiable American interest. He also knew that the precarious peace in Europe was about to break down. Had Napoleon not sold New Orleans in 1803, then Jefferson would have taken it by force in 1804. How exactly the rest of Louisiana would have fallen into American hands is unclear. But once the Stars and Stripes flew over New Orleans, it was only a matter of time until American sovereignty extended up all the tributaries of the Mississippi River.

A similar case can be made for the Peace of Paris in 1783. That conference should not have produced a United States that stretched from the Atlantic to the eastern shore of the Mississippi. America's own allies wanted the fledgling republic hemmed in by the Appalachians. Had they succeeded, the United States would have remained a coastal power. Settlers would still have gone west but might have adapted themselves to Spanish rule or formed precarious breakaway states in the Ohio Valley. In the end, the British decision to gift the new nation control of the Ohio Valley rescued the United States from this fate. Shelburne's choice of trade over dominion was consistent with British policy and vindicated by Britain's subsequent commercial dominance. The decision to strengthen the position of their rebellious former colonies was a triumph of expediency over emotion – and the formative moment in American continentalism.

The fourth and final turning point hinged not on international relations but on domestic politics. The election of 1844 was decided by the votes of a few thousand disaffected abolitionists in New York. The Democrats ran on Texas and Oregon. The Whigs were lukewarm on both. Had the election gone to Clay and not Polk, then the mammoth territorial expansion of 1846–48 would not have happened.

All the same, the Oregon Question would have resolved itself in much the same way under Clay as under Polk, but the shape of the Southwest would have been a different matter altogether.

Clay would not have fostered the crisis along the Rio Grande that Polk precipitated in the spring of 1846. He would have accepted the Texas annexation as a fait accompli and would have offered to purchase the harbour of San Francisco – and probably would have been rebuffed. Relations with Mexico would have been tense, but the grand panoply of Polk's war with Mexico – the siege of Veracruz, Zachary Taylor's stand at Buena Vista, Winfield Scott cantering across the Zócalo – would never have occurred. It is quite possible that Arizona, Nevada, Utah and much of New Mexico would remain Mexican to this day.*

Counterfactuals run both ways. When considering events that happened that might not have, it is helpful to remember events that did *not* happen that could well have come to pass. The most obvious case is Cuba, which the United States salivated over for the better part of a century, at one point offering Spain $130 million for the island. It is as

---

* The complicating factor was gold. John Sutter was in California well before the 1844 election and he would have found gold on his property irrespective of whether war broke out. The California gold rush would still have happened. It seems improbable that any American president could have resisted intervention when tens of thousands of their citizens flooded into a poorly controlled, geopolitically sensitive province filled with mineral wealth on the United States' doorstep. The result may have been a Mexican-American War in California in the late 1840s or an uncontested military occupation justified under the pretext of keeping order and with the actual aim of securing the gold, obtaining the port of San Francisco and pre-empting any similar move by Great Britain.

unlikely that Cuba stayed outside the Union as it is that Alaska became a part of it – and yet that is what happened.

Other examples include the northern portions of Mexico, the southern portions of Canada and various chunks of Central America, most notably those around the Darién Gap.

These failures point towards a general theme in American expansion: the United States had a difficult time absorbing regions that were already thickly settled and politically organized. And in almost every instance where America failed to claim territory, imperial calculation played a decisive role. War with Mexico was one matter; a direct conflict with a European empire was quite another. Fear of antagonizing one or other of the great powers was the only reliable restraint on American avarice. 'The policy of our neighbour to the south of us has always been aggressive,' one Canadian writer observed in 1865. 'There has always been a desire among them for the acquisition of new territory ... They coveted Florida, and seized it; they coveted Louisiana, and purchased it; they coveted Texas, and stole it; and then they picked a quarrel with Mexico, which ended by their getting California ... had we [Canada] not had the strong arm of England over us, we should not now have had a separate existence.'[1]

## NEW VISTAS?

When I began work on this book in 2020 I believed that American expansionism belonged to the past. I was wrong. During his third presidential run, Donald Trump began discussing the annexation of Greenland. After his victory, he added Panama and Canada to his wish list. These claims were repeated during his inauguration, a speech also notable for being the first time the phrase 'Manifest Destiny' was ever used in an inaugural address.

How much of this is sincere and how much of it is bluster is hard to discern. But it has resurrected the prospect of renewed American expansion and has raised with it interesting questions about the project of Trumpism, the strategic imperatives of the United States and the role of territorial aggrandizement in American political culture and in the American imagination.

Trump's loudly proclaimed interest in adding to the United States' land mass might be shocking in the twenty-first century, but it has deep roots in the eighteenth and nineteenth centuries. In that era, size mattered and the rate of territorial expansion was seen as a gauge of the health of the revolutionary experiment. 'The successful establishment of a republican government,' William Seward said, 'adapted to an expanded state, is itself a demonstration of national greatness.' It is not a mystery why a movement guided by the revivalist slogan 'Make America Great Again' would find inspiration in the history of American continentalism.

From the perspective of Trump and his followers, expansion would solve several problems at once. Foregrounded in their arguments are strategic questions: securing the Panama Canal, countering Russian or Chinese influence in the Arctic, protecting sea lanes and strategic choke points. These are credible positions but not sufficient to explain why America needs to occupy land rather than lease airbases, deepen alliances or pursue any one of the other, more conventional, paths available to the world's leading power.

Answers to this riddle can be found in America's expansionist past. The United States expanded in an era of multipolarity. Its territorial acquisitions were made possible because the European powers were either busy fighting with one another or busy recovering from wars just finished. 'The period which elapsed from the year 1789 to 1814,' Luis de Onís reminded the Spanish king in 1821, 'was as flattering and fortunate for the Anglo-Americans, as it was dark and disastrous to the nations of Europe.' Onís was simply telling his royal master what all good strategists know: that periods of flux are periods of opportunity. The United States benefited from the demise of imperial Spain, just as it benefited from Napoleon's need for ready cash in 1803, and would continue to benefit from rupture and distress in Mexico, Britain, China and Russia over the coming decades.

A fluid and uncertain global scene encouraged expediency and opportunism. It also cultivated prudence: it was better to have and to hold than to risk the potential encroachments of a rival at some future date. The acquisitiveness of continentalism was always balanced out by a defensive strain of thinking. Once the United States became a superpower in 1945 it could afford to forget these hard-won lessons. Its military superiority was so great and its economic dominance so insurmountable that it could move confidently on the world stage. There were simply no real rivals. At the time of Jimmy Carter's decision to hand over the Panama Canal, China's GDP per capita was $200; the United States' was a shade under $10,000. It was unimaginable then that China, or anyone else, could pose a threat to American interests in Latin America.

Times have changed. The renewed interest in territorial expansion is a tacit acknowledgement of the return of multipolarity. American statesmen are beginning to rediscover the use of muscles not flexed since the days of Adams, Polk and Seward.[2]

Unshackled from hegemony, the United States will be free to act with bracing cynicism on the world stage. Self-interest will determine policy. The decline of the American-led order, the weakness of former allies and the proliferation of new rivals will all work to justify stridency in foreign relations. Should the United States seek more territory, it will do so in the knowledge that other countries are already on manoeuvres. In the last decade, Turkey, Israel, Azerbaijan and Russia have all claimed new territory. China is perennially on the verge of invading Taiwan.

These realities of twenty-first-century geopolitics will excuse America's return to its old nineteenth-century habits. At the same time, the acquisitions of that earlier period will continue to provide rationalizations for new purchases in the present. One of the recurring themes of political debate in the nineteenth century was of the apparent uselessness of the land acquired. Louisiana was mocked as trackless waste. The Mexican cession was scorned as a desert. Oregon east of the Cascades was damned as arid and uninhabitable. Alaska was spurned as a frozen tundra fit only for walruses and polar bears. Today those regions produce vast quantities of oil, lumber, metals and natural gas.

And they are still revealing new bounties. Just in the period in which this book was written not one but two mammoth lithium reserves (a material vital for the production of electric cars) were found in the United States. Forty million metric tons, worth $1.5 trillion, was found in the McDermitt Caldera along the Oregon–Nevada border. The same year, another deposit was found in the Smackover Formation in south-western Arkansas containing enough to replace all lithium imports into the United States. Amid a global hunt for lithium, the United States found two major sources in a single year in lands secured for the country by James Polk and Thomas Jefferson almost two centuries before. These kinds of discoveries will legitimize further expansion into areas as superficially unpromising as Greenland.

Achieving autarchy, or something close to it, is one of Trump's goals and flows naturally from his suspicion of free trade. But securing resources through sovereign ownership also serves another crucial policy aspiration: to retreat from the United States' position as the global policeman. Trump's scepticism of NATO, his suspicion of 'forever wars' and his indifference to the fortunes of other countries on other continents is well known. It might seem paradoxical – hypocritical, even – that a retreat into isolationism should be married with aggressive expansionist rhetoric towards America's neighbours. But there is no contradiction here: once again, Trump is simply returning to the nineteenth century.

During the revolutionary era, it was common to refer to the United States as a refuge for those who cherished republican ideals. It was a 'Country establish'd in Freedom', as Benjamin Franklin wrote in 1777, destined to 'become great and glorious, by being the Asylum of all the Oppres'd in Europe, and the Resort of … [those] who love Liberty'. These ideas were repeated in Washington's farewell address and Jefferson's first inaugural. This attitude dominated American thinking for the first half of the nineteenth century. It combined a disgust with the endless manoeuvrings of the European great powers (who Jefferson memorably referred to as 'the cannibals of Europe') with a utopian faith in the capacity of the New World to live in pristine isolation from the Old. As John Quincy Adams put it in an 1822 toast: 'The American Hemisphere, and the Declaration of Independence. A new world of matter for a new world of mind.'[3]

Precisely because they wanted to disengage from Europe, Americans became intensely interested in their near abroad. The United States' attitude towards the western hemisphere combined paranoia with idealism and cynicism. Paranoia, because the United States was encircled by European empires; idealism, because it believed it could absorb those territories into an expanding empire of liberty; cynicism, as it appealed to principle while working ruthlessly in its own self-interest. American was a bastion, an exemplar, the last best hope of mankind. What could not be justified in its defence? Surely its flourishing would ultimately be to the benefit of mankind. Liberty was the highest good and America the freest country – therefore anything that perpetuated American interests served liberty. It was this kind of rationale that produced the Monroe Doctrine – a doctrine that Trump and his followers have revamped and refurbished. Talk of annexing Canada, Panama or Greenland can be understood by reference to this older paradigm whereby the United States acts with a free hand in its immediate neighbourhood to help better isolate itself from the toils of great-power politics overseas.

When Trump used the phrase 'Manifest Destiny' in his inaugural he did not use it in reference to Canada, Panama or Greenland – he used it in reference to Mars. This is part of a pattern whereby Trump evokes the mythos of America's expansionist past as part of a political vocabulary rather than as a political programme. Putting a portrait of James Knox Polk in the Oval Office, renaming Mount McKinley and the Gulf of America, sending envoys to Nuuk and the Canal Zone: these are symbolic acts, not necessarily preludes to renewed expansionism.

In his first State of the Union address following his re-election, Trump returned to this mythic past, reminding Congress that 'our ancestors crossed a vast ocean, strode into the unknown wilderness, and carved their fortunes from the rock and soil of a perilous and very dangerous frontier. They chased our destiny across a boundless continent.' Then he went on to list a wide range of policy goals (territorial expansion not among them), before concluding: 'And, through it all, we are going to rediscover the unstoppable power of the American spirit, and we are going to renew unlimited promise of the American dream.'

This emphasis on spiritual rediscovery is the real reason why Trump makes use of expansionist rhetoric. What is distinctive about the MAGA movement is its pessimism about the condition of the contemporary United States. The main theme of Trump's inaugural address in 2017 was 'American carnage'. His former campaign manager Steve Bannon described the country as having been 'eviscerated' by an 'economic hate crime' perpetrated by 'the swamp' and 'the globalist elite'. Those facing the electorate are careful to situate the average American as victims of a sinister conspiracy; other members of the MAGA coalition are not so delicate. Tech billionaire and ideological fellow-traveller Peter Thiel once told an audience that the United States is 'now exceptional in bad ways: We are exceptionally overweight, we are exceptionally addicted to opioids … we are exceptionally un-self-aware, and we are exceptionally un-self-critical.' Whatever language is used and by whom, the broader message is the same: the American people are in a demoralized and degraded condition. The real function of frontier rhetoric is to remind Americans of their glorious past and to revive the vital energies that powered the Scramble for America before they are dissipated and gone forever.[4]

But what were those energies and what kind of nation did they produce? Critics of expansionism invariably complained that by dispersing the population of the United States into the vast interior, the growth of the country's land mass served to weaken the social bonds between Americans. In the 1830s, Alexis de Tocqueville noted the difference between New England, where communities were rooted and stable, and the Southwest, which was raw frontier. In the latter 'social ties are less ancient ... education is not so widespread and ... the principles of morality, religion and freedom are less happily combined'.[5]

This was a common observation. No less an authority than Andrew Jackson made a similar point during his address to Congress promoting Indian removal. 'Doubtless it will be painful to leave the graves of their fathers,' Jackson said of the decision to deport the tribes westward, 'but what do they more than our ancestors did or than our children are now doing? To better their condition in an unknown land, our forefathers left all that was dear in earthly objects. Our children by thousands, yearly leave the land of their birth to seek new homes in distant regions. Does humanity weep at these painful separations from everything, animate and inanimate, with which the young heart has become entwined?' Jackson concluded that they did not, and that in fact this flux was 'a source of joy'. But the very evocativeness of his language betrayed the truth.[6]

The truth, as Jackson well knew, was that the frontier was a place of loneliness, alienation and anomie. Migrants crossing the Appalachians often burst into tears as they left their old lives behind. One pioneer recalled his grandmother arriving in their new home in the Georgia backcountry – 'a lonesome, out-of-the-world' place – and remarking to her son, 'Whitfield, what do you reckon God made this awful, ugly place for?' Travellers to the frontier regularly encountered families and sometimes solitary individuals eking out primeval existences in almost total isolation. The constant churn of peoples forbade the creation of lasting communities and produced a variety of pathologies.[7]

Perhaps the most pernicious of these is the belief that in America everything is disposable. In my research for this book I often found myself visiting towns that once loomed large in the story of America's westward expansion. Almost without exception they have been hollowed out, with beautiful old buildings left empty (if they had not already been demolished) and grand city centres abandoned. Vast tracts of the interior of the United States have essentially been given up on. The legacy of the frontier spirit seems to be a hostility to permanence. 'Generation after generation, those who intended to remain and prosper where they were have been dispossessed and driven out, or subverted and exploited where they were, by those who were carrying out some version of the search for El Dorado,' the great Kentucky writer Wendell Berry has observed. 'If there is any law that has been consistently operative in American history, it is that the members of any established people or group or community sooner or later become "redskins".'[8]

These are words that Donald Trump and J. D. Vance might ponder when they seek to hitch the wagon of national revival to the jaded mules of the frontier mythos. The story of the creation of the continental United States is an important and consequential one. It has its share of drama and glory; it has a cast of heroes and villains; it has its place in global history and in the narrative of the country founded in 1776. But it is not the only American story. It was as productive of American misery and lassitude as it was of American greatness. The United States has a surfeit of dislocation. Those who are currently flirting with expansionism would do well to remember the advice of Daniel Webster: 'We have a republic, gentlemen, of vast extent and unequalled natural advantages ... Instead of aiming to enlarge its boundaries, let us seek rather to strengthen its union, to draw out its resources, to maintain and improve its institutions of religion and liberty, and thus to push forward its career of prosperity and glory.'[9]

# Notes

**INTRODUCTION: 'The Decisive Fact in the Modern World'**
1. Throughout the book all figures for territorial expansion are taken from the 1975 United States government publication *Historical Statistics of the United States, Colonial Times to 1970* accessible here: https://www.census.gov/library/publications/1975/compendia/hist_stats_colonial-1970.html.
2. 'The Rising Glory of America,' Philip Freneau, 1772; Thomas Jefferson to Archibald Stuart, January 25 1786; Gouverneur Morris to Henry W. Livingston, November 25, 1803.

**PART I: THE OHIO COUNTRY**
**Mr Washington Goes to Ohio**
1. Hugh Cleland, *George Washington in the Ohio Valley* (Pittsburgh: University of Pittsburgh Press, 1955), 80–87; Fred Anderson, *Crucible of War: The Seven Years' War and the Fate of the Empire in British North America, 1754–1766* (Faber & Faber, 2000), 52–61; Colin G. Calloway, *The Indian World of George Washington* (New York: OUP, 2019), 87–90; David Dixon, 'A High Wind Rising: George Washington, Fort Necessity, and the Ohio Country Indians', *Pennsylvania History: A Journal of Mid-Atlantic Studies*, 74/3 (2007).
2. Justin Winsor, *The Westward Movement, 1763–1798* (New York: Houghton Mifflin, 1897), 13; Thomas Hutchins, 'A Topographical Description of Virginia, Pennsylvania, Maryland, and North Carolina', Boston, 1787.
3. Eric Hinderaker, *Elusive Empires: Constructing Colonialism in the Ohio Valley, 1673–1800* (Cambridge: CUP, 1997), 44–45; Richard White, *The Middle Ground: Indians, Empires, and Republics in the Great Lakes Region, 1650–1815* (Cambridge: CUP, 2011), 223–27.
4. Anderson, *Crucible of War*, 17–19; 'Report of the Lords Commissioners for Trades and Plantations ... For a Grant of Lands on the River Ohio',

London, 1772; Nick Bunker, *An Empire on the Edge: How Britain Came to Fight America* (London: Vintage, 2015), 99–103.

5. Calloway, *Indian World*, 42, 51, 63–64, 96, 143; Hinderaker, *Elusive Empires*, 3–12, 16, 27, 40–45; White, *Middle Ground*, 187–88, 200–15, 234; *Christopher Gist's Journals*, ed. William M. Darlington (Pittsburgh: J. R. Weldin, 1893), 41.
6. Anderson, *Crucible of War*, 25–32; Calloway, *Indian World*, 54–67; Douglas Southall Freeman, *George Washington*, i (New York: Scribner's, 1948), 270–76.
7. Darlington, *Gist's Journals*, 67–68; Freeman, *Washington*, i, 278–80.
8. Calloway, *Indian World*, 67–80; Freeman, *Washington*, i, 284–324.
9. Calloway, *Indian World*, 80–82; Freeman, *Washington*, i, 328–34.
10. Freeman, *Washington*, i, 341–44; Anderson, *Crucible of War*, 49.
11. Freeman, *Washington*, i, 356–62; Calloway, *Indian World*, 87–89.
12. Cleland, *Washington in the Ohio Valley*, 80–83, 96–100, 104–14; Freeman, *Washington*, i, 403–15, 441.
13. Anderson, *Crucible of War*, 67; 'The Personal and Family Correspondence of Col. John Carlyle of Alexandria, Virginia', accessed from: https://www.novaparks.com/sites/default/files/John%20Carlyle%201720-1780%20Annotated%20Correspondence_0.pdf.
14. Thomas E. Crocker, *Braddock's March: How the Man Sent to Seize a Continent Changed American History* (Yardley: Westholme, 2009), 26–42, 49; Francis Parkman, *Montcalm and Wolfe* (1884), ch 7.
15. Crocker, *Braddock's March*, 71–74, 79–80, 118; Washington to Robert Orme, 15 Mar. 1755.
16. Anderson, *Crucible of War*, 94–96.
17. Douglas Southall Freeman, *George Washington*, ii (New York: Scribner's, 1948), 56–59.
18. Freeman, *Washington*, ii, 60–61; Crocker, *Braddock's March*, 188–96.
19. Freeman, *Washington*, ii, 68–78; Crocker, *Braddock's March*, 208–25; Anderson, *Crucible of War*, 99–104.
20. Freeman, *Washington*, ii, 79–83.
21. Freeman, *Washington*, ii, 73; Crocker, *Braddock's March*, 227–28.
22. Anderson, *Crucible of War*, 158–63; Freeman, *Washington*, ii, 84, 104, 123, 173, 178, 182; Peter Silver, *Our Savage Neighbors: How Indian War Transformed Early America* (New York: Norton, 2008), 42–43, 49–50, 75–78; 'The Journal of Captain Charles Lewis of the Virginia Regiment', accessed at https://tile.loc.gov/storage-services/public/gdcmassbookdig/journalofcaptainoolewi/journalofcaptainoolewi.pdf; William H. Dillingham, *A Tribute to the Memory of Peter Collinson* (Philadelphia, 1852), 28–30.
23. Freeman, *Washington*, ii, 305–06, 314–15, 322–32; Calloway, *Indian World*, 154–59; Washington to Francis Fauquier, 28 Nov., 2 Dec. 1758.

## All He Surveyed

1. George Washington, *Journal of My Journey Over the Mountains* (Albany: Munsell's, 1892).
2. Andro Linklater, *Measuring America: How the United States was Shaped by the Greatest Land Sale in History* (London: HarperCollins, 2002), 11–12.
3. Washington, *Journey Over the Mountains*.
4. Sarah S. Hughes, *Surveyors and Statesmen: Land Measuring in Colonial Virginia* (Richmond, VA: Virginia Association of Surveyors, 1979), 28, 35; John Love, *Geodæsia, or, The Art of Surveying and Measuring of Land* (London, 1688); John Locke, *Two Treatises of Government* (London, 1689); Stuart Banner, *How the Indians Lost Their Land: Law and Power on the Frontier* (Cambridge, MA: Belknap Press, 2005), 39–46; Edmund Burke, 'Thoughts on the Cause of the Present Discontents', London, 1770.
5. Banner, *How the Indians Lost Their Land*, 29–31; Benjamin Franklin, *Observations Concerning the Increase of Mankind* (Boston, 1751); Hughes, *Surveyors and Statesmen*, 72.
6. Douglas Southall Freeman, *George Washington*, i (New York: Scribner's, 1948), 234, 240, 243–44, 268–69.
7. Bernard Bailyn, *Voyagers to the West: A Passage in the Peopling of America on the Eve of the Revolution* (New York: Vintage, 1988), 48–195, 215; Freeman, *Washington*, i, 270–72, 278–84, 327–34, 351–53; Douglas Southall Freeman, *George Washington*, ii (New York: Scribner's, 1948), 322–32; Douglas R. Cubbison, *The British Defeat of the French in Pennsylvania, 1758: A Military History of the Forbes Campaign Against Fort Duquesne* (McFarland, 2010), 92; Francis Parkman, *Montcalm and Wolfe* (1884), 296–98.

## Long Knives

1. John W. Jordan (ed.), 'Journal of James Kenny, 1761–1763', *Pennsylvania Magazine of History and Biography*, 37/1 (1913); *The Papers of Col. Henry Bouquet*, i, ed. Sylvester K. Stevens and Donald H. Kent (Frontier Forts and Trails Survey, 1940), 116–17, 128, 131, 159; Douglas Southall Freeman, *George Washington*, iii (New York: Scribner's, 1948), 89.
2. Colin G. Calloway, *The Indian World of George Washington* (New York: OUP, 2019), 174–76; Fred Anderson, *Crucible of War: The Seven Years' War and the Fate of the Empire in British North America, 1754–1766* (Faber & Faber, 2000), 537–42; Richard White, *The Middle Ground: Indians, Empires, and Republics in the Great Lakes Region, 1650–1815* (Cambridge: CUP, 2011), 288; A. T. Volwiler, 'William Trent's Journal at Fort Pitt, 1763', *Mississippi Valley Historical Review*, 11/3 (1924), 390–413; Bouquet, *Papers*, i, 161.
3. Peter Silver, *Our Savage Neighbors: How Indian War Transformed Early America* (New York: Norton, 2008), 66–71, 141–204; see also Benjamin Franklin, 'A Narrative of the Late Massacres' (Philadelphia, 1764).

4. Bouquet, *Papers*, i, 148; Calloway, *Indian World*, 154–59; White, *Middle Ground*, 253–54.
5. Anderson, *Crucible of War*, 563–69; Colin G. Calloway, *The Scratch of a Pen: 1763 and the Transformation of North America* (New York: OUP, 2006), 90, 92–98.
6. Washington to Robert Stewart, 27 Apr. 1763.
7. Washington to John Posey, 24 June 1767.
8. Calloway, *Indian World*, 188.
9. Colin G. Calloway, *Pen and Ink Witchcraft: Treaties and Treaty Making in American Indian History* (New York: OUP, 2014), 80–98.
10. George Washington to Charles Washington, 31 Jan. 1770; John Page to George Washington, 14 Feb. 1774; Washington to Thomas Lewis, 1 Feb. 1784; Washington to Samuel Lewis, 1 Feb. 1784; Washington to Mercer, 22 Nov. 1771.
11. For description of Braddock's Field, see entry for Monday, 10 Apr. 1775, in *The Journal of Nicholas Cresswell, 1774-1777* (New York: Dial Press, 1924), https://www.loc.gov/item/24030436/; Freeman, *Washington*, iii, 284–85.
12. *Diary of David McClure, Doctor of Divinity, 1748-1820* (New York: Knickerbocker Press, 1899), 118–19.
13. Bernard Bailyn, *Voyagers to the West: A Passage in the Peopling of America on the Eve of the Revolution* (New York: Vintage, 1988), 12–26; 'Diary of John Harrower, 1773-1776', *American Historical Review*, 6/1 (1900), 65–107.
14. Ray Allen Billington, *The Westward Movement in the United States* (Princeton: Van Nostrand, 1959), 156–60; McClure, *Diary*, 107–12; Richard J. Hooker (ed.), *The Carolina Backcountry on the Eve of the Revolution: The Journal and Other Writings of Charles Woodmason, Anglican Itinerant* (Chapel Hill: University of North Carolina Press, 1953), 13–25.
15. David Hackett Fischer, *Albion's Seed: Four British Folkways in America* (New York: OUP, 1989), Part IV; George MacDonald Fraser, *The Steel Bonnets*, 34–49, 57–58, 90–91, 115–16, 125, 169, 173, 200; see also Macaulay's *History of England*, i (1848), ch. 3, and Walter Scott, *Minstrelsy of the Scottish Border* (1802–03).
16. Douglas Southall Freeman, *George Washington*, i (New York: Scribner's, 1948), 132–33; Griffin, P., *The People with No Name: Ireland's Ulster Scots, America's Scots Irish, and the Creation of a British Atlantic World, 1689-1764* (Princeton University Press, 2012), 110–11, 165–66; William Henry Foote, *Sketches of Virginia: Historical and Biographical* (Philadelphia: Lippincott, 1856), 32–37, 123, 295, 359; see also Fischer, *Albion's Seed*.
17. Gage Papers, 91, 153, 328; Alden T. Vaughan, 'Frontier Banditti and the Indians: The Paxton Boys' Legacy, 1763-1775', *Pennsylvania History*, 51/1 (1984), 1–29; Eric Hinderaker, *Elusive Empires: Constructing Colonialism in the Ohio Valley, 1673-1800* (Cambridge: CUP, 1997), 162; White, *Middle Ground*, 345–50; *People With No Name*, 170–72; Lyman Chalkley (ed.),

*Chronicles of the Scotch-Irish Settlement in Virginia, Extracted from the Original Court Records of Augusta County, 1745–1800* (Rosslyn, VA: Mary S. Lockwood, 1912), i, 344.
18. Bailyn, *Voyagers to the West*, 267; Fischer, *Albion's Seed*, 759–65; Henry Nash Smith, *Virgin Land: The American West as Symbol and Myth* (Harvard University Press, 1971), 54; Jack M. Sosin, *Whitehall and the Wilderness: The Middle West in British Colonial Policy, 1760–1775* (Westport: Greenwood, 1980), 313–14; Woody Holton, *Forced Founders: Indians, Debtors, Slaves, and the Making of the American Revolution in Virginia* (Chapel Hill: University of North Carolina Press, 1999), 7–8; McClure, *Diary*, 68; Joseph Doddridge, *Notes on the Settlement and Indian Wars* (Pittsburgh, 1912), 81; Calloway, *Pen and Ink Witchcraft*, 102–06; Uriah James Jones, *History of the Early Settlement of the Juniata Valley* (Philadelphia: Henry B. Ashmead, 1856), 40; *People With No Name*, 172; Kevin Lee Yeager, 'The Power of Ethnicity: The Preservation of Scots-Irish Culture in the Eighteenth-Century American Backcountry', PhD dissertation, Louisiana State University, 2000.
19. C. W. Butterfield (ed.), *The Washington–Crawford Letters* (Cincinnati: Robert Clarke, 1877), 22–26, 33–39.
20. Freeman, *Washington*, iii, 294–96, 327–28, 332, 343–45.
21. McClure, *Diary*, 85, 101.
22. Peter Marshall, 'Colonial Protest and Imperial Retrenchment: Indian Policy 1764–1768', *Journal of American Studies*, 5/1 (1971), 1–17; Sosin, *Whitehall and the Wilderness*, 218–22; White, *Middle Ground*, 340–41, 353; Nick Bunker, *An Empire on the Edge: How Britain Came to Fight America* (London: Vintage, 2015), 99–103; Anderson, *Crucible of War*, 634–36.
23. Thomas Perkins Abernethy, *Western Lands and the American Revolution* (New York: Russell & Russell, 1959), 100; Bailyn, *Voyagers to the West*, 29–56; Calloway, *Indian World*, 210; Edward G. Lengel, *General George Washington: A Military Life* (New York: Random House, 2005), 82–86; Freeman, *Washington*, iii, 353–402.
24. Calloway, *Indian World*, 211; Sosin, *Whitehall and the Wilderness*, 240–45; Holton, *Forced Founders*, 27–35; Thomas D. Curtis, 'Riches, Real Estate, and Resistance: How Land Speculation, Debt, and Trade Monopolies Led to the American Revolution', *American Journal of Economics and Sociology*, 73/3 (2014), 474–626; Matthew L. Rhoades, 'Blood and Boundaries: Virginia Backcountry Violence and the Origins of the Quebec Act, 1758–1775', *West Virginia History: A Journal of Regional Studies*, 3/2 (2009), 1–22.
25. Freeman, *Washington*, iii, 407–09; Lengel, *General George Washington*, 102.

## The Bloody Grounds

1. Matthew L. Rhoades, 'Blood and Boundaries: Virginia Backcountry Violence and the Origins of the Quebec Act, 1758–1775', *West Virginia History: A Journal of Regional Studies*, 3/2 (2009), 1–22; George O. Virtue, 'British Land Policy and the American Revolution: A Belated Lecture in Economic History', University of Nebraska Studies, Sept. 1953; Thomas D. Curtis, 'Riches, Real Estate, and Resistance: How Land Speculation, Debt, and Trade Monopolies Led to the American Revolution', *American Journal of Economics and Sociology*, 73/3 (2014), 552–54, 571–73; Colin G. Calloway, *The Indian World of George Washington* (New York: OUP, 2019), 212; Woody Holton, *Forced Founders: Indians, Debtors, Slaves, and the Making of the American Revolution in Virginia* (Chapel Hill: University of North Carolina Press, 1999), 31–38.
2. *The Journal of Nicholas Cresswell, 1774–1777* (New York: Dial Press, 1924).
3. Edward G. Lengel, *First Entrepreneur: How George Washington Built His – and the Nation's – Prosperity* (Philadelphia: Da Capo, 2016), 123, 134; Jerry A. O'Callaghan, 'The War Veteran and the Public Lands', *Agricultural History*, 28/4 (1954), 163–68; James Sullivan to John Adams and Elbridge Gerry, 11 Oct. 1776; Henry Knox to John Adams, 21 Aug. 1776; John Hancock to George Washington, 24 Sept. 1776; Silas Deane to John Jay, 3 Dec. 1776; see also William Hogeland, *Founding Finance* (Austin: University of Texas Press, 2012), and Charles Beard, *An Economic Interpretation of the Constitution of the United States* (New York: Macmillan, 1913).
4. Reuben G. Thwaites and Louise P. Kellogg (eds), *The Revolution on the Upper Ohio, 1775–1777* (Madison: Wisconsin Historical Society, 1908), 34–67; Randolph C. Downes, *Council Fires on the Upper Ohio* (Pittsburgh: University of Pittsburgh Press, 1968), 177–201.
5. Thwaites & Kellogg, *Revolution on the Upper Ohio*, 24–34, 74–177, 185–7, 207–08; Peter Silver, *Our Savage Neighbors: How Indian War Transformed Early America* (New York: Norton, 2008), 228; Calloway, *Indian World*, 260–62.
6. Thwaites & Kellogg, *Revolution on the Upper Ohio*, 244, 249–50; Reuben G. Thwaites and Louise P. Kellogg (eds), *Frontier Defense on the Upper Ohio, 1777–1778* (Madison: Wisconsin Historical Society, 1912), 126–27, 149, 157–63.
7. Thwaites & Kellogg, *Frontier Defense*, 173–92; Patrick Griffin, *American Leviathan: Empire, Nation, and Revolutionary Frontier* (New York: Hill & Wang, 2007), 153–54; Downes, *Council Fires on the Upper Ohio*, 203–08; Calloway, *Indian World*, 265–66.
8. J. M. Sosin, *The Revolutionary Frontier, 1763–1783* (New York: Holt, Rinehart and Winston, 1967), 37–8; John Filson, *Daniel Boone*.
9. Sosin, *The Revolutionary Frontier*, 73–9; Colin G. Calloway, *Pen and Ink Witchcraft: Treaties and Treaty Making in American Indian History* (New York: OUP, 2014), 109.

10. Eric Hinderaker, *Elusive Empires: Constructing Colonialism in the Ohio Valley, 1673–1800* (Cambridge: CUP, 1997), 215–22; Elizabeth A. Perkins, *Border Life: Experience and Memory in the Revolutionary Ohio Valley* (Chapel Hill: University of North Carolina Press, 1998), 7; Stephen Aron, *How the West Was Lost: The Transformation of Kentucky from Daniel Boone to Henry Clay* (Baltimore: Johns Hopkins University Press, 1996), 34–37.
11. Thomas Jefferson to George Rogers Clark, 3 Jan. 1778.
12. James Alton James (ed.), *George Rogers Clark Papers, 1771–1781* (Springfield, IL: Illinois State Historical Library, 1912), 189–98.
13. Thomas Jefferson to George Rogers Clark, 1 Jan. 17[80]; Lowell H. Harrison, *George Rogers Clark and the War in the West* (Lexington, KY: University Press of Kentucky, 2001), 65–75.
14. Barbara Alice Mann, *George Washington's War on Native America* (Lincoln, NE: University of Nebraska Press, 2008), 127–28; George Rogers Clark to Thomas Jefferson, 22 Aug. 1780; James, *George Rogers Clark Papers*, 476–84; Harrison, *Clark and the War in the West*, 74–75.
15. George Rogers Clark to George Washington, 20 May 1781. For a general overview of the war in the West, see Mann, *Washington's War*, 50–150; Ray Allen Billington, *The Westward Movement in the United States*, 175–90; Justin Winsor, *The Westward Movement, 1763–1798* (New York: Houghton Mifflin, 1897), 166–220.
16. *Diary of David Zeisberger*, ed. Eugene F. Bliss, i (Cincinnati: Robert Clarke, 1885), 3–54; Mann, *Washington's War*, 150–54.
17. Paul A. Wallace (ed.), *The Travels of John Heckewelder in Frontier America* (Pittsburgh: University of Pittsburgh Press, 1985), 190; C. W. Butterfield, *An Historical Account of the Expedition Against Sandusky* (Cincinnati: Robert Clarke, 1873), 9–11, 25–27, 33–37.
18. Silver, *Savage Neighbors*, 204, 250–52; Wallace, *Travels of John Heckewelder*, 190–95; Mann, *Washington's War*, 157–65; Silver, *Savage Neighbors*, 267–77; Jeffrey Ostler, '"To Extirpate the Indians": An Indigenous Consciousness of Genocide in the Ohio Valley and Lower Great Lakes, 1750s–1810', *William and Mary Quarterly*, 72/4 (2015), 587–622.
19. C. W. Butterfield (ed.), *Washington–Irvine Correspondence* (Madison, WI: David Atwood, 1882), 104–09, 118–19, 373; Butterfield, *Expedition Against Sandusky*, 77, 114–19, 223.
20. Butterfield, *Washington–Irvine Correspondence*, 122, 125, 363–67; Calloway, *Indian World*, 276–77.
21. James, *George Rogers Clark Papers*, 80–81.
22. 'Narrative of a Late Expedition against the Indians' (Andover, MA: Ames & Parker, 1798); Edmund De Schweinitz, *The Life and Times of David Zeisberger* (Philadelphia: J. B. Lippincott, 1871), 569–71; see also accounts of the incident in Mann, *Washington's War* and Calloway, *Indian World*.

23. Butterfield, *Washington–Irvine Correspondence*, 126–32.
24. Butterfield, *Washington–Irvine Correspondence*, 377, 384–88; James, *George Rogers Clark Papers*, 80–158; Butterfield, *Expedition Against Sandusky*, 262–77; Calloway, *Indian World*, 278–79.

**Cutting the Knot**
1. Richard W. Van Alstyne, *Empire and Independence: The International History of the American Revolution* (New York: John Wiley, 1965), 162–63; Reginald Horsman, *The Diplomacy of the New Republic, 1776–1815* (Arlington Heights: Harlan Davidson, 1985), 14.
2. Ronald Hoffman and Peter J. Albert (eds), *Diplomacy and Revolution: The Franco-American Alliance of 1778* (Charlottesville: University Press of Virginia, 1981), 164; Alstyne, *Empire and Independence*, 159; George Washington to John Laurens, 9 Apr. 1781.
3. Alstyne, *Empire and Independence*, 62–67; *Diary of John Adams*, iii, In Congress, Fall 1775–Spring 1776.
4. Hoffman & Albert, *Diplomacy and Revolution*, 109–16; Edward S. Corwin, 'The French Objective in the American Revolution', *American Historical Review*, 21/1 (1915), 33–61; Abbé Raynal, *A Philosophical and Political History of the Settlements and Trade of the Europeans in the East and West Indies* (London, 1789), 487; Alstyne, *Empire and Independence*, 204.
5. Samuel Flagg Bemis, *The Diplomacy of the American Revolution* (New York, 1935), 48–64; Corwin, 'French Objective'; Louis-Philippe, Comte de Ségur, *Memoirs and Recollections of Count Ségur*, i (Boston: Wells & Lilly, 1825), 100–02.
6. Bemis, *Diplomacy of the American Revolution*, 76–77, 85–91; Richard B. Morris, *The Peacemakers: The Great Powers and American Independence* (New York: Harper & Row, 1965), 45, 219–40.
7. Philip M. Hamer, 'Henry Laurens of South Carolina: The Man and His Papers', *Proceedings of the Massachusetts Historical Society*, 77 (1965), 3–14; Abigail Adams to John Adams, 12 Jan. 1788; Bemis, *Diplomacy of the American Revolution*, 101–11; Morris, *Peacemakers*, 24–25, 451; James Breck Perkins, 'France and the American Revolution', *Proceedings of the New York State Historical Association*, 4 (1904); Alstyne, *Empire and Independence*, 169, 213; Morris Bishop, 'Franklin in France', *Daedalus*, 86/3 (1957).
8. Alstyne, *Empire and Independence*, 163–64, 174, 214; Bemis, *Diplomacy of the American Revolution*, 174–87; Vincent T. Harlow, *The Founding of the Second British Empire, 1763–1793*, i (London: Longmans, 1964), 240–42.
9. Hoffman & Albert, *Diplomacy and Revolution*, 50–54; Seth Jacobs, *Rogue Diplomats: The Proud Tradition of Disobedience in American Foreign Policy* (Cambridge: CUP, 2020), 24–77.
10. Entry on William Petty by George Fisher Russell Barker, in *Dictionary of National Biography, 1885–1900*, xxxxv; Harlow, *Second British Empire*,

214–20, 223–32; Edmond George Petty-Fitzmaurice, *Life of William, Earl of Shelburne*, ii (London: Macmillan, 1912), chs 5–6.
11. Bemis, *Diplomacy of the American Revolution*, 194–96; Harlow, *Second British Empire*, 232, 245–48; Benjamin Franklin to the Earl of Shelburne, 18 Apr. 1782.
12. John Jay to Robert R. Livingston, 17 Nov. 1782; Alstyne, *Empire and Independence*, 214; Jacobs, *Rogue Diplomats*, 24–77; Harlow, *Second British Empire*, 276–81; Hoffman & Albert, *Diplomacy and Revolution*, 17–18.
13. Bemis, *Diplomacy of American Revolution*, 226–39; Morris, *Peacemakers*, 362–76; Jacobs, *Rogue Diplomats*, 24–77; John Adams to Francis Dana, 17 Sept. 1782; John Adams to Abigail Adams, 22 Feb. 1783.
14. Alstyne, *Empire and Independence*, 222–23; P. Cunningham (ed.), *The Letters of Horace Walpole*, viii (London: Richard Bentley, 1858), 18, 305; Morris, *Peacemakers*, 429–33; Jacobs, *Rogue Diplomats*, 24–77; Ségur, *Memoirs*, 273; Jon Cowans (ed.), *Early Modern Spain: A Documentary History* (Philadelphia: University of Pennsylvania Press, 2003), 234–35; Matthew Lockwood, *To Begin the World Over Again: How the American Revolution Devastated the Globe* (New Haven: Yale University Press, 2019), 174–84, 222–26.
15. Colin G. Calloway, *The Indian World of George Washington* (New York: OUP, 2019), 287.

**Ideal Lines**
1. C. W. Butterfield (ed.), *The Washington–Crawford Letters* (Cincinnati: Robert Clarke, 1877), 77–78; Hugh Cleland, *George Washington in the Ohio Valley* (Pittsburgh: University of Pittsburgh Press, 1955), 278–317; Henry Adams, *The Life of Albert Gallatin* (Philadelphia: Lippincott, 1879), 57–59; George Washington to François-Jean de Beauvoir, marquis de Chastellux, 12 Oct. 1783.
2. Patrick Griffin, *American Leviathan: Empire, Nation, and Revolutionary Frontier* (New York: Hill & Wang, 2007), 187–88; Arthur St. Clair to John Jay, 13[–15] Dec. 1788; Washington to Henry Knox, 5 Dec. 1784; Washington to Hugh Williamson, 15 Mar. 1785; Washington to Richard Henry Lee, 14 Dec. 1784.
3. Gregory H. Nobles, 'Straight Lines and Stability: Mapping the Political Order of the Anglo-American Frontier', *Journal of American History*, 80/1 (1993), 9–35; see also James C. Scott, *Seeing Like a State* (New Haven: Yale University Press, 1998).
4. Payson Jackson Treat, *The National Land System, 1785–1820* (New York: E. B. Treat, 1910), 18–21; Paul Frymer, *Building an American Empire: The Era of Territorial and Political Expansion* (Princeton: Princeton University Press, 2017), 6, 58.

5. Pickering to Elbridge Gerry, 1 Mar. 1785; Peter S. Onuf, *Statehood and Union: A History of the Northwest Ordinance* (Notre Dame: University of Notre Dame Press, 2019), 38, 46–53, 59; Frymer, *American Empire*, 52–9.
6. Malcolm J. Rohrbough, '"A Freehold Estate Therein": The Ordinance of 1787 and the Public Domain', *Indiana Magazine of History*, 84/1 (1988), 46–59; Jack E. Eblen, 'Origins of the United States Colonial System: The Ordinance of 1787', *Wisconsin Magazine of History*, 51/4 (1968), 294–314; Onuf, *Statehood and Union*, 69–72.
7. Brian Balogh, *A Government Out of Sight: The Mystery of National Authority in Nineteenth-Century America* (Cambridge: CUP, 2009), 181–86; Frymer, *American Empire*, 32.

**Quelling the West**
1. *Journal and Letters of Col. John May, of Boston* (Cincinnati: Robert Clarke, 1873).
2. David McCullough, *The Pioneers: The Heroic Story of the Settlers Who Brought the American Ideal West* (New York: Simon & Schuster, 2019), 66–73; May, *Journal*; *Military Journal of Major Ebenezer Denny* (Philadelphia: Lippincott, 1859); Arthur St. Clair, *The St. Clair Papers* (Cincinnati: Robert Clarke, 1882), 1–16, 127–28, 138–48; Clarence E. Carter (ed.), *Papers Relating to the Period of the First Stage of the Government of the Territory Northwest of the River Ohio 1787–1791*, United States' National Archives and Records Service, 1934, 132–33; Peter S. Onuf, *Statehood and Union: A History of the Northwest Ordinance* (Notre Dame: University of Notre Dame Press, 2019), 69, 113; *The Memoirs of Rufus Putnam* (Boston: Houghton, Mifflin, 1903), 104–07.
3. Wiley Sword, *President Washington's Indian War: The Struggle for the Old Northwest, 1790–1795* (Norman: University of Oklahoma Press, 1985), 63–73; Arthur St. Clair to John Jay, 13–15 Dec. 1788; Carter, *Northwest Territory Papers*, 168–69.
4. Colin G. Calloway, *The Indian World of George Washington* (New York: OUP, 2019), 283, 314; Colin G. Calloway, *The Shawnees and the War for America* (New York: Viking, 2007), 75; Mark Savage, 'Native Americans and the Constitution: The Original Understanding', *American Indian Law Review*, 16/1 (1991), 57–118.
5. Sword, *Washington's Indian War*, 28, 38–39; Calloway, *Shawnees*, 76–79, 81–82, 87.
6. Carter, *Northwest Territory Papers*, 119; Calloway, *Indian World*, 381–82; Colin G. Calloway, *The Victory With No Name: The Native American Defeat of the First American Army* (New York: OUP, 2014), 58–70; Sword, *Washington's Indian War*, 126–30; Alexander Hamilton to George Washington, 27 Mar. 1791.

7. Calloway, *Victory With No Name*, 70–75; George Washington to the Miami Indians, 11 Mar. 1791.
8. Calloway, *Victory With No Name*, 77–81.
9. Calloway, *Victory With No Name*, 83–121; St. Clair, *Papers*, 176–77; Denny, *Military Journal*, 164–69; for the accounts of Fowler, Kennan, and Branshaw see 'St. Clair's Defeat', Public Library of Fort Wayne and Allen County, 1954.
10. Calloway, *Victory With No Name*, 122–25.
11. McCullough, *Pioneers*, 170–72; Denny, *Military Journal*, 171–76; Calloway, *Shawnees*, 93–94; William Darke to George Washington, 9–10 Nov. 1791.
12. Calloway, *Shawnees*, 94–106; Benjamin Drake, *Life of Tecumseh, and of His Brother the Prophet* (Cincinnati: E. Morgan, 1841).
13. Calloway, *Victory With No Name*, 154.

## Ohio Fever

1. 'Last Will and Testament of George Washington', U.S. Government Printing Office, 1911.
2. George Washington to David Humphreys, 25 July 1785; Joseph Smith, *Old Redstone, Or, Historical Sketches of Western Presbyterianism* (Philadelphia: Lippincott, 1854), 280; *Journal and Letters of Col. John May, of Boston* (Cincinnati: Robert Clarke, 1873), 41–42, 69, 135–36; John Melish, *Travels Through the United States of America, in the Years 1806 & 1807* (Philadelphia, 1818); John Devereux DeLacy to Thomas Jefferson, 3 Nov. 1801; Elizabeth A. Perkins, *Border Life: Experience and Memory in the Revolutionary Ohio Valley* (Chapel Hill: University of North Carolina Press, 1998), 58; Timothy Flint, *Recollections of the Last Ten Years* (Boston: Cummings, Billiard, 1826), 61–64; Morris Birkbeck, *Notes on a Journey in America* (London: James Ridgway, 1818), 30–32.
3. All quotations from Michaux are from François André Michaux, *Travels to the Westward of the Allegany Mountains* (London: R. Phillips, 1805); Archer Butler Hulbert, *Historic Highways of America* (Cleveland, 1904), xi: *Pioneer Roads and Experiences of Travelers*, i (Cleveland: Arthur H. Clark, 1904), 131–32; Flint, *Recollections*, 7–10; Margaret Van Horn Dwight, *A Journey to Ohio in 1810*, ed. Max Farrand (New Haven: Yale University Press, 1912).
4. Flint, *Recollections*, 11–17; Thomas Ashe, *Travels in America, Performed in 1806* (London: R. Phillips, 1808), 51–52.
5. Reginald Horsman, *The Frontier in the Formative Years, 1783–1815* (Albuquerque: University of New Mexico Press, 1975), 75.
6. Ellen Eslinger (ed.), *Running Mad for Kentucky: Frontier Travel Accounts* (Lexington: University Press of Kentucky, 2004), 262.
7. Eslinger, *Running Mad*, 265, 337–38; Birkbeck, *Notes*, 143; 'Tour to Prairie du Chien, 1829', in *Writings of Caleb Atwater* (Columbus: Scott & Wright,

1833); Melish, *Travels Through the United States*, ch. 74; A. D. Jones, *Illinois and the West* (Boston: Weeks, Jordan, 1838), 20–22, 165–66.
8. John D. Barnhart, *Valley of Democracy: The Frontier versus the Plantation in the Ohio Valley, 1775–1818* (Bloomington: Indiana University Press, 1953), 84–91, 128; Perkins, *Border Life*, 147; 'Three Journals by the Rev. James Smith of Powhatan County, Virginia, 1783–1795–1797', *Ohio Archaeological and Historical Quarterly*, 16 (1907), 348–401; Stewart H. Holbrook, *The Yankee Exodus: An Account of Migration from New England* (Seattle: University of Washington Press, 1950), 29–40; Andrew R. L. Cayton and Stuart D. Hobbs (eds), *The Center of a Great Empire: The Ohio Country in the Early Republic* (Athens, OH: Ohio University Press, 2005), 5.
9. Stephen Aron, *How the West Was Lost: The Transformation of Kentucky from Daniel Boone to Henry Clay* (Baltimore: Johns Hopkins University Press, 1996), 130–40, 164; Wilma A. Dunaway, 'Speculators and Settler Capitalists: Unthinking the Mythology about Appalachian Landholding, 1790–1860', in Mary Beth Pudup, Dwight B. Billings and Altina L. Waller (eds), *Appalachia in the Making: The Mountain South in the Nineteenth Century* (Chapel Hill: University of North Carolina Press, 1995), 50–75; Peter S. Onuf, *Statehood and Union: A History of the Northwest Ordinance* (Notre Dame: University of Notre Dame Press, 2019), 30; George W. Knepper, *Ohio and its People* (Kent, OH: Kent State University Press, 2003), 114–15; Andrew R. L. Cayton, *Ohio: The History of a People* (Columbus: Ohio State University Press, 2002), 35; William Priest, *Travels in the United States of America* (2003), 132–33.
10. Perkins, *Border Life*, 135; Melish, *Travels Through the United States*, ch. 65; John Mack Faragher, *Daniel Boone: The Life and Legend of an American Pioneer* (New York: Henry Holt, 1992), 272–73, 322; Flint, *Recollections*, 55–57; Jones, *Illinois and the West*, 165–66; Cayton, *Ohio*, 43.
11. Horsman, *Frontier*, 50; John A. Jakle, *Images of the Ohio Valley: A Historical Geography of Travel, 1740 to 1860* (New York: OUP, 1977), 123; Timothy Flint, *A Condensed Geography and History of the Western States*, ii (Cincinnati: W. M. Farnsworth, 1828), 364–65.
12. Peter Silver, *Our Savage Neighbors: How Indian War Transformed Early America* (New York: Norton, 2008), 212; Colin G. Calloway, *The Indian World of George Washington* (New York: OUP, 2019), 286–87; Barbara Alice Mann, *George Washington's War on Native America* (Lincoln, NE: University of Nebraska Press, 2008), 151–52.
13. Jakle, *Images of the Ohio Valley*, 92; Perkins, *Border Life*, 172–73; *Ohio Archaeological and Historical Quarterly*, 3 (1895), 296–97.

## PART II: LOUISIANA
### The Door to the House

1. The exact location of Quizquiz is unknown. A 1935 commission appointed by Franklin D. Roosevelt determined that its location was in Sunflower Landing, Mississippi.
2. Edward Gaylord Bourne (ed.), *Narratives of the Career of Hernando De Soto* (New York: A. S. Barnes, 1904); Carrie Gibson, *El Norte: The Epic and Forgotten Story of Hispanic North America* (London: Grove Press, 2020), 36–37; Alan Taylor, *American Colonies: The Settling of North America* (London: Penguin, 2001), 72–74.
3. Paul Schneider, *Old Man River: The Mississippi River in North American History* (New York: Henry Holt, 2016), 91–120.
4. Taylor, *American Colonies*, 382–86; Benjamin F. French (ed.), *Historical Collections of Louisiana*, i (New York: Wiley & Putnam, 1846), 45–50; see also *Lives of Robert Cavelier de La Salle and Patrick Henry* (Paris, 1848).
5. Christopher Morris, *The Big Muddy: An Environmental History of the Mississippi and Its Peoples from Hernando de Soto to Hurricane Katrina* (New York: OUP, 2012), 34–48.
6. D. W. Meinig, *The Shaping of America: A Geographical Perspective on 500 Years of History*, ii: *Continental America, 1800–1867* (New Haven: Yale University Press, 1986), 9–11; Morris, *Big Muddy*, 48–59; Taylor, *American Colonies*, 382–86.
7. Taylor, *American Colonies*, 382–86.
8. Delisle's map can be seen here: https://upload.wikimedia.org/wikipedia/commons/e/e7/Delisle_Carte_de_la_Louisiane_et_du_cours_du_Mississippi_1718_UTA.jpg; Daniel Coxe, *A Description of the English Province of Carolana* (St Louis: Churchill & Harris, 1840), 25, accessible at: https://archive.org/stream/descriptionofengooincoxe/descriptionofengooincoxe_djvu.txt; see du Pratz, *History of Louisiana*, ii, ch. 1, accessible at: https://www.gutenberg.org/files/9153/9153-h/9153-h.htm#book-II.
9. Samuel Flagg Bemis, *Pinckney's Treaty: A Study of America's Advantage From Europe's Distress, 1783–1800* (Baltimore: Johns Hopkins Press, 1926), 181.
10. Thomas Jefferson, *Notes on the State of Virginia*, see reply to 'Query Two'; Washington to Chastellux, 12 Oct. 1783; Joel Barlow, *The Columbiad* (Philadelphia: C. & A. Conrad, 1807), ll. 679–88, accessible here: https://www.gutenberg.org/files/8683/8683-h/8683-h.htm; Gibson, *El Norte*, 119–21.
11. Michaux, *Travels*, 50, 158; J. Hector St. John de Crèvecoeur, *Letters from an American Farmer* (1782), quoted in Anthony F. C. Wallace, *Jefferson and the Indians: The Tragic Fate of the First Americans* (Cambridge, MA: Harvard University Presss, 1999), 197.
12. Thomas Jefferson to Robert R. Livingston, 18 Apr. 1802.

### Thomas Jefferson Dreams of an Empire of Liberty

1. Dumas Malone, *Jefferson the President: First Term, 1801–1805* (Boston: Little, Brown, 1970), 39.
2. William Plumer, *William Plumer's Memorandum of Proceedings in the United States Senate, 1803–1807* (New York: Macmillan, 1923).
3. Merrill D. Peterson, *Thomas Jefferson and the New Nation: A Biography* (New York: OUP, 1970), 399, 762; Donald Jackson, *Thomas Jefferson and the Stony Mountains: Exploring the West from Monticello* (Urbana, IL: University of Illinois Press, 1981), 88; Thomas Jefferson to William Dunbar, 13 Mar. 1804; for slave memoirs, see the oral histories stored at https://www.monticello.org, and Isaac Jefferson, 'Life of Isaac Jefferson of Petersburg, Virginia, Blacksmith' (1847); Annette Gordon-Reed, *The Hemingses of Monticello: An American Family* (New York: Norton, 2008), 267.
4. Dennis Hodgson, 'Malthus' Essay on Population and the American Debate over Slavery', *Comparative Studies in Society and History*, 51/4 (2009), 742–70; Jefferson to Joseph Priestley, 21 Mar. 1801.
5. Jefferson had used this phrase before (on Christmas Day, 1780, he wrote to General George Rogers Clark giving him instructions for his campaign into the Ohio Valley; this campaign, he told Clark, would provide a 'barrier against the dangerous extension of the British Province of Canada and add to the Empire of liberty an extensive and fertile Country') and would use it again throughout his career.
6. Jon Kukla, *A Wilderness So Immense: The Louisiana Purchase and the Destiny of America* (New York: Knopf, 2003), 19; Gordon S. Wood, *Empire of Liberty: A History of the Early Republic, 1789–1815* (New York: OUP, 2011), 287–92; Malone, *Jefferson: The First Term*, 102–04; Roger G. Kennedy, *Mr Jefferson's Lost Cause: Land, Farmers, Slavery, and the Louisiana Purchase* (New York: OUP, 2003), 2–3, 38; Jefferson to C. W. F. Dumas, 10 Sept. 1787; Jefferson to John Taylor, 28 May 1816.
7. Jefferson to William Short, 10 Aug. 1790.
8. Jefferson to Washington, 28 Aug. 1790; Lafayette to Washington, 6 June 1791.
9. 'Jefferson's Outline of Policy on the Mississippi Question, 2 August 1790', in James P. Ronda, *Finding the West: Explorations with Lewis and Clark* (Albuquerque: University of New Mexico Press, 2001), 6–9.
10. Jud Campbell, 'The Origin of Citizen Genet's Projected Attack on Spanish Louisiana: A Case Study in Girondin Politics', *French Historical Studies*, 33/4 (2010), 515–44; Peterson, *Jefferson*, 481–503; Kukla, *Wilderness*, 157–80.
11. Jefferson to Charles Carroll, 15 Apr. 1791; Paul Bingham Willingter, 'A History of the Danville Conventions, 1784–1792', MA thesis, University of Louisville, 1941; Wood, *Empire of Liberty*, 128; Anthony F. C. Wallace, *Jefferson and the Indians: The Tragic Fate of the First Americans*

(Cambridge, MA: Harvard University Press, 1999), 169–70; Charles Gayarré, *History of Louisiana* (New York: W. J. Widdleton, 1867), 176; Jack D. L. Holmes, 'Spanish Treaties with West Florida Indians, 1784–1802', *Florida Historical Quarterly*, 48/2 (1969), 140–54; Elizabeth A. Perkins, 'The Consumer Frontier: Household Consumption in Early Kentucky', *Journal of American History*, 78/2 (1991), 486–510; Kukla, *Wilderness*, 101; Andro Linklater, *An Artist in Treason: The Extraordinary Double Life of General James Wilkinson* (New York: Walker, 2009), 90–91; Christopher L. Leadingham, 'To Open "the Doors of Commerce": The Mississippi River Question and the Shifting Politics of the Kentucky Statehood Movement', *Register of the Kentucky Historical Society*, 114/3–4, (2016), 341–69; Humphrey Marshall, *History of Kentucky* (Frankfort, KY: Henry Gore, 1812), 296.

12. Kukla, *Wilderness*, 189–94; Samuel Flagg Bemis, *Pinckney's Treaty: A Study of America's Advantage From Europe's Distress, 1783–1800* (Baltimore: Johns Hopkins Press, 1926), 265–335.
13. John Quincy Adams to John Adams, 13 Aug. 1796; James Monroe to James Madison, 1 Sept. 1796; Fisher Ames to Alexander Hamilton, 26 Jan. 1797; James Monroe to Pickering, 27 Aug. 1796; Timothy Pickering to Alexander Hamilton, 25 Mar. 1798.
14. Stuart Seely Sprague, 'Jefferson, Kentucky and the Closing of the Port of New Orleans, 1802–1803', *Register of the Kentucky Historical Society*, 70/4 (1972), 312–17; Thomas Fleming, *The Louisiana Purchase* (Hoboken: John Wiley, 2003), 13; Plumer, *Memorandum*; Thomas Jefferson to James Monroe, 13 Jan. 1803.

## This Affair of Louisiana

1. C. L. R. James, *The Black Jacobins: Toussaint L'Ouverture and the San Domingo Revolution* (London: Penguin, 2001), 3–49; Sudhir Hazareesingh, *Black Spartacus: The Epic Life of Toussaint Louverture* (London: Allen Lane, 2020), 7; Donald R. Hickey, 'America's Response to the Slave Revolt in Haiti, 1791–1806', *Journal of the Early Republic*, 2/4 (1982), 361–79.
2. Hazareesingh, *Black Spartacus*, 56–67, 157–58, 212–13, 237–45.
3. Andrew Roberts, *Napoleon* (London: Allen Lane, 2014), 300.
4. Gerald Horne, 'The Haitian Revolution and the Central Question of African American History', *Journal of African American History*, 100/1 (2015), 26–58; Charles Pinckney to George Washington from 20 Sept. 1791; George Washington to Ternant, 2 Oct. 1791; Tench Coxe to James Madison, [ca. 28 Nov.] 1801.
5. U.S. Proclamation Regarding Commerce with St. Domingo, 1799; Hazareesingh, *Black Spartacus*, 190–01, 211; Hickey, 'America's Response'.
6. Jefferson to William Moultrie, 23 Dec. 1793; Jefferson to James Madison, 5 Feb. 1799; Jefferson to Aaron Burr, 11 Feb. 1799.

7. Tim Matthewson, 'Jefferson and Haiti', *Journal of Southern History*, 61/2 (1995), 209–48; Piero Gleijeses, 'Napoleon, Jefferson, and the Louisiana Purchase', *International History Review*, 39/2 (2017), 237–55.
8. Carl Ludwig Lokke, 'The Leclerc Instructions', *Journal of Negro History*, 10/1 (1925), 80–98.
9. James, *Black Jacobins*, 234–44.
10. Jon Kukla, *A Wilderness So Immense: The Louisiana Purchase and the Destiny of America* (New York: Knopf, 2003), 227–43; Thomas Fleming, *The Louisiana Purchase* (Hoboken: John Wiley, 2003), 29–40; Jefferson to Robert R. Livingston, 18 Apr. 1802; *State Papers and Correspondence bearing upon the Purchase of the Territory of Louisiana* (Washington, 1903), 42; Robert R. Livingston to James Madison, 10 Aug. 1802; Rufus King to Alexander Hamilton, 7 May 1802.
11. The disease yellowed the skin of victims, hence the name, and caused serious inflammation of the vital organs, in the final stages practically liquefying them. From the notes from one English doctor's post mortem of a Yellow Fever patient: 'The stomach was found to be the organ which exhibited the strongest marks of derangement. The inner coat was surcharged with blood, appearing very red, and at one spot near the upper orifice it was of a livid hue, and its texture so weakened, that the finger was passed through it, by only a slight pressure' (George Pinckard, *Notes on the West Indies*, 348, 226).
12. Fleming, *Louisiana Purchase*, 39–45; Lokke, 'Leclerc Instructions'.
13. James, *Black Jacobins*, 274–97; Fleming, *Louisiana Purchase*, 45; Julia Gaffield, 'Haiti and Jamaica in the Remaking of the Early Nineteenth-Century Atlantic World', *William and Mary Quarterly*, 69/3 (2012), 583–614; *Oeuvres du Comte P. L. Roederer*, iii (Paris, 1854), 461.
14. This was in line with Jefferson's sentiment, expressed in a letter to Du Pont Nemours on 5 May 1802: 'and at present we should consider an enlargement of our territory beyond the Mississippi to be almost as great a misfortune as a contraction of it on this side'.
15. Thomas Ruys Smith, *River of Dreams: Imagining the Mississippi before Mark Twain* (Baton Rouge: Louisiana State University Press, 2007), 33–34; Kukla, *Wilderness*, 256–57; Fleming, *Louisiana Purchase*, 110–12.
16. Kukla, *Wilderness*, 252–54; *Lucien Bonaparte et ses mémoires, 1775–1840: d'après les papiers déposés aux archives étrangères*, ed. Théodore Iung (Paris, 1882), 129, 148–49.
17. Fleming, *Louisiana Purchase*, 112–17; Kukla, *Wilderness*, 269–80.
18. Merrill D. Peterson, *Thomas Jefferson and the New Nation: A Biography* (New York: OUP, 1970), 768–69; Fleming, *Louisiana Purchase*, 127.
19. Robert R. Livingston and James Monroe to James Madison, 13 May 1803; Andrew Jackson to Thomas Jefferson, 7 Aug. 1803; Hazareesingh, *Black Spartacus*, 324–25; Tim Matthewson, 'Jefferson and the Nonrecognition of

Haiti', *Proceedings of the American Philosophical Society*, 140/1 (1996), 22–48; Gaffield, 'Haiti and Jamaica'.
20. Alexander Hamilton, *New-York Evening Post*, 5 July 1803.

**Committing Louisianicide**
1. Clarence E. Carter (ed.), *The Territorial Papers of the United States*, v: *The Territory of Mississippi, 1798–1817* (Washington, 1937), 235, 263.
2. James Madison to William C. C. Claiborne, 31 Oct. 1803; William C. C. Claiborne to James Madison, 18 Nov. 1803; 'Authority Given to the President to Take Possession of the Territory of Louisiana', 31 Oct. 1803.
3. Henry Adams, *History of the United States of America during the Administrations of Thomas Jefferson*, i, ch. 2, 37.
4. Levi Lincoln to Thomas Jefferson, 10 Jan. 1803; Thomas Jefferson to Pierre Samuel Du Pont de Nemours, 1 Nov. 1803; Thomas Jefferson to John Breckinridge, 12 Aug. 1803; Thomas Jefferson to James Madison, 18 Aug. 1803; Dumas Malone, *Jefferson the President: First Term, 1801–1805* (Boston: Little, Brown, 1970), 316.
5. Raymond Walters, Jr., *Albert Gallatin: Jeffersonian Financier and Diplomat* (Pittsburgh: University of Pittsburgh Press, 1980), 141.
6. Gallatin to Jefferson, 31 Aug. 1803; Walters, *Gallatin*, 153–54; Baring Archives, London, NP1.A 4 Louisiana Purchase Papers.
7. Albert Gallatin to Thomas Jefferson, 18 Aug. 1803; 'An Account of Louisiana', Thomas Jefferson, 1803; Thomas Jefferson to John Dickinson, 9 Aug. 1803; Donald Jackson, *Thomas Jefferson and the Stony Mountains: Exploring the West from Monticello* (Urbana, IL:University of Illinois Press, 1981), 106–12.
8. Jefferson, 'Account'; Jon Kukla, *A Wilderness So Immense: The Louisiana Purchase and the Destiny of America* (New York: Knopf, 2003), 325.
9. Pierre-Louis Berquin-Duvallon, *Travels in Louisiana*, tr. John Davis (New York: I. Riley, 1806), accessed at http://edocs.dlis.state.fl.us/fldocs/FloridaEBOOKS/1106618.pdf; Kukla, *Wilderness*, 293; Abraham Ellery to Alexander Hamilton, 25 Oct. 1803; John Taylor, *Arator* (Georgetown: J. M. Carter, 1814).
10. William Plumer, *William Plumer's Memorandum of Proceedings in the United States Senate, 1803–1807* (New York: Macmillan, 1923).
11. Plumer, *Memorandum*.
12. Plumer, *Memorandum*; William C. C. Claiborne to James Madison, 17 Dec. 1803; William C. C. Claiborne to James Madison, 20 Dec. 1803; Pierre Clément de Laussat, *Memoirs of My Life* (Baton Rouge: Louisiana State University Press, 2003), 88–92.

## Filling in the Map

1. Secretary of War to Amos Stoddard, 7 Nov. 1803, in Clarence E. Carter (ed.), *The Territorial Papers of the United States*, xiii: *The Territory of Louisiana-Missouri, 1803–1806* (Washington, 1948), 8; Floyd C. Shoemaker, 'The Louisiana Purchase, 1803, and the Transfer of Upper Louisiana to the United States, 1804', *Missouri Historical Review*, 48/1 (1953).
2. Thomas Jefferson to James Wilkinson, 23 Feb. 1801; Thomas Jefferson to Martha Jefferson Randolph, 28 May 1801; Thomas Jefferson to Martin Van Buren, 29 June 1824.
3. David L. Nicandri, 'Lewis and Clark: Exploring under the Influence of Alexander Mackenzie', *Pacific Northwest Quarterly*, 95/4 (2004), 171–81.
4. Instructions for Meriwether Lewis, 20 June 1803; Thomas Jefferson to Meriwether Lewis, 4 July 1803 (in the draft of the letter Jefferson wrote 'Missouri' and then crossed it out and wrote 'Mississippi').
5. Meriwether Lewis to Thomas Jefferson, 19 Dec. 1803; A. P. Nasatir (ed.), *Before Lewis and Clark: Documents Illustrating the History of the Missouri, 1785–1804*, ii (St Louis: St Louis Historical Documents Foundation, 1952), 719; Thomas Jefferson to Meriwether Lewis, 16 Nov. 1803.
6. W. Raymond Wood, 'David Thompson at the Mandan-Hidatsa Villages, 1797–1798: The Original Journals', *Ethnohistory*, 24/4 (1977), 329–42; for Nicholas King's map, see https://www.loc.gov/item/98687178/.
7. James P. Ronda, *Lewis and Clark among the Indians* (Lincoln, NE: University of Nebraska Press, 1988), 14, 22, 33–35; Clark's journal, 19 Aug. 1804; Thomas Jefferson to Meriwether Lewis, 22 Jan. 1804; Clark's journal, 25 Sept. 1804; Ordway's journal, 26 Sept. 1804; for the full text of the Indian Commissions see http://www.lewis-clark.org/article/361.
8. Ronda, *Among the Indians*, 62–67, 204; Clark's journal, 5 Jan. 1804; Clark's journal, 30 Mar. 1805; see Eldon G. Chuinard, *Only One Man Died: The Medical Aspects of the Lewis and Clark Expedition* (Glendale: Arthur H. Clark, 1979), 264–65 and 379–80.
9. Clark's journal, 29 Mar. 1805; Meriwether Lewis to Thomas Jefferson, 7 Apr. 1805; Lewis's journal, 7 Apr. 1805.
10. Lewis's journal, 22 Apr. 1805, 3 May 1805; 8 May 1805, 8 June 1805.
11. Lewis's journal, 29 Apr. 1806, 5 May 1805, 11 May 1805, 14 June 1805, 17 June 1805, 28 June 1805.
12. Lewis's journal, 12 Aug. 1805.
13. Thomas Jefferson to William Dunbar, 13 Mar. 1804; Jared Orsi, 'Zebulon Pike and His "Frozen Lads": Bodies, Nationalism, and the West in the Early Republic', *Western Historical Quarterly*, 42/1 (2011), 55–75; Jackson, *Jefferson and the Stony Mountains: Exploring the West from Monticello* (Urbana, IL: University of Illinois Press, 1981), 230–60; Zebulon M. Pike to Thomas Jefferson, 29 Oct. 1807.

14. Noel M. Loomis and Abraham P. Nasatir, *Pedro Vial and the Roads to Santa Fe* (Norman: University of Oklahoma Press, 1967), 186–92; Nasatir, *Before Lewis and Clark*, 725–49.
15. James Wilkinson, 'Reflections on Louisiana' (originally attributed to Vicente Folch), in Paul Alliot and James Alexander Robertson, *Louisiana Under the Rule of Spain, France, and the United States, 1785–1807*, ii (Cleveland: Arthur H. Clark, 1911), 323–47; Loomis and Nasatir, *Pedro Vial*, 236–41; Salcedo to Cevallos, 20 Aug. 1804, in Nasatir, *Before Lewis and Clark*, 749.

## Everything Shifts
1. 'First Trip of the New Orleans, 1811', from I. H. B. Latrobe's address before the Maryland Historical Society, 1882.
2. Alice Crary Sutcliffe, *Robert Fulton and the 'Clermont'* (New York: Century, 1909), 198.
3. Louis C. Hunter, *Steamboats on the Western Rivers* (New York: Octagon, 1969), 22–51.
4. Hunter, *Steamboats*, 4–5; John Tresch, *The Reason for the Darkness of the Night* (New York: Farrar, Straus & Giroux, 2021), 120–21; William Charles Redfield, *Letter to the Secretary of the Treasury: On the History and Causes of Steamboat Explosions, and the Means of Prevention*, 1839, 35; Gregory P. Sandukas, 'Gently Down the Stream: How Exploding Steamboat Boilers in the 19th Century Ignited Federal Public Welfare Regulation', Third Year Paper, Harvard Law School, 2002; Andrew H. Browning, *The Panic of 1819: The First Great Depression* (Columbia: University of Missouri Press, 2019), 75; for steam modernism, see John Darwin, *Unlocking the World: Port Cities and Globalization in the Age of Steam, 1830–1930* (London: Allen Lane, 2020); Timothy Flint, *Recollections of the Last Ten Years* (Boston: Cummings, Billiard, 1826), 108–10; Francis Hall, *Travels in Canada, and the United States, in 1816 and 1817* (London: Longman, Hurst, Rees, Orme & Brown, 1818), ch. 3; Henry R. Schoolcraft, *Personal Memoirs of a Residence of Thirty Years with the Indian Tribes on the American Frontiers* (Philadelphia: Lippincott, 1851), ch. 4; Robert Baird, *View of the Valley of the Mississippi, or, The Emigrant's and Traveller's Guide to the West*,(Philadelphia: H. S. Tanner, 1834), 280.
5. Henry Ker, *Travels through the Western Interior of the United States* (Elizabethtown, 1816); Flint, *Recollections*, 135–36; John Bradbury, *Bradbury's Travels in the Interior of America, 1809–1811* (1819); Fortescue Cuming, *Cuming's Tour to the Western Country, 1807–1809* (Cleveland: Arthur H. Clark, 1904).
6. Flint, *Recollections*, 130–31; John Mason Peck, *Forty Years of Pioneer Life* (Philadelphia: American Baptist Publication Society, 1864), 122, 144–45.

7. Flint, *Recollections*, 23, 52–53, 159–60; for frontier fighting, see Elliott J. Gorn, '"Gouge and Bite, Pull Hair and Scratch": The Social Significance of Fighting in the Southern Backcountry', *American Historical Review*, 90/1 (1985), 18–43.
8. Flint, *Recollections*, 76, 205–06; Peck, *Forty Years*, 145–46; Thomas Nuttall, *Nuttall's Travels into the Arkansas Territory, 1819* (Philadelphia, 1821), 38.
9. Browning, *Panic of 1819*, 91–96; Morris Bien, 'The Public Lands of the United States', *North American Review*, 192/658 (1910), 387–402; Daniel Feller, *The Public Lands in Jacksonian Politics* (Madison: University of Wisconsin Press, 1984), 7–9; see also John R. Van Atta, *Securing the West: Politics, Public Lands, and the Fate of the Old Republic, 1785–1850* (Baltimore: Johns Hopkins University Press, 2014).
10. Anthony F. C. Wallace, *Jefferson and the Indians: The Tragic Fate of the First Americans* (Cambridge, MA: Harvard University Presss, 1999), 221–30; Thomas Jefferson to William Henry Harrison, 27 Feb. 1803.
11. Bray Hammond, *Banks and Politics in America: From the Revolution to the Civil War* (Princeton: Princeton University Press, 1957), 223; James Flint, *Flint's Letters from America, 1818–1820* (Cleveland: A. H. Clark, 1904), 133, 219–23; *Niles' Weekly Register*, xxx, 1826; Peck, *Forty Years*, 84–86.
12. Browning, *Panic of 1819*, 6; Clarence E. Carter (ed.), *The Territorial Papers of the United States*, xix: *The Territory of Arkansas, 1819–1825* (Washington, 1953), 65; Merrill D. Peterson, *Thomas Jefferson and the New Nation: A Biography* (New York: OUP, 1970), 802; Thomas Jefferson to Timothy Bloodworth, 29 Jan. 1804 (the phrase was also used in Jefferson's second inaugural); Flint, *Recollections*, 187–89.
13. Jefferson to Thomas Mann Randolph, 12 Mar. 1802; Thomas Mann Randolph to Jefferson, 20 Mar. 1802; William Dunbar, 'Description of the River Mississippi and Its Delta', *Transactions of the American Philosophical Society*, vi (1809), 165–87; Edward E. Baptist, *The Half Has Never Been Told: Slavery and the Making of American Capitalism* (New York: Basic, 2016), 83; Richard Follett, *The Sugar Masters: Planters and Slaves in Louisiana's Cane World, 1820–1860* (Baton Rouge: Louisiana State University Press, 2005), 19; Henry Bradshaw Fearon, *Sketches of America* (London: Longman, Hurst, Rees, Orme & Brown, 1819), 270–71; Flint, *Recollections*, 308.
14. Follett, *Sugar Masters*, 21, 26–27; J. T. Danson, 'On the Existing Connection between American Slavery and the British Cotton Manufacture', *Journal of the Statistical Society of London*, 20/1 (1857), 1–21; Paul F. Lachance, 'The 1809 Immigration of Saint-Domingue Refugees to New Orleans: Reception, Integration and Impact', *Louisiana History: The Journal of the Louisiana Historical Association*, 29/2 (1988), 109–41; Kelly Houston Jones, '"A Rough, Saucy Set of Hands to Manage": Slave Resistance in Arkansas',

*Arkansas Historical Quarterly*, 71/1 (2012), 1–21; Peter J. Kastor, *The Nation's Crucible: The Louisiana Purchase and the Creation of America* (New Haven: Yale University Press, 2004), 63–64; Walter Johnson, *River of Dark Dreams: Slavery and Empire in the Cotton Kingdom* (Cambridge, MA: Belknap, 2013), 20.

15. Thomas Jefferson to Robert Williams, 10 Feb. 1806; Secretary of the Treasury to John Boyle, 19 Dec. 1807; Secretary of the Treasury to Isaac Briggs, 8 May 1806; Thomas Freeman to the Secretary of the Treasury, 25 Jan. 1812; Clarence E. Carter (ed.), *The Territorial Papers of the United States*, xiv: *The Territory of Louisiana-Missouri, 1806–1814* (Washington, 1949), 93–99.
16. Amos Stoddard, *Sketches, Historical and Descriptive, of Louisiana* (Philadelphia: M. Carey, 1812), 266; Thomas Jefferson to Thomas Mann Randolph, 8 June 1803.
17. Hayden quoted in Harriet Beecher Stowe, *A Key to Uncle Tom's Cabin* (Boston: J. P. Jewett, 1853); Solomon Northup, *Twelve Years a Slave* (Auburn: Derby & Miller, 1853); John Brown, *Slave Life in Georgia: A Narrative of the Life, Sufferings, and Escape of John Brown* (London, 1855).
18. Lewis Garrard Clarke, *Narrative of the Sufferings of Lewis Clarke* (Boston: David H. Ela, 1845); Frederick Law Olmsted, *The Cotton Kingdom*, ii (New York: Mason Bros, 1861), 321; Brown, *Slave Life in Georgia*; see Baptist, *Half Has Never Been Told*.
19. Baptist, *Half Has Never Been Told*, 117, 368; William J. Anderson, *Life and Narrative of William J. Anderson* (Chicago: Daily Tribune, 1857); Ker, *Travels*, 87–81, 126–29, 294.
20. Jacob Green, *Narrative of the Life of J. D. Green* (1864).
21. Brown, *Slave Life in Georgia*.

## The Broom of Destruction

1. Crawford to Gallatin, 27 Oct. 1817.
2. Bray Hammond, *Banks and Politics in America: From the Revolution to the Civil War* (Princeton: Princeton University Press, 1957), 254–55; Murray N. Rothbard, *The Panic of 1819: Reactions and Policies* (Auburn: Von Mises Institute, 2002), 11–13; Monroe to Crawford, 19 May 1819.
3. Crawford to Gallatin, 26 Apr. 1819.
4. James Flint, *Flint's Letters from America, 1818–1820* (Cleveland: A. H. Clark, 1904), 219–23.
5. Howard Bodenhorn, *State Banking in Early America: A New Economic History* (New York: OUP, 2003), 288–89, for case studies of state bank failures see 144 and 241; Rothbard, *Panic of 1819*, 12–15, 25; James Flint, *Flint's Letters from America, 1818–1820* (Edinburgh: James Flint, 1822), 133, 219–23, 273, 288; Amos Kendall, *Autobiography of Amos Kendall* (Boston: Lee & Shepard, 1872), 204; Andrew H. Browning, *The Panic of 1819: The*

*First Great Depression* (Columbia: University of Missouri Press, 2019), 11, 174: Browning estimates nationwide bank failures as potentially as high as 40%.

6. Flint, *Letters*, 129, 187–92, 219–23; Dorothy B. Dorsey, 'The Panic of 1819 in Missouri', *Missouri Historical Review*, 29/2 (1935), 79–91; Browning, *Panic of 1819*, 87–98.
7. Ken S. Mueller, *Senator Benton and the People: Master Race Democracy on the Early American Frontiers* (DeKalb: Northern Illinois University Press, 2014), 89; Hattie M. Anderson, 'Frontier Economic Problems in Missouri, 1815–1828', *Missouri Historical Review*, 34/1 (1939), 38–70; R. Douglas Hurt, *Agriculture and Slavery in Missouri's Little Dixie* (Columbia: University of Missouri Press, 1992), 30.
8. Clarence E. Carter (ed.), *The Territorial Papers of the United States*, xix: *The Territory of Arkansas, 1819–1825* (Washington, 1953), 422; Clarence E. Carter (ed.), *The Territorial Papers of the United States*, xv: *The Territory of Louisiana-Missouri, 1815–1821* (Washington, 1951), 440–43, 594; Timothy Flint, *Recollections of the Last Ten Years* (Boston: Cummings, Billiard, 1826), 199.
9. Anderson, 'Frontier Economic Problems'; Browning, *Panic of 1819*, 47–48.
10. Hurt, *Agriculture and Slavery*, 47–48; Rothbard, *Panic of 1819*, 80–81; Anderson, 'Frontier Economic Problems'; Dorsey, 'Panic of 1819'; Carter, *Territorial Papers* xv, 669.
11. John Holmes to the People of Maine, 10 Apr. 1820; William Wells Brown, *Narrative of William W. Brown, a Fugitive Slave* (Boston, 1847); for more on the characteristics of Missouri slavery, see Diane Mutti Burke, *On Slavery's Border: Missouri's Small-Slaveholding Households, 1815–1865* (Athens: University of Georgia Press, 2010), and Hurt, *Agriculture and Slavery*.
12. *Speech of the Hon. James Tallmadge, of Duchess County, New York, in the House of Representatives of the United States, on Slavery*, New-York Society for Promoting the Manumission of Slaves (Boston: Ticknor, 1849); William R. Johnson, 'Prelude to the Missouri Compromise: A New York Congressman's Effort to Exclude Slavery from Arkansas Territory', *Arkansas Historical Quarterly*, 24/1 (1965), 47–66.
13. *Annals of Congress*, House of Representatives, 15th Congress, 2nd Session, 1170–80; Mueller, *Senator Benton*, 80–82; John R. Van Atta, *Wolf by the Ears: The Missouri Crisis, 1819–1821* (Baltimore: Johns Hopkins University Press, 2015), 80; Rothbard, *Panic of 1819*, 6–13; John Randolph, *Letters of John Randolph, to a Young Relative* (Philadelphia: Carey, Lea & Blanchard, 1834), 36l; Browning, *Panic of 1819*, 333; Tallmadge, *Speech on Slavery*.
14. James Monroe to James Madison, 5 Feb. 1820; James Monroe to Thomas Jefferson, [received 27] May 1820.

15. Browning, *Panic of 1819*, 340; Ronald W. Overley, 'John W. Taylor', MA thesis, Kansas State Teachers College, 1967; John Quincy Adams diary, 13, 24 Feb. 1819.
16. James Madison to James Monroe, 23 Feb. 1820.
17. *Annals of Congress*, House of Representatives, 15th Congress, 2nd Session, 1170–80; Tallmadge, *Speech on Slavery*; *Speech of Mr. M'Lane, of Delaware, on the Following Amendment Proposed by Mr. Taylor, of N.Y. to the Bill Authorising the People of Missouri to Form a Constitution* (Washington, 1820).
18. Frederick Merk, *History of the Westward Movement* (New York: Knopf, 1978), 237–39; Hurt, *Agriculture and Slavery*, 39–41.
19. Patrick Gibson to Thomas Jefferson, 27 July 1818; Thomas Jefferson to Patrick Gibson, 30 July 1818; Thomas Jefferson to Wilson Cary Nicholas, 20 Sept. 1819; Thomas Jefferson to Wilson Cary Nicholas, 2 July 1819; Thomas Jefferson to James Madison, 6 Sept. 1789; Thomas Jefferson to John Wayles Eppes, 30 June 1820; Thomas Jefferson to John Wayles Eppes, 13 Oct. 1820; Thomas Jefferson to James Madison, 17 Feb. 1826; also Alan Pell Crawford, *Twilight at Monticello: The Final Years of Thomas Jefferson* (New York: Random House, 2008), 386; Victor Dennis Golladay, 'The Nicholas Family of Virginia, 1722–1820', PhD dissertation, University of Virginia, 1969, 338.
20. Thomas Jefferson to Albert Gallatin, 26 Dec. 1820; Thomas Jefferson to John Holmes, 22 Apr. 1820; Thomas Jefferson to John Adams, 22 Jan. 1821; Merrill D. Peterson, *Thomas Jefferson and the New Nation: A Biography* (New York: OUP, 1970), 996–1001.
21. Crawford, *Twilight*, 531–33; Thomas Jefferson to William Short, 13 Apr. 1820; Thomas Jefferson to John Holmes, 22 Apr. 1820.

## PART III: THE FLORIDAS
### A Pistol Pointed at the Heart of the Republic
1. After the Louisiana Purchase, the western boundary was modified slightly, such that, in Talleyrand's words, 'the Mississippi, the river Iberville, the lakes Maurepas and Pontchartrain' formed the new limits of West Florida. This left a tongue of Spanish land extending out towards the east bank of the Mississippi, encompassing Baton Rouge, bordered to the north by Mississippi, to the west by Louisiana and to the south by a salient of boggy land containing New Orleans.
2. Jervis Cutler, *A Topographical Description of the State of Ohio, Indiana Territory, and Louisiana* (Boston: Charles Williams, 1812), 154; William Barnett to Huntsville, 12 Mar. 1817, *Florida Territorial Papers*, 67–70; William Bartram, *Travels Through North and South Carolina, Georgia, East and West Florida* (Philadelphia: James & Johnson, 1791); Bernard Romans, *A Concise Natural History of East and West Florida* (New York,

1775), 250–51; Robert D. Bush (ed.), *Surveying the Early Republic* (Baton Rouge: Louisiana State University Press, 2016), 178–84.
3. Frank Lawrence Owsley and Gene A. Smith, *Filibusters and Expansionists: Jeffersonian Manifest Destiny, 1800–1821* (Tuscaloosa: University of Alabama Press, 1997), 22.
4. Alexander von Humboldt, *Voyages*, i & iii; United States Congressional Serial Set, vol. 446, 28th Congress, 1st Session, HoP, 2 Apr. 1844, Rep No. 47, Report from Committee of Military Affairs; Hansard vol. 40, Thursday, 3 June 1819; Arthur Preston Whitaker, *The United States and the Independence of Latin America, 1800–1830* (Baltimore: Johns Hopkins Press, 1941), 107–08.
5. Jefferson to Madison, 27 Apr. 1809.
6. John Sevier to Andrew Jackson, 26 Nov. 1797, in *The Papers of Andrew Jackson*, i: *1770–1803*, ed. Sam B. Smith and Harriet Chappell Owsley (Knoxville: University of Tennessee Press, 1980).
7. Bartram, *Travels*, 138, 450; Claudio Saunt, *A New Order of Things: Property, Power, and the Transformation of the Creek Indians, 1733–1816* (Cambridge: CUP, 1999), 50.
8. James Monroe to JQA, 10 Dec. 1815.

**The Original Lone Star State**
1. Frank Lawrence Owsley and Gene A. Smith, *Filibusters and Expansionists: Jeffersonian Manifest Destiny, 1800–1821* (Tuscaloosa: University of Alabama Press, 1997), 7; Stanley Clisby Arthur, *The Story of the West Florida Rebellion* (1935), 102–11.
2. National Archives, Kew: FO 72/106, FO 72/107, FO 5/70; Rafe Blaufarb (ed.), *The Revolutionary Atlantic: Republican Visions, 1760–1830: A Documentary History* (Oxford: OUP, 2017), 433; Lester D. Langley, *The Americas in the Age of Revolution 1750–1850* (New Haven: Yale University Press, 1996), 178–80.
3. See, for instance, John Adair's letter of 9 Jan. 1809 to James Madison, in which he described the people of the region west of the Pearl as 'ripe fruit; waiting the hand that dares to pluck them; and with them all Florida'. He warned, however, that the Spanish garrison at Pensacola were 'literally Sans culotes without cloathing, rations or money or credit to buy with', while the French creoles were 'attached to french customs, french principles, french Laws; in a word, Bonaparte is their God', and they were 'ready to join any power, who will … make them A dependency of France'. Furthermore, 'British Agents are now amongst these people, labouring to make them believe, that through a connection with the [Bahamas] alone they can prosper.' He concluded, ominously, that 'should the British, during a ferment thus produced, land a Comparatively small force in this District and offer Independence, alliance and Commerce to the People of

the adjoining Territories: It is, difficult for me to say what would be the consequence.'
4. Robert R. Livingston to James Madison, 20 May 1803; Andrew McMichael, *Atlantic Loyalties: Americans in Spanish West Florida, 1785–1810* (Athens: University of Georgia Press, 2008), 85–86; Isaac J. Cox, *The West Florida Controversy, 1798–1813* (Baltimore: Johns Hopkins Press, 1918), 316, 326–27.
5. McMichael, *Atlantic Loyalties*, 127–28.
6. Samuel Fulton to James Madison, 20 Apr. 1810; Holmes to Smith, 20 June and 11 July 1810; see Samuel C. Hyde, 'Introduction: Setting a Precedent for Regional Revolution: The West Florida Revolt Considered', *Florida Historical Quarterly*, 90/2 (2011), 121–32; Cox, *West Florida Controversy*, 326–50; Wykoff letter quoted in full in Arthur, *West Florida Rebellion*, emphasis in the original.
7. Cox, *West Florida Controversy*, 432; full speech accessible here: https://fcit.usf.edu/florida/docs/g/govspch.htm.
8. James Madison Presidential Proclamation, 27 Oct. 1810; Madison to Thomas Jefferson, 19 Oct. 1810; see also *The Philadelphia Repertory*, vol. 1–2, 279.
9. Cody Scallions, 'The Rise and Fall of the Original Lone Star State: Infant American Imperialism Ascendant in West Florida', *Florida Historical Quarterly*, 90/2 (2011), 193–220.
10. William C. C. Claiborne to Thomas Jefferson, 24 Dec. 1810; Samuel Watson, 'Conquerors, Peacekeepers, or Both? The U.S. Army and West Florida, 1810–1811, A New Perspective', *Florida Historical Quarterly*, 92/1 (2013), 69–105.
11. William S. Belko, 'The Origins of the Monroe Doctrine Revisited: The Madison Administration, the West Florida Revolt, and the No Transfer Policy', *Florida Historical Quarterly*, 90/2 (2011), 157–92; No Transfer Resolution. U.S. Congress, 15 Jan. 1811; Hubert Bruce Fuller, *The Purchase of Florida: Its History and Diplomacy* (Cleveland: Burrows, 1906), 186–90.
12. Fuller, *Purchase of Florida*, 213.
13. See Morier's correspondence, Sept. to Dec. 1810 in FO 5/70; also see Admiral Apodaca's letters of Oct. 1810 to Wellesley in FO 72/101.

## Enter Jackson
1. George Robert Gleig, *A Narrative of the Campaigns of the British Army, at Washington, Baltimore, and New Orleans* (Philadelphia: M. Carey, 1821), 84–86; Hansard, Monday, 5 June 1815; AJ to Robert Hays, 26 Jan. 1815, in *The Papers of Andrew Jackson*, iii: *1814–1815*, ed. Harold D. Moser et al. (Knoxville: University of Tennessee Press, 1991).
2. John H. DeWitt, 'Letters of General John Coffee to His Wife, 1813–1815', *Tennessee Historical Magazine*, 2/4 (1916), 264–95; *Niles' Weekly Register*, 7/25, 18 Feb. 1815; Robert V. Remini, *Andrew Jackson*, i: *The Course of*

*American Empire, 1767–1821* (New York: Harper & Row, 1977), 293; John Stokely to AJ, 13 Feb. 1815, Benjamin Hawkins to AJ, 27 Feb. 1815, in *Jackson Papers*, iii.
3. Amos Kendall, *Life of Andrew Jackson* (New York: Harper, 1843), 45; Remini, *Jackson*, i, 2–29, 232–33.
4. Remini, *Jackson*, i, 30; C. Peter Magrath, *Yazoo: Law and Politics in the New Republic* (Providence: Brown University Press, 1966), 11.
5. AJ to the 2nd Division, 8 Sept. 1812, in *The Papers of Andrew Jackson*, ii: *1804–1813*, ed. Harold D. Moser et al. (Knoxville: University of Tennessee Press, 1984).
6. Frank Lawrence Owsley, *Struggle for the Gulf Borderlands* (Gainesville: University Presses of Florida, 1981), 12–13.
7. American State Papers, Indian Affairs, i, 845.
8. Claudio Saunt, *A New Order of Things: Property, Power, and the Transformation of the Creek Indians, 1733–1816* (Cambridge: CUP, 1999), 215; Indian Affairs, i, 846.
9. Indian Affairs, i, 847; Remini, *Jackson*, i, 188–90; AJ to the 2nd Division, 9 July 1812, in *Jackson Papers*, ii; Karl Davis, '"Remember Fort Mims:" Reinterpreting the Origins of the Creek War', *Journal of the Early Republic*, 22/4 (2002), 611–36; Davy Crockett, *Narrative of the Life of Davy Crockett* (Philadelphia: E. L. Carey & A. Hart, 1834), 72.
10. Remini, *Jackson*, i, 184–85.
11. DeWitt, 'Letters of General Coffee'; Crockett, *Narrative*, 88–92.
12. AJ to Robert Grierson, 17 Nov. 1813, in *Jackson Papers*, ii.
13. Remini, *Jackson*, i, 207–09; Susan Marie Abram, '"Souls in the Treetops": Cherokee War, Masculinity, and Community, 1760–1820', PhD dissertation, Auburn University, 2009.
14. Tom Kanon, *Tennesseans at War, 1812–1815* (Tuscaloosa: University of Alabama Press, 2014), 101–06; Remini, *Jackson*, i, 213–17; Abram, 'Souls in the Treetops'; AJ to Thomas Pinckney, 28 Mar. 1814, in *Jackson Papers*, iii.
15. ADM 1/506, 8 June 1814, Captain Hugh Pigot to Cochrane; Frank L. Owsley, 'British and Indian Activities in Spanish West Florida during the War of 1812', *Florida Historical Quarterly*, 46/2 (1967), 111–23; CO 23/61 63–64; Richard K. Murdoch, 'A British Report on West Florida and Louisiana, November, 1812', *Florida Historical Quarterly*, 43/1 (1964), 36–51.
16. 1st–13th Congress. Repr. 14th Congress, 1st Session–50th Congress, 1st Session, vol. 5, 378; James Wilkinson, *Memoirs of My Own Times*, ii (Philadelphia: Abraham Small, 1816), 341; Frank Lawrence Owsley and Gene A. Smith, *Filibusters and Expansionists: Jeffersonian Manifest Destiny, 1800–1821* (Tuscaloosa: University of Alabama Press, 1997), 88–92.
17. Bradford Perkins, *Castlereagh and Adams: England and the United States, 1812–1823* (Berkeley: University of California Press, 1964), 82–83; Nathaniel Atcheson, 'A Compressed View of the Points to be Discussed, in Treating

with the United States of America' (London, 1814), emphasis in the original.
18. *Niles' Weekly Register*, vii, 133–35 (5 Nov. 1814); Matthew J. Clavin, *Aiming for Pensacola: Fugitive Slaves on the Atlantic and Southern Frontiers* (Cambridge, MA: Harvard University Press, 2015), 43–44; Nathaniel Millett, *The Maroons of Prospect Bluff and their Quest for Freedom in the Atlantic World* (Gainesville: University Press of Florida, 2013), 51–52; ADM 1/506, 480–86; WO 1/143, 63–73.
19. AJ to the Cherokee and Creek Indians, 5 Aug. 1814, Big Warrior to Benjamin Hawkins, 6 Aug. 1814, AJ to Rachel Jackson, 10 Aug. 1814, AJ to John Coffee, 10 Aug. 1814, in *Jackson Papers*, iii; Remini, *Jackson*, i, 226–31.
20. Jackson requested direct orders from Secretary of War John Armstrong on 27 June 1814: 'Query – *If the Hostile Creeks have taken refuge in East Florida, fed and armed there by the Spaniards and British; the latter having landed troops within it and fortifying, with a large supply of munitions of war and provisions, and exciting the Indians to hostilities* – Will the government say to me, require a few hundred Militia (which can be had for the campaign at one days notice) and with such of my disposable force in regulars proceed to —— and reduce it?' Armstrong replied on 18 July, writing that 'If [the Spanish] admit, feed, arm and cooperate with the British and hostile Indians, we must strike on the broad principle of self-preservation.' However, this letter did not reach Jackson until some time after he had already moved on Pensacola. The reason for this long delay has never been explained.
21. AJ to William Charles Cole Claiborne, 5 Jan. 1813, in *Jackson Papers*, ii; Thomas Hart Benton to Thomas Flournoy, 5 July 1814, William Charles Cole Claiborne to AJ, 12 Aug. 1814, AJ to William Charles Cole Claiborne, 30 Aug. 1814, in *Jackson Papers*, iii.
22. ADM 101/104/3.
23. WO 1/143.

**Two Trips to London**
1. WO 1/143.
2. Nathaniel Millett, *The Maroons of Prospect Bluff and their Quest for Freedom in the Atlantic World* (Gainesville: University Press of Florida, 2013), 150; WO 1/143.
3. WO 1/143; Frank L. Owsley, 'Prophet of War: Josiah Francis and the Creek War', *American Indian Quarterly*, 9/3 (1985), 273–93; Millett, *Maroons*, 95–100.
4. FO 5/140.
5. Bradford Perkins, *Castlereagh and Adams: England and the United States, 1812–1823* (Berkeley: University of California Press, 1964), 197; John Quincy Adams to John Adams, 24 Feb. 1816; FO 5/110.

6. Both sides ended up accepting an offer from Tsar Alexander to privately and neutrally adjudicate the claims. In 1826, a Russian commission declared Britain owed the United States $1.2 million for slaves liberated by British forces during the War of 1812.
7. JQA diary, 25 Jan. 1816.
8. FO 72/180; Perkins, *Castlereagh and Adams*, 222–28.

**Alabama Fever**
1. Technically, in 1815 Mobile was part of the Mississippi Territory – which included the modern states of Mississippi and Alabama – until it was included in the Alabama Territory when that was created in 1817. Statehood followed in 1819.
2. Powell A. Casey, 'Military Roads in the Florida Parishes of Louisiana', *Journal of the Louisiana Historical Association*, 15/3 (1974), 229–42; Robert V. Remini, *Andrew Jackson*, i: *The Course of American Empire, 1767–1821* (New York: Harper & Row, 1977), 321–22.
3. American State Papers, Military Affairs, iii, 292–93, AJ to Armstrong, 10 Aug. 1814; *The Papers of Andrew Jackson*, iii: *1814–1815*, ed. Harold D. Moser et al. (Knoxville: University of Tennessee Press, 1991): AJ to John Williams, 18 May 1814.
4. Remini, *Jackson*, i, 302–04; Clarence E. Carter (ed.), *The Territorial Papers of the United States*, xv: *The Territory of Louisiana-Missouri, 1815–1821* (Washington, 1951), 63; 'Map of the former territorial limits of the Cherokee "Nation of" Indians' available here: https://www.loc.gov/resource/g3861e.np000155/?r=0.108,0.665,0.266,0.122,0); John Coffee to GLO commissioners, from Huntsville, AL, 14 Feb. 1816 (accessed here: https://digital.archives.alabama.gov/digital/collection/voices/id/1754/rec/7).
5. Remini, *Jackson*, i, 302–04; AJ to William Harris Crawford, 4 June 1816, in *The Papers of Andrew Jackson*, iv: *1816–1820*, ed. Harold D. Moser et al. (Knoxville: University of Tennessee Press, 1994).
6. Remini, *Jackson*, i, 326–31; Charles C. Royce, *The Cherokee Nation of Indians* (Washington, 1887); American State Papers, Indian Affairs, ii, 117; for a map of Alabama land cessions: https://www.loc.gov/item/13023487/.
7. Anne Royall, *Letters from Alabama* (Washington, 1830), 38–55; Daniel S. Dupre, *Transforming the Cotton Frontier* (Baton Rouge: Louisiana State University Press, 1997), 20, 38.
8. Jackson also secured the position of receiver at the Huntsville land office for John Brahan, who had been one of his generals at the Battle of New Orleans.
9. Alabama formally became a territory in August 1817 when it was carved out of the Mississippi Territory – the remainder of which became the state of Mississippi later that year.

10. *Alabama Territorial Papers*, 23, 67–70, 83–85; Gordon T. Chappell, 'The Life and Activities of General John Coffee', *Tennessee Historical Quarterly*, 1/2 (1942), 125–46; 'Letter from the Secretary of the Treasury, transmitting a statement of the sales of public lands in the Alabama Territory', 16 Dec. 1818; Malcolm J. Rohrbough, *The Land Office Business: The Settlement and Administration of American Public Lands, 1789–1837* (New York: OUP, 1968), 99–100.
11. *Alabama Territorial Papers*, 15, 34–35, 67–70, 75, 98, 143; Chappell, 'General John Coffee'; Huntsville *Republican*, 27 Jan. 1818.
12. *Alabama Territorial Papers*, 260, 300; Rohrbough, *Land Office Business*, 124.
13. Sven Beckert, *Empire of Cotton: A New History of Global Capitalism* (New York: Knopf, 2015), 104, 119, 205–06; Thomas Perkins Abernethy, *The Formative Period in Alabama, 1815–1828* (Tuscaloosa: University of Alabama Press, 1965), 35–37, 84–85.
14. Beckert, *Empire of Cotton*, 104, 119, 164, 205–06; Sheryllynne Haggerty, 'What's in a Price? The American Raw Cotton Market in Liverpool and the Anglo-American War', *Business History*, 61/6 (2018), 942–70; Dupre, *Transforming*, 39; Mike Bunn, *Early Alabama: An Illustrated Guide to the Formative Years, 1798–1826* (Tuscaloosa: University of Alabama Press, 2019), 32–33; Chappell, 'General John Coffee'.
15. Frances Cabaniss Roberts, *The Founding of Alabama: Background and Formative Period in the Great Bend and Madison County* (Tuscaloosa: University of Alabama Press, 2019), 44; Huntsville *Republican*, 16 Jan. 1819; John Coffee to Jackson, 12 Feb. 1818; Huntsville *Republican*, 20 Mar. 1819.
16. Rohrbough, *Land Office Business*, 109–11; *Alabama Territorial Papers*, 618; Dupre, *Transforming*, 41, 60, 139; James Jackson to Andrew Jackson, 12 Feb. 1818; Huntsville *Republican*, 20 Mar. 1819, 16 Jan. 1819.
17. Andrew H. Browning, *The Panic of 1819: The First Great Depression* (Columbia: University of Missouri Press, 2019), 102–05; Daniel Feller, *The Public Lands in Jacksonian Politics* (Madison: University of Wisconsin Press, 1984), 27; Murray N. Rothbard, *The Panic of 1819: Reactions and Policies* (Auburn: Von Mises Institute, 2002), 9.
18. Remini, *Jackson*, i, 330–31; Huntsville *Republican*, 20 Mar. 1819; Coffee to Jackson, 12 Feb. 1818.

## Jackson Redux
1. Anne Royall, *Letters from Alabama* (Washington, 1830), 69.
2. AJ to Robert Henry Dyer et al., 11 Jan. 1819, in *The Papers of Andrew Jackson*, iv: *1816–1820*, ed. Harold D. Moser et al. (Knoxville: University of Tennessee Press, 1994).
3. David Sinclair, *The Land that Never Was: Sir Gregor MacGregor and the Most Audacious Fraud in History* (Cambridge, MA: Da Capo, 2004), 173;

*Niles' Register*, 2 Aug. 1817; M. Rafter, *Memoirs of Gregor M'Gregor* (London: J. J. Stockdale, 1820), 87–88; Hubert Bruce Fuller, *The Purchase of Florida: Its History and Diplomacy* (Cleveland: Burrows, 1906), 232–36; David Bushnell, 'The Florida Republic: An Overview', in D. Bushnell (ed.), *La República de Las Floridas: Texts and Documents* (Mexico: Pan American Institute of Geography and History, 1986), 9–23; Frank Lawrence Owsley and Gene A. Smith, *Filibusters and Expansionists: Jeffersonian Manifest Destiny, 1800–1821* (Tuscaloosa: University of Alabama Press, 1997), 145–47.

4. One soldier wrote home to his father describing the incident: 'You cannot conceive, nor I describe the horrors of the scene. In an instant, hundreds of lifeless bodies were stretched upon the plain, buried in sand and rubbish, or suspended from the tops of the surrounding pines ... Here lay an innocent babe, there a helpless mother: on the one side a sturdy warrior, on the other a bleeding squaw. Piles of bodies, large heaps of sand, broken guns, accoutrements, &c. covered the site of the fort.' He added in a postscript: 'First rate land can be purchased in Florida for fifty cents per acre. What speculations! If it should ever be ours, which, I think, will be the case' (Nathaniel Millett, *The Maroons of Prospect Bluff and Their Quest for Freedom in the Atlantic World* (Gainesville: University Press of Florida, 2013), 227).
5. American State Papers, Indian Affairs, ii, 155–59, 616; Millett, *Maroons*, 226–40; John Missall and Mary Lou Missall, *The Seminole Wars: America's Longest Indian Conflict* (Gainesville: University Press of Florida, 2004), 32–37l; John Lewis Thomson, *History of the Second War between the United States and Great Britain* (Philadelphia: Hogan & Thompson, 1848), 499–502; Christina Snyder, *Slavery in Indian Country: The Changing Face of Captivity in Early America* (Cambridge, MA: Harvard University Press, 2010), 218; Owsley & Smith, *Filibusters and Expansionists*, 142–50.
6. James Monroe, State of the Union Address, 16 Nov. 1818; Roger Wendell Anderson, 'Andrew Jackson's Seminole Campaign of 1818: A Study in Historiography', MA thesis, University of Montana, 1956, 47.
7. Calhoun to Jackson, 26 Dec. 1817, Calhoun to Gaines, 16 Dec. 1817 and 16 Jan. 1818, reproduced in *Message from the President of the United States, Transmitting Copies of Documents Referred to in his Communication of the Seventeenth Ultimo, in relation to the Seminole War* (1818).
8. Calhoun to Gaines, 16 Dec. 1817, emphasis added.
9. Anderson, 'Jackson's Seminole Campaign'.
10. Robert V. Remini, *Andrew Jackson and His Indian Wars* (New York: Viking, 2001), 138–39.
11. JQA diary, 26 June 1818; Anderson, 'Jackson's Seminole Campaign'; Harry Ammon, *James Monroe: The Quest for National Identity* (New York: McGraw-Hill, 1971), 543–44; Adam Hodgson, *Letters from North America*

(London: Hurst, Robinson, 1824), 68–92; Remini, *Jackson and His Indian Wars*, 165.
12. Document 8: FO 5/86, Foster to Castlereagh, 15 May 1812; Anderson, 'Jackson's Seminole Campaign'; Deborah A. Rosen, *Border Law: The First Seminole War and American Nationhood* (Cambridge, MA: Harvard University Press, 2015), 36–39, the letter in question is JM to AJ, 19 July 1818.
13. Samuel Putnam Waldo (ed.), *Memoirs of Andrew Jackson* (Hartford: John Russell, 1818), 304; AJ to United States Troops near Suwannee River, 15 Apr. 1818, AJ to John Calhoun, 5 May 1818, AJ to John Calhoun, 2 June 1818, AJ to Rachel Jackson, 2 June 1818, in *Jackson Papers*, iv; Missall & Missall, *Seminole Wars*, 40–42; Samuel Perkins, *General Jackson's Conduct in the Seminole War* (Brooklyn, 1828), 12–23; Charles Fenton Mercer, Speech in the House of Representatives, on the Seminole War, Washington, 1818; Remini, *Jackson and His Indian Wars*, 160–62; Robert V. Remini, *Andrew Jackson*, i: *The Course of American Empire, 1767–1821* (New York: Harper & Row, 1977), 365.

## Giant Steps
1. JQA diary, 7–9 July 1818; Gallatin to Adams, 22 July 1818; Bradford Perkins, *Castlereagh and Adams: England and the United States, 1812–1823* (Berkeley: University of California Press, 1964), 289.
2. Ibid, 12–19 July 1818.
3. J. F. Gallatin (ed.), *The Diary of James Gallatin* (New York: Scribner's, 1916), 4; E. F. Ellet, *The Court Circles of the Republic* (Hartford, 1869), 121.
4. JQA diary, 7 Nov. 1797.
5. JQA diary, 2 July 1815.
6. Roger Wendell Anderson, 'Andrew Jackson's Seminole Campaign of 1818: A Study in Historiography', MA thesis, University of Montana, 1956; Monroe to Madison, 7 Feb. 1819.
7. Monroe to Jackson, 19 July 1818.
8. William S. Belko, 'The Origins of the Monroe Doctrine Revisited: The Madison Administration, the West Florida Revolt, and the No Transfer Policy', *Florida Historical Quarterly*, 90/2 (2011), 157–92; JQA diary, 18 Mar. 1819; Michael Solomon, 'Saving the "Slaves of Kings and Priests": The United States, Manifest Destiny, and the Rhetoric of Anti-Catholicism', MA thesis, Duquesne University, 2009.
9. George Cruikshank satirical print, held in the British Museum: 1868,0808.8438.
10. Hansard, 11 May 1819; William Earl Weeks, *John Quincy Adams and American Global Empire* (Lexington: University Press of Kentucky, 1992).
11. Weeks, *John Quincy Adams*, 246; Nathaniel Millett, *The Maroons of Prospect Bluff and their Quest for Freedom in the Atlantic World*

(Gainesville: University Press of Florida, 2013), 246; William Earl Weeks, 'John Quincy Adams's "Great Gun" and the Rhetoric of American Empire', *Diplomatic History*, 14/1 (1990), 25–42; William S. Belko (ed.), *America's Hundred Years' War: U.S. Expansion to the Gulf Coast and the Fate of the Seminole, 1763–1858* (Gainesville: University Press of Florida, 2011), 90; American State Papers, Foreign Relations, iv, 539.

12. Perkins, *Castlereagh and Adams*, 295; Dexter Perkins, 'Russia and the Spanish Colonies, 1817–1818', *American Historical Review*, 28/4 (1923), 656–72; The Executive Proceedings of the Senate of the United States, on the Subject of the Mission to the Congress at Panama, 1826; Piero Gleijeses, 'The Limits of Sympathy: The United States and the Independence of Spanish America', *Journal of Latin American Studies*, 24/3 (1992), 481–505.
13. JQA diary, 3 Feb. 1819, 15 Feb. 1819, 22 Feb. 1819.
14. Huntsville *Republican*, 20 Mar. 1819, 5 June 1819.
15. Robert V. Remini, *Andrew Jackson*, i: *The Course of American Empire, 1767–1821* (New York: Harper & Row, 1977), 406.
16. William Spence Robertson, 'The Policy of Spain Toward its Revolted Colonies, 1820–1823', *Hispanic American Historical Review*, 6/1–3 (1926), 21–46; David Sinclair, *The Land that Never Was: Sir Gregor MacGregor and the Most Audacious Fraud in History* (Cambridge, MA: Da Capo, 2004), 58–63; Perkins, *Castlereagh and Adams*, 338–40.
17. George C. Herring, *From Colony to Superpower: U.S. Foreign Relations since 1776* (New York: OUP, 2008), 152.
18. Peter Schmidtmeyer, *Travels into Chile* (London, 1824); Philip Ziegler, *The Sixth Great Power: Barings, 1762–1929* (London: Collins, 1988), 101.
19. JQA diary, 26 Nov. 1823.
20. L. M. Penson, *Foundation of British Foreign Policy, 1792–1902* (United Kingdom, Taylor & Francis), 53–65; Harry Ammon, *James Monroe: The Quest for National Identity* (New York: McGraw-Hill, 1971), 477.
21. Jefferson to Monroe, 24 Oct. 1823; Caitlin Fitz, *Our Sister Republics: The United States in an Age of American Revolutions* (New York: Norton, 2016), 127; *Annals of Congress*, House of Representatives, 15th Congress, 1st Session, 1475–76; Alabama *Republican*, 5 June 1819; JQA diary, 29 Mar. 1820, 15 Nov. 1823; M. Rafter, *Memoirs of Gregor M'Gregor* (London: J. J. Stockdale, 1820), 86; North American Pamphlet on South American Affairs, Henry Marie Brackenridge, 40.
22. Arthur Preston Whitaker, *The United States and the Independence of Latin America, 1800–1830* (Baltimore: Johns Hopkins Press, 1941), 335–36; John Quincy Adams to Thomas Boylston Adams, 14 Apr. 1818; Fitz, *Our Sister Republics*, 181; William Spence Robertson, 'The First Legations of the United States in Latin America', *Mississippi Valley Historical Review*, 2/2 (1915), 183–212; Weeks, *John Quincy Adams*, 180; JQA diary, 7 Nov. 1823;

Harry Ammon, 'The Monroe Doctrine: Domestic Politics or National Decision?', *Diplomatic History*, 5/1 (1981), 53–70.
23. Louis A. Pérez, *Cuba and the United States: Ties of Singular Intimacy* (Athens: University of Georgia Press, 2003), 35–43; John Quincy Adams to Hugh Nelson, 28 Apr. 1823.
24. Walter LaFeber, *Inevitable Revolutions: The United States in Central America* (New York: Norton, 1993), 13; Belko, 'Origins of the Monroe Doctrine Revisited'.
25. John Quincy Adams to Louisa Catherine Johnson Adams, 7 Oct. 1822.

**The Widower**
1. Robert V. Remini, *Andrew Jackson and His Indian Wars* (New York: Viking, 2001), 214; John Missall and Mary Lou Missall, *The Seminole Wars: America's Longest Indian Conflict* (Gainesville: University Press of Florida, 2004), 49; Jon Meacham, *American Lion: Andrew Jackson in the White House* (New York: Random House, 2008), 39.
2. Alan Taylor, *American Republics: A Continental History of the United States, 1783–1850* (New York: Norton, 2021), 277; Edward E. Baptist, *The Half Has Never Been Told: Slavery and the Making of American Capitalism* (New York: Basic, 2016), 227; 1830 Census Data; Jedidiah Morse, *A Report to the Secretary of War of the United States, on Indian affairs* (1822).
3. Jackson to Coffee, 13 July 1817.
4. National Archives, FO 5/140, 87.
5. Quoted in Remini, *Jackson and His Indian Wars*, 233.
6. Davy Crockett, *Narrative of the Life of Davy Crockett* (Philadelphia: E. L. Carey & A. Hart, 1834), 206.
7. Jeremiah Evarts, *Essays on the Present Crisis in the Condition of the American Indians* (Boston: Perkins & Marvin, 1829), 87.
8. David W. Haley to AJ, 8 Oct. 1829, William Carroll to AJ, 29 June 1829, in *The Papers of Andrew Jackson*, vii: *1829*, ed. Daniel Feller et al. (Knoxville: University of Tennessee Press, 2007); Mary Elizabeth Young, *Redskins, Ruffleshirts, and Rednecks* (Norman: University of Oklahoma Press, 1961), 15–16.
9. Jackson to Gadsden, 12 Oct. 1829, in *Jackson Papers*, vii; AJ to the Chickasaw Indians, 23 Aug. 1830; AJ to John Pitchlynn, 6 Apr. 1830; AJ to William Berkeley Lewis, 25 Aug. 1830, in *The Papers of Andrew Jackson*, viii: *1830*, ed. Daniel Feller et al. (Knoxville: University of Tennessee Press, 2010).
10. Alexis de Tocqueville, *Democracy in America* (London: Penguin Publishing Group, 2003), 380; Robert Cicero Weems, 'The Bank of the Mississippi: A Pioneer Bank of the Old Southwest, 1809–1844', PhD thesis, Columbia University, 1952, 541.

11. For the classic statement of civilizing policy, see Thomas Jefferson to Cherokee Nation, 4 May 1808; Claudio Saunt, *Unworthy Republic: The Dispossession of Native Americans and the Road to Indian Territory* (New York: Norton, 2020), 54; John Ridge to Albert Gallatin, 27 Feb. 1826; Anthony F. C. Wallace, *The Long, Bitter Trail: Andrew Jackson and the Indians* (New York: Hill & Wang, 1993), 10.
12. Taylor, *American Republics*, 277; Memorial of the Prudential Committee of the American Board of Commissioners for Foreign Missions of Massachusetts, submitted to 21st Congress, 9 Feb. 1831; see Lumpkin, quoted in George William Goss, 'The Debate over Indian Removal in the 1830s', MA thesis, University of Massachusetts Boston, 2011, 18.
13. John Ross to AJ, 28 Mar. 1834, in *Letters of John Ross*, i.
14. Natalie Joy, 'The Indian's Cause: Abolitionists and Native American Rights', *Journal of the Civil War Era*, 8/2 (2018), 215–42.
15. See Circular of the New-York Committee in aid of the Cherokee nation … New York, 10 Feb. 1832, held at the Library of Congress; John Ross to the Cherokee Nation, 21 July 1838, in *Letters of John Ross*, i.
16. Young, *Redskins, Ruffleshirts, and Rednecks*, 90–91.
17. Young, *Redskins, Ruffleshirts, and Rednecks*, 85–86; Christopher D. Haveman, 'The Removal of the Creek Indians from the Southeast, 1825–1838', PhD thesis, Auburn University, 2009.
18. Haveman, 'Removal of the Creek Indians'; Young, *Redskins, Ruffleshirts, and Rednecks*, 85–91.
19. Baptist, *Half Has Never Been Told*, 258; Malcolm J. Rohrbough, *The Land Office Business: The Settlement and Administration of American Public Lands, 1789–1837* (New York: OUP, 1968), 228–32; Joseph Glover Baldwin, *The Flush Times of Alabama and Mississippi: A Series of Sketches* (New York: D. Appleton, 1854), 91.
20. Charles C. Bolton, *Poor Whites of the Antebellum South* (Durham: Duke University Press, 1994), 75–79; Young, *Redskins, Ruffleshirts, and Rednecks*, 99; Rohrbough, *Land Office Business*, 228–32; Baldwin, *Flush Times*, 91, 236–39; former-slave reminiscences taken from Benjamin Drew (ed.), *The Refugee; or The Narratives of Fugitive Slaves in Canada* (Dundurn Press, 2008); William H. Sparks, *The Memories of Fifty Years* (Philadelphia: Claxton, Remsen & Haffelfinger, 1870), ch. 22.
21. AJ to Congress, 8 Dec. 1832; Stanley Lebergott, 'The Demand for Land: The United States, 1820–1860', *Journal of Economic History*, 45/2 (1985), 181–212; Thomas L. Hungerford, 'U.S. Federal Government Revenues: 1790 to the Present', 2006, accessible at: https://www.everycrsreport.com/reports/RL33665.html.
22. John L. Conger, 'South Carolina and the Early Tariffs', *Mississippi Valley Historical Review*, 5/1 (1919), 415–33; for Jackson's views on land policy, see

American State Papers, Public Lands, vi, 618–21; see also Calhoun's *Exposition* and Hayne's speech of 19 Jan. 1830.
23. James Hamilton Jr. to MVB, 19 Feb. 1829, in Martin Van Buren Papers; James Parton, *Life of Andrew Jackson* (New York: Mason Bros, 1861), 580–81; AJ to MVB, 13 Jan. 1833; Meacham, *American Lion*, 219–40; Thomas Hart Benton, *Thirty Years' View* (New York: D. Appleton, 1854), 309–11.
24. Remini, *Jackson and His Indian Wars*, 237–38; *The Liberator*, 5 Feb. 1931, 23 Apr. 1831; George W. Julian, *The Life of Joshua R. Giddings* (Chicago: A. C. McClurg, 1892), 42; JQA diary, 6 June 1830; Joy, 'The Indian's Cause'; Clay, quoted in Merrill D. Peterson, *The Great Triumvirate: Webster, Clay, and Calhoun* (New York: OUP, 1987), 247–48.
25. John and Mary Lou Missall (eds), *In Their Own Words: Selected Seminole 'Talks', 1817–1842*, Seminole Wars Foundation, Pamphlet Series, 1/5, 2009.

## PART IV: THE OREGON COUNTRY
### Consider the Otter
1. Conrad Limbaugh, 'Observations on the California Sea Otter', *Journal of Mammalogy*, 42/2 (1961), 271–73; C. M. Scammon, 'The Sea Otters', *American Naturalist*, 4/2 (1870), 65–74; Victor B. Scheffer, 'The Sea Otter on the Washington Coast', *Pacific Northwest Quarterly*, 31/4 (1940), 370–88; John Jewitt, *A Narrative of the Adventures and Sufferings of John R. Jewitt* (New York, 1815), 119–21.
2. Adam Smith, *An Inquiry into the Nature and Causes of the Wealth of Nations*, i (London: W. Strahan & T. Cadell, 1776); George Dixon, *A Voyage Round the World* (London, 1789), 310; Eric Jay Dolin, *When America First Met China* (New York: Liveright, 2012), 64; A. Owen Aldridge, *The Dragon and the Eagle: The Presence of China in the American Enlightenment* (Detroit: Wayne State University Press, 1993), 96, 155; Amasa Delano, *A Narrative of Voyages and Travels in the Northern and Southern Hemispheres*, i (Boston: E. G. House, 1817), 531.
3. Samuel Shaw to John Jay, 31 Dec. 1786.
4. Dolin, *When America First Met China*, 10–21; Kenneth Scott Latourette, *The History of Early Relations between the United States and China, 1784–1844* (New Haven: Yale University Press, 1917), 13; Matthew Lockwood, *To Begin the World Over Again: How the American Revolution Devastated the Globe* (New Haven: Yale University Press, 2019), 471; Aldridge, *Dragon and the Eagle*, 100–01; Clarence L. Ver Steeg, 'Financing and Outfitting the First United States Ship to China', *Pacific Historical Review*, 22/1 (1953), 1–12; James R. Gibson, *Otter Skins, Boston Ships, and China Goods: The Maritime Fur Trade of the Northwest, 1785–1841* (Montreal: McGill-Queen's University Press, 1992), 52–53.

5. Aldridge, *Dragon and the Eagle*, 125.
6. John W. Swift, P. Hodgkinson and Samuel W. Woodhouse, 'The Voyage of the Empress of China', *Pennsylvania Magazine of History and Biography*, 63/1 (1939), 24–36.
7. Heinrich Zimmermann, *Zimmermann's Account of the Third Voyage of Captain Cook, 1776–1780* (1926), 26; James Cook, *The Three Voyages of Captain James Cook*, vi (London: Longman, Hurst, Rees, Orme & Brown, 1821), 243; John Rickman, *Journal of Captain Cook's Last Voyage to the Pacific Ocean, on Discovery* (London: E. Newbery, 1781), 214–15.
8. Dolin, *When America First Met China*, 10.
9. Cook, *Three Voyages*, 245–46, 271, 454–67; Zimmermann, *Account*, 31–34.
10. 'Even the Muscovites now trade regularly with China, by a sort of caravans which go over land through Siberia and Tartary to Pekin' (Smith, *Wealth of Nations*, i).
11. Jonathan Schlesinger, *A World Trimmed With Fur: Wild Things, Pristine Places, and the Natural Fringes of Qing Rule* (Stanford: Stanford University Press, 2017), 11–52.
12. Dolin, *When America First Met China*, 11; Fred Lockley, *Oregon Trail Blazers* (New York: Knickerbocker Press, 1929), 76–96.
13. Gibson, *Otter Skins*, 44–58.
14. Silas Pinckney Holbrook, *Sketches by a Traveller* (Boston: Carter & Hendee, 1830), 10.
15. Alexander Mackenzie, *Voyages from Montreal on the River St Laurence, through the Continent of North America, to the Frozen and Pacific Oceans, in the Years 1789 and 1793* (London, 1801), 411.
16. James P. Ronda, *Lewis and Clark among the Indians* (Lincoln, NE: University of Nebraska Press, 1988), 151–83.
17. Lewis, 23 Feb. 1806, in *The Journals of the Lewis and Clark Expedition*, ed. Gary Moulton (University of Nebraska Press/University of Nebraska-Lincoln Libraries-Electronic Text Center, 2005): http://lewisandclarkjournals.unl.edu.
18. Meriwether Lewis to Thomas Jefferson, 23 Sept. 1806; Samuel L. Mitchill, *A Discourse on the Character and Services of Thomas Jefferson* (New York: Carvill, 1826), 29.
19. It is not clear whether Lewis was murdered or committed suicide.
20. John D. Haeger, 'Business Strategy and Practice in the Early Republic: John Jacob Astor and the American Fur Trade', *Western Historical Quarterly*, 19/2 (1988), 183–202.
21. Albert Gallatin's son James recorded in his diary an insight into Astor's table manners: 'Really Mr. Astor is dreadful. Father has to be civil to him, as in 1812–13 he rendered great services to the Treasury. He came to dejeuner to-day; we were simply en famille, he sitting next to Frances. He actually wiped his fingers on the sleeves of her fresh white spencer.

Mamma in discreet tones said, "Oh, Mr. Astor, I must apologize; they have forgotten to give you a serviette." I think he felt foolish.'
22. James P. Ronda, *Astoria and Empire* (Lincoln, NE: University of Nebraska Press, 1990), 223, 270, 308.
23. John Denis Haeger, *John Jacob Astor, Business and Finance in the Early Republic* (Detroit: Wayne State University Press, 1991), 121–22, 133; Alexander Ross, 'Adventures of the First Settlers on the Oregon or Columbia River', in Reuben Gold Thwaites (ed.), *Early Western Travels, 1748–1846*, vii (Cleveland: Arthur H. Clark, 1904).
24. Ross, 'Adventures of the First Settlers'.
25. Ronda, *Astoria and Empire*, 235–37; Washington Irving, *Astoria*, i (Philadelphia: Carey, Lea & Blanchard, 1836), ch. 11.
26. J. Ward Ruckman, 'Ramsay Crooks and the Fur Trade of the Northwest', *Minnesota History*, 7/1 (1926), 18–31; Kenneth W. Porter, 'Roll of Overland Astorians, 1810–12', *Oregon Historical Quarterly*, 34/2 (1933), 103–12; Haeger, *Astor*, 126; Irving, *Astoria*, ch. 37; Ronda, *Astoria and Empire*, 177–93.
27. Haeger, *Astor*, 165–66; Barry Gough, *Fortune's a River: The Collision of Empires in Northwest America* (Madeira Park: Harbour, 2007), 308–13; Ronda, *Astoria and Empire*, 245–95.
28. Ronda, *Astoria and Empire*, 301–15; William R. Manning (ed.), *Diplomatic Correspondence of the United States: Canadian Relations, 1784–1860*, i: *1784–1820* (Washington: Carnegie Endowment for International Peace, 1940), 218, 230–32, 262–63.

**The Shape of a Problem**
1. George C. Herring, *From Colony to Superpower: U.S. Foreign Relations since 1776* (New York: OUP, 2008), 134–36.
2. Rush to JQA, 14 Apr. 1819, in William R. Manning (ed.), *Diplomatic Correspondence of the United States: Canadian Relations, 1784–1860*, i: *1784–1820* (Washington: Carnegie Endowment for International Peace, 1940), 907–08.
3. Francis Hall, *Travels in Canada, and the United States, in 1816 and 1817* (London: Longman, Hurst, Rees, Orme & Brown, 1818), 55–59.
4. Hall on the average Canadian farmer: 'Should an inclement season, as was the case last year, disappoint his hopes, he is prepared patiently to confess himself, and die of hunger, fully persuaded that the blessed St. Anne, or St. Anthony, will not fail him in both worlds.'
5. Hall, *Travels*, 60–78, 143–44, 149–54, 163.
6. William Kingsford, *The History of Canada*, ix (Toronto: Rowsell & Hutchison, 1897), 373–74.
7. Lawrence A. Peskin, 'Conspiratorial Anglophobia and the War of 1812', *Journal of American History*, 98/3 (2011), 647–69; Reginald Horsman, 'On to Canada: Manifest Destiny and United States Strategy in the War of 1812',

*Michigan Historical Review*, 13/2 (1987), 1–24; JQA to John Adams, 31 Aug. 1811; JQA to Monroe, 5 Sept. 1814, in Manning, *Canadian Relations*, i, 647–48.
8. See John S. Galbraith, *The Hudson's Bay Company as an Imperial Factor, 1821–1869* (Toronto: University of Toronto Press, 1957), 12–13. James Douglas notes this incompatibility: 'The interests of the Colony and the Fur Trade will never harmonize, the former can flourish, only, through the protection of equal laws, the influence of free trade, the accession of respectable inhabitants; in short, by establishing a new order of things, while the fur trade must suffer by each innovation.'
9. Joseph Bouchette, *The British Dominions in North America*, i (London, 1831), 10–11; H. W. V. Temperley, 'The Later American Policy of George Canning', *American Historical Review*, 11/4 (1906), 779–97.
10. Thomas Tooke and William Newmarch, *A History of Prices*, vi (London, 1857), 340–41; William D. Grampp, 'How Britain Turned to Free Trade', *Business History Review*, 61/1 (1987), 86–112.
11. JQA diary, 29 Aug. 1822.
12. John Floyd, 'Occupation of the Columbia River – Floyd's Report of January 25, 1821', *Quarterly of the Oregon Historical Society*, 8/1 (1907), 51–75; Barbara Cloud, 'Oregon in the 1820s: The Congressional Perspective', *Western Historical Quarterly*, 12/2 (1981), 145–64; Foster Rhea Dulles, *America in the Pacific: A Century of Expansion* (Boston: Houghton Mifflin, 1932), 33, 56; Edward Gaylord Bourne, 'Aspects of Oregon History before 1840', *Quarterly of the Oregon Historical Society*, 6/3 (1905), 255–75.
13. Cloud, 'Oregon in the 1820s'; William R. Manning (ed.), *Diplomatic Correspondence of the United States: Canadian Relations, 1784–1860*, ii: *1821–1835* (Washington: Carnegie Endowment for International Peace, 1942), 462; Richard Rush to JQA, 12 Aug. 1824.
14. Cloud, 'Oregon in the 1820s'.
15. Manning, *Canadian Relations*, ii, 58.
16. Manning, *Canadian Relations*, ii, 907–08; Rush to JQA, 14 Apr. 1819; Manning, *Canadian Relations*, ii, 55–56; JQA to Rush, 22 July 1823; Frederick Merk, 'The Ghost River Caledonia in the Oregon Negotiation of 1818', *American Historical Review*, 55/3 (1950), 530–51.
17. Frederick Merk (ed.), *Fur Trade and Empire: George Simpson's Journal, 1824–25* (Cambridge, MA: Harvard University Press, 1931), xxvii–xxx; James Raffan, *Emperor of the North: Sir George Simpson and the Remarkable Story of the Hudson's Bay Company* (Toronto: HarperCollins, 2007), 107–13, 149, 168, 186, 237–41.
18. Merk, *Fur Trade and Empire*, 6–8, 16, 18, 20, 47, 64–65, 67–68.
19. Merk, *Fur Trade and Empire*, 70–72, 78–79; Raffan, *Emperor of the North*, 187–90.

20. Merk, *Fur Trade and Empire*, 46.
21. Merk, *Fur Trade and Empire*, 124.
22. Alexander Ross, 'Adventures of the First Settlers on the Oregon or Columbia River', in Reuben Gold Thwaites (ed.), *Early Western Travels, 1748–1846*, vii (Cleveland: Arthur H. Clark, 1904), 270; Galbraith, *Imperial Factor*, 83–93; all references to Philip Skene Ogden and William Kittson's journals are taken from https://user.xmission.com/~drudy/mtman/html/ogden.html.
23. Ogden and Kittson journals.
24. Ogden and Kittson journals; Galbraith, *Imperial Factor*, 95.

**Into the Pacific**
1. Charles Wilkes, *Narrative of the United States Exploring Expedition*, iii (Philadelphia: Lea & Blanchard, 1845), 273–85.
2. Wilkes, *Narrative*, iii, 273–85; see Nathaniel Philbrick, *Sea of Glory: The Epic South Seas Expedition 1838–42* (London: HarperCollins, 2004) ch. 10: 'Massacre at Malolo'.
3. Ernest S. Dodge, *Islands and Empires: Western Impact on the Pacific and East Asia* (Minneapolis: University of Minnesota, 1976), 7.
4. Philbrick, *Sea of Glory*, 13–14; Eric Jay Dolin, *When America First Met China* (New York: Liveright, 2012), 149–51.
5. Harold Whitman Bradley, 'Hawaii and the American Penetration of the Northeastern Pacific, 1800–1845', *Pacific Historical Review*, 12/3 (1943), 277–86; Dodge, *Islands and Empires*, 60–62.
6. Dodge, *Islands and Empires*, 59–68; Edward D. Melillo, 'Making Sea Cucumbers Out of Whales' Teeth: Nantucket Castaways and Encounters of Value in Nineteenth-Century Fiji', *Environmental History*, 20/3 (2015), 449–74; Edmund Fanning, *Voyages Round the World: Between 1792 and 1832* (New York: Collins & Hannay, 1883), 463; Herman Melville, *Omoo: A Narrative of Adventures in the South Seas* (New York: Harper, 1847).
7. Jan. 1827, Joshua Bates & J. Baring, Indent for Lace and Other Cotton Goods for Manila. Baring Archive, HC5.1.10a; Graeme Mack, 'Seaborne Sovereignties: Pacific Trade and the Evolution of American Commercial Maritime Imperialism, 1787–1848', PhD thesis, University of California San Diego, 2022, 190–91; Samuel Eliot Morison, *The Maritime History of Massachusetts, 1783–1860* (Boston: Houghton Mifflin, 1921), 90–91, 261–67, 283–84; Richard H. Dana, *Two Years Before the Mast* (Wordsworth American Library, 1996), 61; William Ruschenberger, *Three Years in the Pacific* (Philadelphia: Carey, Lea & Blanchard, 1834), 130.
8. Eric Jay Dolin, *Leviathan: The History of Whaling in America* (New York: Norton, 2007), 201–13, 221; Morison, *Maritime History of Massachusetts*, 314–17, 323; Dodge, *Islands and Empires*, 69; Wilson Heflin, *Herman Melville's Whaling Years* (Nashville: Vanderbilt University Press, 2004),

25–30, 187–89; George Simpson, *An Overland Journey Round the World* (Philadelphia: Lea & Blanchard, 1847), 51–52.
9. Dana, *Two Years*, 73.
10. John Adams to Joseph Bradley Varnum, 5 Jan. 1813; Ernest N. Paolino, *The Foundations of the American Empire: William Henry Seward and U.S. Foreign Policy* (Ithaca: Cornell University Press, 1973), 28.
11. Dolin, *Leviathan*, 214; Frederick Jackson Turner, 'New England 1830–1850', *Huntington Library Bulletin*, 1 (1931), 153–98; Morison, *Maritime History of Massachusetts*, 255–56; Dana, *Two Years*, 61.
12. Paul A. Varg, *New England and Foreign Relations: 1789–1850* (Hanover: University Press of New England, 1983), 130, 143, 154–56.
13. David T. Leary, 'Slacum in the Pacific, 1832–37: Backgrounds of the Oregon Report', *Oregon Historical Quarterly*, 76/2 (1975), 118–34; W. Patrick Strauss, 'Pioneer American Diplomats in Polynesia, 1820–1840', *Pacific Historical Review*, 31/1 (1962), 21–30; see Report of the Secretary of the Navy for 1826, 1827, 1830, 1835, 1841, 1842, available at https://www.history.navy.mil/research/library/online-reading-room/title-list-alphabetically/a/secnav-reports.html; Edmund Roberts, *Embassy to the Eastern Courts* (New York: Harper, 1837), 71.
14. Peter Harvey, *Reminiscences and Anecdotes of Daniel Webster* (Boston: Little, Brown, 1878), 240; Edward P. Crapol, 'John Tyler and the Pursuit of National Destiny', *Journal of the Early Republic*, 17/3 (1997), 467–91; Matthew J. Karp, 'Slavery and American Sea Power: The Navalist Impulse in the Antebellum South', *Journal of Southern History*, 77/2 (2011), 282–324.
15. Jeremiah N. Reynolds, 'Address on the Subject of a Surveying and Exploring Expedition to the Pacific Ocean and South Seas', 1836.
16. Philbrick, *Sea of Glory*, 332–33; Herman J. Viola, 'The Wilkes Expedition on the Pacific Coast', *Pacific Northwest Quarterly*, 80/1 (1989), 21–31; Dolin, *Leviathan*, 241.
17. Charles Wilkes, 'Survey of the Mouth of the Columbia River by the United States Exploring Expedition', available at: https://www.govinfo.gov/content/pkg/SERIALSET-00478_00_00-039-0475-0000/pdf/SERIALSET-00478_00_00-039-0475-0000.pdf; Norman A. Graebner, 'Maritime Factors in the Oregon Compromise', *Pacific Historical Review*, 20/4 (1951), 331–45; Philbrick, *Sea of Glory*, 332–33.
18. Viola, 'Wilkes Expedition'.
19. Charles Wilkes, 'Report on the Territory of Oregon', *Quarterly of the Oregon Historical Society*, 12/3 (1911), 269–99; Viola, 'Wilkes Expedition'.
20. Herbert D. Winters, 'Tyler, Webster, and the Oregon Question', *Quarterly Journal of the New York State Historical Association*, 11/4 (1930), 311–23; Graebner, 'Maritime Factors'; William Sturgis, 'The Oregon Question: Substance of a Lecture Before the Mercantile Library Association', 1845.

## Oregon Fever

1. Hubert Howe Bancroft, *The Works of Hubert Howe Bancroft: 1834–1848. History of Oregon*, i (United States, 1886), 393; Francis Parkman, *The Oregon Trail: Sketches of Prairie and Rocky Mountain Life* (New York: Putnam, 1849), 6, 56–57; Michael B. Husband, 'The Backgrounds and Organization of the great Oregon Migration of 1843', MA thesis, University of Nebraska at Omaha, 1966; Joseph Gaston, *The Centennial History of Oregon, 1811–1912*, i (Chicago: S. J. Clarke, 1912), 244–46; John D. Unruh, *The Plains Across: The Overland Emigrants and the Trans-Mississippi West, 1840–60* (Urbana: University of Illinois Press, 1979), 38.
2. Dale L. Morgan, *Jedediah Smith and the Opening of the West* (Lincoln: University of Nebraska Press, 1953), 322, 343–44.
3. Fred Wilbur Powell, 'Hall Jackson Kelley – Prophet of Oregon', *Quarterly of the Oregon Historical Society*, 18/1 (1917), 1–54.
4. Bancroft: 'If his intellect was not as broad and bright as Burke's, there was at least no danger of the heart hardening through the head, as with Robespierre and St Just.'
5. Powell, 'Hall Jackson Kelley'; Joseph Gaston, *Portland, Oregon: Its History and Builders*, i (Chicago: S. J. Clarke, 1911), ch. 9, accessible at https://en.wikisource.org/wiki/Portland,_Oregon:_Its_History_and_Builders/Volume_1/Chapter_9; Hubert Howe Bancroft, *History of the Northwest Coast*, ii: *1800–1846* (San Francisco: History Company, 1890), 56–58.
6. https://en.wikisource.org/wiki/Marcus_Whitman,_Pathfinder_and_Patriot; Elliott West, *The Last Indian War: The Nez Perce Story* (New York: OUP, 2009), 35–46; Oliver Nixon, *How Marcus Whitman Saved Oregon* (Chicago: Star, 1895), 64–90.
7. Nixon, *How Marcus Whitman Saved Oregon*, 58–59.
8. Nixon, *How Marcus Whitman Saved Oregon*, 120; Jesse Applegate, *A Day with the Cow Column in 1843* (Chicago, 1934); Joseph Ellison, 'The Covered Wagon Centennial: March of the Empire Builders over the Oregon Trail', *Washington Historical Quarterly*, 21/3 (1930), 163–78.
9. Randolph B. Marcy, *The Prairie Traveler: A Hand-Book for Overland Expeditions* (New York: Harper, 1859), 33–42; John Minto, 'Reminiscences of Experiences on the Oregon Trail in 1844', *Quarterly of the Oregon Historical Society*, 2/3 (1901), 209–54; Unruh, *Plains Across*, 406, 410.
10. 'Emigration from Iowa to Oregon in 1843', *Quarterly of the Oregon Historical Society*, 15/4 (1914), 285–99; Marcy, *Prairie Traveler*, 22–25; Lansford W. Hastings, *The Emigrants' Guide to Oregon and California* (Cincinnati: George Conclin, 1845), 9; Applegate, *Day with the Cow Column*; Harrison C. Dale, 'The Organization of the Oregon Emigrating Companies', *Quarterly of the Oregon Historical Society*, 16/3 (1915), 205–27.
11. 'Emigration from Iowa to Oregon in 1843'; Marcy, *Prairie Traveler*, 198–295; Unruh, *Plains Across*, 410; Minto, 'Reminiscences'.

12. Marcy, *Prairie Traveler*, 26–28, 44–46; Unruh, *Plains Across*, 408.
13. Parkman, *Oregon Trail*, 42; James W. Nesmith, 'Diary of the Emigration of 1843', *Quarterly of the Oregon Historical Society*, 7/4 (1906), 329–59; from 'A Report on an Exploration of the Country Lying between the Missouri River and the Rocky Mountains', in John C. Frémont, *The Exploring Expedition to the Rocky Mountains, Oregon and California* (Auburn: Derby & Miller, 1852).
14. Frémont, *Exploring Expedition*; Parkman, *Oregon Trail*, 65–66; Applegate, *Day with the Cow Column*; P. H. Burnett, 'Letters of Peter H. Burnett', *Quarterly of the Oregon Historical Society*, 3/4 (1902), 398–426.
15. Dale L. Morgan (ed.), *Overland in 1846: Diaries and Letters of the California-Oregon Trail*, i (Georgetown, CA: Talisman Press, 1963), 174; Dale L. Morgan (ed.), *Overland in 1846: Diaries and Letters of the California-Oregon Trail*, ii (Georgetown, CA: Talisman Press, 1963), 2, 556, 563; Hastings, *Emigrants' Guide*, 7–8; Unruh, *Plains Across*, 389; Nesmith, 'Diary'.
16. Marcy, *Prairie Traveler*, 124–25; Parkman, *Oregon Trail*, 65–66; Morgan, *Overland in 1846*, i, 173.
17. Parkman, *Oregon Trail*, 96; Unruh, *Plains Across*, 150, 170.
18. Frémont, *Exploring Expedition*.
19. Frémont, *Exploring Expedition*; Marcy, *Prairie Traveler*, 73; Morgan, *Overland in 1846*, i, 126, 177; Morgan, *Overland in 1846*, ii, 685; Minto, 'Reminiscences'; Nesmith, 'Diary'; see William E. Smythe, *The Conquest of Arid America* (New York: Harper, 1900).
20. Nesmith, 'Diary'; George Wilkes, *The History of Oregon: Geographical and Political* (New York: W. H. Colyer, 1845), 82.
21. Wilkes, *History of Oregon*, 82; Minto, 'Reminiscences'.
22. Frémont, *Exploring Expedition*.
23. Nesmith, 'Diary'; Minto, 'Reminiscences'; Jonathan Truman Dorris, 'The Oregon Trail', *Journal of the Illinois State Historical Society (1908–1984)*, 10/4 (1918), 473–547; F. G. Young, 'Journal of Medorem Crawford', *Sources of the History of Oregon*, 1/1 (1897), 1, 3–26.
24. G. Thomas Edwards, 'The Oregon Trail in the Columbia Gorge, 1843–1855: The Final Ordeal', *Oregon Historical Quarterly*, 97/2 (1996), 134–75; John Minto, 'What I Know of Dr. McLoughlin and How I Know It', *Quarterly of the Oregon Historical Society*, 11/2 (1910), 177–200; Hastings, *Emigrants' Guide*, 50–51; Minto, 'Reminiscences'.
25. Minto, 'Reminiscences'; Morgan, *Overland in 1846*, i, 185, 192–96.
26. Morgan, *Overland in 1846*, 188; Hastings, *Emigrants' Guide*, 20–22; Nesmith, 'Diary'.

## The Pioneers and the Politicians

1. John Minto, 'Reminiscences of Experiences on the Oregon Trail in 1844', *Quarterly of the Oregon Historical Society*, 2/3 (1901), 209–54; Jesse Applegate, *A Day with the Cow Column in 1843* (Chicago, 1934); John D. Unruh, *The Plains Across: The Overland Emigrants and the Trans-Mississippi West, 1840–60* (Urbana: University of Illinois Press, 1979), 58, 90, 389; Henry Nash Smith, *Virgin Land: The American West as Symbol and Myth* (New York: Vintage, 1957), 38; Francis Parkman, *The Oregon Trail: Sketches of Prairie and Rocky Mountain Life* (New York: Putnam, 1849), 88–89, 92.
2. Dale L. Morgan (ed.), *Overland in 1846: Diaries and Letters of the California–Oregon Trail*, ii (Georgetown, CA: Talisman Press, 1963), 633; Minto, 'Reminiscences'; Applegate, *Day with the Cow Column*; P. H. Burnett, 'Letters of Peter H. Burnett', *Quarterly of the Oregon Historical Society*, 3/4 (1902), 398–426.
3. Minto, 'Reminiscences'; Elizabeth A. Linn and Nathan Sargent, *The Life and Public Services of Dr. Lewis F. Linn* (New York: Appleton, 1857), 253–56.
4. Edwin A. Miles, '"Fifty-four Forty or Fight" – An American Political Legend', *Mississippi Valley Historical Review*, 44/2 (1957), 291–309; Reginald Charles McGrane, *William Allen: A Study in Western Democracy* (Columbus: Ohio State Archaeological and Historical Society, 1925), 105–08; David M. Pletcher, *The Diplomacy of Annexation: Texas, Oregon, and the Mexican War* (Columbia: University of Missouri Press, 1973), 318.
5. Pletcher, *Diplomacy of Annexation*, 223–25; Appendix to the *Congressional Globe*, 28th Congress, 2nd Session, 1844, 135; John Caldwell Calhoun, *The Papers of John C. Calhoun*, xxv (University of South Carolina Press, 1959), 565–66.
6. Linn & Sargent, *Lewis Linn*, 225; William T. Young, *Sketch of the Life and Public Services of General Lewis Cass* (Philadelphia: E. H. Butler, 1853), 259–60; McGrane, *William Allen*, 110–11.
7. Thomas Hart Benton, 'Letter from Col. Benton to the People of Missouri', 1853, 20; Smith, *Virgin Land*, 26–32; Appendix to the *Congressional Globe*, 28th Congress, 2nd Session, 1844, 135; Norman A. Graebner, 'Maritime Factors in the Oregon Compromise', *Pacific Historical Review*, 20/4 (1951), 331–45.
8. *Transactions of the Annual Reunion of the Oregon Pioneer Association*, xv–xxi (1887), 60; William Kelly, *Across the Rocky Mountains, from New York to California* (London: Simms & McIntyre, 1852), 35; Miles, 'Fifty-four Forty or Fight'; Kenneth R. Coleman, '"We'll All Start Even": White Egalitarianism and the Oregon Donation Land Claim Act', *Oregon Historical Quarterly*, 120/4 (2019), 414–39.

9. Lester Burrell Shippee, 'The Federal Relations of Oregon – III', *Quarterly of the Oregon Historical Society*, 19/4 (1918), 283–305, 307–33.
10. Charles Wilkes, 'Report on the Territory of Oregon', *Quarterly of the Oregon Historical Society*, 12/3 (1911), 269–99; John Suval, '"The Nomadic Race to Which I Belong": Squatter Democracy and the Claiming of Oregon', *Oregon Historical Quarterly*, 118/3 (2017), 306–37; Minto, 'Reminiscences'; Unruh, *Plains Across*, 389; Michael B. Husband, 'The Backgrounds and Organization of the Great Oregon Migration of 1843', MA thesis, University of Nebraska at Omaha, 1966.
11. Minto, 'Reminiscences'.
12. C. J. Pike, 'Petitions of Oregon Settlers, 1838–48', *Oregon Historical Quarterly*, 34/3 (1933), 216–35; Myron Eells, *History of Indian Missions on the Pacific Coast: Oregon, Washington and Idaho* (Philadelphia, 1882), 165; W. H. Gray, *A History of Oregon, 1792–1849* (Portland: Harris & Holman, 1870), 194–95, 292–93.
13. Shippee, 'Federal Relations'; Minto, 'Reminiscences'; Frederick Merk, 'The Oregon Pioneers and the Boundary', *Oregon Historical Quarterly*, 28/4 (1927), 366–88; Suval, 'Nomadic Race'; Leslie M. Scott, 'Oregon's Provisional Government, 1843–49', *Oregon Historical Quarterly*, 30/3 (1929), 207–17; Jackie Gonzales and Morgen Young, 'First Year in Oregon, 1840–1869: A Narrative History', Historical Research Associates, Inc., Oct. 2021, https://www.nps.gov/articles/000/upload/3195_FirstYearInOregon_HistResearchAssociates_Full-FINAL_210928.pdf.

## Careering Towards Compromise

1. Howard Jones and Donald A. Rakestraw, *Prologue to Manifest Destiny: Anglo-American Relations in the 1840s* (Wilmington: Scholarly Resources, 1997), 27–31; Charles Lindsey, *The Life and Times of Wm. Lyon Mackenzie*, ii (Toronto: P. R. Randall, 1862), 147–51.
2. Jones & Rakestraw, *Prologue to Manifest Destiny*, 24–27.
3. Jones & Rakestraw, *Prologue to Manifest Destiny*, 43–67; Jasper Ridley, *Lord Palmerston* (London: BCA, 1979), 269–71; National Archives, Kew, FO 414/305; see the speeches on Oregon of 15 Dec. 1845, 26 Feb., 30 Mar., 6–7 Apr. 1846 in Daniel Webster, *The Works of Daniel Webster* (Boston: Charles C. Little & James Brown, 1851); Jones & Rakestraw, *Prologue to Manifest Destiny*, 1–13; Jesse S. Reeves, *American Diplomacy under Tyler and Polk* (Baltimore: Johns Hopkins Press, 1907), 1–4; National Archives, Kew, FO 414/306; Howard Jones, 'Anglophobia and the Aroostook War', *New England Quarterly*, 48/4 (1975), 519–39; Jones & Rakestraw, *Prologue to Manifest Destiny*, 71–84; Reeves, *American Diplomacy*, 47–48; David M. Pletcher, *The Diplomacy of Annexation: Texas, Oregon, and the Mexican War* (Columbia: University of Missouri Press, 1973), 13–15; Frederick

Marryat, *A Diary in America*, ii (Philadelphia: Carey & Hart, 1839), ch. 4; Pletcher, *Diplomacy of Annexation*.
4. Jones & Rakestraw, *Prologue to Manifest Destiny*, 102–21; Reeves, *American Diplomacy*, 55–56; Pletcher, *Diplomacy of Annexation*, 24–26; JQA diary, 2 Jan. 1843; Sarah Mytton Maury, *The Statesmen of America in 1846* (Philadelphia: Carey & Hart, 1847), 186.
5. Marryat, *Diary*, ii; Ridley, *Palmerston*, 273, 287; Jones & Rakestraw, *Prologue to Manifest Destiny*, 146.
6. William C. Hunter, *The 'Fan Kwae' at Canton before Treaty Days, 1825–1844* (London: Kegan Paul, Trench, 1882), 31–33; Gideon Nye, *The Morning of My Life in China* (Canton, 1873), 17–19; Eric Jay Dolin, *When America First Met China* (New York: Liveright, 2012), 187–88.
7. Julia Lovell, *The Opium War: Drugs, Dreams and the Making of China* (London: Picador, 2011), 2–8.
8. Lovell, *Opium War*, 3–4, 62–73, 132–33, 229–32; Matthew Lockwood, *To Begin the World Over Again: How the American Revolution Devastated the Globe* (New Haven: Yale University Press, 2019), 447–68; Elijah Coleman Bridgman, *The Pioneer of American Missions in China: The Life and Labors of Elijah Coleman Bridgman* (New York: Anson D. F. Randolph, 1864), 119–20; *Panoplist, and Missionary Magazine*, 39–40 (1843), 257; Arthur Cunynghame, *The Opium War: Being Recollections of Service in China* (Philadelphia: Zieber, 1845), 160.
9. Jacques M. Downs, 'American Merchants and the China Opium Trade, 1800–1840', *Business History Review*, 42/4 (1968), 418–42; Stuart C. Miller, 'The American Trader's Image of China, 1785–1840', *Pacific Historical Review*, 36/4 (1967), 375–95; Kenneth E. Shewmaker, 'Forging the "Great Chain": Daniel Webster and the Origins of American Foreign Policy toward East Asia and the Pacific, 1841–1852', *Proceedings of the American Philosophical Society*, 129/3 (1985), 225–59.
10. Macabe Keliher, 'Anglo-American Rivalry and the Origins of U.S. China Policy', *Diplomatic History*, 31/2 (2007), 227–57.
11. Keliher, 'Anglo-American Rivalry'; Thomas Hietala, *Manifest Design: Anxious Aggrandizement in Late Jacksonian America* (Ithaca: Cornell University Press, 1985), 58–62; Samuel Eliot Morison, *The Maritime History of Massachusetts, 1783–1860* (Boston: Houghton Mifflin, 1921), 273–74.
12. William J. Donahue, 'The Caleb Cushing Mission', *Modern Asian Studies*, 16/2 (1982), 193–216; Foster Rhea Dulles, *China and America: The Story of Their Relations since 1784* (Princeton: Princeton University Press, 1946), 25–29; Foster Rhea Dulles, *The Old China Trade* (Boston: Houghton Mifflin, 1930), 187.
13. Keliher, 'Anglo-American Rivalry'; Caleb Cushing, 'An Oration, on the Material Growth and Progress of the United States', 1839.

14. William T. Young, *Sketch of the Life and Public Services of General Lewis Cass* (Philadelphia: E. H. Butler, 1853), 260–62; Wentworth quoted in the *Congressional Globe*, xiv (1844), 135; Pletcher, *Diplomacy of Annexation*, 115, 223–26, 334; also relevant is Sidney Breese, *The Early History of Illinois* (Chicago: E. B. Myers, 1884), 327–32.
15. Albert Gilliam, *Travels over the Table Lands and Cordilleras of Mexico* (Philadelphia: John W. Moore, 1846), 385–86; *Southern Quarterly Review*, viii, 1845, 240; *De Bow's Review*, iii (1847), 148, 446, 489; *Hunt's Merchants' Magazine*, xv (1846), 101; Pletcher, *Diplomacy of Annexation*, 208.
16. Polk diary, 4 Jan. 1846.
17. Norman A. Graebner, *Empire on the Pacific: A Study in American Continental Expansion* (New York: Ronald Press, 1955), 105–06.
18. Polk diary, 29 Nov. 1845; Graebner, *Empire on the Pacific*.
19. Rebecca Berens Matzke, 'Britain Gets Its Way: Power and Peace in Anglo-American Relations, 1838–1846', *War in History*, 8/1 (2001), 19–46; Wilbur D. Jones and J. Chal Vinson, 'British Preparedness and the Oregon Settlement', *Pacific Historical Review*, 22/4 (1953), 353–64; Pletcher, *Diplomacy of Annexation*, 130–32, 238–40; Hershel Parker, *Herman Melville: A Biography*, i: *1819–1851* (Baltimore: Johns Hopkins University Press, 1996), 390; Philip Ziegler, *The Sixth Great Power: Barings, 1762–1929* (London: Collins, 1988), 155; Graebner, *Empire on the Pacific*, 125.
20. The Oregon Pioneer Association wrote, accurately, in 1895: 'Perhaps it would be correct to state that the British lost Oregon by placing "… the beaver paramount to the plow."'
21. Frederick Merk, *The Oregon Question* (Cambridge, MA: Belknap Press, 1967), 246–47; 'Dr. John McLoughlin's Last Letter to the Hudson's Bay Company, as Chief Factor, in Charge at Fort Vancouver, 1845', *American Historical Review*, 21/1 (1915), 104–34.
22. Jones & Rakestraw, *Prologue to Manifest Destiny*, 228–29; Merk, *Oregon Question*, 300; Graebner, *Empire on the Pacific*, 138; Polk diary, 24 Jan. 1846.
23. Frederick Merk, 'British Government Propaganda and the Oregon Treaty', *American Historical Review*, 40/1 (1934), 38–62; John S. Galbraith, *The Hudson's Bay Company as an Imperial Factor, 1821–1869* (Toronto: University of Toronto Press, 1957), 244–50; Merk, *Oregon Question*, 289–314.
24. Howard I. Kushner, 'The Oregon Question Is … A Massachusetts Question', *Oregon Historical Quarterly*, 75/4 (1974), 316–35; Maury, *Statesmen of America*, 142–43.
25. Maury, *Statesmen of America*, 377; Graebner, *Empire on the Pacific*, 126–37; 'Mr Calhoun – War or Peace!', *New Hampshire Sentinel*, 7 Jan. 1846; Ulrich Bonnell Phillips (ed.), *The Correspondence of Robert Toombs, Alexander H. Stephens, and Howell Cobb* (Washington, 1913), 65–66, 70–74.

26. Polk diary, 22 Apr. 1846; JQA diary, 30 Jan. 1846; Merk, *Oregon Question*, 330–31, 382, 391.
27. Merk, *Oregon Question*, 300, 392–93; Hietala, *Manifest Design*, 236–37; Graebner, *Empire on the Pacific*, 222–23; Obama speech: https://obamawhitehouse.archives.gov/the-press-office/2011/11/17/remarks-president-obama-australian-parliament.

## PART V: TEXAS, CALIFORNIA AND THE SOUTHWEST
### The Runaway Scrape

1. Mirabeau B. Lamar, 'Travel Journal', 1835; *Niles' Register*, 6 Aug. 1836; Rena Maverick Green (ed.), *Memoirs of Mary Maverick* (San Antonio: Alamo, 1921), 13; Thomas Maitland Marshall, *A History of the Western Boundary of the Louisiana Purchase: 1819–1841* (New York: Da Capo Press, 1970), 48–77.
2. Gary S. Zaboly, *An Altar for Their Sons: The Alamo and the Texas Revolution in Contemporary Newspaper Accounts* (Buffalo Gap: State House Press, 2011), 30, 56, 110, 155; *Farmer's Gazette*, Barre, Massachusetts, 6 Feb. 1835; *Richmond Enquirer*, 27 May 1836; Noah Smithwick, *Evolution of a State, or, Recollections of Old Texas Days* (Austin: Gammel, 1900), 134–37.
3. Mary L. Scheer (ed.), *Women and the Texas Revolution* (Denton: University of North Texas Press, 2012), 109–10, 163–65.
4. Scheer, *Women*, 163, 165, 170.
5. Scheer, *Women*, 173.
6. Marshall, *Western Boundary*, 170–71.
7. Alan Taylor, *American Colonies: The Settling of North America* (London: Penguin, 2001), 382–86; Paul Horgan, *Great River: The Rio Grande in North American History*, i: *Indians and Spain* (New York: Rinehart, 1954), 780.
8. A. P. Nasatir (ed.), *Before Lewis and Clark: Documents Illustrating the History of the Missouri, 1785–1804*, ii (St Louis: St Louis Historical Documents Foundation, 1952), 743–56; for a history of the American claim, see Marshall, *Western Boundary*.
9. David J. Weber, *The Mexican Frontier, 1821–1846: The American Southwest under Mexico* (Albuquerque: University of New Mexico Press, 1982), 12; Marshall, *Western Boundary*, 104–18.
10. Randolph B. Campbell, *Gone to Texas: A History of the Lone Star State* (New York: OUP, 2003), 100–04.
11. Gary Clayton Anderson, *The Conquest of Texas: Ethnic Cleansing in the Promised Land, 1820–1875* (Norman: University of Oklahoma Press, 2005), 46–47, 70–71; Weber, *Mexican Frontier*, 170; Frederick Merk, *Manifest Destiny and Mission in American History* (New York: Vintage, 1966), 20–21.
12. Horgan, *Great River*, i, 470, 485, 510; Weber, *Mexican Frontier*, 177; Alexis de Tocqueville, *Democracy in America*, 390–91.

13. Andreas Reichstein, 'Was There a Revolution in Texas in 1835–36?', *American Studies International*, 27/2 (1989), 66–86; Scheer, *Women*, 181; Charles Adams Gulick (ed.), *The Papers of Mirabeau Buonaparte Lamar*, i (Austin: A. C. Baldwin, 1921), 292–93; William C. Binkley, *The Texas Revolution* (Baton Rouge: Louisiana State University Press, 1952), 96; Robert F. Karsch, 'Tennessee's Interest in the Texan Revolution, 1835–1836', *Tennessee Historical Magazine*, 3/4 (1937), 206–39; Zaboly, *Altar for Their Sons*, 78, 127, 176.
14. Timothy J. Henderson, *A Glorious Defeat: Mexico and Its War with the United States* (New York: Hill & Wang, 2007), 75–81; Will Fowler, *Santa Anna of Mexico* (Lincoln: University of Nebraska Press, 2007), 5, 19–29, 159–60; Zaboly, *Altar for Their Sons*, 35, 192, 219–21, 301–02; Smithwick, *Recollections*, 133; Dilue Harris, 'The Reminiscences of Mrs. Dilue Harris'.
15. Zaboly, *Altar for Their Sons*, 36, 121; Anderson, *Conquest of Texas*, 80–81; Joanne B. Freeman, *The Field of Blood: Violence in Congress and the Road to Civil War* (New York: Farrar, Straus & Giroux, 2018), 131; Campbell, *Gone to Texas*, 122–23; Donald Day, 'Towards an Understanding of Sam Houston', *Southwest Review*, 29/2 (1944), 276–90.
16. Zaboly, *Altar for Their Sons*, 318–32; Campbell, *Gone to Texas*, 154–56; Fowler, *Santa Anna*, 172–74; Walraven & Walraven, 'Sabine Chute'; Smithwick, *Recollections*, 131–39; Charles Edwards Lester, *The Life of Sam Houston* (New York: J. C. Derby, 1855), 147–52; Smithwick, *Recollections*, 139.
17. Harris, 'Reminiscences'; Eugene C. Barker, 'President Jackson and the Texas Revolution', *American Historical Review*, 12/4 (1907), 788–809; Robert L. Jones and Pauline Jones, 'Occupation of Nacogdoches', *East Texas Historical Journal*, 4/1 (1966); Andrew Jackson, 21 Dec. 1836, 'Statement on the Independence of Texas'; John H. Schroeder, 'Annexation or Independence: The Texas Issue in American Politics, 1836–1845', *Southwestern Historical Quarterly*, 89/2 (1985), 137–64.

## Marching Alone

1. Dilue Harris, 'The Reminiscences of Mrs. Dilue Harris'.
2. Harris, 'Reminiscences'.
3. Andrew J. Torget, *Seeds of Empire: Cotton, Slavery, and the Transformation of the Texas Borderlands, 1800–1850* (Chapel Hill: University of North Carolina Press, 2015), 184; *Times-Picayune*, LA, 29 Mar. 1838; Nancy Nichols Barker (ed.), *The French Legation in Texas* <VOL?>(Austin: TSHA, 1971), 37–47, 67–74.
4. Charles Gulick (ed.), *The Papers of Mirabeau Buonaparte Lamar*, i (Austin: A. C. Baldwin, 1921–27), 531; Rena Maverick Green (ed.), *Memoirs of Mary Maverick* (San Antonio: Alamo, 1921), 34; J. W. Benedict, 'Diary of a

Campaign against the Comanches', *Southwestern Historical Quarterly*, 32/4 (1929), 300–10.

5. *Barre Gazette*, MA, 25 Jan. 1839; *Times-Picayune*, LA, 29 Mar. 1838; New-Bedford *Mercury*, MA, 18 Jan. 1839; Charles C. Bolton, *Poor Whites of the Antebellum South* (Durham: Duke University Press, 1994), 68; J. W. Parker to M. B. Lamar, 17 Mar. 1839, in Charles Gulick (ed.), *The Papers of Mirabeau Buonaparte Lamar*, ii (Austin: A. C. Baldwin, 1922).

6. *Times-Picayune*, LA, 17 June 1838; Joseph Glover Baldwin, *The Flush Times of Alabama and Mississippi: A Series of Sketches* (New York: D. Appleton, 1854), 56, 91; *Portsmouth Journal*, NH, 25 May 1839; *Times-Picayune*, LA, 17 June 1838; A. M. Sakolski, *The Great American Land Bubble* (New York: Harper, 1932), 224–26, 252; *Diary of Philip Hone*, 332–33; *Haverhill Gazette*, MA, 24 Sept. 1836.

7. Wharton to Austin, 11 Dec. 1836, in *Diplomatic Correspondence of the Republic of Texas* (Washington: American Historical Association, 1911), i, 151–54.

8. *Times-Picayune*, LA, 29 Mar. 1839; *Richmond Enquirer*, VA, 2 Nov. 1838; Torget, *Seeds of Empire*, 197–99; *National Register*, TX, 8 May 1845.

9. *Rhode-Island Republican*, RI, 9 Jan. 1839; Green, *Mary Maverick*; Barker, *French Legation*, 66; MBL speech of 21 Dec. 1838, in *MBL Papers*, ii.

10. J. Riddle to M. B. Lamar, 10 Jan. 1839, Inaugural Address, 10 Dec. 1838, in *MBL Papers*, ii.

11. J. M. White to Lamar, 1 June 1839, in Charles Gulick (ed.), *The Papers of Mirabeau Buonaparte Lamar*, iii (Austin:); J. Hamilton to Lamar, 3 Nov. 1838, Anson Jones to Lamar, 19 July 1836, in *MBL Papers*, ii.

12. Harold Schoen, 'The Free Negro in the Republic of Texas, V', *Southwestern Historical Quarterly*, 40/4 (1937), 267–89; *MBL Papers, Ibid*; Randolph B. Campbell, *Gone to Texas: A History of the Lone Star State* (New York: OUP, 2003), 168–70; Gary Clayton Anderson, *The Conquest of Texas: Ethnic Cleansing in the Promised Land, 1820–1875* (Norman: University of Oklahoma Press, 2005), 172–94; Henderson Yoakum, *History of Texas*, ii (New York: Redfield, 1855), 304–05; MBL Inaugural Address, 10 Dec. 1838, Anson Jones to Lamar, 18 July 1836, 'Notes on the Pacific Coast', anonymous letter to Lamar, 1838 (384–85), Samuel Whitcomb to Lamar, 29 Mar. 1839, in *MBL Papers*, ii; A. S. Wright to Lamar, 4 May 1841, in *MBL Papers*, iii; Joe B. Frantz, 'The Sam Houston Letters: A Corner of Texas in Princeton', *Princeton University Library Chronicle*, 33/1 (1971), 18–29; Campbell, *Gone to Texas*, 172; George Wilkins Kendall, *Narrative of the Texan Santa Fé Expedition*, i (New York: Harper, 1844), 67, 146, 253, 392; George Wilkins Kendall, *Narrative of the Texan Santa Fé Expedition*, ii (New York: Harper, 1844), 32; Timothy J. Henderson, *A Glorious Defeat: Mexico and Its War with the United States* (New York: Hill & Wang, 2007),

123–26; Green, *Mary Maverick*, 58; W. J. Jones to Lamar, 8 Feb. 1839, in *MBL Papers*, ii; Josefina Zoraida Vázquez, 'The Texas Question in Mexican Politics, 1836–1845', *Southwestern Historical Quarterly*, 89/3 (1986), 309–44; Will Fowler, *Santa Anna of Mexico* (Lincoln: University of Nebraska Press, 2007), 189–92; FO 203/84.
13. J. Hamilton to Lamar, 11 Apr. 1838, in *MBL Papers*, ii; Anna Muckleroy, 'The Indian Policy of the Republic of Texas, III', *Southwestern Historical Quarterly*, 26/2 (1922), 128–48; Herbert Rook Edwards, 'Diplomatic Relations between France and the Republic of Texas, 1836–1845, I', *Southwestern Historical Quarterly*, 20/3 (1917), 209–41; Torget, *Seeds of Empire*, 196–222; Charles Edwards Lester, *The Life of Sam Houston* (New York: J. C. Derby, 1855), 196–203.
14. *Congressional Globe*, xv, 640.
15. Lester, *Sam Houston*, 204–35; Lelia M. Roeckell, 'Bonds over Bondage: British Opposition to the Annexation of Texas', *Journal of the Early Republic*, 19/2 (1999), 257–78.
16. Duff Green, *Facts and Suggestions, Biographical, Historical, Financial, and Political* (New York: C. S. Westcott, 1866), 188; Robert Remini, *Andrew Jackson*, iii: *The Course of American Democracy, 1833–1845* (New York: Harper & Row, 1984), 493–94; Thomas Hietala, *Manifest Design: Anxious Aggrandizement in Late Jacksonian America* (Ithaca: Cornell University Press, 1985), 18–20; Robert W. Merry, *A Country of Vast Designs* (New York: Simon & Schuster, 2009), 72–74.

**Fortuna in a Frolic**
1. Herman Melville, in *White Jacket* (1850): 'While lying in harbour [in Callao], intelligence reached us of the lamentable casualty that befell certain high officers of state, including the acting Secretary of the Navy himself, some other member of the President's cabinet, a Commodore, and others, all engaged in experimenting upon a new-fangled engine of war. At the same time with the receipt of this sad news, orders arrived to fire minute-guns for the deceased head of the naval department ... I thought it a strange mode of honouring a man's memory who had himself been slaughtered by a cannon.'
2. Amy S. Greenberg, *A Wicked War: Polk, Clay, Lincoln, and the 1846 U.S. Invasion of Mexico* (New York: Knopf, 2012), 15–17; Benjamin Brown French, *Witness to the Young Republic, A Yankee's Journal, 1828–1870*, 158–60.
3. Thomas Hietala, *Manifest Design: Anxious Aggrandizement in Late Jacksonian America* (Ithaca: Cornell University Press, 1985), 24–25; media discussions of the annexation question can be found in *Emancipator and Free American*, Boston, 11 Jan. 1844, and *Telegraph and Texas Register*, Houston, 3 Jan. 1844.

4. Robert James Walker, 'Letter Relative to the Annexation of Texas', 1844; for an extended discussion of the Walker letter and its impact see Hietala, *Manifest Design*, ch. 1.
5. See Christopher J. Leahy, *President without a Party* (Baton Rouge: Louisiana State University Press, 2020), ch. 17.
6. Harriet Martineau, *Retrospect of Western Travel*, i (London: Saunders & Otley, 1838), 148.
7. John C. Calhoun, *A Disquisition on Government* (Columbia, 1851); C. E. Merriam, 'The Political Theory of Calhoun', *American Journal of Sociology*, 7/5 (1902), 577–94.
8. Ray Allen Billington, *Westward Expansion: A History of the American Frontier* (New York: Macmillan, 1949), 504; Thomas Hart Benton, *Thirty Years' View*, ii (New York: D. Appleton, 1856), 590; Leahy, *President without a Party*, 596.
9. Hietala, *Manifest Design*, 40; Benton, *Thirty Years' View*, ii, 590; Anson Jones, *Memoranda and Official Correspondence relating to the Republic of Texas* (New York: D. Appleton, 1859), 343.
10. Robert Remini, *Andrew Jackson*, iii: *The Course of American Democracy, 1833–1845* (New York: Harper & Row, 1984), 496–97; Francis Blair to Andrew Jackson, 2 May 1844.
11. *Emancipator and Free American*, MA, 24 Nov. 1842; John Greenleaf Whittier, 'To a Southern Statesman', in *Anti-Slavery Poems: Songs of Labor and Reform* (Boston: Houghton, Mifflin, 1896), 104.
12. Greenberg, *Wicked War*, 18; Martin Van Buren to William Henry Hammett, 20 Apr. 1844.
13. The other friend Jackson was referring to here was Thomas Hart Benton, who also came out against annexation that month on the grounds that it would involve the republic in a war with Mexico. As Benton put it: 'to incorporate Texas, was to incorporate the war at the same time'.
14. Jackson to Blair, 7 May 1844; Jackson to Blair, 11 May 1844; Greenberg, *Wicked War*, 23–24; Remini, *Jackson*, iii, 496–500.
15. Robert W. Merry, *A Country of Vast Designs* (New York: Simon & Schuster, 2009), 14–47.
16. JKP to Cave Johnson, 15 May 1844.
17. Amos Kendall to MVB, 13 May 1844; Amos Kendall to MVB, 16 May 1844; Alfred Balch to MVB, 22 May 1844; James Kirke Paulding to MVB, 16 Apr. 1844.
18. The nickname was coined by Herman Melville's brother Gansevoort at a speech in New York City during the election campaign: 'As for James K. Polk … we, the unterrified democracy of New York will rebaptise him; we will give him a name such as Andrew Jackson in the baptism of fire and blood at New-Orleans; we will re-christen him. Hereafter he shall be known by the name that we now give him – it is, Young Hickory … We

have had one old hickory tree. Its trunk as yet green and undecayed. Sixteen millions of Americans have reposed under its shade in peace and happiness. It is yet vigorous – but it cannot live forever. And now to take its place is springing up at its very side, a tall and noble sapling. It imbibes its nourishment from the same soil. It flourishes in the same atmosphere. It springs from the same staunch old democratic stock ... We and our children will yet live in prosperity under the broad branches of this one young Hickory tree.'

19. Anonymous to John Van Buren, 21 May 1846; New Hampshire *Sentinel*, NH, 12 June 1844; *Barre Gazette*, MA, 14 June 1844; Greenberg, *Wicked War*, 38–41; Merry, *Vast Designs*, 81–95.
20. Reprinted in the New Hampshire *Sentinel*, NH, 12 June 1844; *Berkshire County Whig*, MA, 20 June 1844; *The Hudson River Chronicle*, NY, 25 June 1844; *Old Warrior*, PA, 1 June 1844.
21. *The Pittsfield Sun*, MA, 6 June 1844; *New Hampshire Sentinel*, NH, 12 June 1844.
22. Alfred D. Chandler, 'Patterns of American Railroad Finance, 1830–50', *Business History Review*, 28/3 (1954), 248–63; Merry, *Vast Designs*, 133–34; Hietala, *Manifest Design*, 197–98; Frederick Merk, *Manifest Destiny and Mission in American History* (New York: Vintage, 1966), 51.
23. Martineau quoted in Amy S. Greenberg, *Manifest Destiny and American Territorial Expansion: A Brief History with Documents* (New York: St Martin's, 2012), 72–73; Ralph Waldo Emerson, 'The Young American', 7 Feb. 1844; Walt Whitman, 'A Visit to a Camp, etc.', 29 Aug. 1846, in *The Gathering of the Forces*, ii (New York: Putnam's, 1920); Herman Melville, *White Jacket* (New York: Harper, 1850); John O'Sullivan, 'The Great Nation of Futurity', 1839; see also Claude Richard, 'Poe and "Young America"', *Studies in Bibliography*, 21 (1968), 25–58, and Robert J. Scholnick, 'Whigs and Democrats, the Past and the Future: The Political Emerson and Whitman's 1855 Preface', *American Periodicals*, 26/1 (2016), 70–91.
24. Diary of Philip Hone, entry of 1 Nov. 1844; Greenberg, *Wicked War*, 51; Webster quoted in *Alexandria Gazette*, 19 Mar. 1844; Ralph Waldo Emerson, 'The Poet', 1841; see also John H. Schroeder, 'Annexation or Independence: The Texas Issue in American Politics, 1836–1845', *Southwestern Historical Quarterly*, 89/2 (1985), 137–64.
25. Charles Dickens, *American Notes*, ii (London: Chapman & Hall, 1842), 145; Michael Burlingame, *Abraham Lincoln: A Life*, i (Baltimore: Johns Hopkins University Press, 2008), ch. 7, 678; Greenberg, *Wicked War*, 55.
26. Barre Patriot, MA, 13 Sept. 1844.
27. Merry, *Vast Designs*, 120–28; Burlingame, *Lincoln*, i, ch. 7, 679.
28. Greenberg, *Wicked War*, 69–71; Benton, *Thirty Years' View*, ii, 638.

## From Intrigue to War

1. Will Fowler, *Santa Anna of Mexico* (Lincoln: University of Nebraska Press, 2007), 239–47; George L. Rives, *The United States and Mexico, 1821–1848*, i (New York: Scribner's, 1913), 706; George L. Rives, *The United States and Mexico, 1821–1848*, ii (New York: Scribner's, 1913), 87; for British perspectives on the negotiations, see Elliott's correspondence in FO 75/22; for detail on the alleged Stockton plot, see Richard R. Stenberg, 'The Failure of Polk's Mexican War Intrigue of 1845', *Pacific Historical Review*, 4/1 (1935), 39–68; see letters of 6 May, 26 May and 15 June 1845 in St. George L. Sioussat, 'Letters of James K. Polk to Andrew J. Donelson, 1843–1848', *Tennessee Historical Magazine*, 3/1 (1917), 51–73; Robert Remini, *Andrew Jackson*, iii: *The Course of American Democracy, 1833–1845* (New York: Harper & Row, 1984), 525.
2. Rives, *United States and Mexico*, i, 708–09; Rives, *United States and Mexico*, ii, 54–59; Peter M. Jonas, 'William Parrott, American Claims, and the Mexican War', *Journal of the Early Republic*, 12/2 (1992), 213–40; John O'Sullivan, 'Annexation', *United States Magazine and Democratic Review*, xvii (1845), 5–10; Seymour V. Connor and Odie B. Faulk, *North America Divided: The Mexican War, 1846–1848* (New York: OUP, 1971), 31; Justin H. Smith, *The War with Mexico*, i (New York: Macmillan, 1919), 123.
3. Remini, *Jackson*, iii, 165–67; Tallmadge to Polk, 30 Mar. 1845; for Polk on California see Glenn W. Price, *Origins of the War with Mexico* (Austin: University of Texas Press, 2014), 91.
4. Jonas, 'William Parrott', 212; Rives, *United States and Mexico*, i, 417–31; see also Polk's first annual message to Congress, 2 Dec. 1845.
5. See Secretary of War Marcy quoted in Norman Graebner, 'The Mexican War: A Study in Causation', *Pacific Historical Review*, 49/3 (1980), 405–26, Secretary of the Navy Banfield in his letter of 29 Mar. 1846, and the diary of Benjamin French Brown, 24 Aug. 1845. Polk made the point repeatedly in his letters and in his diary up until Apr. 1846. In his instructions to Slidell dated 17 Sept. 1845, Secretary of State Buchanan described Polk's position as 'anxious to preserve peace, although prepared for war'; on Polk's personality, see Robert W. Merry, *A Country of Vast Designs* (New York: Simon & Schuster, 2009), and Smith, *War with Mexico*, i, 128–29, for an excellent sketch of Polk's character: 'cold, narrow, methodical, dogged, plodding, obstinately partisan, deeply convinced of his importance and responsibility, very wanting in humor, very wanting in ideality, very wanting in soulfulness, inclined to be sly, and quite incapable of seeing great things in a great way'; FO 75/23/187; see Peña to Slidell, 20 Dec. 1845.
6. Polk, *Diary*, 13, 16 Feb. 1846; for concerns that Taylor's force was too small see Ingersoll to Polk, 26 Aug. 1845, and the diary of George Meade, 26 Apr. 1846; Benton quoted in Smith, *War with Mexico*, i, 130; for a sympathetic portrayal of Polk's actions in this period, see Smith, *War with Mexico*, i,

150; for the comparison to the Vietnam War, see K. Jack Bauer, *The Mexican War, 1846–1848* (Lincoln: Bison Books, 1992); for a hawkish defence of Polk, see Eugene C. Barker, 'California as the Cause of the Mexican War', *Texas Review*, 2/3 (1917), 213–21.
7. Smith, *War with Mexico*, i, 110–11; Graebner, 'Study in Causation'; Gene M. Brack, 'Mexican Opinion, American Racism, and the War of 1846', *Western Historical Quarterly*, 1/2 (1970), 161–74.
8. Smith, *War with Mexico*, i, 105–14; Timothy J. Henderson, *A Glorious Defeat: Mexico and Its War with the United States* (New York: Hill & Wang, 2007), 150.
9. Rives, *United States and Mexico*, ii, 70, 73, 77–80, 141.

**The Mexican Polka**
1. Entry for 11 Apr. 1846, in W. S. Henry, *Campaign Sketches of the War with Mexico* (New York: Harper, 1847), 72.
2. C. M. Reeves, 'Five Years an American Soldier', reproduced in Henry Howe, *Adventures and Achievements of Americans* (Cincinnati, 1858), 429–84; Ulysses S. Grant, *Personal Memoirs of U. S. Grant*, i (New York: Charles L. Webster, 1885), 69–73; George Meade, *The Life and Letters of George Gordon Meade*, i (New York: Scribner's, 1913), letter of 7 Apr. 1846.
3. Reeves, 'Five Years'; Grant, *Memoirs*, i, 95–96; Lester R. Dillon, 'American Artillery in the Mexican War, 1846–1847', MA thesis, North Texas State University, 1969.
4. Meade, *Letters*, i, 9 May 1846; Henry, *Sketches*, 8 May 1846; Peter Guardino, *The Dead March: A History of the Mexican-American War* (Cambridge, MA: Harvard University Press, 2017), 78–82.
5. Meade, *Letters*, i, 9 May 1846.
6. Polk to Gideon Pillow, 20 Apr. 1846; Polk, *Diary*, 25 Apr., 6 May, 9 May 1846; Polk, Message to Congress, 11 May 1846; Amy S. Greenberg, *A Wicked War: Polk, Clay, Lincoln, and the 1846 U.S. Invasion of Mexico* (New York: Knopf, 2012), 102–09; Robert W. Merry, *A Country of Vast Designs* (New York: Simon & Schuster, 2009), 246–52; Guardino, *Dead March*, 85; Calhoun, for instance, claimed that for the Senate to approve the war resolution 'would be to make war on the Constitution': John Caldwell Calhoun, *The Papers of John C. Calhoun*, xxiii (University of South Carolina Press, 1996), speech of 12 May 1846, 99–101.
7. Thomas Hietala, *Manifest Design: Anxious Aggrandizement in Late Jacksonian America* (Ithaca: Cornell University Press, 1985), 240; Polk diary, 13 May 1846.
8. James L. Freaner, *From the Halls of the Montezumas: Mexican War Dispatches*, 15; Ezekiel P. McNeal to Polk, 20 June 1846; Guardino, *Dead March*, 98; John M. Belohlavek, *Patriots, Prostitutes, and Spies: Women and the Mexican-American War* (Charlottesville: University of Virginia

Press, 2017), 22–23; Robert W. Johannsen, *To the Halls of the Montezumas* (New York: OUP, 1985), 11; James M. McCaffrey, *Army of Manifest Destiny: The American Soldier in the Mexican War, 1846–1848* (New York: NYU Press, 1992), 18–19; Paul Foos, *A Short, Offhand, Killing Affair: Soldiers and Social Conflict during the Mexican-American War* (Chapel Hill: University of North Carolina Press, 2002), 42–50; Ernest M. Lander, 'The Reluctant Imperialist: South Carolina, the Rio Grande, and the Mexican War', *Southwestern Historical Quarterly*, 78/3 (1975), 254–70.

9. Johannsen, *To the Halls of the Montezumas*, 28; Samuel E. Chamberlain, *My Confession: Recollections of a Rogue* (New York: Harper, 1956), 30–31; Hietala, *Manifest Design*, 264–65.
10. Guardino, *Dead March*, 105–07; John Reese Kenly, *Memoirs of a Maryland Volunteer* (Philadelphia: Lippincott, 1873), 30–48, 53.
11. David B. Gracy and Helen J. H. Rugeley, 'From the Mississippi to the Pacific: An Englishman in the Mormon Battalion', *Arizona and the West*, 7/2 (1965), 127–60; Valentine Mott Porter, 'General Stephen W. Kearny and the Conquest of California', *Annual Publications of the Historical Society of Southern California*, 8/1–2 (1909–1910).
12. Lisbeth Haas, 'War in California, 1846–1848', *California History*, 76/2–3 (1997), 331–55; Greenberg, *Wicked War*, 121–22; Rockwell D. Hunt, 'Legal Status of California, 1846–49', *Annals of the American Academy of Political and Social Science*, 12 (1898), 63–84; Stockton to Polk, 26 Aug. 1846.
13. Paul Horgan, *Great River: The Rio Grande in North American History*, ii: *Mexico and the United States* (New York: Rinehart, 1954), 721–29; Guardino, *Dead March*, 318–19; Joseph G. Dawson, 'American Civil-Military Relations and Military Government: The Service of Colonel Alexander Doniphan in the Mexican War', *Armed Forces & Society*, 22/4 (1996), 555–72.
14. Kenly, *Memoirs*, 124; Meade, *Letters*, i, 26 June 1846; Ian B. Lyles, 'Mixed Blessing: The Role of the Texas Rangers in the Mexican War, 1846–1848', thesis, University of Texas, 2001; Mary R. Block, '"The Stoutest Son": The Mexican-American War Journal of Henry Clay Jr.', *Register of the Kentucky Historical Society*, 106/1 (2008), 5–42.
15. Will Fowler, *Santa Anna of Mexico* (Lincoln: University of Nebraska Press, 2007), 254–55; Timothy J. Henderson, *A Glorious Defeat: Mexico and Its War with the United States* (New York: Hill & Wang, 2007), 160–64.
16. Chamberlain, *My Confession*, 116–28; Henry, *Sketches*, 310–24; George Wilkins Kendall, *The War between the United States and Mexico* (New York: Appleton, 1851), 12; Fowler, *Santa Anna*, 260–63; Greenberg, *Wicked War*, 158–62, includes an excellent account of Henry Clay Jr's death.
17. McCaffrey, *Army of Manifest Destiny*, 166.
18. Guardino, *Dead March*, 175–89; Tom Reilly, 'Jane McManus Storms: Letters from the Mexican War, 1846–1848', *Southwestern Historical*

*Quarterly*, 85/1 (1981), 21–44; Maria Clinton Collins (ed.), *Journal of Francis Collins: An Artillery Officer in the Mexican War* (Cincinnati: Abingdon Press, 1915), 50–58; Tom Reilly, *War With Mexico!: America's Reporters Cover the Battlefront* (Lawrence: University Press of Kansas, 2010), 101–11; Alan D. Gaff and Donald H. Gaff (eds), *From the Halls of the Montezumas: Mexican War Dispatches from James L. Freaner, Writing under the Pen Name 'Mustang'* (Denton: University of North Texas Press, 2019), 55–78; Robert Anderson, *An Artillery Officer in the Mexican War, 1846-7* (New York: Putnam's, 1911), 93–104; William Jay, *A Review of the Causes and Consequences of the Mexican War* (Boston: Benjamin B. Mussey, 1853), 202–04, 224; Dillon, 'American Artillery'; Reeves, 'Five Years', 453–55.
19. Anderson, *Artillery Officer*, 143; Gaff & Gaff, *From the Halls of the Montezumas*, 90–162; Johannsen, *To the Halls of the Montezumas*, 166.

**The Ordeal of Peace**
1. Bancroft to Polk, 18 May 1847, 3 June 1847, 18 Nov. 1847; for a domestic perspective on how the war impacted Transatlantic relations, see Vernon K. Stevenson to Polk, 29 May 1847: 'We are taking all Mexico with our Glorious army & France can say nothing since her tricks for the Infanta & we have silenced England by small presents to her starving populace so it seems that the balance of Power so much talked of in annexing Texas, fails to act, even when we are reaching to the very city of Mexico.'
2. Robert W. Johannsen, *To the Halls of the Montezumas* (New York: OUP, 1985), 19, 145; Tom Reilly, *War With Mexico!: America's Reporters Cover the Battlefront* (Lawrence: University Press of Kansas, 2010), 2–3, 92–93.
3. Peter Guardino, *The Dead March: A History of the Mexican-American War* (Cambridge, MA: Harvard University Press, 2017), 106–07, 128–31; William Starr Myers (ed.), *The Mexican War Diary of George B. McClellan* (Princeton: Princeton University Press, 1917), 18–19; Amy S. Greenberg, *A Wicked War: Polk, Clay, Lincoln, and the 1846 U.S. Invasion of Mexico* (New York: Knopf, 2012), 194, 199; Mary R. Block, '"The Stoutest Son": The Mexican-American War Journal of Henry Clay Jr.', *Register of the Kentucky Historical Society*, 106/1 (2008), 5–42.
4. Charles T. Porter, *Review of the Mexican War* (Auburn: Alden & Parsons, 1849), 112, 164–65; Abbott quoted in William Jay, *A Review of the Causes and Consequences of the Mexican War* (Boston: Benjamin B. Mussey, 1853), 257; 'Popular Responsibility for the Present War', *Advocate of Peace*, 7/13–14 (1848), 145–48; Jane Grey Swisshelm, *Half a Century* (Chicago: Jansen, McClurg, 1880), 93; Henry David Thoreau, *Civil Disobedience* (1849); *National Anti-Slavery Standard* (NY), 31 Dec. 1846; 'Speech of Mr Giddings of Ohio upon the Resolution to Refer so Much of the President's Message as Relates to the Mexican War', 1846.

5. Lincoln's speech and resolutions are in Arthur Brooks Lapsley (ed.), *The Writings of Abraham Lincoln*, ii: *1843–1858* (New York: Lamb, 1888); Webster quoted in 'Politicians Against the War', *Advocate of Peace*, 7/13–14 (1848), 159–65; 'Speech of Mr. Corwin of Ohio in the Senate', 11 Feb. 1847; Charles Sumner, *His Complete Works*, ii (Boston: Lee & Shepard, 1990), 207–15; Greenberg, *Wicked War*, 168; Frederick Merk, *Manifest Destiny and Mission in American History* (New York: Vintage, 1966), 153.
6. Robert W. Merry, *A Country of Vast Designs* (New York: Simon & Schuster, 2009), 381; Merk, *Manifest Destiny*, 122–26; Thomas Hietala, *Manifest Design: Anxious Aggrandizement in Late Jacksonian America* (Ithaca: Cornell University Press, 1985), 155, 166; 'Conquest of Mexico. Interesting Discussion in the Senate', in the *Barre Gazette* (MA), 7 Jan. 1848; 'Speech of Gen. Houston, of Texas at the Great War Meeting at Tammany Hall', 29 Jan. 1848.
7. Eric Foner, 'The Wilmot Proviso Revisited', *Journal of American History*, 56/2 (1969), 262–79; Thomas Hart Benton, *Thirty Years' View*, ii (New York: D. Appleton, 1856), 695; Bill and Explanation of Preston King, 4–5 Jan. 1847.
8. Hietala, *Manifest Design*, 128; Albert G. Brown to JKP, 20 June 1846; James W. Chalmers to JKP, 27 June 1846; Jefferson Davis to Charles J. Searles, 19 Sept. 1847; Merk, *Manifest Destiny*, 162; Benton, *Thirty Years' View*, ii, 698.
9. Greenberg, *Wicked War*, 91–94, 174–76.
10. Greenberg, *Wicked War*, 218–21.
11. *The Diary of Philip Hone*, ii, ed. Bayard Tuckerman (New York: Dodd, Mead, 1889), 13 Mar. 1848; Benton, *Thirty Years' View*, ii, 710.
12. Calhoun to Andrew Calhoun, 23 Feb. 1848; there is a good description of John Quincy Adams's death in Benton's memoir and in the *Farmer's Cabinet* (NH), 2 Mar. 1848.
13. Daniel Walker Howe, *What Hath God Wrought: The Transformation of America, 1815–1848* (New York: OUP, 2007), 811.

**Gold Fever**

1. Hubert Howe Bancroft, *History of California*, xxiii (San Francisco: History Company, 1888), 26–47.
2. Frederick J. Teggart and C. S. Lyman, 'The Gold Rush: Extracts from the Diary of C. S. Lyman 1848–1849', *California Historical Society Quarterly*, 2/3 (1923), 181–202.
3. Ralph P. Bieber, 'California Gold Mania', *Mississippi Valley Historical Review*, 35/1 (1948), 3–28; Ralph J. Roske, 'The World Impact of the California Gold Rush 1849–1857', *Arizona and the West*, 5/3 (1963), 187–232; Mason's report quoted in Edwin Bryant, *What I Saw in California* (New York: Appleton, 1849).

4. Sucheng Chan, 'A People of Exceptional Character: Ethnic Diversity, Nativism, and Racism in the California Gold Rush', *California History*, 79/2 (2000), 44–85.
5. JKP, State of the Union, 5 Dec. 1848; Malcolm J. Rohrbough, *Days of Gold: The California Gold Rush and the American Nation* (Berkeley: University of California Press, 1997), 173, and *California Historical Society Quarterly*, 77 (1922), 21; Bieber, 'California Gold Mania'.
6. Rohrbough, *Days of Gold*, 52–53; John O. Holzhueter and Edwin Hillyer, 'From Waupun to Sacramento in 1849: The Gold Rush Journal of Edwin Hillyer', *Wisconsin Magazine of History*, 49/3 (1966), 210–44; Ray Allen Billington, *The Westward Movement in the United States* (Princeton: Van Nostrand, 1959), 566, 590–91.
7. Samuel Locke diary, NYPL Diaries [Unbound] 1833–1850, box 2.
8. Jessie Benton Frémont, *A Year of American Travel* (New York: Harper, 1878), 65–67.
9. NYPL, Henry Hunter Peters Papers.
10. Gary Clayton Anderson and Laura Lee Anderson (eds), *The Army Surveys of Gold Rush California* (Norman: University of Oklahoma Press, 2015), 49–51, 54, 60–61; Walter Colton, *Three Years in California* (New York: A. S. Barnes, 1850), 272, 279, 293; Billington, *Westward Movement*, 590–91; J. D. Borthwick, *Three Years in California* (London: William Blackwood, 1857), 103, 119, 224.
11. Daniel B. Woods, *Sixteen Months at the Gold Diggings* (New York: Harper, 1851), 35–38; Josiah Royce, *California* (Boston: Houghton, Mifflin, 1886), 238–39; Anderson & Anderson, *Army Surveys*, 70–73, 169–71; Leonard Pitt, 'The Beginnings of Nativism in California', *Pacific Historical Review*, 30/1 (1961), 23–38; Randolph Roth, *American Homicide* (Cambridge, MA: Belknap Press, 2009), 355, 361.

**Trying Conclusions**
1. Taylor's plantation was just north of Natchez. Originally named Cypress Grove, he later renamed it Buena Vista, after his famous victory.
2. Sean Wilentz, *The Rise of American Democracy: Jefferson to Lincoln* (New York: Norton, 2005), 635–36.
3. Allan Nevins, *Ordeal of the Union*, i: *Fruits of Manifest Destiny, 1847–1852* (New York: Collier, 1992), 240–42, 260; Edward M. Steel, *T. Butler King of Georgia* (Athens: University of Georgia Press, 1964), 71–73.
4. Report of the Debates in the Convention of California, on the Formation of the State Constitution, in September and October, 1849, 143–44, 148.
5. J. F. H. Claiborne (ed.), *Life and Correspondence of John A. Quitman* (New York: Harper, 1860), 35; James M. McPherson, *Battle Cry of Freedom* (New York: OUP, 1988), 66–68; William J. Cooper, *Jefferson Davis, American* (New York: Knopf, 2002), 199; Ronald C. Woolsey, 'A Southern Dilemma:

Slavery Expansion and the California Statehood Issue in 1850 – a Reconsideration', *Southern California Quarterly*, 65/2 (1983), 123–44.
6. Nevins, *Ordeal*, i, 246, 255–59; Wilentz, *American Democracy*, 638–39.
7. Merrill D. Peterson, *The Great Triumvirate: Webster, Clay, and Calhoun* (New York: OUP, 1987), 458.
8. Nevins, *Ordeal*, i, 279–302.
9. Nevins, *Ordeal*, i, 301–02, 314; Wilentz, *American Democracy*, 645; Robert Rhett, *The Death and Funeral Ceremonies of John Caldwell Calhoun* (Columbia: A. S. Johnston, 1850).
10. Nevins, *Ordeal*, i, 252, 308, 310, 319; Joanne B. Freeman, *The Field of Blood: Violence in Congress and the Road to Civil War* (New York: Farrar, Straus & Giroux, 2018), 152–67; Walter Stahr, *Seward: Lincoln's Indispensable Man* (New York: Simon & Schuster, 2012), 244.
11. Nevins, *Ordeal*, i, 327–32; Holman Hamilton, *Prologue to Conflict: The Crisis and Compromise of 1850* (University Press of Kentucky, 2005), 108–10, 151; L. M. Ganaway, 'New Mexico and the Sectional Controversy, 1846–1861, II', *New Mexico Historical Review*, 18/3 (2021), 205–46; Hudson Strode (ed.), *Jefferson Davis: Private Letters, 1823–1889* (New York: Harcourt, Brace, 1966), 62–64; Peterson, *Great Triumvirate*, 473.
12. Hamilton, *Prologue*, 161–65; Peterson, *Great Triumvirate*, 469; Cooper, *Jefferson Davis*, 203; Abridgment of the Debates of Congress, from 1789 to 1856: 7 Dec. 1846–30 Sept. 1850, 591.

## Mesilla, USA

1. *Daily Atlas*, MA, 9 May 1853; Odie B. Faulk, 'The Controversial Boundary Survey and the Gadsden Treaty', *Arizona and the West*, 4/3 (1962), 201–26; C. Gilbert Storms, *Reconnaissance in Sonora: Charles D Poston's 1854 Exploration of Mexico and the Gadsden Purchase* (Tucson: University of Arizona Press, 2015), 22–26.
2. Ray Allen Billington, *The Westward Movement in the United States* (Princeton: Van Nostrand, 1959), 394–98; Ralph Waldo Emerson, *The Complete Works of Ralph Waldo Emerson*, xi: *Miscellanies* (Boston: Houghton, Mifflin, 1906), 125–26; Edward E. Baptist, *The Half Has Never Been Told: Slavery and the Making of American Capitalism* (New York: Basic, 2016), 350–53.
3. George Fitzhugh, *Sociology for the South, or, The Failure of Free Society* (Richmond, VA: A. Morris, 1854), 87, 139; *De Bow's Commercial Review of the South & West*, iii (New Orleans, 1847), 138–40; Robert F. Durden, 'J. D. B. De Bow: Convolutions of a Slavery Expansionist', *Journal of Southern History*, 17/4 (1951), 441–61; Kevin Waite, *West of Slavery: The Southern Dream of a Transcontinental Empire* (Chapel Hill: University of North Carolina Press, 2021), 56–57; Lewis Cecil Gray, *History of Agriculture in the Southern United States to 1860*, ii (Gloucester, MA: Peter Smith, 1958),

932–34; Steven G. Collins, 'Progress and Slavery on the South's Railroads', *Railroad History*, 181 (1999), 6–25; John Franklin Kvach, 'The First New South: J. D. B. De Bow's Promotion of a Modern Economy in the Old South', PhD dissertation, University of Tennessee – Knoxville, 2008; Billington, *Westward Expansion*, 399–402.

4. R. S. Cotterill, 'Memphis Railroad Convention, 1849', *Tennessee Historical Magazine*, 4/2 (1918), 83–94; Lewis H. Haney, *A Congressional History of Railways in the United States*, i (Madison: Democrat, 1910), 13–18; *Journal of the Proceedings of the Commercial Convention*, Charleston, 1854, 79; Robert R. Russel, 'The Pacific Railway Issue in Politics Prior to the Civil War', *Mississippi Valley Historical Review*, 12/2 (1925), 187–201; also see Kvach, 'First New South'.

5. United States War Department, *Reports of Explorations and Surveys, to Ascertain the most Practicable and Economical Route for a Railroad from the Mississippi River to the Pacific Ocean*, vii, 19–20.

6. Louis Bernard Schmidt, 'Manifest Opportunity and the Gadsden Purchase', *Arizona and the West*, 3/3 (1961), 245–64; Kvach, 'First New South'; Paul Neff Garber, *The Gadsden Treaty* (Philadelphia: Press of the University of Pennsylvania, 1923), 16–30.

7. J. Fred Rippy, 'The Negotiation of the Gadsden Treaty', *Southwestern Historical Quarterly*, 27/1 (1923), 1–26; Schmidt, 'Manifest Opportunity'.

8. *San Antonio Ledger*, TX, 1 June 1854; *Daily Democratic State Journal*, CA, 2 Aug. 1854; *National Anti-Slavery Standard*, NY, 27 Aug. 1853; *Farmer's Cabinet*, NH, 8 Mar. 1855.

9. Will Fowler, *Santa Anna of Mexico* (Lincoln: University of Nebraska Press, 2007), 308, 345; *Progreso*, TX, 29 Oct. 1876; *Tampa Guardian*, FL, 22 July 1876; *Salt Lake Tribune*, UT, 15 July 1876; *Philadelphia Inquirer*, PA, 28 Sept. 1876.

10. George Griggs, *History of Mesilla Valley* (Mesilla: Bronson, 1930), 87; *Pittsfield Sun*, MA, 25 Jan. 1855; *Boston Daily Atlas*, MA, 11 Jan. 1855; *Farmer's Cabinet*, NH, 1 Mar. 1855.

11. Joanne B. Freeman, *The Field of Blood: Violence in Congress and the Road to Civil War* (New York: Farrar, Straus & Giroux, 2018), 31; Robert E. May, *The Southern Dream of a Caribbean Empire, 1854–1861* (Athens: University of Georgia Press, 1989), 219.

12. D. W. Meinig, *The Shaping of America: A Geographical Perspective on 500 Years of History*, ii: *Continental America, 1800–1867* (New Haven: Yale University Press, 1986), 478; Jefferson Davis, *The Rise and Fall of the Confederate Government*, i (New York: D. Appleton, 1881), 316; the various secession declarations can be accessed here: https://www.battlefields.org/learn/primary-sources/declaration-causes-seceding-states; William Carey Crane, *Life and Select Literary Remains of Sam Houston of Texas* (Dallas: William G. Scarff, 1884), 600.

13. May, *Southern Dream*, 238.
14. Kevin Waite, 'Jefferson Davis and Proslavery Visions of Empire in the Far West', *Journal of the Civil War Era*, 6/4 (2016), 536–65; W. H. Watford, 'Confederate Western Ambitions', *Southwestern Historical Quarterly*, 44/2 (1940), 161–87; Imogene Spaulding, 'The Attitude of California to the Civil War', *Annual Publication of the Historical Society of Southern California*, 9/1–2 (1912), 104–31; Waite, *West of Slavery*, 1; Charles Lining, 'The Cruise of the Confederate Steamship "Shenandoah"', *Tennessee Historical Magazine*, 8/2 (1924), 102–11.

## PART VI: ALASKA
### Young Russia Greets Young America
1. *The Pilot*, vol. 26, no. 42, 17 Oct. 1863.
2. *Harper's Weekly*, 17 Oct. 1863; Albert A. Woldman, *Lincoln and the Russians* (Cleveland: World Publishing, 1952), 140–53; Norman E. Saul, *Distant Friends: The United States and Russia, 1763–1867* (Lawrence: University Press of Kansas, 1991), 345–49.
3. Saul, *Distant Friends*, 34; Matthew Lockwood, *To Begin the World Over Again: How the American Revolution Devastated the Globe* (New Haven: Yale University Press, 2019), 192–94, 208, 220.
4. Saul, *Distant Friends*, 32–47; Ronald J. Jensen, *The Alaska Purchase and Russian-American Relations* (Seattle: University of Washington Press, 1975), xiii–xv; James R. Gibson, *Imperial Russia in Frontier America: The Changing Geography of Supply of Russian America, 1784–1867* (New York: OUP, 1976), 99–101, 142–44.
5. Saul, *Distant Friends*, 133–57, 181–84; Sven Beckert, *Empire of Cotton: A New History of Global Capitalism* (New York: Knopf, 2015), 243.
6. Saul, *Distant Friends*, 163, 176–77, 227; Walter Stahr, *Seward: Lincoln's Indispensable Man* (New York: Simon & Schuster, 2012), 270.
7. Saul, *Distant Friends*, 180, 230–31, 253.
8. Saul, *Distant Friends*, 187–90, 201, 213–22, 268–72, 328; Jensen, *Alaska Purchase*, 4–10.
9. Lee A. Farrow, *Seward's Folly: A New Look at the Alaska Purchase* (Fairbanks: University of Alaska Press, 2016), 23–28; Jensen, *Alaska Purchase*, 4–14.
10. Jensen, *Alaska Purchase*, 62; Doris Kearns Goodwin, *Team of Rivals: The Political Genius of Abraham Lincoln* (London: Penguin, 2005), 66–91; William H. Seward, *William H. Seward's Travels Around the World* (New York: Appleton, 1874), 13, 771–72.
11. Frederic Bancroft, 'Seward's Ideas of Territorial Expansion', *North American Review*, 167/500 (1898), 79–89; Stahr, *Indispensable Man*, 193–95, 275, 342–46.

12. Bancroft, 'Seward's Ideas'; William H. Seward, *Life and Public Services of John Quincy Adams* (New York: Derby, Miller, 1849), 382; Ernest N. Paolino, *The Foundations of the American Empire: William Henry Seward and U.S. Foreign Policy* (Ithaca: Cornell University Press, 1973), 11–23.
13. Paolino, *Foundations*, 10–14; Bancroft, 'Seward's Ideas'; 'The True Greatness of Our Country. A Discourse Before the Young Catholic Friends' Society at Baltimore', 22 Dec. 1848, William Henry Seward, 1848; Joseph A. Fry, *Lincoln, Seward, and US Foreign Relations in the Civil War Era* (Lexington: University Press of Kentucky, 2019), 178.
14. Paolino, *Foundations*, 26–44; Seward, *Travels*, 771–72; 'The Whale Fishery and American Commerce in the Pacific Ocean, Speech of William H. Seward, in the Senate of the United States, 29 July 1852, 1852, Stahr, *Indispensable Man*, 157.
15. The islands would eventually be sold to the United States in 1917, for $25 million, and became the United States Virgin Islands.
16. George C. Herring, *From Colony to Superpower: U.S. Foreign Relations since 1776* (New York: OUP, 2008), 256–57; David E. Shi, 'Seward's Attempt to Annex British Columbia, 1865–1869', *Pacific Historical Review*, 47/2 (1978), 217–38.

**Winning Walrussia**
1. Lee A. Farrow, *Seward's Folly: A New Look at the Alaska Purchase* (Fairbanks: University of Alaska Press, 2016), 23.
2. Sven Beckert, *Empire of Cotton: A New History of Global Capitalism* (New York: Knopf, 2015), 246–64.
3. Norman E. Saul, *Distant Friends: The United States and Russia, 1763–1867* (Lawrence: University Press of Kansas, 1991), 315–51; Ronald J. Jensen, *The Alaska Purchase and Russian-American Relations* (Seattle: University of Washington Press, 1975), 27–29; Gorchakov to Stoeckl, 10 July 1861, at https://history.state.gov/historicaldocuments/frus1861/d203; Harold E. Blinn, 'Seward and the Polish Rebellion of 1863', *American Historical Review*, 45/4 (1940), 828–33.
4. Ernest N. Paolino, *The Foundations of the American Empire: William Henry Seward and U.S. Foreign Policy* (Ithaca: Cornell University Press, 1973), 41–60, 67–68; Perry McDonough Collins, in 'Statement of the Origin, Organization and Progress of the Russian-American Telegraph', Western Union Telegraph Company, 1866, 144; Tyler Dennett, 'Seward's Far Eastern Policy', *American Historical Review*, 28/1 (1922), 45–62.
5. Paolino, *Foundations*, 67–69.
6. Farrow, *Seward's Folly*, 18; Jensen, *Alaska Purchase*, 39–44; Joseph Florimond Loubat, *Narrative of the Mission to Russia, in 1866, of the Hon. Gustavus Vasa Fox, Assistant-Secretary of the Navy* (New York: Appleton, 1879), 89–96.

7. George Simpson, *An Overland Journey Round the World* (Philadelphia: Lea & Blanchard, 1847), 79; Farrow, *Seward's Folly*, 26–31; Jensen, *Alaska Purchase*, 47–51.
8. Saul, *Distant Friends*, 388–96.
9. Farrow, *Seward's Folly*, 45–51; Frederick W. Seward, *Autobiography: Seward at Washington* (New York: Derby & Miller, 1891), 348.
10. Farrow, *Seward's Folly*, 63–65; Charles Sumner, 'Speech of Hon. Charles Sumner, of Massachusetts, on the Cession of Russian America to the United States', 1867.
11. Nelson A. Miles, *Personal Recollections and Observations of General Nelson A. Miles* (Chicago: Werner, 1896), 417; Farrow, *Seward's Folly*, 67–68; Corry O'Lanus [pseudonymous], *Corry O'Lanus: His Views and Experiences* (New York: Carleton, 1867), 58–60.
12. Farrow, *Seward's Folly*, 77–78.
13. William H. Seward, *William H. Seward's Travels Around the World* (New York: Appleton, 1874), 403–14.
14. Seward, *Travels*, 415–23.
15. Seward, *Travels*, 415–33; Seward's Sitka speech can be accessed here: https://tile.loc.gov/storage-services/service/gdc/gdclccn/48/03/13/88/48031388/48031388.pdf.
16. Farrow, *Seward's Folly*, 125; Eric T. L. Love, *Race over Empire: Racism and U.S. Imperialism, 1865–1900* (Chapel Hill: University of North Carolina Press, 2004), 44, 58; for America's 'pointillist' imperial strategy, see Daniel Immerwahr's *How to Hide an Empire* (London: Vintage, 2020).

## CONCLUSION: The Scramble for America

1. Max M. Edling, *A Hercules in the Cradle: War, Money, and the American State, 1783–1867* (Chicago: University of Chicago Press, 2023), 4.
2. Luis de Onís, *Memoir upon the Negotiations between Spain and the United States of America* (Washington, DC: De Kraafft, 1821).
3. Benjamin Franklin to Jonathan Williams, Sr., 27 May 1777; Thomas Jefferson to John Adams, 1 June 1822.
4. The relevant portion of Thiel's speech is quoted here: https://www.econlib.org/peter-thiels-pivot/.
5. Alexis de Tocqueville, *Democracy in America*, 233.
6. Andrew Jackson, 'Message Regarding Indian Removal', 15 Feb. 1832.
7. J. D. Anthony, *Life and Times of Rev. J. D. Anthony* (University of Georgia Libraries, 1896), 22–34.
8. Wendell Berry, 'The Unsettling of America' (1977), reproduced in Paul Kingsnorth (ed.), *The World-Ending Fire: The Essential Wendell Berry* (London: Allen Lane, 2017).
9. Webster's speech is reproduced in full in the *Richmond Dispatch*, 4 Jan. 1895.

# List of Illustrations

13 – 'A new map of the western parts of Virginia', Thomas Hutchins, London, 1778, (Library of Congress)
18 – George Washington's map, accompanying his 'journal to the Ohio', 1754, (Library of Congress)
32 – 'A plan of Alexandria', George Washington, 1749 (Library of Congress)
74 – 'A map of the British and French dominions in North America', John Mitchell, 1755, (Library of Congress)
90 – 'Map Showing the Principal Meridians and Base Lines of the United States', North West Publishing Co., 1913
92 – 'Plat of the seven ranges', Thomas Hutchins, 1796 (Library of Congress)
93 – John Martin Land Warrant, 1782 (General Land Office)
100 – Seal of the North West Territory, Charles Burleigh Galbreath, (1907) (Public domain)
130 – 'Carte de la Louisiane', Guillaume Delisle, 1718, (Library of Congress)
133 – Hydrological map of the USA, (Alamy)
144 – 'Port of New-Orleans shut', handbill, 1802, (Library of Congress)
186 – 'Alluvial Valley of the Mississippi River', Army Map Service, 1930 (Library of Congress)
203 – 'Reynolds's political map of the United States', 1856, (Library of Congress)
210 – Map of the southern boundary, Andrew Ellicott, 1800 (Library of Congress)

213 – 'The West Indies', John Cary, 1783 (Library of Congress)
229 – Battle of New Orleans, Albert Hoffy, 1840 (Library of Congress)
259 – Plat of Andrew Jackson's land on the Tennessee River, (General Land Office)
278 – 'American Justice!!', George Cruikshank, 1819 (British Museum)
281 – 'Map of the United States', David Burr, 1839 (Library of Congress)
320 – 'Map of the United States of America', John Melish, 1816, (Library of Congress)
356 – 'Map of the Oregon Territory', Charles Wilkes, 1844(Library of Congress)
364 – 'Map of an exploring expedition to the Rocky Mountains', John Charles Frémont 1845, (Library of Congress)
414 – 'Map of Texas', Stephen Austin, 1830
427 – Republic of Texas currency, 1830s (Texas State Library)
435 – 'Awful explosion of the "peace-maker"', N. Currier, 1844 (Library of Congress)
439 – 'Map showing the distribution of the slave population', Edwin Hergesheimer, 1861 (Library of Congress)
452 – 'The Marriage of Texas', (Texas State Library)
466 – 'Volunteers for the Mexican War!', broadside, 1846 (Star of the Republic Museum)
499 – 'Map of the gold regions of California', James Wyld, 1849 (Library of Congress)
545 – 'William the Glutton', cartoon, Frank Leslie's Illustrated Newspaper, September 28, 1867 (House Divided: The Civil War Research Engine at Dickinson College)

# Acknowledgements

This book took six years to research and write and was made possible by the generosity of dozens of people and institutions. It is constructed from material made available to me in libraries, archives, and private collections on both sides of the Atlantic. I would like to thank the British Library, the National Archives, the New York Public Library, the New York State Historical Society, the Library of Congress, the Baring Archive, the London Library, and the Bodleian, among others, for granting me access to their collections and to thank their employees for being so helpful and welcoming.

As this book was commissioned in the summer of 2020, the first few years of its research took place under lockdown conditions. Consequently, I was heavily reliant on digitised collections accessible online. I swiftly gained an appreciation for how much has been made available to the public through the largely unacknowledged work of countless anonymous people who have collectively digitised a vast amount of material. I would be remiss if I did not thank them here, although I do not know their names.

That this book was ever conceived of is due to the influence of Gary Savage and Jay Sexton, who on separate occasions, many years ago, inspired a fascination with American history in me that ultimately gave rise to this project.

Researching this subject afforded me the opportunity to travel widely in the United States in pursuit of my subject. Ten thousand miles of asphalt later, I gained a renewed appreciation for the country, its people, and its past, and learned a huge amount directly and indirectly relevant to this book from generous and well-informed strangers I met along the way. Those trips were made more enjoyable, if less rigorous, by the presence and participation of Greg Sgammato, Homa Deilamy, Zach Harris, Jack Priestman, and Will Siguler.

In London I would like to thank the Society of Authors whose generous grant gave this project a vote of confidence when it was much needed. I owe, as ever, a great deal of thanks to my judicious and worldly agent, Sophie Scard, for her hard work and unfailing support over all these years and for the assistance in various capacities of her *confrères* at United Agents. At William Collins, I am indebted to the leadership and vision of my editor Arabella Pike whose tolerance of the somewhat chaotic manner in which this book has taken shape is matched only by her skill in helping it assume its final, and I think better, form. I am similarly obliged to Alex Gingell and Sam Harding who exhibited exceptional patience as this book went through the editorial process as well as to Anne Rieley, Tim Waller, and Nic Nicholas. I am also extremely grateful for the enthusiasm and professionalism of Laura Meyer, Paul Erdpresser, and Anna Derkacz.

Lastly, I owe a greater debt than can be properly conveyed to Carlotta Bonafini for her forbearance, good humour, and support over the course of these long years.

# Index

Illustrations are denoted by the use of italic page numbers.

Abenaki Indians 15
Aberdeen, Lord 392–3, 404, 440, 441
*Active* steamboat 557
Adams, Abigail 78, 84
Adams, John 78–80, 286–7
  on Britain 73, 75
  family 274
  Franklin and 82, 83–4
  French embargo 148
  Jefferson and 136
  lawyer 349
Adams, John Quincy 273–7, 279–81, 286–7
  background 272
  on Calhoun 393, 437
  Castlereagh and 248–9
  Clay and 289
  death of 493–4
  Declaration of Independence and 569
  on First Opium War 398
  J. Canning and 328
  on J. Floyd 333–4
  on Jackson 305
  on Monroe 267, 288
  Oregon Question 336–7
  on partition by foreign nations 284
  'poet' 168
  on Russia 536
  on slavery 200–1
  Texas and 415

Adams-Onís Treaty (1819) 281, *281*, 282, 328, 411, 415, 493, 537
Addington, Henry 161
Agua Nueva massacre (1846) 483
Akron 117
Alabama 215, 216, 250–60, 261, 293, 301–2
Alabama River 215, 243
Alamo, Battle of the (1836) 411–12, 418, 420
Alaska 4, 8, 380, 531–61
Alaska Purchase (1867) 556, 559–60, 564
Albuquerque 528
Aleutian Islands 316, 536, 553, 560
Alexander I, Tsar 274, 283, 284, 328
Alexander II, Tsar 535, 548, 551
*Alexander Nevski* ship 533, 534
Alexandria 20, 32, 56
'All Mexico' lobby 482, 486, 493, 543
Allegheny Mountains 17, 113
Allegheny River 12, 26, 71
Allen, William 379, 380, 400, 406, 407
Allouez, Claude-Jean 127
Almonte, Juan 456–7, 461
Alta California 457, 492, 496
Alvarado, Luis de Moscoso 126
Ambrister, Robert 263–4, 269, 279
Amelia Island 262–3, 265
American Fur Company 322, 333, 340, 370
American Peace Society 484
Ames, Fisher 163

642    INDEX

Amherst, Jeffery 37–8
Amiens, Treaty of 143, 152
Ampudia, Gen Pedro de 462–3
Amur River basin 537, 544, 549, 552
Anderson, William 190
*Andrews* steamboat 533, 534
Antarctica 353
Apalachee Indians 125, 211
Apalachicola River 214, 239, 240–1, 263, 264
Appalachian Mountains 12, 14, 30, 39, 74, 86, 112, 117, 132
Appalachian Ridge 12, 17
Applegate, Jesse 378, 384, 386
Aranda, Conde de 82–3, 84
Arapahoe Indians 366
Arbuthnot, Alexander 263, 268, 269, 279
Argentina 219, 283
'Argonauts' 502–4, 505, 506, 539
Arista, General 455, 462, 464
Arizona 4, 470, 522, 523, 527–8
Arkansas 178, 181, 184, 187, 291
Arkansas River 127, 133
Aroostook War (1838–9) 392
Articles of Confederation (1781) 89, 98, 332
Ashburton, Alexander Baring, Lord 393
Astor, John Jacob 321–6
Astoria 321–7, 540
Augustus (Moravian) 69
Aury, Louis-Michel 263
Austin, Moses and Stephen 117, 416, 426
Australia 2, 501

Bacon, Francis 136
Bagby, Senator 489
Bahamas 74, 216, 263, 392
Baja California 486, 522
Balize, the 214
Baltimore 229–30, 230, 343, 445–7, 481
Bancroft, George 445, 481–2
Bancroft, Hubert Howe 361
Bannon, Steve 570
Barbé-Marbois, François 153, 154, 155
Barings' Bank 160–1
Barlow, Joel 131, 136
Barnes, Richard 36
Barren River 115

Bartram, William 211–12
Bates, Edward 335–6
Bathurst, Earl 247, 279
Baton Rouge 221, 224, 226, 243
Baylor, John R. 527
Baylor, Mary 412
Bear Flag revolt (1846) 471
Bear River Valley 372
Benton, Jesse 235–6
Benton, Thomas Hart 235–6, 452–3, 487–8
  Floyd and 333
  Foote and 514
  on 'gunpowder popularity' 468
  Linn and 379, 385
  Maine and 393
  on Mesilla 523
  Oregon Question 407
  Polk and 406, 493
  *Princeton* incident 434
  on slavery 441
  Texas and 384
  Webster and 394
Bering, Vitus 316, 536
Bermuda 74, 246
Berrien, John 513
Berry, Wendell 572
Biddle, Capt James 326
Biloxi 128, 211
Bismarck, Otto von 559
'Black Belt', Deep South 215, 242, 299, 301
Black communities 145–8, 279, 293, 436
Black, William 326
Blackfeet Indians 325, 340, 366
Blainville, Pierre-Joseph Céloron de 16
Blair, Francis 441, 442
Blount, William 232
Blue Jacket (Shawnee leader) 103–9
Blue Licks, Battle of the (1782) 72
Blue Ridge Mountains 30, 35–6
Bluegrass 114, 115, 118
Bolívar, Simón 219, 262, 285
Bonaparte, Joseph 154, 218–19, 277
Boone, Daniel 25, 45, 48, 61, 72, 119
Boone family 45, 59, 88
Boone's Lick 194–5, 196, 198
Boonesborough 59, 61, 62
Boston 51, 77, 346–7

INDEX 643

Boston Tea Party (1773) 24, 52, 311–12
Boudinot, Elias 297, 298
Bouquet, Col Henry 29, 37–8
Bradbury, John 180
Braddock, Maj Gen Edward 22–9, 108, 113
Braddock's Field 121
Brazos River 411, 424
Breese, Sidney 379, 447
British Columbia 329, 541, 546
British Empire
  Astoria and 325–6
  Canada and 95
  China and 395–401
  Confederacy and 547–8
  Corn Laws 382, 404, 407
  the Floridas and 248–9
  foreign policy 284
  France and 143
  fur trade and 318
  government 53
  manufactures 14
  Nicoll and 238–44
  Ohio Country 13–14, 20, 37, 39, 51
  Oregon and 381–3
  Russia and 540
  South America and 283
  Spain and 77, 140, 249, 280
  Tea Act (1773) 311
  Texas and 431, 441
  US and 226, 392, 545
  War of 1812 227–9, 234
Brown, John 142, 188, 189, 190–1
Brown, John H. 537
Brown, William Wells 190, 198
Bryant and Sturgis 347
Buchanan, James 466–7, 492, 537, 539
Buena Vista, Battle of (1847) 472–5, 475
Buffalo 391
Burgesses, House of 42, 43
Burgettstown 121
Burke, Edmund 34
Burnett, Peter 378–9
Butler, Anthony 413
Butler, William Orlando 469

Cabeza de Vaca, Álvar Núñez 125
Caddo Indians 125
Cahaba 256

Calaveras 505
Caldwell, Capt Matt 'Old Paint' 424
Calhoun, John C. 200–1, 437–41, 465–6, 493–4
  on Cass 381
  death of 513–14
  J. Q. Adams on 393, 437
  Jackson and 269, 270, 303–4
  Lamar and 428
  Monroe and 266
  Oregon and 406
  'Peace and Free Trade' 405
  Secretary of War 265, 273
  Upshur and 433
  vindicated 489–90, 510
  Wilmot Proviso and 511–12
California 455–61, 465–7, 470–2
  annexation 4, 408, 486, 492–3
  Calhoun on 512
  free state 516–17
  gold fever 495, 496–507
  Jackson and 415
  Seward and 513
  slavery and 510
  Taylor on 509
*Californios* (Hispanic) 350, 497
Callava, Col José 282
Campbell, Israel 188
Campbell, John 258
Campeche 431
Canaan, American ('land of promise') 111–22
Canada 2, 330–2, 381–2, 390–1
  Britain and 95, 152, 566
  France and 76
  Ohio and 121
  Sumner and 555
  trade in 187
  Trump and 566
  uprising in 403
  US and 83
  waterways 173, 320
  *See also* New France (*now* Canada)
Canning, George 284, 286, 288, 332–3
Canning, Stratford 328
Canton *see* China
Canton System 312–13, 396–8
Caribbean littoral map (1803) *213*
Caribbean, the 212–14, 216
Carlisle 38, 48

*Caroline* crisis (1837–42) 390–2, 400
Carroll, Billy 235
Carroll, Harry 195–6
Carson, Kit 471
Carter, Jimmy 567–8
Cascade Mountains 319–20, 374
Cass, Lewis 379, 380–1, 384, 393, 406, 445, 513
Castiglione, Giuseppe 310, 314
Castlereagh, Viscount 248–9, 273, 279, 280, 285
Catherine the Great 167, 536
Catholicism 53, 98
Central America 130, 288, 527, 566
Cerro Gordo 478
Chamberlain, Samuel 468, 469, 474
Charles III, King of Spain 84
Charleston 75, 81, 262
Cherokee Indians 296–9
  Dragging Canoe 61–2
  in Georgia 215
  Jackson's army 236, 237
  in Kentucky 15, 42
  kidnap Boone's daughter 59
  Michaux and 116
  'removal' 294–5
  signed treaties 251, 252, 291
  Spain and 141
Chesapeake 35, 187, 188
Cheyenne Indians 366, 556
Chicago 468
Chickamauga 533
Chickasaw Indians 141, 180, 215, 251, 252, 295
Chihuahua 175, 518, 522
Childress, George Campbell 412
Chile 283, 347, 501
Chilkat Indians 558
Chillicothe 117
China 310–14, 345–7, 395–401
  Collins and 550
  connecting with 350
  fur imports 315, 316–18, 327, 338
  GDP 568
  gold fever 501
  trade with 321, 351
Chinook Indians 172, 319, 557
Chippewa (Ojibwe) Indians 15, 175, 390
Choctaw Indians 125, 141, 215, 227, 237, 250, 252, 294, 295, 300–1

Chuinard, Eldon G. 172
Cincinnati 108, 117, 120
Civil War, American (1861–65) 547
Claiborne, William C. C. 158–9, 164, 178, 222–3, 224, 225, 226
Clark, George Rogers 61–5, 66, 72, 74, 102, 141, 167, 195
Clark, William 167–74, 183, 318, 319, 322, 333
Clarke, Lewis 189
Clay, Cassius Marcellus 469
Clay, Henry 289–90, 449–51, 484–5
  Adams and 200
  Calhoun and 437, 513
  Gallatin and 336
  Ghent negotiator 276
  Missouri and 202
  national debt and 304
  Polk and 565
  presidential candidate 432, 444, 446
  slave-owner 520
  on slavery 305
  South America and 285, 286
  Taylor and 514
  Texas and 442, 445
  Wilmot Proviso and 511, 512
Clay, Henry Jr 469, 475, 483, 484, 485
Clayton, John 509
Clearwater River 362
*Clementine* ship 496
Cleveland 117, 190
Clinch River 45, 116
Coacoochee (Wild Cat) 306
Coahuila 460, 522
Cochrane, Admiral 238–9, 240, 245–6
Cochrane, Thomas 283
coffee 146, 147, 478
Coffee, John 228–9, 235–6, 237–8, 254–7
  Indians and 251, 252, 259, 295, 301
  Jackson and 242, 244, 254, 258–60, 259, 290, 291
Coffee, Mary 228–9, 437
Colbert, Brown 188
Cold War 287, 564
Collins, Perry McDonough 549–51
Coloma 497, 498, 501
Colombia 283, 286
Colorado 133, 175
Colorado River 133, 411

Colton, Rev Walter 505
Columbia Bar 322–3
Columbia District 338–9
Columbia River 133, 174, 318–20, 326, 355–7, 363, 407
  mouth of 170, 322, 324, 325
*Columbia* ship 317
Columbia Valley 385
Columbus 117
Columbus, Christopher 145
Comanche Indians 413, 424
*Comet* steamboat 178
Conecuh River 209, 214
Conestoga people 38, 47
Congreve rockets 343
Connecticut 345, 349
Constantine, Grand Duke 552
Constitution of the United States (1789) 98, 159, 201, 527
Constitutional Convention (1787) 98
Continental Congress 52, 57, 75, 89, 91–4, 96
Continental Divide 174, 280, 318, 325, 334, 370, 521, 527
Cook, Capt James 314–15
Cooper, James Fenimore 377
Coosa River 296
Corn Laws 382, 404, 407
Cornstalk (Shawnee chief) 57–8, 59, 60
Cornwallis, Lord 80
Corps of Discovery *see* Lewis and Clark expedition (1804–6)
Corpus Christi 455, 462
Corrêa da Serra, José 170
Cortés, Hernán 476
Corwin, Thomas 485
cotton 252–4, 256–8, 405–6
  'cotton famine' 547–8
  France and 147
  -growing regions 214, 215, 249, 301–2, 423, 432
  harvesting 158
  for Liverpool 185, 189, 249, 382, 394, 428
  Russian imports 538
Cooper, James Fenimore 377
Council Bluffs 361, 364, 556
Coxe, Daniel 130

Crawford, William 41–3, 49, 54, 58, 59, 69–71, 86
Crawford, William H. 192–3, 267
Creek Indians 215–16, 239–45, 251–2
  Jackson and 232, 291
  leaders 270, 292
  Mad Dog 209–10, 216, 306
  Nicolls and 246–7
  and removal 294–5
  removal treaty and 299–300
  Soto and 125
  Spanish support 141
  *See also* Red Sticks (Creeks)
Cresswell, Nicholas 56–7, 66
Crimean War (1853–56) 540
Crockett, Davy 235, 236, 293
Croghan, George 24, 26
Cruikshank, George, *'American Justice'* 278–9, *278*
Cuba 125, 214, 216, 224, 287, 565–6
Culpeper County 32, 35, 36
Cumberland County 48
Cumberland Gap 14, 61, 87
Cumberland Mountains 116
Cumberland River 12, 43, 116
Cuming, Fortescue 180
Curtice, Jimmie 420
Cushing, Caleb 398–400, 468
Custer's Last Stand (1876) 108
Custis, Peter 175
Cutler, Jervis 211
Cuvier, Georges 137
Cypress Land Company 257, 258

Dalles, The 319, 361, 374–5
Dana, Francis 274, 536
Dana, Richard Henry 348, 350
Daniel, Jesse 121
Daoguang Emperor 396
Darién Gap 566
Darke, Col William 105, 107, 108
Davis, Jefferson 468–9, 474, 482, 489, 511, 515, 516–17, 521, 525–6, 527
Dayton, Jonthan 164
De Bow, James 519–20
de Lassus, Carlos de Hault 169, 217, 221, 223
De Villiers, Coulon 21, 22
Declaration of Independence (1776) 55, 317

Decrès, Admiral 150, 153
Delaware Indians
  attack settlers 104
  British and 58
  Crawford and 70, 71
  flee to Ohio 15
  French and 25
  leaders 24, 29, 37, 48, 67
  pacifists 47
  raiding parties 66
  Shawnee and 103
  US and 60
  *See also* Moravians
Delisle, Guillaume 130, *130*
Denny, Ebenezer 106, 108
Dessalines, Jean-Jacques 156–7
Detroit 52, 62, 65–6
Dickens, Charles 450, 496
Dinwiddie Proclamation (1754) 40, 42–3, 54, 86
Dinwiddie, Robert 16–17, 19–20, 22, 27, 36
Dollar, the 56–7
Donelson, Andrew Jackson 433, 454
Douglas, Stephen 379, 516
Downman, Raleigh W. 248
Dragging Canoe (Cherokee) 61–2
Drew, Andrew 390
Dunbar, Col David 24, 26–7
Dunbar, William 185
Duncan, Stephen 301
Dunmore's War (1774) 53, 54, 57–8, 61
Duquesne, Marquis 16

East Florida 75, 210–12, 243, 262–3, 265–6, 279
East India Company 311, 332–3, 395
Eaton, John 295
Econfina River 269
Eells, Myron 383, 384, 386
Elder, John 47
Elk River 375
Ellicott, Andrew 209, 210, 211
Emerson, Ralph Waldo 297, 349–50, 448–50
*Empress of China* ship 311–12, 313–14
Emuckfaw 237
Enotachopco 237
Eppes, John Wayles 204
Everett, Edward 286, 350, 356–7

Fairfax, George 52
Fallen Timbers 102–9
Falls of the Ohio 194
Farnham, Thomas Jefferson 388
Fauquier, Francis 29
Fearon, Henry 185
Ferdinand VII, King 218, 219, 221, 222, 226, 277, 282
Fernandina 210, 262–3, 265
Field, Cyrus 550
Fiji 343–4
Fillmore, Millard 516
Fischer, David Hackett 46
Fithian, Philip 34
Fitzhugh's Mill 359
Flint, James 193–4
Flint River 264
Flint, Timothy 180, 181, 185
Florida Keys 214, 470
Floridablanca, Conde de 77
Floridas, the 207–306, 438
Floyd, John 333–6, 378
Floyd, Michael 333
Folch, Vicente 209, 212
Folsom, Capt Joseph L. 500
Foote, Henry 514, 515
Forbes, Brig Gen John 28
Forbes, John M. 283
Formosa 546
Fort Adams 158–9
Fort Baton Rouge 217–18, 223
Fort Blount 116
Fort Bowyer 243–4
Fort Brown 462–3
Fort Clatsop 319
Fort Cumberland 23, 24, 27, 29
Fort Duquesne 20, 24, 25, 26, 29, 36
Fort Fauntleroy 527
Fort Gadsden 268, 269
Fort George 326, 337
Fort Harmar 99, 100, 102
Fort Henry 59
Fort Jackson 242
Fort Jackson, Treaty of (1814) 251, 264
Fort Kearny 556
Fort Laramie 370
Fort Le Boeuf 19
Fort Mims 234–5
Fort Necessity 22, 42
Fort Pitt 29, 38, 48, 50, 57, 58, 59, 71

Fort Randolph 59, 60
Fort Ross 536, 539
Fort Scott 263, 264, 268
Fort Southwest Point 116
Fort Stanwix 42
Fort Vancouver 339, 341, 361, 364, 386, 388–9, 403
Fort Washington 104, 105
Fossett, Peter 137
Fowler, Maj Jacob 107
Fox, Gustavus Vasa 551
Fox Indians 183
Fox River 127, 325
Franklin, Benjamin 14, 23, 34, 48, 76, 79–80, 82, 83, 132, 569
Frazier, John 17, 22
Freaner, James 479–80
Free Soil Movement 488–9, 509
Freeman, Thomas 175
Frelinghuysen, Theodore 292–3, 449
Frémont, John C. 364, 371, 459, 471
French Empire 11–29, 75–8, 145–56
  bankrupt 84
  Confederacy and 547–8
  Ferdinand VII and 282–3
  Franklin and 79–80, 82–3
  Louisiana Purchase and 160–5
  Mexico and 430
  Mississippi Valley 129–31
  Poland and 549
  shipping insurance 273
  Spain and 140–1, 143
  Texas and 431
French Revolution (1789–99) 146
Freneau, Philip 312
Fulton, Robert 178
fur trade 309–27

Gadsden, James 522–3
Gadsden Purchase (1854) 523, 528
Gage, Gen Thomas 24, 51–2
Gaines, Gen Edmund Pendleton 225, 263, 264, 265, 411, 413
Gallatin, Albert
  banking and insurance 183, 273
  Clay and 336
  Crawford and 192, 193
  federal land policy reform 182
  Ghent negotiator 276
  Jefferson and 139, 160, 204
  Lewis and 170
  Louisiana Purchase and 161, 165, 187
  Ridge and 296
Galveston 428
Gardiner, Julia 434
Gardner, Johnson 341
Garland, Gen John 524
Garrett family 264
Garrison, William Lloyd 305
*Gaspee* affair (1772) 52
Gates, Horatio 24
*General Jackson* steamboat 178
General Land Office (GLO) 182, 195, 196, 254, 255–6, 258–9, 301
Genêt, Edmond-Charles 141
George III, King 39, 56, 58, 80, 239, 241
George, Prince Regent 248
Georgia 75, 188, 215, 294, 296, 297, 298, 305, 571
Ghent, Treaty of (1814) 227, 245, 248, 251–2, 264, 276, 326
Giddings, Joshua 484
Gifford, Francis 463, 464
Gilmer, Thomas Walker 434
Gilmore (Virginian soldier) 60
Gist, Christopher 16, 17, 21, 24
Gist, Thomas 86
Gleig, George Robert 228
Gnadenhutten 66, 68, 71
Goff, Capt Peter 469
gold fever 495, 496–507, 499
Goliad massacre (1836) 412
Gorchakov, Alexander 548, 549
Gowens, Henry 301
Grand Pré, Lt Louis Antonio de 217
Grant, Ulysses S. 468
Gray, Capt Robert 170, 317, 322, 405
Grays Harbor 320
*Great Eastern*, SS 550
Great Kanawha River 12, 43, 86
Great Kanawha Valley 45, 57, 61
Great Lakes 14, 15, 133, 233
Great Meadows 17, 21, 27, 43
Great Migration (1843) 363
Greathouse, Daniel 57
Greeley, Horace 359
Green, Jacob 190
Green River 372
Greencastle 38

Greenland 546, 566, 570
Greenough, Horatio 59
Greenville, Treaty of (1795) 109
G.T.T. (Gone to Texas) 424–6, 425
Guadalupe Hidalgo, Treaty of (1848) 492, 518, 522, 539
Guadalupe River 411
Guadeloupe 151
Guam 97
Guatemala 218–19
Gulf Coast 210, 214, 250, 266, 287
Gulf of California 133
Gulf of Mexico 128, 133, 213, 216, 245, 416, 455, 570
Gulf Plains 215, 216, 250, 252, 291, 300–1, 304
Gunter's chain 31, 90

Hacket, Nelson 187
Hadjo, Hidlis 243, 247, 249, 263, 268–9
Haiti 145–8, 156–7, 157, 204, 546
Hall, Francis 179, 330–1
Hamer, Thomas L. 469
Hamilton, Alexander 98, 104, 157, 160
Hamilton, Gen Henry 63–4
Hamilton (Virginian soldier) 60
Hampton, Wade 301
Hangtown 505–6
Hanna's Town 71
Hannegan, Edward 379, 403, 406
Hardin, John J. 469, 475
Harmar, Gen Josiah 104
Harris, Dilue 420, 422
Harris, John 59
Harrison, Eastwick and Winans 538
Harrison, Joseph 538
Harrison, William Henry 351–2, 426
Harrodsburg 62
Harrower, John 44–5
Hawaii 315, 322, 346, 347, 348, 351, 496, 501, 505
Hayden, Lewis 188
Hays, Stockley 235–6
Henry, Patrick 55, 60, 62
Herrera, Joaquín de 461
Himollemico (Red Stick leader) 268
Hispaniola (*now* Haiti) 145–8, 156–7, 204
Holmes, David 222

Holston River 45, 116
Holt, Thomas 375
Hone, Philip 492–3
Hope & Company 160
Horseshoe Bend (Tohopeka) 237
Houston 422–3
Houston, Sam 412, 418, 419–21, 428, 431–3, 443–4, 487, 526
Howe, General 60
Hudson River 178
Hudson's Bay Company (HBC) 332–3, 337–40, 388–9, 403–4
  'bribes' and 386
  Britain and 382
  Columbia River and 407
  Oregon and 341, 374, 385
  posts 372
  Simpson and 348
  supply chain 316
  Wilkes and 354
Humboldt, Alexander von 137, 212
Hunt, Wilson Price 324–5
Hunter, Capt Sherod 528
Huntsville 253–4, 255–6, 258, 282
Hutchins, Thomas 91

Iceland 546
Idaho 329, 408
Illinois 14, 37, 52, 63, 96, 119, 121, 180, 520
Illinois River 127–8, 178
Independence, Missouri 358, 363–4
Indian Removal Act (1830) 292, 301, 305
Indiana 96, 119, 121, 520
Indians 215–16
  British and 240, 241
  'Indian removal' 183–4
  Jackson and 290–302
  Ohio 11, 19, 23, 25–6, 28, 29, 37–40, 42, 47, 50–1, 57–73, 101–4, 120–1
  St. Clair's Defeat 106–8
  in Texas 431
  Thorn and 323–4
  Upper Louisiana 179–80
  *See also individual peoples*
Indonesia 346
Ingersoll, Charles Jared 382
Innes, Harry 142
Iowa 519

Ireland 44, 45–6, 482
Iroquois (Mingo) Indians 15–16, 21, 25, 42, 57, 58–9, 64–5, 70, 341
Irvine, General 69, 71
*Isaac Tod* ship 325
Issaquena County 301

Jackson, Andrew 227–44, 261–71, 272–4, 276–82, 289–98
  Alabama 250–60
  'American Justice' cartoon 278
  on Calhoun 441
  Coffee and 235, 242, 244, 254, 258–60, 259, 290, 291
  on Indians 290–1
  Lamar and 428–9
  on Louisiana Purchase 156
  Polk and 443–5, 454–5
  as president 300, 301, 302–5
  prize colt stud 285
  on Russia 538
  S. Houston and 419
  slavery and 249, 383, 456, 571
  Tennessee militia and 459
  Texas and 415, 421, 426, 433, 435, 442–3
  on the Webster–Ashburton Treaty 393
Jackson, Donald 175
Jackson family 231
Jackson, James 163–4
Jamaica 263
James River 188
Japan 347
Jay, John 78, 80, 82, 83, 102, 313
Jefferson, Isaac 136
Jefferson River 174
Jefferson, Thomas 55–6, 135–44, 203–5
  Astor and 322
  Claiborne and 224
  Clark and 64–5
  Dunbar and 185
  on expansion 184
  The Floridas 220
  French and 145, 148, 152, 157
  fur trade and 318
  on Indians 105, 183
  Lewis and Clark expedition (1804–6) 167–72, 320–1
  Louisiana and 150, 156, 158–62
  Madison and 159, 204, 214, 223–4
  Monroe and 143–4, 155, 200, 205, 267
  on New Orleans 134
  on Northwest Territory 97
  Pike and 175
  as president 139
  proposes decimal system 89–90
  on slaves 188
  on Texas 415
  Trist and 491
  on waterways 131
Johnson, Andrew 551, 554
Johnson, Cave 444
Johnson, George 301–2
Jolliet, Louis 127
Jones, Anson 429
Jones, James, J. 444
Jonesborough 116
Jumonville, Ensign 21, Ohio Country

Kamchatka 537, 540, 552
*Kamchatka* ship 537–8
Kanawha River 43, 58
Kansas River 368
Kaskaskia 52, 63
Kearny, Gen Stephen 470–1, 497, 507
Kelley, Hall Jackson 360–1, 362
Kelly, William 367, 384
Kemper, Nathan and Samuel 220
Kemper, Reuben 220, 224–5, 227
Kendall, Amos 445
Kendrick, John 317
Kennebec River 350
Kentucky 61–5, 118–19, 181–2
  annexation 94
  frontier in 57, 59
  hunting in 13, 15, 42
  militia 72, 103, 106, 227
  Newport 416
  populations 88, 121
  Spain and 142
  trade in 132
Kentucky River 12
Ker, Henry 179
Kickapoo Indians 15
King, James 315, 316
King, William 513
Kiowa Indians 366

Kittson, William 341
Knight, Dr John 70–1
Knox, Henry 104
Knoxville 116
Kodiak Island 536
Kossuth, Lajos 539

La Salle, René-Robert Cavelier, Sieur de 127–8, 415
*Lady Washington* ship 317
Lafayette, Marquis de 140
Lake Miccosukee 264, 268
Lake Michigan 127
Lake Pontchartrain 128
Lamar, Mirabeau Buonaparte 428–31, 431
Lancaster County 38
Land Acts (1796–1820) 109, 182, 202
Land Ordinance Act (1785) 89–91, *90*, 92–3, 95, 97, 139
Las Casas, Bartolomé de 126
Latin America 278, 284, 286, 568
Laurel Mountain 86
Laurens, Henry 78, 81–2, 84
Laussat, Pierre-Clément 150, 152, 164–5, 166
Lawrence, Maj William 243–4
Leclerc, Gen Charles 149, 150–1
Ledyard, John 167, 316–17
Lee, Jason and Daniel 361, 362
Lee, Richard Henry 55, 88, 110
Lee, Robert E. 478
Lewis and Clark expedition (1804–6) 167–74, 183, 318, 322
Lewis, Meriwether 167–74, 175, 183, 318, 320–2
Lexington 114–15, 116
Licking River 72
Limestone (*later* Maysville) 114, 117
Lincoln, Abraham 449, 451, 469, 485, 524–6, 535, 551
Lincoln, Levi 159
Lincoln, Mary Todd 535
Linn, Lewis 378–80, 385, 386
Lisovski, Admiral 533, 534
lithium reserves 568
Liverpool, Lord 332–3
Livingston, Robert 150, 152, 153–6, 178, 212, 220
Locke, John 33–4, 49, 136

Logan (Mingo leader) 57, 58–9
Logstown 19
Long Island 75, 349
Los Angeles 471, 472
Louis XIV, King 127, 128
Louis XV, King 131
Louis XVI, King 80, 84
Louisiana 14, 95, 123–205, *130*, 227
Louisiana Purchase Treaty (1803) 153–7, 160–5, 201–2, 204–5
  disputes after 329
  Floridas and 212, 220, 222
  'Indian removal' 291
  limits 170, 174, 176
  parts of 173
  payment for 192
  terms 166
  test of system 184, 564
Louisville 117, 132, 177
Lower Louisiana 162
Lower Mississippi Valley 185, *186*, 187–8, 215, 240
lumberjacks 346, 392
Lyman, Chester Smith 498–9
lynching 506

McClure, David 44–5, 49, 50–1
McDonald, Finan 340
McDougall, Duncan 323, 324
MacGregor, Gregor 262–3, 283
Mackay, Alexander 408
Mackenzie, Alexander 167, 318
Mackinac Island 324–5
McKinley, Mount 570
McLeod Affair (1840) 391–2, 546
McLoughlin, John 339–40, 342, 354–5, 362, 386, 388–9, 403–4
MacNab, Allan 390
Mad Dog (Creek chief) 209–10, 216, 306
Madison County 253
Madison, James
  Claiborne and 158–9
  on the Constitution 201
  Fossett on 137
  Gallatin and 183
  Holmes and 222
  Jefferson and 159, 204, 214, 223–4
  Lafayette and 95
  Livingston and 220

No-Transfer Resolution 225
  Wilkinson and 239
Maine 297, 349, 392, 393, 438
Maksutov, Prince Dmitry Petrovich 556
Malolo Island 343–4
Malthus, Thomas 138
Manchuria 537
Mandan villages (*now* Bismarck) 170, 171–3
Mangum, Willie 513
Manifest Destiny 455, 468, 483, 506, 539, 541, 552, 566, 570
Manrique, Mateo González 244
Marietta 100–2, 104, 114, 117
Marquette, Jacques 127
Marryat, Frederick 394–5
Marshall, James 497–8
Marthasville 198, 199
Martin, John 92, 94
Martineau, Harriet 437–8, 448
Maryland 89, 188, 438
Mascouten Indians 15
Mason, Col Richard Barnes 500–2
Mason, George 55
Mason, Robert 511
Masot, Governor 269
Massachusetts 349, 393, 436, 449
Matamoros 455, 462, 463, 464
Maumee River 65
Maury, Sarah Mytton 382, 405
*Mayflower* ship 99
Maysville 117, 426
McLeod Affair (1840) 391–2
Meade, Lt George 462, 464–5
Melville, Gansevoort 403
Melville, Herman, *Moby-Dick* 344, 346, 347, 348, 349, 354, 449, 468
Merrimac River 350
Mesilla 518–29, 522
Methodism 112, 361
Mexican–American War (1846–48) 458–81, 466, 484–5, 489–93, 497, 501, 506, 524
Mexico 415–119, 430–32, 481–95, 509–11, 515–16, 565–6
  annexation 380, 427, 451, 508
  Argonauts and 506
  Gadsden Purchase and 523–4
  Polk's plan 456–8

Sutter and 496–7
Texas and 421, 429, 442, 452, 453
Venegas and 219
war with 405
waterways 411
Mexico City 219, 416–17, 472–3, 476, 479, 487, 490–2, 494, 522
Miami River 12, 15, 65, 72, 119
Michaux, François 112–17, 132, 134, 167
Michigan 96, 119
Michilimackinac 52
Midway Atoll 546
Milledgeville 250, 254, 256
Miller's Place 209–10
Miller's Run 87
Mingo Bottom 69, 70
Mingo (Iroquois) Indians 15–16, 21, 25, 42, 57, 58–9, 64–5, 70
Minto, John 365, 366, 371, 378, 384, 385–6
Miranda, Francisco de 286
Miro, Esteban 142
Mississippi 216, 220, 234, 293, 295, 301, 474, 489
Mississippi River 125–34, 139–42, 177–8
  basin 162
  extent of *133*, 211
  Flint on 181
  'Indian removal' 292
  Indians along the 180
  Indians and 39
  land around 74, 116
  path of 14, 470
  US and 143
Mississippi Valley 183
Missouri 178, 181, 184
Missouri Compromise (1819–20) 194–200, 202, *203*, 488, 493
Missouri River 128, 132, 162, 168–70, 172–4, *173*, 318
Mitchell Map 73–4, *74*, 82–3, 392
Miwoks 505
Mobile 128, 211, 215, 221, 225, 239–40, 243–4, 250
Mobile River 133, 215, 252
Mohawk River 14
Moluntha (tribal elder) 103
Monongahela, Battle of the (1755) 25–8, 43

# 652  INDEX

Monongahela River 12, 16, 17, 25, 71
Monroe Doctrine (1823) 287, 467, 569–70
Monroe, James 153–6, 264–8, 276–7
  Adams and 267, 288
  'American Justice' cartoon 278–9
  Calhoun and 303
  Canning and 286
  Crawford and 193
  flees Washington 272
  Floridas and 212, 216
  Huntsville and 285
  Jackson and 282
  Jefferson and 143–4, 155, 200, 205, 267
  meets Napoleon 152
  Northwest Ordinance 97
Montana 408
Monterrey 472, 489, 500
Montezuma 468, 476
Morales, Don Juan Ventura 143, 152, 476, 477
Moravians 15, 38–9, 66–9, 70, 71–2
Morgan, Daniel 24–5
Morier, William 226
Mormon Island 504, 505
Mormons 459, 497, 498, 541, 556
Morrison, Robert 384
Morse, Samuel 446–7
Motte, Jacob Rhett 300
Mount Sterling 121
Mount Vernon 22, 43, 50
Muscle Shoals 215, 242, 252, 257
Muskingum River 12, 66, 67, 69, 99
Mystic River 350

Nanking, Treaty of (1842) 397, 398
Nantucket 347, 348
Napoleon I 152–4, 155–6, 159–61
  exiled 238, 248
  Floridas and 216, 218, 221
  Leclerc and 149, 151
  Louisiana and 564
  Louverture and 147
  Spanish and 143
  US and 567
Nashville 115–16, 178, 232, 235
Natchez 128, 177, 185, 233, 295, 301
Natchitoches 175, 455
Nebraska 180, 369

*Neptune* steamboat 188–9
Nesmith, James 369, 371, 372, 376
New Bedford 348, 349
New Echota 296
New England 55, 114, 118, 156, 348, 350, 382, 383, 393, 407
New France (*now* Canada) 14, 16, 29, 37, 53
New Granada 262
New Hampshire 349
New Madrid 177, 195
New Mexico 4, 430, 457, 470, 472, 492, 516, 523
New Orleans 140–3, 152–5
  diversity of 162–3
  French and 129–30, 134, 147, 149–50
  goods to 132, 213, 417, 422, 520
  Jefferson and 158–9
  militia 227, 467–8
  mining 501
  Monroe and 212
  port shut off 144
  Santa Anna and 413
  slavery and 188
New Orleans, Battle of (1815) 228–30, 229, 282, 304
*New Orleans* steamboat 177, 178
New York 51, 75, 262, 350, 382, 391, 451, 533–5
New York State 199, 438, 541–2
New Zealand 2, 501
Newcastle, Duke of 22
Newfoundland 78, 550
Newton, Isaac 136
Nez Perce Indians 360, 362
Niagara 52, 102
Niagara Falls 390, 391, 535
Nicholas I, Tsar 537–8
Nicholas, Wilson Cary (W. C. N.) 203–4
Nicolls, Edward 240–2, 243, 244, 245–7, 249, 264
No-Transfer Resolution (1811) 225–6, 239, 265, 287
Nootka Sound Crisis (1789) 140, 317, 536
North Carolina (*now* Tennessee) 116, 181, 231–2, 438
North, Lord 80, 84

North West Company 175, 322, 324–6, 332, 340, 540
Northup, Solomon 188, 189
Northwest Ordinance (1787) 96–8, 101, 488
Northwest Territory 96–8, 99–102, *100*, 120
Nott, Josiah 300
Nueces River 411, 455, 461, 462
Nueva Helvetia 496–7
Nuevo León 522
Nullification Crisis (1832–33) 303–4, 429, 437, 441
Nuttall, Thomas 182

Ogden, Philip Skene 339–41, 405
O'Higgins, Bernardo 283
Ohio Country 9–122, *18*, 183, 194, 438, 520
Ohio River 12–13, 39, 43, 64, 83, 91, 118, 120–1, 132
Ohio Valley 14–16
Ojibwe (Chippewa) Indians 15, 175, 390
Oklahoma 205, 291
Omaha Indians 171
Onís, Luis de 226, 277, 281, 567
*Ontario*, USS 326
Opdyke, George 534
Opium War, First (1839–42) 396–8, *397*, 400
Opium War, Second (1856–60) 552
Oregon Country 307–408, 320, *356*, *363*, *381*, 387
Oregon Question 328–42, 355–6, 357, 380, 382, 385, 401, 403–8, 565
Oregon Trail 364–76, *364*, 503
Oregon Treaty (1846) 408, 539
Oregon ultras 378–85, 386, 394, 399, 400–2, 405–7, 546
*Orleans* steamboat 188
Orme, Robert 24
*Orpheus*, HMS 238
O'Sullivan, John 447–8, 449, 455
Oswald, Richard 81–2, 83–4
Ottawa Indians 15, 37
otter, sea (*Enhydra lutris*) 309–10, 345, 537
Ouachita River 132
Outer Manchuria 552

Pacana Indians 211
Pacific Northwest 140, 167, 172, 281, 283, 316–17, 328, 334
Packingham, Hezekiah 371
Pakenham Letter (1844) 440
Pakenham, Maj Gen Sir Edward 227, 228–9, 240
Palmerston, Lord 391–2, 394, 396, 402, 548
Panama 544, 566
Panama Canal 567, 568, 570
paper money 56–7, 183–4, 193–4, 258, *427*, 431
*Paragon* steamboat 179
Paredes, Mariano 461
Paris, Treaties of (1763/1783) 37, 56, 72, 73, 87, 563–4
Parker, Peter 397–8
Parker, Theodore 485
Parkman, Francis 368, 369, 370, 377, 378
Pascagoula Indians 211
Pascagoula River 214
Pastry War (1838) 430
Paulet affair (1843) 400
Pawnee Indians 368
Paxton Boys 38–9, 47–8
Peale, Charles Willson 175
Pearl River 214, 220, 243, 399
Peck, John Mason 180, 181–2, 184
Peel, Sir Robert 392, 402, 404, 407–8
Peking, Convention of (1860) 552
Peña y Peña, José Manuel de la 492
Pendleton, Edmund 55
Pennsylvania 12–17, 121, 160, 183, 438
Penobscot River 350
Pensacola
  Black communities 233
  Britain and 221, 240
  Jackson and 243–4, 269, 272
  Nicolls and 241, 249
  Spain and 225, 277, 282
Perdido River 211, 214
Perry, Cdre Matthew 538
Peru 283, 501
Peters, Henry Hunter 504
Philadelphia 23, 77, 132, 140, 232, 262
Philippines 346
Pichon, Louis-André 145, 147, 148, 150
Pickering, Timothy 148

# 654  INDEX

Pierce, Franklin 468, 522
Pigot, Capt Hugh 238, 239
Pike, Zebulon 174–6
*Pilgrim* ship 348, 350
Pillow, Gideon 445
Pinckney, Charles 142–3
Pinckney Treaty (1795) 142, 210
Piqua, Battle of (1780) 65
Pitt, William (the Elder) 28, 81
Pittsburgh 43, 45, 50, 65–6, 86, 87, 91, 112–14, 117
Platte River 132, 180, 368–70, 377
Plymouth Colony 99–100
Poinsett, Joel 304
Point Isabel 463
Point Pleasant 43, 58, 59
Poland 549
Polk, James Knox 401–2, 443–7, 450–3, 454–8
  Aberdeen and 404
  Bancroft and 482
  Clay and 565
  'The Devil' letter 483
  G. Melville and 403
  gold fever and 501–2
  Mexican–American War and 464, 465–7, 470, 471, 472–3, 482, 485, 489
  Oregon and 336, 405, 406–7
  as president 494–5
  slave-owner 520
  Trist and 491–3
  Trump and 570
Pontiac's War (1763–66) 37, 39, 47–8
Pontotoc County 301
Porter, Charles T. 483–4
Portneuf River 372
Posey, John 40–1
Potawatomi Indians 15
Potomac River 17, 30, 434
Poughkeepsie 330
Poyais, Kingdom of 283
Preemption Act (1841) 379
Presbyterianism 47, 181, 361–4
Prescott, William H. 468
Priestley, Joseph 138
*Princeton*, USS 434–5, *435*, 471
Pringle, Virgil 370, 371, 375, 376
Proclamation Line, Royal (1763) 39, 40, 41–2, 51, 82

Prospect Bluff 246, 263, 268
Puerto Rico 97
Puget Sound 355, 357, 405, 557
Puritans 34
Putnam, Rufus 99–100, 104, 105

Qianlong Emperor (1736–96) 310, 312, 314
Qing Dynasty 396, 398, 552
Quakers 34, 48, 191
Quebec 52
Quebec Act (1774) 53, 56
Quincy, Josiah 79
Quizquiz 125–6

*Raccoon*, HMS 325–6
railroads 90, 448, 519–24
Raleigh Letter (1844) 442–3, 451
Randolph, Anne Cary 175
Rappahannock River 248
Rayneval (Vergennes' private secretary) 83
Rebellions of 1837–38 (Canada) 391
Red River 128, 132, 175, 178, 179, 188, 190
Red Stick (Creeks) Indians 233–8, 242, 264, 268
Redstone Creek 16, 22
Relief Act (1821) 202
Rhode Island 75, 349, 502
Richmond 142
Ridge, John 297, 298
Rio Grande River 126, 133, 411, 418, 455, 457, 461, 462, 465, 492
Robinson, Charles 538
Rochambeau, Donatien 151, 152, 156
Rockies, the 173, 281, 322, 329, 334, 359–60, 361, 366, 382
Roosevelt, Nicholas 178
Ross, Alexander 323
Ross, John 296, 297–9
Rousseau, Maj Gen Lovell H. 556
Royal Navy 152, 156, 221, 227, 228, 248, 325
Royall, Anne 253–4, 261
Royce, Sarah 370
Rush, Richard 284
Russell, John 404
Russia 274, 283, 315, 316, 533–41, 547–61

INDEX 655

Russian-American Company (RAC) 536–7, 539–40, 549–50, 552
Russo-American Treaty (1824) 329

Sabine River 162, 411, 413
Sacramento 459, 556–7
St Asaph's 62
St Augustine 210
St Charles 195
St. Clair, Arthur 100–2, 103–8
St Croix River 392
Saint-Domingue 145–8, 149–51, 152, 156–7
St Francisville 224
St John's Plains 221
St Joseph 364, 365, 366, 377
St Louis 130–1, 166, 170, 172, 176, 194–5, 325, 383–4
St Marks 210, 268, 269
St Mary's River 264
St Stephens 254, 256
Salcedo, Nemesio de 175, 176
Salem 66, 346
Salish Sea 355
Saltillo 472, 473, 489
Sampson, William 116
San Antonio 411–12, 424, 431
San Antonion River 411
San Diego 408
San Francisco
  Alaskan ice 539
  Clay on 485
  harbour 355, 408, 455, 456, 565
  Lyman on 498
  Seward and 557
  Sutter and 496
  Webster on 353
San Ildefonso, Treaty of (1800) 143
San Jacinto, Battle of (1836) 418–21
sandalwood 345–6
Sandusky River 15, 65, 67, 69, 70
Sandwich Islands 400–1
Santa Anna, López de 411–12, 413, 417, 418–21, 430, 473–5, 478–9, 522–4
Santa Fe 430, 459, 470, 528
Sante Fe 515
*Sarah* ship 395
Sasanare, Frasier 341
Saskatchewan River 133
Sauk Indians 183

Savanna 74, 214, 262
Savannah 262
Scandinavia 275
Schäffer, Georg Anton 536
Schonbrunn 66
Schoolcraft, Henry Rowe 179
Scioto River 12
Scotland 44, 45–6
Scots-Irish 45–9, 86–7, 94–5, 119, 180, 230
Scott, Dred 190, 201
Scott, Gen Winfield 391, 475, 476–9, 483, 486–7
Scott, Lt Richard W. 264, 268
sea cucumbers 346
seals 345, 348
Second Bank of the United States (SBUS) 183, 192–3, 199
Ségur, Comte de 77, 84
Seminole Wars (1816–58) 269–70, 303, 306, 460
Seminoles 141, 211, 261–2, 263–4, 269, 295
Sentmanat, Don Francisco 462
Seven Years War (1756–63) 28, 36, 75, 113
Seward, William H. 349, 509, 512–13, 535, 539, 541–6, 545, 547–51, 553–61, 567
Shaw, Samuel 311–13
Shawnee Indians
  British and 102
  Delawares and 103
  Dragging Canoe and 61–2
  Knight and 70, 71
  leaders 57–8, 59, 60, 233–4, 382
  raiding parties 64–5, 66
  settlements 15, 42, 72, 121
Shelburne, Earl of 81–2, 83, 84, 565
Shenandoah Valley 35, 36
Shields, James 469
Sibley, General 528
Simmons, Colonel 378
Simpson, George 337–40, 342, 348, 389, 403, 552
Sioux Indians 366, 370
Sitka 536, 552, 556–61
Skipwith, Fulwar 223, 224
slavery 145–8, 162–4, 185–90, 197–205, 301–2, 305–6, 383–5

656    INDEX

abolishing 96, 157
Adams County 295
  in the American South 439
  British and 245
  Davis and 527
  the Floridas 212, 222
  at Fort Adams 158
  in Guadeloupe 151
  Indians and 296
  Jackson and 249, 383, 456, 571
  Jefferson and 137
  lasting 520
  Louisiana 129
  Ohio country 114, 118
  Seward and 543
  slave-owners 184, *186*
  Texas 421
  Virginia 248
  Wilmot Proviso and 512-13
Slidell, John 457, 458, 461
Sloat, Cdre John D. 471
Smith, Adam 81, 82, 310
Smith, James 26
Smith, Jedediah 360
Smith, John 164
Smith, Robert 226
Snake Country 340-2
Snake River/Valley 325, 340, 372
Snakes 366
Soda Springs 372
'Song of the West Floridian Army in 1810' 225
Sonora 505, 506, 522
Soto, Hernando de 125-6, 127
South America 249, 262, 280, 283, 285-6, 288, 338, 345, 550
South Carolina 302-5
South Pass 360, 361, 370-1
South Umpqua River 375
Southwest, the 409-529
Spalding, Henry and Eliza 361-2
Spanish Empire 217-26, 277-8
  blocking American expansion 77-8, 83, 139-43
  ceding claims 328
  Colonel José 210
  the Floridas and 125, 264-5, 282
  Louisiana and 95, 126, 131-2, 158, 176, 277
  Mesilla and 529
  Mexico and 415
  Southwest and 415
Spanish Florida 210, 217, 241, 246, 262, 265, 268
Stamp Act (1765) 51, 76
Stanwix Treaty (1768) 45, 48, 58, 59
'The Star-Spangled Banner' 282, 313, 343
State of the Union addresses 167, 279, 291, 402, 406, 501, 509, 570
Stephens, Alexander 508, 515
Stiles, Ezra 120
Stockton, Cdre Robert F. 434, 471-2
Stoddard, Capt Amos 166
Stoeckl, Eduard de 541, 551-4, 556
Storms, Jane McManus 486-7
Strait of Juan de Fuca 355, 357
Straits of Florida 213-14, 249, 287
Sturgis, William 357
sugar 146, 147, 185, 187, 227, 346, 412
Sumner, Charles 554-5
Susquehanna 60-1
Susquehanna Valley 38
Sutter, John 496, 565
Sutter's Fort 497, 498, 539
Suwanee River 264, 269
Swisshelm, Jane 484

Tabasco 476
Tahiti 347
Talladega 236
Tallapoosa River 238
Talleyrand, Charles-Maurice de 150, 153, 155-6
Tallmadge, James 197-8, 200, 202
Tallushatchee 236
Tamaulipas 460, 522
Tampico 476, 486
Tanaghrisson (Half King) 12, 19, 20, 21
Taylor, John 198, 200
Taylor, Zachary 508-11, 514-16
  Buena Vista 472-5
  leading his army 462, 463, 464, 465
  Polk and 458, 483
  as president 468
  in Texas 455
tea 310-13, 317, 345, 395
Tea Act (1773) 52
Teal, Anne Fagan 413

technological innovation 447–8
Tecumseh (Shawnee leader) 233–4, 382
telegraph lines 446–8, 482, 501, 538, 549–51
Tenisaw Indians 211
Tennessee 45, 115–16, 118, 181–2, 183, 232, 252, 293, 451
  militia 227, 234–5, 261–2, 459
Tennessee River 12, 133, 215, 251, 252, 253, 254
Texas 411–56, 526–8
  annexation 4, 384–5, 408, 457, 459, 484–5, 493, 494–5
  border 492
  claims to 280
  emigration to 423
  Lewis and Clark expedition 175
  map *414*
  'marriage' cartoon *452*
  railways 519
  support of 515
  Tyler and 352
the Sea of Japan 552
Thiel, Peter 570
Thompson, David 170, 324
Thoreau, Henry David 378, 484
Thorn, Jonathan 322–4
Thornton, Capt Seth 463
Thornton, Jessy 365, 366
Tobey, William C. 476
Tocqueville, Alexis de 295, 416, 571
Tombigbee River 215, 243, 252
*Tonquin* ship 322–4
Tonti, Henri de 127
Tookaubatchee 233
Toombs, Robert 405–6, 407, 510
Toussaint Louverture 146–8, 152, 153
Townshend Acts (1767–68) 24, 311
Transcontinental Treaty (1819) *see* Adams-Onís Treaty (1819)
Travis, William Barret 411
Trent, William 19, 20, 38
Trias, Gen Angel 524
Trinity River 411, 420
Trist, Nicholas 490–2
Trump, Donald 566–7, 569, 570, 572
Trump, Frederick 560
Tunica Indians 211
Tyler, John 352–3, 432–3, 451–2
  eye on China 398, 399, 401
  marriage 434
  as president 379, 391, 426, 441, 450

Unalaska Island 315
Underground Railroad 190, 191
United States Exploring Expedition (U.S. Ex. Ex.) 343–4, 353–5
Upper Louisiana 128, 162, 170–4, 179–80
Upshur, Abel 433, 436–7
US Navy 351, 471, 476
Utah 516
Utes 366

Van Braam, Jacob 17, 22, 42
Van Buren, Martin 351, 421, 426, 432, 441, 442–3, 444, 445
Vance, J. D. 572
Vancouver Island 314, 355, 402, 403
Varnum, James Mitchell 100
*Velocipede* steamboat 178
Venango 19
Venegas, Francisco 219
Venezuela 219, 262, 285, 286
Veracruz 430, 458, 476–8, 481
Vergennes, Charles Gravier, Comte de 75–7, 80, 82–3, 84
Victor, Gen Claude 150, 152, 153
Villeré, Jacques 227, 244
Vincennes 63–4
Virginia 19, 34–5, 55–60, 94, 114, 118, 188, 205, 438
  militia 11–12, 16, 17, 21, 22, 23–9, 59

Wabash 104–9
Wabash River 12, 15, 63–4, 178
Walker, Robert J. 433, 435–6, 445, 486
Walla Walla Valley 362
Wallace, Roger 67
Walpole, Horace 84
Wanghia, Treaty of (1844) 400, 401
War of 1812 (1812–15) 227–9, 302, 325
Ward, Ensign Edward 20
Wasco-Wishram Indians 319
Washington 197, 198, 329, 408
Washington family 34–6
Washington, George 17–29, 30–6, 86–8
  Clark and 66
  Crawford and 49, 50, 58

        in despair 75
        on foreign entanglements 349
        Genêt and 141
        Irvine and 71
        Jefferson and 140
        'land of promise' 111–12
        last days of the colonial frontier 50, 52–4
        legacy 55, 110–11
        maps by *18*, *32*
        meets Jumonville 12
        a noble estate 40–4
        as president 98, 136
        on rivers 131
        St. Clair and 103–4, 105, 108
Washington, John 34–5
Watauga River 45
Watson, Henry 189, 190
Watson, James C. 299, 300
Wayne, Gen Anthony 108–9
Webster–Ashburton Treaty (1842) 393–4
Webster, Daniel
        on America 449, 572
        British elite and 393
        Calhoun and 438, 513
        Cushing and 399
        Maine and 394
        on Mexican–American War 485
        resigns 432
        on San Francisco 353
        Taylor and 514, 516
        Wilmot Proviso and 512, 513
        writes to Everett 356–7
Wellesley, Marquis 219
Wellington, Duke of 227, 275, 284, 407
Wentworth, John 400, 403
West Florida 155, 211, 212, 218, 220–5, 240
West, John 32
western world, the 12–17, *13*
whaling 347–8, 349, 350

Wharton, William 426–7
Wheeling 59, 72, 114, 117
Whistler, George Washington 538
Whistler, James Abbott McNeill 538
Whitman, Marcus and Narcissa 361–4
Whitman, Walt 449
Whitworth, Robert 470
Wilkes, Lt Charles 343–4, 353–7
Wilkinson, Gen James 143, 158, 165, 239, 415
Willamette Valley 361, 375–6, 388–9
William Darke, Col William 105
Williamsburg 19, 62, 64
Williamson, David 68, 69
Wills Creek 16, 17, 20, 23
Wilmot, David 487, 488–9
Wilmot Proviso (1846) 487–90, 495, 507, 510–12
Winthrop, Robert 405
Wirt, William 297
Wisconsin 96
Wisconsin River 127, 325
Wolfe, Gen James 331
Wood, James 58–9
Woodbine, Capt George 238–9, 263
Wood's Creek 504–5
Worth, Gen William J. 306, 494
Wyandot Indians 15, 64–5, 66, 67, 69, 70, 103, 104
Wykoff, William 222–3
Wyoming 408

Yamassee Indians 211
Yazoo Delta 301
Yell, Archibald 469, 475
Yellow Creek 57
Yellow Hair (tribal chief) 239
Yoholo, Opothle 300
York Express 338
York Factory 338
Yorktown 25, 66, 75, 80
Youghiogheny River 17, 20, 41, 43, 86
Younger, Philip 301